MW01632635

GORDON B. HINCKLEY

SHOULDER FOR THE LORD

GEORGE M. MCCUNE

HAWKES PUBLISHING INC.
5947 SOUTH 350 WEST
P.O. BOX 65735
SALT LAKE CITY, UT 84165
801-266-5555
FAX 801-266-5599

 Published in the United States of America
by Hawkes Publishing Inc., Salt Lake City

Appreciation is given
Utah State Historical Society
Special Collections, University of Utah Library
Daughters of Utah Pioneers Memorial Museum
LDS Historical Department Archives
and
LDS Business College
for use of photographic collections

Library of Congress Cataloging Data

McCune, George Moody
Gordon B. Hinckley – shoulder for the lord. – 1st ed.

p. 608 cm.

ISBN 0-89036-583-0
1. McCune, George Moody, 1943-
–Biography.
2. Religious Leaders, American–20th Century–Biography
I. Title

Manufactured in the United States of America

First Printing May 1996
Second Printing June 1996

SECOND PRINTING
IMPROVED TEXT

Dedicated
to
Matthew McCune, 1811-1889
and
Sarah Elizabeth Caroline Scott, 1812-1877
the founders
of my
Latter-day Saint
Heritage

"Let us learn to anoint our friends
while they are yet among the living.
Post-mortem kindness does not
cheer the burdened heart;
flowers on the coffin cast no
fragrance backward over
the weary way."
– *George Childs*

Contents

PREFACE

The public life of Gordon B. Hinckley is well documented and Gordon B. Hinckley himself has woven a story of his own life through these sources. This journalistic diary of the man has been a large source of food for this biography. Within the same speeches and reports is Gordon B. Hinckley's own daily diary entries of his personal life interspersed to make a certain point in his discourses.

Brought together in sequence of events, we can draw closer in knowing the man. To me it has been as though Gordon B. Hinckley has purposely been giving me fodder for this life story of his ministry.

Gordon B. Hinckley is the 15th prophet of the Church of Jesus Christ of Latter-day Saints officially established in New York State on April 6, 1830. He is the second LDS Church prophet in this dispensation born in the 20th Century.

My pleasure in bringing this information together has been an acquaintance going on 31 years before publication with a man and leader whose life has parallelled my own father's life. President Hinckley was born only eight months after my own father. My father was born in November 1909 and Gordon B. Hinckley in June 1910. My father was born in Eureka, Utah and Gordon B. Hinckley in Salt Lake City—only 60 miles apart. They lived in the same age, in the same environments, and experienced much of the same society.

I was companion to one of President Hinckley's nephews, Bryant Hinckley Wadsworth, one of 11 children of President Hinckley's youngest sister Sylvia. While Elder Wadsworth's companion in Japan, I first met Elder Hinckley as he visited Tokyo in missionary conferences and was one of the thousands of missionaries interviewed by him.

On another of his visits, I was called into the mission president's office as mission secretary to take down in shorthand a letter from the lips of Gordon B. Hinckley to aid in obtaining a visa for a Mexico citizen having trouble obtaining a visa to enter Japan where he had been assigned to fill a Latter-day Saint mission. From those experiences and many thereafter has grown a great love and respect for this special individual.

Truly Gordon B. Hinckley can be called a "shoulder for the Lord." He has always been a strong man willing to take the burdens put on his shoulders. During several administrations of LDS prophets, he has often been left sole member in the First Presidency healthy enough to carry on the heavy administrative, ceremonial and speaking duties of the highest echelon of LDS Church Government.

Many have been cooperative regarding my effort to be anxiously engaged. They have opened their files and added their great support to me in preparing this manuscript. Not all can be mentioned. But a couple of special mentions are Bill Slaughter, Photographic Archivist of the LDS Historical Department; Linda Haslam, Jim Kimball, Mary Gifford, Karen Bolzendahl, Larry Skidmore, JoAnn Bitton, J. Michael Hater, all of the archivists and librarians at the LDS Church Historical Department; personnel at the University of Utah Special Collections Library; and Craig Nelson, Public Affairs Director of the LDS Business College. Last but not least is John D. Hawkes, my publicist, who has had faith in me and my literary creativity for over 20 years.

Thanks to all of you for your enlightened perspective of history and biography. To examine the chronicles of a worthy human being's life is to step up one more link towards Divinity.

I lay this book on the altar and present it to Gordon B. Hinckley and the Lord with my love, hoping that you and all of us may be enriched by reading the sojourns of Gordon B. Hinckley and his ancestors in this the dispensation of the fullness of times.

As there are four separate records of the Savior preserved in the New Testament, all directed at a different audience, I present this as one of the records of the ministry of Gordon Bitner Hinckley. I have tried to write it for all, for those who would like to gain a better understanding of their Latter-day Saint neighbors as well as for Latter-day Saints themselves.

As the testimony of two or more witnesses is better than one, I present this work as one of the many testimonies which surely will be given of Gordon Bitner Hinckley's life and ministry.

May this contribution to understanding not only Gordon B. Hinckley, but also the church he serves, help everyone who reads it enjoy his life and find greater purpose in their own life. May the information as presented be of use to you in your quest for truth.

The Biographer
February 1996
Salt Lake City, Utah

TOKYO

"Are any of you sick?" he said as he looked into the faces of 83 missionaries. They were seated on aluminum folding chairs opened on top of the rice stem tatami mat floor. Rice shoji screens framed in dark brown wooden squares was the backdrop. Along the entire room to the left more shoji screens, filled with milk colored rice paper, separated the assembly from the Japanese garden immediately outside.

Their dress was typical. White shirts, ties, suit coats and trousers. These were missionaries of the Church of Jesus Christ of Latter-day Saints, about 19-24 years of age. Soft skin. Clear complexions. Budding young men and some ladies. Even several native Japanese filled their ranks. They had been prepared by their leaders for the apostle's visit. And intently they looked towards the speaker.

Then he burst into tears.

"We need one another's faith. We need one another's strength in this work. I hope you are praying for Brother and Sister Andersen, for one another, for your parents."

Tears began streaming down the cheeks of President Dwayne N. Andersen of the Northern Far East Mission. The weeping apostle was Elder Gordon Bitner Hinckley. The place was a two story wooden home built considrably before World War II by some affluent Japanese family and purchased by the LDS Church shortly thereafter. Central Branch. Aoyama District, on the famous Omote-sando Boulevard, Tokyo. It was Saturday morning, November 21, 1964. It was crisp outside.

"Your parents pray for you. The Lord loves you."

Tears continued to flow down the apostle's cheeks. His words quivered. But his characteristic deliberate soft speech still emerged.

"You can't do the Lord's work alone. Someday we are going to have to stand in the presence of God and give an account of our lives, including our lives in Japan. Think of the words, 'Thy scepter an unchanging scepter of righteousness and truth. Thy dominion an everlasting dominion.'"

This was Elder Hinckley's eighth visit to Japan, his sixth year as an LDS general authority and his third year as an apostle. His wife Marjorie sat by his chair on the stand along with Sister Peggy Andersen and President Andersen.

"I appreciate you. I cried when I saw you here because the harvest is great and the laborers are so few. Oh, the responsibility that is yours!

You few, you carry a responsibility for all the vast multitudes of Japan.

"God bless you, each of you. I humbly pray that His spirit will go before you to be on your right hand and on your left hand and that you will walk with a devotion that will shine on your faces. 'The rights of the Priesthood are inseparably connected with the powers of heaven,' and, '. . . the powers of heaven cannot be controlled nor handled only upon the principles of righteousness.'"

He then asked once again for any who were sick to come forth. A folding chair was placed in front of the room facing the missionaries.

An elder with a very serious back injury came forward. Elder Hinckley and the mission presidency came forward. The elder was anointed by one of them and then Elder Hinckley, standing behind the elder, placed his hands on the crown of the elder's head followed by the hands of all three mission presidency circling the missionary. The LDS apostle sealed the anointing by "power of the Melchizedek priesthood" and then spoke words of blessing upon the elder. The elder was blessed. One could see Paul at Lystra nineteen hundred years before healing the cripple.

A sister missionary then came forward. Likewise she received an anointing which was then sealed with a blessing by Elder Hinckley.

"President McKay said in his feeble voice as I was leaving the upper room in the temple to come here, 'God bless you. Give my love and my blessings to the missionaries and the saints wherever you find them.'

"That is as close, I don't like to say this, but that is perhaps as close as you will get to President McKay in this life. I do it with love in my heart for you in the name of Jesus Christ. Amen."[1]

Fifty-four year old Gordon B. Hinckley then commenced personally interviewing all 83 missionaries individually in a small room on the second floor of the Central Branch chapel for the rest of the day. Three blocks up the wide boulevard, the 1964 Tokyo Olympic games recently raged at the Sports Dome by Meiji Jingu Park. The US Air Base at Bienhoa, Saigon was recovering from a Viet Cong attack which destroyed six of its B-57's November 1st. US President John F. Kennedy had been assasinated by rifle bullets in Dallas a year minus one day before.

Such was a day in the life of Elder Gordon B. Hinckley.

HERITAGE

On the 128th birthday of the Church of Jesus Christ of Latter-day Saints, Gordon B. Hinckley stepped to the pedestal-podium of the April 6, 1958 LDS World General Conference in the Tabernacle at Salt Lake City's Temple Square in his acceptance speech as the newest assistant-to-the-twelve apostles. Into the old-style watermelon shaped microphone he spoke with his hands gripped tightly to both sides of the stand.

"Humbly I seek the blessings of the Lord. I am overwhelmed with a sense of inadequacy. I feel shaken. I would like to express appreciation to my father, who lies very critically ill in the hospital. No son ever had a better father. I'd like to express appreciation to my mother.

"I say these things because I'd like to make the point that all of us in our various situations are the result largely of the lives that touch ours. Today I feel profoundly grateful for all who have touched mine."[1]

Gordon B. Hinckley's legacy is rich in diverse heritage preparing him for his position as LDS seer, revelator and prophet in what members of the Church of Jesus Christ of Latter-day Saints call "the dispensation of the fullness of times."

It is impossible to know the man without knowing the fathers and mothers who prepared the path. If for any reason, you do not desire to explore this rich heritage, turn to page 109 of this book on "Boyhood."

Trusted Followers of William the Conqueror

When Norsemen Vikings moved down from Scandinavia to Gaul (future France) in 856 A.D., they established what is now dubbed "Normandy, France" and adopted the culture, ways and language of the local residents.

For as long as colonists occupied North American Massachusetts until the American Revolution, the Normans assimilated into Gaelic life until the great-great-great grandson of the original Norman King Rollo, assumed the Norman throne in 1035. This 3rd great grandson William, destined to be surnamed "the Conqueror", began 39 years of conquest from age 20.

By his side were always his "henchmen" (taken from *hengestman*, Middle English meaning "a groom", derived from *hengest*, meaning "stallion", hence "the groom for a stallion"). These henchmen stood by the haunch of William the Conqueror's horse and horses of his fellow soldiers, rendering assistance and aid not only in controlling the horse, but also in encouraging and supporting their warrior riders. Thus, over the ages of antiquity, "henchmen" came also to be used for "trusted followers."[2]

When William the Conqueror invaded England in 1066, one of these henchmen was Hugh de Grentesmenil with whom William the Conqueror was so pleased he gave a plat of real estate to him following subduing of England. It was later named "Henchman's Meadow" or "Hinc" (meaning "hauncy" and "lys" meaning "tract", thus "tract of land of a henchman").[3] This meadow became the genesis of the future surname of a prophet of God. Whether Hugh was of pure Norman blood, pure Gaelic blood, or a mixture of the two is not known.

This real property was devised to de Grentesmenil's posterity to the 1200's when Simon de Montfort inherited it. But he and his son both died in a battle against the King of Evesham fighting to secure representation rights for English Shires. Eventually, the House of Commons was organized as a result of that 1265 battle.

By 1280, Montfort's descendants first adopted the surname "de Hinckley" (the "de" being a carryover of the Norman French meaning "of").

The de Hinckley's became prominent in the area of Stafford, England. One was High Sheriff of County Stafford. Another was a justice of the peace, another a member of Parliament, others officers in the army or sergeant-at-arms to King Edward III, or body guard to a prominent Earl of Stafford named Hugh.

The sergeant-at-arms for Hugh accompanied him on a pilgrimage to "the Holy Sepulchre" in Israel and brought the Earl of Stafford's heart back in a silver casket when Hugh died on the trip. The Earl Hugh mentioned this de Hinckley in his will.

1st Generation - John de Henclyne, abt. 1326-

In 1348, John de Henclyne paid 16£ to the steward for the Archbishop of Canterbury for lease of real property in Mellefeld, Tenham, Kent County. He also paid an assessment for knighting the "Black Prince" in 1346. This gentleman is the first known ancestor of the pedigree leading to the prophet Gordon Bitner Hinckley. He also participated in the privileges from the crown extended to inhabitants of the Canterbury area who provided ocean vessels when needed for war.

England and County Kent, lower right hand, Leicestershire center

This association originated under French influence at the time of the Norman conquest. It was called the Cinque Ports organization (literally "5 seaports). Later three more port cities were added to the organization which still exists in England even today.[4]

2nd Generation - John Henclyf, abt. 1356-

John de Henclyne's son was also called John but he spelled his surname Henclyf (variant "Henclive"). Evidentally it was custom to name your first son at this time after the father. And if a son, even though not first born, died, several times in the Hinckley pedigree, the next or another son was given the same name, apparently in an effort to perpetuate that name as well as for fondness. Nothing further is known about John Henclyf, born about 1356.

3rd Generation - John Henclyf, abt. 1378-

But no doubt he was a devout Christian or how else would his son John Henclyf, born before 1401 around Tenham, Kent County have been so devoted. In the last will and testament, of this 3rd John in the long line of John's of the pedigree, he directed his sons to use "Johnthomas" and "Lytyl" gardens from his estate to "glaze a long window on the North bed of the Chyrche at Tenham." His sons did so and the bequest evidentally caused the parishioners to name the chancel after the benefactor. It is still called "Hincley Chancel." He is listed in a 1463 last will and testament listing his wife Jane and sons.

By 1433, the great majority of Hinckleys in Stafford had likewise moved to Kent County on the southeast tip of England. On the way from London to Dover they settled in such hamlets as Lenham, Harrietsham, and Tenham.

And in Leicestershire County close to the center of England, there is a small town called Hinckley and a "Hinckley Castle" evidencing additional Hinckley family presence. From Kent-County-Hinckleys came the first Hinckley family to immigrate to America.

4th Generation - John Henclyf, abt. 1400-

The unbroken chain of Johns continued with John Henclyf of Tenham, England, born about 1435, of Lenham, Kent County.

5th Generation - John Henkele, abt. 1435-

Next in line is John Henkele, first to be of Lenham, Kent County. His wife was named Marjorie and his three sons were John, Robert and Thomas. He is also documented in his will dated 1483/4 in which he requests interment at the St. Mary's churchyard in Lenham and devises his messuage and garden in Tenham with Choemarsh marsh and three acres called Cooneer to his wife for life, then to his son Thomas. To his son Robert he devised his messuage in Lenham and two acres of land next to Lovegrove.

6th Generation - John Henkle, abt. 1460-

The next son in the descendant blood-line is John Henkle, also of Lenham, Kent County. Although no will is presently extant for him, he was overseer of the will of his younger brother Robert.

7th Generation - John Hynckleye, abt. 1514-1577

His son John Hynckleye married Johane who bore two sons and a daughter to him. Robert, the direct ancestor of Gordon B. Hinckley, was the second son. John's first wife died June 23, 1563/4 and he remarried Aves Elles July 3, 1570 who bore him one daughter.

He executed a will one and a half months before his death. In it he requested burial in the "Haryetsham" churchyard and made a bequeath "to the poor."

He provided meticulously for the care of his surviving second wife and five year old daughter by providing life estates of his "tenement" on "Steden strete," where he last dwelled together with the adjacent barn and six acres called "Stylles feylds." He did likewise with two other parcels of land called Newman and Chawke. After a determinant time, the real property went to his son Robert, the next direct ancestor of President Gordon B. Hinckley.

8th Generation - Robert Hinckley, abt. 1537-1606

It is not known why Robert Hinckley, second son of John Hynckleye, 1514-1577, was bequeathed all of his father's realty. More than likely the first son John predeceased Robert. In any event, in addition to looking after his stepmother and stepsister in his probable birthplace of Harrietsham, Kent County, he started his own family by marrying Elizabeth Leese, widow of Thomas Leese of Throwly. Three sons were progeny. But Elizabeth died in 1574.

Robert remarried. And Katherine, his second wife, bore him four sons and four daughters starting February 2, 1575. The third son and seventh of these eight children was Samuel, who immigrated to America in 1635.

On April 6, 1605, 225 years to the day before organization of the Church of Jesus Christ of Latter-day Saints, Robert executed a will at age 68. He requested burial in the Harrietsham churchyard. And then the next thing he requested was that following his burial bread be made with funds from his estate and distributed to the poor people of the parish of Harrietsham and that an additional five shillings each be distributed to each of them.[5] This bequest is very significant for it shows the kind of devout Christians Gordon B. Hinckley's ancestors were. They were not misers nor insensitive to the needs of their fellowmen. These traits and feelings of the heart have carried forward to the 15th prophet of the LDS Church.

Next Robert devised 33 acres of woodland, messuage and barn in Harrietsham to his fifth son Stephen. To Samuel he bequeathed 30£ and to his youngest son John, then 14, he bequeathed 20£. All of his other possessions were given to his son Stephen from his second wife and surviving sons Thomas and Isaac of his first wife.

Eleven months after making his will, Robert was buried on March 27, 1606.[6] It is interesting to note that not only in Robert's case, but just about all of his ancestors above who died testate executed their wills just short weeks before their deaths. They all appeared to know when their mortal period was ending.

The Hinckleys in England were given a coat of arms with the motto "*Je ne change quen mourant* (French for "I only change in dying").[7] It is reproduced below as follows:

HINCKLEY

Hinckleys in America

9th Generation - Samuel Hinckley, 1589-1662

Samuel Hinckley, 1589-1662, was the 9th generation progeny from the earliest known Hinckley progenitor of Gordon B. Hinckley. He was baptized in St. John's Church in Harrietsham, Kent County, on May 25, 1589 and became a follower of the Puritan divine John Lothrop.

Samuel married Sarah Soule of Hawkhurst, Kent Copunty, born in 1600. Samuel was 24, Sarah almost 17 on their marriage day of May 7, 1617.

Their first of 16 children, a son named Thomas, was born in Hawkhurst, some 30 miles southwest of Harrietsham. Eight of the 16 children were born in England but four died there before the family migrated to the Americas.

By 1622, they had established their home at Tenderden, Kent County, half way between both of their respective parents' homes in Harrietsham and Hawkhyrst. Two years prior, when Samuel was 31 and Sarah 20, a group of Puritan immigrants had landed at a point on the North American Atlantic Coast and named it Plymouth. The passengers while on the ship *Mayflower* which carried them there had signed a "compact" while on the seas pledging in simple and short language a mutual covenant to live together in unity and good will.

John Lothrop had started out a pastor of the Church of England but disaffected to Puritanism and was imprisoned two years for his disloyalty to the Church of England. As a condition for his release, he agreed to leave Britain and in 1634, did so, traveling to this new little enclave of English Puritans establishing themselves in what was then the new Plymouth Colony.

The same year, while still living in Tenterden, Samuel, then 45, his wife Sarah, 34, and their four surviving children Thomas, Susannah, Sarah and Mary followed Lothrop with a group of others, sailing on the ship *Hercules* for the New England coast in America. His firstborn and son Thomas was 16; Susannah, 9; Sarah, 5; and Mary, 3.

The *Hercules* was a 200 ton sale ship captained by one John Witherly. The manifest included 103 men, women, children and servants. Thirty eight of these passengers were from Samuel and Sarah's home town. Included was a surgeon from Ashford with three children and three servants. There were 10 couples, 41 children, 10 singles, 17 servants, and 15 officers/sailors/staff. Samuel is listed on the ship's manifest as "gentry", or a "landowner" by profession. Sarah was about three months pregnant with her ninth child when they set sail March 25, 1634 from Sandwich, Kent County, England. On the open sea, Elizabeth was born before the ship and passengers arrived in Boston Harbor on September 18, 1634. They had been on the Atlantic Ocean for almost six months[8].

More than half of the passengers, including the Hinckley family, went to a small settlement established by Reverend John Lothrop called Scituate located on the the Atlantic shoreline about half way between Boston and Plymouth. They erected a home on lot 19 on a road dubbed "Kent Street", named after their former county of residence in England.

In 1637, two years after arriving in America, Samuel took a "freeman's oath", giving him rights to vote and exemption from municipal taxes. Then, after Samuel was born, the family moved 32 miles south and a little east down the coast of Cape Cod to a point where the cape curves like the front of bell tipped shoes to a settlement called Barnstable. There, Samuel lived out the rest of his life farming a large area and developing a new residential area called West Barnstable.

Samuel died and another son born was given the same name. Then a daughter came, then twin sons. All of these children died young, however, possibly due to the harsh environment and living conditions of the raw wilderness of New England.

It was at this time that Samuel's oldest son Thomas, now 22, married his bride Mary Richards from Weymouth, a small settlement about half way from Boston and the Hinckley's first home in Scituate.

Thomas located his home beside his father and mother's one story thatched roof home. West of Samuel and Sarah's small home was Rowley's Pond.

Samuel was called and served as a juror many times. He also surveyed roads, cutting the first paths in the pristine Massachusetts wilderness. He was kindly to strangers. But this was not tolerated by the Puritan rule. So two times he was charged with "entertaining strangers."

His friends Cudwerth, Hatherly and Rovinson were of the same mind. They, too, were of the liberal temperment. Reverend John Smith, temperment. Reverend John Smith, who married his first daughter Susannah when she was 18, also joined the same liberal group.

Cape Cod - Scituate between Boston & Plymouth, Barnstable on the shoe
Weymouth between Boston and Scituate

One time Samuel was also penalized ½ shilling for "keeping various swine unringed." But all this was part of life.

He dabbled in the sale of real property and his name is listed as Grantor many times in the land records. One such development was West Barnstable. Some time after Samuel moved to Barnstable, Reverend John Lothrop, Samuel and some 30 other men placed their eyes on another spot of land near Barnstable and incorporated it as West Barnstable.

Four miles west of Barnstable on the way to Plymouth is the site of Samuel's family farm. It was known as Goodspeed farm and a hearthstone from his home, demolished about 1870-80, was procured by a 9th generation descendant for conversion into an engraved monument to Samuel in 1917.

Samuel and Sarah's last two children, Samuel (the 3rd son so named as the other two had died), and John (the 2nd so named as the first had died young) both lived long lives and married.

Son Thomas had already started his public career when the 15th and 16th children of the first Hinckley couple in America were born. Grand jury duty and surveying roads were Thomas' involvement as he studied the practice of law.

At age 56, after a very prolific life as mother and spouse, Sarah died on August 18, 1656. Samuel was then about 67 years old. About one year four months later, he and Bridget, a widow of Robert Bodfish, joined in marriage December 16, 1657. They lived together about four years when Samuel executed a will at age 73, just 23 days before his death.

In his last testament, his second wife Bridget is given his home, the garden, a parcel of real property and his two cows named Prosper and Thrivewell together with "all the household stuff she brought with her."

His surviving daughters were presumably given portions of his estate at the time of their marriages. His sons Thomas, Samuel and John were given large tracts of his real estate. And the remainder of his estate was given in specific legacies to his son Thomas' children Samuel, Thomas, Mary and Bathsheba and to additional grandsons Samuel Cobb and Jonathan Cobb. His personal possessions were valued at 162£, 16 shillings. He died on October 31, 1662.[9]

Hinckley Line Pedigree of Gordon Bitner HINCKLEY

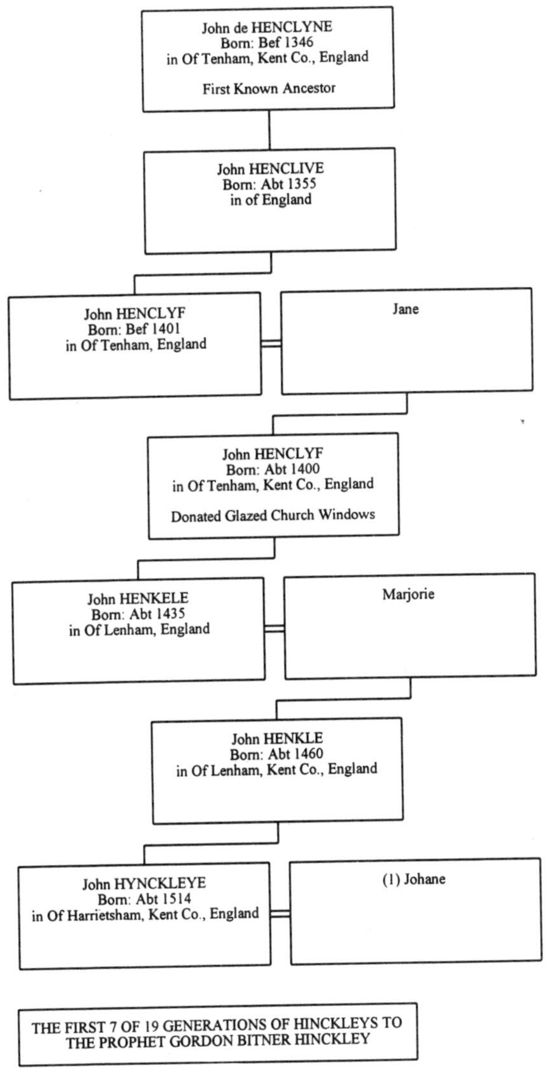

Hinckley Line Pedigree of Gordon Bitner HINCKLEY

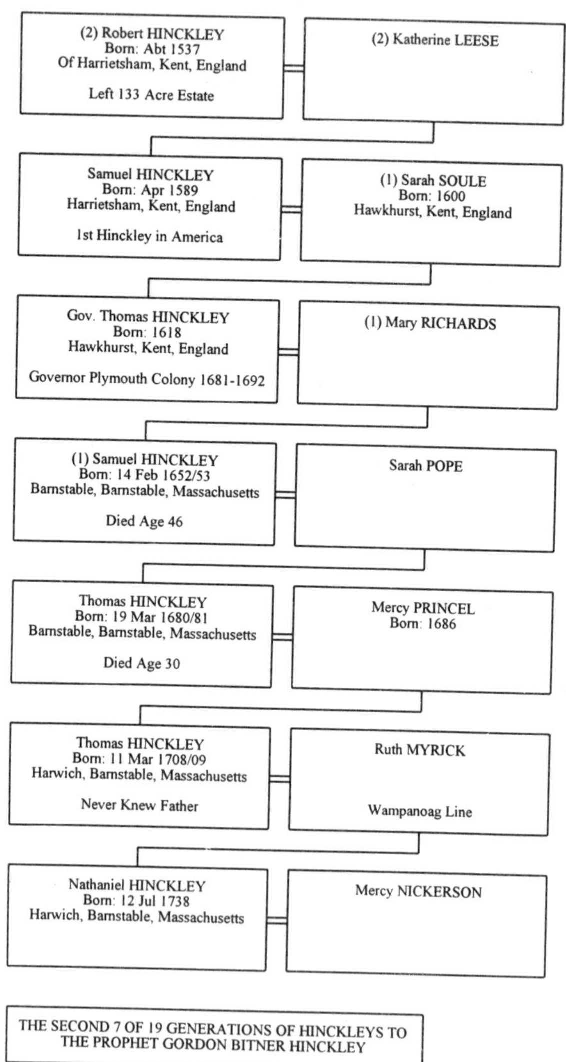

Plymouth Colony
Governor 1681-1692
Thomas Hinckley

10th Generation - Thomas Hinckley, 1619-1706

Thomas Hinckley was the first child and first son of Samuel and Sarah Soule Hinckley, baptized March 19, 1619 in Hawkhurst, Kent County, England. He spent his childhood and early teens in England. From Hawkhurst, his mother's home town, his parents and family moved to Tenterden, Kent County, located half way in between their respective parents' homes in Harrietsham and Hawkhurst. What education he received is not known. But when he immigrated to America with his parents and three sisters at age 16, it was not long before his appeared.

On March 25, 1634, he embarked on a six month sailing voyage across the Atlantic Ocean with his parents and sisters in the ship *Hercules* bound for religious freedom amongst the new Puritan colony established just 15 years before by *Mayflower* pilgrims at Plymouth in present day Massachusetts.

An additional sister Elizabeth was born at sea. The family and most of the 103 passengers immediately went to a new settlement called Scituate located on the seacoast of Cape Cod about half way between Boston and Plymouth. Here the family established a home on Kent Street on Lot 19.

Thomas was approaching manhood and became interested in Mary Richards from Weymouth, a settlement located a few more miles towards Boston from Scituate. Her parents were Thomas and Welthian (variant "Welthena") Loring Richards who first immigrated to a town called Dorchester in 1630 and moved to Weymouth, Massachusetts Colony, around 1639. Thomas Richards became an important miller for the Pilgrim colonists until he died in 1650 and his wife Welthian lived to at least 1679.

It is from this Richards line that the prophet Gordon Bitner Hinckley and Franklin Delano Roosevelt, 1882-1944, 32nd president of the United States of America, gain common heritage. Both have Thomas and Welthian Loring Richards as direct progenitors, each in nine descending generations from the couple.[10]

Thomas married Mary Richards on December 4, 1641 and they had eight children. The fifth child and first son Samuel, 1652/3-1697, is

President Gordon B. Hinckley's direct progenitor.

Thomas had moved with his family when 18 from Scituate to Barnstable, along the coast to the south and on the Cape Cod shoe as the coast bends east. Here he established his home to the side of his parents. It was near Rowley's Pond to the east of his parents thatched roof one story home.

When Thomas married, he was 22 years old and entered public service for the first time. He first served on the Grand Jury in 1641. Also, he started work as a surveyor, continuing this profession along with others until 1673. He further studied the law and after being on the Company Rolls in 1643, started the practice of law in 1644. He also once again commenced service on the Grand Jury, a service which did not terminate until 1685 when he was four years into his service as governor of the Plymouth Colony.

He and his father Samuel took the "freeman's oath" allowing them rights of suffrage and exemption from municipal taxes in 1645. In 1646, Thomas was elected deputy, a post as representative of Barnstable to the Plymouth Colonial Court, equivalent to a legislature in colonial America. He was reelected representative of Barnstable in 1649, 1654 and 1655.

Tragedy struck Thomas in 1859 when his wife Mary Richards passed away just three months from giving birth to the couple's 8th child. A family of eight children, all still young in age, were left. They were 15, 13, 11, 9, 7, 5, 2 and 3 months old.

However, providence provided a new mate for both Thomas and his new wife Mary Smith (Glover), a young 29 year old mother of two who had recently been widowed through the death of her first husband Nathaniel Glover of Dorchester. The two joined together in holy matrimony bringing together her two young children and the 8 young children of Thomas.

Although 12 years younger than Thomas, who was 41, Mary was said to have been very beautiful and refined, virtuous and praiseworthy. She continued in 43 years of marriage to Thomas and when she died in 1703, Thomas penned some of his heartfelt poetry to her memory.

During their marriage, nine children were born to their union, bringing to 17 the total natural children fathered by Thomas in his lifetime and 19 when you add the additional two children brought to the marriage by his second wife.

Through Thomas' public service, he acquired increasing familiarity with the government administration of Plymouth Colony until he rose in 1658 to the office of Assistant Governor to Governor Thomas Prince, 4th of the 6th governors to serve the Plymouth Colony. This post he continued through 1679 through the administration of the 5th governor Josias Winslow.

While Assistant Governor, Thomas also was tax collector of the minister's taxes in 1670 and a member of the Barnstable Town Council in 1675. These germinations of the free democratic spirit which burst into 1776 American independence 100 years later are very inspiring. He also was a member of the Central Board of the Massachusetts and Plymouth Colonies from 1673 to 1692. This board coordinated the two colonies' affairs.

In 1675, war was declared on the Wampanoag Indian Tribe after their leader, Philip, formed an alliance with 10,000 warriors of surrounding tribes and by surprise massacred 600 colonists in 13 towns. Philip was the second son of the Great Chief Massasoit who first made a treaty of peace with the 1620 Mayflower pilgrims. Governor Josias Winslow retaliated by taking the Indian's fort at Narraganset Swamp and Thomas, his assistant governor, was made commissioner over all of the Plymouth Colony's military war forces in what was called King Philip's War.

In August 1676 at the last great battle when chief Philip, given the English name by his father, was slain and the rebellion ended, Thomas Hinckley was present and participated.

In 1680, Governor Josias Winslow died at age 43 and Thomas' official title was changed from Assistant Governor to Deputy Governor. He was 61 years old at the time and performed all of the duties of governor until 1681 when he was officially elected to the office as the 6th and last real governor of the Plymouth Colony.

Thomas administered the affairs of Plymouth Colony until 1686. The prior Duke of York had ascended to the throne of England as James II in 1685 and rescinded the Plymouth Colony and many other colonial charters.

It took a year, however, before King James II sent formal commission to Sir Edmund Andros, appointed by James II as Governor of New York in 1674, to take over administration of all of the colonies in the north including Massachusetts, Maine, Plymouth, Rhode Island, Connecticut and New Hampshire under one consolidated "Dominion of New England" with headquarters in Boston. In 1688, New York and

Jersey were added to the dominion.

Governor Hinckley governed Plymouth Colony until Andros arrived with his credentials but was asked, along with several of his assistants, to sit on a Governor's Council with Andros in Boston. Elections were stopped, however and leaders were appointed by Andros during the short three years he was governor of the New England Dominion.

When William, prince of Orange, and his wife Mary, rightful heiress to the throne of England, entered England from the European Continent in 1689 to assert her rights as queen, King James II quickly fled to France and abdicated his throne. Andros' "imperious disposition" in his manner of management caused great resentment among the colonists.

So when news of William and Mary's ascension to the throne of England reached them, Andros was seized by patriots in Boston with many of his followers and imprisoned. He was then sent back to England for trial. The tide towards independence was rising in Boston, the birthplace of United States freedom.

Governor Thomas Hinckley was once again elected to administer Plymouth Colony in 1689 and also served on the Council of "King William's War." For the next three years he attempted to obtain a renewed charter for the colony from the new king and queen.

"If any colony was entitled to a royal charter," Governor Hinckley wrote, "Plymouth was, for it was the first that broke the ice and underwent ye brunt . . . for the inlargements of his Majestie's dominions in this heretofor most howling wilderness, amidst wild men and wild beasts."

But the future looked bleak for Plymouth. Thomas tried everything he could, however, asking Mr. Increase Mather, a delegate on his way from Massachusetts Colony to carry a petition for new charter to England, "Please also plead Plymouth's case."

Governor Hinckley wrote, "I see little or no likelihood of obtaining a Charter for us unless their majesties, out of their Royal bounty and clemencie graciously please to grant it . . . to their poor and loyal Subjects of this colonie."

Such was the case. Mr. Increase Mather, rather than pleading the cause of Plymouth, had Plymouth Colony merged with Massachusetts Colony in 1691 "on the pretext that the old colony had no hopes of procuring one of its own."[11] And the Plymouth Colony ended its 70 year existence.

Boston Patriots lead prisoner Sir Edmund Andros
through Boston Streets
after deposing him as
New England Dominion
Governor in 1689

Governor Hinckley then was asked to become a counselor to the combined colony, the equivalent of the Upper House of Parliament in governmental administration of the American Colonies. He filled his position as counselor as long as he was able.

Thomas kept a diary and avidly wrote poetry. He was said to have been the best read lawyer in the Plymouth Colony. He was studious in habits and taste and has at least three volumes of writings on deposit in the Boston Public Library and at least one segment of official and private correspondence and prose published in *Massachusetts Historical Collections*, Vol. 4, 4th section, (Boston: New England Historical Society, 1861).

But the real revelation of his true nature is given in the unique names he and his second wife Mary Smith (Glover) gave four of their daughters: Admire, Experience, Thankful, Reliance.[12] Two of these daughters married ministers. One other daughter, Abigail, also married a minister.

On October 16, 1700, at the age of 81, Thomas executed his last will and testament. His second wife Mary Smith had not yet passed away. So he gave her his "dwelling house, Eastern part" and profits from the "old house and orchard, all Cattle, horesekind, sheep and swine, with all my Personal estate" and profits from the north part of the barn.

To John, one of his three surviving sons, he devised the "Western part" of his "dwelling house."

He indicated he had already given each of his married children portions of his estate and the" greatest part of my lott whereon he built his dwelling house, et al "to his son Samuel, sole surviving son of his first wife Mary Richards. Therefore, he gave his surviving sons from his second marriage, John and Ebenezer, "all the rest of my lands and houseing."

It is incitive to read his indirect counsel in wisdom to his youngest sons, who were already 33 and 27 years old while his older son Samuel was then 48. "John and Ebenezer to maintain fence dividing their lands . . . and be Careful to prevent damage and discord between them."[13]

Almost three years later, his second wife Mary Smith predeceased him on July 29, 1703, almost 73. Thomas penned some of his heartfelt poetry to her memory. It evidentally was a tremendous loss. Then almost three years later, he passed away on April 25, 1706 at the age of 87.

Moore, in his *Lives of the Governors of Massachusetts* sumarizes Governor Thomas Hinckley's tenure as follows:

> During half a century he held offices of trust and power in the Old Colony, and had a controlling influence over the popular mind. He was the architect of his own fortune in life; the builder of his own reputation. He was a man of good common sense, and of sound judgment; honest and honorable in all of his dealings; industrious, persevering and self-reliant; and, if it be any praise, he was the best read lawyer in the Colony. He had some enemies–it would have been a miracle if so prominent and independent a man had none. Barren trees are not pelted. The Quaker influence was arrayed in hostility to him. He examined every question submitted to him in its legal aspects, and, viewing his acts from that standpoint, he was seldom wrong. He was a rigid independent in religion, and his tolerant opinions, though in advance of the times, did not come up to the standards of the present. Some of his acts I shall leave for others to defend, but that he was the intolerant and cruel man that some infatuated bigets of his time represented him to be, the facts will not sustain. He was a living man and never allowed his faculties to rust by inaction, and, to the last, could draft an instrument with as much clearness and precision as in his early manhood. A monument was erected to his memory in 1829.[14]

His burial place is in the cemetery on the hill in between Barnstable and West Barnstable where an elaborate tombstone is a marker. Sadly there appears not to be any portrait or sketch of his likeness found to date.

Colony Governor to Latter-day Saints

11th Generation - Samuel Hinckley, 1652-1697

Plymouth Colony Governor Thomas Hinckley's firstborn son Samuel came into the world on February 14, 1652 at Barnstable, Plymouth Colony. He spent his childhood with his large family of brothers and sisters from his mother Mary Richards and also 11 additional children, two from the first marriage of his father's second wife Mary Smith (Glover) and nine new brothers and sisters she bore his father.

Then at age 24 he married Sarah Pope, daughter of Thomas and Sarah Jenning Pope, of Sandwich, Plymouth Colony. She evidentally was illiterate and signed her name with an "X" on documents.

Samuel was given a large tract of land on his father's farm called the Timber Lands on which he built his family home and had 11 children. His first son and third child Thomas became the direct ancestor to the prophet Gordon B. Hinckley. All of Thomas and Sarah's children were born by the end of 1697.

Samuel's mother Mary Richards passed away three months after giving birth to her eighth child Mehetable in 1659. Samuel was only seven at the time so had little time to be with her. But Mary Smith, a young widow of 29 filled in well. She married Samuel's father the following year.

Samuel evidentally farmed to support his family. In 1675, he did serve as a militiaman in the war against King Philip and his alliance of 10,000 renegade indians.

Shortly before Samuel passed away, he executed a will dated March 12. He states, "First I comitt my soul to God in Christ who gave it me and my body to decent burial when God shall please to call me hence."[15]

Then he died rather young on March 19, 1697 at age 46. His estate included livestock, oxen, horses and swine. Wool and flax, "loomes and geers" were also there. Total estate value was 135£.

Following his death, his wife Sarah Pope remarried in a year to Thomas Huckins. Sarah and her second husband Thomas had one daughter in addition to raising the rest of Mr. Huckins eight children from his previous marriage.

Apparently the 11 children of Samuel and Sarah were raised by others. Accordingly, Samuel Hinckley's children moved to Harwich, Massachusetts; then to Truro, Massachusetts and some later to Maine.

When Sarah executed her will of January 5, 1726 or 7, she mentioned her daughter Hannah and granddaughter from the Huckins marriage and eight children and two granddaughters of the Hinckley marriage including son Thomas Hinckley who had died prior to her death. She died sometime between Jan. 5 1726 and July 5, 1727.[16]

12th Generation - Thomas Hinckley, 1680/1-1710

Even though Thomas Hinckley, the first son and third child born to his parents Samuel Hinckley and Sarah Pope, was mentioned in his mother's will, he actually predeceased her 16 years before. He died at the young age of 30.

But from his birth in Barnstable, Plymouth Colony, on March 19, 1680/1 it appears he moved further out on the peninsula of Cape Cod to the town of Harwich, located very close to the front of the shoe shaped cape. His wife Mercy Princel was born 1686 and they had two sons after their marriage in 1705.

The first son was Joshua, born March 29, 1707 in Harwich, Massachussetts and the second Thomas, Gordon B. Hinckley's direct ancestor, born the next year or the following year, also in Harwich.

On one occasion after his father had died in 1697, Thomas and his mother Sarah signed a document with an "X" indicating both had little opportunity for formal education.

But it appears in Thomas's short 30 year life, he sustained himself and small family through farming like his father Samuel.

Thomas died in 1710 leaving his 24 year old wife. Administration of his estate was granted his widow October 11, 1710. Six months later, she remarried her second husband William Crosby April 26, 1711 at the hands of a justice of the peace. Mr. Crosby gave her two young sons, only three and one or two years old, a father to raise them.

13th Generation - Thomas Hinckley, 1708/9-1789

Thomas Hinckley, who had been born March 11, 1709/9 in Harwich, Barnstable, Massachusetts, never remembered his natural father for he was only one or two years old at the time of his death. But undoubtedly he knew his stepfather William Crosby who married his mother Mercy Princel shortly after Thomas' father died.

Not much is presently known of his personal life. But undoubtedly he grew up and lived in Harwich, Massachusetts at least until 1737 when the first Nathaniel Hinckley in Gordon B. Hinckley's pedigree was born there.

Harwich is located on the southern side of the great cape named Cod, at the bottom of the front of the shoe shaped cape separating Cape Cod Bay to the north from Nantucket Sound on the south. These bays and sounds of the Atlantic Ocean are only two miles to the south, five miles to the north and 5½ miles to the east of Harwich, Massachusetts. Cranberry bogs, wild and uncultivated, grew rich in the area. They invited their new inhabitants to partake of their deliciousness in late Fall.

At age 25½, Thomas married 19 year old Ruth Myrick in Chatham, Massachusetts, located just five miles directly east of Harwich and only one-half mile from the Atlantic Ocean. Ruth was the 3rd great-granddaughter of the Wampanoag chief Quadequina, young brother of the "great chief" Massasoit who befriended the first permanent Pilgrims with a treaty of peace. Through her, Gordon B. Hinckley derives his Native American heritage.

And Ruth gave her father's first name Nathaniel to her son, Gordon B. Hinckley's direct progenitor.

The exciting times of Thomas and Ruth's lives were also monumental. Thomas lived through the American crescendo for freedom. The American patriot & diplomat Benjamin Franklin was born only three years before Thomas and had left Boston for Philadelphia by 1723. By 1732, he was publishing his *Poor Richard's Almanac* along with the forrunner of the *Saturday Evening Post* magazine.

Thomas lived when the French and Indian War was being fought from 1756 to 1763 to basically determine control over Canadian and Eastern North American soil. Young George Washington engaged in his first diplomacy and military campaign during this time. In 1763, possession of all of Canada and all territory east of the Mississippi River was given Britain. Thomas died just six years later at about 60 years of age.

14th Generation - Nathaniel Hinckley, 1738-?

Nathaniel was 31 years old when his father Thomas passed away. His life was also one of excitement. The acquisition of the eastern territory and Canada by Britain through the treaty ending the French and Indian War actually strengthened colonist's desires for independence and rumblings for freedom from Britain continually increased until Paul Revere made his famous horeride to Lexington on

April 18, 1775 advising Minutemen militia along the way of approaching British troops. The first battle of the American Revolutionary War started at Lexington. Nathaniel would have been 37 at this time. The apprehensions and anxieties of revolutionary war surely resided in every heart in Massachusetts at that time.

Nathaniel could have lived to witness the declaration of independence of July 4, 1776 and finally the promulgation of the constitution of the United States and ratification by the last colony Rhode Island in 1790.

He had been born in Harwich, Barnstable, Massachusetts on June 25, 1738 and was almost 23 when he married Mercy Nickerson at Chatham, Barnstable, Massachusetts on January 21, 1761. Just as his father Thomas had married a resident of Chatham, so did Nathaniel. He had been named after his mother's father, the first "Nathaniel" in what would prove to be a name which would carry down to also become the middle name of Gordon B. Hinckley's grandfather. Thomas' death date is not known.

Nathaniel and Mercy had a son they also named Nathaniel, born in the summer of 1769 in Harwich.

15th Generation - Nathaniel Hinckley, 1769-1849

When the second Nathaniel was born on July 12, 1769 at Chatham, Cape Cod, Massachusetts, the Boston Tea Party was about to occur three years later. He, too, lived during a period of exciting American history during which the patriots declared independence and uncertain war commenced. During these war years and carving of the American Constitution, Nathaniel matured.

He was 22 years old when he married Rhoda Barber at Elizabethtown, Essex, New York on December 29, 1791. She was born September 3, 1773 in New York Colony at Elizabethtown Essex. This birth in New York was to influence the migration of the future Hinckley progenitors of the Prophet Gordon B. Hinckley from the new state of Massachusetts .

Nathaniel passed away March 22, 1849 at Port Jackson, Clinton, New York. Before his death, on December 5, 1794, he fathered the third Hinckley given the name Nathaniel in Elizabethtown, New York.

16 Generation - Erastus Nathaniel Hinckley, 1794-1831

This great-grandfather of the future prophet Gordon B. Hinckley married Lois Judd in January 1821 when he was 27. She was the sixth of 10 children born at Bastard, in Leeds, Ontario, Canada to Arza Judd

Hinckley Line Pedigree of Gordon Bitner HINCKLEY

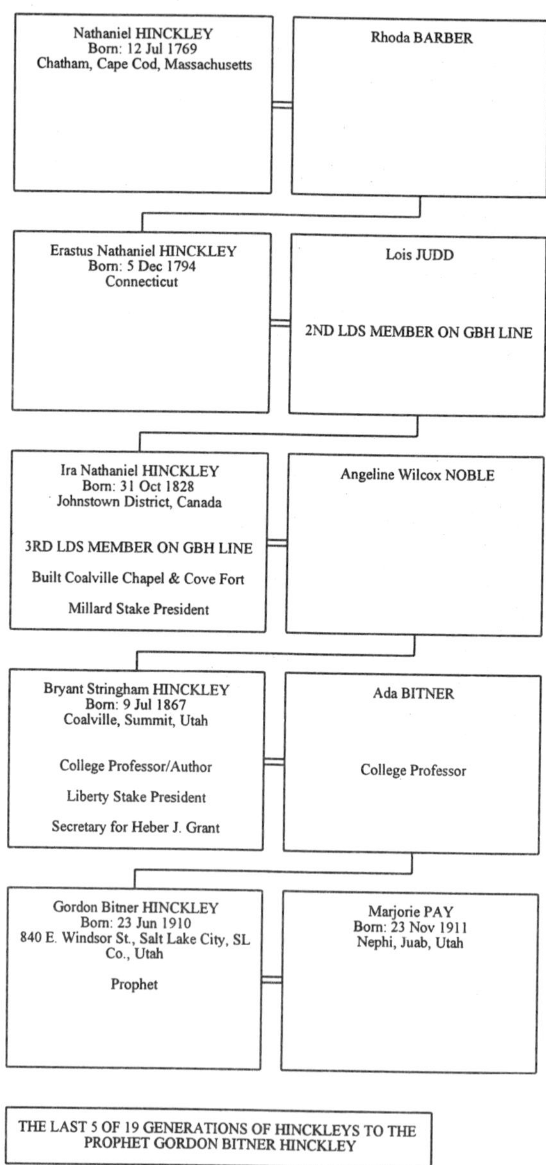

and Lois Knapp on September 15, 1805 and was 16 at their marriage, 11 years younger than Erastus.

Erastus broke from agrarian livelihood and obtained employ as a boatman on the Great Lakes near his home. One chronicle says he was born in Connecticut. In any event, his youth and early manhood was spent in and around New York and the Great Lakes of Ontario and Erie.

At times in his life, he also was a mechanic, probably connected with his boatman work. In addition, he became a shoemaker.

The couple resided in Rochester, New York for a while and then moved to Lois' home town of Leeds, Ontario, Canada. There five children were born including four sons and a daughter. The third of their sons is Gordon B. Hinckley's grandfather Ira Nathaniel Hinckley, born in Leeds, Canada on October 30, 1828[17].

Two years later, Erastus, at the untimely age of 36, died of tuberculosis on September 8, 1831 at Leeds. His widow Lois was destitute with five extremely young children. She was not yet 26.

As Providence would provide, however, she remarried but also died just 12 years later in 1845 at age 38. However, Providence also would in about five years give her, her parents and family, her relatives and Gordon B. Hinckley's grandfather and grandfather's brother an opportunity to receive knowledge of the Church of Jesus Christ of Latter-day Saints before Lois died.

Mayflower and Wampanoag Progenitors

In 1609, Stephen Hopkins, age 29, signed on as minister's clerk with the *Sea Venture* sailing from London June 2 for Jamestown, Virginia Colony. He was born in 1580 and baptized at Wotton Underedge Parish in Wortley, Gloucester County, England. He married Constance Dudley sometime around 1604 and had a young daughter Constance, age 4, and son Giles, age 2, at the time he sailed. Giles is Gordon B. Hinckley's direct ancestor. Stephen's father was probably Stephen, a clothier, of Wortley.

The first colonists had arrived in Jamestown, Virginia Colony in May 1603 and were beginning their creation of the first permanent colony of English on the Eastern coast of North America.

Stephen appears to have been of a very adventuresome spirit coaching him into taking this voyage which would prove a precursor to becoming one of 102 famous pilgrims who sailed to Plymouth in 1620.

The Wampanoags at Plymouth

At this same time, a federation of native American tribes living at Cape Cod and vicinity were experiencing culture shock from contact with white skinned sailors who occasionally visited their shores. The first visitor was Gosnold Bartholomew in 1602 and then Samuel de Champlain in 1604.

The nine chiefs who governed the federation of some 30 tributary tribes of the Wampanoag native Americans included Quadequina, a tall young man of very modest and seemly countenance.[1] He was called "Atauskawaw", meaning "Lord."[2]

His younger brother Akkompoin, called "Vucumpowet" was another chief. And his older brother Ousamequin, meaning "Yellow Feather", was head of the Chiefs Council, also called "Massasoit" or "Great Chief."[3] These chiefs were to play a great part in the colonization of the Plymouth Colony in 1620 and Quadequina was to become the direct ancestor of Gordon B. Hinckley.

Marooned on Bermuda

Stephen Hopkins displayed his independent spirit and alternate meekness when the ship he rode entered a hurricane and was washed ashore on Bermuda 600 miles directly east of North Carolina. The 150 survivors were marooned on the island nine months until they built two ships ultimately taking them to Jamestown.

Stephen read the Psalms on the Sabbath and acquired a good knowledge of the scriptures during the nine months, but also became an outspoken advocate for freedom from the King of England arguing the Virginia Colony jurisdiction was limited to Jamestown and the shipwreck on Bermuda separated the survivors from control of the Government of England.

The majority felt otherwise, however, and placed him in manacles where he was sentenced to death by court-martial. "But so penitent hee was and made so much moane, alleadging the ruine of his Wife and Children in this his trespasse," William Strachey records, friends obtained pardon from the governor to be appointed over Jamestown Lord De la Warr who was with the marooned group along with official instructions for Jamestown and his lieutenant-governor, high marshal, admiral and vice-admiral. The two new vessels *Patience* and *Deliverance*, fitly named by the passengers who suffered the tribulation they endured, once completed, arrived in Jamestown just three years and 10 days after the first colonists there.[4]

Stephen spent about two years in Jamestown learning much including the ways of the native American. He then returned to his home in England located outside London Wall on the high road entering the city at Aldgate near Heneage House. There he associated with the group called Merchant Adventurers. Thomas Weston was the manager. Future Mayflower passengers John Carver and William Bradford were neighbors. Additional promoters of the future pilgrim voyage Robert Cushman, London agent for the Pilgrims, and Edward Southworth, a future immigrant to New England, all influenced Stephen and his family in their future decision to join the Mayflower passengers.

Stephen worked as a tanner and leathermaker up to the time his family left for America. His wife Constance died sometime before 1617, however.

The Whaler Visitors and Wampanoag Plague

Back at Cape Cod and future Massachusetts and vicinity, John

Smith visited in 1614. He made one of the first maps of the area but also kidnapped 24 native Americans and took them back to Spain and England for slave trading. One of these kidnapped Wampanoags was Squanto, called Tisquantumi, later to figure prominently in the diplomatic and economic development of the Plymouth Colonists. Jamestown had brought the first black slaves to American shores the year before.

Who knows but what John Smith's "whalers" also brought the small pox and yellow fever to the New England coast natives for the very next year in 1615 a great plague hit the people of the Wampanoags. Their great population of 100,000 was almost completely annihilated by either small pox or yellow fever or both leaving only approximately 5,000 survivors by 1617.

The Mayflower Voyage

Stephen Hopkins remarried around 1617 to Elizabeth Fisher and had one of their eventual seven children by her two years before the ship *Mayflower* made its historic voyage to the northern coast of America. Elizabeth was expecting their first son at the time Merchant Adventurers' manager Thomas Weston convinced the Hopkins family to join the pilgrim group going to America. The child was the only one born at sea during the voyage and therefore christened "Oceanus" after the sea. He lived only a few years in the hostile environment of Plymouth, however.

Stephen was one of three "Masters", commanding officers assisting the ship's Captain, during the voyage. But he was one of the "strangers" on the voyage, not a strict separatist desiring to split from the Church of England's orthodoxy. He held particular views and undoubtedly was one of the independent thinkers desiring no control by others. His attitude regarding regimentation was displayed clearly in his previous campaign for mutiny while marooned on Bermuda. But his acquired skills and knowledge of the Americas, marinering, and diplomacy with the native Americans made him much more the asset for the pilgrims.

The free spirit of the "strangers" on board prompted promulgation of the "Mayflower Compact", one of the important precursors to America's eventual freedom documents. William Bradford, future second Governor of the Plymouth Colony, chronicled this written compact was "occasioned partly by the discontented and mutinous speeches that some of the strangers amonst them had let fall from them in the ship."

The voyage was originally supposed to land the passengers in the vicinity of Virginia territory close to Jamestown. But it hit shore much further north. This prompted those advocating individualism to express their wish to "live as they wished and to take orders from no one."[5]

The disputed opinion is corroborated by Winslow who wrote "some [were] not well affected to unitie and concord, but gave some appearances of faction [and thus] it was thought good . . . that we should combine together in one body, and to submit to such government and governours, as we should by common consent agree to make and choose."[6]

So while the *Mayflower* stood in Provincetown Harbor before setting foot on Plymouth Rock, the men who were free on board, including Stephen Hopkins, were solicited to sign in the Captain's cabin a very short and succinct document later to become known as the Mayflower Compact which condensed simply stated "that the individual would subject himself to majority rule."[7] Stephen was 14th signer.

Meeting with the Wampanoags

Only 99 stepped off the Mayflower. One died at sea, four while at harbor, one was born at sea (Stephen's son Oceanus Hopkins), and one was born at harbor before debarking. Only 52 of the 99 were still alive 11 months later when the next ship from England arrived. Contrary to many misconceptions, the *Mayflower* never returned to Plymouth again. Other ships came, but not the *Mayflower*. Stephen Hopkins' son Giles was 11 when they arrived at Plymouth in December 1620. His second wife Elizabeth Fisher, daughter Damaris and newly born infant son Oceanus were also with him along with two male servants.

The pilgrims were unaware of the disastrous epidemic which had plagued the Wampanoags and the Wampanoags were similarly incognizant of the rapidly declining numbers of the original pilgrims. So both groups, fearing for their survival, were well conditioned to cooperate in peace.

During the first months after arrival of the *Mayflower* pilgrims, Massasoit (the Great Chief) of the Wampanoags and his other chiefs sought out those who might help them communicate with the new Whitemen. One of these was Samoset, a native American chief of the Pemaquid tribe in Maine. Samoset had acquired some English by association with white sailors fishing along the shores of Maine.

Also among the Wampanoags was Squanto who had been kidnapped by John Smith in 1614 and sold into slavery in Spain. He had somehow obtained his freedom and lived in England where he acquired remarkable English until he was taken back to New England in 1619 by friendly sailors..

The Spring came and with it the first overture of peace from the local Wampanoags. Samoset was selected as the first emissary. He approached the camp of the pilgrims in March 1621 and the pilgrims quickly turned to Stephen Hopkins for help. Samoset was placed for the night in the home of the Hopkins.

Samoset surprised the colonists when he greeted them, "Much welcome, Englishmen, much welcome, Englishmen." He told of a "great chief" who would like to visit the camp with his other leaders. One week later, Massasoit came into camp. He was accompanied by Samoset and Squanto and his brother Quadequina and Akkompoin and others of the Council of Chiefs of the Wampanoag Federation of tribes. Other warriors also came creating a total entourage of 20 visitors.

Great was the impression and indelible the memory of the event. The chiefs were all elaborately dressed with skins and plumes of brilliant colors.[8] Massasoit, representing the chieftains, welcomed the colonists and offered to assist and support them in their new settlement. He also offered an agreement of friendship which was reduced to English parchment and signed by all of the chieftains present including Quadequina. The excellent English of Squanto facilitated easy communication between the groups.

Cooperation with the Wampanoags

In July of 1621, Stephen Hopkins was once again called upon to assist by visiting Massasoit. He assisted Miles Standish in a mission to make amends with the Wampanoags for corn he and his men had taken during his first exploration trip of Cape Cod. Trumpery presents were presented to Massasoit and much good will created at little expense.[9]

Stephen also was one of three to assist in the first land expedition away from shore. How much language he knew is not exactly known, but it is certain he was called upon continuously to interpret when meeting with the Wampanoags.

November 1621 brought the first harvest and with it the gratitude which turned into the first Thanksgiving in America. Quadequina and his brother Massasoit were there along with many other native Americans who enjoyed the bounties of wild turkey and corn which the

Wampanoags had taught the colonists how to grow fertilizing each stock with a fish from the sea.

During these meetings, numerous exchanges were made. Quadequina was given a knife and jewel to hang when he took custody of Edward Winslow on one occasion as hostage to guarantee the safety of some of his own warriors until they returned from a visit to the colony settlement. "Pots of liquor, a good amount of Bisket and some butter were also willingly accepted."[10]

Life at Plymouth

At Plymouth, Stephen became a merchant and farmer. He built the first wharf and then turned around and sold it for 60£. He received six acres of land in an allocation of 1623 which he farmed and cultivated. At a settlement in Yarmouth, he built a house but then gave it to his oldest son Giles and returned to Plymouth. He maintained his first home built at the east corner of Main and Leyden Streets and there ran both a general merchandising store and tavern.

The Governor of Plymouth Colony made him his assistant during the years of 1633 through 1636. But although he was "intelligent, robust and enterprising, practical, quick to see a point and fertile in expedients, . . . he was touchy and not at all averse to settle with anybody who crossed his path."[11]

As a result, these traits got him in dutch with authority. He got in a fight with a John Tisdale and on June 7, 1636 was found guilty of battery, paying 5£ fine and 40 shillings damages to Mr. Tisdale. On several occasions in 1637 and 1638, he was punished for allowing excessive alcoholic consuption in his house by his servants and others on the Sabbath and at other times. He also was fined for allowing servants and others to play "shovel board" in his house. On one occasion he was "committed to ward" in contempt of court for failing to take responsibility for one of his servants Dorothy Temple until he accepted maintenance and support for her for the remaining term of her servitude to him.

As an aggressive enterpriser, he also was fined several times for selling beer, wine and nutmeg at exhorbitant prices.

But, in 1642, he, possibly as much for punishment as well as for praise, was given the responsibility to take charge of a repetitive delinquent named Jonathan Hatch "and the said Mr. Hopkins to have a speciall care of him."[12]

Mayflower Pilgrim Line Pedigree of Gordon Bitner HINCKLEY

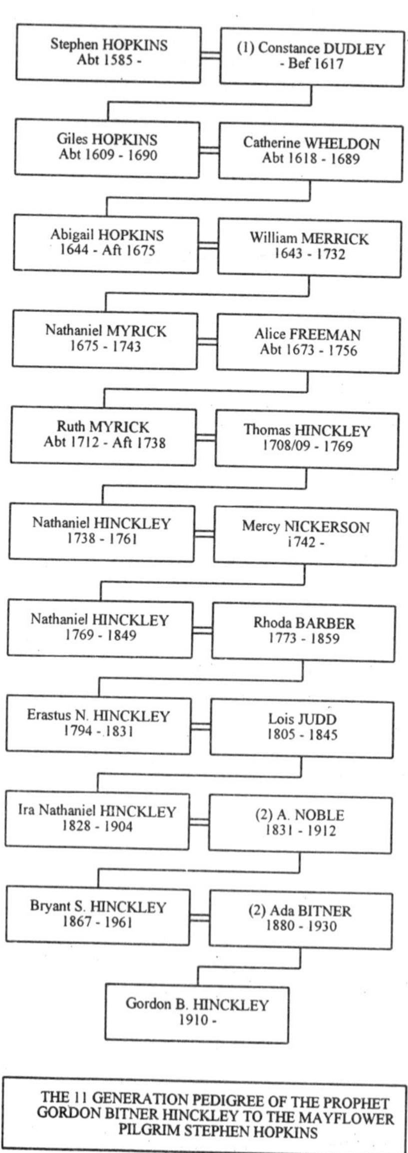

Margaret of Quadequina

Two of the early immigrants to Plymouth Colony were Gabriel Wheldon, of Arnold, Nottingham, England, and his brother (name unknown). Gabriel had been married in England before sailing to America but his first wife named Margaret evidently was deceased at the time of his migration.

Both brothers had a free spirit much like Stephen Hopkins and found their way to the camps of the Wampanoags. There they both fell in love with two of the daughters of chief Quadequina, younger brother of the Great Chief. They each married and Gabriel gave his second wife the English name "Margaret" after his first spouse.

The two counseled with their father-in-law and his older brother Massasoit regarding what to do. The Plymouth Colony would probably punish them for their intermarriage. Massasoit advised them to return to the colony and all would be well.

The Plymouth Colony tribunals saved face by banishing the couples from Plymouth for life but did not send them back to England. Gabriel and Margaret established their home in Barnstable where the Hinckleys came in the late 1630's and here Gabriel and Margaret raised a large family of girls.[13]

One of these was Catherine "Catone" Wheldon who married Stephen Hopkins' oldest son Giles on October 9, 1639. Giles had been given the home his father had built in Yarmouth and the couple established their home and raised four children there. When Giles' father Stephen passed away about July 1644, his father left an estate worth 130£ by testamentary disposition including bulls, cattle, a horse, home, household goods, clothing, tools and 17£ plus in accounts receivable.

The fourth of 10 children and second of five daughters Abigail Hopkins was born October 1644 in Eastham, Barnstable, Plymouth Colony just a few months after his father's death.

Giles was conveyed 100 acres by his younger brother Caleb about the time of Abigail's birth and shortly thereafter established residence in Eastham. He was a surveyor of highways in 1660, 1662 and 1671. He was slandered by one William Leverich sometime before October 1654 and won a demation suit aagainst him October 3, 1654. He then served on juries in 1667 and 1668. He also left a will and a codicil admitted to probate April 16, 1690.

Wampanoag Line Pedigree of Gordon Bitner HINCKLEY

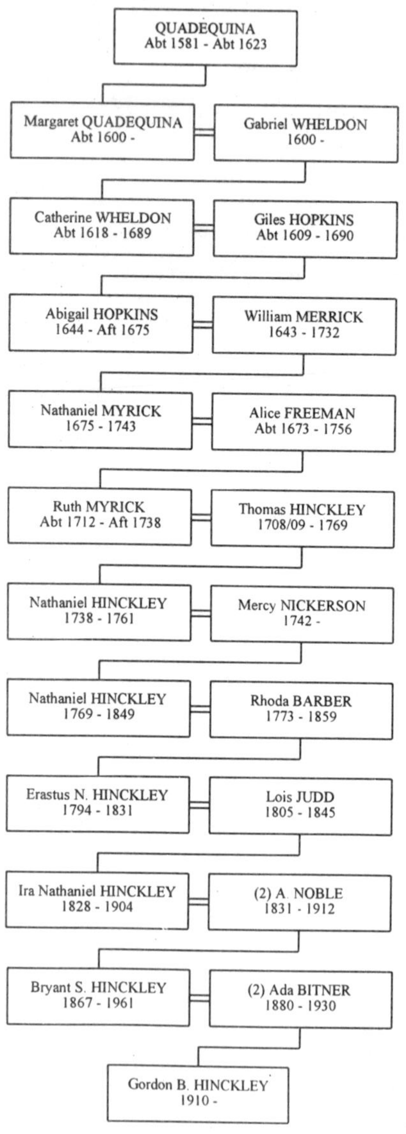

THE 12 GENERATION PEDIGREE OF THE PROPHET GORDON BITNER HINCKLEY TO THE NATIVE AMERICAN WAMPANOAG FEDERATION OF THE ALGONQUIN NATION

Mayflower Pilgrim & Wampanoag Kinship

of Gordon Bitner HINCKLEY

Name	Relationship with Gordon HINCKLEY
BARBER, Rhoda	2nd great-grandmother
BITNER, (2) Ada	Mother
DUDLEY, (1) Constance	8th great-grandmother
FREEMAN, Alice	5th great-grandmother
HINCKLEY, Bryant Stringham	Father
HINCKLEY, Erastus Nathaniel	Great-grandfather
HINCKLEY, Gordon Bitner	Self
HINCKLEY, Ira Nathaniel	Grandfather
HINCKLEY, Nathaniel	3rd great-grandfather
HINCKLEY, Nathaniel	2nd great-grandfather
HINCKLEY, Thomas	4th great-grandfather
HOPKINS, Abigail	6th great-grandmother
HOPKINS, Giles	7th great-grandfather
HOPKINS, Stephen	8th great-grandfather
JUDD, Lois	Great-grandmother
MERRICK, William	6th great-grandfather
MYRICK, Nathaniel	5th great-grandfather
MYRICK, Ruth	4th great-grandmother
NICKERSON, Mercy	3rd great-grandmother
NOBLE, (2) Angeline Wilcox	Grandmother
QUADEQUINA	9th great-grandfather
QUADEQUINA, Margaret of	8th great-grandmother
WHELDON, Catherine "Catone"	7th great-grandmother
WHELDON, Gabriel	8th great-grandfather

Abigail and William Merrick

Abigail married William Merrick on May 23, 1667 in Eastham and mothered Nathaniel Merrick in 1674/75. The family resided in Eastham, Plymouth Colony, where William was also a surveyor of highways in 1678 and 1679 and a grand juror in 1684.

The family then moved to Harwich before 1694 and petitioned for incorporation of the town. A church was built in the city in 1700 by seven residents including himself. Abigail, however, passed away and William remarried a widow by the name of Elizabeth whose first husband was Jabez Snow. William then passed away testate by will proved November 29, 1732.

Nathaniel & Alice Freeman Merrick

Nathaniel married Alice Freeman about 1699 in Hardwick, Massachusetts Colony and fathered Ruth Myrick about 1712. He was a yeoman in February 1741/2, which was a small farmer.

Ruth Myrick married into the Hinckley family on March 31, 1730 to Thomas Hinckley, born March 11, 1708/9, the great-grandson of Governor Thomas Hinckley.

Through this chain of descent, President Gordon Bitner Hinckley claims good Mayflower passengers and native American ancestry.

President Franklin Delano Roosevelt Relationship

Not only do the genes of native Americans and Plymouth Colony founders run through President Gordon Bitner Hinckley, he also possesses common genes with Franklin Delano Roosevelt, longest term president of the United States of America.

The relationship arises from the marriage of Thomas Richards to Welthian Loring. This couple first arrived in America in 1630 and settled in Dorchester. They then moved to Weymouth, Massachusetts Colony, around 1639. Thomas Richards became an important miller for the colonists until he died in 1650. His wife Welthian, variant "Welthena", lived until at least 1679.

Thomas and Welthian had two daughters who take their blood to President Hinckley and President Roosevelt. Daughter Mary became the first wife of Plymouth Colony Governor Thomas Hinckley on December 4, 1641 and daughter Alice bore a daughter named Anna who married Ephraim Hunt.

From the Hunt marriage, Elizabeth Hunt was born, who bore a daughter Mercy Pope, who bore a son Joseph Church, who bore a daughter Deborah Church, who bore a son Warren Delana, who bore a daughter Sarah Delano, who was the mother of President Franklin Delano Roosevelt, born January 30, 1882 in Hyde Park, New York to a wealthy railroad vice president.

President Roosevelt was the 5th cousin of another American president Theodore Roosevelt, 1858-1919. The relation actually helped "FDR"'s political career, but not in the way expected. Theodore Roosevelt served as United States president from 1901-1909 but then made another bid for the presidency as a third party candidate in the campaign of 1912. But FDR, as a young 30 year old New York State senator, lent his support to democratic candidate Woodrow Wilson who won the election because of the divided republican party.

As a reward for his support, Woodrow Wilson made FDR Secretary of the Navy, a position he enjoyed. He was an avid sailor and loved ships. During World War I, he was widely publicized when he visited

Kinship of Gordon Bitner Hinckley & Franklin Delano Roosevelt

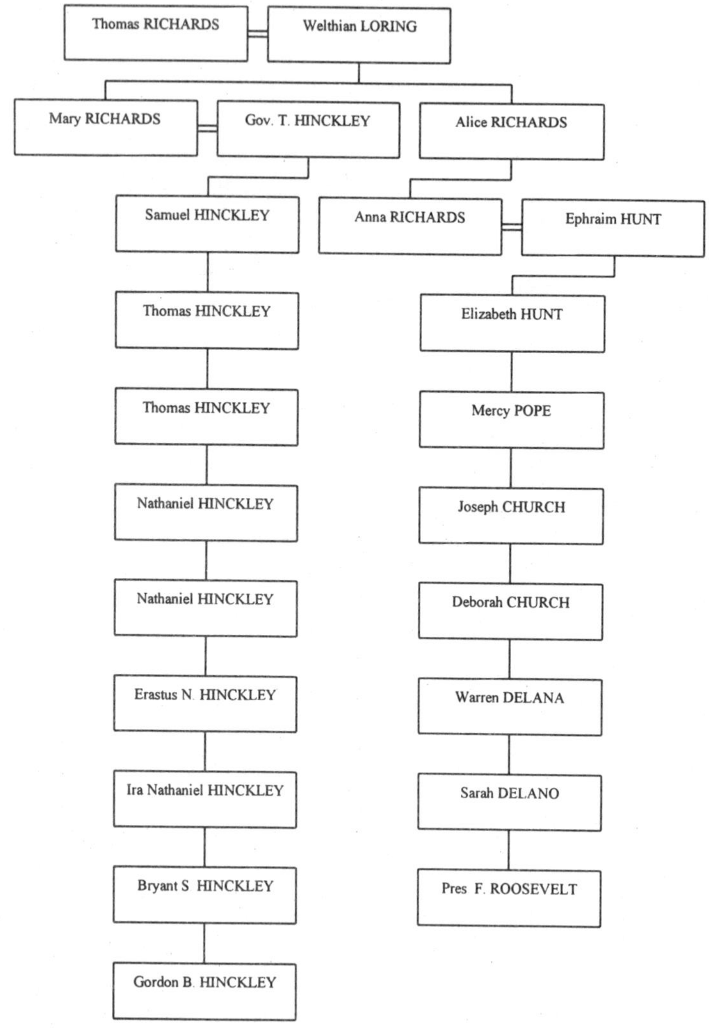

THE PROPHET GORDON BITNER HINCKLEY AND THE 32ND PRESIDENT OF THE UNITED STATES FRANKLIN DELANO ROOSEVELT ARE RELATED THROUGH THE RICHARDS AND LORING FAMILIES AS SHOWN ABOVE

Pres. Franklin D. Roosevelt Kinship to

Gordon B. HINCKLEY

Name	Relationship with Gordon HINCKLEY
CHURCH, Deborah	5th cousin 4 times removed
CHURCH, Joseph	4th cousin 5 times removed
DELANA, Warren	6th cousin 3 times removed
DELANO, Sarah	7th cousin twice removed
HINCKLEY, Bryant Stringham	Father
HINCKLEY, Erastus Nathaniel	Great-grandfather
HINCKLEY, Gordon Bitner	Self
HINCKLEY, Gov. Thomas	7th great-grandfather
HINCKLEY, Ira Nathaniel	Grandfather
HINCKLEY, Nathaniel	2nd great-grandfather
HINCKLEY, Nathaniel	3rd great-grandfather
HINCKLEY, Samuel	6th great-grandfather
HINCKLEY, Thomas	4th great-grandfather
HINCKLEY, Thomas	5th great-grandfather
HUNT, Elizabeth	2nd cousin 7 times removed
HUNT, Ephraim	Husband of the 1st cousin 8 times
LORING, Welthian	8th great-grandmother
POPE, Mercy	3rd cousin 6 times removed
RICHARDS, Alice	7th great-grandaunt
RICHARDS, Anna	1st cousin 8 times removed
RICHARDS, Mary	7th great-grandmother
RICHARDS, Thomas	8th great-grandfather
ROOSEVELT, Pres. Franklin Delano	8th cousin once removed

the battlefields in Europe.

He was nominated for vice president on the democratic ticket in 1920 but republican Warren Harding captured the election. Shortly thereafter, FDR was stricken with polio after a spill into cold water while sailing. He lost use of his legs at this young age of 33.

Personal determination led FDR to exercise daily gaining enough strength to stand and use braces and crutches. Warm Springs, Georgia mineral baths were purchased for his own therapy and also offered at reduced price to other polio victims.

In 1928 FDR ran for governor of New York and won. Innovative initiatives were implemented by him for his state when the 1929 Stock Crash and resulting depression occurred.

He ran for the presidency of the United States in 1932 at a time when America was in the bottom pit of the worst depression in history. His campaign promise was to provide the American people a "new deal." Upon inauguration on March 4, 1933, at age 51, he commenced famous "fireside chats" one week after becoming president, drawing the nation around their radios on a regular basis with down to earth talks to "My fellow Americans." With public works projects and many other acts of legislation, America's economy gradually revived and he won re-election by a landslide in 1936.

The next challenge he faced was war. He gradually prepared the American people in his "fireside chats" to prepare to defend themselves and help England and the other European powers fighting against the Axis powers by providing desperately needed weaponry and supplies.

When Japan bombed Pearl Harbor, the United States manufacturing machinery was well on its way to ever increasing production enabling rapid creation of armaments for a worldwide Allied Forces resistance and ultimate offensive ending the war in Europe. He, with his charisma and sincerity, was able to rally the entire United States into action.

But, he literally wore himself out and suffered a fatal stroke dying on April 12, 1945, a few months before Allied victory in Germany and a few more before victory in Japan. His unprecedented fourth term as president had commenced in 1945. Total years as president were 12 years one month and eight days.[1]

President Franklin Delano Roosevelt's traits can be seen in President Gordon Bitner Hinckley.

Grandfather Ira Nathaniel Hinckley

All of the foregoing was a precursor setting the stage for a miraculous meeting for a young man named Ira Nathaniel Hinckley, last of four sons and five children born to Nathaniel Hinckley and Lois, named after her mother Lois Judd, in Bastard, Leeds, Ontario, Canada, on October 30, 1828.

Lois' father was Arza Judd, Sr. From this progenitor came the name "Arza" for future Hinckleys.

Ira was the fourth Hinckley in succession to be given "Nathaniel" as one of his names but the first on the Hinckley family tree to receive the first name Ira. "Ira" was given to him from his mother's younger brother of the same name.

His sea captain father, mechanic and shoemaker, holding the first name Erastus and middle name Nathaniel, spent the majority of his short life on the waters of the Great Lakes. When he passed away at age 36 of tuberculosis, Ira was 2 years 10 months old. Therefore, Ira never knew or remembered his natural father personally.

This family tragedy left his oldest brother Harvey Judd, age 8; his next older brother Levi Silas, age 7; his next brother Arza Erastus, age 5; Ira himself, age almost 3; his younger and only sister Rhoda Lurinda, age 1 year 5 months; and Ira's young mother, age a week shy of age 26.

What a pitiful sight it was. Luckily, however, the Judd family were numerous in the Leeds area. They had moved there shortly after the 1770's when free land was offered by Britain's new Canadian colony following firm determination of possession of the territory by England after William's Treaty with France was signed ending the French and Indian War of 1765.

Lois' parents were compassionate people of faith coming from the Connecticut area of the United States and one of her uncle's sons took special attention to Lois. His name was Levi Judd, variant "Evi", actually her first cousin through her Uncle Joel Judd. Shortly they were married.[1]

However, Levi had the poor trait of criticizing. Ira could not seem to do anything right. He was constantly criticized and treated cruelly by his stepfather and suffered in self esteem for it. This experience of his

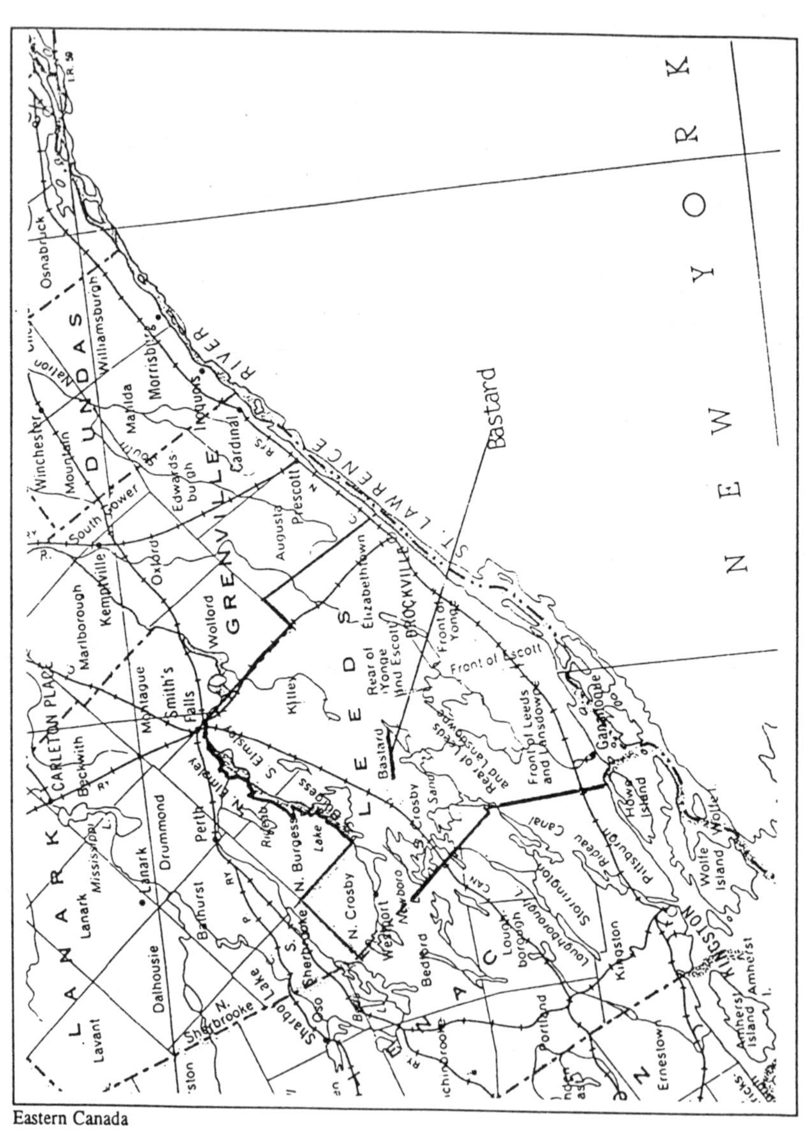

Eastern Canada

youth, however, was to inculcate a value in him which would bless the lives of not only his future children but the generations of his progenitors after them. [2] Kindness was Ira's trademark.

Education was not a part of his life. Only four months of sitting down at a school desk ever was experienced by Ira. His learning was acquired by his mother while she was alive, the experiences he had with his stepfather and brothers, the associations he had with his grandparents Judd and great uncles and aunts, and good old hard knocks. But he gradually grew to young manhood in this environment in Bastard, Leeds, in the province of Ontario, Canada, located not much more than 50 miles south of Ottawa, Canada south, southwesterly and just northeast of the northeast end of Lake Ontario of the Great Lakes.

Leeds was a land of many waters in its own right with many lakes and streams weaving through its territory. The St. Lawrence River was its south border line and on the other side of Lake Ontario near Rochester, New York, was the little town of Palmyra which Ira would learn of not too many years hence. But its climate was harsh, warm months continuing only from about July, August and September.

The Judd family were to play a big part in Ira and his next older brother Arza Erastus' lives. It was through their listening ears that a message was heard and not rejected and lives and generations changed forever.

Coming of the Restoration Message

Religion in the new Ontario Province of Canada was limited to circuit preaching and neighborhood gatherings in the early 1800's. No permanent chapels existed. When the roving ministers would come, "marriage bees" of as many as 50 couples at the same time were performed. Also, almost everyone would assemble to hear any preacher who came.

Amidst this environment traveled a young 30 year old man named Brigham Young to tell his brother Joseph in Kingston about a new faith he had discovered. He went to Kingston, Ontario, located about 40 miles south and west of Bastard. There he exuberantly related his experience.

Brigham had been given a book to examine by another brother Phineas. It was about 500 pages long and bound in a light tan leather. Inside the print date read 1830 and the spine contained the words "Book of Mormon." The book related the history of an ancient people who had lived in America from about 590 B.C. together with an even

Ira Nathaniel Hinckley

earlier people who had inhabited North America about 2300 B.C. All in all, it contained about 2,400 years of history in condensed form.

The amazing thing was it paralleled the Bible in its recording of doctrines of Christians, contained portions from the Old Testament's segments of the revelations of Isaiah, and recorded a visit of Jesus Christ to the ancient inhabitants of the Americas shortly after his crucifixion.

Undoubtedly these words of unusual and newly published scripture imparted to Joseph Young filtered through the territory of Leeds because Joseph himself was one of the roving ministers for the Methodist faith. Then in 1835 additional embracers of the "new Bible" held a conference in the town of Loughborough, about 20 miles south and west of Bastard. They consisted of six men who called themselves "latter-day apostles" of the Church of Jesus Christ of Latter-day Saints.

They spoke of a living prophet residing in a small community called Kirtland in Ohio, located just east of Cleveland not far from the southern banks of Lake Erie. His name was Joseph Smith, Jr., and he was only 29 years old.

But they said through the graces of God this young adult had been schooled by angels and visited by God the Father and his Son Jesus Christ in vision, had been told none of the faiths of Christianity were sanctioned by God at that time due to apostasy from the true doctrines and principles originally taught by Christ, and had personally been restored Heavenly authority or "priesthood" by angels through which he had in turn "restored" the pristine Church of Jesus Christ to the earth in the same fashion it had originally existed when Jesus Christ walked on the earth.

This was a revolutionary doctrine espoused by preachers. It undoubtedly reached the ears of the Judd family clans in Bastard and surrounding Leeds. An additional "apostle" from this new "American church" named Parley P. Pratt further went to Toronto in 1836 and the surrounding area espousing the same doctrine of the "restoration."

Back in Kirtland, 37 year old John E. Page, another convert to this new church, was approached by this "living prophet" Joseph Smith, Jr. and asked to preach his new religion to the people of Canada.

John's immediate reply was, "But I can't go on a mission to Canada, Brother Joseph. I don't even have a coat to wear."

Joseph Smith looked at John and said, as he removed his own coat from his back, "Here, take this one and the Lord will bless you abundantly."

John, without further excuse, travelled to Upper Canada with a companion by the name of William Harris on May 31, 1836 and ended up in Leeds, Ontario, where they experienced much interest in their message. Later a James Blakesley joined John Page as his companion and then Henry G. Sherwood. These preachers called themselves "elders" after ancient officers established by Jesus Christ when he organized his church in 30 A.D.

Elders Page, Blakesley and Sherwood expounded the same knowledge Brigham Young had told his brother Joseph and the other six apostles had told the curious in Loughborough and added much other detail. They told of a new "quorum" of 12 men specially called by the prophet Joseph Smith to be especial witnesses of the Lord Jesus Christ as in ancient times. They told of imperfections which had crept into translations of the Bible, of "doctrines of men" which had supplanted the original pure doctrines of Christ in such a way that God could no longer sanction their ways.

They told of the gradual withdrawal of God's authority from the Christian believers as they became filled with inaccuracies and half-truths in their practices and corrupt in their dealings with the rest of mankind. They told of the "falling away first" the apostle Paul had prophesied would occur before the Savior returned to the earth [3] and of the time of "refreshing " and "restitution of all things" further predicted by the ancient apostle Peter.[4]

They told of the "new Bible" called the Book of Mormon, translated from ancient records recorded on gold plates given to Joseph Smith, a new prophet like Moses in their day, to be the servant of God commissioned to restore lost truth and bring forth the additional record prepared by God to come forth at that time to serve as a second witness of the divinity of Jesus Christ. They told of restored "keys" of authority and power called the "priesthood" which had been withdrawn from mankind due to their apostasy from the pure truth of the doctrine of Christ, but now restored to the earth again so men properly chosen and ordained as in Christ's time could administer and preach in the Lord's name with authority and approval from God.

All of this intrigued Lois Judd Hinckley's father Arza Judd, Sr. and her mother Lois Knapp Judd, her large family of brothers and sisters, her father's brothers and sisters and their families, and also Ira Nathaniel Hinckley and his brothers and young sister Rhonda.

The Leeds area became a fertile plot of ground for Elder John E. Page and his companions. Numerous hearers of their words felt touched by a divine spirit to investigate further. Many were so convinced of its truth at the moment they heard the elders' message, they asked for membership in this new found faith.

Baptism into the LDS Church

Ira Nathaniel Hinckley was young when all of these events started. His mother Lois Judd Hinckley probably was baptized along with her parents and many others of her Judd family brothers and sisters and cousins and uncles and aunts in the Summer of 1836, just six years after the Church of Jesus Christ of Latter-day Saints had been officially chartered in New York State, Fayette Township, on April 6, 1830.[5] Suffice it to say, Arza Judd, Sr. and his wife Lois Knapp earn the distinction of being the first converts of Gordon B. Hinckley's known Hinckley line to join the LDS Church. Adams family members also were baptized into the LDS Church in December 1836. They were related through Arza Judd, Jr.'s wife Lucinda Adams.

The next Spring, however, Rhoda, only sister of Ira, passed away at age seven on March 6, 1837.[6]

Arza Erastus Hinckley states in his personal diary he was not baptized until en route to Far West, Missouri in the early part of 1838. Arza was 11 and Ira would have been 9 at that time.

Ira was only eight at the time his Judd grandparents joined the new faith and even though under the doctrine of the new religion, little children reached the age of accountability and could be baptized when eight, it appears from genealogy records of his parents' family, he was not baptized until July 1, 1843 at age 14¾ while living in Nauvoo when more mature.[7]

Migration to the United States and "Zion"

Elder Page and Elder Sherwood enjoyed great success in Leeds and surrounding areas. Between September 25 and November 17, 1836, a full 97 baptisms were realized. All in all, when Elder Page ended his mission to Canada, he reported almost 600 baptisms to his credit and remembered the promise given him by the prophet Joseph Smith.

Local ministers of other faiths became concerned over the success of the "Mormon philosophy" as they called it due to the faith's use of Mormon's book as well as the traditional Christian Bible. Mormon was said to have been an ancient prophet who lived in America and abridged the voluminous records of his people into one concise record and gave it to his son Moroni before dying in a battle against an enemy group called Lamanites. Moroni was said to have preserved the record by burying it in a stone box in the side of a small hill called Cumorah located by the little village of Palmyra, New York where Joseph Smith recovered the record in 1827 after being shown its location by Moroni who appeared as an angel to Joseph.

The ministers in Leeds did not need to fear the popularism of "Mormonism", however, for another of the new-found-faith's doctrines espoused at that time was to "gather" to a new spot designated as "Zion" located in the low lying hills of Missouri just east of the Missouri River and Kansas City. Zion was to be a place of refuge and peace for the new believers who were at that time also being proselyted in England by the apostles who had been called by Joseph Smith in 1835.

John E. Page organized the migration of his Canada converts. The Judd family and the Hinckley boys Arza and Ira and their mother and stepfather left in the Winter of 1837 by wagon in considerable deep snow. They arrived at the banks of the St. Lawrence River, borderline between Canada and the United States, in four to five days. A river pilot was enlisted to guide them over the partially frozen river. Pine boughs were placed over the spots of thin ice or air pockets and the six wagons containing the Arza Judd, Sr. family, his son Arza Judd, Jr.'s family (including Lois Judd Hinckley, Levi Judd and the two Hinckley sons) and his son Ira Judd's family and they were guided over the river. They stayed the Winter in a one room cabin located four miles from the St. Lawrence River banks.

The rest of Elder Page's group came across the river and were joined by the Judd families in the Spring of 1838. Apparently the two older brothers of Ira Nathaniel Hinckley and Arza Erastus Hinckley did not accompany the group. Harvey Judd Hinckley, 15, and Levi Silas Hinckley, 14, were living with an Uncle Judd who was raising them.[8]

The wagon train of LDS converts from Canada originally planned on stopping in Kirtland, Ohio where they supposed Joseph Smith still resided. They found when they arrived at Kirtland that Joseph Smith had fled apostate enemies in Kirtland on January 2, 1838 and faithful Latter-day Saints had largely evacuated Kirtland and left for Independence, Missouri. Just a few days before a group of over 500 called the "Kirtland Camp" had left the city July 6, 1838.

John Page's group followed the Kirtland Camp and communicated with them regularly as they jointly travelled the some 800 miles through hostile groups of settlers to a small settlement called Far West. The new Christian religion created through Joseph Smith, Jr.'s work received strong opposition from the beginning. Those who received the faith and were baptized, were readily ostracized by their neighbors, even their own family members, including parents, on occasion.

Along the route, eggs were thrown at the wagons. They were heckled. The elements smothered them with humid heat in the day and unpleasant cold in the nights. Added to their distress were rumors from those met when they arrived at the Mississippi River of war raging between the LDS believers and local Missouri settlers. But they still pushed on and in October 1838 arrived at Far West. There they first saw in person the 6 feet 2 inches tall prophet Joseph Smith, Jr., only 32 years of age. He was "well built, strong and active; of a light complexion, light hair, blue eyes, very little beard, and of an expression peculiar to himself, on which the eye naturally rested with interest, and was never weary of beholding.

"His countenance was ever mild, affable, beaming with intelligence and benevolence; mingled with a look of interest and an unconscious smile or cheerfulness, and entirely free from all restraint or affectation of gravity; and there was something connected with the serene and steady penetrating glance of his eye, as if he would penetrate the deepest abyss of the human heart, gaze into eternity, penetrate the heavens, and comprehend all worlds."[9]

Ira Nathaniel Hinckley was just turning 10 years old about the time of arrival in Far West. On the day of Ira's 10th birthday, October 30, 1838, persecutors of a group of settlers who had stopped at a location called Haun's Mill a short 12 miles distance to the north and east of Far West fired upon the settlers and slaughtered many.

Ira and his relatives had jumped from a hot pan into a burning fire of persecution and turmoil. Just as they had arrived at Far West, Missouri militia anti to the LDS populace were gathering around its little city to force the "Mormons" to leave their state. They had been given color of authority by what has now been labeled an infamous "extermination order" signed by the governor of the state who himself was grossly subjective in his hatred for Latter-day Saints and had used the excuse of unconfirmed rumors of "Mormon" uprising to execute an order to his state militias to remove the LDS populace from his state or "exterminate" them.

Ira's brother Arza as a youth of 12 was given permission by militia surrounding the town of Far West to feed their livestock and horses.[10] But then on Wednesday, October 31, the leader of the LDS defenders betrayed his leaders and allowed Joseph Smith, Jr., his counselor Sidney Rigdon and three other leaders to be captured by the anti-LDS militia.

In the pre-arranged betrayal, General Samuel D. Lucas, temporary commander of the Missouri militiamen, haughtily rode into Far West and without speaking to the five men assembled for what their LDS military leader had said would be a peace conference, ordered his guards to surround Joseph Smith and the others. It happened so abruptly, no one knew what was happening. When the prisoners were immediately marched into a camp of the anti-Mormon militia, it seemed like thousands of savage looking beings dressed and painted like Indian warriors surrounded them and began bloodcurdling screams of conquest.[11]

The shrieks of these persecutors continued through the night creating terror in the hearts of the remaining Far West occupants. During the night a secret "court martial" was conducted by General Lucas sentencing Joseph Smith and the other four men to be executed the next morning in the hollow square at Far West. But the general told to carry out the orders, General Alexander Doniphan, refused.

"It is cold-blooded murder. I will not obey your order. My brigade shall march for Liberty tomorrow morning, at 8 O'clock; and if you execute these men, I will hold you responsible before an earthly tribunal, so help me God."[12]

Ira Nathaniel Hinckley and Arza Erastus Hinckley, his two year older brother, were at Far West when these historic events in the LDS Church's history transpired.

Hyrum Smith, the prophet Joseph's older brother, and Amasa Lyman, two other leaders of the Latter-day Saints, were found and arrested and the city of Far West ravaged with destruction and rape on November 1st. But the prophet Joseph and the others were not executed. They were dragged to dungeons in Richmond, Missouri and Liberty, Missouri where they languished until April 1839.

At the same time as Joseph Smith and his brethren were being hauled off to Richmond, Missouri's dungeon, every LDS man at Far West was taken to the hollow square in the town and one by one told with a bayonet pointed close to his stomach, "Either leave the Mormons and live and do as us or sign over your property and leave the state forthwith or be shot down."[13]

Exodus to Illinois

Almost no sooner than they had come, and in the harsh winter months of the Missouri Winter, wagons were loaded and the Judd families, including Lois Judd Hinckley and her two Hinckley sons and daughter, participated with the other saints in the exodus from the area. They backtracked approximately 250 miles east in rain and cold to the northeast across the mighty and broad Mississippi River into the State of Illinois.

John E. Page's first wife and two children all died during the persecutions in Missouri but John looked to Mary Judd, first daughter of Arza Judd, Jr., just turned 20, to fill the void. He had known her undoubtedly since his first proselyting to Leeds, Ontario, Canada when she was 18.

Elder Page was appointed and ordained to take the place of one of four apostles on December 19, 1838 and married Mary Judd just one week later on December 26. Mary later authored lyrics to a Latter-day Saint hymn "Ye Who Are Called to Labor."

Some of the Judd families went to St. Louis. Others went to the town of Quincy, Illinois where the local populace generally opened their arms to the destitute LDS saints. Arza Judd, Sr. and his wife Lois went to a farmhouse five miles east of Springfield, Illinois. Ira and Arza Hinckley and their mother and step-father also resided in this area called Bloomfield.

Corn was cultivated on 25 acres in 1840 and 35 acres in 1841. In 1842, the two brothers went to the city of Nauvoo to associate with the blossoming populace who had converted the lowlands at the bend of the Mississippi River into a city reaching the population of 20,000–largest city in Illinois at the time. "Nauvoo", meaning "the beautiful", was chosen by Joseph Smith, Jr. to replace the old name of Commerce in early 1839 when the saints started relocating there. It now had beautiful brick homes along straight streets and square blocks. Arza Erastus Hinckley was now 16 and Ira 14. Ira helped with the guard protecting the prophet Joseph Smith, Jr. from his enemies.

The youth heard the prophet Joseph Smith, Jr. deliver many of his addresses in the grove by the site of a "temple" the LDS believers had begun building on the top of a knoll overlooking the lower previous marshland swamps at the banks of a bend in the Mississippi River.

Family genealogy records record Ira Nathaniel receiving baptism at the time of residence in Nauvoo on July 1, 1843.[14]

Arza records in his diary, "Herd [sic.] Joseph Smith preach many times. His preaching was all inspiring."[15] Ira also told his son Ira Noble of standing under a tree one time in Nauvoo while hearing the prophet Joseph Smith speak.[16]

Parley P. Pratt, a contemporary apostle at the time, most eloquently described the prophet's charisma. "He possessed a noble boldness and independence of character; his manner was easy and familiar; his rebuke terrible as the lion; his benevolence unbounded as the ocean; his intelligence universal, and his language abounding in original eloquence peculiar to himself–not studied–not smoothed and softened by education and refined by art; but flowing forth in its own native simplicity, and profusely abounding in variety of subject and manner.

"He interested and edified, while, at the same time, he amused and entertained his audience; and none listened to him that were ever weary with his discourse.

"I have even known him to retain a congregation of willing and anxious listeners for many hours together, in the midst of cold or sunshine, rain or wind, while they were laughing at one moment and weeping the next. Even his most bitter enemies were generally overcome, if he could once get their ears."[17]

On June 27, 1844, persecution, which seemed to follow the Latter-day Saints wherever they were to go, raised its intolerant sting so fully again, Joseph Smith and his older brother Hyrum were murdered at the two story red brick jail in Carthage, Illinois, just 20 miles east of Nauvoo. Brigham Young, who had first taken the message of the Book of Mormon to his brother Joseph in Kingston, Ontario, Canada, took over leadership of the LDS Church as senior apostle of the 12 man quorum of 12 apostles.

About the same time, Ira Nathaniel Hinckley's mother died at Bloomfield, five miles east of Springfield, Illinois of small pox. Ira was about 16 and his older brother Arza approximately 18. The two brothers worked on the temple construction in Nauvoo at the request of the apostles in fulfillment of the admonition of Joseph Smith to complete the temple and dedicate it. Persecution continued against all Latter-day Saints in Illinois and ultimatums were given for them to leave the state as they had left Missouri.

A temple had been first built in Kirtland and dedicated in 1836 as a special edifice similar to that of the temple of Solomon and temple of Herod built in ancient Jerusalem before the birth of Christ. But this temple had been abandoned and another commanded to be built through revelations received by the prophet Joseph Smith when the saints arrived at Nauvoo. Temples were contemplated in Missouri, too, but the Latter-day Saints were prematurely expelled from that state before they could be built.

This time, the saints in Nauvoo and Illinois were determined to fulfill the command of what they considered "the God of Heaven" to build a special "house of the Lord" where special ordinances could be performed. Joseph Smith had disclosed these ordinances as the "new and everlasting covenant" required of all faithful disciples of Christ in order to return to heaven following mortal life. Regular worship services were not held in temples. Rather, special ordinances and instruction were received.

Connected with this "new and everlasting covenant" was a resumption of ordinances for deceased ancestors once performed by the ancient Church of Christ as recorded by Paul the apostle in 1 Corinthians 15:29. "Else what shall they do which are baptized for the dead, if the dead rise not at all? why are they then baptized for the dead?" And crowning the ordinances to be performed there were the binding together for eternity of husbands and wives and parents and children through what Latter-day Saints believe is the special power of God or priesthood just like Adam and Eve were joined together by God in the Garden of Eden. This "celestial marriage" or "eternal marriage" is essential to their ultimate return to Deity they believe.

Even though the persecution persisted and the pressure to leave Nauvoo strengthened, the temple was hurried to completion and dedicated to the Lord. In it were performed baptisms for the dead and also "sealing" ordinances of husbands and wives and parents to children and the related making of sacred covenants and receipt of special education for faithful saints called the "endowment".

Pioneer Immigration to the Rocky Mountains

A commitment with Illinois persecutors was made by the leaders of the LDS Church to leave the beautiful city of Nauvoo they had built. Ira Nathaniel Hinckley and his brother Arza Erastus Hinckley assisted their grandparents to make the exodus from Illinois by creating an outfit of gear and materials needed. But Arza Judd, Sr. and wife Lois were aging and appeared not sturdy enough to make the planned journey to the Western United States. Joseph Smith, Jr., before he was killed had predicted the Latter-day Saints would go to the Rocky Mountains in the West and build a great settlement.

So the two brothers, their grandparents and cousin Ira Judd determined they could stay with Ira for now and the boys would go and prepare a way for them with some of the first companies of saints going to the Rocky Mountains.

The two brothers walked the 108 miles to Nauvoo by foot where Arza went west to Mount Pisgah, Iowa, a staging area established by the future "pioneers" to the Rockies to regroup and prepare for the trek West. He then went to Council Bluffs, Iowa, a staging area further West.

Ira Nathaniel Hinckley separated from his brother at this time and assisted his Aunt Constance, a Judd family relative, prepare for the trek West. He traveled with her to Winter Quarters, another staging area located about 380 miles west across the State of Iowa and over the Missouri River near Omaha, Nebraska. There he built a home for her to await her turn to go to the Rocky Mountains.

Wedlock with Eliza Jane Evans

Then he travelled south 250 miles on the Missouri River, probably by riverboat, to Platte County, Missouri, located just northwest of the scene of the persecutions and expulsions of eight years before. Here he met 20 year old Eliza Jane Evans, daughter of David Evans who would be the captain of the wagon train they would take to the Rocky Mountains in 1850. They were married in June 1848, probably in Platte County. Ira was almost 20 and now full grown to his height of 6 feet 1 inches. His weight was 175 lbs. And "there was nothing coarse or rugged about his appearance. He was always well-dressed, well-groomed and affable. He wore a white shirt when he worked in the field."[18]

All during these years, Ira had been acquiring several skills. He had built a home for his Aunt Constance. He had farmed and cultivated the ground. He learned the blacksmith trade, he learned the art of toolmaking, and he constructed wagons, all important abilities which would benefit him, his family and the LDS Church throughout the rest of his life.

At Platte County, Missouri, Eliza Jane became pregnant and gave birth to a child on July 16, 1849 whom they named after her mother

Eliza Jane Hinckley.

Then in April 1850, Ira, Eliza Jane and their baby daughter Eliza left with 54 wagons, Eliza's father as captain, to cross the plains to the Valley of the Great Salt Lake on the west side of the Rocky Mountains where an initial party of 149 LDS pioneers had established a settlement 24 July 1847. The Valley was east of a large lake much like the Dead Sea in the Holy Land with no outlet for drainage. Its consequent brine water filled with salt and minerals left by the evaporating lake water caused Mountain Men to name it the "Great Salt Lake." It was so filled with minerals and salt, you could not sink when you swam in it.

The wagon journey of 1,000 miles always took months to complete. Average progress was between 11-15 miles a day by wagon. Buffalo was encountered. But also were native Americans, some more hostile than others. Prairie hens abounded as well as other wild game. There was no lack of things to do from early dawn to late evening.

But dreaded sicknesses for which no cure was known at the time also plagued the pioneer wagon trains. And sadly as the group reached a location two-thirds the way across Wyoming, 750 miles along their journey and only some 200 miles out from their destination of Great Salt Lake Valley, cholera struck the wagon train. It moves with such speed that within a day victims can be dead.

Such was the tragic fate of Ira's young 23 year old wife Eliza Jane. She perished on the plains of Sweetwater County, Wyoming on June 27, 1850 along with Ira's younger brother Joel Judd born to Ira's mother and his stepfather Levi Judd, also struck with the disease at the same time.

Ira was left with their 11 month old daughter in his arms after he built a coffin for his beloved wife and laid her and his brother Joel to rest on the prairie on the south side of the Platte River, Wyoming.

The John Beers Company came along during the epidemic and Ira and his infant daughter continued the balance of the trek to Salt Lake with them. On September 22, 1850, the party reached the summit of the mountain called Big Mountain, first spot where the "Valley" could be seen, and gazed out over the vast wasteland they would call Zion.

It was a majestic view with the surrounding tree leaves of the aspens and oak turning their oranges and reds and brows and yellows. The Great Salt Lake could faintly be seen on the distant right horizon. Then the pioneers tied tree trunks behind their wagons to slow their descent to safe speed and drove over the summit and down the steep incline into the Valley where several thousand other saints now made their home.

First Life in Salt Lake City

First life in Great Salt Lake City, as it was called, was primitive. Almost everything had to be created. With the exception of what goods and supplies you were able to bring with you from the East, food had to be grown and raised, clothes had to be spun and sewn, furniture had to be carved and glued, virtually everything had to be made by yourself.

Salt Lake had only been first reached by the pioneers a little over three years before. Much had to be done. A steady stream of new immigrants was also continuously coming over the summit of Big Mountain and down the narrow Emigration Canyon into the shallow bowl valley of the Great Salt Lake. The Valley had originally been part of a much larger lake bed forming the bottom of ancient Lake Bonneville but that lake had gradually dried up leaving the remains now known as the Great Salt Lake, still over a hundred miles long north and south and the largest body of water inland in the Western half of the United States.

The now dry portion forming the Salt Lake Valley traversed about 24 miles from the Rocky Mountains to the east to the smaller Oquirrh Mountains to the west and 22 miles from the north to the "Point of the Mountain" knoll dividing it from another valley to the south. So the Valley was essentially 24 miles wide and 22 miles long.

The pioneers were spreading out to various sections all through the Salt Lake Valley and beyond. Brigham Young was embarking on an ambitious vision to populate not only the Salt Lake Valley but all of the surrounding Western Territories.

For Ira's first years in the Rocky Mountains, however, he provided sustenance for his daughter Eliza Jane and built a house which later was the first home of St. Mark's Hospital. His brother Arza arrived back in Salt Lake after first arriving in 1847 four days after the original pioneers. He had marched in the Mormon Battalion to Santa Fe and Pueblo, a volunteer group of LDS men recruited by the United States Government in July 1846 to aid in a war with Mexico to determine possession of Texas and the Western territories of the United States. Then they had tried to catch the initial pioneer group and almost did.

Ira and Arza had met briefly a short time before on the "Mormon Trail" about 200 miles west of Winter Quarters. Both brothers embarked on many similar assignments together. Both became city policemen. Ira continued the policing for five years and Arza for seven. They also protected the U. S. Mail. This duty involved travel across the route of the Mormon pioneers from Winter Quarters to the Valley of the Great Salt Lake.

Marriage to Adelaide and Angeline Wilcox

The "saints" not then having a temple in which they might perform their eternal marriage sealings, erected a house in the northwest corner of one of the large square blocks laid out by Brigham Young for the city of the Great Salt Lake. It was named the Endowment House by Brigham Young who permitted the sealing ceremonies and related endowment to be performed there until the saints could build their temple in the Salt Lake Valley. The prophet Brigham Young designated the middle east portion of the same block as the place where their permanent temple would be built and construction commenced in 1852. Ira helped with excavation for the temple foundations.

Sometime after arriving in the Salt Lake Valley, Ira was blessed to meet a young 20 year old maid by the name of Adelaide Cameron Noble. On December 11, 1853 Ira and Adelaide were sealed in the Endowment House for time and all eternity as husband and wife. Eleven children were eventually born to them, the first a daughter Martha Adelaide, born August 12, 1854.

The Latter-day Saints were at this time adherents to plural marriage as practiced by Abraham, Isaac and Jacob in ancient Israel. If a wife gave permission as Sarah had done to Abraham for her husband to take another wife and Brigham Young or one of the other presiding authorities of the LDS Church authorized it, it was permitted to enter into polygamy.

Adelaide, Ira's second wife, had an older sister by almost two years named Angeline Wilcox Noble who was still unmarried. Adelaide gave her permission for Ira to take her sister Angeline as his plural wife and Angeline, the grandmother of President Gordon B. Hinckley, was sealed to Ira, also for time and all eternity, at age 23½, in the Endowment House on July 22, 1855, his third wife.

Adelaide and Angeline Wilcox had come to the Great Salt Lake Valley on October 6, 1850 with their parents Lucian and Emily Wilcox Noble. They and their parents lived in Lovonia, Michigan in the 1830's when their father Lucian and a friend, out of curiosity, went to hear two LDS missionaries preach. Something in their "manner and

Ira Nathaniel Hinckley
and
Angeline Wilcox Noble

message" appealed to them, so they returned "again and again" to their meetings. They soon received conviction of their doctrine and both families were baptized. Their relatives thought they were crazy but later they returned to Lavonia, Michigan to visit their relatives and an 85 year old brother of Lucian Noble said, "We all thought Lucian was crazy, but we have lived to see the time when we *know* he was the only one in the family who was *not* crazy."[19]

Angeline was blue eyed with brown hair, small and in later years about 145 pounds. She had a high forehead and a prominent nose.[20] She bore Ira eight children, the first being born on March 31, 1856, Emily Angeline. There eventually were a total three daughters and five sons mothered by her, the sixth child and third of the five sons being Bryant Stringham Hinckley, the father of President Gordon B. Hinckley.

Angeline "was a deeply religious woman, absolutely free from duplicity, who taught her children to walk uprightly before the Lord. She was a woman of leadership and a good deal of native ability as a public speaker. Her prayers were beautiful."[21] She was fine looking, loved to read church books and newspapers, was a good cook, seamstress, ironer and housekeeper and a "natural born aristocrat." Her son Ira Noble said of her, "She was a high spirited woman and extremely proud, but very tender hearted. Her most outstanding quality was her absolute loyalty. She was completely frank, honest, and devoid of any deceit. She frequently would quote scripture to me."[22]

Building Horseshoe Bend Fort

Latter-day Saints practiced their religion through lay membership as in the days of the ancient Church. When the prophet gave a responsibility to a Latter-day Saint, they considered it a call from God. So when Ira was asked by Brigham Young to go to the horseshoe bend on the North Platte River 30 miles west of Ft. Laramie, Wyoming and superintend the building of a fort, he readily complied.

After this was completed, he once again guarded the U.S. mail and assisted in the building of new roads in the territory. Many other public works projects were assisted by him.

Call to Build Fort & Chapel in Coalville

One of the pioneer settlements started by President Brigham Young was a small town called Coalville located northeast of Salt Lake up in a little valley in the Rocky Mountains about 35 miles from Salt Lake and 40 miles from Evanston, Wyoming.

In 1863, Brigham Young next asked Ira Nathaniel Hinckley to go to the small community of Coalville and build a chapel to serve as the saints place of worship and also as a place of safety from any hostile native Americans. He readily packed up and moved there.

He built the chapel of native rock and also built a small log home for his family while there. His brother Arza also came and assisted. Both the chapel and the log home are still in existence. The chapel has been removed to the Frontier Village portion of Lagoon Amusement Park located in Farmington, Utah, about 20 miles north of Salt Lake City, and the old Ira Nathaniel Hinckley home has been removed to Cove Fort, Utah and reconstructed on land just east of the old fort.

While engaged in this calling for the Prophet Brigham Young, the birth of President Gordon B. Hinckley's father Bryant Stringham Hinckley was nearing. But before that birth occurred, Ira received another call.

Cove Fort

Ira's children thought Coalville would be their permanent living place. But about April 14th, 1867, a horeseman from Salt Lake rode up to the fence surrounding his home, let down the two wooden poles at the front gate, led his horse inside, replaced the two bars, mounted the horse and rode up to the blacksmith shop where Ira was working.

The messenger handed Ira a letter from Brigham Young. Ira took it and examined it carefully, then said to an assistant at the blacksmith shop, "Take care of the horse for him."

"Come with me."

Ira introduced the messenger to his family and a meal was prepared for him. Then Ira said, "Say to the President I will be there on the appointed day with conveyance prepared to go."

The letter asked, "Elder Ira Hinckley, Dear Brother, we wish to get a good and suitable person to settle on and take charge of the Church Ranch at Cove Creek, Millard County. Your name has been suggested for this position. As it is some distance from any other settlement, a man of sound practical judgment and experience is needed to fill the place. Cove Creek is on the main road to our Dixie, Pahrananget & Lower California, some 42 miles south of Fillmore & some 22 miles north of Beaver. If you think you can take this mission, you should endeavor to go south with us. We expect to start a week from next Monday. It is not wisdom for you to take your family there until after a Fort is built, etc."[23]

Ira was in Salt Lake a week from the next Monday to travel with

Brigham Young to the site for the fort and began measuring and staking the land. Lava rock was obtained and lime kilns built. Timber was gathered and a sawmill constructed. A shingle mill was completed and craftsmen gathered. By November, the fort was being constructed.

In addition to the fort was a large barn and stable built to the north for the livestock and horses. The lava rock went into the four feet thick walls and the interior from the sides of each wall were made into living quarters with considerable open space left in the center. Lookout posts were made at the top with stairs and a walkway constructed near the top of interior rock walls for access.

Gordon's father was born July 9, 1867 in the log home in Coalville built by Ira. Ira's children and two wives eventually moved to Cove Fort. Meanwhile, Ira's brother Arza had been made probate judge in Coalville in 1868. Seven native Americans visited the fort a few mornings after the first family of children arrived and greetings were exchanged. The visitors were then given breakfast.

Life at the fort continued for the Hinckleys well into the late 1870's. On February 15, 1875, President Brigham Young visited the fort and was entertained there. Then just a month before Brigham Young died, another call came.

Call to be Millard Stake President

As mentioned by Brigham Young in his letter calling Ira to build Cove Fort, there was another small community 42 miles northwest of Cove Fort called Fillmore. It was the site of the first Utah Territorial Government seat and home of the Millard Stake of Zion.

A "stake" is an ecclesiastical unit composed of a group of LDS members residing in a certain area. It represents the stakes of a tent, the overall tent representing Zion as a whole. Thus, instead of diocese or parishes, Latter-day Saints take the symbolism of a tent as espoused by Isaiah in his prophecy (Isaiah 33:20) which they believe speaks of the "latter-days" and call their major ecclesiastical units "stakes" and the smaller portions within each stake "wards" or "branches."

On July 22, 1877, Ira was asked to take over the responsibility as president of the Millard Stake from its first stake president Thomas Callister. This necessitated another move, that to Fillmore.

Today stake presidents in the LDS Church serve on the average nine or so years. Ira served, as did others during his time period, for much longer. This calling continued for 25 years until his son Arza Alonzo Hinckley, and younger brother of Gordon B. Hinckley's father

Coalville Chapel
Now at Pioneer Village
Lagoon Amusement Park, Utah

President's Office
Great Salt Lake City
April 12th 1867.

Elder Ira Hinkley
Dear Bro:—

We wish to get a good and suitable person to settle and take charge of the Church Ranche at Cove Creek Millard County. Your name has been suggested for this position as it is some distance from any other settlement, a man of sound practical judgement and experience is needed to fill the place. Cove Creek is on the main road to our Dixie, Pahranagat & Lower California some 42 miles south of Fillmore & some 22 miles north of Beaver. If you think you can take this mission you should endeavor to go south with us. We expect to start a week from next Monday. It is not wisdom for you to take your family there until after a fort is built there. There is a mail and Telegraph station there. Should you conclude to go let me know by the bearer of this letter and when you start come prepared with conveyance to accompany us.

Your Brother in the Gospel

Brigham Young

P.S. The object of building a fort at Cove Creek is to afford protection from Indians to the Telegraph & mail stations and to travelers who are almost constantly on the road. Also to furnish feed and protection from bad weather to this latter class. There is farming & hay land plentifully, also herding facilities good, with fire wood in abundance, close by.

B.Y.

CALL FROM BRIGHAM YOUNG—This is the letter sent by President Brigham Young to Ira N. Hinckley calling him to go to Cove Creek, Millard County and build a fort. Mr. Hinckley left his family and answered the call.

Inside Cove Fort
Utah

Bryant, was made his successor.

The duties of a stake president were heavy. In a letter to his son Ira Noble Hinckley, Ira once remarked, "It takes two thirds of my time in the stake among the people."[24] A stake president had charge of the temporal needs as well as spiritual welfare of all Latter-day Saints living within the boundaries of his unit. He also had responsibility for seeing the gospel was offered everyone who lived within his stake but was not a member of the LDS Church. He had two counselors and 12 additional men called a "high council" to aid him in the administration of his stake. And within each stake were a number of wards whose leader was called a "bishop", as in the ancient Church of Christ, over which he presided. Membership in a stake could be from one to many thousand. There were many meetings and lots of ministering to the needs of the poor and wanting as well as to those who for one reason or another fell away from strong faith.

While holding this call as a stake president, Ira was also elected mayor of the city of Fillmore two times. This added additionally to his portioning of time. But the two major families were brought to Fillmore and separate homes established for them. Ira would spend one week with Adelaide's family and the next week with Angeline's. A farm five miles west of Fillmore with a farmhouse attached was also obtained for ranching. Ira loved fine horses and made sure they had some. He had his boys rub them down, including their legs, and curry them an hour and a half each evening. Also, by 1884 they were milking 30 cows at the ranch.

Back at the fort, Ira's two oldest sons Ira Noble, son of Angeline, and Lucian, son of Adelaide, now 17 and 15, were leased the some 320 acres of ranchland and fort and Ira's brother Arza Erastus also came and assisted. One day, Ira Noble remarked, "You have no idea of the amount of work that it requires to keep that place up!"

Ira burst into laughter and said, "Oh, don't I have?!"

With his church responsibilities, Ira regularly traveled to LDS Church general conferences held the first part of every April and October in Salt Lake City. On the trips north, he stopped regularly at the home of a fellow "brother", a label by which Latter-day Saints respected men and women as their spiritual brothers and sisters, as all children of God or "Father in Heaven." Females were called "sisters" and males "brothers". Here at Brother Harley's in the town of Nephi, 90 miles south of Salt Lake City, he met his only daughter Margaret,

25 years old and single.

On October 9, 1884, Ira took Margaret Harley as a second plural wife and fourth marriage. As in all four of his marriages, this marriage too was sealed for time and all eternity in the Endowment House in Salt Lake City. Margaret bore one child of Ira, his last child.

Education & the Millard Stake Academy

In the late 1880's LDS Church leadership directed each stake to establish an academy for higher education. This was certainly consistent with Ira's desire to give each one of his children a formal education he never was able to have. So now President Ira N. Hinckley was the leader in organizing the Millard Stake Academy.

Much earlier he had purchased $160.00 "life scholarships" for his two oldest sons Ira Noble and Lucian and had sent them to school in Salt Lake. Wife Angeline also went with other children and took care of them while they attended the John Morgan School. He and his wives had a special desire that their children would not be deprived of good education as they had been deprived. On this point, Ira's childhood experience had a profound effect on the raising of his children and has equally positively affected his posterity since.

"I do not know of anything I could do in this world that would give me more satisfaction than to help educate my children in the right direction and then to have them make good use of it when they get older. It will be a blessing to them that no one can take from them," Angeline wrote in a letter to her son Ira Noble when he was on a mission to New Zealand in March 1884.[24]

Regarding his devotion to educating his children, Ira wrote to his missionary son Ira Noble in May 1884, "All the times are hard so far as money is concerned here, but I must educate my children as far as possible, for that is all I can do for them."[25]

Education was so important for their children, Angeline moved to Provo, Utah arriving November 3, 1883 with three heavy wagons filled with household goods, furniture and bedding and five sons and a housemaid. Hayracks were on the wagons to hold feed for several horses and two milk cows. Three days had elapsed from the time they left Fillmore traveling up and over the steep Scipio Hill just to the north of Fillmore and down rocky, rough, dusty and muddy roads the 100 miles to Provo. There a home with six rooms located one block away from Brigham Young Academy was rented and the boys sent to the academy. Sons Frank, Edwin, Bryant Stringham, Arza Alonzo and

Elmer went to school and Angeline took in as many as 11-13 boarders to pay for coal, wood, coal-oil, sugar, groceries, $2.00 a week for their hired girl, school tuition and other necessities.[26]

Angeline remained in Provo assisting her children go to B.Y. Academy for nine years until 1892.

Principles

It is said that Ira always had "unfailing kindness to those in distress, a love and respect for education, and a quiet, sober, consistent manner of living."[27]

The principles he taught his children are well evidenced by the manner in which he treated them and the wise counsel he imparted to them. Ira Noble Hinckley, Ira's oldest son, was called "Bub." When he was very young, while working with some logs, Ira asked his son, "Bub, go get the hammer."

"I don't want to get the hammer," Bub replied.

"Bub, get the hammer."

"I don't want to get the hammer," came the reply.

"You sit down on that log and don't move, and I will go for the hammer. Nervy (nickname for his second oldest daughter Minerva), you stay here and watch him while I am gone."

Ira did not hesitate to do as his father asked after that.[28]

One time, his two oldest boys Ira Noble and Lucian Noble succumbed to the temptation of smoking the unused portions of cigars non-LDS travelers discarded beside the stages before they went into the fort to eat dinner. LDS were taught in a revelation received by Joseph Smith in 1833 not to smoke or chew tobacco in what is called the "word of wisdom." Tea, coffee and alcoholic drinks were also discouraged as bad for your health.

But Ira Noble and Lucian were curious boys. They also would buy tobacco to chew making the excuse they were going to ride the range. Their father knew what was going on but waited until the right moment to counsel his sons. When his son Lucian was about to herd some cattle to the area called Green River, father Ira Nathaniel came to him and said, "Here, Lucian, is some money. If you must chew tobacco, do not beg it, buy it." He inspired good actions by talking kindly to his sons and explaining why tobacco was bad for them.[29]

In reference to criticizing authorities over you, he always said, "Never crack the whip above your head."[30]

Referring to those angry or in distress, he counseled, "Let them empty everything out before you try to put anything in. You can't put anything in a vessel which is already full."[31]

Referring to stray cattle found on the range from time to time, he said, "If you are not absolutely sure of it, do not put your brand on a calf or colt."[32]

Regarding sexual virtue, he told his sons, "I would rather have us dead than immoral, and would rather put us in our coffins than have us ruin a girl."[33]

His wise admonition to oldest son Ira Nobel after close to a year on his mission is both wisdom and an affirmation of Ira Nathaniel Hinckley's own conviction of the truth of his religion. Speaking of those missionaries who had gone without "purse or scrip" to preach the gospel who were good and great men, he said, "And that is what I would like you to be, and I believe you can if you choose to be. Of course, it is an unceasing labor. But it pays well in the outcome for it is life everlasting. . . . In this kingdom is power, dominion and eternal increase which is worth living for . . . . I beseech of you to be prayerful and watchful that the destroyer may not have power over you for he will do his best to lead the servants of the Lord astray. Let's set our marks high and climb for it. May we have the blessing of the Lord to help us is my prayer in the name of Jesus. Amen."[34]

Ira's daughter Minerva said of him, "He would never scold or argue with his children. There was no talking back. When he corrected them, it was done in a very quiet tone of voice. He had a very sweet, lovely disposition and was unusually dignified. Everyone looked up to him, even those employed by him. He was never late for an appointment. He possessed a quality of natural refinement."[35]

Angeline also shows her wisdom and convictions in other letters to her missionary son Ira Noble off in New Zealand. She wrote him on May 28, 1884, "Praying that your path may be strewn with thorns enough so you can appreciate the sweet and learn how to battle with the opposite so as to qualify yourself . . . ."[36]

Then on July 22, 1884, Angeline wrote, "It is just 29 years today since I was married. When I look back, I wonder if there are many that can look with as good a degree of satisfaction on the past as I can, not but what I have been sorely tried in some ways, but my children have been such a comfort. So far they have not disgraced me in any way, but on the contrary they have been an honor to me and a comfort as well, which I feel thankful to my Heavenly Father for."[37]

Evading the U.S. Marshalls

In the 1880's increasing pressure was being placed on the Latter-day Saints to discontinue polygamous marriages. The latter part of 1879, the United States Supreme Court had upheld a conviction of George Reynolds for having more than one wife. The Edmunds Act passed by the United States Congress defined "unlawful cohabitation" as not only living with but merely supporting and caring for more than one woman.

John Taylor, successor to Brigham Young who had died in 1877, spoke of the nation's bitter prejudice against the Latter-day Saints and said the saints would "contend inch by inch" for their liberties and rights as American citizens.[38]

Church leaders who had more than one wife were left with the dilemma. Should they forsake their wives and children or should they continue to support them. Ira was one of the great majority who chose to avoid the marshals as they tried to capture them. A plan was implemented where Ira often slept in remote ditches in parts of his ranch fields and field glasses were used to examine any visitors coming the way of the ranch. A horse was always kept saddled day and night.

But sometimes he did sleep in the ranch house. One such night between 1888 and 1890, Ira was asleep in his bed with false teeth in a glass of water and his boots by his bed. Alarm was given some marshals were at the gate of the ranch.

Ira pulled on his trousers and some slippers and putting the house between him and the marshals, made way to the barn where he mounted his horse and was off. The marshals were surprised to see his false teeth and boots by his bed but no Ira.

Shortly before the fourth prophet of the LDS Church, Wilford Woodruff, issued a manifesto in 1890, declaring the termination of the practice of polygamy by the Latter-day Saints, Ira was recognized on the streets of Provo by a marshal who took him to court where he was fined $50.00 and that was all the punishment from the U.S. Government he ever received.[39]

Final Years

Ira came to Fillmore with a net worth of about $100,000.00 but through his liberal and philanthropic efforts to improve the Fillmore community and other areas at large, was left with little of it when he was released from his stake president assignment in 1902. He donated much to building of two temples in the towns of St. George and Manti, Utah and encouraged his sons to do likewise. He financed the Millard Stake Academy much.

Following his release as stake president, Ira moved to Provo, Utah, located 40 miles south of Salt Lake City. And six months before his death, he was attacked with pleurisy, an inflammation of the membrane that lines the chest and covers the lungs, and passed away in Provo, Utah in the afternoon on April 10, 1904 at age 75½. His older brother Arza Erastus had passed away three years earlier in Rexburg, Idaho at almost the same age. Both of them had been faithful to their new religion until the end.

Ira Nathaniel Hinckley had sired a total of 21 children during his lifetime, a daughter from his first wife Eliza Jane Evans, 11 children by his second wife Adelaide Noble, and eight by his third wife Angeline Noble, older sister of Adelaide. One child was born of his fourth marriage to Margaret Harley.

Eulogies were profuse regarding Ira Nathaniel Hinckley. Funeral services were held at 1:30 P.M. in the tabernacle building in Provo, Utah, larger buildings than usual chapels where stake gatherings could be held for several thousand people.

Brigham Young Academy, the academy established in Provo, and predecessor to Brigham Young University, was located on a campus just three blocks north on University Avenue. Two of Ira's sons, including Gordon B. Hinckley's father Bryant Stringham Hinckley, had taught there and about all of them attended there. Accordingly, the administration of the academy dismissed all classes during the services so students and faculty could have an opportunity to attend.

Three "general authorities", a title given to full time officers appointed to watch over the church worldwide, were there including Francis M. Lyman of the 12 apostles; Seymour B. Young of the seventy, another priesthood office instituted by Jesus Christ in the ancient church whose special responsibility was to prepare the way and preach and spread the gospel of Jesus Christ to every nation, kindred, tongue and people (the martyr Stephen was a seventy when he was stoned to death); and John Smith, church patriarch, a position designed to bless LDS church members with special personal blessings of potential as ancient Jacob blessed his 12 sons, the fathers of the 12 tribes of Israel.

Elder Seymour B. Young said, "He has gone to the reward of a man who has never betrayed a trust, never betrayed his brethren and never betrayed his God; a man who scattered blessings along his pathway through life; not only to his loved ones, but to all with whom he came in contact."[40]

Elder Francis M. Lyman said, "Every son bids fair to become his father's equal. You can not expect to excel him in devotion to the work, but you might become his equals, and you have enjoyed better advantages in life than your father. You daughters, also, are devoted to the principles to which your father was devoted through life.

"Elder Hinckley has lived a very worthy life, and has been abundantly rewarded and the family with which he has been blessed will cause him great honor. Neither he nor the mothers of his children will ever have cause to blush for the actions of their children."[41]

Such statements seem to be a prophetic statement from an LDS apostle pertaining to President Gordon B. Hinckley and many other posterity of Ira Nathaniel Hinckley.

Uncle Apostle Arza Alonzo Hinckley 1870-1936

Many do not know, even Latter-day Saints, that Gordon B. Hinckley is not the first of his family name to be a Latter-day apostle. As rich in the blood of the Native Americans and English and Normans as he is, President Gordon B. Hinckley also has a full uncle Arza Alonzo Hinckley 40 years his senior, who was first called to the LDS apostleship. He was an LDS apostle for two years before his death.

Gordon's father had four brothers and three sisters, one of each who died as children. Three years after President Hinckley's father was born in Coalville, Utah, the first of two younger full brothers was born at Cove Fort, Utah just when construction of the fort was being completed.

Arza Alonzo was born at the fort in April on the 23rd day in 1870. He lived there with his other brothers and sisters helping at the fort until 1877, the year the second leader of the LDS faith Brigham Young died.

The Continental Railroad had then come and railroad spurs were being completed to southern areas of the Utah Territory. The last real confrontation with native Indian tribes had ended with the Black Hawk War of 1870. Use of the fort where he was born for protection from Ute indians was largely past although the facilities were a ready way station for decades later for buggy and horse and stage travelers.

When his father was then called to be president over the LDS Millard Stake, Alonzo moved north 42 miles with his father to Fillmore, territorial capital of Utah Territory from 1851 to 1857. A south wing of a contemplated larger capitol building had been completed in 1857 but the territorial legislature met in it only once in 1855. Further construction of the other contemplated three wings and central rotunda dome was postponed until federal appropriations were received but they never were and the original plans were reversed and the capital established in Salt Lake City.

In the completed south wing of the old territorial capitol, Arza Alonzo received formal education along with his other brothers and sisters. President Hinckley's father was only three years older than

Elder Arza Alonzo Hinckley, 1870-1936

Pres. Gordon Bitner HINCKLEY Kinship to Elder Arza Alonzo HINCKLEY, 1870-1936

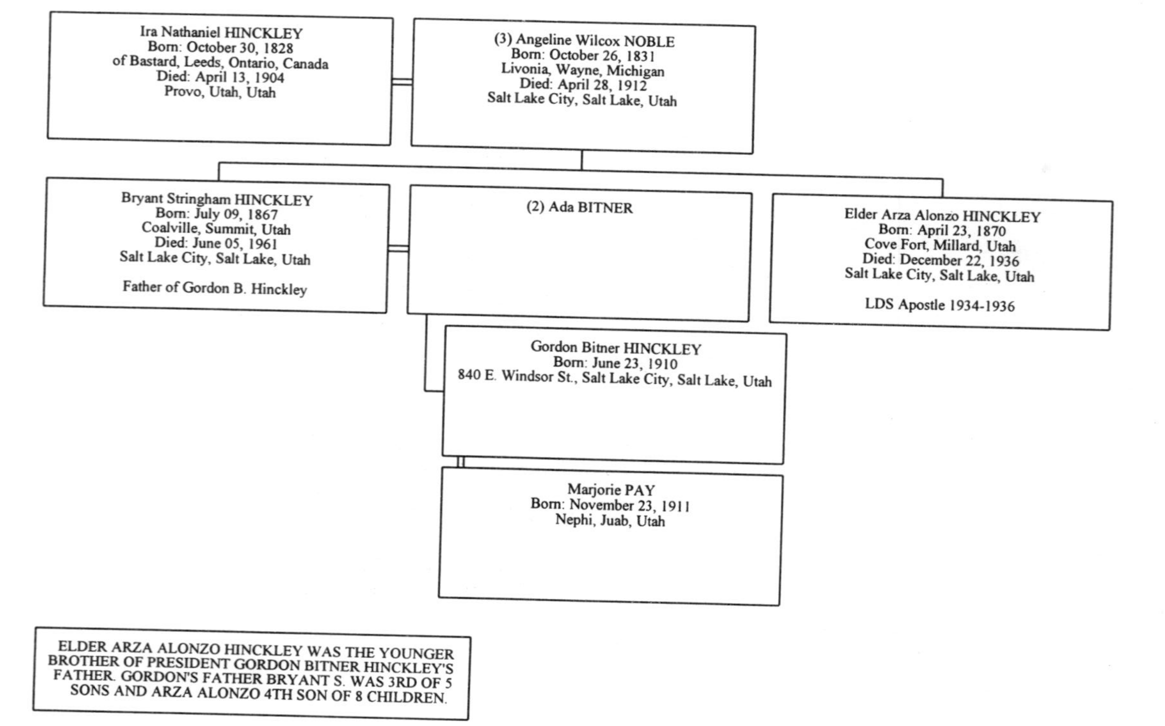

Arza. LDS Academies arose in the late 1880's and onward at enclaves of LDS population for education of youth through college.

The BY Academy, father of future Brigham Young University, was located in the city of Provo just 40 miles south of Salt Lake City. An Academy was also established in Fillmore and Arza studied there some.

In 1892, at the age of 22, Arza Alonzo married Rose May Robinson. They had 14 children. The second was born while Arza filled a foreign LDS mission away from his wife and children in the Netherlands.

During his mission, Arza was blessed to learn the Dutch language and was blessed with the healing power. A lame boy was blessed and healed. A woman cut a hole in the ice of a baptismal site in Winter at Arza's promise she would be healed of an affliction if she did so and was baptized and it was so. She later came to Utah and bore 11 children.

When his father was released as president of the Millard Stake after 26 years service, Arza was chosen to replace him. Shortly thereafter, he received a blessing from the stake patriarch stating in part, "If you continue faithful in this calling, wherein you are called to labor, you will . . . be numbered with the Twelve Apostles of the Church of Jesus Christ of Latter-day Saints."

He then outserved his father as stake president over the same stake for 27 years, was next called to be mission president over the LDS California Mission, and was then called on October 11, 1934, while still serving as mission president in California, to be a member of the LDS Quorum of the Twelve Apostles.

His clear thinking reflected the same genes of President Gordon B. Hinckley and his Uncle Arza Alonzo Hinckley's forebear Governor Thomas Hinckley of the Colony of Plymouth. Men said he was "the outstanding figure at meetings of boards of directors, stockholders, as well as public gatherings." He had good judgment expressed in a dignified manner but forcefully.

While performing his church assignments, he also found time to serve the community as a state legislator and Utah State Agriculture Commissioner. Large arid parcels of soil in and around Fillmore were turned into productive farmland through his leadership and efforts.

When called to be an LDS apostle, Arza, who liked to be called his middle name "Alonzo" and actually signed his name "Alonzo A. Hinckley", was declining in health. The brief two years and two months he served as an apostle before his passing found him, according to the First Presidency of the LDS Church, "unwavering in his testimony of the Living Christ." On December 22, 1936, he died at age 66.[1]

Parents
Bryant Stringham Hinckley
&
Ada Bitner

Bryant Stringham Hinckley, father of President Gordon B. Hinckley, was the 13th in chronology of the 21 children sired by Ira Nathaniel Hinckley, 1828-1904. He was the third of five sons given to Ira Nathaniel by his third wife Angeline Wilcox Noble, older sister to his second wife Adelaide Noble.

Bryant was born in Coalville, Summit County, Utah on July 9, 1867 while his father was away in Central Utah making preparations for construction of Cove Fort on the banks of Cove Creek, 42 miles southeast of Fillmore, Utah Territory. He was born in the home which now has been removed from Coalville to Cove Fort and reconstructed as a memorial to his father and other Hinckley family of Arza Erastus who did so much in the early days of pioneer settlement in Utah. The home was constructed by his father at the same time his father superintended the construction of the rock chapel and haven for safety in Coalville at the request of LDS President Brigham Young.

When Cove Fort had been constructed, Bryant moved with his mother to the fort and spent his first cognitive years there. It took 10 days to travel from Coalville, up in the Rocky Mountains northeast of Salt Lake City, to the volcanic rock fort now established at Cove Fort. Eliza Jane, Ira's first child born in Missouri, was the oldest child at about 18 when his two families all arrived at the fort.

Quarters were spacious in the 100 foot square fort. Six rooms were lined along the north and six along the south interior walls of the fort. Fireplaces were in every room and each room was connected to each other by interconnecting doors. Large and heavy wooden gates eight inches thick swung open to admit visitors at the east entrance.

The oldest child of the Noble sisters was 14 year old Martha Adelaide, daughter of Adelaide. Next was Emily Angeline, age 12, daughter of Angeline. Then came Minerva Angeline, daughter of Adelaide, also about 12 and Lois Electa of Adelaide, age 11. Then came Adelaide's next daughter Luna Adell, about 8.

Ira Noble was the oldest boy, son of Angeline, also about 8 at the time. Lucian Noble, Adelaide's son, about 6, was next in age. Then came Amelia Clarisa, about 7, Angeline's daughter. Harvey Noble, son of Angelina, was only about 3 and Frank Noble, son of Adelaide about the same. Then came Bryant Stringham, just a year old.[1]

The eight daughters and five sons made for a lively family. On top of that there were ranch hands, a telegraph operator and additional helpers. And then came the first baby born at Cove Fort, son Edwin Smith, born to Adelaide on July 21, 1868.

Schooling was conducted at the fort for those who were of age by a Mrs. Dobson whose husband was one of the ranch hands. Local indians visited the fort regularly as well as travelers going south or north. It was a lively way station for everyone travelling on what had come to be known as the "Mormon Corridor", a trail bending slowly to the west from Salt Lake City down to the Nevada desert, the Las Vegas area, and to San Bernadino, California. Believe it or not, LDS pioneers had first been sent by Brigham Young to colonize those two spots. In 1857, most of both groups withdrew from those two areas, however.

Next baby to be born at the fort was Bryant's young brother Arza Alonzo, born April 23, 1870 when Bryant was only 2¾ years old. And then Adelaide had a daughter Nellie born just six months later. Arza Alonzo was destined to serve as an LDS apostle for the last two years of his life.

Two stages, the Salisbury and Gilmore, stopped at the fort each day. They were very heavy and carried Wells Fargo Express Co. strongboxes as well as every type of traveler imaginable. The prominent, the vagabond, the educated, the ignorant, the humble, the proud, the refined, the ruffian all had to pass by Cove Fort. This was the age of the Wild West.[2] Some were traveling west for adventure, some for gold. Others were returning East in disappointment. Others routinely traveled back and forth.

Prayer was held in a north room by the Hinckleys every day.

Visits of Brigham Young

Brigham Young made regular stops at the fort on his way to or from visits to Southern Utah and his Winter home in the town of St. George located in a red soil low elevation area where the climate was warm even in Winter. Adelaide did the hosting and supervised cooking of the daily 12 loaves of bread and other food. The children remember the long table covered in white linen and set just right for the prophet Brigham Young and the group traveling with him.

Entertainment was performed after dinner. Extra beds were made, even on the floors if needed. Lots of home made butter and cheese were prepared.

The Fugitive Native American

At one time a native American named Cissicks and two squaws lived in wickiups west of the fort. The wives worked for the fort washing and performing other domestic chores. The native American was cruel looking and rash tempered. He was hard to manage and once left for several days. He returned one morning and Adelaide prepared his breakfast. While he was eating, Beaver police officers appeared and asked Ira if the native American Cissicks was there.

"Yes," Ira replied.

"Put all his squaws and family in a corner room of the fort and lock the gates. We must take him prisoner. He is wanted for killing two men in the mountains east of here."

They tied his feet under an extra horse and his hands behind him and rode off. His wives were terrified and hid. One put herself in a clothes basket under dirty laundry. The other hid under the floor in one of the rooms of the fort. The native American was taken to Beaver where he was duly executed for murder.[3]

Wrangling and the Misfired Pistol

Bryant Stringham's first remembrances of the fort are the corralling by the wranglers. Horses were needed for the stages and ranch. When new horses were to be broken, the ranch hands would mount in the corrals and put their spurs to the shanks. The contest between man and beast was right out of the Old West. Cowboys in their chaps hung on for dear life as the wild mustangs kicked and bucked. Dust flew in every direction as the critters twisted and turned.

Equally thrilling was the round up of steers and cattle. Bringing them all together to the corrals was a feat in itself. Once again the ranch hand's horses were worked to a lather as they maneuvered this way and in circles coaching a hesitant steer to move in a certain direction. One can almost smell the manure scented dust rising in circles from the stomping hoofs of the horses and cattle.

Then when Bryant was about seven, he and his six year old brother Edward Smith and the fort's telegraph operator Maycock got a little too bold and curious. Pistols were kept under the pillows of beds for safety and the two boys and young telegraph man pulled one out one day. Ed and Maycock took the pistol outside the fort and walked to the window of the room where Bryant was located. As they fidgeted with the pistol,

Ed accidentally pulled the trigger. The pistol was pointed in such a direction, the discharged bullet hit Bryant's left knee.

The doctor in the small town of Beaver 26 miles away was summoned and he commenced a daring needle probe for the bullet but could not find it. So he poured "Jacob's oil" in the wound and bandaged it. The leg ached for nights. Bryant cried and cried. He couldn't sleep. But his father Ira took him in his arms and comforted him. Bryant learned the virtue of kindness from his father. Bryant states he has the distinction of being the only person shot at Cove Fort.[4] He is also the only Hinckley who carried a ball of lead in his leg for the rest of his life.

The Scholar Instinct

In his autobiography, Bryant states he was bashful and retiring as a youth. One time he was asked to give a speech on a segment of the Book of Mormon. He was terrified but still performed.

But his hunger for education and academics manifested itself from the very beginning. His first school teacher was his older sister Minerva, daughter of Adelaide and 10½ years his senior. Bryant had lived at Cove Fort until age 4, then went with his mother to Salt Lake City where she aided other children to attend the John Morgan School. In 1874, they returned to Cove Fort.[5] Following Bryant's encounter with the mischarged pistol, he moved to Fillmore, 42 miles north of Cove Fort, for his first school.[6]

His sister Minerva was 17½ and Bryant about 7. He loved learning the multiplication tables by singing, so much so that he preferred going into the school and singing his M tables rather than being out in the playground.

In 1875, Bryant was baptized into the LDS Church by Millard Stake Patriarch John Ashman.

His second teacher was "Jean", actually Emily Angeline, oldest daughter of his mother Angeline and eight months older than her sister Minerva. He received a third teacher and at about age 10 was awarded the prize for geography from this teacher.

On October 21, 1879, Thomas A. Edison successfully invented the electric light bulb. This momentous event in world history occurred when Bryant was 12 years old. About this time, Bryant was ordained a deacon in the LDS Aaronic Priesthood, another name for the lesser or Levitical Priesthood which ancient descendants of Jacob's son Levi had received from the prophet Moses. This priesthood gave authority to perform temporal ordinances as the ancient Levites did in the Tabernacle of the Congregation during the days of Moses.

Deacon quorums, or groups, were organized with up to 12 deacons each and in each quorum, a president was appointed by the bishop of the ward in which the deacons resided. A bishop was a leader similar to Timothy in ancient times who was charged with the temporal welfare of a group of Latter-day Saints and presided over the group, called a "ward." In addition to the quorum president, two counselors and a secretary were also appointed to oversee the members of the quorum.

The duties of a deacon in the LDS faith were primarily to assist the bishop when called upon to gather "fast offerings", alms given to the poor through donation of at least the equivalent of the uneaten food saved through abstaining from two meals a month; also the passing of the Sacrament at regular Sunday "Sacrament Meetings" held by each ward.

The Sacrament was the ordinance established by Jesus Christ at the Last Supper with his 12 disciples or apostles where bread and pure wine of the vine was first blessed and then distributed or "passed" to those disciples in the upper room during the Israelic Passover in 33 A.D.

Water instead was substituted for wine at this time due to a revelation the prophet Joseph Smith, Jr. had received during his lifetime from a visiting angel which told him in part "it mattereth not what ye shall eat or what ye shall drink when ye partake of the sacrament if it so be that ye do it with an eye single to my glory."[7] Passing the sacrament was considered a very sacred duty and opportunity.

At this time, Bryant received his first ecclesiastical position of leadership in his faith by being appointed president of his deacon's quorum. His leadership talents were already recognized.

He attended Millard Stake Academy one year and two years at the Point of the Mountain and graduated. While in Fillmore, he became a worker (teaching) in the LDS primary, an organization in the LDS faith for training children three to 11 years of age.

His next progression in holding the Aaronic Priesthood was being ordained to the office of teacher. This privilege was given to young men around the age of 14 or 15. It authorized not only the passing of the sacrament but also its sacred preparation and also gave teachers the charge to "watch over the church always and be with and strengthen them; and see that there is no iniquity in the church, neither hardness with each other, neither lying, backbiting, nor evil speaking; and see that the church meet together often, and also see that all the members do their duty.[8] Instead of 12 there could be as many as 24 in teachers quorums.

On October 31, 1883, at age 16, Bryant Stringham Hinckley accompanied his mother and brothers Frank, Edwin, Arza Alonzo and Elmer together with a hired girl named Sena Rasmussen in three heavy wagons laden with household goods, furniture and bedding on a move to Provo, Utah. His mother Angelina took the boys to Provo for schooling at Brigham Young Academy, a school of higher education established for education of the LDS mind as well as the soul.

Here he and three of his brothers registered at the intermediate department at the academy.[9] And in his religion, he received the third office in the Aaronic Priesthood, once again by the "laying on of hands" as when he had been made a deacon and teacher. Men holding the same or greater priesthood gathered around him and placed their hands on his head, one acting as mouth, and pronounced the prayerful ordinance on him as Jesus had "chosen and ordained" his apostles in ancient times.[10]

This new office of "priest" in the Aaronic Priesthood gave him authority not only to pass and prepare the sacrament but now also bless it before its distribution to LDS members. It also authorized him to perform the ordinance of baptism.

At Brigham Young Academy, he entered and won the oratorical contest. He also at one time won a prize for being the handsomest man.[11] In 1889, he met his future first wife Christine Johnson at the commissary at BY Academy. During this time his first published article entitled "The Pioneers" was printed in two LDS periodicals entitled *The Contributor* and the *Juvenile Instructor*. In May 1889, just before he turned 22, he was awarded the degree of Bachelor of Pd. and a B.D. degree from the General Board of LDS Church Schools.

Frisco Challenge

His degree was earned and now it was time to use it. Bryant went to the boom town of Frisco in Beaver County about 40 miles southwest of Fillmore to teach school. There he stayed for three years carrying the mail on Saturdays on the horse "Old George" from the railroad depot to the post office and contending with Harry Houston, a rowdy student, in battles for three weeks and a lot of yearly persuasion.

Bryant counts this teaching challenge as his hardest experience.[12]

He returned to Fillmore after his first teaching experience much wiser and patient and looking towards some advanced educational training in the Northeast, an interesting choice considering the future call he would receive some 44 years later to preside over an LDS mission in the same area. He received the Melchizedek Priesthood, the Higher Priesthood, allowing a man to administer in not only temporal but also all spiritual ordinances of the gospel of Jesus Christ.

Then on August 24, 1892, he was "set apart", a special ordinance where authority and a blessing to perform certain work or callings in the LDS Church is given by priesthood leaders, not only to study at college in Chicago but also as a missionary in the Northern States Mission. He was admonished to spread the message of the restored gospel to all with whom he came in contact.[13]

At Eastman National College, Poughkeepsie, New York,[14] he studied and in less than a year returned Provo, Utah where he married his first wife Christine Johnson for time and all eternity on June 28, 1893 in the temple just completed and dedicated in Salt Lake City after 40 years construction. This marriage also allowed him to receive his "endowment" in connection with his temple marriage sealing.

By this time Bryant Stringham Hinckley had reached his full stature of 6 feet. He was one inch shorter than his father Ira. He was slender in build and only about 135-150 lbs. But he always dressed neatly and stood erect. Good suits and white shirts were worn to work and white or khaki shirts and trousers were worn in farm work.[15]

Professor at Brigham Young Academy

The newlyweds returned to Provo where Bryant was given a teaching position at the Brigham Young Academy. The opportunity gave him increased experience in dealing with people and imparting acquired knowledge to them. For seven years he continued teaching at the academy. He became a father on July 10, 1894 with the birth of a son the new parents named Bryant Stanford. Two daughters and another son were born in Provo to the new family.

The other son was named Heber Grant Hinckley after a good young friend of Bryant's named Heber Jeddy Grant. Heber was at that time in his 16th year as an LDS apostle, having been ordained to that high calling at the age of 25. Heber, 11 years Bryant's senior, was asked by Bryant to name and bless Heber Grant Hinckley, another ordinance of the LDS faith where a Melchizedek Priesthood holder will act as voice while holding an infant in his hands and, often joined with a number of other priesthood holders, pronounces a name upon the baby's head and gives a blessing.

In January 1896, Utah was granted statehood by the United States Congress six years after LDS prophet Wilford Woodruff had issued his "Manifesto" terminating the practice of plural marriage by the LDS Church. This was a momentous occasion for the residents of Utah. It restored to them the privileges they had been denied due to the polygamy controversy. It also gave them new impetus for development.

Then Bryant was approached to become dean of the business school at the LDS College in Salt Lake City. He accepted, moved to Salt Lake City and began March 4, 1900 overseeing the business courses taught at the Templeton Building, a six story structure located at that time on the southeast corner of Main Street and South Temple. The Salt Lake Temple just completed in April 1893 was located diagonally to the northwest across the street in the block which was now known as "Temple Square."

At the time Bryant assumed leadership of the business school at LDS College, there were 45 states in the union of the United States. Population of the country was 76,000,000 and the average wage was 22¢ per hour. Automobiles were appearing although there were only 150 miles of paved highway in the entire United States.[16]

Tithing buildings designed as points for storage and accounting of donation of one tenth of each Latter-day Saints' increase in "kind" or currency were still located just across the street to the north and the famous home of Brigham Young which also served as the first LDS Church office in the Salt Lake Valley, called the Beehive and Lion Houses, was located just one block to the east on the north street side.

Here a young 20 year old woman by the name of Ada Bitner was instructing with her sister Della. Another teacher was a young man by the name of J. Reuben Clark, Jr. These associations with each other daily were destined to profoundly affect not only professor Hinckley but President Gordon B. Hinckley's life in future years. A small faculty composed of only about a half dozen teachers, this LDS business school was only part of a larger campus just then forming on the northwest corner of the block just east of the temple.

LDS College, called LDS University from 1901 to 1926, was growing under the direction of the LDS general authorities out of its 1886 forerunner the Salt Lake Stake Academy into an institution for high school and higher education. In the next 10 years, four buildings would be completed forming the school's campus.

With the turn of the century, many other progressive projects had also been recently completed or started in Salt Lake. The old tithing buildings were razed across the street immediately north of the Templeton Building for construction of the future 10 story Hotel Utah and for a "grand gym" by its east side.[17]

The first phase dark stone two story Italian Renaissance Alta Men's Club building had been completed at the southeast corner of 100 East South Temple Street in 1898 diagonally across the street from Brigham Young's Beehive House. A large mansion of red sandstone built by railroad and mining magnate Alfred William McCune and his wife Elizabeth Ann Claridge was reaching completion on the hill overlooking the Salt Lake Temple at 200 North Main Street.

Preparations were moving forward for construction of a Catholic Cathedral of the Madeleine two blocks east on South Temple Street. Talk of building a fine capitol building was being had and the fourth LDS prophet Lorenzo Snow was implementing a revelation received in St. George the last part of 1899 giving new emphasis to Latter-day Saints in paying one's "tithes" in order to retire his church's debts.

Trolley barns were now in use at 700 East and 500 South housing the now electrified old mule drawn trolleys which wound around miles of tracks in the growing streets of the city.

The business courses in 1900 were not only taught on the sixth floor of the Templeton Building but also in the Social Hall constructed in 1851 by the early pioneers as the first gathering place for socials and theater. It was located up a block to the east of the Templeton Building and down south one half block on about 51 South 100 East. Also, some courses were taught at the west part of Brigham Young's old home called the Lion House. Bryant taught algebra, history, theology, political science, economics, and some other courses.[18]

Bryant was ordained a seventy in his LDS faith, giving him membership in the 42nd quorum of seventy.[19] This office gave him special charge to spread the gospel message he so fervently believed.

Then in April 1900, just a month after assuming head of the business school of LDS College, he was asked by the general authorities of the LDS Church to serve on one of its general boards. This important position was to assist the youth of the LDS Church as a member of the General Board of the Young Men's Mutual

Improvement Association. The position required considerable time working with other general board members in organizing and implementing activities and programs supporting male youth and encouraging them in their social and spiritual growth.

"General boards" had been established for four organizations: An organization formed by Joseph Smith, Jr. in the Nauvoo days for women before he died called the "Relief Society", designed to perform compassionate Christian service; the Young Men's Mutual Improvement Association; a corresponding organization for young women called the Young Ladies Mutual Improvement Association; and the Primary organization for teaching young children. Another organization for Sunday school coordination and textbook generation had developed in 1872 first called the Deseret Sunday School Union.[18]

But this was not all for Bryant. In addition to his position as head of the business school at LDS College and his new assignment on the general board of the YMMIA, Bryant was called to serve as an alternate high councilor on the high council of the Salt Lake Stake. Twelve men filled the council in each stake of Zion and a substitute or two were also called to fill the vacancy of a regular high councilor in meetings when they might be absent much like an alternate juror filled the place of jurors when needed. In order to receive this calling, another priesthood office was conferred upon Bryant by ordination–that of "high priest."

This office was like that of "elder" and "seventy" held by Melchizedek or "higher priesthood" holders but its special duty was that of "presiding" and spiritual administration. Thus high councilors were given the Melchizedek Priesthood office of high priest. Stake presidents, bishops and most of their counselors were also given this priesthood office. The ordination was performed on March 12, 1901 and Bryant was contemporaneously "set apart" as an alternate high councilor in the Salt Lake Stake of Zion.

Joseph F. Smith, son of the prophet Joseph Smith, Jr.'s older brother Hyrum, became sixth prophet of the LDS Church on October 17, 1902 following the death of Lorenzo Snow one week earlier.

Additional children were born to Bryant and his first wife Christine Johnson Hinckley while they were in Salt Lake. A daughter was born January 23, 1902 but on the very same day their last daughter born in Provo, Grace Hinckley, passed away at only two years of age.

In 1903, the LDS Church, through generous renewed tithing

contributions by members of the Church, paid the first of two $500,000.00 bonds it had issued to pay off its debts.[19] Orville and Wilbur Wright also made their first successful 12 second flight in their airplane on December 17, 1903.

The first subway in the United States opened in New York City in 1904 and in March 1904 a Bureau of Information Building, forerunner of LDS visitor centers, was opened on the south end of Temple Square. Then two sets of twins, one set males and one set females, were born in 1904 and 1905 respectively. One of the female twins was stillborn, however. Then on May 11, 1908, their last child, a daughter, was born.

The family's first home was at 723 East 700 South in Salt Lake. There the two sets of twins were born. The first set arrived February 1, 1904. Twenty-five days later the Liberty Stake was formed February 26 out of the Salt Lake Stake. And it encompassed the boundaries where Bryant and Christine's family resided. Bryant was called to the first high council of the new Liberty Stake by its initial president Hugh J. Cannon, son of George Q. Cannon who had been a counselor to four prophets in succession–Brigham Young, John Taylor, Wilford Woodruff, and Lorenzo Snow.

Hugh J. Cannon had apprenticed the printing trade from his father and was recommended by Bryant to the LDS Church to become editor of the LDS owned newspaper called the *Deseret News*. The word "deseret" was taken out of Mormon's history and meant "honey bee" to ancient inhabitants of America named therein. When Brigham Young first named the territory inhabited by the Latter-day Saint pioneers, he called it "Deseret," although the state which eventually formed was named "Utah" by the United States Congress.

One of the fellow high councilmen was Fred M. Michelsen. They were assigned to one of several committees organized to assist the work of an LDS stake. Many hours were spent working together on the Aaronic Priesthood high council committee.

January 1, 1905 saw the opening of the LDS Hospital built on the hills north and east overlooking the Salt Lake Temple and on January 10, 1907, the second and last bond of indebtedness in the principal sum of $500,000.00 was paid by the LDS Church making it essentially debt free from that time forward.

On April 21, 1907, both Bryant and Fred Michelsen started working together as stake president counselors when Bryant was called to be 2nd counselor to President Hugh J. Cannon.

Everything was going rather wonderfully for Bryant and Christine in 1907. They purchased a large two story home at 700 South Windsor Street (840 East) for $3,600.00. The LDS General Priesthood Committee on Outlines was established April 8, 1908 and moved to establish age groups for the ordination to offices in the Aaronic Priesthood. This move set the average age for becoming a deacon, teacher or priest.

However, shortly thereafter, while Bryant and Christine were visiting Provo after birth of their last child and daughter Christine, Bryant's wife Christine suffered an attack of appendicitis. She was operated on but did not survive and died July 11, 1908 at age 38 exactly two months to the day from the day she had given birth to her daughter Christine.[20] This event was devastating to Bryant.

After a short 15 years of marriage, Bryant had suffered almost the identical tragedy his grandmother Lois Judd Hinckley had experienced in 1831 at age 26. But he had eight of his ten children surviving–Bryant Stanford, just 14; Josephine Levina, 12; Heber Grant, 9½; Caroline, 5½; Wendell J., 4¼; Ralph Waldo, 4¼; Venice, 2½; and Christine, 2 months–and Bryant himself was almost but not yet 41.

On October 1, 1908, Henry Ford introduced his mass produced Model-T automobile and the clamor for gas driven cars was on. Bryant made arrangements following his wife's death for her parents, Niels and Josephine Caroline Mathia Johnson, to care for 5½ year old Caroline and 2 month old Christine. His mother Angeline and his mother's sister Adelaide, both still alive, assisted with the remaining six children at the family home on Windsor Street. Additional housekeepers were also enlisted from time to time while Bryant thought through his future and the future of his young family.[21]

Courtship of Ada Bitner

While teaching, Bryant would read the statement about the virtuous woman found in Proverbs, last chapter.[22] "Who can find a virtuous woman for her price is far above rubies."[23] Then he looked at one of his co-teachers, Miss Ada Bitner, single and age 28.

He started courting her. One of his visits was to his stake president Hugh J. Cannon. President Cannon felt she was a beautiful character and he and his wife rejoiced in the prospects Bryant would win her.[24]

Ada was a petite young woman around 5 feet four inches tall with large blue eyes and an oval face. She was between 110-120 lbs. in weight and of "almost translucent" skin.[25] Her hair was warm, rich, and slightly red. Modest and quiet, she had a light heart. Bryant had seen her cheerfulness and the spring in her step.[26] And she was smart. First teacher in the Utah Territory to teach the Gregg method of shorthand, she also was an accomplished pianist.

Bryant had known her now for almost nine years since he came to the business school in early 1900. He saw there were many similarities in their makeup. Both loved knowledge. Bryant had been accumulating a large number of books and so had Ada. They were both academians, professors on a university level. And they both loved culture and the arts.

Their differences were mainly in social pleasures. Bryant had through the years overcome his shyness and timidity. He had taken oratory at B.Y. Academy and had the growing experience with rowdy students in Frisco. Now he was molded as a powerful public speaker. As early as September 13, 1903, at age 36, he had stood at the pulpit in the Tabernacle on Temple Square and delivered a message on "Mormonism is Practical" during the quarterly conference of the Salt Lake Stake. This pulpit was the same pulpit where Brigham Young had stood in LDS general conferences as well as every prophet since him.

Ada on the other hand was very shy before audiences although she enjoyed dancing and playing the piano and entertaining guests. She had acquired a baby brand piano and a nice alto voice.[27]

The Bitner Heritage

Sometime between September 1639 and 1673, Reverend Hans Herr migrated with his wife Elizabeth Mylin Kendig from Zurich, Switzerland to Lancaster County, Pennsylvania. There, their daughter Maria was born at Strasburg in 1673. Maria married another reverend named Benedict Brackbill about 1690 produced Barbara Brackbill in Strasburg May 10, 1714 who married Jacob Groff about 1734. Jacob had been born at Earl, Lancaster County, Pennsylvania. Anna was one of their progeny, born July 20 1740 at Camago, Lancaster County, Pennsylvania. She married Christian Barr whose ancestors had resided as early as 1692 in Pennsylvania. Christian Barr and Anna Groff became the parents of Anna Barr.[28]

At least one other minister exists on the ancestral line of Ada Bitner. Hans Herr, born before 1655, was from Switzerland. Benedict Brackhill also was a reverend, born 1665, and Melchior Brenneman, born 1726 in Pennsylvania was a minister, whose father Christian had come from Germany.[29] It appeared some power higher than man was

Bryant Stringham Hinckley, 1867-1961
About when He Courted Ada Bitner

Ada Bitner, 1880-1930
About the Time She Courted Bryant S. Hinckley

preparing the way for the future parents of President Gordon B. Hinckley to be nurtured and inculcated with principles and values of faith.

Ada's Bitner heritage stemmed not only from Switzerland but also from France where other progenitors moved to Germany, then Holland, then America when William Penn, an early American patriot, was alive.[30]

It was Anna Barr who has the distinction of being the first progenitor on Ada Bitner's line to join the LDS faith. She was born the December 4, 1803 in Bart Township, Lancaster County, Pennsylvania the sixth of 13 children, six sons and seven daughters, of her parents. She first married Samuel Musser in Lancaster County, Pennsylvania on January 27, 1824 and had children by Samuel. But Samuel died young.

Abraham Bitner, to be Anna's second husband, had been born May 23, 1782 in Manor Township, Lancaster County, Pennsylvania and had married his first wife Catherine Schneider on August 3, 1806. But his first spouse also died young. Abraham's parents had come to America in the mid 1800's from Sheffield, Yorkshire, England.

Both Anna Barr (Musser) and Abraham Bitner, 22½ years her senior, met and brought their families together in a family union in Harrisburg, Dauphin County, Pennsylvania on May 12, 1835. Their first of three children was born in Washington, Lancaster County Pennsylvania on June 25, 1836 but she died at only eight months of age. And then their only son and future father of Ada Bitner, named Breneman Barr Bitner after Anna Barr's maternal Brennaman surname ancestors, was born December 15, 1837 by the Susquehana River, in Washington Borough, Lancaster County, Pennsylvania. [31]

After Breneman was born, Abraham Bitner took his new wife Anna and the combined Musser and Bitner children west to a fine prairie near Quincy, Illinois "covered with flowers of various colors, standing forth as so many witnesses, proclaiming with thousands of voices to the traveler as he moves along."[32] There, one more daughter, their last child Martha Ann Bitner, was born November 13, 1840 near Quincy, Adams County, Illinois.[33] But Abraham Bitner's health was waning at the time of his daughter Martha's birth so the family returned to Philadelphia to surrounding relatives where he died at age 58½ on November 18, 1841.[34]

Anna Barr (Musser) Bitner was one month from turning 38 when her second husband died. Now she had not only the Musser children

Breneman Barr Bitner, 1837-1909
Father of Ada Bitner Hinckley

but also two surviving Bitner children to raise alone. Ada Bitner's future father Breneman was not quite four years old. His younger sister was just a year old.

At this delicate time in Anna's life, the message of the restored gospel came to her. She and her Musser children were old enough to understand the message and when the LDS missionaries preached in the nation's famous city where independence had been declared in 1776 and the United States constitution crafted in the 1780's, Anna and some of the Musser children entered the waters of baptism in Philadelphia, Pennsylvania in October 1843 becoming Latter-day Saints.

The LDS elders counseled to "gather" with the rest of the saints in Nauvoo, Illinois so she with her children went back to the plains near Quincy where they had previously briefly lived. Then she moved to Nauvoo after the majority of the saints had been expelled. About 1847, she too was compelled to exit Nauvoo and took her children across the Mississippi and across Iowa where the family lived in several locations for some two years.

In 1849, the family took a wagon and two oxen loaded with all they owned and crossed the plains with another group of LDS pioneers. Breneman Barr Bitner was about 11½ years old and helped drive the oxen. "I drove two yoke of oxen and a heavily laden wagon through heat and cold across the deserts and rivers and mountains to this valley. We had no tipovers, lost no cattle, and were free from molestation by Indians. The Lord is ever mindful of the widow and the fatherless," he wrote.[35] They arrived at Big Mountain's summit and gazed out towards the Great Salt Lake Valley in October 1849. As soon as the family arrived, Breneman was baptized in Salt Lake City on October 27, 1849.[36]

Life in Salt Lake & Move to Big Cottonwood

When Breneman, his mother and fellow siblings arrived in the Salt Lake Valley, it was fast turning Winter. A few settlements existed in the Valley but most was still covered with the wild sagebrush unique to the semi-arid Western territories. The Rocky Mountains to the east of the Valley were a distinctive chain from which one could orient himself. First from the little Salt Lake City development moving south was a rock slated majestic mountain the pioneers named "Mount Olympus." Next to the south came a single mountain named "Lone Peak" and towards the southern end of the Valley was a mountain with two summits named "Twin Peaks."

Bitner Line Pedigree of Gordon Bitner HINCKLEY

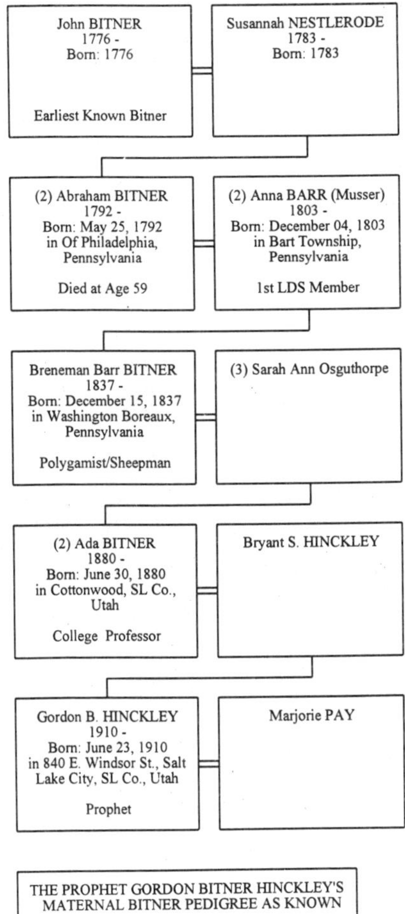

Maternal Bitner Kinship of Gordon Bitner Hinckley

Name	Relationship with John BITNER
(Musser), (2) Anna BARR	Daughter-in-law
BITNER, (2) Abraham	Son
BITNER, (2) Ada	Great-granddaughter
BITNER, Breneman Barr	Grandson
BITNER, John	Self
HINCKLEY, Bryant Stringham	Husband of the great-granddaughter
HINCKLEY, Gordon Bitner	2nd great-grandson
NESTLERODE, Susannah	Wife
Osguthorpe, (3) Sarah Ann	Wife of the grandson
PAY, Marjorie	Wife of the 2nd great-grandson

The Musser and Bitner children and their mother Anna went first to downtown Salt Lake City and lived for six years. In 1855, they moved south along the foothills of the Rocky Mountains on the east side of the Valley past Mt. Olympus mountain to an area in between Mt. Olympus and Lone Peak. Here a stream flowed out of a canyon separating these two mountains. There were lots of cottonwood trees along the stream's banks and so both the canyon and the area where the stream entered the Valley were named "Big Cottonwood" by the early Latter-day Saint settlers.

Here the family moved. Breneman was now going on 18 and helped establish a farm. "It was a time of great scarcity although we did not suffer unduly because we lived on game. Many people, though, were in dire need of food,"[37] Breneman wrote in his diary. That year grasshoppers had plagued the saints crops causing much damage.

Two years later, a crisis arose between the United States Government and the LDS people. Rumors and gossip were reaching the East accusing the "Mormons" of rebellion and intent to create their own government. US President James Buchanan initially believed the rumors and ordered an army under the command of General Johnston to take Albert Cummings and establish him as the territorial governor of Utah.

Brigham Young called out all able bodied men to serve in a state militia to slow the arrival of the army until the true facts could be made known to the US Congress and President. Breneman served as well as Ira Nathaniel Hinckley's older brother Arza Erastus Hinckley in this campaign.

Breneman records, "In the winter of 1857 I went out with a large company of others to meet Johns[t]on's Army. We crossed the mountains in the depth of winter with the snow four feet deep, and often we had to help the horses pull the wagons. We wore very scanty clothing but lived well on bread made of flour and water and some beef we secured from Government freighters."[38]

Breneman progressed in the offices of the LDS priesthood and was to turn 27 five days later when he took a bride by the name of Mary Esther Benedict and was married for time and all eternity to her in the Endowment House on December 10, 1864. His young wife, however, died a short time later without bearing him any children.

Breneman next married Marjory Martina Halseth on April 10, 1866 who bore him 12 children and then entered into plural marriage by marrying Sarah Anne Osguthorpe.

Ada Bitner's Mother Sarah Anne Osguthorpe

Sarah Anne Osguthorpe moved with her parents Lydia Roper and John Osguthorpe from Sheffield, England when she was 1½ years old. Since her birth on May 23, 1847, the family had planned the trip to America, arriving seven weeks after the ship they were traveling on suffered a leak and smallpox broke out and killed several passengers. Her parents took her to Philadelphia, Pennsylvania where they, like Breneman's mother Anna Barr, heard the LDS missionaries' message and were converted. When she was six, her family, now with one other child, left for the Rocky Mountains with the Charles Welkin Company in April 1853.

Indians stampeded their cattle and buffalo would spook the oxen. But after three months, they too reached the summit of Big Mountain and made the steep descent into the Valley. When Sarah saw the still desolate sagebrush valley she is said to have grieved, "Oh! Let's go back to Philadelphia!"[39]

But the Osguthorpe family settled like the Bitners on the east foothills of the Valley. However they were a little closer to the main settlement of Salt Lake by another small stream which flowed from a canyon on the north side of Mt. Olympus mountain. A mill had been constructed on the stream and so the canyon, stream and area was named "Millcreek" by the early settlers. Sarah's parents there built a good farm close to the mouth of the canyon with orchards. Her father purchased a sawmill.

Sarah had a sweet voice and was asked to sing at various activities. She also nursed the sick through scarlet fever and smallpox. But she never contracted these diseases. Schooling was only a few months at a Mrs. Brown's but she learned to read and had a happy, serious but "often gay" adolescence. At 19, an engagement with a young man was broken and she turned to her faith in prayers for peace and consolation.

Then she was approached by Breneman Barr Bitner to be his plural wife. She prayed diligently for guidance and finally felt this was what her God desired. She became Breneman's plural wife on January 4, 1869 for time and all eternity in the Endowment House in Salt Lake.

"The Bitner Girls"

Sarah bore Breneman seven children. All in all Breneman sired four sons, two from each wife, and 15 daughters. Sarah moved to the Big Cottonwood farm three years after her marriage and there mingled with and helped Marina, Breneman's second wife, and her children. The

John Osguthorpe
Father of Sarah Anne Osguthorpe Bitner

Lydia Roper Osguthorpe
Mother of Sarah Anne Osguthorpe Bitner

farm was a place of beauty with a nice flowing well, orchards, shade trees, meadows and fields of grain. While babies slept, Sarah and Martina would often dance for rest and relaxation, sometimes until 4 A.M. Breneman meanwhile was a foreman at some of the Big Cottonwood sawmills in the canyon, raised sheep and fine horses, including a pure strain of Hambletonian stock, purchased property elsewhere in the Valley, built new roads and bridges, was a commissary in the Black Hawk Indian War of 1867 when two of his comrades were ambushed and killed by indians and became an assessor which he performed late into his life.[40]

His religion did not let him rest either. He was made a Sunday School superintendent and then bishop of the Big Cottonwood Ward. In 1871, he also was called on a mission to the Eastern States Mission, leaving his wives and children to survive on their own industry as the "brethren" often did at that time when the general authorities asked them to preach the gospel in the missionfield.[41]

Breneman was said to have been consistently kind, a man of great faith, impartial to children, just, loving to children and friendly. He stood tall and straight even when old and a shock of white hair gave him a look of poise and dignity. His integrity was said to have been absolute. He did not receive education beyond grade schools but educated himself by reading good books. Politically he actively worked in the Republican Club for young men.[42]

The 15 daughters he fathered became known as the "Bitner Girls" and Ada Bitner became the 13th of the 15. Ada was born June 30, 1880 to Sarah Anne Osguthorpe Bitner in the large two story brick home which had been built out of the original adobe structure. Its design resembled those in Pennsylvania from where Breneman originated. The actual street address today is about 4800 South and 1500 East. The farm contained a full 65 acres of land.

The Bitners were said to be the ideal polygamous family. At the end of Sarah and Marjory Martina's lives, they lived together in the same home. Ada's two older brothers, mothered by Sarah, purchased the Kimball Station, a Pony Express stop. All but two of the children received college education. The three oldest daughters took singing lessons from their grandfather Osguthorpe and came home one day singing, "The angels were sing-ging, the bells were ring-ging." Grandfather Osguthorpe was teaching them not only singing but also correct diction.

Breneman's second wife Marjory Martina Halseth, of Norwegian ancestry, had a nice Norwegian accent at first but was tutored by Breneman to pronounce proper English "v" sounds. "W's" were also mastered.[43]

Ada attracted to sister Della, daughter of Marjory, and both got along well. The Bitner girls visited the "city" from time to time. There were mule-drawn streetcars. Buggys and wagons were needed to get to the city. No high-rise buildings yet existed. It was about 12 miles to downtown Salt Lake City from Big Cottonwood.

When their father took them to town, usually on Monday mornings, he often would recite hymns and poetry. "God moves in a mysterious way, His wonders to perform. He plants His footsteps on the sea, and rides upon the storm," and then after singing the verse, would add, "Behind a frowning providence, He hides a smiling face."[44]

The family had family prayers in the morning and sometimes in the evenings. And the girls were taught to ride "like gentlewomen" on his Hambletonian breed horses. Daughters Erma and Madeline were especially good riders. At supper one evening, a maid set and removed the tableware and plates. Until the crumbs were removed, dessert was not served. The dessert was one peach each.[45]

Ada Bitner's Childhood

Ada lived at the farm the first seven years of her life. Then she and her mother and her two brothers and four sisters by mother Sarah moved in to downtown Salt Lake City at 274 East 400 South. There her mother Sarah took care of her grandmother Starr. A cow was cared for as well as mushrooms grown. A room was added for Anna, daughter of Marjory, and Mary, Sarah's oldest daughter, where they could conduct a dress making business. They both became successful seamstresses through this trade until they both married.

Sarah and those that lived with her, including Ada, later moved to a home at 200 South Hawkes Court and then about November 9, 1901, moved to a home purchased for $2,500.00 at 259 Center Street. From this location, both Sarah and Marjory Martina's children attended high school, college or went to work in central Salt Lake.[46]

Ada received early schooling from the local stakes who had been given charge for the education of youth within their boundaries through establishment of Stake Academies. She, like her future husband Bryant Stringham Hinckley, thrived on education and learning. At the age of about nine, she was given a dictionary in recognition for achievement.

She had obtained recognition from her teacher "for excellence."[47] Then on September 3, 1889, at age nine, she was baptized and confirmed a member of the Church of Jesus Christ of Latter-day Saints.

In September 1894, at age 14, she received schooling at the Oquirrh School which later became the Fremont School. Then, desiring additional skills and knowledge, she went to a school in Chicago and studied business courses, including the newly developed Gregg shorthand. She was an exceptional student with great penmanship.[48] One of her school friends was the daughter of LDS apostle Frank Y. Taylor.[49]

After graduating from the school in Chicago, Ada returned to Salt Lake City and obtained employment along with her close sister Della at the Salt Lake Business College teaching Gregg shorthand, English and typing.[50] The business college was soon acquired by the LDS Church and assimilated into the developing LDS College at the time her future husband Bryant S. Hinckley was brought from the B.Y. Academy to take over its direction.

At one time her sister Erma also taught at the LDS College & University. The head of the shorthand department was J. Reuben Clark, Jr., later to be a US ambassador and first presidency member of the LDS Church. One of her students during the 10 years she taught was LeGrand Richards, also destined to be one of the greatest evangelic LDS apostles and the author of *A Marvelous Work and a Wonder*.[51]

During these years she developed an abiding testimony of the LDS doctrines, studied piano, sang, and acquired the skills which would make her a very good mother and mate. Cooking, sewing, ironing were all developed. Her grammar was excellent. She had a good vocabulary and reading was exciting for her. She is said to have been brilliant.

The Formation of the Bryant S. & Ada Bitner Hinckley Family

Through this background, it was not hard to see Bryant and Ada, although Bryant was almost 13 years her senior, were meant to be husband and wife. Someone had arranged and planned this long before the generation of Bryant and Ada came. Ada was excellent with English. Bryant took up the slack in mathematics and history.

The year 1909 was a momentous year in Utah, too. Utah was discovering its vast mineral and mining resources. Copper was being mined from a large open pit mine on the west hills of the Valley. The town of Eureka along the same chain of western mountains about 60 miles to the south of the Salt Lake Valley was a booming silver mining town.

Construction of the Hotel Utah on what was to become "Administration Block" was started across the street north of the Templeton Building and on the northeast corner of Main Street and South Temple Street.

A large sandstone Union Pacific Railroad Depot was completed in French Renaissance style at the west end of 100 South Street at 400 West. Increased railroad traffic was continuously traveling through Salt Lake which was rapidly becoming known as "the crossroads of the West" due to its strategic location between Eastern cities and growing Los Angeles and San Francisco. To go to Los Angeles you traveled south from Salt Lake. To go to San Francisco, you traveled immediately west.

The Cathedral of the Madeleine was also opened in 1909. And the First Presidency, composed of the LDS prophet and at least two counselors, issued a statement on the origins of man advocating man's divine parentage by a loving spiritual Father in Heaven and a divine atonement of man's sins by God's literal son Jesus Christ for those who believed on Christ and live all of his teachings including that of being born "of water and of the spirit" by baptism administered through valid priesthood holders.[52]

During this exciting time in Salt Lake City, Bryant and Ada continued their courtship. But on April 10, 1909, her father Brenneman Barr Bitner passed away in Salt Lake City at age 72. Still betrothal to Bryant ensued and Ada received her endowment in the Salt Lake Temple on June 24, 1909. Bryant, almost 42, and Ada, age 29, were then sealed as husband and wife in the Salt Lake Temple for time and all eternity on August 4, 1909.[53]

Instantaneously she became the mother of six children at home and two others being raised by their grandparents Johnson in Provo, Utah. The children at home were 15, 10, 5 and 5 year old sons and 13 and 3 year old daughters.

She terminated her employment at the LDS University business college and devoted all of her time as housewife and mother. She brought all of her books and her baby grand piano to the Hinckley home at 700 South Windsor Avenue (840 East) where she placed it in the parlor.

On April 14, 1910, Bryant was recommended by Elder Hyrum M. Smith, a son of the then prophet Joseph F. Smith, to fill the position of general secretary for an LDS owned health and sports complex soon to be completed on the Administration Block to the south of the now completed LDS University campus.[54]

One day before the appointment, Bryant was called and sustained to be President High J. Cannon's 2nd counselor in the Liberty Stake Presidency replacing Philip Maycock who had died. The formal sustaining and setting apart transpired at services on April 21, 1910.[55] The next day on April 22, 1910, official announcement of Bryant's appointment to direct operations at the new Deseret Gym were made.

Bryant visited the East on $500.00 to study gymns. He examined those at the University of Chicago, Boston, Dayton and New York City.[56]

BOYHOOD

With all the foregoing ancestral background, Latter-day Saints believe God's final preparations were made to bring Gordon Bitner Hinckley into this world. One of the Latter-day Saint doctrines is that everyone is foreordained to do certain works on this earth–not predestined. To be predestined would mean God has taken away man's moral agency to choose.

But Latter-day Saints believe every woman and man placed on this world is capable of making choices independent of his divine parentage. If he or she chooses, he or she can follow the path designated to bring him or her to full experience with the calls God prepared and "ordained" them to do while their mortal test continues on this earth. But if each woman or man so lists, they can reject the opportunities God prepared for them and forfeit the blessings which could have been theirs.

Gordon B. Hinckley lived past the 38 years of the LDS Church's first leader Joseph Smith, Jr. and its second prophet-leader Brigham Young's 71 years for what Latter-day Saints believe is some divine purpose. The revelations received by Joseph Smith, Jr. in his short 38 years of mortality include a statement "Your days are known and thy years shall not be numbered less."[1] The stage had been set for the birth of Gordon Bitner Hinckley, destined to be the 15th prophet of the Church of Jesus Christ of Latter-day Saints.

Ada had conceived about September 1909 and the son in her womb had matured to full term when on June 23, 1910 she gave birth to a healthy baby boy on the second floor of the Hinckley family home located on the southwest corner of 700 South and Windsor Street (840 East), Salt Lake City, Salt Lake County, Utah.

The parents named him Gordon Bitner Hinckley and he was formally named and blessed at their local LDS 1st Ward in Liberty Stake where they were members.

The population of Salt Lake City was 92,777 when Gordon was born and the entire population of the Salt Lake Valley was 131,426.[2] William Howard Taft was president of the United States and then campaigning for a second term on the Republican Party ticket. Woodrow Wilson was challenging for the Democratic Party and Theodore Roosevelt was the wild card, running independently on his own "Bull Moose Party" when he did not obtain the Republican nomination. The divided Republican Party aided Woodrow Wilson's victory.[3]

Anti-Mormon propaganda was beginning to surge, particularly about Senator Reed Smoot, accused of polygamy, who had been seated in the United States Congress after three years of investigation of LDS Church officers about political involvement. Life expectancy was about 50.[4]

Samuel Clements, alias Mark Twain, had died at age 74 in April and O. Henry on June 5 at age 38. Halley's Comet made one of its closest ever approaches to Earth in 1910.

The day after Gordon was born, Japan invaded Korea. The Boy Scouts of America was also organized on February 8, 1910. In Salt Lake City, an addition to the Alta Men's Club was completed to the east of the first phase. A "Bishop's Building" was also opened at 50 North Main Street on Administration Block just east across the street from the Salt Lake Temple.[5] And the Deseret Gym opened officially September 20, 1910 after nine months delay.

While Gordon was an infant, his father Bryant was busily involved in directing the Deseret Gym's first years. An "anti-Mormon" P. E. director named William E. Dayas was employed.[6] He also had a good secretary named Della Caffery who was efficient and devoted.

In religious service, Gordon's father was still actively serving as a general board member for the LDS Church YMMIA. Three LDS apostles oversaw the board as an executive committee. Hyrum M. Smith, who recommended Bryant to be director of the Deseret Gym; Bryant's good friend and future next prophet Heber J. Grant; and Stephen L. Richards, with whom Gordon would later work for 35 years, were the supervising general authorities.[7] Gordon's father, now 47 at the time of Gordon's birth, loved Heber J. Grant and the prophet at that time, Joseph F. Smith, was one of his heroes.[8]

The Hinckleys' Home

Ada loved to entertain. She was skillful and beautiful at it. Haviland China and cut crystal tumblers with silver plated silverware were brought into the dining room off of the main hall. Beautiful linen adorned the table topped with nice serving pieces when company came or the family's weekly Sunday dinners were had. The daughters in the home were trained as servers.[9]

As guests entered the main door from the north off 700 South, they saw a gray and white two story wood structure with a long porch supported by carved poles typical of the architecture of the time. The porch extended all along the north and east sides of the home so one could walk all of this distance on the porch from the front of the home to the back of the home where there were an old shed and outhouse. A railing around the porch also enhanced the Victorian 1890's flavor.

Inside the front door was a long hall with a front stairway leading to the second floor. Guests went past the parlor, first door to the right, containing mahogany furniture and Ada's baby grand piano. The parlor was left cold most of the time. Only when family activity or guests appeared was it opened and heated.

Guests entered the second door to the right where a coal stove heated for dining and a round oak dining table with buffet and chairs sat. Ada had her white peddle sewing machine and a rocking chair here, too. And by the window to the west was a built in window seat containing storage space underneath.[10] Not only was this room for dining, but it served as the family living room.[11]

Across the hall to the east was a large library with bookshelves on all four walls. On the shelves were Bryant and Ada's accumulated books of knowledge totalling over 1,000 volumes. In the center of the room sat a large table with two chairs, a couch and an easy chair or two.

To the south of the library was the large kitchen with a "monkey stove" for heating water and a hot water tank in a corner. A gas range, sink and a kitchen table and chairs also were there. Then there was a pantry for food storage.

Sliding doors between the library and kitchen and the parlor and dining room made it very convenient to open up these rooms into larger areas when desired.

Six doors on the first floor led to the east porch, the west porch, the pantry, the dining room, a "shelf basement" and rear stairs. The stairs in the rear went up to the second floor and down to the basement.

In the basement was a coal burning furnace with coal bin. On the second floor was a long hall similar to the first floor with stairs on the north and south ends leading to the first floor. Four large bedrooms accommodated the family that lived there and one of these rooms was assigned to Gordon as he grew. A bathroom also was on the second floor with stairs leading to the attic.[12]

Like at Brigham Young's Beehive House on South Temple Street, the Hinckley home also had a "fairy window" located half way up the front stairway allowing the Hinckley children to look out from the

Home Where Gordon Bitner Hinckley Was Born and Raised
700 South Windsor Street, Salt Lake City, Utah

second floor as if they were in a streetcar and see guests arriving or going below. The staircase had a banister and the stairs were carpeted. The children would slide down the bannister and spy on company or dates of Bryant's older daughters from his first wife Christine Johnson.[13]

The home was set back from the corner of 700 South and 840 East with a large lawn in between and trees surrounding the house.[14] Truly it was a very nice home Gordon's father had bought for $3,600.00. This was not all that influenced the infant life of Gordon. As he became increasingly cognizant of life, he realized that around him were many children living in his home much his senior. The instant family of two teenagers and four other children from 10 to 3 certainly told him he was not the only child in the family.

Gordie's Infancy

As with most American families, nicknames were given to most. Bryant's sister Minerva Angeline, daughter of Adelaide, was called "Minnie." And Gordon, "spindly and frail", was quickly dubbed "Gordie." [15] His features and traits began to mirror his mother.[16]

Shortly after Gordie was born, Bryant and Ada took a well deserved trip away from home. Five year old sister Venice and Gordie were placed in the care of Lucile. When Gordie's parents returned home, Gordon had forgotten his mother and would have nothing to do with her. He cried and Ada cried. She was heartbroken he would not come to her.[17]

But this was soon remedied and Ada became Gordie's mother again. Ada was a careful manager of the home and exhibited courage in the face of situations like this. She was loyal to husband, family and friends, and most especially her faith. Her faith was full with an anxious desire to serve church and mankind.[18]

So callings from the LDS Church were not slow in coming. Ada was asked to work with the youth of her church in the Mutual Improvement Association and became a teacher in the Sunday School. One of the classes she taught was the Literary Class and students loved it.[19]

When she was not serving her church and community, she was busy baking many loaves of bread each day, quilting, tatting, chrocheting, sewing, and painting pictures and delicate china. She grew a flower garden and bottled condiments and all varieties of fruit. Cooking was mastered, too.[20]

In this environment, Gordie began to grow. But Gordon says he was a shy lad, poor in stamina and health and ordinary.[21] His first major illness was whooping cough, a dread disease of the time, requiring much attention and nursing. He was only two at the time and this illness of his caused a great deal of concern to his parents about a year after a younger brother Sherman, Ada's second child, had been born in October 1911. His father Bryant's mother Angeline had passed away April 28, 1912 about the same time, too, at age 83.

At this time, LDS sponsored "seminary" first was allowed during "released school time" at the Salt Lake Granite High School. Here young Latter-day Saints could study their religion at the same time they attended high school in the community. This event marked the start of phase out of the LDS Academies for high school and junior college students.[22]

At this time also, a young LDS Apostle by the name of David O. McKay was on November 8, 1912 appointed the first ever chairman of a new LDS Correlation Committee of LDS general authorities.[23]

Ada was told by her doctor Gordon needed fresh air and pristine environment to fortify his constitution. So Gordon's parents pondered and meditated and prayed what to do. Ada's childhood home in Big Cottonwood afforded farmlike surroundings untouched yet by the city but the stream flowing from the mouth of Big Cottonwood Canyon was violent and swift. She had learned this in her own youth.

Establishment of the Family Farm

A little further to the north towards the main city of Salt Lake was her grandmother Osguthorpe living in the orchards and farm at the mouth of Millcreek Canyon. Bryant and Ada went out to look at the surroundings, still mostly open spaces with farmland and a few homesteads forming the nucleus of what was then being called "East Millcreek."

As Ada looked up at the Rocky Mountains to the East, her eyes fell upon majestic Mount Olympus towering above the little community of East Millcreek as a sentinel with its jagged rock slate exposed to the sky. "This is the place," she thought and asked her husband to purchase it with funds Ada had saved during her teaching career. Five acres were purchased from Sam Cornwall in 1912 containing a large "hollow" through which flowed a nice slow stream of spring water and a little house and fruit trees.

The downpayment was paid with Ada's savings and the family

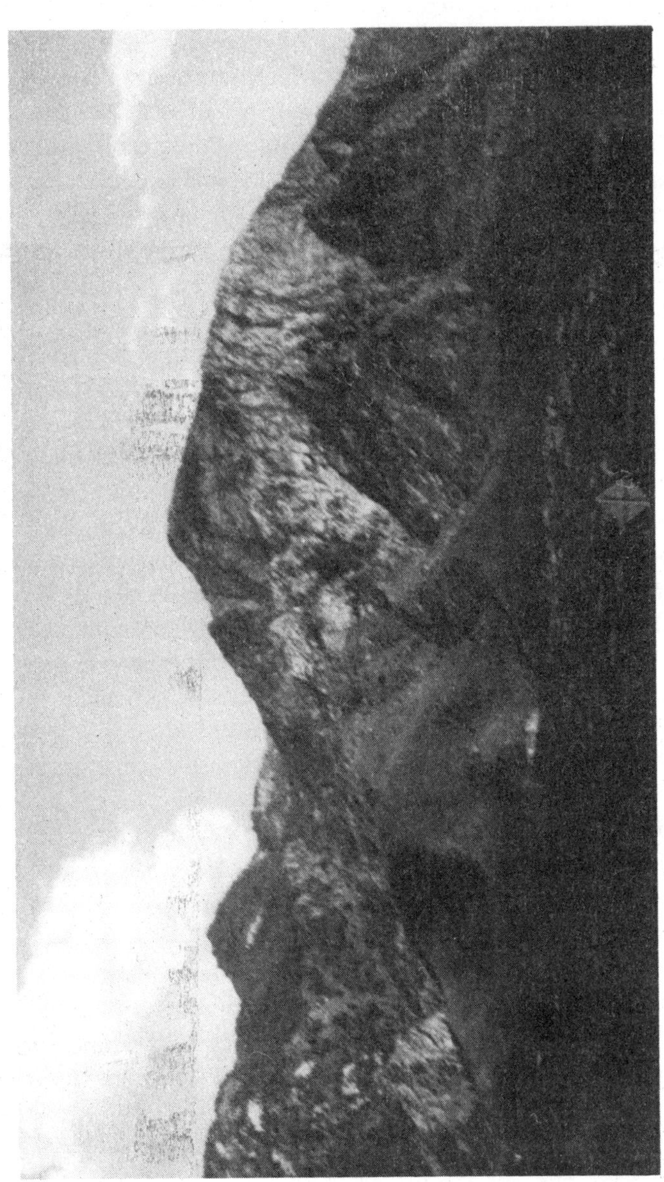

Mount Olympus As Seen by Ada Bitner Hinckley
When the Location for the Hinckley Farm Was Selected

moved there for the first time during the following Summer. The farm was located 8½ miles from the family's Windsor Street home and only ⅓ mile south from the main Millcreek stream flowing from Millcreek Canyon.

On February 25, 1913, the United States Constitution was altered by ratification of the 16th amendment authorizing an income tax. Also, the same year, Gordon's father, as a member of the Athletic Committee of the LDS General Board of the Young Men's Mutual Improvement Association, made a formal motion to LDS Church President Joseph F. Smith favoring LDS Church affiliation with the Boy Scouts of America.[24] This was approved and adopted May 21, 1913.[25] Additional acreage was added to the family farm in 1913, too.

By 1914, a new house was built for $500.00. Ruth, Ada's third child and Gordon's first younger sister, had arrived February 4 of that year. A long narrow road 1,000 feet long connected the farm house from the dirt road leading to the city.

The farm home had a front porch, a fireplace in a front room, a rear kitchen with a coal stove and no electricity or piped water. Two small bedrooms and a bath took off from the kitchen and one other bedroom completed the original layout. A back hall left space for an ice box. Small and inconvenient, Ada still loved this home which reminded her of the Cottonwood home of her childhood.[26] Light was provided at night by kerosene lamps and the coal range stocked with wood and coal provided cooking and heat.

It was in 1914 when Gordon recalls his first cognitive memory. A stonemason was erecting what appeared to Gordon to be a great rock fireplace. He was in the narrow living room watching. "The floor joists were in place with loose boards on them, and Mr. Hubbard, the stonemason, was laying up the rock fireplace, the design of which Mother had approved."[27]

Nineteen fourteen proved to be a year of many happenings. Not only did the Hinckley family settle into their new farm home during the summer, the LDS Church started construction of the first temple outside the United States in Cardston, Alberta, Canada. Also, tensions were mounting in Europe culminating in war during the Fall. World War I was happening and America, though far away, was concerned.

In New York City, Harlem became the capital of Black Americans and Coney Island saw a million people throng to its beach.[28] Back at the new Hinckley farm, Gordon had overcome his whooping cough but received some unwelcome freckles. Big round blue eyes peered out of his triangular face as he ran barefoot among the fields, deep oak and other vegetation surrounding his parents' new summer farm. There were lots in the family, now nine in all together with mom and dad. And there was lots to do.

Gordon, 4, and his one year younger brother Sherman, 3, were too young to be harnessed for much of the toil yet so it was a time of romping and playing with themselves and neighbors. The Bennion family lived next door and they were good and happy friends with contagious laughter of small boys having a good time.[29]

Barefoot felt so good and while Gordon's older siblings took walks to the streetcar station in Holladay two miles away, the boys discovered the "hollow" was just like a jungle. Native vegetation in its pristine state lined the source of its strength along the channel of the slow flowing spring water.

Mother was in the kitchen much of the time cooking. The wood and coal burning stove required chopped kindling which warmed up a naturally hot kitchen into an oven itself while Ada baked bread or bottled fruit from the orchard trees surrounding the home. The icebox was cooled by blocks of ice placed in a top compartment and though located in the basement, required what seemed like constant disposal of melted water accumulated in the collecting pan at the bottom of it.

There were two cows, a brown cow named "Polly" and a Jersey named "Babe." The men did the milking and Gordon, along with his brother Sherman, soon learned how to squeeze the udder to extract the rich contents. Cream was skimmed and much of the skim left fed to a family pig. Cottage cheese was made cooking the milk until solid separated from whey and cheesecloth was used to strain the curds from the watery whey. Still there was left over cream which was shaken into butter after it soured.[30]

Back at Windsor Street

The family stayed on the farm during the Summer and then returned to the Windsor Street home just in time for school to start. Gordon came down with an earache and was in great pain. His mother took two bags of salt and heated them on the coal stove in the dining room. Then she held a bag against Gordon's aching ear. The comfort was wonderful and when the one cooled, she replaced it with the other. All night she did this until Gordon was somewhat relieved.[31]

The older girls from Bryant's first wife were given some piano lessons and the boys and girls could all take as many classes as they liked at the Deseret Gym managed by their father. [32] This provided an opportunity for all the Hinckley children. Mom was a sweet tooth and often asked the kids to buy some broken candy from Keeleys on Main Street in downtown Salt Lake or bitter chocolate from Lindsay Candy Co. on 800 South and 500 East.

Ada was not pretentious. She had a plain gold wedding band and a few real genuine jewelry pieces. A cameo pin, gold locket, two pearl rings, one turquoise and some coral beads were the extent of her treasure chest. But she did collect spoons from various places she travelled. These were the kind of things the children remembered. Especially was it nice to hear their mother play the piano and sing.

These were the good times remembered by all and then the major event awaited by those in Utah for some time occurred. The State Capitol Building situated on the top of a hill at the end of 100 East Street was completed. This building was similar in design to the Nation's Capitol Building in Washington, D.C. and had a huge rotunda and round dome in the middle. It was made out of huge blocks of grey granite speckled with black chips. In honor of the capitol building, 100 East was renamed "State Street."

This same year, LDS Church Prophet Joseph F. Smith asked all Latter-day Saints to commence having at least one evening association with their family. Monday nights were designated for the event to be called "family home evening." Bryant and Ada, being the faithful Latter-day Saints they were, took the prophet at his word when he promised family's blessings for doing so and therefore the Hinckley family launched into the program.

There were trying moments as the family began to have a formal family home evening together. At the beginning, the children would often laugh and make cute remarks about each other as each child was asked to participate in giving a reading, singing a song, playing the piano or doing some other presentation. But the cold parlor where the family home evenings were held and Ada's grand piano stood, began to warm with family togetherness and love as well as with the coal stove and as the parents persisted, everyone found they were singing together, praying together more often and listening quietly as their mother read from the Bible or Book of Mormon story book.

Their father Bryant told stories from memory and one stuck in the mind of Gordon. It was about two boys who decided to play a trick on an old man who was working barefoot in his field. They put a silver dollar in his shoes as they lay by the side of the field. When the man returned and found a dollar in his shoe, he was elated. He immediately dropped to his knees and prayed out loud, "Thank you, Father, for answering my prayer. My wife is sick and my children had no bread to eat. Thou hast been benevolent to me."

President Hinckley has stated this consistent and faithful striving to hold family home evenings as the prophet had requested reaped enormous blessings for his family. "Love for our parents was strengthened, love for brothers and sisters enhanced, love for the Lord increased, appreciation for simple goodness grew in our hearts."[33]

Gordon's mother also was a gentle teacher. She carefully corrected manners and eating habits and the children's posture and grammar.[34] Whenever a neighbor child said "ain't" or other grammar mistakes, she got upset.[35] But the displeasure was not anger. It was academic disappointment conveyed to her children so they would develop better traits of communication and social graces.

On Sunday, first the children dressed for Sunday School. Then for lunch, the dining room table was set with linen and silverware from the buffet drawers. An aroma of good food pervaded the home as Ada brought forth roast, potatoes, gravy, and banana cream cake or similar desserts.[36]

On cold Winter nights, Ada would read stories to the children from a 1911 book called *Mother Stories from the Book of Mormon* by William Albert Morton.[37] This practice remained in the children's hearts all through their lives.

And every Spring and Fall, the family was called upon to houseclean. They did not do a great sparkling job but it taught them the value of cleanliness and some sense of industry.

Many guests visited the home regularly due to Bryant's positions in his stake presidency, the YMMIA General Board and his management of the Deseret Gym. John A. Widtsoe, one of the renowned LDS apostles, and stake president Hugh J. Cannon were only a couple of the visitors.[38] This early exposure to LDS Church leaders all had an influence on young Gordie Hinckley.

Then there was the influence of good books. As the children matured, Ada started reading to the children from the actual Book of Mormon. Such tutoring developed within Gordon and his other brothers and sisters a "love for this sacred volume and for other wonderful pieces of writing" Ada shared with her children.[39]

The library was a fixture in Gordon's life from the very beginning. The library was waiting for him and for any other member of the family or visitor to enjoy. Not only were the books on the shelves rising from the floor to the ceiling, there were also many magazines and the *Deseret News*, all good literature with positive ideas and encouragement for life's challenges.

There was the solid table in the center of the library always abutted with a good lamp for reading. The invitation was there and eventually was accepted by all family members to feast upon the knowledge of great men gone before. Included in the works were a 50 volume set of the *Harvard Classics* and the *World's Best Histories*.[40]

"In those days, of course, we had no television, and radio was not even available during most of those earlier years. I do not wish to convey the idea that as children we read extensively in our father's books. But they provided an environment. We saw our father and mother read, and they read to us. It did something of an indefinable nature. It gave us a familiarity with good books. We felt at home and at ease with them. They were not strangers to us. They were as friends, willing to give to us if we were willing to make a little effort.

"In addition to such books we had the Church magazines. Our parents read them and read to us from them.

"We likewise had the *Deseret News* in our home. This was long before publication of the *Church News*. We read the newspaper and felt a certain kinship with it." There was little risque or vulgar literature, movies or other material that came into the Hinckley children's contact. Maybe they were living in a sheltered society but the benefits were multitudinous in future years.[41]

All was not pleasure either. The furnace had to be fed. There was coal to shovel and stokers to be removed from the coal burning furnace. Gordon and Sherman were put to the task along with their other brothers. There was also an automatic duty to wash dishes. If you dirtied it, you cleaned it.

Gordon's parents were both intelligent and well educated, intellectual and refined, and disliked the coarse or uncouth. They had senses of humor but never vulgar. There were always enough good funny stories to tell without the sordid. His parents also taught through their actions their displeasure for gossip. Instead, they relished in the arts and cultural arts.[42]

Gordon's father had a good salary but barely enough for the necessities and a few little luxuries. He worked hard and showed through his example and statements the need and benefits of work. Even before the family purchased their first five acres of the summer farm in East Millcreek, Bryant was busy speculating. He bought and sold parcels of real estate in the developing areas surrounding Salt Lake proper. He was a moving force in the Utah Reclamation Company, owning 600 acres in the Valley, 10 acres in the Cottonwood area, and 35 acres in East Millcreek. Later he purchased the two homes in back and to the south of their family home on Windsor Street.[43]

Gordon's mother was compassionate. When a beggar came to the door, she would always give him something like a bacon and egg sandwich.[44]

When Gordon's younger sister Ruth was about one and Gordon 4½, their mother Ada went to California for a month's rest. While Ada was away, and after Gordon and Sherman had attended primary that day, Gordon's father wrote to her on February 9, 1915, "Gordon has been asking some very wise questions." After they washed their hands and faces clean before bed, he wrote they "looked just beautiful. I am very proud of them."[45]

Then on May 7, 1915, world war drew closer to the United States when a German submarine torpedoed the British luxury liner *Lusitania* killing 1,153 persons including 114 US citizens.[46] LDS Prophet Joseph F. Smith then began construction of the first LDS temple outside the Continental United States in the Hawaiian Islands in a village called Laie on the Island of Oahu where he had served an LDS mission as a 17 year old boy early in his youth.[47]

Sunday church services and other activities for the Hinckley family were held at the 1st Ward in the Liberty Stake where the chapel had a curtain down the center which could be pulled to divide the area in two. An old coal heater was in the room's center until a new chapel was built.[48] And Gordon faithfully attended.

First at his age there was primary, designed for LDS children 3 to 11 years old. Here the fundamentals of his religion were conveyed to children which came naturally owing to his parents' regular practice of the same principles at home with family home evening, with regular prayer as a family each day, blessing of meals at dinnertime, and similar acts of faith such as reading from the scriptures regularly.

Ramona, Ada's fourth child and second daughter, was born on

January 13, 1916. Then on April 21, 1916, Bryant, Gordon's father, was sustained as second counselor of the Salt Lake Liberty Stake.[49]

The New 1916 Model T Ford

What a jubilant surprise it was for all in the family when one night in the Summer of 1916, their father came to the farm home in the evening driving a brand new black Model T Ford straight off the factory lines of Henry T. Ford's mass production lines. Bryant was so "skittish" about driving up the narrow lane to the farm house that he parked the first night at neighbor Ferry Young's.

The Ford started with a crank and you had to be careful for it had a terrific kick back when you retarded the spark. Also, although really convenient for the time compared to the horses, buggies and home made cart the family had been using as transportation up to the time, the coils would on occasion get wet and not start.

But that didn't matter. You put some canvas over the cowl and exercised a little care in retarding the spark and everything worked swell. It jumped into life. Gordon says through the simple experience of the family's Model T Ford, he learned the simple lessons about "making preparation to save trouble." And since there was no battery, the magneto only generated electricity when the motor was turning. Thus the higher the speed of travel, the brighter the lights shown at night. If you slowed down, the glow of the lights got progressively yellow and dim.

Through this experience, Gordon learned "that if you want to see ahead as you go down the road, you had to keep the engine running at a fast clip. Industry, enthusiasm and hard work lead to enlightened progress. You have to stay on your feet and keep moving if you are going to have light in your life."[50]

When the family received their Model-T Ford, their father and mother took them on a trip to Yellowstone National Park about 220 miles north of Salt Lake in Wyoming and Montana. There were no paved roads at the time and few of them were even gravelled. And although the cars of that time clipped along at what then was thought as a tremendous pace on flat ground, they had a very difficult time going up inclines. It was out of the car and helping to push the lovely "Duster" as Ada called it up the steep hills.

The family stopped one night at Pocatello, Idaho and then camped along the side of the road with bonfire meals for nurishment. Early cars coupled with unpaved roads also were hard on the primitive rubber tires. They gave out regularly and needed substitution. All of these experiences provided memories for the children even 60 years later.

At the park they saw many animals including bears, moose, deer and elk. Also at Mammoth Hot Springs, a large training camp for army recruits preparing for World War I action was seen.

While in Idaho, the family visited an Uncle Breneman and wife living in rough conditions. Later, Gordon's parents talked to the family about how hard the lot of Uncle Breneman was.[51]

Lessons at East Millcreek

Gordon says he never felt adequate as a young boy. He felt shy and ordinary. "I have a feeling for the rank and file of the Church because I am one of them," he says.[52] No doubt this is a manifestation of one of his strongest traits–that of humility. But there is something you can learn by getting close to the soil.

And Gordon and his brother Sherman and sisters did that every Summer they went out to East Millcreek and cultivated the orchards and ground there. It might be you can't learn it hardly any other way. You get close to God's creations. Your hands feel the touch of the raw earth. Your palms get black with terra. It clings to the fingers that work the soil. It does wonders for your feeling of affinity to God and His creations. And it helps you be meek knowing all we have comes from Him and His marvelous creations.

No better way can be found to draw closer to God than to be alone in His fields, to ponder and meditate as did Isaac before his bride to be arrived from Canaan. East Millcreek was a test tube for the boy Gordon as he matured into a prophet.

The family started to get into an annual routine at the farm. Each year they would go out about May and return to the city about October. On the farm, they often rose at 5 A.M. and picked raspberries in the cool and quiet of the Summer mornings. The girls would weave baskets out of burrs, dolls from hollyhocks and beads from wild rose berries and rolled up magazine strips glued together. Paper dolls were made from Sears catalogs and doll furniture from shirt laundry cardboard.[53]

There was no washing machine so the family sent shirts to a laundry and had the rest "wet washed" and sheets and linen "iron flat." No piano was at the farm but a Victrola record player was there where the family listened to records from Caruso, Galli-Curci, Fritz Kreisler, Alma Gluck, etc. The kids got their first taste of classical music.

The boys were taught by Bryant how to plant gardens. Irrigating was a necessary skill. And so was cow milking, horsemanship, egg gathering and chicken feeding. A horticulturist from the State Agricultural College in Logan was called to teach each boy how to prune and graft trees for the expanding farm was richly planted with fruit trees of every kind–apple, pear, peach, cherry, apricot, plum–you name it and you were almost bound to find it among the orchards. Through this knowledge, Gordon says he not only learned that fruit needs space between the branches for sunlight and air but also that new young wood produces the best fruit.[54] The Master's parable of the olive tree bore practical reality to the young Gordon.

Gordon remembers distinctly one time climbing up in the high branches of a cherry tree and looking out on the Valley of the Salt Lake. A train was just traveling along the iron rails puffing steam high in the air from its locamotive. Gordon thought, "Some day I'd like to see the world."[55]

The art of getting the water to the end of the row was another invaluable lesson.[56] Without this knowledge, the trees would dry up and shrivel. The shovel and lantern on a dark night were the boys' guide and sword of the soil as they took turns on watering days making sure the irrigating water made its proper course.

Through the farm experience, Gordon and his siblings grew to appreciate natural things, the wonders of nature and its processes including the miracle of creation and birth.[57]

The draft horses were common at the time. And knowledge of how to bridle them was learned. Blinders were put by their eyes to keep their attention. A practical parable was learned by Gordon through this.[58] They often harnessed their two horses to the small cart they had made and travelled around East Millcreek in it.

In the morning each day, the Hinckley's turn to take water was seized early. A key was turned on to fill kettles and buckets and anything else which needed filling. But the water was not in any way purified. Then it was turned off. A neighbor down below named Horace Eldredge would get excited from time to time when the flow ceased but Bryant would gently appease him.

Ada knew not only how to sing but also yodel so when dinner was ready, there was a big "Yoo-hoo" and sometimes more to boot. She also sang "Little Boy Blue" by Eugene Field and another tune which went:

We are a happy family; sitting on the
floor galore.
We haven't any chairs to sit on;
So we have to sit on the floor.
They've taken all the chairs and the table.
There's a mortgage on the rolling pin.
And all we've got is a big round pot,
And a frying pan to wash the baby in.

Gordon and Sherman would dress in short pants and shirts with big oversized hats and wide brims on their heads as they explored the rich greenery of the "hollow" and rest of the farm. And then there were the swimming holes. One was in the orchard, a pool lined with rocks and filled with irrigation water. But the best was the little dam built by Gordon and Sherman in the middle of the stream of the "hollow." Their mother Ada taught her children another verse for that one:

Mother, may I go out to swim?
Yes, my darling daughter.
Hang your clothes on a hickory limb
But don't go near the water.

Both Sherman, who was destined to become an engineer, and Gordon seemed to have mechanical talents. They relished in building things in the "hollow" out of old wheels, wood, and farm machinery parts. One of these was a shower. They put a shower head on a large old water tank and filled it with water. The summer sun would heat it quite nicely during the day and then they would let each family member take their brief turn under the nozzle.[59]

These early dablings with things mechanical continued not only through Sherman's life and career but also with Gordon. He became a handyman par excellance. Anything seemed to be fixable by him. Cars that wouldn't run, appliances, all types of gadgets were conquerable by him and his ingenuity or logic.

At the "reservoir", the name given to the swimming pool in the orchard, Bitner cousins would come and associate. Many aunts, uncles and cousins would visit. And not just family but many from the city would come out to be with Gordon's parents.

The children would play numerous games including finding the first ripe fruit and largest vegetable. Nests of birds eggs ready to hatch also existed and carloads of fruit and vegetables were harvested and sold including watermelons. Cherries were abundant. Apricots, peaches and pears were likewise. And corn, carrots and beans were plentiful.

Also in the "hollow" by the cool spring, it was "mumblety peg" the children would go play for hours in the afternoons after the day's farm work was over. Marbles were also a favorite sport for Gordon.[60]

Time for School

When the family returned to Windsor Street, Ada always made new dresses for her daughters for school. Aunt Minnie always used to come and help out, too.[61] Gordon was now six, too, and of age for school. But he did not want to go. Walking barefoot and in open spaces fancy free the last four years of his life had really gotten to him. Like Mark Twain's fictional Tom Sawyer, "I could not bear the thought of wearing shoes to school and being cooped up in a classroom most of the day."[62]

So when his mom and dad told him it was school time, he put up a terrific fuss. One thing his parents never did was use force. Somehow, they were able to influence their children in other ways. This time, no influence could persuade Gordon to go to school so the parents gave up. Gordon was given a reprieve from school, at least for 1916. On October 8 of that year, Gordon's father spoke on "The LDS Church and Salvation through Obedience to the Gospel" from the pulpit at the LDS Church's World General Conference in the Tabernacle on Temple Square.[63]

Chirstmases at Home

On Christmas at the Hinckleys, Gordon and Sherman got involved again making numerous ornaments for the Christmas tree. Luxury items were never under the tree but mainly practical items such as clothing. One special Christmas, however, a beautiful Flexible Flyer sleigh was left by Santa. It was the pride and joy of the family for many years.

Ada went all out for Christmas providing pounds and pounds of "fondant" rolled on marble slabs, fruit cake, plum pudding, and simple but tasteful gifts for many, many people.

During good weather, "kick the can", run sheepy run, no bears out tonight, and Andy-I-Over" were favorite games. In the house, their father Bryant would play "automobile" and "Bear" with the lights out. Older sisters and brother (Venice, Lucile and Al) would buy ice cream cones and whole candy bars and give them to the younger kids.

Family prayer was held in the dining room. Little Ruth would sometimes trace her fingers on the figures on back of the chair when prayers got a little long to her. But their mother was always cooking and singing and the children learned many hymns.

In the evening, it was time for homework and the kitchen table was the spot. Ada would help as she worked in the kitchen baking eight loaves of bread every other night while teaching her daughters her techniques.

Venice taught the "Charleston" to her younger sisters while doing the dishes and once in a while brought a big dill pickle or a boyfriend's chocolate to share. On the table each day were lots of cheese, bottled fruit, dry fruit, milk and oat and wheat cereals.

Their mother Ada rocked her babies and sang many lullabies to them. She would take the children to visit her sister Mary Bitner Sheets from time to time. They were always treated to goodies on such occasions.

And through all of these experiences, Gordon learned frugal habits.[64] And in addition a great love for his parents developed. It was a quiet strength which Gordon did not have the courage to express verbally much. But the awareness of a family who prayed together and worked together and helped one another solidified deep in his soul.[65]

The big event at the farm in 1916 was the moving of the old shed and out house from the back of the Windsor Street home to the East Millcreek farm on two hay racks.[66] The 8½ miles by horse drawn wagon was a slow show.

World War I

On April 6, 1917, right on the 87th birthday of the LDS Church, Gordon and Sherman were with their mother in front of their Windsor Street home when a newsboy came up crying "Extra! Extra!" It was Clark Fallas who brought a paper with big bold letters on the first page indicating World War I had started with the United States Congress formally declaring war on Germany.[67]

And it was not long before Stan, oldest brother and son of Bryant's first wife, was enlisted in the army. Bryant Stanford was 23 and just married. His wife Beulah Jenkins Wilcox was expecting. The baby was weak at birth and Beulah's grandpa Dr. Wilcox could not save it. Stan came home to visit after the baby died and then left for Europe. It was the last time the family saw him.[68]

Hamilton School

Sherman was almost age six in time to start school in the Fall 1917 and it was time for Gordon to start, too. But his desire for formal schooling was no stronger than a year before. On September 1, 1917, when school began, Gordon hid out. But his parents found him later and this time would not relent. Gordon was taken crying to school at the Hamilton School just one block south and a half a block west at the corner of 800 South and 800 East in Salt Lake.

But breaking Gordie into school life was not just that easy. A few days after school begun, Gordon put up another fuss and ran around the house trying to escape. He was captured, however, and taken to school.[69]

One month later on October 2, 1917 the four story LDS Church Administration Building at 47 East South Temple Street in Salt Lake, which would become his home office for so many years of his future life, was dedicated and opened to use by the LDS First Presidency, Quorum of the Twelve, Presiding Bishopric and Historian's Office.[70] The rest of the Hinckley children had been attending Hamilton School and Sherman started the same time, too.[71] The Hamilton School was a 3½ story building named after Alexander Hamilton, famous American Patriot. Here Gordie began acquiring the three R's, reading, writing and arithmetic. And here it was that he found he could associate with boys and girls he never had met and tolerate confined classrooms.

A nice little uniform of shirt and tie and short pants and long black stockings were also worn to the knee. But they were cotton and wore out frequently, requiring darning frequently. From this experience, Gordon learned "a lesson on the importance of personal neatness and tidiness, and that has blessed my life ever since."[72]

In his first year, he had a boy friend with an obsessive fixation. He would chew his tie until it became wet and stringy. But later in life, this friend became a "man of substance." Gordon learned from this event "never to underestimate the potential of a boy to make something of his life, even if he chews his tie."[73]

And even Gordon was amazed. He could study and remember what he studied. Slowly but consistently he started to catch up to those his own age. Two special promotions were given him putting him in line with his own age group and actually ahead one year from the regular pace of study if he had progressed one grade each year at a time.[74]

Each day at Hamilton School, the students assembled in front and pledged allegiance to the flag of the United States of America. Then they marched in orderly manner to their respective rooms.

Just almost around the corner was home and Gordon's mom and dad had a special tradition. Once a year they invited the teachers of their children at Hamilton School for a "Teacher's Lunch" at their

Hamilton School Where Gordon B. Hinckley
Attended the First 7 Years of His Schooling

home. A very nice invitation was sent by Ada. The table was beautifully set. Everything was prepared. For the short lunch period, the Hinckley girls did the serving after rehearsing with their mother. The children felt a little bit of extra pride for parents who would be this thoughtful and appreciative.[75]

About this time Gordon learned a little rhyme he and his classmates recited in Sunday School.

What is tithing?
I will tell you every time.
Ten cents from a dollar,
And a penny from a dime.[76]

The rhyme was consistent with the principle which had been taught in his home by his parents. The Lord gives us everything. He only asks us to return 10%. Gordon remembers walking to the home of the bishop in those days, in trepidation, to see Bishop John C. Duncan and give him his 25¢ tithing. He felt it an obligation and duty to assist.

Tithes received in this way were used to fund the general projects of the LDS Church such as temple building and administration. The principle was consistent with Abraham's payment of tithes to Melchizedek, King of Salem, and Malachi's admonition to bring tithes into the storehouse of God to receive blessings poured out from the windows of heaven.[77] His parents had placed faith and love for the restored gospel and a desire to do the right thing in Gordon.[78]

On February 14, Valentine's Day, students at school exchanged paper hearts and in the evening dropped them at doors of friends, stomped on the porch and ran to hide. Sometimes they would tie fishline to a card and pull when the receiver went to pick it up.[79]

July 13, 1918 found a new Women's Department completed in remodeling of the Deseret Gym. Now Gordon was 8 years old and of baptismal age. But this ordinance was postponed for another nine months. World War I was drawing to a climax and it looked like Stan would be home soon.

Then a tragic telegram was received about October 20, 1918 from General Young informing the family Stan had died of pneumonia in France on October 19.[80] He was only 24 and the oldest child of Bryant S. Hinckley. The entire family was shocked. He was buried in France in the fields of Normandy with other war casualties and the family never saw him again. This tragedy affected Gordon and the rest of his family for life. More tragic was the fact the war ended less than a month later on November 11, 1918.

Eight days after the worst war in the world's history ended, LDS prophet Joseph F. Smith died on November 19, 1918 at age 80. And in four days the Hinckleys' special friend and apostle Heber Jeddy Grant was set apart in the Salt Lake Temple as the 7th prophet of the LDS Church.[81]

Baptism & Flu Epidemic

It was about this time Ada took 8 year old Gordon to the old Social Hall, then still standing, at about 51 South State Street for a puppet show with other family members. Dolls that moved and spoke fascinated them.[82] At home, the family had a small dog which Gordon pampered while wearing a round nit cap, bowl shaped. Even in youth, he had a broad forehead.[83]

Then came a momentous day. Gordon Bitner Hinckley was baptized into the Church of Jesus Christ of Latter-day Saints by his father Bryant Stringham Hinckley at the 1st Ward of the Salt Lake Liberty Stake on April 28, 1919. The next Sunday, May 3, 1919, his father Bryant Stringham Hinckley confirmed Gordon a member of the LDS Church and gave him the Gift of the Holy Ghost at the 1st Ward in Liberty Stake.[84]

Latter-day Saints believe the ordinance of baptism, if received in sincerity through someone having authority, cleanses one of his previous sins and makes one able to return to their Heavenly Father if they continue to take upon them the name of Christ, live his teachings, and remember Christ. So now all of those fusses he had had about going to school were washed away and Gordon felt good.

On October 19, 1919, Gordon's father was released as 2nd counselor and sustained as 1st counselor in the Salt Lake Liberty Stake Presidency.[85] On November 27, 1919, the LDS temple in Hawaii was dedicated by new LDS prophet Heber J. Grant, the first temple located outside the continent of North America.[86] These events all tended in their own way to impress the young Gordon Hinckley as he continued to grow.

At home, the prophet Joseph Smith, Jr. was lauded by Gordon's parents and the environment was one which conveyed a feeling of appreciation for the prophet Joseph's deeds and sacrifices.[87]

At this time, there was more sickness than today. Pasteurized milk had not been perfected. The spread of diseases was not hampered. Immunizations for childhood diseases had yet to be invented. Therefore, the only line of defense essentially was quarantine of those with communicable diseases. Signs were regularly placed in windows of homes where chickenpox or measles had broken out.

A bright orange sign with black letters was posted if it was smallpox or diphtheria. Later in life, Gordon indicates these childhood signs taught him "to watch for signs of danger and evil and stay away."[88]

But it was not only the regular childhood diseases that plagued America in 1919 and early 1920. A massive flu epidemic also hit the country. In Utah, many were struck with the flu. Many died. Schools and churches were closed. The populace went around with masks over their nose and mouth.

Gordon, his father, and sisters Venice and Ruth were struck with the virus. Accordingly, Ada, who was expecting her fifth child, nursed the four invalids with a Sister Reiser and the rest of the family's help.[89]

In Gordon's home, all the children just knew that their father loved their mother. There was no recollection of either speaking unkindly to or of the other. Bryant encouraged Ada in her church activities and neighborhood and civic responsibilities and Ada was as loyal a helpmate to a husband as anyone. Ada had much natural talent and Bryant helped her use it. Her comfort was Bryant's constant concern. We see then that Gordon's parents treated each other as equals and companions, loved and appreciated. Ada encouraged Bryant and did everything to make him happy, too.[90]

Although seemingly inconceivable, Gordon and his brothers and sisters never saw their parents argue or use sharpness with one another in their presence. They probably had differences of opinion, but they were never known by their children. And physical force was never used on any of the kids. If Ada asked someone to do something and they didn't do it after a couple of requests, she would do it herself no matter how tired she was. That hurt the guilty child worse than anything else ever could.[91]

President Hinckley said of his parents in October 1994, "I will be forever grateful for a father who never laid a hand in anger upon his children. Somehow he had the wonderful talent to let them know what was expected of them and to give them encouragement in achieving it."[92]

But there was in contrast in the neighborhood around Windsor Street a man whom Gordon "detested" at the time. President Hinckley says he has since repented of that emotion but at that young time in his development, seeing this man whip "his children with strap or stick or whatever came to hand as his vicious anger flared on the slightest provocation" caused to well in him an intensity of feeling against this man as he physically punished Gordon's neighborhood friends.[93]

What a contrast the practice of Gordon's parents was with that of his uncontrolled neighbor. And the fruits appear today. Gordon has seen his childhood friends who were whipped by that father in troubled lives of temper and harshness towards their own children.

But there were many varieties of neighbors around him, a close-knit group, who seemed to know everyone else. And soon a very important neighbor was to move into his neighborhood at 807 South 800 East.

Two sayings Gordon's father Bryant imparted to his children revealing his genuine character were:

"Cynics do not contribute, skeptics do not create, doubters do not achieve," and "Be somebody."[94]

On March 7, 1920, Ada gave birth to her fifth and last child and third daughter, Sylvia Bitner Hinckley.

Back at East Millcreek

In the Spring, it was back to the farm. "Snip" and "Bish" were the work horses there. They hauled and pulled when needed and handled the wagons and buggies when used. Now due to problems with renters of the Windsor Street home, the library and parlor had been padlocked and kept from use by tenants while the Hinckleys were at the farm.

At the farm one day Ada cranked the Model T and drove thru the narrow lane on her way to an appointment downtown. But the car ran into the side ditch and stuck. She missed her appointment but the car was not damaged.

Such was the sample of experiences at the farm called "Glenada" by Gordon's parents. Each year the boys or father milked a cow or two morning and evening. Each year horticulture was mastered more and more.

The pruning began way before Summer. As early as January or February, the boys would go with their father to the orchards and even with snow on the ground, prune. From these Winter experiences preparing the trees for the coming Spring, Gordon learned "you can pretty well determine the kind of fruit you would pick in September by the way you pruned in February."[95]

Clipping and sawing the right places and shaping the trees so the sun would touch leaves and fruit in Spring and Summer determined the yield of fruit at harvest.[96]

At the farm house, it was a wonderful day when electric power was brought from the road a thousand feet away. An arrangement with the power company was made to pay for the line over time and light fixtures and a three coil electric kitchen stove came to life.

Also another kitchen appliance fascinated "Gordo", as he was also called. The "fireless cooker" had two deep wells inside a well insulated wooden chest. Aluminum kettles with tight lids were placed in the wells and the chest clamped shut. Artificial stone fitted each well bottom. After the stone was heated on an electric hot plate, the stones were placed under each well, thus slowly cooking an "especially delicious" meal.[97]

The regular regimen which had developed at the farm was work in the morning, lunch at Noon and play in the afternoon.[98] In the evenings Gordon and Sherman would often sleep out under the stars and look up at the Big Dipper with its handle, cup pointing to the North Star. Gordon would note the position of the North Star, positioned over the axis of the Earth. It never changed location. This "polar star" was constant. This experience was a lesson to him. It taught him to be "constant" and taught him that God is "constant" and unchangeable.[99]

Gordon also was taught and believed he had a guardian angel who could watch over him and help him, whose knowledge was far greater than his, who could see ahead when he could not, who could influence him in one direction or another to save him from mistakes and tragedies if he lived worthy of his guidance and protection.[100] This gave him comfort and solace but did not make him perfect.

As brothers will do, especially when they are only just one year apart in age, Gordon and Sherman squabbled quite a bit. Finally, their father Bryant brought two pair of boxing gloves to them one day and said, "If you've got to spat, here. Go to it." That had a sobering effect on both boys.

Every year Gordon's parents entertained. Some would come for breakfast and gather around the farm house where Ada had planted trees and flowers making it a beautiful place. Fresh fruit in large bowls was served. Strawberries, raspberries, peaches, all with cream. Hot rolls, bacon, liver, fried chicken, ham and side dishes. What a feast.

Cream was never wasted. Home made ice cream was churned or sour cream cake, sour cream salad dressing, butter and cottage cheese

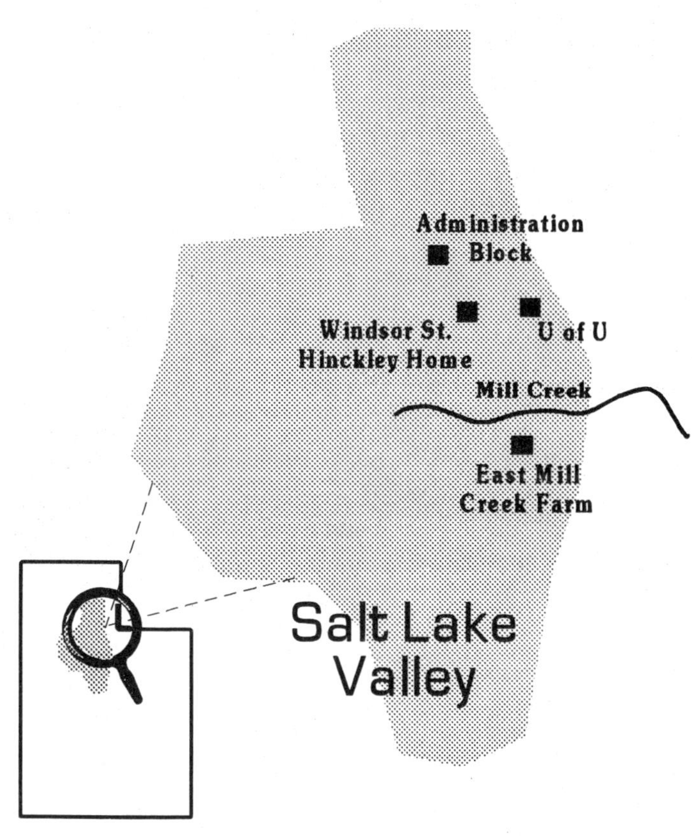

Salt Lake Valley with Approximate
Locations of Windsor Street Home & East Millcreek Farm

were products.

After cleaning up in the afternoon, there were usually visitors. They were treated to such things as tomatoes, homemade bread, onion sandwiches, bottled fruit, dried apricots, and strawberry jam cooked on the tar roof of the house.[101]

In Cottonwood, the 10 acres owned by Gordon's father were planted with wheat and harvested by father and sons. Gordon remembers going with his father to the West Jordan Flour Mill with a load of wheat for grinding to flour which was used at home for bread making.[102]

Sixth through Junior High

Gordon turned 10 while at the East Millcreek farm in June 1920. Then when the family returned to Windsor Street and school, Gordon's father essentially became acting stake president for Liberty Stake when Liberty Stake President Hugh J. Cannon was asked to accompany LDS apostle David O. McKay on a world survey of LDS missions for the LDS First Presidency.

The tour was projected to last a year and visit Polynesia, New Zealand, Australia and Asia with additional stops in India, Egypt and Palestine before visiting LDS missions in Europe. At this time, LeGrand Richards was serving as one of the 12 high counselors in the Liberty Stake.[1]

The Winter of 1920, Gordon's younger sister Ruth contracted whooping cough. When the quarantine official visited the home, he could not get her to give him a cough so he had her run around the house outside. When she came in she really sounded sick.[2]

And Gordon continued school at Hamilton School up to the 6th grade. He had the same essential friends from the 1st to the 6th grades but one always seemed to be in trouble. He had difficulty with concentration. In the Spring, at 11 A.M. he disturbed the class in Miss Spooner's room.

"Get in the closet," she said.

When the Noon bell rang, his friend came out of the closet licking the last of Miss Spooner's lunch. The class couldn't help laughing.

Sadly, this classmate went on clowning throughout his life. He "learned too late that life is a serious thing in which serious choices are to be made with much of care and prayer."[3]

It was about this time the Phillip LeRoy Pay family moved into Liberty Stake to a house at 804 South 800 East, just across the street from the Hamilton School. They had three children including a 9 year old daughter named Marjorie. Liberty Stake was one of the largest stakes in the LDS Church and the 1st Ward had 1,500 members. Still those who actively attended had chance to meet each other. It was in primary that Gordon first saw Marjorie Pay. She gave a reading and Gordon's first thought was she was a good reader with confidence.[4]

Following June 1921 when Gordon was 11, Gordon received his patriarchal blessing, a blessing privileged once in one's life, in which a stake patriarch or the Patriarch of the Church declared a Latter-day Saint's lineage to the House of Israel (Abraham's grandson Jacob who was given a new name "Israel" by God and sired 12 sons who became the fathers of the 12 tribes of Israel).[5]

The patriarch who gave him his blessing, a blessing believed by Latter-day Saints to be personal revelation for guidance of one's individual life, was Thomas E. Callister of Liberty Stake. He said in part to Gordon:

> "Thou shalt grow to the full stature of manhood and shall become a mighty and valiant leader in the midst of Israel . .
>
> "The Holy Priesthood shall be thine to enjoy and thou shalt minister in the midst of Israel as only those can who are called of God. Thou shalt ever be a messenger of peace; the nations of the earth shall hear thy voice and be brought to a knowledge of the truth by the wonderful testimony which thou shalt bear. . .
>
> "You will lift your voice to the nations of the world and testify of truth . . . ."[6]

The patriarchal blessing is not believed by Latter-day Saints to be a prediction nor a prophecy bound to happen. It is believed by LDS believers to be a statement of potential–a blueprint which may come to pass if one makes the right choices in righteous living and adhering to Christ's teachings.

Gordon did have faith in God at the time but not a conviction of the absolute validity of the restored gospel. Yet he kept nurturing his faith with faithful attendance at his church meetings and family gatherings and prayers and he had no inclination to commit criminal acts.

Indeed you could say he followed the young prophet Joseph Smith, Jr. when he wrote of himself, "I frequently fell into many foolish errors, and displayed the weakness of youth, and the foibles of human nature; which, I am sorry to say, led me into divers temptations, offensive in the sight of God. In making this confession, no one need suppose me guilty of any great or malignant sins. A disposition to commit such was never in my nature. But I was guilty of levity, and sometimes associated with jovial company, etc., not consistent with that character which ought to be maintained by one who was called of God as I had been."[7]

At the time, the Baldwin Radio Plant at 3470 South 2300 East, not far below the Hinckley family's East Millcreek farm, and on the north bank of the stream of Millcreek, was just starting to boom manufacturing literally the first headsets for listening to the early radio station broadcasts just coming on line en masse throughout the United States. Utah was starting to enter the radio broadcast era also with stations starting broadcasts from the top of the Hotel Utah and the top of the Newhouse Hotel.

The M-Men and Gleaner program of the LDS Church's Young Men & Women's Mutual Improvement Association for 17 to 23 year olds also was launched in 1921. Through this program, young adults were helped in their crucial years of young adulthood.

In 1922, membership in the LDS Church reached the milestone of 500,000 and a hospital for children opened on the side of the hill of the north "Avenues" streets called the Primary Children's Hospital.[8] Gordon continued, also, to learn more and more about the man Joseph Smith, Jr. who had founded the church his parents so fervently championed[9].

Praise to the Man Who Communed with Jehovah

The 12th year of Gordon B. Hinckley's life was a landmark. He became a Boy Scout and moved from Primary into the Young Men's Mutual Improvement Association. He learned "Be Prepared" and "Do a good turn daily" which stuck with him.[10] In addition he was challenged by his father to memorize the words from the 13th Section of the *Doctrine & Covenants*, a compilation of 136 revelations the LDS prophet Joseph Smith, Jr. and prophets following him had received during their lifetimes for the benefit of those living in the "latter days." The section was short but significant. It stated:

> "Upon you my fellow servants, in the name of Messiah I confer the Priesthood of Aaron, which holds the keys of the ministering of angels, and of the gospel of repentance, and of baptism by immersion for the remission of sins; and this shall never be taken again from the earth, until the sons of Levi do offer again an offering unto the Lord in righteousness."[11]

The source of the words is believed by Latter-day Saints to be John the Baptist, the cousin of Jesus Christ, who baptized the Savior when the Messiah turned 30 prior to the beginning of His mortal ministry of three years. In May of 1829, Joseph Smith, Jr. and his scribe Oliver

Cowdery were in the process of translating the Book of Mormon from the ancient gold plates Joseph had been lent by a heavenly messenger named Moroni when pages repeatedly were translated talking about the ordinance of baptism.

They became intensely desirous of receiving baptism and inquired in unison to God pleading for light and knowledge on how they could receive the baptismal covenant. On May 15, 1829 they went to a beautiful green foilaged area on the banks of a river called Susquehanna in a little settlement called Harmony, State of Pennsylvania in an area where there were many streams and beautiful fresh water lakes. As they prayed, John the Baptism, as a heavenly messenger, manifested himself to them and laid both of his hands on both of their heads and pronounced the words recorded in D.&C. 13 above and then told the young men to go and baptize each other.

The Priesthood of Aaron was first conferred giving the two young men the same authority John the Baptist had possessed when the Baptist had baptized his cousin, the Messiah, and then the young men could baptize each other. Joseph was told to baptize Oliver first and then for Oliver to baptize Joseph. These two baptisms were the first two baptisms of Latter-day Saints.

Aaron in ancient Israel was the younger brother of the prophet Moses and as posterity of the Israelic tribe of Levi, having descended from Jacob's son Levi, was given a Levitical priesthood (or power) by his older brother Moses to administer the temporal ordinances of the Israelic Tribes. This authoritative power (or priesthood) is believed necessary by LDS disciples in order to perform the ordinance of baptism.

Gordon was asked to memorize John the Baptist's words in order to gain a clearer appreciation for the Aaronic Priesthood which he could now receive at age 12. The day came and Gordon was ordained to the Aaronic Priesthood and given the office of deacon within its quorums.[12]

As a deacon, he became a member of the deacons quorum of the 1st Ward of the Salt Lake Liberty Stake and began functioning in the office. He began to be a messenger for the bishop of his ward in collecting fast offerings. He also now was given the privilege of passing the sacrament to members of the LDS Church after it was blessed by others holding the office of priest in the Aaronic Priesthood or those holding the Melchizedek (or "Higher") Priesthood.

Shortly after his ordination, Gordon's father took him to his first group meeting with the combined priesthood holders of the Liberty Stake. Gordon was somewhat unwilling to go but still went with his father.[13] The gathering was held at the 10th Ward chapel. The Liberty Stake was now the largest stake in the entire LDS Church. A full 15,000 LDS members resided within its geographical boundaries.

Gordon sat at the back row as his father walked to the front of the room and assumed his position as 1st counselor with the stake presidency on the stand. There were 400 men there, all men. And Gordon felt "a little alone and uncomfortable in a room filled with strong men."[14]

The opening song was "Praise to the Man" written by an early LDS Church pioneer leader named William W. Phelps. It revered the memory of Joseph Smith, Jr. and was sung with deep feeling and volume by the men present, many of them being European converts with their native countries' accents. Vigorously but with deliberateness they sang:

"Praise to the man who communed with Jehovah!
Jesus annointed that Prophet and Seer.
Blessed to open the last dispensation,
Kings shall extol him, and nations revere.
Hail to the Prophet, ascended to heaven!
Traitors and tyrants now fight him in vain-nn-nn-nn.
Mingling with Gods, he can plan for his brethren;
Death cannot conquer the hero again.

"Praise to his memory, he died as a martyr;
Honored and blest be his ever great name!
Long shall his blood, which was shed by assassins,
Plead unto heav'n while the earth lauds his fame.
Hail to the Prophet, ascended to heaven!
Traitors and tyrants now fight him in vain-nn-nn-nn.
Mingling with Gods, he can plan for his brethren;
Death cannot conquer the hero again.

Suddenly Gordon began to shiver and a tingle went down his spine. They continued:

"Great is his glory and endless his priesthood.

Faithful and true, he will enter his kingdom,
Crowned in the midst of the prophets of old.
Hail to the Prophet, ascended to heaven!
Traitors and tyrants now fight him in vain-nn-nn-nn.
Mingling with Gods, he can plan for his brethren;
Death cannot conquer the hero again.

"Sacrifice brings forth the blessings of heaven;
Earth must atone for the blood of that man.
Wake up the world for the conflict of justice.
Millions shall know 'Brother Joseph' again.
Hail to the Prophet, ascended to heaven!
Traitors and tyrants now fight him in vain-nn-nn-nn.
Mingling with Gods, he can plan for his brethren;
Death cannot conquer the hero again."[15]

Before the song had been finished, Gordon knew something had happened to him. No longer did he just believe Joseph Smith, Jr. was a prophet of God. Now he knew! He knew! He knew. There was no longer any doubt. The conviction burned deep in his soul. The Holy Ghost had communicated with him.[16]

"It touched my heart. It gave me a feeling that was difficult to describe. I'd never had it previously in terms of any Church experience. There came into my heart a conviction that the man of whom they sang was really a prophet of God, and I am grateful to say, that conviction which I believe came by the power of the Holy Spirit, has never left me."[17]

About this time, Gordon also began his first paying job. He acquired a paper route for the *Deseret News* and delivered papers and collected subscriptions.[18] This employment did not bring in a lot but it was enough to pay school expenses.[19]

The "Demonstration" at Hamilton School

Sixth grade passed and Gordon and his classmates were ready to move on to 7th grade at Roosevelt Junior High School, a school just newly built and opened in September 1921. But the graduating 6th graders were sent back to Hamilton School when Roosevelt filled to capacity.

The boys were insulted and furious. They deserved to go to Roosevelt. And they wanted to do something about it. A meeting was held after school and a plan determined to boycott school the next day. Rather than doing something constructive, the boys basically wandered and wasted the day. The truant officer Mr. Clayton didn't catch anyone though.

The next day, Principal Stearns stood at the entrance to the school. He was bald on the front half of his head, had round wire rimmed glasses and a tight lip covered by his mustache. He was "stern."

"Striking is no way to settle a problem.

"You are expected to be responsible citizens. If you have a complaint, you can come to my office and discuss it."

Then he laid the bombshell. "Each of you will not be let back into school until you bring me a note from your parents."

There was nothing Gordon could do but walk drudgingly home and ask his mother for a note. He felt very "sheepish" as he entered the house during normal school hours.

"Gordon, why are you home?"

"Well, aaaa, you see, I and the boys didn't go to school yesterday to protest."

"What protest?"

"Well, they sent us away from Roosevelt. Will you write me a note? Mr. Stearns won't let us back to school until we . . ."

There's more to what was said and the above is just one guess of the conversation, but after the humiliation and self introspection wisely dished out by the school principal was over, Gordon got his note.

His mother Ada wrote:

"Dear Mr. Stearns:

"Please excuse Gordon's absence yesterday. His action was simply an impulse to follow the crowd.

Sincerely, Ada Bitner."

To Gordon, his mother's note was the most stinging rebuke he ever received. It hurt him to the core and he learned "I would make my own decisions on the basis of their merits and my standards. That decision has blessed my life many times, sometimes in very uncomfortable circumstances. It has kept me from doing something which if indulged in could at worst have resulted in serious injury and trouble and at the best would have cost me my self respect."[20]

Gordon also learned that "it is not the building that made a difference; it was the teachers." Seventh grade went by just fine at Hamilton School.

And by November 1922, Gordon's father had acquired the "hollow" area for their farm and the total acreage had reached 30 acres, five acres larger than the famous Knotts Berry Farm in Buena Park, California.

It was not long before Gordon also became president of his deacon's quorum, the first quorum over which he would preside in his church. This calling caused him spiritual and mental reflection. He desired to do a good job.[21] He had received a witness that Joseph Smith, Jr. truly was a prophet of the living God. He thus knew that the Book of Mormon was scripture and that all of the teachings his parents had imparted to him during his short 12 years on earth were in reality true. So he tried his best to do a good job. Through this first presiding position in his church, Gordon learned the principles of brotherhood, service, and faithfulness before the Lord.[22]

The LDS temple which had been commenced 10 years before in Cardston, Alberta, Canada was finally finished and dedicated by LDS prophet Heber J. Grant on August 26, 1923.[23] This provided temples for the Latter-day Saints in Utah, Hawaii and Canada.

Roosevelt Junior High School

Then in September 1923, Gordon finally got his chance to attend Roosevelt Junior High School, situate at 900 East and 1400 South in Salt Lake City and named in honor of former US President Teddy Roosevelt.

The school had cost $224,602.73 to build and had been first opened for students in November 1921. It was still very, very new, a decided contrast to the older Hamilton School. But, as Gordon had learned the year before, it was not the surroundings but the teachers that counted. He also had to apply himself. This was a good year in the 8th grade at Roosevelt.

No auditorium had been completed yet so school assemblies were held outside while there was good weather on the top of a slope backdropped by tall thin poplar trees while the audience of students sat or stood on dust or mud on the lower athletic field.[24]

In late Winter 1922, Gordon's younger brother Sherman contracted scarlet fever. Gordon and his father and family with the exception of Sherman, mother Ada, Ramona and Sylvia, decided it was best to remove themselves to the East Millcreek home until quarantine was lifted. The move lasted six weeks after which Sherman learned to walk

Roosevelt Junior High School
900 East 1400 South, Salt Lake City, Utah
About 1921

again. All of his old skin peeled from the disease revealing a new pink layer which gradually became white and normal. His teeth also were full of cavities.

Wendell, one of the twins from Bryant's first wife Christine Johnson, was then 18 and suffering from a heart condition which worried the entire family. But family prayers continued as well as faith in their God.

In 1923, the Bronx, New York became the sixth largest city in the United States with a population of 1,000,000.[25] About this time, Gordon started regular visits each Saturday morning to the Deseret Gym his father managed. It was a little distance from home but not extremely great. The LDS Church Administration Building was located just to the southwest of the gym and Gordon's good friend George Homer Durham regularly worked out there as a "leader." Calisthenics, swimming, and other games were played in swim clothes with jerseys.[26]

Little Orphan Annie was created in the comic strips of the American newspapers in 1924 as Gordon studied in 9th grade. His high school years had started and he was to be influenced all the more by the high school days.

High School at LDS College

Gordon transferred to the LDS University for high school. It was the outgrowth of the original Salt Lake Academy organized in 1886 and changed to LDS College in 1890. From 1901 at the time Gordon's father became director of the business school portion of the school, the name was changed to LDS University and in 1927, a year before Gordon graduated from high school, it was once again changed back to the LDS College until 1931 when all but the business college closed its doors as a result of the Great Depression.[1]

The college had not only junior college curriculum, it also had a high school and had been solidifying ever since 1901 when the old three-story tithing grain bin, vacant some time, was renovated into a gymnasium, chemistry/biology laboratory, rest rooms and boiler room at 70 North Main Street across the street east of the Salt Lake Temple and Temple Square.

The Deseret Gym completed in 1910 added to the campus. The Joseph F. Smith Memorial Building was completed in 1919 at about 40 East North Temple Street. A business College Building was built by 1901 facing west just to the south of the Joseph F. Smith Building. Barratt Hall, gathering place for school assemblies, was completed in 1902 facing northwest and diagonally southwest of the business college. And the Brigham Young Memorial Building was constructed at about 60 North Main Street immediately across the street just a little north of the Salt Lake Temple.

This campus with its half circle stream of buildings surrounded almost a quarter block of lawn and trees on the northwest corner of what now is Administration Block just east of Temple Square in Salt Lake City. In the back of the campus to the east was a sports field shaped much like a football field and surrounded with essentially open space on the northeast quarter of the Administration Block.

George Romney and George Homer Durham were fellow students with Gordon. George Romney was destined to become one of the major contenders for the United States Presidential Election in the future and G. Homer Durham was destined to become President of Arizona State University, first Commissioner of Education in Utah and a 70 general authority in charge of directing the LDS Church Historical Department.

LDS College Campus, Salt Lake City, Utah, in 1935
Left to right, Joseph F. Smith Memorial Building (then the Genealogical Society Building), Business College Building, and Barratt Hall

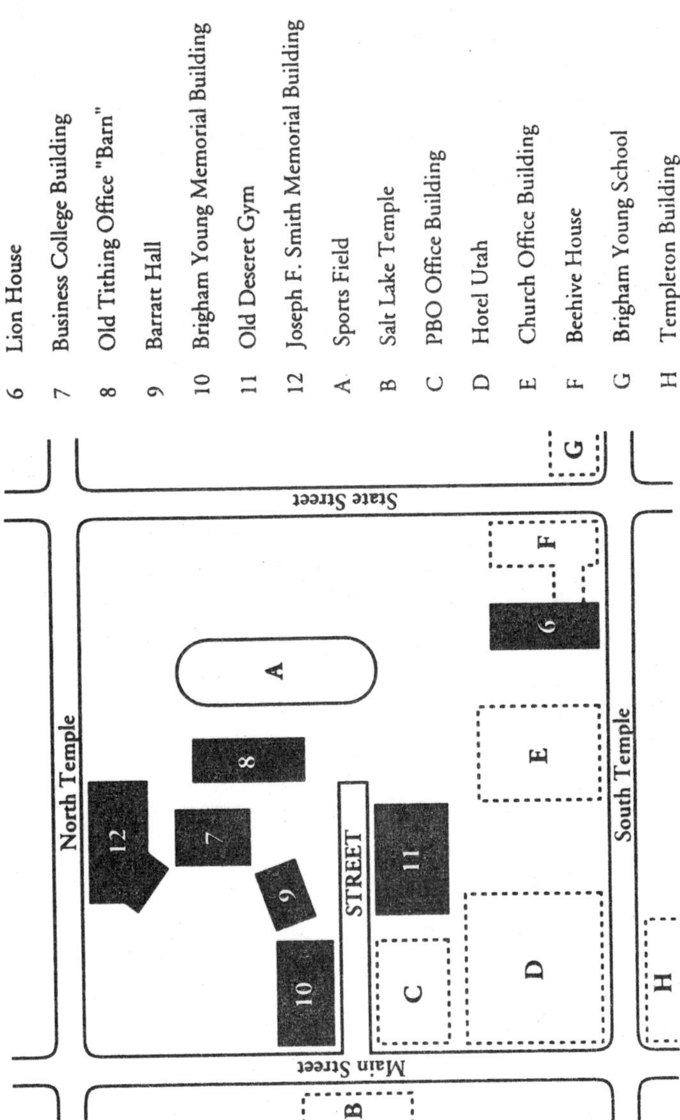

LDS College Campus, 1901-1931, Salt Lake City, Utah

It was here Gordon went to a different environment of school. This school was LDS Church sponsored much like the Brigham Young University developing on the east hills of the city of Provo, Utah 40 miles to the south. Brigham Young's Lion House and the Beehive House were also used as campus classrooms from time to time as well as the McCune School of Music located a block up the street at 200 North Main, Salt Lake City, Utah on what was being now called "Capitol Hill."

When Gordon entered the LDS University, which would be called the LDS College when he graduated from high school, America was in search for the "ebullient" life in the middle of the "Roaring Twenties" with the "Charleston" and its high speed jazz music, flappers, double breasted suits and straw hats and bow ties. It was an exciting time to grow up. Cars were becoming increasingly sophisticated.

Calvin Coolidge was now president of the United States. Adolf Hitler had just been freed from jail after serving eight months of a five year term for high treason in a failed "beer hall coup" to topple the German government.

The "Charleston" had been introduced from Charleston, South Carolina in an all black American review in New York in 1923. Middle-aged danced it in 4/4 time and those who disliked moving had fun standing perfectly still "while criss-crossing the hands back and forth across the knees."[2]

At this time, Gordon's father was made president of the Salt Lake Liberty Stake on May 28, 1925 when Hugh J. Cannon was called to preside over the German Mission for the second time.[3] He was released about the same time as General Board Member of the YMMIA after serving in that capacity for 25 years and 5 months.

In 1925, Principal of the university was Feramorz Young Fox. Fox was a former student of LDS High School, head of the LDS Business Department and an insurance agent. He had obtained a Phd. at Northwestern University in Chicago.[4] By 1925 there were 2,195 students at the university of which 42% were business college students.

Devotionals were held daily and on Wednesdays for about an hour at Barratt Hall, named after Samuel M. Barratt. About 1,000 could be seated in the auditorium on the second floor. General authorities from the adjacent offices in the Church Administration Building would speak. Religion classes were also part of the curriculum as is the practice at Brigham Young University in neighboring Provo.

Students were required to take at least one religion class each semester. On the high school level, these classes were the equivalent of released time seminary held usually adjacent to public schools and to institute classes for higher education students which commenced at non-LDS colleges and universities in 1926 at the University of Idaho.[5]

LDS standards of morality and behavior were required which included no profanity, obscenity, tobacco, alcohol, games of chance, disturbances at devotionals, gambling, improper conduct at parties or sluffing devotionals. [6]

What could be considered the mission statement of LDS College in 1927 as stated in the *Deseret News* of September 6, 1927 by Dr. Adam S. Bennion was: "Reverence for things sacred, respect for superiors, tolerance for those of different opinion, helpfulness, cooperation, friendship, continuance of habits of prayer, worship, service to God and man, of clean living, right thinking, good reading, wholesome recreation, vigorous study, regularity and dependability, thrift and self examination."[7] Little did they know they were molding a future prophet for the nations, "The shoulder for the Lord."

Gold and Blue were the school colors, adopted in November 1893, and also was the name of the school song.[8]

Gordon took a year of Latin at the high school and literature was catching his attention. He enjoyed reading and found he was developing an interest in writing.[9]

As for activities, there were many. In addition to student body and class elections, there were outings, hikes, parties, dances, stomps, competitions, student court, dramatic productions, business skill speed contests, college music, club meetings and athletics. [10]

The Romantic Courting Friends

While at LDS College High School, Gordon met a male student from a country town and a girl from the city. The boy, a brown paper bag carrier for lunch usually with a bologna sandwich inside. He cleaned the school to pay his tuition. His asset was a personality and smile that "seemed to sing of goodness." The girl was beauty contest material and from a comfortable home. She was freckle faced and quiet but her hair and dress were attractive.

"Something of magic took place between them. They fell in love." An odd couple most thought. But to them, they were inseparable. Dancing, studying, just laughing together brought this couple great joy. Forty-five years later, Gordon met them on a plane. In a dark airplane

LDS College Rally North and East of
LDS Church Administration Building
About 1928

LDS College Inside Barratt Hall, About 1928
l. "The Hope of the Nation - Art - Science - Revelation"
r. "The Strength of the Nation - Integrity - Service - Fidelity

LDS College Coeds
1928, the "Roaring '20's"

LDS College Pep Rally Parade, 1928

LDS College Typical "Roaring '20's Dance, 1928

LDS College Baseball Game on Field in 1928 where East Portion of 28 story LDS Church Administration Building was completed in 1973

LDS College Typical Coeds, 1928, Salt Lake City, Utah

LDS College, Salt Lake City, Utah, Business College Building, 1928

cabin, he walked down the aisle and saw her, now white-haired, nestled in his shoulder with their hands clasped.

They had followed Gordon to college and eventually married. She supported while he struggled. But it paid off. He went to a professional school and graduated near the top of his class. She had children. On the plane 45 years later, they were coming from New York where he had just delivered a professional paper to a prestigious group. She was proud of his accomplishments and Gordon wished he could have caught her face on an instant camera.

Returning to his seat, Gordon thought, "Their friends of high school saw only a farm boy from the country and a smiling girl with freckles on her nose. But these two saw in each other love, loyalty, peace, faith, and the future. . . a flowering of something divine, planted there by the Father who is our God. . . . They had lived with virtue and faith, with appreciation and respect for self and one another," in those school days. Now they were reaping the rewards of their fidelity and integrity in peace and quiet satisfaction after having long ago married in one of the LDS temples, there making "covenants" for eternity and promises never broken.[11]

Substitutes for Senator Reed Smoot

During the LDS College High School days, an event occurred which was quite remarkable. Senator Reed Smoot, also an LDS apostle, was scheduled to speak at the Salt Lake Liberty Stake 1st Ward but Senator Smoot notifed the ward bishop, John Duncan, he would be late. To fill in time, Bishop Duncan asked two young men in his ward to speak. One was Robert Sontag and the other was Gordon B. Hinckley.

Gordon was at the farm irrigating the day of the conference but promptly completed the water turn and rushed to the chapel after changing. There, both talked. For some reason Reed Smoot never arrived but the speeches of the two young men were well received and proved a worthy substitute.[12]

Family Felicity and Family Tragedy

A joyful event occurred for the Hinckley family on Christmas day, December 25, 1926. Venice, next to the youngest children of Bryant's first wife Christine Johnson, united in marriage with Lester John Nielson when she was age 21.[13] Venice was the surviving twin of her father's twin daughters. Her twin sister Virginia had been stillborn on October 25, 1905. Venice and her husband went to the LDS temple and received their endowments and were sealed for time and all eternity six years after their civil marriage. This is a common practice permitted in the LDS faith when a couple initially marry civilly without a temple sealing ceremony. Normally this can be done twelve months after an initial civil marriage.

But this experience of felicity was to be followed by two very trying times in the lives of the Hinckleys. Just two days and a month following Venice's marriage, brother Wendell Johnson Hinckley succumbed to heart failure on January 27, 1927, four days short of being 23 years old. He had never married. Wendell was one of the twin sons Bryant had sired by his first wife Christine. His twin brother Ralph Waldo went on to marry Glays Lavern Kroff just eight months later September 20, 1927 but not before some horrific news was disclosed to the children of Ada Bitner Hinckley.

During the Summer of 1927 while the family was on the East Millcreek farm, Gordon's younger brother Sherman was with his father in the fields one afternoon. All of a sudden his father Bryant Stringham Hinckley broke down and started to cry. Sherman was told that a growth had been found on one of Ada's breasts and that it had been diagnosed malignant.[14]

The family soon all knew the situation and commenced fervent prayers and fasting. Elder Frank Young Taylor, son of former prophet John Taylor and a member of the LDS 12 apostles, helped administer to Ada several times before Ada eventually went to California. Administration is a priesthood ordinance performed normally by at least two or more Melchizedek Priesthood holders. As in the ancient Church around the time of Christ, it was conducted in two parts.

First one of the "elders" (holders of the Melchizedek Priesthood) poured a drop or two of pure olive oil on the crown of the afflicted brother or sister's head. The oil had been previously dedicated by an elder for the specific purpose of healing "in the household of faith." After the oil was rubbed into the scalp, the elder stated orally the oil was being placed on the afflicted's head in an act of faith and by the power of the priesthood he held for the purpose of healing the sick and ended by stating he did so in the name of Christ.

Then all elders present placed their hands on the afflicted brother or sister and with one acting as voice for all "sealed" the anointing by once again stating their authority and stating the previous anointing by consecrated oil was being sealed by their combined Melchizedek Priesthood power. Then was pronounced whatsoever blessing the one as voice felt inspired to say.

This was believed by Latter-day Saints to be a continuation of the same acts of faith and "exercise" of authority and power from Christ the Savior as that exercised by the Savior himself and his disciples following his crucifixion as recorded in the Acts of the Apostles and Gospels of the New Testament.

Before Ada was 47, she had known her prognosis of cancer and once it was disclosed to Sherman, all of the children were told she was going to have the lump removed. A Dr. Middleton was called in to perform the surgery. He removed an entire breast and the tissue down Ada's left arm. Following the surgery, she also undertook radium treatments, then in their infant development. They made her sick. She returned home and launched into physical therapy exercise to restore the use of her left arm. She was not despondent and the family was grateful the cancer had been arrested, at least for the time being.

During this time, the twins Wendell and Waldo worked at the Deseret Gym. The LDS temple in Mesa, Arizona was also dedicated by Heber J. Grant on October 23, 1927. Then Gordon got involved in working at Deseret Gym. This work would prove to be a Godsend to Gordon as shortly the Great Depression of 1929 was about to take away all regular employment for a vast majority of laborers and professionals alike.

But God seemed to be watching over Gordon, now 17, for a great and wise purpose. The potential for his life had been stated to him by his stake patriarch six years before in his personal patriarchal blessing. If he was faithful, the realization of those possibilities would come.

Along with his brother Wendell, Gordon helped after his brother Waldo passed away. He was assigned to the "Key Room" where maintenance and electrical chores were solved. Plumbing was another part of the job. But as in the "hollow" and at other places on the farm, Gordon seemed to have the same engineering acumen as his younger brother Sherman, and could find a solution to just about any handyman task thrown his way.[15]

It was in the Spring of 1928 when Gordon graduated from the LDS College High School. At that time they danced to Irving Berlin's "Always" wherein was the refrain:

"I'll be loving you, always, with a love that's true,
always.
When the things you've planned, need a helping hand,

Gordon B. Hinckley
LDS College High School Graduation Picture, May 1928

I will understand, always, always."[16]

About the time he became a high school graduate, the first regular TV broadcast was made by WGY in Schenectady, New York [17] Although technology had not been perfected and mass production achieved yet allowing the masses to afford the phenomenon, it was truly a milestone in world history.

At the time of Gordon's graduation, the *"S" Book*, official student yearbook for the school, stated his senior group was the "peppiest" class in school. They promoted school spirit, good will and pep. The Senior Commencement Dance during the 1st semester of the school year was said to have outdone the Junior Prom for originality and novelty. Four mirrors had been placed at the entrance of the Roof Garden as the Senior gift. A Senior Assembly had been held 2nd semester. And they danced to a tune with lyrics which went:

"Is love like a rose that blossoms and grows,
Then withers and goes when stars don't?"[18]

Thus ended the high school days of Gordon and his friends, among which were George Romney and G. Homer Durham.

COLLEGE

Literature began to strongly interest Gordon as he went through his high school years. And with it was an increasing interest in putting down the written word himself. So when it came time to make decisions regarding his plans following high school, he looked to studying something which would increase his knowledge of the written word.

Up on the east foothills of north Salt Lake Valley was developing a nice university. It had started as the first university established west of the Mississippi, named the University of Deseret, by the LDS Church in 1850 and later transferred to the Territory of Utah for operation when its name changed to the University of Utah.

Since 1900, an increasingly growing complex of buildings had been developing as a newly located East Bench campus around what was dubbed "President's Circle" at about 220 South and 1350 East. The first four buildings completed were the "L" Building or first library in 1900, in 1901 the Normal Building housing "normal classes" and industrial education, and in 1902 the Sciences Building housing math, physics and chemistry and the Museum Building housing biology and geology together with museum items.

Next came the Administration Building right on the east apex of the circle and directly in line with 200 South completed in 1912-1914. At the time Gordon was completing his junior and senior years in high school, other facilities enhancing the campus were finished. One was Kingsbury Hall, a drama and music building containing a nice theater and classrooms, completed in 1927 and a football stadium completed in October 1927 south of the President's Circle.

In 1928, the Mines Building on the circle was completed along with the Engineering School. And a student "Union" was started on the northwest corner of the circle.[1] George Thomas was president of the university and quite an impressive faculty had been developed. President Thomas was a 1901 graduate of Harvard's school of administration and held a 1903 Ph.D. from Halle. Assisting him was a faculty of 224, nine of which were on sabbatical. The English Department had 21 professors and teachers with one on sabbatical.[2] The university also had a classical languages department.

Perhaps a great influence, aside from natural talent and ability, was the example of Gordon's mother and father on his decision to major in English. They were academians. Mother Ada was a disciplined language and grammar believer who had taught all of her children to speak and write with dignity and correctness. And the library presence in Gordon's home from the very inception of his life cannot be discounted in his decision. Later Gordon stated he felt his mother nurtured and consciously or otherwise shaped his direction.[3]

Also, his religion certainly cannot be ruled out in its influence on his decision to minor in Greek and Latin ancient languages.[4] These were two of the languages in which the ancient texts of the Holy Bible were written and from which the English versions had been translated. He had taken one Latin class during high school which whetted his appetite.

The University of Utah campus was just 3 miles from the family Windsor Street home and just 2 miles from the Deseret Gym where he continued to work during the Summer of 1928. The 28th Summer Olympics were held in Amsterdam in August where the United States topped most points received at 437.

On September 28, 1928, Gordon went with 1,200 other freshman to the University of Utah campus and registered for his first quarter as a freshman with English major and Greek & Latin minor. On that same day in Germany, Prussia lifted the public speaking ban on Adolf Hitler.

During the same month, then American president Herbert Hoover predicted on September 11 an end to poverty in America was near. On September 15, Alexander Fleming, a bacteriologist at the London University School of Medicine, accidentally discovered penicillin when some airborne mold had killed a culture of staphylococcus wherever it had fallen. This tremendous discovery was to change the course of medicine and drastically reduce mortality from pneumonia and similar diseases.

"Mortimer" had his name changed to "Mickey" the mouse and started talking in a squeaky voice in his second animated movie "Steamboat Willie" released by Walt Disney. Chiang Kai-shek had the titles of "Chairman of the Nationalist Government of China" plus "Commander-in-Chief" of the Chinese forces given to him.[5]

Also at the time, a briefcase cost between $5.85 to $11.50, a Parker pen cost $3.50 and narrow brim hats, starting to come into vogue, cost $6.00. Frank Sinatra, 13, was singing "I'll be seeing you in all the old familiar places" with the Tommy Dorsey Band and the "big band" era was on its way.

Deseret Gym, Salt Lake City, Utah

Courses Gordon could complete at the U. of U. in order to be an English major included freshman English, business letters, chronological survey of English literature, masters of fiction, expository writing, masterpieces of drama, English masterpieces, modern English grammar, advanced English composition, journalistic writing, the short story, the one act play, development of the English novel, the essay, principles of poetry, romantic poets, Victorian poets, English prose writers of the 19th century, American literature, contemporary poetry, lyrics, development of English drama, and Shakespeare.[6]

Of the above courses, Gordon had to complete 36 to 45 credit hours beyond his freshman year from the School of Arts & Sciences. Required courses in the curriculum were a chronological survey of English Literature, advanced English composition, Shakespeare and Chaucer, Old English or history of the English language. General education requirements included classes in physical education, hygiene, math and physical science, biological science, language and social science.

Physics in math and physical science; zoology in biological science; speech and English in languages and anthropology, economics, philosophy and sociology in social science were options[7]

Classes and Teachers

The actual classes taken by Gordon included four classes of English, two of speech, Latin, sociology, zoology, history, physics, Greek, geology, economics, philosophy and anthropology.[8]

English courses included virtually all of the English literature including intensive Shakespeare for two quarters and Victorian writers. He took a poetry composition class, too, and read good English and American anthologies.[9]

Of his professors, there was the first Jewish teacher ever to teach in a university in Utah. This teacher spoke of his admiration for the Salt Lake Temple and its east spire on top of which sat a gold leaf statue depicting the heavenly messenger Moroni blowing a trumpet.

This figure sits on a spire of almost all of the temples built by the LDS people and represents to them the messenger heralding the "everlasting gospel" spoken of by John the Revelator in Revelations 14:6-7. This professor never ceased sounding praise for the workmanship and symmetry of design of the Salt Lake Temple which had taken LDS pioneers 40 years to complete.[10]

English professors on the faculty included S. B. Neff, G. M.

Marshall, B. Roland Lewis and assistant professors Quiney, Richards Angleman, Zucker. Instructors were Hubbard, Snow, Rohrbough, Austin, Crabtree, Christensen and Caux. Ghiselin, Chapman, Maughan, Horst, Birney, Singer and Clapp also assisted.[11]

Speech faculty consisted of professor Babcock, assistant professors Maw and Smith, Mr. Bane, Mrs. Webster, Miss Redd, Mr. Plummer, and Mrs. Brimhall.[12]

From among the above Gordon was tutored in secular knowledge and skills which would benefit him throughout his life.

The "Great Depression" of 1929

Although the greatest depression in American and world history lasted much longer than two months in 1929, the stock market crash which marked its rapid acceleration started in the Fall of that year.

It was a year of unassumed pending affliction. The U. of U. football team garnered its second championship in three years in the Rocky Mountain Conference. The 10 story Newhouse Hotel on Salt Lake's downtown Main Street and 400 South boasted 400 rooms at $2-4 per night for a single room.

Will Durant gave a talk to the U studentbody in which he said, "One of the problems facing young people is that marriage in our society must be postponed from the natural age to the financial age." Gordon came to conclude that was a true statement. Marriage requires self-discipline.[13]

Transcontinental Air Transport started the first coast to coast air service across the United States on July 7, 1929. It took two days and two nights, flying during the day, sleeping on trains at nights, and cost $351.94 one way. The choir of over 300 LDS members organized in Salt Lake City for many years started weekly live radio broadcasts from the Tabernacle on Temple Square over KSL Radio on July 15 of the same year also.[14] And the happiest time for the Hinckley family during the year was the marriage on September 16, 1929 of Gordon's older sister Christine, youngest child of his father's first wife Christine Johnson, at age 21, to Oliver Preston Robinson in the LDS temple for time and all eternity.[15]

Then came the crash. On October 29, 1929, the New York City Stock Market collapsed in frantic trading. Several weeks before "Black Thursday" large trust managers were rumored to be divesting numerous stock portfolios. Perhaps this incited some fear in fellow stock investors. In any event, the declines created a reported 11 suicides by some grief stricken speculators.

The crash had repercussions throughout the country of America and in overseas industrialized nations. In Salt Lake City, it hit LDS College hard as well as other institutions of higher learning. The other two major universities in the state were Brigham Young University and the Agricultural College in a little community called Logan about 60 miles northeast of Salt Lake in the tops of the Cache Valley segment of the Rocky Mountains.

Gordon's father took a reduced salary of 80% as patronage of Deseret Gym plunged.[16] Gordon was now 19 as the depression deepened in the economy of the entire United States. The gym's situation continued through 1933.

In the midst of all this despair, Sonja Henie, the Norwegian ice skating queen, won her crown for the second year and Marlene Dietrich stared in the movie "Blue Angel" and was arrested for it.

Gordon had progressed in the offices of the Aaronic Priesthood since being given the initial office of deacon and on March 3, 1930, as he neared the end of this sophomore year in college, was ordained to the Melchizedek Priesthood (the higher priesthood) in his LDS Church.

In the same ordination, he was given the office of an "elder" by John A. McDonald in the 1st Ward of Salt Lake Liberty Stake.[17]

This was a momentous step for Gordon because it gave him all of the authority of the Melchizedek Priesthood. Latter-day Saints believe that once a man obtains the higher or Melchizedek Priesthood, if he is faithful in "magnifying" it, he has all of the authority from Jesus Christ to perform ordinances and act in other ways for and on behalf of Jesus Christ so long as he exercises the priesthood he has in accordance with the guidance and permission of leaders appointed.

Other than the higher priesthood, he is only given different offices, which have certain spheres of responsibility, and the eternal sealing to spouse in a temple of God. Whether one is given the office of elder, seventy, high priest, patriarch, bishop, apostle or even prophet-president, each Melchizedek Priesthood holder holds just as much authority and power as the other only with different ranges of responsibility.

Well, Gordon had this higher priesthood now and he would find in the trying times ahead that it would be a marvelous power and strength to him. He was 19¾ years old when he received the Melchizedek Priesthood from Brother McDonald.

Mother's Death

For about two and a half years after Gordon's mother had received a mastectomy of her left breast, the children at least did not know of any recurrence of their mother's cancer. But in March of 1930, Ada and Bryant went on a trip to Chicago returning with Ada's left arm impaired in movement and swollen. The family expected the worst and the doctor confirmed a relapse of the malignancy.

Radium treatments were resumed. They made Ada extremely ill but she did not complain. Daughter Ruth observed both her mother and father conversing on a bench at the East Millcreek farm that Summer. It was very emotional watching them as it was apparent her mother's stamina was weakening and her parents loved each other so very much.

In July 1930, a group of women whose family or relatives fought in World War I organized a tour to visit the graves in Europe of their loved ones who died in the war and Ada determined she desired to see her son Bryant Stanford's grave. Stanford's widow Beulah had also decided to go. Both departed July 18, 1930 and returned in August. No one on the trip was told of Ada's condition nor received a hint of her inward suffering but a personal entry penned in the leaves of a small book while she was on this trip revealed her self will and faith.

"The God Power within me is stronger than my weakness," she wrote.

Also when she returned, she left a manuscript of the women's journey which was published posthumously in the *LDS Improvement Era* magazine, official monthly magazine of the LDS Church at that time.

At the farm, the children busily tidied up the farm house, bottled much fruit, weeded the grounds and scrubbed. But Ada acted lethargic to their overtures of love and kindness when she returned when in normal health she would have lavished her children with praise and although she manifested a "brave front" at the train station when she returned from Europe, her children knew her well enough to immediately recognize her progressing illness.

In the Fall, the family returned to the Windsor Street home where fervent family prayers continued from the Summer months and priesthood administrations in the household of faith were performed. But another Latter-day Saint teaching expressed in a revelation received by the prophet Joseph Smith, Jr. in 1831 said, "And again it shall come to pass that he that hath faith in me to be healed, and is not appointed unto death, shall be healed."[18] So everything is conditioned upon the "will" of the Father in Heaven.

Ada accepted any and all offers and suggestions to help. Her daughter Ruth hotpacked her with mineral baths. Health foods, herbs, and mineral water were received. And then in October, she heard of the Coffey-Humber treatment being administered by two doctors in California, hoped by many of the time to be a cancer cure or at least inhibitant or relievant of pain. Ada's husband was desirous of doing anything for his beloved wife and asked her to receive the treatment.

Ada's sister Mary accompanied Ada to Los Angeles where lodging was obtained across the street from the clinic where the treatment was given. Neighbors knew she was going and commenced a profuse expression of affection for the Hinckley family. The Liberty Stake members over which Bryant presided and many others called by phone. Invitations to dinner were unending and donated food filled the kitchen.

Ada kept up courage and concern for her family. She wrote a letter addressed to her daughter Ruth and "the Rest" on October 15, 1930 asking her to do some tidying and house straightening jobs such as brushing her husband's tuxedo and placing it in a cedar bag. Ramona was admonished to wear her coat and the entire family requested to eat good meals.

Then on November 1st, Ada's sister Mary suggested Bryant come to California for the treatment. Ada desired for him to wait until the least expensive train fares became effective but Bryant packed and left immediately.

At Los Angeles, he wrote of his faith on November 4th to his family, "Mamma seems a little more weary, otherwise not much change this morning. We are hoping for an improvement but are reconciled to what ever may come. Thus far we have done all that we could do and we seem powerless. She is in the hands of the Lord. He can spare her life and raise her and if it is his will, she will live. If not, all will be well. There is a very tranquil and sweet influence here."[19]

The same morning, the family joined the block long line of automobiles waiting for their scheduled appointment to receive the 6cc. of liquid hope. Bryant recorded the experience. "Out on the sidewalk is a small table, two nurses and a doctor. The cars drive up in their turn and it takes about one minute for a shot in the right arm and they pull away hoping for the better. The doctor and nurse come over here when the car patients are served. Expect them in about a half hour.

"I am waiting in the room. Patients of all ages and conditions are in this line. The doctor is a man of about 30 - bare headed and bald headed, with an apron on and his sleeves rolled up carrying a clip with the patient's history on. The nurses are young, have their caps on and a hypo needle. As the car approaches they get the patient ready and in a minute it is all over. They gave Mamma 6 cc. They never talk about the condition of the patient."[20]

Bryant assisted Ada several times during the night, lifted her, rubbed her feet, moved her legs and otherwise helped for the next five days as more of Ada's sisters arrived to her flower filled room. Then on a beautiful Sunday morning in the presence of her husband Bryant and sisters May, Della, Libby and Erma, she passed away November 9, 1930 at 10:00 A.M.

Bryant and her sisters made the necessary preparations and boarded the train to return to his children. All of his children from his first wife Christine Johnson were 21 or older. Gordon was 20, Sherman 19, Ruth 16¾, Ramona almost 15, and Sylvia 10½.

As the train pulled into the Salt Lake City depot, the hearse stood silently waiting to transport Ada's remains to the funeral home as Ada's children waited. The children were grief stricken and Bryant was "ashen and weary" knowing he faced the same situation he had done in 1908 with five children depending upon him. The children walked solemnly down the station platform to the casket in the baggage car and saw the mortician unload and carry it to the hearse.[21]

Gordon came to know at that moment even more the tenderness of his father's heart. It has affected him all of his life. He "came to know something of death, the absolute devastation of children losing their mother, but also of peace without pain, and the certainty that death cannot be the end of the soul."[22]

The next day Sherman went to the Registrar's Office at the University of Utah where he had enrolled as a freshman in engineering a year after Gordon. He asked for an excuse along with Gordon. When the registrar, who was Brother Norton, a Liberty Stake high councilman, heard their request, tears filled his eyes.[23]

The funeral was held November 13, a Thursday, at 2:00 P.M. in the Liberty Stake 1st Ward Chapel. Not only were ward members present, a profusement of affection was displayed by numerous other stake members and general authorities of the LDS Church led by their prophet leader President Heber J. Grant.

1st Ward Chapel, Liberty Stake, Salt Lake City, Utah
Where Ada Bitner Hinckley's Funeral Was Held
and the Hinckley Family Worshiped

Joseph Anderson, personal secretary to President Heber J. Grant also was in attendance and took down the entire course of proceedings in shorthand. The pulpit was profuse with flowers as Bishop John C. Duncan conducted. An opening prayer was offered by Fred J. Pack and a violin duet given by the Lindsay Sisters. Then Fred M. Michelsen, who served on the high council and as a fellow counselor in the Liberty Stake Presidency with Gordon's father Bryant Stringham Hinckley spoke. "I know that no words of mine can help to take away the sorrow that comes in parting, but I sometimes think that it is a beautiful thing that we sorrow in parting, because true sorrows sometimes bring our deepest and lasting joys."[24]

Former stake president Hugh J. Cannon, with whom Gordon's father had served for 25 years, as long as he had presided over Liberty Stake either as one of his high councilors or as his stake presidency counselor, next spoke. "Brother Hinckley–we know that he will meet this trial with the same courage, faith and devotion that he has met every trial which has come into his life. His eyes are fixed on the future. He understands the Gospel of the Lord Jesus Christ, and I can well believe that without that faith, that hope and that absolute knowledge which he has in his heart, this blow would literally crush him. But no blow, no calamity, howsoever severe, can completely crush a thorough Latter-day Saint."[25]

Gordon and his brother Sherman and sisters Ruth, Ramona and Sylvia all sat at the front pews of the congregation with their father. They acted brave but inside their hearts were paining greatly. Even Gordon, oldest of his natural siblings, now 20 years old, pained tremendously.

Then Brother Wilson McCarthy stood. He was a former student of Gordon's father Bryant when Bryant taught at the LDS College. He recalled that Bryant quoted the last chapter of Proverbs and talked about it in his teaching about the value of a virtuous woman. In reading that proverb "it seemed to me that they were written for Ada. . . . I would only pray that I might have the power to be an instrument in bringing the comfort to President Hinckley that he has brought to the hearts of hundreds of people. I can just hear him tell on an occasion of this kind how that all is well, and the cheer and the blessing that he has brought to the lives of hundreds. I think I can say this and I know he would not appreciate it perhaps, that when the next historian writes the history of the great teachers and spiritual leaders of this generation he

Interior Chapel of 1st Ward, Liberty Stake, Salt Lake City, Utah

must to be honest write high the name of Bryant S. Hinckley."[26]

When Brother McCarthy would visit in the Hinckley home "what a joy," he said. "What a joy it was to sit around their table and visit them in their home! You felt good about it. A fine spirit came over you. You felt good in his humor, geniality, everything that went with the sweetest and loveliest of companionship. . . . I know that the greatest heritage that can come to these young children of hers is the fact that they are the children of Ada Hinckley. The greatest assurance of their success in life is the fine love and care and companionship which this great mother gave to them."[27]

LDS apostle Frank J. Cannon next spoke. "I want to say to you that these two families are in favor with God the Eternal Father and he will always be mindful of them because of the devotion and faith of their fathers and their mothers. These boys and these girls are proving true to the heritage that they so nobly and honorably bear."[28]

Then the living LDS prophet Heber J. Grant rose to the stand. "I know that no true Latter-day Saint mourns as do the people of the world. I never think of my mother, my wives, my two sons and my daughter as being in the graveyard. I think only of the joy and the peace and the happiness they are experiencing in having gained salvation and eternal life. It is like being born to joy and happiness from a world of care and sorrow when the faithful pass away. There is no sorrow, only in parting temporarily with those we love, when death enters our home."[29]

President Grant stated he knew Ira Nathaniel Hinckley when President Grant was a boy and felt he was one of the choicest and finest men it was ever his lot to know. When President Grant was made an apostle, he became more intimately acquainted with Ira as Ira presided over the Millard Stake. President Grant also indicated he knew Bryant S. Hinckley from the time Bryant studied at the B.Y. Academy.

"I rejoice in the wonderful family of men and women of integrity and devotion to God, to their families, to their country such as he [Ira Hinckley] left as the heritage of his posterity."[30]

Then as was his custom at funerals, President Grant turned to the 76th Section of the Doctrine and Covenants and read "speaking of the resurrection of the dead, concerning those who shall hear the voice of the Son of Man, . . . these are they whose bodies are celestial."[31]

Following the LDS prophet Heber J. Grant's words, Senator William H. King, US Senator representing Utah, was called upon impromptu to say a few words. "I was not aware until the announcement was just made by the bishop that I would be called upon for a word on this sad occasion . . . We feel that we have been brought into the valleys of the mountains where we might learn more of the ways of the Lord and become equipped to become ambassadors and messengers to the nations of the world . . . I have known Brother Bryant Hinckley and his family since he was a child . . . No nobler man exists than he. His heart is pure, and he has aspirations for service and for devotion to the cause of Christ . . . The tributes paid to our departed sister were well deserved. We cannot add anything to her glory and to the crown of righteousness which she has earned.

"May God bless those who mourn. May he bless all of us. May we go forth from this building determined to serve God with more faithfulness and devotion in the future than in the past. May our testimonies be strengthened, and when we are brought face to face with death, may we feel that it is just a short separation between the living and the so-called dead, and that if we are devoted to the Lord here we shall rise in the first resurrection and shall have joy, happiness and eternal life throughout the endless ages. May God comfort our hearts and bless us and strengthen us and increase our faith and strengthen our testimonies, and in the end save us all, through Jesus Christ. Amen."[32]

A vocal solo "I know that my Redeemer Lives" was sung by Brother Charles R. Pike and after over two hours of service, normally only one hour at most LDS funerals, the benediction was offered by Stringham A. Stevens.

Thus was a typical LDS memorial service ended. All were asked to arise while Ada's casket and her family and relatives left the chapel first. The pallbearers placed the coffin in the hearse and a cortege travelled to the Wasatch Lawn Cemetery located in the Salt Lake Valley at 3401 South Highland Drive. There another LDS ordinance was performed.

After the family and friends had assembled at the grave site and the casket placed at the grave, a holder of the LDS Melchizedek Priesthood stood at the head of the grave and bowing his head as if in prayer stated he dedicated the gravesite before him by authority of the Melchizedek Priesthood which he held and in the name of the Savior Jesus Christ as a sacred and final resting place for Ada Bitner Hinckley and pronounced such other words of dedication as he was inspired to utter. The casket was then lowered into the grave for burial.

Continued University Studies

Gordon's mother and father had been married for 21 years. During Gordon's 20 short years, his mother had taught him to love the Lord, love one another, render service gladly, appreciate the finer things, endeavor to have good health, engage in righteous living, aspire to fulfill our responsibilities to the best of our ability, be honest and fair, and seek knowledge concentrating on the beautiful aspects of life.[33] This legacy was a rich addition to Gordon's heritage. He was going to need these gifts in the next crisis of faith to bear upon his life.

LDS Church membership had doubled by 1930 since Gordon's birth and now stood at 1,000,000 and growing.[34]

At the time of the last illness and passing of Gordon's mother, he and his siblings had put on a brave front, fought back the tears, but the wounds were deep and painful. The experience of his mother's passing gave Gordon a deeper understanding of all who lose a mother.[35]

Back at his university studies, Gordon, although his mother's absence weighed heavy on his soul, plunged into continued studies. A rally was held at the RKO Theater before the University of Utah and BYU game. And on January 8, 1931, Admiral Byrd visited the U campus. The admiral had ended a vast Antarctic air survey in November 1929 completing the first flight over the South Pole. In February 1931, Pope Pius XI of the Roman Catholic Church denounced trial marriage, birth control and divorce. The next month in March of 1931, a St. Patrick's Day Ball was held in the rotunda of the Utah State Capitol by the studentbody of the University of Utah.[36]

The comic strip Dagwood made its debut as well as Dick Tracy in 1931. And junior college and high school classes were cancelled at the LDS College due to depleting enrollment from the depression.[37] University of Utah enrollment also decreased dramatically from 1931 due to the depression.[38] But Gordon, blessed with continued employment at the Deseret Gym, was able to pay the $19.00 per quarter tuition together with other expenses for school.

Nineteen thirty one was also the year Japan invaded Manchukuo without warning launching a great war in China.[39] It was a year of dancing and dating and lots of fun while students at the U worried about life with cynicism.[40]

Gordon, 20, also got up enough courage to phone the girl living just across the street from him at 827 East 700 South. Her name was Marjorie Pay. She was 19 and had moved around the block from 804

Aerial View of University of Utah Campus About 1932
From the Northwest Looking Southeast

South 800 East with her father and mother and several younger brothers and sisters in 1926 to the red brick home across the way where Gordon and she could see each other entering and leaving their individual homes just about every day. They had seen each other at church regularly too where Marjorie had become a Sunday School teacher at age 17 and had held just about every office in the Mutual Improvement Association for young men and women.[41]

"Yes, I'd be glad to go to the Gold & Green Ball," she answered when Gordon asked.

That Spring the Empire State Building was opened in New York City on May 1, 1931, the tallest human made structure in the world at the time.[42] Rumble seats were standard now on the new sporty coupes of the faster than ever automobiles. The cowboy comedian Will Rogers said, "Give me a Dr. of Applesauce."

Enrollment at the University of Utah totalled 3,600 in 1931, Gordon's senior year at the university.[43] On September 20, 1931, Gordon's father invited Liberty Stake patriarch Joseph Keddington to the family's home for dinner. [44] And Bryant was now also courting a school teacher named May Green.

The season was dark to Gordon in many ways. There was 30% unemployment in the United States. Savings which the family had in the bank had been lost through bank closures. There seemed among many nothing to live for. But those "of great faith held on tenaciously in spite of the poverty."[45] The cynicism started to get to Gordon, too.

In September of 1931, the unemployed rioted in London and over 5 million were without work in Europe. In October Al Capone went to prison in the US. There was little opportunity for employment. There was no minimum wage. The pay was extremely small. A wage of $50.00 a month was fortunate. If you received $100.00 monthly you could consider yourself rich.[46] Men were in soup lines. Many committed suicide. Some succumbed. It was not hard to be pessimistic. He began to look gloomily and was caught up in the negativism of the time.

He had studied philosophy and anthropology, history, Emerson, Carlyle, geology, and biology and heard the whole Darwin theory of organic evolution. He wondered about it. He thought about it much but didn't let it throw him. He remembered the scriptures telling about the origins and relation of God.[47] Gordon had also studied T. E. Lawrence's (alias "Lawrence of Arabia's") *Seven Pillars of Wisdom*, the title having been taken from Proverbs.[48] But even though he had almost an ideal father and mother "I began to question some things in slight measure, the faith of my parents."[49]

This test of his faith, a faith he had felt with strong conviction in that room with 400 men in the 10th Ward chapel of Liberty Stake when 12 years old, compelled him to read and study to make certain for himself. Later he was to remark to the studentbody of the Brigham Young University in one of almost a dozen occasions speaking there at their weekly devotionals and Sunday firesides, "All go through the same test."[50]

He also recalled all of the teachings of his faithful parents, the testimony of the living prophet Heber J. Grant at his mother's funeral, and several other events which had given him the same feeling. Several times he had been touched with the same spirit he felt when he was in that meeting with 400 men at the Liberty Stake 10th Ward as he heard LDS prophet Heber J. Grant speak.

One time Gordon heard President Heber J. Grant tell of reading the Book of Mormon as a boy. He spoke of Nephi and the great influence it had on President Grant's life. Then with a voice ringing with conviction Gordon will never forget, President Grant quoted a passage from that Book of Mormon in the book of 1 Nephi 3:7:

> "I will go and do the things which the Lord hath commanded, for I know that the Lord giveth no commandments unto the children of men, save he shall prepare a way for them that they may accomplish the thing which he commandeth them."

There came into Gordon B. Hinckley's heart a similar feeling he had when 12 years old, "a resolution to do what the Lord has commanded."[51]

Another time, Gordon was sitting in the Tabernacle on Temple Square and heard one of the general authorities say that peace can come only through an acknowledgment of Jesus Christ. Gordon doubted that would ever occur but later glimpsed a vision of how it could happen when he found himself in Hiroshima, Japan in the 1960's.[52]

One other time, Gordon similarly heard Heber J. Grant's voice ringing with conviction bear witness of the sacred law of tithing and the marvelous promises the Lord had made to those who honestly pay it. Gordon was impressed.[53]

And another instance, Gordon heard President Grant testify with conviction of the "little white slaver" which imprisoned those who used tobacco. He had resolved never to partake of that habit.[54]

All of these cumulative experiences really helped Gordon at this juncture in his life. He later said the decisions of his generation are essentially the same as those of subsequent generations. "And I have been through many of them. They are often complex and difficult and fraught with tremendous consequences."[55]

The trial of his faith, the problem of whom to marry and when, the decisions of career choices, the action of social contacts, and a myriad of other choices such as eats, drinks and clothes all were his to make just as they are for all in their own lives when they were the same age.

Senior Year at the U

As Gordon worked out his test of faith, his last year of study at the university came. The writers of the school yearbook *Utonian* wrote of their year, "At high Noon youth invades the campus! Here, there is life; here, there is life; here, jollity and gaiety; here, going enthusiasm and spirit; here, youth supreme! Even the copious and abundant leaves dance in the playful breeze, and now the stately building looks austere, seen in this sportive atmosphere."[56]

Coeds wore waved hair, many parted near the center with hair down to the neck. As students walked to campus from the west, they met the "boulder rock" across President's Circle in front of the Administration Building at the foot of the flag pole. The Union Building for students was completed and opened Thanksgiving night.

The three level building on the north side of President's Circle boasted a beautiful dance hall on the main floor running along the north side of the building. When one climbed the steps and entered the main floor, the garden type doors to the ballroom met their eye ahead. Ornate decorative motifs enhanced the decor in a strip at the top of the walls where they met the ceiling.

The military ROTC (Reserve Officers Training Corp.) marched on President's Circle, even when it snowed. Football, basketball, track, tennis, polo, wrestling, and swimming were available to men. Dance, basketball, swimming, and volleyball were offered to women.

There were student assemblies every week. Their themes were educational, serious and lighter entertainment. Matinee dances were held at the Union and also on Christmas, Prom Week and Founders Day.

Before home football games, there were rallies and songfests on the

"U" mountain and a parade of floats during Homecoming activities followed by a special dance. There were many sororities and fraternities available to the students.

During the Homecoming Parade, every organization entered a float "expressive of school spirit." Bedecked cars served as portions of the parade. The school year 1931-1932 was a wondrous year for the football team. The Thanksgiving Rally was held the day before the annual Utah vs Aggie game. The U football uniforms consisted of white shirts with three vertical stripes on the front and three dashes on the ribs. The helmets were leather and shaped like watermelons.

Utah beat BYU 38-0 with numerous substitutions. In their two basketball games of the season, both schools split a game each, 44-36 BYU and 40-39 U. of U. Other football scores were U vs CAC, 60-6; U vs Boulder, Colorado, 32-0; U vs Washington Huskies, 6-7; and U vs Denver, 46-0.[57]

In the Valley, the Utah Copper Company owned the Bingham Copper Mine, Utah Power & Light Co. had 40 generating stations in the State, natural gas was on line, and there was an Ambassador Hotel in addition to the Newhouse and Hotel Utah. Local men's clothier Arthur Frank was selling suits for from $25.00 and the Bamberger Electric Railroad was running regularly from Brigham City to the north to Provo 40 miles south of Salt Lake City.[58]

February 1932 found the Rockerfeller Center in downtown Manhattan, New York City, under construction. In March of that year, Charles Lindbergh's baby was kidnapped. That same month Brigham Young's Lion House was converted into a social home for young women, joining Brigham Young's main Beehive House which had been converted into such a young women's dormitory some time before.[59]

On February 22, 1932, Gordon's father married his third wife, May Green, in the Salt Lake Temple for time and all eternity.[60] And on April 2, 1932, LDS prophet Heber J. Grant began his campaign against smoking.[61] A huge block "U" had for some time been created on the side of a small hill immediately northeast of the main U campus and on May 13, 1932 was whitewashed by the students. Two days later, Utah Governor George H. Dern declared a special "fast day" for the poor during the depths of the depression.[62] Citizens, LDS and others alike, were all requested to refrain from eating two meals and donate the unused food money for use by the poor.

U-BYU Football Game 1932-33 Season

It was June 7, 1932 when Gordon B. Hinckley proudly and happily marched in a processional in graduation robes and hat and listened to a commencement address "of which I remember absolutely nothing." He was conferred the degree of Bachelor of Arts in English with a minor degree in Greek and Latin from the Arts & Sciences Department of the University of Utah.[63] There were 81 graduates from the Arts & Sciences Department out of the total 293 graduates.[64]

Gordon's friend G. Homer Durham was also one of the 1932 graduates from the Arts & Sciences Department. James L. Gibson had been dean of the department since 1915 and George Montanye Marshall was the head professor of English. Professor Marshall had round glass lenses worn down on the nose, a rounded short collar, wide dark eyeglasses, darker stems on the spectacles and whitened hair.

Many of Gordon's college classmates remained faithful during these trying times but others' faith and testimony was traded for a "gaudier garment woven of inferior fabric."[65] And the interesting thing has been over the years Gordon's cling to his faith and convictions established as early as at age 12 have proved more stable than many of the facts taught dogmatically as proven fact during his university years.

The facts of that day, dogmatically set forth, have in many instances become fiction in the areas of medicine, physics, chemistry, even political science. Attitudes have changed. There have been changes in law. And literature and art have experienced shifts in standards. Everywhere there has been change and modification "except eternal verities."[66]

Gordon's interest of literature had grown into a love during his college years. And not only that, he desired to create his own written word. That desire churned his ambitions. He looked at a school, well respected and prominent, where his sites fixed. Columbia. That is where he desired to go.

Columbia was a long standing institution of higher learning chartered in 1754 as King's College by King George II in New York City until after the American Revolution when its name was changed to Columbia College. It was located on Morningside Heights since 1897 when it was first made a university and a journalism school was endowed there by Joseph Pulitzer, the German emigrant journalist who greatly developed and expanded the *Saturday Evening Post* into a major magazine. The Pulitzer Prize in journalism is named after him. Gordon set his sites on attending graduate school in journalism there.[67]

Gordon Bitner Hinckley
University of Utah Graduation June 1932

At this time, Gordon continued his employment at Deseret Gym in order to save funds for his contemplated studies at Columbia. In July 1932, Siam was taken by a military coup and Franklin Delano Roosevelt, then Governor of New York State, was nominated by the Democratic party for President of the United States. In his acceptance speech, he said, "I pledge you, I pledge myself to a new deal for the American people."

Also in July of the same year, Ziegfeld, the creator of Ziegfeld's Follies, died. The "Bonus Army" was driven out of Washington, D.C. as they demonstrated on behalf of World War I veterans for a "bonus" for service in the Great War. General Douglas MacArthur and Major Dwight D. Eisenhower commanded government troops who dismantled and set fire to the makeshift shanties and tents of the demonstrators.

The Summer Olympics were held in Los Angeles in August 1932 where a crowd of 95,000 watched ceremonies in the LA Coliseum. The United States scored more points than in any previous Olympics–740.5 to the next runner up's 262.5 points for Italy. Unemployed in America rose to 11,000,000 the same month.[68] The artist Picasso painted *Girl Before a Mirror* this year.

Franklin D. Roosevelt won the presidential election by a landslide of 472 electoral votes to 59. Before Roosevelt was installed as the 32nd president of the United States, however, Hitler became chancellor of Germany on January 30, 1933 after 10 years of rise to power. February 1933 saw Japan withdraw from the League of Nations and Mae West star in "She Done Him Wrong."

On March 4, 1933 Franklin D. Roosevelt was officially inaugurated. The depression-tired-citizens of his nation looked upon him much as a prophet favored to deliver the United States from their deepest depression in history. Population of the United States was 120 million while over 13 million were still unemployed. At the east plaza of the Capitol building in Washington, D.C., President Roosevelt in ringing tone said, "The only thing we have to fear is fear itself."[69]

Two days before President Roosevelt broadcast his first fireside chats, an earthquake killed 123 people in Southern California at Long Beach and Orange County.

The earthquake, however, did not stop Roosevelt from stating the objective of his government was to "restore commodity price levels." He then began his fireside chats before the radio sets of the American people on March 12.[70] Setting the neighborly and familiar tone for the

31 "fireside chats" he would broadcast to the American people during his 12 years as president, he began his first chat with, "My friends, I want to talk for a few minutes with the people of the United States about banking."[71]

On March 23, Hitler was granted dictatorial powers in Germany and in April his Nazi party boycotted Jewish business establishments in retaliation for world boycott of German goods.

MISSION

The depression had precipitated a large decrease in the number of LDS missionaries called. But there was a select group of faithful brethren and some sisters who still were being asked to fill missions. Rather than volunteering for missions as is now the usual practice, in the earliest days of the LDS Church beginning with Joseph Smith, Jr., often brethren, married or unmarried, were named without warning by the prophet of the LDS Church to serve missions.

An instance was recorded where Brigham Young visited a stake conference in Nephi, Utah and all of a sudden read off a list of names of brethren who were asked to fill missions. Several of Gordon's ancestors had been so called including his grandfather Ira Nathaniel Hinckley.

It was not quite as instantaneous in the 1930's, but priesthood leaders, mostly the bishop of one's ward when inspired, often called men in and asked them to serve. So when Gordon was asked by his bishop John C. Duncan to come into his office in the early part of 1933, Gordon had a pretty good idea of what he was going to ask.

Gordon now had graduated from college and was accumulating a savings for graduate school at Columbia's school of journalism. And sure enough, Bishop Duncan, a tall man, posed the question. "We would like you to go on a mission, Brother Hinckley. Will you go?"[1]

Like fictional George Bailey in the 1949 movie "It's a Wonderful Life", Gordon was put on the spot. What shall he say? This will interfere with his education plans and girlfriends. Will he follow his own plan and go to Columbia or will he accept the call of the Lord? He could not refuse. His faith, his values, the love he had for his father, and especially the precepts which had been instilled in him by his parents regarding the Savior of the world and His atonement could not be denied. The love he had for his Father in Heaven and the prophet Joseph Smith, Jr. also urged him to agree to a mission.

It did not take long to receive his official letter signed by President Heber J. Grant calling him to serve in the European Mission just moved from Liverpool to headquarters in London, England. He was to enter the Mission Home for a week's training in June.

All designations for missions are considered by Latter-day Saints to be made by inspiration and revelation of the prophet of the Church or delegated apostles given the specific commission from the prophet of the Church. At that time there were 28 LDS missions opened in the world plus the European Mission designed to administer the affairs of all of the missions in Europe. Those called to the European Mission worked with missionaries in the British Mission when proselyting.

The European Mission, because it was administrative, was presided over by one of the Quorum of the Twelve apostles. Under its administration in 1933 were the British, French, Swiss, German-Austrian, Netherlands, Armenian, Swedish, Danish, Norwegian, and Czechoslovak Missions.

Finances were the problem. It was not only the middle of the depression, he had some debts as other young men, and the little savings which had been in the family was wiped out with bank failures of the depression. Also, the British Mission area where he would be living was not just another mission. It was the most expensive mission at the time in the world with a very unfavorable dollar to pound exchange rate. Still he exercised his faith and the Lord stepped in.

Later he said that this decision blessed him with gratitude of those that helped and the friendship of those that he helped and he became less selfish and was blessed knowing he was doing the will of the Lord.[2]

First gratitude went to his dear mother. It was discovered she had through the years been placing pennies and nickels and dimes and quarters in a pot as she brought groceries and pocket change home from shopping. The amount had accumulated to around $600.00, a very large sum in those days.[3] After his mother's death, Gordon had felt his mother's nearness and now he felt it more than ever.[4] His dear mother had the foresight to create a savings account separate and apart from the regular institutional depositories which would fail. This money became more sacred than ever to him and he used it with extreme discretionary care.

Next gratitude went to his brother Sherman, who was in his senior year at the U in 1933. Sherman graduated with a Bachelor of Science degree in Mines and Engineering from the University of Utah in the Spring of 1933 and went to work almost immediately at the Lark Mine of U.S. Smelting Company and then mines near Gold Springs, Nevada; Drum Mountain near Delta, Utah; and Park City, Utah where silver was still being extracted. He contributed greatly to Gordon's mission funding.[5]

Mission Preparation and the Mission Home

All LDS missionaries, whether they are male or female, married or unmarried, are entitled to receive their endowments in an LDS temple before they leave on their missions. Gordon had this great privilege on Friday, June 9, 1933 in the Salt Lake Temple.[6]

After making the five sacred covenants each endowed Latter-day Saint makes with God in the endowment and receiving the higher light and knowledge available only in LDS temples, Gordon was prepared to be set apart for his mission. This was accomplished the next Tuesday on June 13, 1933 where he was set apart by LDS apostle George Albert Smith as a full-time missionary for the Church of Jesus Christ of Latter-day Saints to labor for two years in the European Mission.[7] George Albert Smith was destined to be the next LDS prophet in 1945 upon the passing of Heber J. Grant.

Gordon then entered the Mission Home located at 31 North State Street just north of the Beehive House on Administration Block, Salt Lake City, Utah. Here all new missionaries were given a week's instruction on their high and sacred callings as LDS missionaries from general authorities of the LDS Church. Such men as LDS apostle David O. McKay instructed them.[8] When Elder McKay spoke, he gave each missionary an assignment to write a theme paper on "What it Means to be a Missionary."

Now Elder Gordon B. Hinckley (all full-time male LDS missionaries are called "elder") went to the task and turned in his paper. A few days later, Elder David O. McKay (apostles are also called "elder" in the LDS Church) called 22 year old Gordon B. Hinckley to come to his office. Elder Hinckley did not know the purpose of the request but he hurried over to Elder McKay's office in the Administration Building just through the block.

"Congratulations," Elder McKay said. "You submitted the finest paper I have ever received from the missionaries." Elder McKay, destined to become President McKay in 1951, made note of this promising young man with a bachelor's degree in English who evidentally had already so mastered the art of his college major he had indelibly impressed this prominent apostle McKay, a former college educator himself.

As Gordon prepared to depart by train on June 20, 1933 for the East Coast and his mission in England, his father handed him a little card. On it was written just five words: "Be not afraid, only believe."[9]

The words were taken from Mark's record of the Savior's own words recorded in Mark 5:36. The sentiment touched Elder Hinckley. He placed it in his suit pocket and kept it there throughout his mission, looking at it frequently. In April 1989, as a member of the LDS First Presidency, he wrote about the slogan in his First Presidency message in the *Ensign,* the official LDS Church magazine, and expanded upon it.[10] Four days before on June 16, President Franklin D. Roosevelt had signed the National Industrial Recovery Act into law.

Train to Chicago and 1933 World's Fair

Elder Hinckley traveled three days on the trains with a missionary companion Elder Kent Bramwell. "I felt very lonely on the train ride," Elder Hinckley said.[11] When they arrived at Chicago, they stopped for a short visit to the 1933 Chicago World's Fair which had just opened. They took a Parmley transfer bus between stations passing many tall buildings in the heart of Chicago.

One lady asked the driver, "What building is that?"

"That's the Board of Trade Building. Nearly every day some man, whose stock has gone down, jumps out one of those windows."[12] The depression certainly was still raging.

But despite the depression, America and the world went on with the world's fair exhibition themed "A Century of Progress" focusing on world improvements from 1833 to 1933. The fair exhibition was held on three miles of Lake Michigan's shore located on the east side of Chicago. An impressive Avenue of Flags met the visitors as they entered the fair. Red on the tops with yellow stripes at the bottom, the flags were draped on aluminum poles, approximately 12 on the left and 12 on the right and pointed into the main public promenade on a 45○ angle forming a sort of arch of flags as visitors to the fair walked down the corridor. It was very impressive. At the end of the wide promenade were four American flags waiving in the breeze in front of the long reflecting pool in front of the Adler Planetarium.

There were many exhibits to be seen once the visitors paid the 50¢ entrance fee for adults or 25¢ for children. The exhibits were situate around a man-made lagoon on the lake front. A walkway from the west side of Chicago's mammoth railroad tracks took one into the park on the south, center and north parts of the fair. A "sky ride" took one up two tall towers at which point a "rocket car" suspended high in the air carried observers from one tower to the next allowed visitors to see the entire park and man-made lagoon from the air as well as the entire

Chicago area and four states on a "clear day." Fair visitors wore long dresses, suits and ties or at least white shirts with flat straw hats.

Then one could visit many other exhibition spots such as the Hall of Science, Field Museum of Natural History, Soldiers Field Stadium, the Electrical Group, General Motors Building, Administration Building, Admiral Byrd's Polar Ship *The City of New York*, the Golden Temple of Jehol, Street of Paris, the Sinclair Dinosaur Exhibit, Enchanted Island, "Old Heidelberg", and the Travel and Transport Building.[13] At the transport exhibition, displays of the last 100 years of railroad trains were there including the Royal Scot London Midland & Scottish Railway of Great Britain, which Elder Hinckley, unbeknownst to him, would ride soon once he reached London, England.

The view of the fair and the large city of Chicago fascinated Elder Hinckley. He had never seen such skyscrapers, so many people in one place and such a large scale exhibition. He did not know then that in just six short years he would be displaying his own designed exhibition in San Francisco at a similar fair.

New York City and the Voyage to England

Young Gordon Hinckley celebrated his 23rd birthday on his way to New York City. The elders arrived in New York and found the *SS Manhattan* bound for Plymouth, England. One other elder went with them making a party of three. This was a time of deep introspection for Gordon B. Hinckley. He pulled out a copy of his patriarchal blessing he had brought with him and read it.[14] He thought about the first LDS elders who in 1837 had taken the same voyage long ago for the first time to England at about the same time of the year, except he was traveling on a nice steamship and they had been on a sail ship. He would be in England in a few days. It had taken them 18 days and 18 hours on the open sea to reach Liverpool.

He thought about the first seven elders' encounter with the English citizens when they first preached their new religion. One of the seven elders named Joseph Richards had lived in England until 1832 when he had emigrated to Canada and subsequently been converted to the LDS Church. Elder Richards had a brother James Fielding who was an independent minister in Preston, England, formerly of the Methodist clergy. James had written his brother Joseph and invited Joseph to "come and preach your new religion in my chapel." So the seven elders had immediately traveled the 30 miles from Liverpool to Preston after they arrived in England.

The seven elders arrived in Preston three days after the coronation of Queen Victoria. The streets of Peston were alive with local election banners. All of a sudden one of the banners was opened on the street of Preston and the elders saw it. It read "Truth Will Prevail." Like a message from Heaven, ths message gave them courage. They found the sturdy brick Vauxhall Chapel of Elder Fielding's brother and preached to three overflow crowds on July 23, 1835. Several of Reverend Fielding's parishoners requested baptism. The first was George D. Watt, expert in phonography (shorthand), who was baptized along with eight others July 30, 1835 in a river called Ribble running through the city of Preston. It was just one week after their arrival.[15]

Would he be as effective a missionary? The question weighed heavy on Elder Hinckley's soul. But the words of his patriarchal blessing gave him comfort.

First Assignment to Preston

The elders' vessel pulled into Plymouth, England situated on the south and west end of England in the evening of July 1, 1933. As the elders' ship docked at port near Midnight, they heard the song "Danny Boy" being sung. Gordon looked towards the source of the beautiful music and saw an Irish tenor bellowing out the lyrics. President Hinckley has loved that song ever since.[16]

The elders transferred to a boat train circling the some 300 miles around the southern end of England & up the English Channel & the Thames River to London. There he stayed at the European Mission Headquarters for a day meeting the mission president LDS apostle John A.Widtsoe & is wife. Gordon knew them from visits to his home.

Elder Widtsoe had been presiding over the administration of the European missions for several years. He was born in Norway & was well fit for his position. His wife counselled the new missionaries on what food to eat. Next morning, Gordon was put on a train to go to Preston. Preston! The same town the first elders Heber C. Kimball, Joseph Fielding, Orson Hyde, Willard Richards, John Goodson, Isaac Russell and John Snider had first preached in on July 23, 1835. The other two elders were told to remain in London for the time being.

Elder Hinckley boarded the train with tremendous worry. He had always felt inadequate and the feeling had not left him. His father's card and patriarchal blessing rested in his suit pockets, however. The train ride was lonely along the 209 miles to Preston. North he traveled out of the metropolis of London, past Rugby, to Stafford, then Crew.

Britain with London marked "L", lower right hand, Lancashire by Yorkshire

Elder Hinckley's companion Elder Bramwell, the District Leader of their Liverpool District, met him at the Preston station and took him to the "digs", the nickname of the missionaries for their apartment at 15 Wattam Road close by the brick Vauxhall Chapel.[17]

There were 85 missionaries in Britain at the time and the total missionaries called worldwide by the LDS Church in 1933 totalled only 525.[18] There were no permanent LDS chapels in England at the time except one in Sheffield. The rest were rented and branches were small and struggling.[19] Total LDS members in Britain in 1933 was about 6,604 and membership increased to only 7,069 by the end of 1935.[20]

Britain was not a very fertile field at the time. Elder Hinckley was apprehensive. Then in the very evening Gordon arrived in Preston, his companion announced they were going down to Market Square and hold a street meeting. The area was a market square marked by a large obelisk, a four sided pillar tapering to the top and ending in a pyramid, in its center. Significant three story buildings cornered all sides and trees with park benches and slate walks surrounded the Obelisk monument in the middle of Market Square.

At the Obelisk the two elders sang a hymn and then said a prayer. Passersby started to stop and an audience congregated. But the people were poor. It was the bottom of the depression in Britain, too. Wooden clogs were worn for shoes. Their clothing was reflective of their economic condition.

Also, Gordon thought he was in a country speaking a foreign language. Their dialect was British and more than that, Lancashire dialect. They were difficult to understand and Gordon was as difficult to understand to them with his Utah dialect. But the elders started to preach. Gordon was very timid. It was difficult to plunge into that first street meeting. The Obelisk marked the same spot where 96 years before the first LDS elders to arrive in England had preached their own street meeting in Preston. No one seemed interested in their message. In fact, Elder Hinckley quickly learned there was "intense opposition."

As the days and weeks started to go by, Elder Hinckley's health deteriorated and that probably was aggravated by his mental state. He had good old discouragement which produced depression. He was disillusioned. No open arms or receptive hearts seemed to be left in not only Preston but also the surrounding area where the first elders in England had experienced so much success. In fact, rather than apathy, there was much antagonism and prejudice displayed.[21]

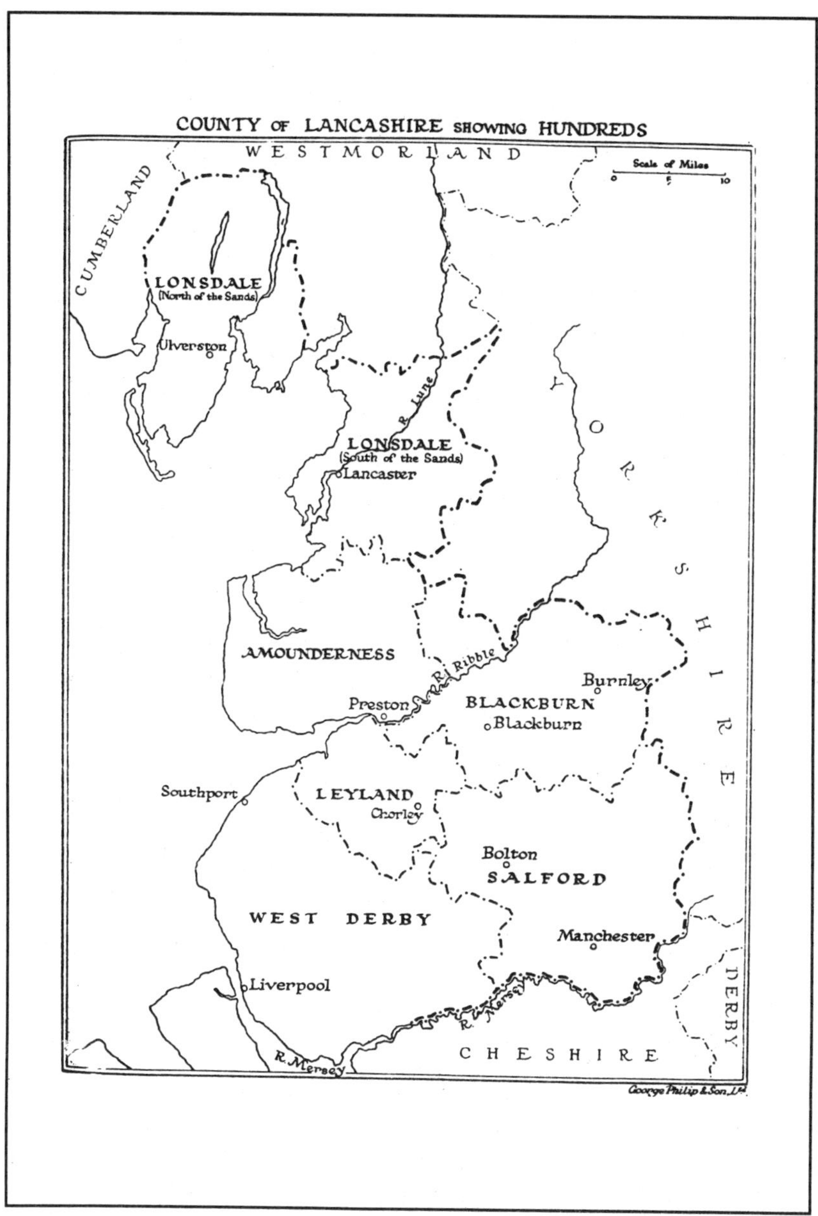

Lancashire County, England showing Westmoreland to North

Finally young 23 year old Elder Hinckley wrote his father a letter.

"Dear Dad,

"I feel I am wasting my time and your money. I don't see any point in my staying here. No one will listen."

Two weeks later the missionaries in his district read a scripture in their regular morning group study class. It was taken from the New Testament, Matthew 16:25, words of the Savior:

> "For whosoever will save his life shall lose it: and whosoever will lose his life for my sake shall find it."

When study class was over, the day's mail came and in it was a letter to Gordon from his father. Gordon ripped the edge of the envelope and took out the letter. As he unfolded it, a very short one paragraph from his father on the single sheet enclosed blared out at him.

> "Dear Gordon,
>
> "I have your letter.
>
> "I have only one suggestion. Forget yourself and go to work.
>
> Love, Dad"

Gordon felt a surge of enlightenment. He took the letter in his hand and walked upstairs to his second floor bedroom and beside his bed bent to his knees.

"Dear Father,

"I am sorry.

"I pledge and covenant that I will try to forget myself and lose myself in thy service."[22]

As he rose from his prayer, the fog of Lancashire seemed to lift from his eyes and heart. "The sun began to shine in my life. I had a new interest. I saw the beauty of this land. I saw the greatness of the people. Everything that has happened to me since, that's been good, I can trace to that decision made in that little house . . . in Preston, Lancashire."[23]

Selfless service! That's the key. The combination of the two messages from his two fathers–one in heaven and one on earth–caused Elder Hinckley to recognize his error, decide to repent and resolve with immutable commitment to be better. That was the turning point in Elder Hinckley's mission and for that matter in his life, a commitment to be selfless like the Savior.

From that moment on, proselyting in and around Preston was edifying though difficult. The surroundings of Preston became familiar. Down Fishergate Road and Friargale Road, across the old Flagstone Market where street meetings were held by Elder Hinckley and his fellow missionaries (and where the 1837 missionaries had so held them), the old cock-pit where the first missionaries of 1837 had also preached, the old tram bridge across the Ribble River and the river itself all became indelible landmarks to him.[24]

On July 22, 1933, Donald Douglas successfully tested its new DC-1 airplane made of aluminum alloy for TWA. The airplane could remain airborne even though one of the two engines died. Earlier, United Airlines purchased the new all metal trimotor 247 aircraft produced by Boeing. The public were finally starting to be convinced safe and practical air transportation could be a reality.

Elder Hinckley and his companions labored through September in and around Preston. People regularly rejected them but a few listened. Thomas L. Martin was one who opened his heart. His father was a pit miner; he, too. The gospel brought light and life into his life and opportunity and goodness and truth.[25]

Later President Hinckley said of this initial few months of his mission, "I feel especially fortunate to have been sent to Preston as my initial assignment . . . . I am profoundly grateful that while laboring on the ground which [the 1837 elders] hallowed by their efforts, there came into my heart a great consuming love for this work of God and for His Beloved Son, the Redeemer of the world, in whose name we all serve as members of His Church."[26]

About October 1933, Elder Hinckley was transferred to another town called Nelson located north of Preston but still in the County of Lancashire. The elders lived at 10 Wickworth Street, once again on the second floor of a two story apartment house.[27] He was about two months there tracting and mingling with the local populace. On occasion they would tract with local LDS members. And one such brother Elder Hinckley companioned with was Robert Pickles.[28] What a "cheeky lad" Bob Pickles would say of Elder Hinckley.[29] Gordon had reached his full height now of 5 feet 10 inches, two inches shorter than his father but somewhat taller than his mother. And he was quite the dark and handsome lad. Brother Pickles was one year older than Gordon.

On October 14, 1933, LDS apostle Joseph F. Merrill assumed the presidency of the LDS European Mission from John A. Widtsoe.[30] He became an apostle in October 1931 at the age of 63 and now was 65 years of age. He had been a physics and electrical engineering professor at the University of Utah prior to his apostleship and principal of the Utah State School of Mines. His education had been extensive, studying at several major American universities including Cornell, University of Chicago and John Hopkins. His original research in physics had been published in Germany, thus lending himself to assist administration in Europe.[31]

On October 22, 1933, back at home, President Franklin D. Roosevelt reported his "new deal" had put four of 10 million unemployed workers back to work as he broadcast his fourth fireside chat by radio from the White House in Washington, D.C. "How are we constructing the edifice of recovery–the temple which, when completed, will no longer be a temple of money changers or of beggars, but rather a temple dedicated to and maintained for a greater social justice, a greater welfare for America–the habitation of a sound economic life?" he said.[32]

Back in England, the LDS missionaries in Lancashire County visited and slept on the grassy meadow rising from Lake Windemere northeast of Preston. Elder Hinckley looked from the lake to the sky in the quiet, lovely place and remembered William Wordsworth's poem penned at that place in Grasmere, Morcombe Bay, almost 100 years before. For Elder Hinckley, it was an exhilbarating environment to behold.[33]

Wrote Wordsworth at that place:

"Our birth is but a sleep and a forgetting.
The soul thaat rises with us, our life's star,
Hath had elsewhere its setting
And cometh from afar.
Not in entire forgetfulness,
And not in utter nakedness,
But trailing clouds of glory do we come
From God, who is our home."

At this time, the LDS First Presidency was dedicating a new chapel, showcase of the LDS Church's presence in Washington, D.C. at the corner of Columbia and 16th Street. The cream marble chapel rose with a large obelisk shaped tower on the pinnacle of which was placed the typical gold leafed statue of the heavenly messenger Moroni, usually affixed only to the tops of LDS temples.[34] Extracts from select LDS scriptures were etched in gold letters in a few of the marble blocks around the outside walls of the church. The chapel was an impressive presence of the LDS Church established on the north hills of the Nation's capital city on 1600 Street. Following 1600 Street down the hill twelve streets to the south brought you directly in front of the White House where the President of the United States lived.

About the end of November 1933, Elder Hinckley received a letter of transfer from the European Mission office in London. The new mission president Elder Joseph Francis Merrill requested he come to the European Mission office to become one of his assistants.

Transfer to the European Mission Office

After Elder Hinckley read the transfer letter, he turned it over to his companion. After his companion had read it, he turned to Gordon and said, "Well, you must have helped an old lady across the street in the pre-existence. This has not come because of anything you've done here."[35] President Hinckley has used this quote several times since he has become an LDS general authority to emphasize he considers himself to be just an ordinary man called for some reason to extraordinary responsibility.

Gordon travelled down the same train tracks he had taken in the other direction five months before when going to Preston. This time he was returning to the large metropolis of London, located on the southeast area of the big island of England. The city of London was the largest city in the world at the time, a city of art, music, drama and commerce. It was established probably well before Christ as the first Roman soldiers who came to England in 43 A.D. found a flourishing market on the banks of the Thames River.

There were tremendous buildings in pre World Ward II London. Many museums of substantial influence, the British Museum being the most prominent, displayed specimens from early civilizations of the world acquired by the hundreds of years of British colonization. In addition St. Paul's Cathedral with its huge dome is seen from all part of the city. Westminster Abbey built in the 1000's and the Tower of London started by Julius Caesar are other prominent landmarks.

Many historic parks including Kensington Garden, Hyde Park, Green Park and St. James Park broke up the huge complexes of many centuries old "flats" and merchant establishments. And there were lots of automobiles, double decker buses, subways, trolleys and railroads.

The European Mission office was located fairly close to Hyde Park, probably the most famous park in the metropolis. Hyde Park consisted of 360 acres in the 1930's. It was the ancient haunt of monastic friars and a royal preserve and royal hunting ground. Through the centuries it had been the spot of many romances, duels, banqueting by kings and queens and the site of gallows there many a condemned criminal met his final demise.

Hyde Park was a beautiful place in the 930's. A manmade lake was constructed on the grounds in 1733 called "The Serpentine" due to its wavy shape where swimming in the Summer and ice skating in the Winter was enjoyed. Hundreds of wooden benches were placed throughout the park and near the marble arch corner was a spot where "itinerant orators" took their place especially on Sundays to the entertainment and amusement, and sometimes, serious contemplation of those who came to watch and listen.[36] It was to this group of "itinerant orators" the local LDS missionaries in London regularly added their voices.

Now the quiet clog of horse drawn carriages down the many lanes through the trees and greenery were replaced by "snorting motorcycles and thousands of motor cars" and buses, swift lorries and bicycles.

Hyde Park is "the most truly democratic spot in London," wrote Mrs. Alec Tweedie in 1930 in her 237 page treatise on the park. "Hyde Park is common heritage of all . . . It is surprising what tolerance there is, what good feelings pervade the throng made up of such extraordinary mixture and contradictions."[37]

Missionary Life in London

When Elder Hinckley arrived in London, he found he and one other full time missionary assisted President Joseph F. Merrill in administration of the European missions. He also found his good friend George Homer Durham who had arrived in the British Mission and was serving as president of the YMMIA of the British Mission. Elder Hinckley and Elder Durham, with the other missionaries in London, lived in the same building and ate at the same place in the basement dubbed the "Skullery" by the LDS missionaries.

Elder Hinckley and his companion worked in the European Mission office each week day and did missionary proselyting in the evenings and at other times the opportunity would arise. They often taught in the weak branches of the LDS Church in the area and each Sunday took from the closet a little folding stand, walked to Tottenham Court Road, boarded the red bus to Hyde Park, set up the stand, sang hymns and preached.[38] It was amazing. Elder Hinckley's timidity started to dissolve as he proclaimed in strong voice the mission which had been performed by Joseph the Prophet and the divinity of Jesus Christ and the restoration of His Church on the earth.

One particular heckler of many stands out in Elder Hinckley's mind. It was a gentleman with a cane who would try and annoy the missionaries by putting his cane as close as possible to the nose of the elder preaching. If he had touched the elder, it would have been a criminal offense, but otherwise he was just "teasing."[39]

Elder Hinckley and his fellow missionaries joined the London Central YMCA where they obtained some regular exercise. As Elder Hinckley entered the foyer, the words emblazoned on the wall in front of him also became emblazoned in his mind:

"With all thy getting get understanding.
Proverbs 4:7"[40]

Out on the streets in London, you learned to "hop fast" and look to your right before stepping into the road. The autos sped around the streets on the left rather than the right side of the street. There were also many fine stores and merchandise. Elder Hinckley especially frequented one where they sold quality shirts.[41] Fish and chips were a favorite of Elder Hinckley. And he began to realize he was having "great and marvelous experiences with wonderful people" in England[42]

In 1934, another U grad was now in the British Mission. Wendell J. Ashton, who had graduated magna cum laude the same year as Gordon B. Hinckley, Utah's finalist as a Rhodes scholar, and a future prominent jounalist in Utah was with them but there were only 65 in the mission now.[43]

Baseball was a great proselyting tool. It had mushroomed in the mission by chance when two elders in Liverpool took a baseball and started throwing and hitting it to each other in the Liverpool Botanical Gardens during 1932's Summer. A young Canadian, Mr. Holland, saw them playing and asked if he could join. Word spread that a baseball team was being organized. Those three men became the focus of attention and the Canadian became field rep of the National Baseball Association of Great Britain when Elders William R. Houston and Harvey F. Freestone were transferred.[44]

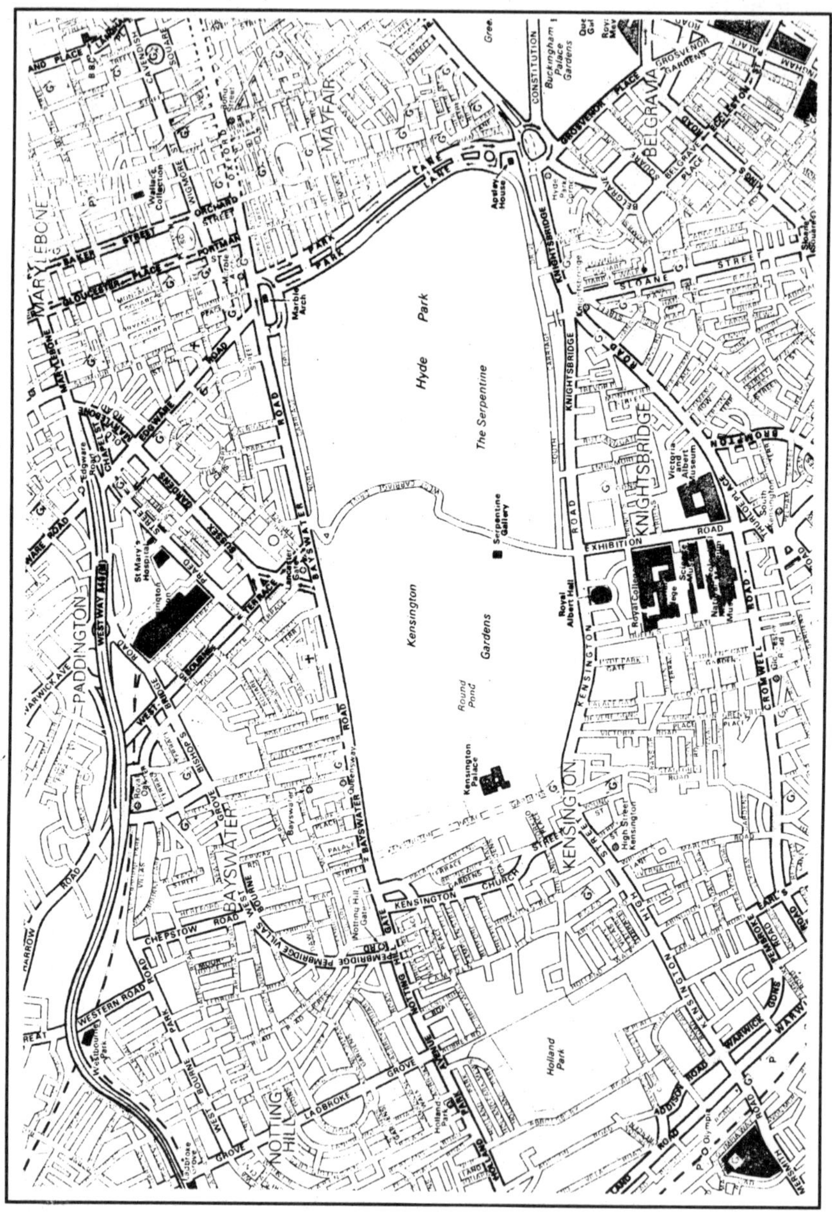

Hyde Park, London, England

The baseball craze started in England through the LDS missionaries in Liverpool and soon a league of 16 teams was organized with one of them the "Latter-day Saint" team. All members of the LDS team were respectfully called "Elder" by his teammates and also opposing teams. A big "L.D.S." in gold letters was sewn on their uniforms. And conspicuous among the league, the LDS team did not play on Sundays.

In London, the European and British Mission office staffs and other missionaries in the London District played on the team. And through "kindness of good men" the expenses of their uniforms, shoes, mitts and bats were largely absorbed through donations.

Elder Hinckley had been given responsibility as Director of Publicity in the British Mission and endeavored to place paid advertisements of upcoming LDS Church conferences in one paper which refused to print the ads. But when the softball teams gained favor with the public, the same paper began publishing lengthy articles on the work of the LDS Church in England including praises for the young Americans "who preach as well as play ball."[45]

The baseball craze soon spread to softball, even more inexpensive to play. Teams were quickly seen among the English and in Scotland. The "M" Men's young adult program of the LDS Church took up softball and played it in the parks of England, Ireland, Scotland and Wales. Courteous invitations were extended to youth and adults alike to learn the sport. A great many chose "to enjoy the fellowship and become associated in the environment of young men who are willing to sacrifice to preach a happy, practical religion."[46]

Another form of proselyting was developed by Elders J. Ridge Hicks, Ralph Hardy, Park Smoot and Earle C. Harmson. They mounted bicycles and traveled up and down Britain visiting each Boy Scout troop "telling the fascinating story" of native Americans and of the "book which is a record of the forefathers of at least some of them."[47] Two elders went before and made appointments with Scout groups. Then all four "frankly explained their purpose" as LDS missionaries, sang a native American song, and performed part of the Snake Indian dance in full native costume.[48]

Not to be denied, the Newcastle District pioneered a series of exhibitions on the Word of Wisdom practiced by Latter-day Saints. Halls were rented and vendors of quality foods and drinks "in agreement with the principles of the Word of Wisdom were invited to exhibit their products." Cereal manufacturers participated for a small fee, created attractive booths and offered free samples. Health officials "responded to invitations to speak."[49]

Through the ingenious proselyting methods of the LDS elders, people were heard to say, "I like the way you fellows play that baseball game of yours," when the LDS missionaries knocked on doors.

Or, "I have a son who'd learned to play your new game. He's told me what a wonderful fellow you are."

Or, "Tell me about the Book of Mormon. My husband saw two of your men give an American Indian dance at his club the other night."

Or, "Do you know that we had one of your Word of Wisdom dinners yesterday?"[50]

The Christmas Eve of 1934 was one of the most delightful for Elder Gordon Hinckley. The six LDS missionaries present gathered around a piano as George Homer Durham played carols. Playing the piano seemed to come easy to him. All sang and spoke together quietly of the Son of God. Homer then had short hair, a boyish face and thin figure.[51] Gordon was equally thin, with fine wavy hair. He had never looked more debonair. The comeraderie was intense and the feeling of oneness inspiring. Homer talked frequently about Eudora, the daughter of the previous European Mission president John A. Widtsoe, whom he eventually wooed and married. Gordon's faith constantly grew and solidified during these times.[52] Then another great test faced him.

The Obstinate Publisher

One day President Joseph F. Merrill called Gordon into his office. He told Gordon he was concerned about several newspaper articles recently published about the re-print of an old fictional novel depicting the LDS Church in an untrue light.

"I want you to go down to the publisher of this book and protest."

Elder Hinckley was humbled and struck with great apprehension. He thought about suggesting Elder Merrill a much better person to visit the book dealer than himself but true to his principles and faith, accepted the assignment and went to his room. As he had done on the second floor of his flat in Preston, Gordon fell to his knees in unexperienced meekness and contrition.

The book which Elder Hinckley had been asked to protest was a fictional novel purporting to be a history of the LDS people. It contained snide and ugly untruths. Elder Hinckley's "stomach was churning" as he left his apartment, walked to the Goodge Subway Station and took the subway to Fleet Street.

The office of the publisher was located and Elder Hinckley went in. He presented his calling card to the receptionist and asked to see Mr. Skeffington.

"Mr. Skeffington is very busy."

"Well, I've come about 5,000 miles and I'll wait for him," Elder Hinckley replied. Elder Hinckley sat down.

Then the waiting game began. The secretary went into Mr. Skeffington's office from time to time and then after an hour and two or three such visits, Gordon was finally taken to the publisher's office.

The room contained a big desk in back of which Mr. Skeffington sat. He had a big cigar in his mouth and looked at Elder Hinckley as if to say, "Don't bother me."

Gordon held the book review articles President Merrill had given him. He sat down and began explaining the purpose of his visit.

Mr. Skeffington at first was belligerent. But Elder Hinckley continued on. He did not know what he was telling Mr. Skeffington. He cannot remember. But there seemed to be a power speaking through him. Then Mr. Skeffington's defensive and belligerent manner began to change.

The publisher softened and at the end of their meeting agreed he would recall all of the books and have a statement placed in the sleeve of each volume stating the book was not to be considered history, that it was fiction, and that "no offense was intended against the respected Mormon people." This was done at considerable expense.

Gordon left the publisher's office with renewed gratitude to God. He learned that day "if you put faith in the Lord and go forward in trust, He will lead the way even when there appears to be no way."[53]

Later this same publisher did another great favor for the LDS Church and each year Gordon found Christmas cards in his mailbox from Mr. Skeffington until the publisher died.

Experiences with Members and Companions

One night in the rain, the door of Elder Hinckley's room sounded. Gordon opened the door and saw a young brother, a recent convert to the LDS faith, in the entrance.

"Brother, come in."

"I've got to talk with someone, I'm all alone. I'm undone."

"What's your problem?"

"When I joined the Church a little less than a year ago, my father told me to get out of his home and never come back, and I've never been back.

"A few months later the cricket club of which I was a member read me off its list, barred me from membership, the boys with whom I had grown up and with whom I had been so close and friendly.

"Last month my boss fired me because I was a member of this Church and I have been unable to get another job and I have had to go on the dole.

"And last night the girl with whom I have gone for a year and a half said she would never marry me because I'm a Mormon."

Elder Hinckley said, "If this has cost you so much, why don't you leave the Church and go back to your father's home, and to your cricket club, and to the job that meant so much to you, and to the girl you think you love?"

The brother did not immediately respond. He was silent for a long time. Then he put his head down between his hands and began to sob. He sobbed and sobbed.

Elder Hinckley started to cry, too.

At last, the brother looked up at Elder Hinckley and said, "I couldn't do that. I know this is true, and if it were to cost me my life I could never give it up."

He picked up his wet cap and walked to the door and out into the rain. He was lonely, trembling and full of fear. But he was resolute. Elder Hinckley thought of "the loneliness of conscience, the loneliness of testimony, the loneliness of faith, and the strength and comfort of the Spirit of God."[54]

Another friend was one of Elder Hinckley's missionary companions. After their missions in England, time passed and this former companion served in World War II. He allowed himself to associate with bad company, married a spouse who was not LDS, and took habits which caused him to feel outside the LDS Church. He moved around the country.

Elder Hinckley, in the 1970's was attending a stake conference in California. The phone rang in the foyer of the chapel where he was speaking. It was his long lost companion. He had seen Elder Hinckley's picture in the paper and it had caused him to call. Elder Hinckley excused himself from a meeting he was to attend and waited for the brother. They embraced as "brothers long separated."

After awkward beginnings, reminiscing of the best days in England broke the barriers. He talked of his experiences separated from church activity as if they were nightmares and expressed a desire to return. He felt it would be difficult and embarrassing. But he agreed with Elder Hinckley to try. Not long thereafter, Elder Hinckley received a letter from him. "I'm back. I'm back, and how wonderful it feels to be home again," he wrote.[55]

Another conversion occurred at the end of Elder Hinckley's mission. He and his companion met a young man in a remarkable way and spent many hours teaching him. The investigator had a struggle within to decide to join but he had great joy in finding the Church. He was a gifted man, educated, sincere and prayerful. After the elders had taught him a long time he was baptized and then both Elder Hinckley and his companion returned home.

The new convert was shy and sensitive. Members of the branch where he went were not as sensitive and empathetic as *they* should have been. Someone criticized him for a small mistake. The critic had a "salty tongue and a short temper." Sadly the convert left the evening meeting and never came back. He was hurt and wounded. Elder Hinckley kept track of him through correspondence. The brother served in the army during World War II, married and the wife died. The brother never returned to the LDS Church.

Such were some of the good and bad of missionary work. But through it all, Elder Hinckley says, "The power of faith came to me when I was a missionary in England."[56]

At a Zone Conference of the London District LDS missionaries, the mission president asked the missionaries, "Brethren, what is the greatest, most significant testimony we have to give the people of the British Isles?"

Many proposed answers were given such as "Joseph Smith is a prophet, the Book of Mormon is true, the Priesthood has been restored to the earth, etc."

After all of these, the President said quietly, "These are all great truths of which we bear witness. But over and above all of these is our testimony that Jesus is the Christ, the Son of God; that He lives, our resurrected Lord and Savior, the Redeemer of mankind."[57]

At another conference at the Kidaminster Hotel in June 1935, Elder Gordon Hinckley was the featured speaker at the Young Men and Women's meeting. The conference was historic for the British Saints. It was a great occasion for missionaries and had been planned by Elder G. Homer Durham.

In the evening after the regular meetings, the missionaries gathered in an upstairs hotel room. They chatted informally and then an idea surfaced. When they returned to the United States they would form a club. The name of "Windsor" was proposed. And future wives of the 30 elders who became the membership would be dubbed the "Merry Wives of Windsor." When they did return to the States, this group did meet. They have had meetings monthly and continued for over 60 years![58]

Visit to Europe and the Eastern U.S.

Italy invaded Ethiopia without warning in 1935, the year Elder Hinckley's mission was over.[59] George Homer Durham, Heber J. Bowden and Gordon Bitner Hinckley were to be released at the same time and had about $100.00 each to see Europe. So they went across the Channel of England to the Continent and climbed aboard 3rd class trains all night, walked during the day, and saw the sites.

G. Homer Durham was the "tour guide." He knew all of the sites and the historical background regarding them. He also knew where the historic treaties of Europe had been signed. They visited some of these historic halls, the Louvre Art Museum in Paris and also a Paris opera.

They went to Berlin, Germany and also saw the Tomb of the Unknown Soldier of World War I. Hitler had held a rally only a few days before and the city was electrified by his recent visit. An elderly woman came to the unknown soldier's tomb, poorly dressed, and walked directly to the shrine, face wrinkled with age and stress, with a handful of flowers clutched in her hand and placed them at the feet of the figure of the soldier. She then knelt and prayed and arose with tear filled eyes, then slowly walked away. Nearby, the three returning elders heard drill drums of marching youth of a new generation of Germans.[60]

As the elders visited France and Germany, they bore testimony in the meetings of the LDS saints they attended. Then they returned to England and boarded the same ship, the *SS Manhattan*, which had taken Elder Hinckley to England two years ago.

When they arrived in New York City, Elder Hinckley went to Columbia University by bus at 116th Street. Here he went through the gate and walked across the campus "just to see what I had missed." It was a thoughtful visit. Next they travelled to Washington, D.C., once again bearing their testimonies as they met with LDS saints. They saw the Mall, the Capitol, the White House and the LDS Chapel on the hill north of 1600 Pennsylvania Avenue with the golden leafed statue of Moroni on the top.

Next they travelled to Palmyra, New York, about 23 miles east of Rochester. They had learned that a new statue of the heavenly messenger Moroni was to be dedicated by President Heber J. Grant just at the right time for them to attend. At this sacred time of dedication, one of the Eastern States Mission's missionaries by the name of Bruce R. McConkie was present. He was to become one of the greatest scriptorian LDS apostles the LDS Church has ever known. At the foot of the Hill Cumorah, the spot where Latter-day Saints believe the gold plates from which the Book of Mormon was translated were buried, Gordon witnessed the unveiling of a large statue of the golden leafed heavenly messenger Moroni unveiled. And then as sort of a spiritual climax to their missions, the elders heard the living LDS prophet Heber J. Grant bear testimony of personal knowledge of the Angel Moroni.[61]

From Palmyra, the trio of returning missionaries travelled to Detroit, Michigan where Gordon's father had arranged for him to pick up a new Plymouth automobile for $740.00 and drive it home for Gordon's parents.[62] The car was obtained and the three elders drove across the country the 1,600 miles to Salt Lake City in the new car.

When Gordon arrived at home, he was tired and worn out. He weighed only 126 pounds when he should have weighed at least 150. He felt his patriarchal blessing had been fulfilled when it said he would lift up his voice of testimony to the nations. He had done that in Britain, Paris, Germany, New York, Washington, D.C., etc. So when his parents invited him to go with them to Yellowstone, he said, "No, I'm tired of traveling. I never want to travel again."[63]

Some wonderful things had happened to Elder Gordon B. Hinckley, though, while he was on his mission. Doubts and questions were replaced by a firm testimony. "I came to know my Father in Heaven and my Savior to a degree unrealized before."[64]

"My mission was a marvelous experience. I am eternally grateful for it. It set anchors and guideposts in my life."

What did he gain in his mission? "A solid and enduring testimony of the divine origin of the Book of Mormon and a solid and enduring testimony of the divine calling of the Prophet Joseph Smith."[65]

Returns to England

President Gordon B. Hinckley returned to England many times following his mission there. In 1958 he visited Preston for a few hours.

He walked the old cobbled streets, the flagstone walks. He went by the Vauxhall Chapel, strolled beside the Ribble River and went past the cock-pit. He felt a new appreciation for missionaries.[66] The history of Britain and its Isles has been the subject of his intense reading.[67]

In 1994, he returned to Preston, that town where almost no one would listen, and broke ground for an LDS temple to be built there. Brother Robert Pickles was there in a wheelchair. When President Hinckley learned one of the members of the LDS Church he tracted with back in 1933 was there, he asked to be shown where he was. When President Hinckley saw him, he embraced him and tears streamed down both of their cheeks.[68]

After President Hinckley was set apart as LDS prophet, he made another visit to England, visiting many areas in 1995. He bore testimony to all he met of the strength of his missionary experience.

Personal Testimony of the Benefits of Missionary Service

On September 30, 1995, President Hinckley spoke to the priesthood holders of the LDS Church during the regular semiannual World General Conference. His powerful statement to young men is also a reflection of the benefits which accrued to himself through his own mission in England.

> "I throw out a challenge to every young man within this vast congregation tonight. Prepare yourself now to be worthy to serve the Lord as a full-time missionary. The Lord has said, 'If ye are prepared ye shall not fear.' (D.&C. 38:-30) Prepare to consecrate two years of your lives to sacred service.
>
> "That will in effect constitute a tithe on the first twenty years of your lives. Think of all that you have that is good–life itself, health, strength, food to eat and clothing to wear, parents, brothers and sisters, and friends. All are gifts from the Lord.
>
> "Of course your time is precious, and you may feel you cannot afford two years. But I promise you that the time you spend in the missionfield, if those years are spent in dedicated service, will yield a greater return on investment than any other two years. You will come to know what dedication and consecration mean.
>
> "You will develop powers of persuasion which will bless your life. Your timidity, your fears, your shyness will

gradually disappear as you go forth with boldness and conviction. You will learn to work with others, to develop a spirit of teamwork.

"The cankering evil of selfishness will be supplanted by a sense of service to others. You will draw nearer to the Lord than you likely will in any other set of circumstances. You will come to know that without His help you are indeed weak and simple, but that with His help you can accomplish miracles.

"You will establish habits of industry. You will develop a talent for the establishment of goals of effort. You will learn to work with singleness of purpose. What a tremendous foundation all of this will become for you in your later educational efforts and your life's work. Two years will not be time lost. It will be skills gained. You will bless the lives of those you teach, and their posterity after them. You will bless your own life. You will bless the lives of your family, who will sustain you and pray for you. And above and beyond all of this will come that sweet peace in your heart that you have served your Lord faithfully and well.

"Your service will become an expression of gratitude to your Heavenly Father. You will come to know your Redeemer as your greatest friend in time or eternity. You will realize that through His atoning sacrifice He has opened the way for eternal life and an exaltation above & beyond your greatest dreams.

"If you serve a mission faithfully and well, you will be a better husband, you will be a better father, you will be a better student, a better worker in your chosen vocation. Love is of the essence of this missionary work. Selflessness is of its very nature. Self-discipline is its requirement. Prayer opens its reservoir of power. And so, my dear young brethren, resolve within your hearts today to include in the program of your lives service in the harvest field of the Lord, as a missionary of the Church of Jesus Christ of Latter-day Saints."[69]

MASS COMMUNICATIONS

Elder Joseph F. Merrill, president of the LDS European Mission, asked Gordon B. Hinckley to report condition of the European missions and needs for printed materials and other concerns to the LDS First Presidency when he returned from his mission in July 1935.[1] This same month, the Nazi's intensified their repression of Jews in Germany. The following month, the Social Security Act became law in the United States joining many other industrialized nations providing comprehensive care for the elderly, handicapped and unemployed.

When Gordon climbed the grey granite steps and entered the LDS Church Administration Building at 47 East South Temple in Salt Lake City, little did he know that soon he would have an office there continuing the rest of his life (with the exception of three years). He walked through the large swinging stainless steel doors, across the marble entryway and past the main reception room to the president's office in the first floor's northeast corner.

He was escorted into the presence of LDS President Heber J. Grant and his two counselors J. Reuben Clark, Jr. and David O. McKay. J. Reuben Clark, Jr. had been made President Grant's 2nd counselor in 1931 at the passing of Charles W. Nibley but did not actively fill the position until April 1933 when his government appointment as U.S. Ambassador to Mexico could be terminated. In September 1934 while Elder Hinckley was in Britain on his mission, 1st counselor Anthony W. Ivins also died and J. Reuben Clark, Jr. was made 1st counselor in his place and David O. McKay assumed membership in the First Presidency for the first time as 2nd counselor.

Gordon was already known to President Grant through the prophet's long friendship and association with Gordon's father and mother and J. Reuben Clark, Jr. knew Gordon's mother through teaching with her at the same business college in the early 1900's. David O. McKay remembered Elder Hinckley from that special experience receiving Gordon's exceptional missionary essay in the Mission Home two years before.

But, pressed for time, President Grant told Gordon he could have 15 minutes. Gordon quickly began. He explained the situation of the missions in Europe and their great need for improved printed materials in the various languages for proselyting and spreading the restored gospel message. The time quickly passed. Fifteen minutes soon went. The First Presidency saw this young man was well informed and articulate. His mission had done great things for him. They commenced asking him questions, particularly President Grant, about facts, opinions and his background. Soon not only 15 minutes had passed but one hour and the First Presidency were grateful for his consultation with them.

Gordon went home feeling relieved. He felt for the first time the burden of his mission was over and he could begin his own life now. Then Brother Hinckley received a phone call the next day from First Presidency counselor David O. McKay asking Gordon to see him.

Brother Hinckley, now just 25, entered the LDS Church Administration Building again, this time finding President McKay's office. As they greeted and sat down, President McKay interviewed him more about his background and desires.

This meeting with President McKay, led to Gordon being told the LDS Church was just forming an Executive Committee (executive committees were formed from general authorities, particularly from members of the Quorum of the 12 Apostles, for guidance of certain facets of church activities) to stir up greater use of mass media, particularly through the air, printed materials and other forms of publicity for the LDS Church and its missions. The executive committee was to be called the Church Radio, Publicity and Mission Literature Committee and would consist of six of the 12 apostles. It would be chairmaned by LDS apostle Stephen L. Richards who had been handling such matters much on his own for some time.

Then President McKay said, "We need an executive secretary for the committee. Will you come work for the Church as that secretary?"

A salary of $65.00 per month was the salary for those with college degrees. Gordon accepted and then shortly was also contacted by Dr. John A. Widtsoe, former president of the European Mission when Gordon had first arrived in his mission in England. LDS apostle Widtsoe was now, as one of his many duties as an LDS apostle, the LDS Church Education Commissioner in charge of overseeing all of the schools then operated by the LDS Church as well as all of its secondary education seminaries and high education institutes.

Elder Widtsoe asked Gordon to become a part-time seminary teacher for students nearby downtown Salt Lake. "Just teach one hour a day and we will give you $35.00 a month," he said. Gordon took the additional employment making a total monthly income of $100.00.[2]

Radio, Publicity & Mission Literature Committee

First of all, the name of the committee was anti-productive to sound advertising principles. It was just too long. And the scope of the committee's responsibility was extremely broad.

But, the LDS Church was a baby when it came to utilizing the media effectively. Oh, it had its own LDS Church organs, several magazines directed to internal membership. And it had a radio station which was broadcasting weekly live presentations of the LDS choir which had become known as the Mormon Tabernacle Choir and some LDS Church sponsored radio programs on Sunday evenings. And a few pamphlets were in print. But overall, there was no unified direction in a growing church. Missions at that stage were pretty much left to create their own printed materials and proselyting techniques.

The infrastructure of the United States was just barely coalescing. Paved roads had not started in the United States until Union Square in New York City was asphalted in 1872. Paris, France had pioneered the first asphalt street in 1854. By 1916 there were only 20 streets paved in Salt Lake City from the first start in 1892. But from 1928 to 1936, State Street from 9th South to 17th South had finally been asphalted and part of the "Mormon Corridor" from Salt Lake towards Los Angeles from Provo to Springville and from Nephi to Levan had the black stuff.[3]

Aviation was taking off with development of the Douglas and Boeing air passenger planes. And railroads were continuing their importance as people and freight movers.

The recording industry had started off solidly in 1888 when Columbia Records started, moving into prominence in 1927 for the next 19 years as CBS. Victor Records had started in 1901, later becoming RCA Victor.

When vacuum tubes for radio transmission were invented in 1906, use of the little boxes with headphones became increasingly popular with the broadcast of the first world series over radio on October 5, 1921. Salt Lake City got involved with DDYL, situated atop the Newhouse Hotel, in 1922. The LDS College had an experimental station for students for a while about the same time and then KSL began full time commercial broadcasting, the first of such sort West of the Mississippi River, on April 21, 1922. The LDS Church had taken advantage of this on October 3, 1924 when they first broadcast one of their world general conferences over the broadcast area of Utah.

"KSL" had not been the call letters of the LDS Church's radio station until 1925 although they had been on the air. The National Broadcast Corporation purchased WEAI in New York in 1926 and other expansion of radio nationally gradually prompted the US government to pass the 1929 Radio Act requiring radio station licensing. Gordon's father Bryant S. Hinckley had delivered a radio address on KSL in 1928.

Watts at KSL were 5,000 in January 1929 and were increased to 50,000 in 1932 when an affiliation with the Columbia Broadcasting System was made.

In the way of major Church publications, LDS seventy Brigham Henry Roberts had been commissioned by the LDS First Presidency and published a multi-volume work called a *Comprehensive History of the Church of Jesus Christ of Latter-day Saints* on the eve of the Latter-day Saints' 100th anniversary April 6, 1930. Then on March 21, 1931, a 10 reel LDS Church history motion picture film was completed. On the Church's birthday April 6, 1931, the Church's newspaper *Deseret News* began publishing a weekly insert called the *Church News*.

The LDS faith had tried a 500 foot exhibit in the Hall of Religions at the 1933 Chicago World Fair prepared by an LDS artist Avard Fairbanks.

But this was about the extent of the LDS Church's mass media use. Elder Stephen L. Richards had been an LDS apostle since 1917 when he was only 37. He had a short career as a lawyer in Salt Lake before his call. But his LDS Church service had been great. He was the grandson of Willard Richards, one of the two LDS apostles present with Joseph Smith, Jr. and his brother Hyrum Smith in Carthage, Illinois when the two Smith brothers were murdered in 1844. He had served as a counselor in the LDS Deseret Sunday School Union with David O. McKay in 1909, becoming his good and close friend.

Since becoming an LDS apostle, Elder Richards had been an assistant to the LDS Church Education Commissioner, chairman of Utah State's Civil Works Administration, a member of the Board of Regents at the University of Utah, and on the Missionary Committee and now Church Radio, Publicity and Mission Literature Committee.[4]

Prior to Elder Hinckley's assumption of the position of executive secretary to the RPML committee, Elder Richards had made responses to non-members of the LDS Church when requested.[5] He also was handling the KSL Sunday evening radio broadcasts and other activities.[6]

First Projects

The six LDS apostles met for the RPML committee with newly employed Gordon B. Hinckley and set out a general plan. Gordon was to be given a wide range of discretion to create uniform pamphlets for use by the LDS Church's worldwide missions. He was also to oversee preparation of the weekly radio programs. He was also to look in to the production of a new series of programs for radio depicting history and life of the Latter-day Saints and to make recommendations for use of the rapidly developing mediums of communication he felt appropriate.

In effect, Gordon was given the license and also the responsibility of being the LDS Church's producer, director, script writer and narrator for virtually all printed literature for the missions, radio publicity, and any other innovative uses of the rapidly developing audio/visual and printed mediums he could think of subject to the committee's approval. He essentially was also to be the LDS Church's public relations department. Brother Hinckley recommended steps and projects to the six member committee and upon their approval, went to work.

Brother Hinckley did not waste any time. He hunted up a missionary companion's father who operated a furniture store and obtained a reject table with one short leg and a warped top. He then brought his own typewriter from home and set them up in a room on the upper floors of the Church Administration Building he was given permission to use. Then he went down to the secretary on the first floor and asked for a ream of paper.

"A whole ream?" the secretary asked.

"Yes, please."

Then he went upstairs and sat at his typewriter, inserted a piece of paper and started to compose.[7] The first creations which came from his inspiration were leaflets which could be used by the missions of the Church in a uniform manner. One was on the Sabbath Day.[8] Others treated all aspects of the missionary endeavor. Elder Richards became a teacher and helper of great influence, a tutorage which would last for almost 25 years.[9]

The Fullness of Time Series

Next was the momentous task of creating a radio program series. The "Golden Days of Radio" were just emerging. Radio was taking hold of the entire country. Especially with the big band music, the sports broadcasts, the comedians, dramatic actors and even the President of the Unites States' use of this medium, the time seemed right for such a series.

First there were outlines to create, writers to find, musical scores to be written, actors to secure and radio production companies to discover. It was determined the series would be entitled "The Fullness of Time." Why the Fullness of Time? Well, Latter-day Saints believe that their church was organized in the last period of the world's present existence, that in this dispensation or period, all of the fullness of God's plan for his earthly children would be restored and brought forth fully and completely, and so this was in very deed "the fullness" of time.

Segments compatible with 30 minute radio programs would be created. They would start with a segment about the Book of Mormon, then the first vision of the prophet Joseph Smith, Jr. An outline for a total 39 episodes treating the entire history of the Latter-day Saint Church up to the present time was submitted and approved.

Brother Hinckley was plunged into the books. He did much research and reading, sifting through every item of information he could put his hands on to find the true facts. The whole history of the Latter-day Saint religion had to be well researched and well known. Then he put his fingers to the typewriter, came up with a manuscript, took it to Elder Stephen L. Richards for review and came back for revisions and re-drafting. The critiques were sent to others, too. And a fellow by the name of Chase Varney was also enlisted to help with the episode scripts. But most of the scripts were eventually authored by Gordon B. Hinckley and Brother Hinckley was responsible for production.

Next, a producer was needed. Correspondence was generated to radio program producers in Los Angeles. Three boxes and 35 files were created by Gordon B. Hinckley pertaining to all facets of the creation, production and distribution of the series.

Trips were taken to Los Angeles to interview prospective producers and finally Mertens and Price, Inc. and George Logan Price, Inc. were selected for the recording. It took until 1938 before the first episodes were ready for airing.

A local LDS brother named Roscoe A. Grover gave suggestions on the "announcement" of each episode. Professional actors were selected for the dramatic recordings. The famous organ located in the Salt Lake Tabernacle on Temple Square was chosen the instrument for playing the dramatic background music of each production. Scripts were created in such a fashion that advertisements or station identifications could be inserted like any other radio programs.

The beginning of each episode began with two bars of the familiar Christian hymn "A Mighty Fortress" played by the resonate Tabernacle organ following which a narrator said in deep and bold words "The Fullness of Time" followed by a 15 second leader of additional background music. The narrator then continued, "The Church of Jesus Christ of Latter-day Saints presents 'The Vision', one of a series dealing with modern prophecy and its fulfillment."

The first series of episodes contained 13 programs. They were:

1 - The New Promised Land
2 - The Vision
3 - Words Which Have Slumbered
4 - The Word Restored
5 - The Glad Tidings
6 - The Call Westward
7 - The Tents of Kirtland
8 - A Dream of Zion
9 - Founding of Nauvoo
10 - The City Beautiful
11 - A People of Destiny
12 - A Testimony Sealed in Blood
13 - Hope Rises in the West

The second series of episodes were:

14 - The Camp of Israel
15 - Planting for Other Reapers
16 - The Mormon Battalion
17 - The Fall of Nauvoo
18 - Winter Quarters
19 - The Exodus
20 - The First Winter
21 - God, Rather than Gold
22 - Unto Every Nation, Tongue & People
23 - Zion Spreads Her Branches
24 - Handcarts West
25 - The Lamanites

26 - With Fire and Sword
27 - Patriotism Through Fire
28 - A Token to the Nations
29 - A Witness Returns
30 - Twilight of a Great Life
31 - Years of Endurance
32 - Whosoever Believeth
33 - Dawning of a Brighter Day
34 - The Windows of Heaven
35 - The Vindication of the Years
36 - The House of the Lord
37 - The Great Tabernacle
38 - A Plan for Human Welfare
39 - The Sunshine of Good Will[10]

The first series was completed between 1938-1939 and the second series in 1940 and 1941. Brother Hinckley also had the work of finding places where the episodes would be played. Due to the quality of the productions, Brother Hinckley's persuasive manner of approach coupled with the Spirit of the Lord working in him, and the increased good will towards the LDS religion, over 100 radio stations consented to air the series.[11] Copies of the large 78 rpm records were also sent to each LDS mission. Others were distributed to the stakes and wards so all could benefit from them, especially the youth of the Church. Use in "cottage meetings" by missionaries, the Sunday School, seminary and institute were made. Public sale of the records were also made in retail outlets.

The records were created so professionally and the script so natural, the gospel restoration story came alive. While listening to the episodes, they seemed logical, reasonable and true. A great step had been taken by the Church. With the exception of six radio broadcasts of the weekly Sunday LDS Church broadcasts called "Church of the Air" nationwide on CBS radio beginning March 3, 1935 and the weekly 30 minute live broadcasts of the Mormon Tabernacle Choir over CBS, no such broad dissemination of LDS doctrine had ever been achieved, and certainly not in dramatic form. It truly was a most momentous step forward for the LDS Church.

Weekly Sunday Radio Broadcasts

Regular radio broadcasts were also produced and coordinated by Brother Hinckley. Scripts were obtained, speakers scheduled and numerous other details looked to for the smooth execution of these broadcasts. The series was called "Church of the Air" and utilized Gordon's father and Stephen L. Richards and other known speakers among church leaders of the LDS faith. Even Gordon prepared and delivered some of the addresses.

There were other radio programs on KSL radio designed and similarly supervised by Brother Hinckley, too.[12]

Film Strips

Film strips had never been used by the LDS faith to promulgate their message. But this time they would be. Gordon recommended film strips be prepared for use not only by missionaries but also by the priesthood quorums and auxiliary organizations of the Church.

Each filmstrip took much research and contemplation. Sometimes, resources had to be tapped from many places. Photographs for the strips were needed. And the scripts had to be written and packages put together with a printed booklet of dialogue. Copyright permissions were requested from some who might lend their photography or other material for use. All of this took time but was rewarded with finished products adding to the Church library of the Latter-day Saints. "Teachings of Mormon Leaders Today" was one of the first completed. "Chronology of Significant Events in Church History" was another.

"Latter-day Saint Leadership", "Accomplishments of the Mormon People", "The Apostacy", and "The Abundant Life" were some of the film strips produced in 1936. "Fascinating Salt Lake City" also treated the founding and growth of the city established in the tops of the "Everlasting Hills."

The prolific outpouring of filmstrips in 1936 also included a 50 slide presentation entitled "Forgotten Empires" designed to "excite the curiosity of listeners" to want to know more about early American civilization. Over 27 sources were sought for information. Much was taken from the book *Seven Claims of the Book of Mormon*. The slide program was quite a deep study of the ruins and ancient inhabitants of South America. It masterfully compared the similarities of South American calendars, astronomy, and language to Semitic and Egyptian, particularly Egyptian language, pyramids, statues and mummifying. Symbols, temples, altars and boats were compared, impliedly indicating the origin of the culture of the Americas came from Semitic and Egyptian origins as the historical Book of Mormon record states.

In part of the script, Brother Gordon Hinckley wrote:

"Our church believes this account–known as the Book of Mormon–to be a true chronicle of an important part of the civilization of early America. We believe the book to be a translation of records engraved on sheets of gold by native historians, records which came to light a little over a century ago and were translated into the English language, and later translated into 16 other languages. It is our belief in this book which has prompted our interest in American archeology and has made fascinating science the piecing together of the picture of early American culture."[13]

In 1938, the "Forgotten Empires" film strip was combined with an additional 50 slide presentation entitled "Before Columbus" and the two used to convey the origin and authenticity of the Book of Mormon history.

Another film strip entitled "Landmarks of Church History" also contained 50 slides. This strip required contacting the US Army Air Corps., Rand McNally Co, Utah Photo Materials, and Fellowcraft Studios for permission to use various photos. Tremendous sourcing techniques were required to assimilate proper slides.

In the "Landmarks" script, Brother Hinckley talked about how the national highways of the United States converge at Salt Lake City and the railroad expresses regard Salt Lake as their most important stop. He talked of the busiest airport for "giant airliners" west of the "modern city with wide streets and perfect square blocks of 10 acres" and the mosaic of homes and buildings, trees and broad shrubs cupped in surrounding hills like a painting "on the bottom of a bowl."[14]

Many other film strips were created. A "Scenic Utah" 16 millimeter movie was produced in 1937 and a new release in 1942. Other subjects were "Accomplishments of the Mormon People", "The Apostacy", "The Abundant Life", "Welfare", "King of Kings", "In the Tops of the Mountains", "Historic Highlights of Mormonism", "The House of the Lord", "With Power to Act", and "The Word of Wisdom." All of these productions were completed in the years 1936-1941 and the first part of 1942 before Gordon B. Hinckley quit church employment for about three years to help with America's World War II effort.[15]

Father's Mission Presidency in the Northern States

In December 1935, Donald Douglas successfully tested its new 21 passenger DC-3 airplane. Now increasingly larger numbers of airplanes were being produced, gradually reducing the cost of air travel and creating an increasingly affordable alternative to long distance travel.

Hollywood was the movie capital of the world generating an increasing variety of films. The Marx Brothers were popular. Clark Gable, Greta Garbo, Errol Flynn, Marlene Dietrich, Katharine Hepburn and Cary Grant were just some of the stars. "Mutiny on the Bounty" with Laughton and Gable came out. "Captain Blood" starred Flynn. There was just about any subject you desired–the classics, romance, comedy, adventure.[16]

At the same time, President Heber J. Grant asked Gordon's Father to assume the mission presidency of the Northern States Mission when the president serving at that time suffered a fatal heart attack. Bryant S. Hinckley was set apart for the calling on January 5, 1936.[17] And at the "farewell" held during a regular Sunday Sacrament meeting at the 1st Ward in Liberty Stake, the outpouring of love and affection shown to him was tremendous. There was an extremely large crowd.

Bryant, now 68, his new wife May, and the youngest remaining of his children Ramona, 20, and Sylvia, 15¾, took the train to their new calling headquartered in Chicago, Illinois. Through the calling, Bryant was released as president of the Liberty Stake after 18 years in the stake presidency and 10 years as its president.

Bryant had really been guiding a momentous missionary effort even before his call to be a mission president. Under his leadership, his Liberty Stake had realized a whopping 1,800 baptisms during a period when the concept of "stake missionaries" in the LDS faith began. During his presidency, his stake was also the first in the LDS Church to start holding priesthood meeting on Sunday morning for male members of the Church.[18]

Up to his mission presidency call, Bryant had also superintended the Deseret Gym for 25 years since its opening, served on the LDS College Board of Trustees for nine years from 1927, been a member of the LDS Hospital Board of Directors a year and two months, spoken in the Salt Lake Tabernacle at least 19 times (one of the times in LDS general conference and one time before the LDS Deseret Sunday School Union), and authored at least two articles, not to mention his 25 years service as a General Board Member of the LDS YMMIA. Gordon could certainly be proud of the father going before him. He was an inspiration.

Miscellaneous Endeavors

Additional ideas surfaced and were presented by Gordon, approved and implemented. Souvenir records of the Tabernacle Choir were prepared for use by the Information Bureau on Temple Square. Large numbers of tourists visited the Salt Lake Temple and its surrounding grounds encompassing an entire block called "Temple Square." The numbers were ever increasing. The architectural wonder of the large silver dome shaped Tabernacle where the Tabernacle Choir sang before the mammoth pipe organ within was also a great attractor.

The Tabernacle building had been constructed prior to completion of the first Intercontinental Railroad in the United States. Thus building materials were scarce and therefore, in place of nails, the timbers of the huge oblong shaped dome ceiling had been joined together with pegs and wet rawhide which shrank into a tight harness once dry.

The acoustics of the Tabernacle were also earning world fame. Architectural awards were given. One could drop a pin at the front of the stand and it could be heard in the rear of the Tabernacle. So having recordings of the choir music available as souvenirs for visitors was one way to create refreshed memories and engender increased respect and interest in the LDS Church.

Also produced were special recordings of Tabernacle Choir selections for missions. These recordings could be used to acquaint others with the accomplishments and beliefs of the LDS people, particularly their fostering of the arts and music.

Book of Mormon dress was also examined. How could the covers of the Book of Mormon be more attractive? What was the ideal typesetting and layout? All of these questions were asked and pondered. And new printings saw new styles of covers.[19]

In February 1936, the first "beetle" shaped all-steel Volkswagen automobile was introduced in Germany. Italy took over Ethiopia. Civil war erupted in Spain. The British oceanliner Queen Mary "recaptured" the treasured "Blue Riband" by crossing the Atlantic at an average 30.7 knots. And in August, the black American runner Jesse Owens implicitly challenged Nazi theories of Aryan race supremacy by capturing four gold medals in track and field at the Olympiad in Berlin, Germany.[20]

In 1936, the LDS Tabernacle Choir also began a new format during their weekly live radio broadcasts. Music by the choir from that time was complemented by a short inspirational reading called "the Spoken Word" delivered by a young 30 year old host and moderator named Richard L. Evans.

Franklin D. Roosevelt won a second term as President of the

United States in November 1936 and shortly thereafter Japan, Italy and Germany formed the Axis states of fascism using anti-communism as their excuse. The innovative American architect Franklin Lloyd Wright finished his "Falling Water" home in Bear Run, Pennsylvania at age 68. The home revealed very modernistic design blending with surrounding trees, shrubbery and stream flowing on the hill where it was built.

FDR was inaugurated on January 20, 1937, beginning the practice of installing American presidents on January 20 instead of the first week in March. In March 1937, Benny Goodman and his big band began to take "the country by storm." His swing music "not only had them tapping their feet and snapping their fingers, but dancing with wild abandon in the aisles." Gordon became a husband the following month in the Salt Lake Temple, marrying his teenhood neighbor Marjorie Pay.

The shining red Golden Gate Bridge across San Francisco Bay became the world's longest spanning bridge of the time at 4,200 feet when it was completed in April 1937, the same month of Gordon's marriage.[21] The dirigible balloon Hindenburg burst into flames the next month as it landed at Lakehurst, New Jersey, killing 33 of its 97 passengers. Walt Disney's "Snow White and the Seven Dwarfs" hit the movie houses in December 1937.

Gordon submitted estimates of slide film production and suggestions on recording equipment purchases. He also conducted a survey of radio listeners after "The Fullness of Time" broadcasts began in 1938. Music transcriptions were also another of his responsibilities.[22]

He also had been working on a book. *A Short History of the Church of Jesus Christ of Latter-day Saints* was approved and completed for distribution published through the Church Radio, Publicity and Mission Literature Committee in 1938. George E. F. Eyston set a world land speed record at the Bonneville Salt Flats (smooth salt beds from the ancient Lake Bonneville) located 100 miles west of the present Great Salt Lake traveling 357 miles per hour.

Western Airlines Express advertized a one way flight from Salt Lake to Los Angeles for $34.75 and $17.37 for return on a two prop aircraft in September's *Utah Magazine*. A round trip flight to Pocatello, Idaho was between $12.00-30.00, an average 4¢ per mile, said to be cheaper than driving.[23] Hitler occupied Austria without warning in March this year, then moved into Czechoslovakia in October. The 30th of October, Orson Welles fooled the United States people with his realistic broadcast of "War of the Worlds" over nationwide radio.

The year 1939 was the subject of two major exhibitions. Brother Hinckley had been working some time directing the construction of a 50 seat pavilion fashioned to look like a mini-Salt Lake Tabernacle on the Treasure Island in San Francisco Bay for the World Exhibition being held there. On February 18, 1939 1,400 attended the exhibit of the LDS Church on the first day. This was a tremendous undertaking and required much work and organization.

Then shortly after Gordon's father received release on April 18, 1939 from his Northern States Mission presidency, the 1939 New York World's Fair opened its gates on April 30. As the new crystal "Perisphere", a round spherical building, and gold "Trylon", a tall slender pyramid spire, gleamed in the chilly Spring air, President Franklin D. Roosevelt formally dedicated the exhibition. Almost 20,000 armed servicemen marched along with native costume clad Europeans, Asians and Americans.

When Brother Hinckley's father Bryant returned to Salt Lake, LDS prophet Heber J. Grant asked him to head up a new Church Department of Education as secretary but the department never developed. Instead, Bryant went to work for President Grant answering and drafting correspondence and delivering numerous radio talks from January to August 1940 and July to October 1943. He also was asked by President Grant to write a biography on the life of Daniel H. Wells, one of the counselors to former LDS prophet Brigham Young. He did this and then suffered a bout with pneumonia. But due to the discovery of penicillin, it was not fatal.

Nineteen thirty-nine found Gordon working on various projects besides the Golden Gate International Exhibition in San Francisco. But these activities and responsibilities in the LDS Church and family are treated in other chapters in this book.

Suffice it to say, 1939 was a year America looked on as Europe inflamed into war. In September 1939, Western Europe leaders were shocked when Russia entered into a non-aggression treaty with Germany. Then Germany invaded Poland without warning on September 30 and Britain and France declared war on Germany. One week later, LDS missionaries were pulled from Germany.[24] On October 6, 1936, LDS prophet Heber J. Grant also delivered a message from the First Presidency on world peace. But it did not stop Russia from attacking Finland regarding the strategic Karelian Isthmus.

In a brighter light, nylon stockings started their popularity and the Rockefeller Center in New York was completed on November 1st, 1939. The epic movie "Gone With the Wind" was released on December 15 in Atlanta, Georgia.

In 1940, Gordon worked on investigator records and radio licenses in addition to the other projects in which he was involved. During 1940, the war in Europe expanded. Hitler invaded Norway, Denmark, the Netherlands, Belgium and Luxembourg without warning. Italy attacked France and later Greece without warning. And in June 1940, France fell to German occupation.[25]

Selective Service (the involuntary draft of males to military service) was re-instituted by President Franklin D. Roosevelt on September 16, 1940 for the first time in peacetime.

In his December 29, 1940 fireside chat, FDR said, "Never before since Jamestown and Plymouth Rock has our American civilization been in such danger as now . . . . The Nazi masters of Germany have made it clear that they intend not only to dominate all life and thought in their own country, but also to enslave the whole of Europe, and then to use the resources of Europe to dominate the rest of the world . . . . Frankly and definitely there is danger ahead—danger against which we must prepare . . . . I want to make it clear that it is the purpose of the nation to build now with all possible speed every machine, every arsenal, every factory that we need to manufacture our defense material. We have the men, the skill, the wealth, and above all, the will."[26]

With this kind of world situation, 1941 began. April LDS General World Conference saw President Grant name the first assistants to the 12 ever called. These men were to assist the regular LDS apostles in the rapidly growing administration of the LDS Church.[27]

World War II

The Japanese bombed Pearl Harbor, Hawaii on Sunday, December 7, 1941 putting the wheels in position for declaration of war by the United States. Gas and rubber restrictions were imposed and President Roosevelt went to the air again. "Together with other free peoples, we are now fighting to maintain our right to live among our world neighbors in freedom, in common decency, without fear of assault. . . We are now in this war. We are all in it—all the way. Every single man, woman, and child is a partner in the most tremendous undertaking of our American history. We must share together the bad news and the good news, the defeats and the victories—the changing fortunes of war.

"Every citizen, in every walk of life, shares this same responsibility. The lives of our soldiers and sailors—the whole future of this nation—depend upon the manner in which every one of us fulfills his obligation to our country . . . .

"And in these difficult hours of this day—through the dark days that may be yet to come—we will know that the vast majority of the members of the human race are on our side. Many of them are fighting with us. All of them are praying for us. For in representing our cause, we represent theirs as well—our hope and their hope for liberty under God."[28]

With this mandate to the nation, the call to service in the war was loud and clear. On January 4, 1942, the LDS Church participated in a special day of prayer declared in the United States by President Roosevelt. On January 17, 1942, the LDS leaders discontinued all institutes, conventions and auxiliary stake meetings to help LDS members meet wartime restrictions imposed on travel and help in payment of increased war taxes.

General Conferences of the LDS Church were restricted to leaders only and the Tabernacle on Temple Square closed until World War II was over. The LDS leaders met in an adjacent meeting hall south of the Tabernacle called the Assembly Hall and in an assembly room on the 4th floor of the Salt Lake Temple.[29]

The missionary force plummeted as the LDS Church agreed with the US Government not to call draft age men to missions. As a result, 1,257 had been called in 1941 but only 261 were called two years later and most of those in 1942, 1943 and 1944 called on missions were sisters or elderly men.[30]

Patriotic response to the call of President Roosevelt for help from everyone prompted 31 year old Gordon B. Hinckley to assist in any way he could. The need for the literature, films and other materials in the missions was not as needed now except for assistance to LDS servicemen who rapidly started joining military units voluntarily as well as through the draft. Brother Hinckley desired to enter the service also and was supported in his desire by his church leaders.

But before he left Church employ, he completed a publication for priesthood ordinances to be used by LDS members servicing in the military. Other loose ends were finished such as record labels, a revision of a *Picture Story of Mormonism* first published in 1940, "Fullness of Time" radio broadcasts, and a revision of the film "Scenic

Utah."[31]

Employment at D & R G

Then he went down to the local Naval Recruiting Office and applied for officer candidate school. He was examined by the doctors and medical history taken. But they rejected him upon the grounds he had asthmatic episodes in the past. So he looked for some other way in which he might assist the war effort.

The railroad was a vital system needed to carry the implements of war and soldiers quickly and efficiently to the areas needed both East and West and North and South. And Salt Lake, as Gordon had written in his script for "Landmarks of Church History", was the most important railroad crossroad in the West. He then went to the Salt Lake City Union Depot and Railroad Company, owned jointly by the Denver & Rio Grande Railroad and Western Pacific Railroads, to see if they needed any help.

They hired Gordon to help with the traffic control. After a few months, he went to Denver for a supervisory conference and from that meeting was offered a position as assistant superintendent of mail, baggage and express traffic in Denver. He and his family remained in Denver until after the war.[32]

Return to the Radio, Publicity & Mission Literature Committee

After the war was over, Brother Hinckley made a visit to Salt Lake City and while there went to the Church Administration Building to visit his former employer Elder Stephen L. Richards. Elder Richards asked Gordon to return to LDS Church employment and assist him.

When the railroad learned they might lose Brother Hinckley, they offered him a package of benefits and salary it was very difficult to reject. But Gordon did refuse the offer at the railroad and returned to Church employment.

Back at the Church Offices, Gordon once again essentially began where he left off. The missions were now very low in numbers but with the end of the war, now missionary work could be rejuvenated. The missions in Europe gradually began to reopen and the Occupation in Japan opened even other doors to spreading the gospel there.

General Conferences were resumed in the Tabernacle and Gordon set up the network where they could be broadcast to many more locations than just Utah. Where radio waves could not be used, private wire hookups were arranged.[33]

While the war had raged, Gordon's father had been busy helping

President Grant and had also been prolific in writing numerous articles published in LDS Church magazines. His father was still right in the Church Administration Building and Gordon and he could regularly associate together. This was a nice situation Brother Gordon Hinckley enjoyed.

As in the earlier days of employment for the Church, the projects Gordon participated in crossed many lines of Church involvement. Particularly was this true with mass communications activities and mission work. One of the first projects Brother Hinckley was given was to supervise the translation and printing of missionary literature into foreign languages and shipment of audio-visual material and literature to the various missions.

He also proposed tracts and pamphlets for the missions and was asked to oversee the translation of the Book of Mormon, the Doctrine and Covenants, the Pearl of Great Price (the three volumes of literature in addition to the Bible which were considered part of the "Standard Works" or canonized scripture used by the LDS religion). Hymnbooks also were needing foreign translation. In fact, there was a resurgence of religion felt in post-war Europe, South America and Asia. With it came the opportunity for the LDS Church to increase the dissemination of its "glad tidings" of the gospel restoration.

One of the first foreign translation projects was the Portuguese translation of the D.&C. and Pearl of Great Price for Brazil. Choir records were also produced in 1947 for Japan. Then an extensive number of translation projects began. They included a large number of projects beginning in 1947 and 1948 translating the Standard Works, pamphlets and even some books into the respective languages for Argentina, Denmark, Holland, Germany, Finland, France, and Japan.

Additional literature projects were enlisted for the California, Canadian, Central American, Central Atlantic States, Central States, Eastern Central States, Eastern States, Hawaiian, and Northern California Missions. He also assisted in such projects as music library transcriptions, shipments to stake and full-time missions, and radio program broadcasts on CBS. In 1950, a mission literature survey was performed to determine needs. He reported to Elder Stephen L. Richards pertaining to all of these matters.[34]

What of the Mormons?

A major project for the Church Radio, Publicity and Mission Literature Committee was the writing of a 231 page volume destined

Gordon B. Hinckley
Sharing a Translation of the Book of Mormon
with President David O. McKay

to be disseminated in part indefinitely in numerous languages worldwide. Gordon put together all of the history and knowledge of the Church he had acquired in his 37 years and condensed it into a book entitled *What of the Mormons?*

He divided the book into two major portions: The Mormons Today and The Mormons Yesterday.

The Mormons Today treated: Who are they? What do they believe? What is their program? and What is their organization?

The Mormons Yesterday treated: Genesis, an angel and a book, the power of God among men, the church organized, Mormonism in Ohio, the Church in Missouri, Nauvoo the beautiful, the martyrs, exodus, to the promised land, pioneering the wilderness, years of conflict, years of endurance, and the summer of good will.

At the end of the text, Gordon wrote:

"The men and women of that pioneer era are gone. Gone are the days of forced winter marches, of burning homes and desecrated temples, of lonely graves on the prairie. Another generation has come to whom these trials are but words of history. But this generation also has its problems. Never was there a greater need for religion. Seldom if ever have men and nations been more abjectly destitute of the principles of Christianity applied to living.

"And now, as never before, the Church of Jesus Christ of Latter-day Saints is endeavoring to meet this challenge and this opportunity. It has ever had but one purpose, and it is now trying to pursue that purpose more vigorously than at any time in its history. That objective is to bring men and women to the Savior and Redeemer of the world and to a realization that only through the cultivation of faith which actively manifests itself in good works can men and nations enjoy peace."[35]

The original 1947 printing, released on the 100th year anniversary of the first LDS pioneers arrival in the Salt Lake Valley, experienced some foreign translations and several new editions until 1972 when the part "The Mormons Yesterday" was printed separately in a new 4½" X 7" soft cover volume of 154 pages called *Truth Restored*. It has been translated and published numerous times since in many, many languages as a missionary tool and Church history primer for new LDS members.

Gordon B. Hinckley Reviews Translation
of Japanese Book of Mormon
with Watabe Family and John D. Chase,
an RM from Northern Far East Mission

General Conference TV Broadcasts

In April 1948, another innovation was first implemented, that of broadcasting LDS general conference by closed circuit TV from the main Tabernacle on Temple Square to other buildings such as the Assembly Hall on Temple Square.[36] This same year, another industry in Utah started when an oil well in Vernal, Utah started production. Vernal is located in the eastern portion of Utah and certainly used to be the home of numerous dinosaurs. A large quarry of dinosaur bones right at Vernal is home of the United States Dinosaur National Park.

One year later in October 1949, another first occurred. At general conference that month, the first broadcast of conference sessions were made over KSL TV.[37] All of these innovations were implemented by Gordon B. Hinckley.

Radio Programs

Gordon wrote and produced a new radio series in 1950 called "A New Witness for Christ" which aired regularly.[38] This program continued on the air for several years until 1957. In 1950, a catalog of music transcriptions was also prepared.[39] Ideas for future broadcasts constantly had to be thought up when one of these series began. Gordon became very versed in the art of radio program production and script writing.

In June 1950, another conflict began, this time in Korea when North Korean armed forces invaded South Korea. US President Harry S. Truman ordered US forces into Korea on June 27 but the next day North Koreans captured Seoul. On July 8, General Douglas MacArthur, designated commander of the unified United Nations forces, established a Pusan beachhead, took back Seoul in August and September and moved on to the North Korean capital of Pyongyang in October. Then Chinese Communists entered the war on October 26 and forced United Nations retreat toward the 39th parallel in December.[40]

Publication of James Henry Moyle Biography

Despite all of his other activities, Brother Gordon B. Hinckley still found time somehow to complete a biography on James Henry Moyle, father of LDS general authority Henry D. Moyle. The biography was completed and published in 1951.

The original biographer had been John Henry Evans who died in 1947 after accumulating voluminous notes and manuscript material including the subject's diaries and writings. When Mr. Evans died in 1947, the family with four sons and two daughters came to Brother

Hinckley who had been well acquainted with John Henry Evans. They asked him to complete the biography.

Gordon Hinckley did not refuse. He went to work with what free time he had and wrote the 339 page book. On page 325 of his book, published by Deseret Book, Gordon revealed some of his own objectives followed by President Hinckley throughout his life. He wrote, "But President Moyle was quick to realize the possibilities of radio, newspapers and exhibits to erase old ill-founded prejudices against his people."[41]

The New Sub-Committee of the Missionary Committee

The intertwining relationship of the missionary work of the LDS Church with the publicity, literature and audio and visual communications of the Church caused a major change in the Executive Committees in 1951. The Radio, Publicity and Mission Literature Committee was brought under the umbrella of the Missionary Committee and Gordon was given the official title of Executive Secretary of the Missionary Committee, thus becoming the official administrator of both although in many respects he had been such since 1935.

Gordon continued his public relations for the LDS Church as well as essentially guiding the "Missionary Department" of the Church although it was not officially called such yet.

Such radio programs as "Faith in Action" commenced broadcast in 1951 and continued until 1957. The December 18, 1955 broadcast was particularly significant, broadcast five days before the LDS prophet Joseph Smith, Jr.'s 150th birthday. All of the radio programs being produced required multitudinous detail. Requests were made for radio material. Business was conducted with the Pan American Broadcasting Company. Speakers were constantly being arranged. Music was also needed for the productions. In 1957, a program was produced for radio treating the "Mormon Missionary." But these efforts were only a fraction of what Brother Hinckley was doing.

Numerous recording companies became well known to Gordon B. Hinckley, also. Among them were Allied Record Manufacturing, Co.; Califone Corp.; Century Record Manufacturing; Columbia Records; Recorders Lab Inc.; Sawyer's Inc.; Sumner Productions; and Telefilm, Inc.[42] With these companies, the radio programs were preserved and disseminated. Also, there were records made of the Tabernacle Choir and other groups.

Gordon B. Hinckley
The Radio, Publicity and Mission Literature Committee Days

Brother Hinckley's expansion of communication within the LDS Church also continued. On April 5, 1952, General Priesthood, the one session of general conference not normally broadcast to the general public was first broadcast to LDS chapels in numerous areas by closed circuit wire transmissions.[43]

The next year in October 1953, LDS world general conference was expanded beyond the central Rocky Mountain area to even a wider broadcast area.[44] And this broadening of general conference coverage continued on and on and on.

On December 18, 1955 "A Modern Witness for Christ" was released. Then the transistor was invented in 1956. This breakthrough in radio and television technology really moved mass communication forward. It greatly enhanced the clarity of transmission and the manufacture of receivers of almost any size.

Post 1957

When Gordon B. Hinckley became an Assistant to the Twelve in the April 1958 LDS General Conference, it was by no length a stop of his public relations and mass communications contributions to the LDS Church. He will always be involved. He has been a powerful force in creating a healthy and favorable image for his church.

In 1961, the purchase of WNYW and shortwave transmitting radio stations in Boston was made. WRUL in Boston and New York City were acquired for Europe and South American broadcasts of church programs in 1962.

The Summer 1964 New York World's Fair contained the most sophisticated Latter-day Saint exhibit ever before presented in a public exhibition. Not only was a large "Mormon Pavillion" in the form of the Salt Lake Temple constructed, an elaborate display of newly developed paintings depicting the Old Testament prophets and the life of Christ were artfully displayed and a 20 minute film created called "Man's Search for Happiness."

It was 1969 when the last ⅔ of Brother Hinckley's book *What of the Mormons?* was first published in paperback form as *Truth Restored.* The name of the official monthly LDS Church magazine was changed to *Ensign* after being called *The Improvement Era* for many decades.

Nineteen seventy two found the LDS Church formally organizing a Church Public Communications Department with Gordon's old fellow schoolmate and British Mission returned missionary Wendell J. Ashton named as its first director.[45]

The Mormon Tabernacle Choir was invited to America's Bicentennial Celebration program at Washington, D.C. in 1976 through the aid of LDS member J.W. Marriott, founder of Hot Shoppes, airline in-flight meals and then the worldwide Marriott Hotel chain.[46] By September 1, 1978, Elder Hinckley had lead out in using the Church media and audio/visual aid materials largely produced through his insight and assistance in many stake conference and other religious situations, seeing tears fill the eyes of the viewers, enlightened officers and, most important, a strengthening of "the work."[47]

As then Elder Hinckley spoke to the 25th Anniversary Party at the BYU Media Production Studios at the Brigham Young University, Provo, Utah, on the 1st day of September in 1978, he shaped the direction of LDS Church's policy and values pertaining to movie and video production when he declared:

"Now we have come to the wonders of today's wide screens, magnificent color photography, the magic of animation, the lifelike quality of quadraphonic sound and many other wonderful things.

"The technique is here, and it is wonderful to behold. The tragedy is that so much of what is produced is filthy, degrading and demeaning to human dignity and morality.

". . . That only increases the challenge to use these marvelous technologies for that which teaches truth, which builds faith, which motivates improvement in behavior, and which stirs the soul to a sense of the eternal nature of man as a son of God.

"This is the studio established and designed to accomplish His purposes . . . . This studio was established 25 years ago for the purpose of building the kingdom of God. And for that purpose it has been added to and defined in the years that have followed."[48]

In April 1980, Elder Hinckley was present at the special broadcast of a portion of LDS general conference from the site of the organization of the LDS religion 150 years before. In fact, he was one of the major instigators and planners of the event on the reconstructed homesite of the Peter Whitmer family home in Fayette township, New York State. This was a moving and tremendous media first for the LDS Church.[49] A year and a half later found the Church first utilizing its own satellite channel transmitting General Conference from Temple Square to stake centers (major meeting halls for stake members) from a relay satellite 22,300 miles above the equator.[50]

In April 1983, Elder Hinckley was now "President Hinckley" as a counselor in the LDS First Presidency and in that influential and administrative role continued his gentle persuasion of improvements in LDS organization and practices. In April 1983, the First Presidency announced a change in broadcast of the General Priesthood session of LDS general conference from 7:00 P.M. to 6:00 P.M.[51] The move was another strategic public communications move allowing all LDS members to view the session on TV satellite transmissions at a reasonable time in the various time zones of America.

A Diplomat Par Excellence

President Hinckley has always been a diplomat par excellence for his religion. He has always been consistantly and effectively implementing effective journalistic techniques to promote the good image of his church. Removing misunderstandings and conveying a clear and correct picture of LDS Church doctrines, culture and values has always been his objective.

In the accomplishment of this goal, President Hinckley has exercised his "astute knowledge of public and political matters."[52] One such accomplishment was joining the interfaith network of an 18 religion organization on a cable TV channel called VISN on September 17, 1988.[53] By 1991, the LDS Church was not only producing public service spots on TV and radio, it was to receive awards for the quality of its "Home Front" series of over 1,000 positive media signets focusing on social issues. In 1991, the spots centered on the subject of drug abuse and in 1992 on the environment.[54]

How has President Hinckley influenced all of this? It has not been possible all by himself. But through the numerous steering committees and boards of directors he has served on making suggestions and influencing and inspiring the executive opinion which results in direction, much has been realized of his ideas and vision. On April 23, 1992, he reflected upon the 60 years of refinement of the application of radio and TV while speaking to another of the LDS Church's institutions of higher learning at Rick's College located in Rexburg, Idaho.[55]

The "councils" in which President Hinckley has served will be treated in more detail in the chapter with that name in this book. The board of the Deseret News was one influential one, however. Also, Bonneville International, an outgrowth of an earlier Church organized company designed to produce audio and visual media products and act as a holding company for its Church owned radio and TV stations, was another board served. The ex-president of Bonneville spoke of President Hinckley's "quick insight and panoramic view of any media situation" in an hour long masterfully produced April 1995 documentary video on recently installed new LDS prophet Hinckley.[56] G. Donald Gale of the KSL Editorial Board spoke on March 14, 1995's regular KSL Editorial Comment of President Hinckley as "informed and somehow able to find time for reading many newspapers and magazines."[57]

"We know him to be a man of understanding, wisdom, wit, compassion, and humility. He amazes colleagues with his knowledge of history and events of the day," Mr. Gale continued further. "Surely, no one knows more about the operations of The Church of Jesus Christ of Latter-day Saints than President Hinckley. His entire life has been dedicated to church service."[58]

Since his presidency as the 15th prophet of the LDS faith began March 14, 1995, President Hinckley did not cease the same objective promulgated during his entire life since his mission and even before. His objective was to eventually give every member of the LDS Church and every one living on this globe, for that matter, the opportunity to participate in the conferences and other activities of his church.

To 17,328 saints at a Regional Conference in Tacoma, Washington before September 30, 1995 he remarked "the broadcast studio of the Church" was continually increasing and it was hoped conference would be available to the islands of the Pacific and Atlantic soon and Central and South America. He also expressed appreciation for the many translators who so selflessly volunteer their talents to simultaneously interpret the proceedings of general conference and other periodic firesides and meetings sent by satellite. And he did not forget those desirous but not yet able to hear live satellite transmissions by saying they "will participate by the voice of the Spirit."[59]

Neal A. Maxwell, an LDS apostle called to the apostleship at the same time President Hinckley moved from that quorum to the First Presidency on July 23, 1981, spoke of President Hinckley's "simplicity and directness", of his "compassion and empathy", of his ability to see "beyond the moment and below the surface", and his discernment of "flattery" and capacity to "keep institutional perspective" while implementing "fixed principles." Elder Maxwell spoke of "good" as the adjective which always attached to President Hinckley's "judgment, humor, will, and nature."[60]

Truly President Hinckley has been a master at the art of mass communication realizing the true statement "communication is the foundation of all human relations." He did not realize his dream to attend graduate journalism school at Columbia, but in his own way has been a professor of the art of communications throughout his life through his example of its use and promotion of its possibilities.

President Hinckley's own statement regarding his belief regarding mass commuinications is a fitting conclusion to this chapter of his life:

"I think we can use the media more and more to disabuse the minds of false notions concerning the LDS people."[61]

MARRIAGE

It is remarkable how similar the first impressions of Marjorie Pay and Gordon B. Hinckley were when they first noticed each other existed.

Marjorie states, "When we first met, I thought he was a very unusual man. He was different. He did everything with a little flare."[1]

The first time Gordon B. Hinckley remembers Marjorie was when she gave a reading in the Liberty Stake 1st Ward primary. He thought her to be a good reader with confidence.[2] She probably was about nine.

Little moments lead to big things. And these mental impressions and feelings planted in these two individuals' minds and hearts would lead to a day when Gordon, at age 26 and Marjorie, at age 25, would kneel at the altar in the Salt Lake Temple and seal their love for time and all eternity as husband and wife.

Marjorie started her sojourn on earth in the little town of Nephi, Utah on November 23, 1911, the oldest of an eventual seven children, including five daughters and two sons, of LeRoy Phillip Pay and Georgetta Paxman. Nephi was a little settlement founded in 1851 by LDS pioneers on the banks of a small creek which they named "Salt Creek" due to the salty taste of the water acquired from salt deposits as it flowed down a little canyon connecting Nephi's Juab Valley with Sanpete Valley to the East. On Christmas Eve, December 24, 1911, she was given her name and a blessing in Nephi, Utah by her father.[3]Her first four and a half years were spent in Nephi where she was her parent's sole child.

Then in 1916 she and her parents moved to Salt Lake City where her father obtained employment as a warehouseman for Salt Lake Hardware and her first brother Harold George was born July 18, 1916. The family first lived on 4 Rigby Court in Salt Lake but moved to 223 North West Temple in 1917 when Marjorie's father became clerk at Salt Lake Hardware.

They next moved to 745 Lake Street in 1918 until 1919 while LeRoy, also called "Roy", became bookkeeper for Beveridge Motor and while he was still employed by Beveridge Motor, moved to 804 South 800 East just across the street south from the Hamilton School located within Liberty Stake where the Hinckley family resided and Gordon Hinckley attended elementary school.[4] Marjorie was about nine when the family moved to Liberty Stake and she had both of her younger brothers, Harold and Douglas, with her and her parents by that time.

In her childhood bedroom, on a wall facing her bed, was a picture of the Savior at 12 years of age teaching the wise men in the temple. It was the first thing she saw every morning. She thinks this is one reason why her love of the Savior started early in her life.[5] Also, Marjorie was taught about the Savior as a young girl at her mother's knee.[6]

According to Marjorie, her parents were "humble people" but had a home "filled with faith."[7] She was taught of her ancestors, noble people who had followed the dictates of their conscience and joined the Latter-day Saints in the mid-1800's Westward trek across the plains to the Valleys of the Rocky Mountains.

Pay Line Heritage

Her heritage stems from the four families of Pay, Goble, Paxman and Evans. The known Pay pedigree to date begins in Shropshire County, England in about 1560 and moves after several generations to County Kent by about 1723 to towns in Folkstone and Dover. In her pedigree there are three Richard Pays, born respectively in 1765, 1794 and 1821. The second Richard Pay, Marjorie's great-grandfather, married Sarah Prescott in the quaint and historic town of Dover with its cobblestone streets, the Dover Castle on a hill dating back to 1125 A.D., the old stone church in the middle of town and the White Cliffs which became so famous during World War II.

To Richard and Sarah Prescott Pay was born Marjorie's grandfather, the third Richard Pay on her line. He was the first born child of his parents and at 24 married Eliza Hurst Gibbins, 20, on September 16, 1845 but she died five years later on April 5, 1850 without issue. But before her death, both Richard and Eliza heard the restoration message and accepted baptism on February 26, 1849. About a year before Eliza's death, Elder Thomas Caffel baptized her at Dover.

Richard received the Aaronic Priesthood the next month and progressed to the Melchizedek Priesthood and office of elder by 1850. From 1850 to 1853, Richard served a mission "without purse or script" in the southern counties of England and Eliza died while he was preaching the gospel.

He went home to Buckland and married his first cousin Sarah Pay on April 30, 1854. Sarah, too, had joined the church at Dover in 1850, baptized by an Elder Theubury. She bore Richard one son and one daughter but the boy died in infancy. Richard and Sarah emigrated to the United States from Liverpool, England on May 25, 1856 when

Pay Line Pedigree of Marjorie PAY

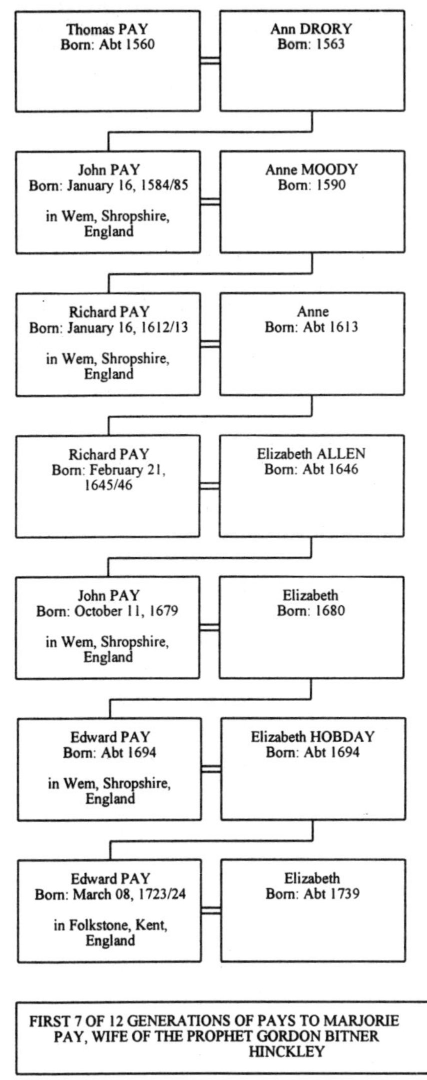

Pay Line Pedigree of Marjorie PAY

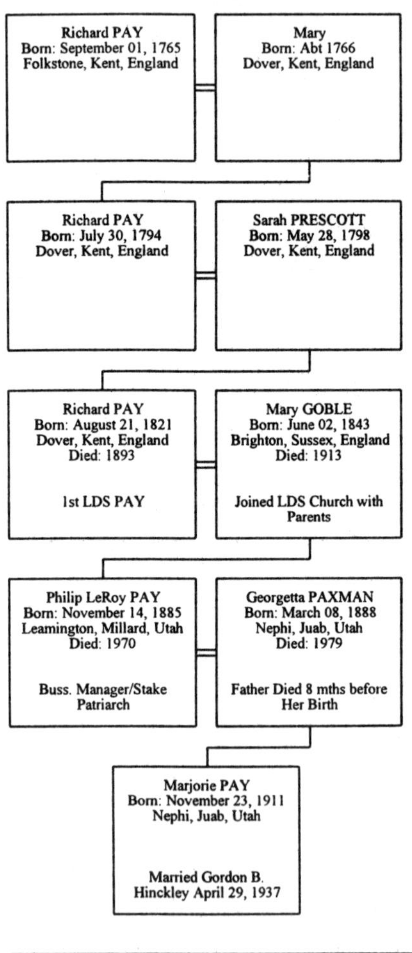

LAST 5 OF 12 GENERATIONS OF PAYS TO MARJORIE PAY
WIFE OF THE PROPHET GORDON BITNER HINCKLEY

Sarah was seven months pregnant. The sea voyage on the *Horizon* took six weeks and was fraught with mutiny, a chasing shark, deaths, seasickness, and an almost disastrous collision with an iceberg. But the children among the 900 passengers passed most of the time happily while playing games and singing "songs of Zion."

After arriving in Boston, the party took a train to Iowa City, Iowa where their daughter was born July 10/11, 1856. But wife Sarah contracted "mountain fever" and their daughter also passed away October 4 at Chimney Rock, Wyoming. Richard could not find anyone to assist digging his daughter's grave when a Brother William Goble came up and helped. Brother Goble, his wife and six children, including their oldest daughter Mary, had crossed the ocean together on the same ship as Richard and Sarah. A bond was formed which was never broken. Later in the trek, Richard helped Brother Goble bury one of his little daughters when she died along the roadside at Sweet Water.

Shortly thereafter, Sarah also died when they arrived at Fort Bridger, Wyoming at age 30 years and 10 months. When he arrived in Salt Lake City, December 13, he stayed the Winter in a settlement south of Salt Lake called American Fork and tied all he owned up in a handkerchief the next Spring and walked 50 miles South to Salt Creek, later changed by Brigham Young to "Nephi", and there married his third wife Mary Goble, a surviving daughter of Brother Goble who had helped him bury his daughter at Chimney Rock.

From their marriage in Nephi by Bishop Jacob G. Bigler on June 26, 1859, Mary bore Richard 13 children, 10 of whom were sons, from 1860 to 1885. The last and 13th child was Marjorie's father Phillip LeRoy Pay, born November 14, 1885 in a small settlement west of Nephi called Leamington. Seven and a half years later, Richard died in Leamington on April 18, 1893 at age 71⅔ years, a year and three months after their oldest son died of pneumonia at age 21.[8]

Goble Line Heritage

Marjorie Pay Hinckley's "Goble" heritage is equally noble. The Gobles were living in Sussex, England in the early 1800's. William and Harriet Johnson Goble bore a son William Goble in Singleton, Sussex, England on February 25, 1817. He had matured and married Mary, the daughter of John and Sarah Penfold on January 12, 1841.

In 1855, the William and Mary Penfold Goble family, with their six children, were proselyted by the Latter-day Saint missionaries and mother and father baptized in March of that year. Their first child, a

Goble LDS Line Pedigree of Marjorie PAY

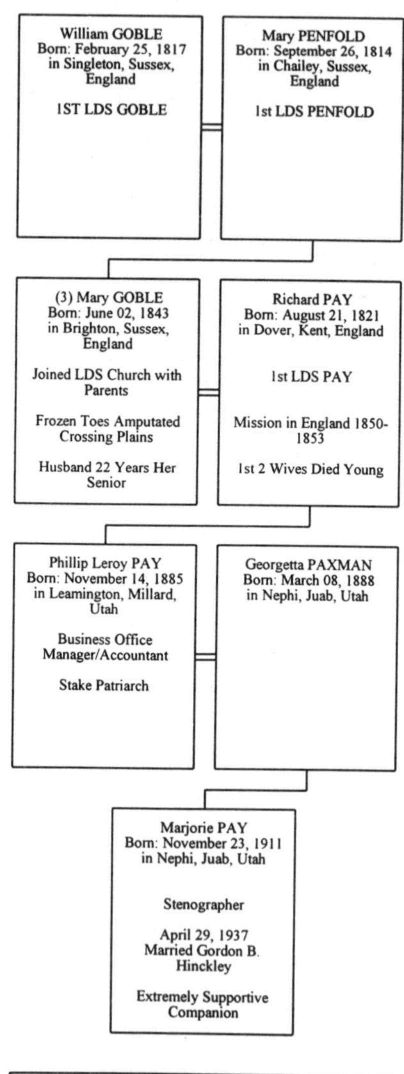

LATTER-DAY SAINT GOBLE GENERATIONS TO MARJORIE PAY, WIFE OF THE PROPHET GORDON BITNER HINCKLEY

son, had died two and a half months after birth and their first daughter Mary Goble, born June 2, 1843, was the oldest living child. She received baptism on November 5 at age 8½.

The family almost immediately started plans to gather to "Zion" in the tops of the Rocky Mountains and left on the same ship as Richard Pay and his wife in May 1856, the ship *Horizon*. After arriving at Iowa City, however, the tragedies began. Two year old Fanny broke out with measles. A thunderstorm toppled their quilt tent fastened to handcarts and Fanny's additional exposure to the rain complicated her illness and she died July 19. On the 1st of August 1856, a wagon train started West with unbroken oxen, passing Fanny's grave as they left.

They crossed the plains of Iowa to Nebraska and across Nebraska to Wyoming. There the Platte River was full of icebergs but the trail required a river crossing at this point. The frigid water coupled with the bitter cold weather so injured the party 14 of their number died in the night. The same night, Mary Penford Goble gave birth to a baby girl but little Edith lived only six weeks due to malnutrition. The pioneer group were destitute of food. Water was also gone. Snow water was used for several days.

Oldest daughter Mary, then a few months over 13, was asked by her mother to go with another sister to a spring a few miles from camp for some fresh water the wagontrain captain told them existed. The two females discovered an elderly brother fallen in the snow and the older woman explained where to travel and she would return to obtain help for the man before he froze to death. Mary became frightened thinking of hostile Indians and panicked. She began running around in the snow and became disoriented. Her toes, then her feet, then her legs gradually began to numb. However, the men at camp became concerned when she did not return by 11:00 P.M. and sent out a search party who found her. But her feet, legs and toes were frozen.

The pain was terrible when her legs were put in water and her body rubbed with snow. The feet and legs were okay but the toes did not revive. Next to die in the family was James, 4½. He had probably feasted too much on an injured oxen killed and eaten by the camp the night before. The next morning he was dead.

Edwin, 11, and Caroline, almost 7, were by now also suffering from frostbite. The ground was so frozen, tent pegs could not be pounded so snow was pushed on the tent edges as a substitute. Not enough flour was left for bread so "thin gruel" called "Skilly" filled in.

The mother was weakening with illness. Just as the company approached Big Mountain before their final descent into the Salt Lake Valley, Mary Penford Goble died December 11 leaving her 13 year old daughter Mary the oldest female in the family. The body was kept in the wagon and taken to Salt Lake.

When Brigham Young visited, he burst into tears at the plight of the family of eight now reduced to the family of four–William Goble, 13 year old Mary, 12 year old Edwin, and 8 year old Caroline.

A doctor was there at the same time and determined to cut both of Mary's feet off at the ankle, but Brigham said, "No, just cut off the toes, and I promise you, you will never have to take them off any further. The pieces of bone that come out will work out through the skin themselves."

So while the sisters prepared Mary's mother for the grave, the doctor amputated Mary's toes on both feet using a saw and butcher knife. Her father walked from the room where Mary's mother was being dressed for burial to the room there Mary's surgery was proceeding during these two tragic experiences. "He could not shed a tear," due to the anxiousness of the moment. Then Mary and the other two frostbitten children walked into the room where their mother lay to see her for the last time before her burial the next afternoon in the Salt Lake Cemetery.

Rather than getting better, however, Mary's feet got worse until the following July 1857 when Dr. Wiseman took Mary into his home to give her close and constant care. But when he uncovered them, he said, "I can do no more for you unless you consent to have your feet cut at the ankle."

"But Brigham Young promised me I would never have to take off more than the toes."

"All right, sit there and rot. I will do nothing more until you come to your senses."

Mary endured, cried, suffered the pain as her feet pained and pained. Then there was a knock at her door one day. An elderly sister stood at the doorway. "I felt that some one needed me for a number of days. May I help you."

Mary started to cry.

"What is the matter, child?"

Mary showed her her stubbed feet with no toes and told her Brigham Young's promise.

"Yes, the woman said, "with the help of the Lord we will save them yet!"

The senior sister prepared a poultice and placed it on Mary's feet and each day after the doctor's inspection, she came to Mary's home and changed it. Finally, after three months, Mary's feet were healed.

Dr. Wiseman saw her one day and said, "Well, Mary, I must say you have grit. I suppose your feet have rotted to the knees by this time."

"Oh, no," Mary replied. "My feet are well."

"I know better. It could never be."

So Mary removed her stockings and showed her healed feet to Brother Wiseman.

"My girl, it is surely a miracle. What did you do?"

"Never mind that. They are healed."

Mary went home to her father and when he saw the fulfillment of President Young's prophecy, both father and daughter cried together. He rubbed her atrophied leg muscles with oil and attempted to straighten them every way he knew but without success. Then one day, he said, "Mary, I have thought of a plan to help you. I will nail a shelf on the wall and while I am away to work, you try to reach it."

Mary tried to touch the shelf during the entire day every day for several days. Finally she could reach it. Then her father moved it a little higher and she struggled to touch it and then it was raised again. In about another three months, her leg muscles had strengthened and straightened and she commenced learning how to walk again.

Richard Pay, although 22 years her senior, wooed and won Mary to become his third wife. They were married June 26, 1859, he almost 38 and she just 16. Their progency consisted of 13 children, the last of which was Marjorie Pay Hinckley's father LeRoy Phillip Pay.[9]

Paxman Line Heritage

Marjorie Pay Hinckley's Paxman line heritage known to date stems from a known Robert Paxman born in 1748 of Ashfield-cum-Thorpe, Suffolk County, England. The family generations moved to Sweffling in County Suffolk and then to Colchester, Essex County, England where William Paxman was born on October 23, 1836 at Hemstead near Colchester, Essex County, England, the third child and second of four sons of James and Esther Reynolds Paxman's nine progeny.

When 14, William's mother died and the children were scattered. William went to London and obtained employ first as an errand boy

Paxman Line Pedigree of Marjorie PAY

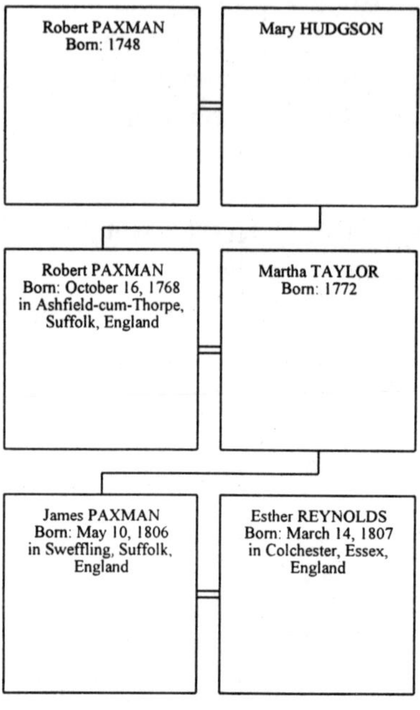

FIRST 3 OF 7 GENERATIONS OF KNOWN PAXMANS TO MARJORIE PAY, WIFE OF THE PROPHET GORDON BITNER HINCKLEY

Paxman Line Pedigree of Marjorie PAY

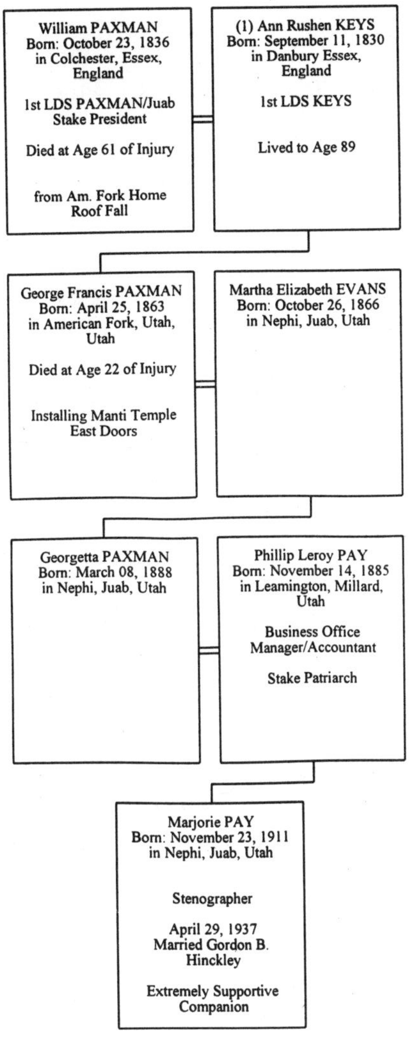

LAST 4 OF 7 GENERATIONS OF KNOWN PAXMANS TO MARJORIE PAY, WIFE OF THE PROPHET GORDON BITNER HINCKLEY

and then as a tinsmith apprentice. Through "his industry and application to duty," it is said he "made his way to first hand in the large establishment."

But William's heart ached and mourned the greatest loss of his early teenage years, his wonderful mother. He pined for something to fill the void of his lost family. He was truly made ready, meek and contrite to receive the message of the restoration. Soon he came in contact with Latter-day Saint missionaries and mingled and sang with them. He absorbed their message readily and joyfully and was baptized by Elder Edmond C. Brand on June 15, 1852 at the age of 16.

William immediately immersed himself in complete faith striving to live the gospel. He progressed in the offices of the priesthood and served in various callings. One service was the distribution of the local Britain church publication called the *Millennial Star*. One day he distributed a *Millennial Star* to a fellow sister five years older than him with blue eyes and long brown hair by the name of Ann Rushen Keys. Her hair "hung in natural ringlets so long that when they were straightened out she could sit on them" and were often tied with blue ribbons.

Ann had been baptized with her parents Joseph and Mary Rushen Keys and three others of the total five daughters and four sons of her parents. Brother John Holland had performed Ann's baptism on September 13, 1851. Her mother had been the first of the family to join after first giving the LDS elders a very hard time, shaking her finger in the face of Elder Penrose as she said, "False prophet!" to him.

At age 23, Ann had obtained employ as a maid for a vehemently anti-Mormon family. But she remained faithful in Church attendance and took care not to upset her source of sustenance. As friendship turned to courtship with William, however, one time she allowed him to visit her kitchen while the owners of the home were gone but while she prepared dinner for them, the wife unexpectedly returned with some fish. William was quick enough to dash into the coal chute located on one of the kitchen walls and into the bin but then the woman of the house went directly to the coal bin and shoveled out some coal. Luckily, however, she did not discover William. And the two "love birds" never did that again!

Marriage ensued and migration to America. They travelled on the very *same* vessel and voyage as Richard and Sarah Pay and the William and Mary Penford Goble families, the *Horizon*, departing May 25,

1856, two more of the 900 passengers on board. Their first child, a son, only 3½ pounds, was born midway in the Atlantic and named "William" after his father, "Reed" after the ship's kind captain, and "Horizon" after the steamer on which they travelled. But when the ship arrived in Boston, rather than immediately traveling on to the Rocky Mountains, they stayed in Boston.

William obtained work as a clerk in a stove manufacturing establishment and there learned the soldering or "tinkering" trade. Another son and their first daughter were born in Boston during their five years there. Then when the US Civil War began, following counsel of the brethren LDS general authorities, they made their way to the Rockies and eventually ended up in the settlement of American Fork, about 30 miles south of Salt Lake City.

After extreme hardship of several years living first for a year in a dugout not better than a "pig litter" and almost starving during a severe grasshopper plague in 1864, William built a molasses mill on the banks of the stream flowing out of American Fork Canyon and also a home which eventually contained nine rooms and a storage closet, orchards, lawn, trees, grape arbors, and shrubs. He also entered into plural marriage during 1864, as Gordon B. Hinckley's grandfather had done, taking a widow with three children named Susan Horsley into his care.

In the interim two other sons, James and George Francis, had been born together with a daughter. George Francis was to become the grandfather of Marjorie Pay Hinckley. And when the beautifying of the new home began, the young boys James and George were "set to work clearing rocks from the ground."

But when they thought their work was done, their mother asked them to move the rock pile to another location. "The boys, full of indignation, pouting and mumbling that they didn't see why rocks had to grow and they wished they'd never seen a rock, saw the one pile gradually diminish while the other grew taller and taller as the hours slowly rolled by."

William served as superintendent of the local Sunday School and later obtained employment in nearby Provo at the Abraham O. Smoot Lumber Company. Then when he took his third wife Emily Abel by whom he eventually sired six children and when all 11 of William's children by his first wife Ann were born, he was called to fill an LDS mission to Britain.

He was away from his wives and families for two years during which time he was made president of the London Conference for over a year. One fellow missionary wrote of him, "His personality and language commanded strict attention. His simplicity, and above all, his perfect faith as an humble Elder, seemed to me his outstanding quality. His knowledge of the gospel bore witness to all who listened to his testimony. He was honest and conscientious. The Elders admired him and were willing to fill all duties required by him."

Upon return from his mission, William was called to be an assistant bishop for LDS presiding bishop Edward Hunter in 1878 until he was next called in 1883 to move to Nephi and become the Juab Stake President. The persecutions which had beset Gordon B. Hinckley's grandfather Ira regarding plural marriage also came to William and his wives. They were forced to hide and move to and from Utah & Idaho.

Shortly after William took his fourth wife Katherine Ann Love in 1884, who eventually bore him five children, the LDS general authorities deemed it best for his safety and also worthy of his character to call William and his new wife Katherine to preside over the New Zealand Mission. Work on the third LDS temple to be built in Utah was nearing completion in Manti, across the hills east of Nephi, at the time and his fourth son George Francis aided in its completion.

While on his 3½ year mission to New Zealand, William became as endeared to the local Maori Latter-day Saints as he had with the saints in Britain. They lavished great love and respect on him as he led the small missionary force there and guided the first translation of the Book of Mormon in the Maori language.

His son George Francis, back in America, also married Martha Elizabeth Evans on September 18, 1885 in the Logan LDS Temple while his father was in New Zealand but when Martha was barely expecting her second child, George injured himself severely while helping lift the east doors of the Manti temple to their hinges. In just a few days, he died back at Nephi. His widowed wife Martha bore him his second child and second daughter, eight months after his death on March 8, 1888 in Nephi. Her mother christened her "Georgetta" in honor of the father she never knew. Georgetta became the mother of Marjorie Pay Hinckley.

William and Katherine returned to Nephi from their mission the last part of 1889 where William resumed his position as president of the Juab Stake. Then in 1897, anticipating attending October LDS general conference, he visited his home in American Fork on the way and built a scaffold to perform repairs to its roof. While replacing the shingles, however, the scaffold gave way, plummeting William to the ground. He did not feel any pain at first although one leg was broken. But within a few days, his nervous system was affected and he passed away on October 12, 1889 just 11 days before turning 62.[10]

Evans Line Heritage

The pedigree of Marjorie Pay Hinckley's Evans line also goes to England and the County of Cambridge. Richard Hugh and Sarah Jarrold Hyder were from there. In the city of Cambridge, Cambridge County, England, Sarah had matured in refinement and education. Richard desired his children to be raised in the influence of faith and took their son and three daughters to the Church of England.

But then Richard died at the untimely age of 32. Widow Sarah continued on raising her children and became acquainted with a Brother Goates, an LDS convert, when he delivered dairy and bakery products together with eggs to her home. Their conversations drifted to religion from time to time and she admired his knowledge of the Bible. Eventually she asked what church he attended and he told her he was a Latter-day Saint.

Brother Goates then gave her pamphlets and she began a serious study of the Bible to determine the validity or falsity of the doctrine printed in the literature. Her children, however, objected to her association with the baker and were embarrassed and humiliated when she took them to an LDS meeting at the town hall. But as time passed, her daughters were convinced of the truth of the restoration message and were baptized with Sarah, the first baptisms in Cambridge. Three days later, her son suddenly died.

The four women consisting of three daughters and a mother left for "Zion" on February 23, 1851 after turning down 300£ offered by Sarah's parents as an enticement to stay and place her daughters in Cambridge College. "I am sorry, Mother and Father," she replied. "I cannot take the money. I feel compelled to gather with the Saints."

True to their faith, the four women left well-to-do relatives, friends, comforts, Cambridge College educations, and a successful business for their new beliefs and crossed the ocean to America. Daughter Charlotte Jarrold Hyder, 17, recorded in her diary, "The sea is calm and beautiful. The wind is in our favor and although I long to see my friends in Cambridge, I console myself in the thought that I am going

Evans Line Pedigree of Marjorie PAY

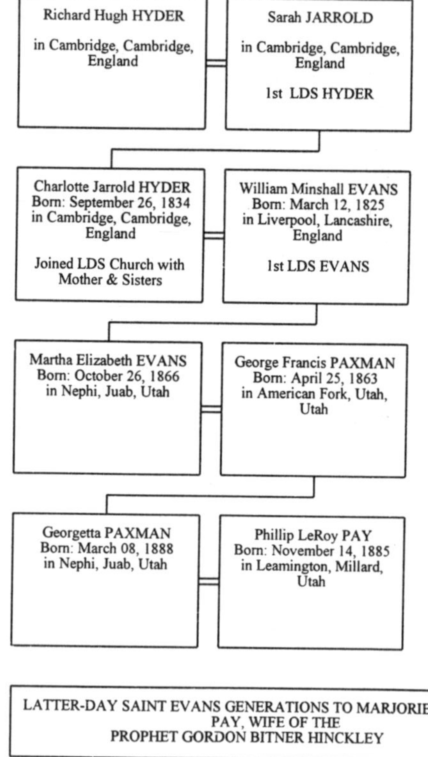

to Zion, the promised land. Oh! Glorious thought!"

While crossing the 1,000 miles to the Salt Lake Valley, Charlotte met William Minshall Evans, a bugler and convert born in Liverpool, England on March 12, 1825. William had discovered the LDS Church one Sunday morning by accident as he was walking to his Baptist Church services to sing in their choir in Liverpool. That day he overheard the "most beautiful singing he had ever heard" as he walked. He followed it to an alley and then up a stairway where LDS missionaries were singing. He listened to their sermon and when he returned home, his brother said, "Where were you this morning? You were not in your place in the choir."

"I was where you should have been, and I will never be satisfied until you hear the beautiful truth that I heard this morning."

Both brothers were converted and baptized into the Church of Jesus Christ of Latter-day Saints.

William and Charlotte immediately fell in love and married July 15, 1852 in Salt Lake City, sealing their marriage for time and all eternity 11 days later on July 26, 1852 in the LDS Endowment House.

From William and Charlotte's union came 12 children, the ninth of which was Martha Elizabeth Evans, born to the family on October 26, 1866 after they had emigrated to Salt Creek (later Nephi) shortly after they arrived in Salt Lake City.

William and Charlotte lost their third son David on July 6, 1872 at age 12 and their second son Charles 10 months later on May 3, 1873 at age 14. Charlotte did much charitable service soliciting donations for construction of the Manti LDS temple, gleaning storage wheat for the LDS relief society, sewing burial clothes, nursing the sick, and cultivating mulberry bushes for the production of silkworms.

William was then called on a mission to England but returned ill just 13 months later and passed away a few weeks later two months shy of 52 on January 5, 1877. Charlotte was only 42.

Their daughter Martha Elizabeth, however, grew to womanhood and was courted by George Francis Paxman. They married in the Logan LDS temple on September 18, 1885 and had two children, Marjorie Pay Hinckley's mother being the second child Georgetta bore eight months after George's untimely death, at age 24, from a strangulated hernia received as he worked on the Manti Temple.

Martha was not quite 21 when her husband died. She demonstrated extraordinary courage by moving into a one room adobe home by the side of her mother and developed the talents of a seamstress to support herself and two daughters. She remained single for the remaining 66 years of her life.

Faith and good books were taught her daughters through example and reading "the best books." Tithing was scrupulously paid.

When her daughters graduated from high school in Salt Lake City, the three women moved to Salt Lake, rented a home and while the two daughters attended the LDS Business College and University of Utah, Martha worked in the alterations department of ZCMI department store. When almost 88, she died in Salt Lake City on September 21, 1954.

Teen Years

Marjorie remembers the unconditional support and love her mother Georgetta gave to Marjorie's father. Particularly she vividly remembers sitting by the stove in the dining room waiting with her mother for her father to come home from his MIA assignment with the LDS youth. They would talk and laugh about the activities he had witnessed and Marjorie "thought his being the MIA president must be the most wonderful thing that could happen to a family."

Additional church assignments were the same as the years passed and her father's employment settled to the Taylor Richards Motor Company where he was first cashier, then deputy manager, cashier, accountant and bookkeeper. The family moved across the street from Gordon B. Hinckley's home in 1926. Their home was of red brick and couldn't be missed when you came out of the Hinckley home front door and looked across the street.

When 17, Marjorie became a Sunday School teacher and as the years went by held almost every ward MIA calling including president. In later years, she also served as primary president and relief society president.[11]

Following high school, she enrolled in a business course studying in 1928 and 1929 to be a stenographer. She then began a stenographer job in 1930 at Owens-Illinois Pacific Coast Glass Co. When Gordon B. Hinckley left for his mission to England in 1933, the Pay family was still living across the street from the Hinckleys but in 1935, the year Gordon returned from his mission, the family moved to another red brick home at 632 Hollywood Avenue (1955 S.). Here Gordon went to court his sweetheart following return from his mission.[12]

Marjorie Pay Home Across Street from Hinckley Home
from 1925-1934
827 East 700 South, Salt Lake City, Utah

Home of Marjorie Pay
from 1934-1937
632 East Hollywood Avenue (1922 South)
Salt Lake City, Utah

Marjorie's father started employment as manager at the Super Window Shade Company about this time and then switched to the Judkins Company as their manager. He then worked as a warehouseman for the LDS Salt Lake Pioneer Regional Council Welfare Department except for one year work for the Salt Lake City Welfare Department.

Marjorie's father later was ordained to be an LDS patriarch and her mother would "have the house in immaculate order, with fresh flowers and an air of happiness permeating every room" when LDS brothers or sisters came to their home to receive their patriarchal blessings from Patriarch Pay.

Marjorie states the devotion and support of her mother for her father's callings in the LDS Church "prepared me, without realizing it, to live happily with a man whose total commitment to the Lord has dictated our lifestyle."[13]

Courtship and Marriage

Marjorie Pay and Gordon B. Hinckley's courtship started when he was 20 and she 19. She was serving as the popular brown eyed Liberty Stake Gleaner President. The phone rang and it was Gordon Hinckley from across the street. To his question she said, "Yes, I'd be glad to go to the Gold and Green Ball." They associated with each other occasionally at first but their courtship really didn't blossom until after Gordon returned from his mission in the Summer of 1935. But from then on, they met often.[14]

One of Marjorie's friends was Eudora Widtsoe, daughter of LDS apostle John A. Widtsoe. Eudora called a spade a spade, always gave an honest appraisal and was loyal. Gordon B. Hinckley and G. Homer Durham soon were fast friends wooing both Marjorie and Eudora respectively.[15]

Finally Marjorie decided Gordon "was going places" and consented to his proposal of marriage.[16] In 1936, they dated, danced, and had lots of fun while they worried about life. It was the actual start of wars and constant crises shook the entire world in Europe and other spots in Asia.

Then they set the date and place. It would be in the temple and Brother Hinckley's boss Elder Stephen L. Richards of the LDS apostles would seal them. Gordon's wife Marjorie looked beautiful as she knelt across the altar in the temple from him. He was bewitched with the "wondrous aura of young womanhood upon her."[17] They were sealed as husband and wife for time and all eternity on Tuesday, April 27,

1937 in the Salt Lake Temple.

Afterwards Gordon expressed gratitude he married a woman "who wanted a temple marriage and who was worthy of a temple marriage."[18] He reflected to himself his wife is a daughter of God engaged with him in the great creative process of bringing to pass God's eternal purposes. Then he mused, "A woman can keep the love for her husband by looking for and emphasizing his godly qualities. Each man has them."[19]

First Family Home

About August of 1937, the year of Gordon and Marjorie's marriage, sodium vapor street lights came on in Salt Lake City.[20] This was a marvelous advance for the city. It helped if only to light the meager income of Gordon's early marriage years. But however meager the earnings, the couple were wonderfully happy. Poor in the world's eyes, "we were as happy as if we owned the whole world," President Hinckley said.[21]

The first home of the newlyweds was the old family homestead at the East Millcreek farm. It was located at 2595 South 3700 East in Salt Lake City.[22] Here they stayed for the first two or three years of their married life and here they brought home their first baby girl, Kathleen, after her March 31, 1939 birth.

President Hinckley has since talked about why his marriage had been a success. He says first he from the beginning has had an anxious concern for the well-being of his companion. Next he has practiced four "cornerstones" which have built their house: Respect, a soft answer, honesty and family prayer. He believes the following admonition of Psalms 127:1 pertaining to happy marriages: "Except the Lord build the house, they labor in vain that build it."[23]

FAMILY

The first family home of Gordon and Marjorie Hinckley was located 10 blocks south of the mouth of Millcreek Canyon on a level plateau "lip" above a slopping hill descending into the bottom of Salt Lake Valley. Looking the other way, from 1625 East to the East, appropriately named "Highland" Drive by the early inhabitants, starts the gradual incline called the "East Bench" of the Salt Lake Valley.

To the southeast stood the majestic cliffs of Mount Olympus. To the extreme north lay the campus of the University of Utah. To the west was the lower base of Salt Lake Valley. It was truly a beautiful place. And the memories of youth gone by certainly reigned in the mind of Gordon as he and his new bride set up their own home in the house of memories.

When the couple moved into the homestead, Gordon fixed it up. He bought a furnace and through his skills acquired at the maintenance shop at Deseret Gym, hooked it up. Other remodeling was also done. There seemed always to be an improvement in Gordon's brain for his homes. And there seemed always to be areas left for future doors but the family seemed to always grow one or two years ahead of the improvements. There was always an unfinished part at the homes or yard.[1]

Membership for both Gordon and Marjorie was then transferred from the LDS 1st Ward of the Liberty Stake to the East Mill Creek Ward in Grant Stake on March 20, 1938. [2] The next month, Gordon heard J. Reuben Clark, Jr., now an LDS apostle of 3½ years, give his now famous general conference talk on "interest" on debt. [3] It reminded him of the relentless increase of interest when money is borrowed and placed a signpost of caution in his memory.

About June 1938, Marjorie was expecting and gave birth to Kathleen on March 31, 1939 in Salt Lake. A month later Gordon was ordained a 70 on May 1st by John H. Taylor at East Mill Creek Ward, Grant Stake. This calling was a stake calling at the time. Each stake had Melchizedek Priesthood seventies quorums. The basic privilege of seventies was to do missionary work. Then another month later Gordon blessed his first child and daughter Kathleen at the same place on June 4, 1939.[4]

Gordon did not shy from community service at age 28 either. He soon was serving on one of his first civic "councils" as one of the directors of the East Mill Creek water company.[5] Equitably allocating the water resources of the community was a very important issue for all residents of the area. Gordon helped with this admirably, particularly with his long acquaintance with the water and irrigation needs of the community from the family farm days.

So admirable were his contributions, the community elected him president of the East Mill Creek Betterment League, "the highest civic office in the community."[6] In his late 20's and early thirties, Gordon guided the economic, aesthetic and social development of East Mill Creek. Community action was also one of his early demonstrated values.

Building a Family Home

Gordon next turned 29 years old on June 23, 1939. The new family seriously commenced plans to build their own home. The concept appears to be influenced from Gordon's years spent in England. A lot at 3703 South 2700 East, Salt Lake City, just a block south of the old farm homestead was selected with orchard space to the south. The parcel was part of the East Millcreek family farm. The attractive bungalow style home was placed back from 2700 East enough to provide a nice front lawn.

Marjorie was expecting her second baby about the time Germany, Italy and Japan signed their Axis agreement September 27, 1940. And the war deepened in Europe as the Hinckley home was being built. Yugoslavia and Greece were invaded, the Balkans dominated and Russia invaded during 1941 when the Hinckley home was being constructed. The couple's first son Richard Gordon was born May 2 of that year.

Brother Gordon B. Hinckley excavated the footings for his home and with the help of friends, constructed it. The old "hollow" where Gordon and his brother and sisters had grown up in the Summers was in the back and part of the property. The gullies and trails were the same. Over 250 trees were next planted. They grew with the children and enhanced the green apples, cherries, peaches, fields, trees, huts, and "hidden places" Gordon and Marjorie's own children would enjoy in their own childhoods.

Morning glory had supreme control over the lot when they began, however, and required lots of work trying to eradicate. Great old native oak trees were complemented with additional maple, birch, ash, linden, hawthorne, locust, spruce and cedar trees. Broad lawns and shrubs were also planted including flowering and evergreen. One tree which would

Gordon B. & Marjorie P. Hinckley Family Home
3703 South 2700 East, Salt Lake City, Utah

become the subject of a parable Gordon would speak later was a thornless honey locust, a spindly little whip from the plant nursery. It was planted on the south side of the house.

The grounds acquired a very natural and wild appearance. To the south were fruit trees which Gordon loved to cultivate as in days of youth. Marjorie developed the scattered violets, tulips, pansies, myrtle and other flowers.[7]

Missionary work almost stopped when Pearl Habor was bombed on December 7, 1941. Gordon desired to help with the war effort and with the blessing of his LDS Church leaders, went to the local Navy recruiting center and applied for officers training. He was rejected as a soldier due to allergies and asthma experiences as a youth.

When January 24, 1942 came, Gordon visited the gravesite of Rebecca Widers at Scollsbluff, Nebraska, one of the few known graves of pioneers who died on the trail to Utah, in connection with his preparation of the lecture "Historic Highlights of Mormonism." Said Gordon, Rebecca Widers' resting place was "a sacred spot" kept green and lovely by "those who appreciate its significance" and "a token of the faith of men and women who sacrificed their all to reach and build that Zion."[8] Rebecca had died of cholera on August 15, 1852.

Maybe the travel to Nebraska affected Gordon's decision to try and find some employment at the railroad to assist in the World War II effort. The pioneer grave of Rebecca Widers was located right to the side of the railroad tracks and in part of its right-of-way. In any event, railroads were crucial to the success of the war and so Gordon applied and was given the job as assistant superintendent of the Salt Lake City Union Depot at 270 South Rio Grande, the railroad station serving the Rio Grande Railroad and Western Pacific Railroad. Soon he was promoted to stationmaster supervising all of the important cargo and passengers being transmitted by rail across the country. Much military cargo and many servicemen were passengers on the trains.

Later, a supervisory conference was held in Denver which Gordon was to attend. At the conference, the abilities and talents of Gordon B. Hinckley became readily apparent by the executives present and soon an offer of advancement and appointment to assistant manager of all mail, baggage and express traffic for the entire Denver & Rio Grande Railroad was made. Gordon accepted and took his family to Denver.

The Orchard by the Hinckley Home

On one occasion, a careless switchman in St. Louis "moved a piece of steel four inches" and a baggage car due in Newark, New Jersey went 1,400 miles away to New Orleans, Louisiana. Later, Gordon used this memory of his railroad days to teach the principle of concentration and constancy in one's work. Gordon certainly was constant.[9]

During the Hinckley family's residency in Denver, their third child Virginia Lee was added to their family on February 8, 1945. In August of 1945, World War II ended and on a visit to Salt Lake City, Gordon visited Elder Stephen L. Richards, his old boss, who asked him to return to work. When the D & R G Railroad found out about it, they offered Gordon a very attractive benefits and salary package to stay with them. It was "very hard," Gordon says, to turn down their offer, but he did.

Return to Salt Lake City

Back in Salt Lake City, the Hinckleys moved back into their cottage home on 2700 East and 3703 South in East Mill Creek. Family life got exciting about this time with a daughter 6, a son 4 and an infant daughter. Christmas became exciting from then on. A neighbor Al "Olie" Langston visited the Hinckleys on Christmas Eve as Santa Claus. He was a good Samaritan who gave of himself throughout his life.[10]

Al Langston used to irrigate the orchards of the family farm when Gordon was a child and used to pick fruit from its trees. In addition to Olie's association, Mark E. Petersen, a newspaperman at the *Deseret News* who later become an LDS apostle, also lived in the same East Mill Creek Ward.[11]

Salt Lake City in the 1940's

The family had big Christmas trees with lots of presents.[12] Christmas gifts were bought in two main shopping areas–Sugarhouse or Downtown. In Sugarhouse, named after the sugar refinery which originally was there, many smaller shops and a Keith O'Brien Department Store existed. The Salt Lake Granite Stake Tabernacle was also just north of 2100 South, the main street in Sugarhouse. Granite Furniture also was at the center of the Sugarhouse shopping district on the corner of 1100 East and 21st South.

But the main shopping was still accomplished downtown at the ZCMI Department Store, first department store west of the Mississippi, with its five story building just south of South Temple on Main Street. A regular potpourri of fine chocolates and pastries could be purchased in the basement, too. And a fast food cafeteria was located there along with a small grocery corner and lower priced budget items. Up from the first floor was the now famous ZCMI restaurant where finer dining could be realized.

The streets on both sides of Main were lined from ZCMI right on down to Broadway (300 South) with lively and well frequented shops and stores. Keeley's ice cream, candy and snack shop was on the way on the west side of Main. LDS apostle David O. McKay and later LDS prophet liked to frequent Keeley's for lunch. Arthur Frank's men's suit and clothier was also there.

Further down on the east side of Main was Lamb's Restaurant located in the south half of the old *Salt Lake Herald* newspaper building at 169 South Main, the oldest continuing restaurant establishment in the State of Utah with its dark mahogany booths, tables, wainscot, backbar, counter, counter stools and fresh fruit in the glass deli display case to the left immediately following the cashier counter as you entered the long hall with mahogany booths on the right wall. George P. Lamb had started his restaurant in 1919 in Logan as a Greek immigrant and moved his very successful business to the old *Herald* Building in 1931.

And then there was the Woolworth's 5 & Dime on the east side just before you got to the corner of 300 South and Main. The store was complete with the traditional snack bar traditional with Woolworth's and Kress 5 & Dime stores consisting of a long counter with swivel chairs along the south side of the store as you entered. Waitresses in white uniforms and white nurse style hats pinned to the tops of their heads busily hurried forward and backward filling the many and varied orders of the shopping customers, particularly at the Noon hour, with hot and ice drinks, sandwiches and desserts of ice cream and pies.

You could get to the other main shopping area on Broadway at 300 South two different ways from Main Street–either walk directly to the corner of 300 South and turn east or take the shortcut through Woolworth's which actually occupied quite a segment of the block in an "L" shaped pattern at about the middle of Main from about 250 South, running back into the block to the east, and then curving to the south about 50 East with the entrance on to Broadway emerging at that spot right between Main and State Streets.

When you emerged from the south entrance of Woolworth's on Broadway, you could immediately see the Paris Department Store across the street on the street's south side and just up to the east at the corner of Broadway and State Street was the four story white brick Auerbachs Department Store, the two other major department stores in the city.

Across from Auerbach's to the north was Ding Ho Restaurant, always taking in a large crowd of downtown shoppers for Chinese or American food, and diagonally to the northeast from Auerbachs was the Capitol Theatre with its high cylindrical steeple and its long broad walkway running diagonally northeast up to the entrance of the main movie theater in the downtown Salt Lake area at the time besides the Utah Theater across the street from the 11 story Tribune Building at 143 South Main.

Malls had not yet come to Salt Lake City so the main concentration of shopping was still in Downtown or Sugarhouse with interspersed shops, hotels and motels, restaurants and grocery supermarkets from downtown Temple Square to 3900 South.

Ordination to High Priest

Before a month had passed after Gordon turned 36, he was brought in and extended the call to be new second counselor to East Mill Creek President LaMont B. Gunderson. The calling came before Gordon had ever been a bishop over a ward, a branch president or even a counselor in either a bishopric or a branch presidency. In the middle of the Summer, LDS apostle Charles A. Callis came to stake conference July 21, 1946 and conferred the office of High Priest upon Gordon B. Hinckley, then set him apart as the stake president's second counselor.[13]

This position of high administration and ministry over the entire membership of the East Mill Creek Stake was Brother Hinckley's beginning in service on executive ministering "councils" of the LDS Church. Thus began the never ending period Marjorie says when Brother Hinckley never was able to sit with the family in church when the children were growing up.[14]

One of the first things he did was to write a concise and succinct sketch of the history of East Mill Creek for the official program of a stake bazaar held just a month after he was made second counselor. The carnival included two days of "fun and frolic" the 23rd and 24th of August including music, dancing, games, side shows, entertainments, eats, and "everything" at the Grandview Ward chapel at 2930 South 20th East in Salt Lake. In addition to working with President Gunderson, Gordon served with first counselor Ralph S. Barney and stake clerk Kline P. Barney.[15]

The next February, Marjorie was expecting her fourth child. Kathleen was baptized on the last day of April 1947. The Centennial celebration of the arrival of the first pioneers to the Salt Lake Valley was observed on July 24, 1947 and Gordon's book *What of the Mormons?* was released. Clark Bryant Hinckley, Brother and Sister Hinckley's second son, was born October 30.

Through these years and thereafter, whenever something needed fixing, Gordon was to the job. He taught his children through example to "dig in" and get the job done. Confront it, read the instructions, and go to work to solve the challenge. "Dad could fix anything, whether it was the gearbox of the washing machine or a lawn mower or a family car," his son Richard has said. "Such resourcefulness, coupled with an unusual degree of pragmatism and good sense, has paid great dividends in Dad's life. I imagine there have been many challenges over the years which may have seemed impossible to less imaginative men, but for which he has found unique solutions."[16]

Equally, Marjorie guided the traffic at home. She also was a good listener. As "Grand Central Station" developed at the Hinckley abode, the kids always knew mother would give them time and an ear, no matter how busy things got. She imparted compassion liberally and laughed with the children out of many happenings.

Next family landmark was baptism of Richard Gordon Hinckley, oldest son of the family, on August 3, 1949. Next came Virginia Lee, baptized April 22, 1953. As the 50's emerged, so did Elvis Presley and the kids got as involved as anyone with the wave of new "rock and roll" music and dancing. Gordon was managing the missionary work of the LDS Church at this time and traveling with Elder Stephen L. Richards and himself throughout many missions of the LDS Church. He also traveled with his family.

In 1953, Gordon and Marjorie, together with their four children, now 14, 12, 8 and 6, visited Cove Fort with Gordon's father Bryant S. Hinckley.[17] Bryant was now 85, about the same age President Hinckley was to be when he became 15th prophet of the LDS Church. Gordon, with the great knowledge he had acquired from his father and mother and his own personal study resulting in the numerous historical radio broadcasts, filmstrips and books about LDS history and doctrines created by him, was a fit tour guide for his children.

Gordon Bitner & Marjorie Pay HINCKLEY Family

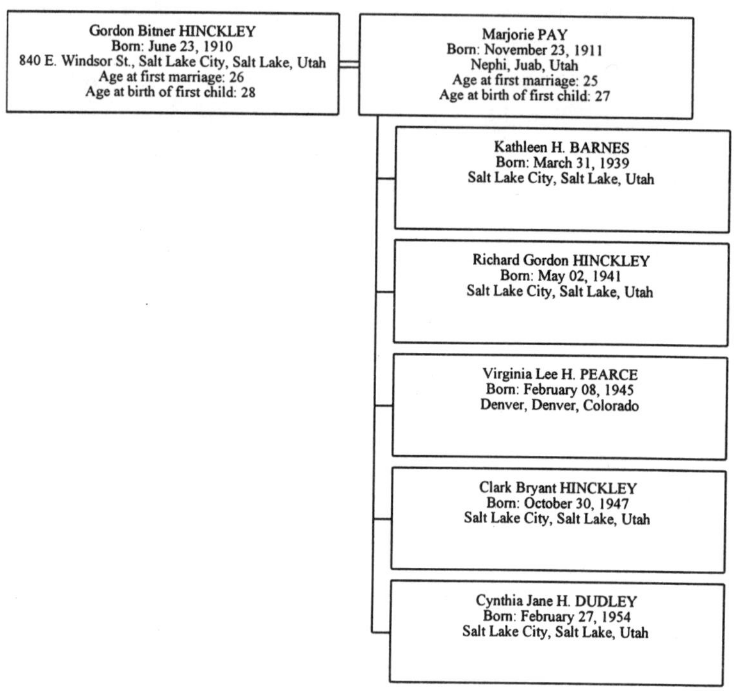

GORDON B. HINCKLEY WAS:

BAPTIZED INTO LDS CHURCH	28 APRIL 1919
ENDOWED IN THE SALT LAKE TEMPLE	9 JUNE 1933
MARRIED FOR TIME & ALL ETERNITY	29 APRIL 1937

Family Group Sheet

Husband: Gordon Bitner HINCKLEY

Born:	June 23, 1910	in: 840 E. Windsor St., Salt Lake City, Salt Lake, Utah
Married:	April 29, 1937	in: Salt Lake Temple, Salt Lake City, Utah
Father:	Bryant Stringham HINCKLEY	
Mother:	(2) Ada BITNER	

Wife: Marjorie PAY

Born:	November 23, 1911	in: Nephi, Juab, Utah
Father:	Philip Leroy PAY	
Mother:	Georgetta PAXMAN	

	CHILDREN		
1 F	Name:	Kathleen H. BARNES	
	Born:	March 31, 1939	in: Salt Lake City, Salt Lake, Utah
2 M	Name:	Richard Gordon HINCKLEY	
	Born:	May 02, 1941	in: Salt Lake City, Salt Lake, Utah
3 F	Name:	Virginia Lee H. PEARCE	
	Born:	February 08, 1945	in: Denver, Denver, Colorado
4 M	Name:	Clark Bryant HINCKLEY	
	Born:	October 30, 1947	in: Salt Lake City, Salt Lake, Utah
5 F	Name:	Cynthia Jane H. DUDLEY	
	Born:	February 27, 1954	in: Salt Lake City, Salt Lake, Utah

The family regularly took vacations touring Utah and the surrounding Western States, stopping at every historical marker they came to, where Brother Hinckley always had something to say and explain about the significance of the spot and the events which had transpired there.

The spots came alive when the past events on the very spots were told. Marjorie would also read to the children in the car, always two to three books during a vacation. No radio was turned on. One time in the late 1950's, the family listened to their mother read *Where the Red Fern Grows*. Tears started to flow among the children and before they stopped, their father drove them around the block so they could dry their tears before they were seen in public.[18]

The last of the five children for Gordon and Marjorie arrived February 27, 1954 and was christened Cynthia Jane. By this time, oldest child Kathleen was in high school and active in modern dance. She toured across the United States one time with the Virginia Tanner groups.

Boeing's 707 four engine airliner inaugurated the jetliner age with a passenger capacity of 219 passengers and a cruising speed of 600 miles per hour.[19] In April 1955, the scientific genius Albert Einstein passed away in New Jersey at age 76. Disneyland came to life in Anaheim, California in July of 1955, the dream of proud Walt Disney.

Clark, second son, was baptized January 27, 1956, the year before Kathleen entered Brigham Young University as a freshman. Richard graduated from high school in 1958 but before he graduated, had a part in a very significant event in the lives of the Hinckley family.

It was Saturday, April 5, 1958. In the morning the phone rang. Richard answered and recognized the voice of President David O. McKay who had assumed the position of 9th prophet of the LDS Church exactly seven years before. President McKay asked for Brother Hinckley.

Richard immediately ran out in the yard where Gordon was working and told him President McKay was on the phone. It was the morning of the second day of LDS General Conference. Richard followed his father into the house and watched as he took the phone and talked to the prophet. He saw his reaction.

"Yes, sir, I'll be right there."

Silently Gordon went and showered, put on his suit and tie and left. That day Brother Hinckley became "Elder Hinckley" as a newly called

Assistant to the Twelve. Virginia, second daughter, then just a fresh new 13 teenager, was aware of the human weaknesses of her parents. She regarded them at her discriminating teen infancy as nothing more than average and "sometimes lacking" as any adolescent.

At the dinner table that day she said, "Well, I guess the Lord's got to work with what He's got."

That was really an expression of her faith, a belief the Lord would turn her father into "something more than my father, and He has."[20]

The Hinckley family had a tradition of gathering around the table at home for dinner and conversation. Elder Hinckley, from early times, enjoyed relating amusing events experienced during the day at work. Work at a religious institution's office, in the LDS Church at least, was not monastic stoicism by any means. The workers went about their jobs with a sense of joy and gladness.

Indeed one of the prophet Joseph Smith, Jr.'s epistles to his fledgling flock of Latter-day Saints in the closing years of his life stated, "Let your hearts rejoice, and be exceedingly glad."[21] The Hinckley family was a glad family around the dinner table. Elder Hinckley would tell of a humorous experience or joke and then laugh, and laugh and laugh. The family reacted the same.

Family Life

Family life in the Hinckleys was typical of any "together-family" in the '50's. Each member of the family was very busy with their own activities. There was gardening to be done, too, and good books to read. Marjorie also became involved in continuing education taking a class or two at the U. She was teaching literature or social science in the ward and stake. Home at the Hinckleys was a happy place where friends and youth loved to be.[22]

Later it was said, "Marjorie is to be given full credit for getting her children to feel each is a part of Gordon B. Hinckley's ministry and sustaining parts," and "Marjorie's influence has as much as anything brought her husband to the presidency."[23]

Family Home Evening and family prayer were a regular routine. There were not many heavy gospel discussions. Brother Hinckley was not dictatorial. However, each member of the family knew where their father stood.[24] Richard, called "Dick", didn't discuss many concerns with his father but knew his father knew the truth of the restored gospel. He was an anchor to the family. "God was real and personal to him," Richard said.[25]

Gordon B. Hinckley's prayers revealed the "depth of his faith." He prayed for his children, for the downtrodden, for the oppressed, for the lonely, for the afraid, and a frequent phrase was, "We pray that we may live without regret."[26] He was "beautiful and articulate in daily prayers" and eternally optimistic.[27]

Later President Hinckley reflected upon the power of family prayer in his life when he declared with conviction in the *Ensign* magazine First Presidency message of February 1991, "The inclination to be unholy and unthankful is erased when family members thank the Lord for life and peace and all they have. And as they thank the Lord for one another, there is developed within the family a new appreciation, a new respect, a new affection, one for another.[28]

Kathy remembers their home was a "home where life was stable." You knew "Dad's values and commitments would never change." You felt secure, cared for and free to live, grow, develop, and become what you wanted to be.[29] Can we see any reflections from the generations of Gordon and Marjorie's heritage?

Marjorie said of her husband, he "never hesitated to do whatever was needed to make me and the family more comfortable." She appreciated his "integrity and loyalty" and the way he always expressed "his complete confidence in his wife and children." Family members were encouraged causing them "to reach beyond themselves." Gordon was positive. He reassured concerned individuals with the phrase "things will come out well in the end." And love of music, literature and life by both Gordon and Marjorie has "made being with him a great adventure."[30]

However, brothers quarrelled with brothers, sisters with sisters and sisters with brothers from time to time. Richard was 17 and his younger brother Clark 11. One day in June, Richard was going somewhere and Clark wanted to go with his big brother. Richard said, "Get lost."[31]

Gordon was not immune to sickness either. In the Summer of 1958, he was home with the flu when his 11 year old son Clark came and said, "Dad, have you seen Dr. Popenoe on TV?"

"No."

"Well, you ought to see it. It's killing."

About 2 P.M., Elder Hinckley turned on the TV and witnessed a show where a couple married 29 years were swearing at each other. Another couple married 11 years were doing the same. Elder Hinckley thought, "What a travesty."

He thought of the statement of President Stephen L. Richards, "The answer to marital problems is not divorce but repentance."

He later said regarding this incident, "If people had a true understanding of who they are, these things would not happen."[32]

The same year in the Fall, Kathleen returned to Salt Lake and transferred her university studies to the University of Utah. She lived at East Mill Creek and became a mutual teacher (MIA teacher) for young women in the East Mill Creek LDS Ward.

The same year Richard entered the U of U and also began six years in the US Army Reserves. The uranium boom in Southern Utah ended in November of 1958 and the heretofore booming Moab area in the southeast corner of the state began to dry up and later experience a significant amount of cancer, felt in years to come to have precipitated from exposure to radioactive material.

Kathleen found her one and only and agreed to marriage in 1959. The lucky man was Nicholas Alan Barnes whom she married in the Salt Lake Temple for time and all eternity on November 13, 1959 after receiving her endowments on November 9. She and her husband stayed in the East Mill Creek Ward where Kathleen became primary president for five years while she ran an import and gift shop at 232 South Main Street in Salt Lake.

In April 1960, Elder Hinckley took his first trip to the Far East. He flew on one of the new four-engine 216 passenger Boeing 707's. John F. Kennedy was nominated in July by the Democratic Party to run for President of the United States and Richard M. Nixon by the Republican Party. Richard turned missionary age in 1960 also and put in his papers with his bishop for a mission call towards year's end. The call from the prophet David O. McKay came, personally signed. It read:

> "Dear Elder Hinckley:
>
> "You are hereby called to be a missionary of the Church of Jesus Christ of Latter-day Saints to labor in the Central German Mission.
>
> "Your presiding officers have recommended you as one worthy to represent the Church of our Lord as a Minister of the Gospel. It will be your duty to live righteously, to keep the commandments of the Lord, to honor the holy Priesthood which you bear, to increase your testimony of the divinity of the Restored Gospel of Jesus Christ, to be an exemplar in your life of all the Christian virtues, and so to conduct

yourself as a devoted servant of the Lord that you may be an effective advocate and messenger of the Truth. We repose in you our confidence and extend to you our prayers that the Lord will help you thus to meet your responsibilities.

"The Lord will reward the goodness of your life, and greater blessings and more happiness than you have yet experienced await you as you serve Him humbly and prayerfully in this labor of love among His children.

"We ask that you please send your written acceptance promptly, endorsed by your presiding officer in the ward or branch where you live.

Sincerely yours, David O. McKay, President"

Richard received his endowment on January 6, 1961 and went in the mission home for training. Before he came home two years later, he was to become assistant to the president like his father. Gordon and Marjorie became grandparents the same month, too, when on January 27 Kathleen and her husband Nicholas became the parents of a daughter they named Heather.

Bryant S. Hinckley, Elder Hinckley's father, was now almost 94. He had suffered a heart attack in 1957 and then a series of illnesses and hospitalizations. On June 5, 1961, he passed away after a disabling stroke. He had worked for President Heber J. Grant answering his correspondence, filling many of President Grant's speaking engagements and writing many periodical articles at his request. After President Grant's death, he had continued answering much of the First Presidency's mail under LDS prophet George Albert Smith's presidency and spoke a great deal until his heart attack.[33]

Elder Hinckley surely was proud of his noble father. When he passed away, Bryant Stringham Hinckley had an unbelievable number of books and articles published. He truly had endured in faithfulness to the end. His funeral was held on the 7th of June.[34] Almost at the same time, Kathleen graduated from the University of Utah with a degree in education and taught school for one year. Later she substitute taught in the Granite School District in Salt Lake for several years.

Four months later to the day from his father's passing, Elder Hinckley was called to the holy apostleship when a vacancy in the 12 man quorum was created by President David O. McKay's call of LDS apostle Hugh B. Brown as a third counselor in the First Presidency in June of that year.

Marjorie answered the phone this time on Saturday, September 30, 1961. It was President David O. McKay. Forty-five minutes later Gordon B. Hinckley was presented in LDS general conference for sustaining vote as a member of the Quorum of the Twelve Apostles of the LDS Church. He spoke of his grandfather Ira and his father Bryant with great affection indicating when he was extended the call to be a member of the 12 he was overwhelmed. Marjorie knew he was very humbled by it.[35]

He went home and knelt at his bed and cried and pled with his Father in Heaven to help him with this heavy burden. Immediately thereafter, Major Yuri Gagarin became the first man to ever fly in space when the Soviet Union successfully plummeted him in a space capsule on April 12 above the earth in the Vostok ("East") rocket.[36]

Family Life During the Apostleship

Malls came to Salt Lake City in 1962 and with the first in the Big Cottonwood area around 4800 South Highland Drive (1870 East), merchandising in the Salt Lake Valley was changed forever. Rather than having to go downtown now and search for a parking spot before going to the three major department stores, now shoppers could drive to the spacious free parking lots surrounding the large acreage of shops anchored by a ZCMI and Penney's on each end at the Cottonwood Mall. It was a revolutionary innovation for the Salt Lake Valley and for the State of Utah, too. With the opening, others started planning, too, for additional enclosed malls in satellite areas of the Valley but they were not to open for another eight to 10 years.

In the meantime, merchants in downtown Salt Lake could see the future. Malls would take away at least a part of their traditional business. New innovations and adjustments were inevitable. During this time, the Hinckleys' youngest child Cynthia Jane was baptized on March 30, 1962. John F. Kennedy was in his second year as president of the United States.

Even before Elder Hinckley had assumed his place in the Quorum of the Twelve LDS Apostles, his wife Marjorie had accompanied him on his assignments. She went with him whenever permitted and was by his side. This practice continued until and after Gordon B. Hinckley assumed the presidency of his church, great companionship.

Through their parents' travels and the tales their mother related to them of the places they had seen and the memories they had generated, all of the Hinckley children acquired a love of travel and a desire to meet new people. "It's in our blood," said Kathleen. "From Dad we got the sense . . . nothing was too big to tackle, no distance too far to go."[37] From Mom they were told every detail of experiences their parents partook around the world. Marjorie always wished the children could see the same places she had seen and meet the same men and women she was privileged to meet. Then they would know and love them the same way she and Elder Hinckley loved them.[38]

The great burden of the apostleship certainly was stressful on Gordon. He now was acquainted with jet lag and its product of instant languishness, at least until the body's brain clock adjusted to the new time zone. Papers seemed to pile up on his desk relentlessly, never ending, just like the compounding of interest, begging for attention. Humor and a happy outlook on life provided a scapegoat to routine and hobby hours at home remodeling the home, improving the yard and rapping the hammer in his work clothes gave him the refresh of spirit and mind he and all of us need.[39]

Nineteen sixty three came and with it graduation from Granite School District high school for Virginia. Richard's two and a half year mission also was over and he returned from Germany to studies at the University of Utah. Virginia also entered the U of U. Elder Hinckley, responsible now for LDS work in the Orient, was making frequent trips to Asia. At this time President John F. Kennedy was assassinated and his vice president Lyndon B. Johnson was sworn in as his replacement.

Clark, youngest son, graduated from Olympus High School in 1964, a member of the first graduating class of the new high school. In August, North Vietnam torpedo boats reportedly attacked U.S. destroyers in the Gulf of Tonkin and US President Johnson ordered retaliatory air strikes. On August 7, the US Congress passed a resolution authorizing the president to take necessary steps to "maintain peace."[40]

Clark entered Brigham Young University the same month of August 1964 for two years study of mathematics. Kathleen's husband Nicholas Alan Barnes became an executive for Quantas Airlines this year and the family moved to Hawaii where they became members of the LDS Kahala Ward with Kathleen soon being asked to serve in LDS relief society, Cub Scouting and MIA.

Richard graduated with a B.A. in economics from the University of Utah in 1965 and then worked the Summer in Alaska. In the Fall, he entered Stanford University in Palo Alto, California for a Masters in

Business Administration. Virginia also ended her sophomore year at the U and received her endowments on September 3 and was married a week later to James Richard McGhie Pearce in the Salt Lake Temple for time and all eternity on September 10, 1965.

Immediately, she and her husband went to Nebraska where her husband entered the University of Omaha Medical School for studies in internal medicine. They lived in Omaha where Virginia also continued her own college at the University of Omaha. US military in Vietnam had risen from 23,000 in June to 184,000 by the end of the year and Elder Hinckley was continuously visiting them on his frequent visits to Asia.

Clark received a call to serve an LDS Mission in Argentina in 1966 and during his two years proclaiming the LDS faith was transferred to the new Spain Mission among one of the first four missionaries to be sent there. He was their zone leader during the call.

Elder Hinckley occasionally went to his 12 inch square metal box sitting on the top of his desk at home and turned the six knobs and two dials on the shortwave band radio. He was excited to hear the broadcasts from ordinary people from all over the world.[41]

On May 11, 1967, Virginia Lee and Jim Pearce brought Elder and Sister Hinckley another grandchild. A daughter Rosemary was born in Omaha, Douglas County, Nebraska. The last of the Pearce's five daughters (including a set of twins) was born in Salt Lake City on September 7, 1975.

Richard also graduated from Stanford with his MBA degree in 1967 and went to work for Touche Ross, an accounting and management consulting firm. On July 28, 1967, he also married Jane Everett Freed, a temple marriage for time and all eternity. Clark returned from his successful mission in Argentina and Spain to studies at BYU this year and was admitted to the honors program of mathematics at the university. He also joined the US Army Reserves for a six year stint.

Virginia and her husband Jim returned to Salt Lake City in 1968 where Jim interned at the LDS Hospital while Virginia completed her studies and was awarded a degree from the U. Clark's graduation from the Y in Provo occurred in 1969 when he was granted a Bachelor of Science degree in mathematics. Richard began two retail merchandising outlets with his brother-in-law in California in 1969 and was called to be Elders Quorum President in his local LDS Studio City Ward.

Clark was accepted to Harvard for his MBA schooling in 1969. He also married Kathleen Hansen in the LDS temple for time and all eternity. Not long thereafter, Richard returned to Salt Lake City and began employment as the financial VP for the Dahnken merchandising chain.

The LDS University of Utah University Stake soon had him on their high council and later made him branch president (a smaller unit of members in the LDS Church not yet strong enough in numbers to have the full slate of programs found in LDS wards) of the U of U University 14th Branch organized for college students attending the U.

Tragedy struck the family of Elder Hinckley's youngest sister Sylvia on February 2, 1970 when she succumbed to cancer in Cedar City one month before turning 50.[42] She had been diagnosed over a decade before and seemed to have the same gene as her mother Ada which caused both to die at 50.

She left a husband and almost a dozen children, many of them still young. And to compound the tribulation, her husband passed away just a year later, leaving all of the children orphaned. Gordon and Marjorie attended both funerals in the small ranching town of Panaca, Nevada where the family made their agricultural living and spoke at both memorial services.

On March 15, 1970, Richard became a father with the birth of a daughter named Jennifer in Los Angeles, California. Clark then began work at the National City Bank in New York City in 1971 and was put into the LDS bishopric of the LDS Manhattan 2nd Ward. Clark graduated in the honors program at BYU and was accepted for graduate school at Harvard, Stanford, Michigan University and BYU. Marjorie Pay Hinckley kept busy in service as the co-director of the cancer drive in Salt Lake County. By June 1971, they gathered a record sum for such a drive in the entire United States![43]

Virginia and her husband Jim moved to New Haven, Connecticut in 1971, too, for Jim's residency. Virginia became a counselor in the local relief society of her LDS ward. Cynthia Jane was now through high school and entered BYU in the Fall of 1971.

After 1971, Clark came to Salt Lake City and sub-divided the old East Millcreek farm and engaged in other land development. He was also made Ensign Stake high councilor. Virginia returned to Salt Lake City in 1973 and her husband entered private internal medicine practice. They settled in the LDS Parley Ward where Virginia was made a relief society counselor. Then Virginia and Kathleen joined forces and co-authored five successful children's books.

Cynthia Jane graduated from high school in 1972.

Roger Davis Dudley was the lucky man to marry Cynthia Jane on June 10, 1975. About this time, Elder Hinckley and Marjorie moved into a condominium and Jane and her husband Roger moved into the family home at 3703 South 2700 East. "At last," Marjorie said, "brick walls Dad cannot knock out or change."[44] Gordon called it a "filing cabinet" where a man, woman and children were not meant to live all their days.[45]

Kathleen had her last of five children (four daughters and one son) on April 14, 1977 in Honolulu, Hawaii. Then she and her husband moved to Chicago in 1977 when her husband was made manager of Quantas Airlines for the Central States and Mexico. They moved to the North Shore LDS 1st Ward where she was installed as relief society president. The same year, Clark moved to Detroit as an associate at the Michigan National Bank.

In October 1978, Elder Hinckley took some of his grandchildren to the circus and had extreme pleasure in watching them.[46] By 1982, he had 21 grandchildren.[47] They were bright eyed, beautiful, smiling and touched the heart. And they all loved to call Marjorie their "groovy grandma."[48]

He was proud his daughters and daughters-in-law loved and honored their husbands and nurtured, trained and treasured their children. They had taught and directed them to the LDS church and with unselfishness had attended the temple. They loved life, faced challenges and adversities and drank deeply of life's enriching experiences with laughter and scintillating discussions.

In 1982, Elder and Sister Hinckley also attended the graduation at the University of Utah where he reflected it was his 50th anniversary from his graduation. He contemplated there were many in his graduation class who had become prominent men and women who have looked for the positive in life through prayer, faith, work and diligence.[49]

Lois Anderson Hinckley, the fourth wife of Gordon's father Bryant, passed away May 7, 1983 at age 93. She had married Bryant S. Hinckley on June 20, 1944 after Bryant's third wife had passed away in 1943.[50] Her memorial service was held in the East Mill Creek Stake 12th Ward.

Family Trip to the Orient

As Elder and Sister Hinckley's 50th wedding anniversary approached, Gordon asked Marjorie where she would like to go or what remembrance she would like. She said, "I would like to go with our children to the places I have desired so long to show them."

Arrangements were made and in 1987, their children saved up for a trip to Hong Kong. They had always desired to see the places their parents had told them about. Elder Hinckley had official assignments there so the children met their parents in Hong Kong. When Kathy stepped onto the streets, it seemed like she was coming home. Virginia remembers they followed their dad's style. They acted themselves and did not appear to be more than they were.[51]

After tiring meetings and dinner, Marjorie would slip away quietly and see if the children were ok. Memories were created, interaction accomplished and dreams fulfilled.

As was almost always the case, Gordon's birthdays were usually observed with work and assignments. His 77th birthday on June 23, 1987 was no exception. He attended a Mission President's Seminar at the LDS Missionary Training Center in Provo, Utah and then had dinner with his family.[52]

The next year, Virginia was honored to be chosen a member of the LDS General Board of the YWMIA, the corresponding body for women Gordon's own father had served on for 25 years.[53] Then two years later and on President Hinckley's 80th birthday, oldest son Richard had the honor of becoming the 4th Hinckley in succession to become a stake president.[54]

As great-grandparents, President and Sister Hinckley sat at their dinner table in early 1992 and looked into each other's eyes. Each saw wrinkles and white hairs in the object of their affection for almost 53 years. But to Gordon, Marjorie was no less beautiful than when they married in 1937. In fact she was more so beautiful with wrinkles with her inherent strength, integrity and love.[55] Just a few months thereafter, their daughter Virginia was made first counselor in the YWMIA General Board of the LDS Church on April 4, 1992.[56]

For President Hinckley's 82nd birthday, 25 of his family members met for a barbecue on the back lawn of the family home now occupied by his daughter Jane Hinckley Dudley. The orchard trees were still to the south of the home together with a garden. Prunes and additional new trees had been planted. It was also a welcome home party for

President and Sister Hinckley's grandson Jeff Barnes, just returned from an LDS mission to the newly opened mission in Poland.[57]

When President and Sister Hinckley were on their way to England, they stopped in Detroit and visited with some of the Barnes grandchildren as well as spending 1½ hours with the daughter of a nephew.[58] And after President Hinckley assumed full presidency of the LDS Church in March 1995, Carol Hinckley Cannon, fifth child and third daughter of the first wife Christine Johnson of President Hinckley's father, died August 27, 1995 at the age of 93.

Such is only a sample of the rich and varied family life of the LDS prophet Gordon B. Hinckley. Though away from the family for extended periods from the very beginning, still great fruits have been poured out upon President Hinckley and his wife Marjorie. As a fitting closing to this chapter, Marjorie has said, "A father's activity in the Church is nothing but a blessing to his children."[59]

TEMPLES

Little did Gordon B. Hinckley know at the time his parents first imparted their knowledge and faith regarding LDS temples to their children that he would some day dedicate or rededicate more temples in the latter-day dispensation than any other single person in history. But the sacredness of these special shrines called the House of the Lord burned deep in his soul from an early age.

When he was called on his mission at age 23 to Great Britain, he entered the Salt Lake Temple for his own endowments. At an earlier age, he had the opportunity to visit the same temple, go to the special baptismal font located in its basement, and with others 8 years of age or older (now 12), perform baptisms for the dead. He saw the golden colored oxen, 12 in number representing the 12 tribes of Israel, bearing up the large basin of water where the holy ordinance was performed.

Following return from his mission and employ for the LDS Church as executive secretary for the Radio, Publicity and Mission Literature Committee, he had opportunity as a regular temple recommend holder to attend any LDS temple as frequently as circumstances allowed to perform additional endowments for deceased ancestors.

A vital belief of the Latter-day Saints is they cannot be saved without their dead receiving the same saving ordinances of baptism along with the endowment and sealing of families together for time and all eternity. These are considered temporal ordinances which must be performed for everyone who has lived on this earth for the atonement of Jesus Christ to be efficacious in their lives, but millions and billions of ancestors have lived on this earth without the opportunity to even hear of Jesus Christ, let alone be baptized by someone holding the authority of the priesthood received from Jesus Christ.

Then in 1937, Brother Hinckley was privileged to go to the temple and be sealed to his wife Marjorie Pay.

Such were the experiences of Gordon B. Hinckley with LDS temples for the first 27 years of his life. At the time he was married, there were a total seven operating LDS temples in the entire world, four of them located in Utah. One was in Canada, one in Hawaii and the other in Mesa, Arizona. So temple building for the Latter-day Saints was still in its babyhood. From 1927 to 1945, a period of 18 years, no other temples were constructed by the Church of Jesus Christ of Latter-day Saints until a House of the Lord in Idaho Falls, Idaho was dedicated the month World War II was over.

The Swiss Temple

Seven years after the war ended, LDS prophet David O. McKay travelled to Europe for six weeks visiting Holland, Denmark, Sweden, Norway, Finland, Germany, Switzerland, Wales, Scotland and France, and while in Europe announced in June 1952 the selection of a site in Berne, Switzerland where a temple would be built, the first LDS temple on the European Continent.[1] A year later, President McKay travelled to Switzerland again and broke ground for construction of the Berne temple. Five days later, he selected a site outside London for an additional temple.

It was at this time that Gordon, then working as executive secretary for the Missionary Committee of the LDS Church with the sub-committee of Radio, Publicity and Mission Literature now under Missionary Committee jurisdiction, was called into President McKay's office. The prophet told Brother Hinckley a temple in Berne, Switzerland was to be built but would be different from any other temple to date. It would serve many people on the European Continent from different nations speaking different native languages.

President McKay said, "I would like you to find a way to present the temple ceremonies in various languages without multiplying the number of temple workers.[23]

"You will work under the direction of Joseph Fielding Smith and Richard L. Evans."[4]

Brother Hinckley, from that time on, was not only a regular patron attending the temple to perform ordinances for deceased ancestors, he was an innovator who took temple building in the LDS faith in a new direction.

From his experience with the mass media, he could see the opportunity to use the rapidly developing technology of film and recorded sound to aid in making the Swiss Temple truly a temple for all nations. Conceptionalization, production and directing once again came to play in planning an audio/visual presentation taking the place of live display of the knowledge imparted during the endowment.

Also enlisted were translators who could literally "transfer" the words of the temple ordinances into their native tongues. The German language, the French language, the Swiss language, Dutch, Spanish, all received attention. This was truly going to be the temples of all temples for God's children. This work led to the preparation of the temple ceremony in 14 languages.

As the tall spire in the front of the temple in Switzerland started to rise from a rectangular shaped concrete structure covered with creamish gray terra cotta, Gordon worked on developing the films in several languages which would transform the temple ceremonies into numerous different tongues for the first time in LDS Church history. At the same time, he was heavily involved in supervising the translation of the Book of Mormon, other Standard Works and LDS literature into numerous foreign tongues, many for the first time. So his resources were nicely in place. But there were many details and much unforeseen matters to attend before such a new modernization became reality.

Then the installation supervision began with trips to the site. Installing of modern up-to-date speaker systems, projector and other equipment was a novel thing in temples. While working there prior to the dedication, Brother Hinckley came down with a heavy cold. The cold turned to pneumonia about the time of the openhouse and dedication dates in September 1954. President David O. McKay came for the dedication and "was so solicitous for my welfare. He was the epitome of kindness and concern."[5] Gordon gradually recovered.

In between January and February 1955, President David O. McKay had selected a site for another temple in New Zealand while on a 45,000 mile tour of the LDS missions in the South Pacific. And a few days before the openhouse to the Swiss Temple began, President McKay dedicated the site for the London Temple in Newchapel, Surrey County, England and broke ground for its construction August 27, 1955.

Brother Hinckley was 45 years old when he witnessed his first temple dedication.[6] The proceedings of the event were great schoolteachers to him, setting the way in which he himself would direct the dedication of numerous Houses of the Lord in future years. The finished temple was first opened to the public for viewing. Any responsible person was allowed to enter and view the various rooms and interior and many came.

The temple was located in a beautiful open space surrounded by green lawns and wooded areas. It was of modern-contemporary design while still maintaining a semblance to its earlier predecessors. Square footage was 34,750 square feet broken into three floors of 82 rooms.

The Tabernacle Choir made a significant tour of Europe at the time.[7] Europe, recovering from the despoil of all out war, took a fresh new look at the church which had started in America and brought back the Christian religion as it existed nearly 2,000 years before. The establishment of a permanent temple on European soil with its benefits available to peoples in their 14 diverse languages was the establishment of the Church of Jesus Christ of Latter-day Saints' "beachhead" of new understanding and respect in the Old World.

Despite his sickness, Brother Hinckley still participated in the dedication services where President David O. McKay offered the first prayer of dedication on September 11, 1955. Gordon sensed the majesty and marveled at the destiny of "this great kingdom" as he shook hands with men and women from Finland, Sweden, Norway, Denmark, Britain, Belgium, France, Germany, Switzerland and Austria.[8]

Los Angeles Temple

The next temple reaching completion was the Los Angeles LDS Temple dedicated March 11, 1956. It was a mammoth temple located on property in Santa Monica, California just west of the famous beach and downtown area and right on the famous Santa Monica Boulevard. The property was a knoll rising above the boulevard which formerly belonged to 1920's Hollywood movie maker Harold Lloyd.[9]

Brother Hinckley and wife Marjorie paid as much attention to installation of its media innovations as they had done with the temple in Switzerland. In contrast with the modest 35,000 square feet of the Swiss Temple, this LDS edifice contained 146,000 square feet. Its endowment rooms were as large as some LDS chapels and its steeple topped by a golden Angel Moroni statue still is a major landmark in the Los Angeles area. Twenty three acres of lawns, palm trees and other fountains and shrubs surrounded the temple.

A Lesson in Spirituality in Berne

Brother Hinckley went back to Berne Switzerland for the temple's first anniversary check-up in December 1956. He arrived at the railroad station in Berne at 11 A.M. Just as he exited, bells began to ring from the many Christian chapels in the ancient city. As he stepped out onto the street, every auto, bus, railroad train, and other vehicle stopped. It became deathly still. Gordon was in awe. What was happening, this spontaneous unity of humanity in this picturesque Swiss city?

The "cavernous" railroad station seemed like a cathedral. Brother Hinckley next looked across the plaza from the station. Men situate on construction scaffolding for a new multi-story building stood still with bare heads. Bicycles stopped. Every man and woman and child dismounted and stood with heads bowed and bare.

The stillness continued for three minutes. It seemed like eternity. Then the populace began to move again. Brother Hinckley asked the purpose of this most impressive display of humble unified silence.

"We are sending trucks to Hungary today for the brave Hungarian people. Russian soldiers have been slaughtering them in Budapest with machine guns."

Switzerland, long standing nation of "peace", opened their arms and hearts once more to the downtrodden. Their borders opened to refugees from Hungary being oppressed by communist iron fists. The convoys began to cross through Austria on their way to Hungary that day. From Berne, Basel and Zurich they also departed.[10] Brother Hinckley thought as he experienced this extraordinary event, "What a contrast—communism and Christianity." From that experience, Gordon brought back with him a pack of Edelweiss seed which he kept ever since to remind him of that special event on the streets of Berne in 1956.[11]

New Zealand Temple Dedication

The next temple to be completed was the temple in New Zealand, another first for the LDS Church. It was officially dedicated by LDS prophet David O. McKay on April 20, 1958. Gordon and wife Marjorie were there, the inseparable couple, at the openhouse and before fixing the temple for use by 11 different Polynesian languages. New Zealand, land of the steel-cliffed snow-capped peaks, land of the Maori people and Australian immigrants, land of extreme beauty and decided contrast.

The Hinckleys shook hands with the Pakehas, Maori, Australia, Tasmania, Tonga, Samoa, Rarotonga, Fiji, Tahiti, and Hawaiian people.[12] They came from everywhere in a great expression of yearning for the place where they could go and be sealed as eternal families and learn more about their Father in Heaven.

One family traveled the entire width of Australia, then crossed the Tasman Sea to Auckland, then traveled to the temple. They first thought they could not pay for such a trip but the father looked at his wife and children and determined they were more precious than car, and furniture and dishes. Such things could be earned again but to be sealed together as an eternal family would happen only once. So they came.[13]

Another family from Tonga spent all of their money for a plane ride to New Zealand after boating from Tonga to Fiji. Though cold at night, they stayed in tents. Gordon went in the evening during the temple openhouse and visited them. He saw them cold and shivering but very faithful indeed.[14]

Another little widow came to the temple with 17 children. She knelt at the altar and wept. Her husband had died plus a number of her children. But all that were there wept. The breadth, depth and devotion of the members was overwhelming. David O. McKay had visited Polynesia as an LDS apostle in 1921. When an elderly man and woman saw him again, they broke into tears of happiness.[15] Brother Hinckley was amazed at the inspiration of President McKay as he directed sessions of the dedication in 11 different languages. Many were the inspiring experiences during the dedication.

London Temple Dedication

Immediately after the New Zealand Temple was dedicated, Gordon labored the same way to prepare the London Temple for language diversity. The dedication took place September 7, 1958 and was once again presided over by David O. McKay. The saga of faithful members was the same this time, too. Gordon was so pleased a temple was being finished in the land and city where he had labored so hard in 1933-1935. It was exciting to him.

Some LDS saints residing in South Africa did without necessities in order to travel 7,000 miles from the southern tip of their continent to the temple dedication and saving ordinances they believed were there.[16] Thousands of the curious stood in long lines for the pre-dedicatory openhouses. Eventually 76,000 non-LDS attended the open houses. One policeman said, This is the first time I have ever seen English so eager to get into any church."

Everyone asked varied questions and after the complete tours those with additional questions met with missionaries in the evenings to talk. Brother Hinckley stood with the missionaries in the evenings.

One couple came to the front steps of the temple. Brother Hinckley volunteered, "May I help you in any way?"

"Yes, what about this 'marriage for eternity' to which reference was made in one of the rooms?"

The three sat on a bench below an ancient oak tree near the temple gate. A wedding band was on the young lady's finger and the couple tightly squeezed each other's hands.

"Now to your question," Brother Hinckley said. "I suppose you were married by the vicar."

"Yes, just three months ago."

"Did you realize that when the vicar pronounced your marriage he also decreed your separation?"

"What do you mean?"

"You believe that life is eternal, don't you?"

"Of course."

"Can you conceive of eternal life without eternal love? Can either of you envision eternal happiness without the companionship of one another?"

"Of course not."

"But what did the vicar say when he pronounced your marriage? If I remember the language correctly, he said, among other things, 'in sickness and in health, for richer or for poorer, for better or for worse, till death do ye part.' He went as far as he felt his authority would permit him and that was till death separates you. In fact, I think that if you were to question him, he would emphatically deny the existence of marriage and family beyond the grave."

"But," Brother Hinckley continued, "the Father of us all, who loves his children and wants the best for them, has provided for a continuation under proper circumstances, of this most sacred and ennobling of all human relationships, the relationships of marriage and family.

"In that great and moving conversation between the Savior and his apostles, wherein Peter declared, 'Thou art the Christ, the Son of the living God,' the Lord responded, 'Blessed art thou, Simon Barjona: for flesh and blood hath not revealed it unto thee, but my Father which is in heaven.' The Lord then went on to say to Peter and his associates, 'And I will give unto thee the keys of the kingdom of heaven: and whatsoever thou shalt bind on earth shall be bound in heaven: and whatsoever thou shalt loose on earth shall be loosed in heaven.' [Matthew 16:13-10]

"In that marvelous bestowal of authority the Lord gave to his apostles the keys of the holy priesthood, whose power reaches beyond life and death into eternity. This same authority has been restored to the earth by those same apostles who held it anciently, even Peter, James, and John.

"Following the dedication of the temple on the following Sunday, those same keys of the holy priesthood will be exercised in behalf of the men and women who come into this sacred house to solemnize their marriage. They will be joined in a union which death cannot dissolve and time cannot destroy."[17]

The young newlywed bride was surprised and interested in the truths expressed.[18]

To others it was explained these same ordinances available to the living are also available to ancestors who have lived before us on this world. Though they were not privileged to live when such sealing power was on the earth or unable to receive the sealing ordinances during their mortal lives, relatives and posterity could perform them on their behalf by standing in as proxy for them just as the Savior of all Mankind stood in the place of all humanity before the Father as the greatest proxy since the world began and atoned for our sins.

In contrast, Brother Hinckley later met a man who smugly said, "I am saved."

"What about your father?"

"I guess he isn't saved."

"Can you believe that in the justice and mercy of God he would make it possible for you to enjoy all the blessings which you claim you have and deny those same blessings to your father and your mother, who gave you all that you have of life and body and mind?"

To Brother Hinckley, it was "one of the serious anomalies" of life that the "great religious systems of the world, which teach equity and justice and mercy and kindness, have in their theology nothing of this great principle" of "universal salvation and exaltation."[19]

Some people from all of the nations of Finland, Sweden, Norway, Denmark, Belgium, Holland, Germany, Austria, France, England and South Africa were at the dedication. They looked pure, noble and virtuous. Soon to be "Elder" Hinckley reflected when he met and saw them, "We see the miracles of the work through the everyday lives of its disciples."[20]

Brother Hinckley witnessed David O. McKay's news conferences with newspaper and TV reporters and heard him testify to them. President McKay's counsel was inspiring.

When the time came for the dedication prayers, Brother Hinckley was moved by the solemn and beautiful and moving prayers of the several sessions–not just one session. Numerous sessions were held repeating the dedication prayer as during the previous dedications in Berne, Los Angeles and New Zealand accommodating all those who desired to participate in the dedications.[21]

Following the dedication of the London Temple, Brother and Sister Hinckley went to Preston, County Lancashire, where he first labored as a missionary 25 years before. He met the saints and saw the clearness, the light in their eyes, the indefinable something that came from the restored gospel.

In contrast, he looked into the faces of the people of Lancashire who had not the gospel in their hearts. He felt sorry for them. The majority of their forebears rejected the gospel 121 years before. He felt sorry they rejected the glad tidings when he was there 25 years ago and was sorry they were rejecting it now.[22] Little did he realize that in little over 35 years later he would come to that same community and dedicate ground for a future LDS temple in Preston.

It was now almost six months since Gordon had become a general authority for the LDS Church when he returned to Salt Lake City from the London Temple dedication.

Japanese Saints Visit to Hawaiian Temple

It was seven years later before the first group of the then 10,000 LDS members in Japan went to the nearest temple in Hawaii. Elder Hinckley mingled with the group of 165 saints on this historic occasion. As supervisor over the Far East at the time, Elder Hinckley had the privilege of seeing the preparations of several years reach fruition. Fund raising had been the focus of attention for some time. A Japanese Saints Choir recorded a record for sale and small pearl tie pins had been sold. The temple ceremonies had been translated by Tatsui Sato who had also re-translated the Book of Mormon in Japanese when LDS missionary work resumed in Japan following World War II. Some LDS faithful still went without necessities to afford the trip.

Sealing of the Soldier Serving in Vietnam

As a general authority for the LDS religion, Elder Hinckley was given the sealing power from the LDS prophet, the custodian in whom this sealing power resided. With this power, he was authorized to perform eternal marriage sealings for time and all eternity in Houses of the Lord. He also was by 1967 visiting the LDS servicemen in Vietnam on a regular basis. One handsome US air force officer, a jet fighter pilot, and his wife came to him. They had joined the LDS Church a little over a year before in the Southern States. Now he was to go to Vietnam.

The future was uncertain for them but this family with their children asked to be sealed in the temple. Elder Hinckley performed the sealing. It was a sanguine experience as the husband and wife knelt across the altar of the temple and joined hands and by the authority of the restored Melchizedek Priesthood were sealed. Then the children joined around the altar and each placed their hands on their parents' hands and were sealed to their parents as their children for time and all eternity.

Husband and wife and children all embraced after the ceremonies and then the mother looked into the eyes of her husband and said, "Come what may now, dear, you are ours and we are yours, forever."[23]

Increased Temple Building

The momentum of LDS temple building continued next with completion of a beautiful and large temple on the hills east of Oakland, California on November 17, 1964. Elder Hinckley and his wife Marjorie were present in between trips to the Orient.

Then another temple was completed in Ogden, third largest city in Utah, located about 23 miles north of Salt Lake City. Joseph Fielding Smith had assumed the presidency of the LDS Church by this time after David O. McKay's passing and offered the dedicatory prayer on January 18, 1972. Then a temple almost identical to Ogden's was dedicated on February 9, 1972 in Provo, Utah. "We look forward to the day, O Our God, when Thou wilt reveal unto Thy servants where other temples shall be built in all the nations where Thy saints increase in numbers and serve Thee in righteousness," the dedicatory prayer said in part.[24]

Washington, D.C. Temple

Elder Gordon B. Hinckley assumed the chairmanship of the LDS Temple Committee in October 1972 and served in that capacity until May 1976. This responsibility gave supervision to all of the temples of the LDS Church worldwide. O. Leslie Stone was executive secretary.

At the time, another majestic temple was being completed in Bethesda, Maryland at a point where the completed interstate beltway surrounding Washington, D.C. made a sharp bend to the left as it swerved north.

The temple was placed in a wooded glen just in front of the path of the beltway in an ideal location. When you came around another bend in the freeway further west, immediately the six majestic spires of the edifice burst into your view and then you drove directly towards the temple until just before it you once again turned to the left driving by its spires nestled in surrounding treetops. In daytime it was magnificent. At night when illuminated, the spires representing the Melchizedek and Aaronic Priesthood sliced into the night sky creating a breathtaking experience. If you looked at the temple, you couldn't help but receive a big boost in spirit no matter how depressed you might have been. The tallest spire in the center facing east was 288 feet high with the familiar golden leafed heavenly messenger Moroni on its top.

Being the master public relations man he is, Elder Hinckley was not about to let this opportunity pass without utilizing it for all it was worth. As Temple Committee Chairman, he made sure Wendell J. Ashton, director of the new LDS Public Communications Department, planned everything he possibly could to bring the temple to the attention of the leaders of government, domestic and international, and all of the citizens in the surrounding area of Washington.

In August 1974, Elder Hinckley completed a detailed article published in the LDS official magazine *The Improvement Era* entitled "Why These Temples?"[25] Therein was depicted the sacred and selfless service performed in the LDS shrines called Houses of the Lord.

Then the activities of over two months culminating in dedication of the new Washington Temple began. The temple was completed on September 9, 1974 after expenditure of $15,000,000. The site had been selected by David O. McKay in 1952 and construction had begun on January 18, 1969. Spencer W. Kimball had assumed the position as 12th LDS prophet after a brief 1½ year administration of 11th LDS prophet Harold B. Lee.

Around 2,000 college students from the East Coast universities and colleges were the first to visit the almost completed temple on August 18. Then a cornerstone ceremony was arranged for 300 specially invited guests and the press. A local choir sang and the visiting prophet, his counselor and Elder Hinckley each explained one facet of temples and LDS doctrine.

Elder Hinckley said in part, "Temples stand as a living witness of our conviction that life is eternal. As we live here so shall we live after we leave here." He also gave the closing prayer at the ceremony held September 9, 1974. He also helped President Spencer W. Kimball and his counselor Marion G. Romney apply mortar around the cornerstone.[26]

Following the cornerstone ceremony, the largest press conference ever held by the LDS Church convened in the "Bridge", a room connecting the main body of the temple with an annex building. Statements were made and then questions answered by the LDS prophet Spencer W. Kimball as well as all LDS church leaders present.

On September 12, 1974 through the auspices of eight LDS US representatives, Elder Gordon B. Hinckley went to the US Capitol Building. He walked through the halls where the prophet Joseph Smith, Jr. possibly walked in the late part of 1839 when visiting Congress for redress of persecution of the saints in Missouri. As he was guided into the chambers of the US House of Representatives, Speaker Carl Albert, of Oklahoma, introduced him as an LDS apostle here to participate in the finishing of the LDS Church's new temple in Bethesda. Elder Hinckley was then asked to offer the prayer for the afternoon session.

"Our beloved Father in Heaven, we praise Thy holy name.

"We thank Thee for the beauties of this good land, for the inspired Constitution under which we are governed, for the servants of the people, these Representatives, who here meet to consider and legislate.

"Please, Father, give them understanding. Give them inspiration that they may be prompted in all they do by principles of mercy, equity, and justice.

"May they have in mind always the preservation and the enhancement of the freedom and the prosperity of the people. May they look to Thee as the source of all true wisdom, that through them all of the Nation, and even the entire world, may be blessed, we humbly pray in the name of Jesus Christ. Amen."

Then Congressmen Wayne Owens and Gunn McKay, both representatives from Utah, invited all the United States Representatives to visit the open house for the temple. President Spencer W. Kimball had visited the US Senate Wednesday, the day before, and offered the opening prayer there.[27]

For the rest of the week, Elder Hinckley served as one of the hosts to over 100 US congressional leaders, the president's wife, supreme court justices, senators, ambassadors, clergy, educators, and business executives. The First Lady had her picture taken with President Spencer W. Kimball.[28] Said Mrs. Gerald Ford, "This is truly a great experience for me. It's an inspiration to all." One leader of the Nation looked up at the spires of the temple in the evening and said, "This beautiful structure is a symbol of those virtues which have made up a great nation and a great people. We need such symbols."[29]

The LDS Tabernacle Choir arrived on two charter planes Friday, September 13 and the next evening on Saturday performed for the President of the United States Gerald R. Ford and his wife in the Kennedy Center in downtown Washington, D.C. LDS prophet Kimball and his wife were invited to sit in the presidential box .[30]

Nothing was spared to make the dedication of the Washington Temple the biggest event ever for the LDS Church in the Nation's Capitol since Joseph Smith, Jr. had preached there in late 1839.

Next open houses began for six weeks during which 300,000 visitors toured the inside and outside of the new temple. On November 19, 1974, the temple was dedicated by President Spencer W. Kimball.

President Kimball said a very significant thing during the September 9 cornerstone ceremony: "The pace of constructing new temples will accelerate in the future. We are a temple building people. We believe in eternity; we believe in permanence. When we build a temple we build it forever; when we perform temple ordinances we perform them forever."[31] Indeed, President Kimball would start many temples which Elder Hinckley would dedicate beginning 1983.

Elder Hinckley returned to Washington, D.C. for the final two days of ceremonies and spoke of the temple ordinances, praised the builders, and indicated this was the 8th temple dedicated in which he had participated. "God lives and we are all His children," he said.[32]

Constantly on his mind during the temple dedication was the early days of the LDS religion when the believers could obtain no respect from the government and the present where respect and confidence had changed in the LDS Church's favor.[33]

Arizona Temple Rededication

On March 17, 1975, Elder Hinckley was in Mesa, Arizona assisting with the rededication of the Arizona Temple. Three Million Dollars had been used to renovate and enlarge the temple. Elder Hinckley spoke five times to groups of over 100 each. He saw more clergymen than ever and was receptive to their questions.

A Protestant minister asked Elder Hinckley, "I have been all through this building, this temple which carries on its face the name of Jesus Christ. But nowhere have I seen any representation of the cross, the symbol of Christianity. I have noted your buildings elsewhere and likewise find an absence of the cross. Why is this, when you say that you believe in Jesus Christ?"

"I do not wish to give offence to any of my Christian brethren who use the cross on the steeples of their cathedrals and at the altars of their chapels, who wear it on their vestments and imprint it in their books and other literature," Elder Hinckley answered. "But for us, the cross is the symbol of the dying Christ, while our message is a declaration of the living Christ."

"If you do not use the cross, what is the symbol of your religion?" the minister said.

"The lives of our people must become the only meaningful expression of our faith and in fact, therefore the symbol of our worship," Elder Hinckley replied.[34]

There were 200 media representatives at the temple prior to its rededication. To them he said in part, "Temples supply the ordinance of eternal marriage which cement the family relationship throughout eternity."

He then emphasized that this was an ennobling concept creating better husbands, better wives, better neighbors and better citizens where women play a key part. He then introduced the Relief Society and Young Women and Primary Association organizations to those listening.[35]

At the dedication, Elder Hinckley spoke with four other LDS apostles present and then the temple rededicatory prayer was offered by Spencer W. Kimball after choir members who had sung at the first dedication in October 1927 sang.[36]

A couple, Peter & Nancy Blaine, were baptized through going to the open house the first day where they listened to Elder Hinckley speak at a nearby stake center.[37]

The Tokyo Temple

Announcement of building of the Tokyo Temple, first LDS temple in Asia, was made in the *Japan Times* on August 10, 1975. There were 64,000 LDS members in Asia at the time and 25,000 in Japan. It was to be the 18th operating temple of the LDS faith and was expected to take 18 months to construct. But when building started in the first half of 1976, it actually took until 1980 to complete even though the smallest temple built to that date.[38] It contained 18,000 square feet of space and took the place of the previous LDS mission home which had stood there since 1948.

But before that temple was completed, Elder Hinckley was found at the LDS St. George Temple located in the little community in the

counselor Nathan Eldon Tanner had given brief remarks on October 14, 1975 and then took the Governor of Nevada on a tour of the renovated building leaving Elder Hinckley to answer further newsmen questions.

Elder Hinckley explained that the renovation would double the work capacity of the first temple completed by the early pioneers in 1877. Electrical wiring and plumbing had been raised to modern standards and the entire temple refurbished from wear. Murals which had originally adorned the walls of several of the rooms had been removed for use elsewhere.[39] He also indicated the Hawaiian Temple, the Manti and the Logan temples were scheduled for similar renovation.

The rededication of the Logan LDS Temple took place on March 13, 1979 and Elder Hinckley was there. There were 1,258 in the priesthood room of the temple and 450 in other rooms. Seventeen hundred others were listening on remote TV sets in the Logan Tabernacle and 350 in the Logan LDS 18th Ward Chapel. In the priesthood room, Gordon B. Hinckley sat with the LDS First Presidency and seven other general authorities on the Melchizedek Priesthood side of the hall on tiers or levels. Elder Hinckley's childhood friend G. Homer Durham was also present.

Elder Hinckley spoke of the unselfish nature of temple service quoting from a March 26, 1907 proclamation of the First Presidency which stated "Our purposes are not petty or earthbound."[40]

Back in Tokyo

The temple in Tokyo finally reached completion and Dwayne Nelson Andersen and his wife Peggy Jean Huish Andersen were called to be its first temple president and matron. They had served as mission president and mission mother over the Northern Far East Mission from 1962-1965 when the mission home sat on the spot of the new temple.[41]

The temple resembled the architectural design of the Ogden and Provo Temples and was located in the exclusive district of Hiroo surrounded by numerous embassies and across the street from the Arisugawa Park. At the dedication by President Spencer W. Kimball on October 27, 1980, Marjorie P. Hinckley wept for joy. She felt the veil was very thing. It was a very spiritual experience to her.[42]

Jordan River

The Salt Lake Valley had a Jordan River just as the Holy Land. It was the small narrow stream which leisurely meandered from the Provo Lake north past the Point of the Mountain, demarkation point between the end of Utah Valley and beginning of Salt Lake Valley, flowing through the Salt Lake Valley and ending up as a tributary to the Great Salt Lake. At a point about one-third the way north into the Valley, a site had been selected for the second temple in the Salt Lake Valley and because it was located close to the river called Jordan, it was called the Jordan River Temple.

Sessions for the dedication began with a cornerstone laying on August 15, 1981 and Gordon B. Hinckley was there, this time in his new capacity as a third counselor to ailing LDS President Spencer W. Kimball. Twelve thousand attended.

"The Jordan River Temple is a testimony to all who see it of the faith of the LDS in the immortality of the soul. Every purpose for which it is built is an affirmation of our conviction that life continues after death for all of our Father's children. If there is no faith in eternal life, there is no need for temples." he said.[43]

He then praised the members for paying for the temple, for the faith displayed through their deeds and for the testimony displayed through their sacrifice. Open houses continued through Tuesday, August 31 and a dedication held November 16 with additional dedicatory sessions through November 20.[44]

Groundbreakings

In February 1982, President Hinckley wrote in his First Presidency message in the *Ensign* magazine that he has regularly contemplated the millions who serve in the temples as proxies. He marvels and gives thanks God has provided a way for all and a faith generated by the "selfless service" presented in LDS temples.[45]

The next month President Hinckley announced a temple would be built in Guayaquil, Ecuador and on August 25, 1982 was in Manila, Philippines breaking ground for a temple. Despite a typhoon threat, 2,000 attended. The next day he was in Taiwan breaking ground for a temple in Taipei and on the 29th in Tokyo installing President and Sister Adney Y. and Judy N. Komatsu as second temple president and matron of the Tokyo Temple.[46] Gordon B. Hinckley's extraordinary implementation of temple building had begun.

The next January 1983, Gordon could be seen at Dallas, Texas as the key speaker on a chilly day breaking ground for a temple in that city. In fact there was a slight snow falling in the evening before he spoke to 90 LDS regional representatives and stake presidents.[47]

His prayer of dedication contained a plea that the animosity experienced by the cold attitude in the community would soften. "Cultivate the habit of a generous heart," he said.[48]

Dedications and Dedications and Dedications

Then began the unprecedented saga where President Gordon B. Hinckley began dedicating 22 new temples and four rededicated temples *before* he was even set apart as 15th prophet of the Church of Jesus Christ of Latter-day Saints.

The first began in Atlanta, Georgia where on June 1, 1983, due to LDS prophet Spencer W. Kimball's poor health and the equally ill health of his first counselor Marion G. Romney, now second counselor Gordon B. Hinckley was left in the First Presidency to perform the dedication. It was raining during the cornerstone laying. President Hinckley presided over 11 dedicatory sessions speaking at the first and five more and personally gave six of the 11 prayers[49]

Two months later President Hinckley was in Apia, Samoa for his second temple dedication. Six thousand six hundred were present on August 7, 1983. President and Sister Hinckley had arrived on the 4th of August to a traditional Samoan welcome.

The entourage immediately flew to Tonga where King Taufa'Ahau Tupona IV greeted the group. Elder Groberg of the 70 and his wife together with D. Arthur Haycock, all participated in the cornerstone laying of August 9 and the first dedicatory service of the Tonga LDS Temple. Dedicatory services continued until August 11.

Two days later, on August 13, 1983, President Hinckley was in Chicago breaking ground for a temple there. The groundbreaking had been delayed due to local resident opposition to the location. President Hinckley presided and told the group, "We promise that what we do here will enhance rather than diminish the charm of this lovely area.[50]

One month later, President Hinckley was in Santiago, Chili dedicating the temple there. Members quiet and subdued came fasting and praying to the dedication. President Hinckley exclaimed regarding the ill prophet Spencer W. Kimball, "I have felt a terrible loneliness in his absence," but he carried on. At 4 P.M. the temple was dedicated after a cornerstone ceremony.

A gathering of 3,600 witnessed the proceedings. The Hinckleys' plane was delayed by fog and arrived Thursday morning, the day of the dedication. But his own fatigue did not seem to be on his mind. As he began 10 dedicatory sessions held 15, 16 and 17 September, he also said, "I feel deeply touched as I reflect on President Kimball's condition."[51]

The dedication was a sensitive, touching moment. Members frequently shed tears and lines an hour long waited for the second LDS temple in South America to be dedicated. Brazil had been the first South American nation to receive a temple and a temple in Peru was under construction.

The Hinckleys flew back from Chile all night. President Hinckley had given 15 speeches in the last 10 days with no speech writer. He had been almost constantly involved in spiritual services. His voice was weak and subdued but he still delivered the 16th speech the next day. September 19, at a BYU Devotional before thousands of students in Provo, Utah.[52]

It was next back to Polynesia where the Papeete, Tahiti Temple was now ready for dedication. On October 27, 1983 this temple was dedicated by President Gordon B. Hinckley. Immediately, travel was taken to Mexico City, Mexico. Here LDS apostle Boyd K. Packer had broken ground for a temple on November 25, 1979.

The beautiful temple designed in harmony with the ancient culture of the Americas, was dedicated by President Hinckley on Friday, December 2, 1983. He also spoke at the cornerstone ceremony and applied the mortar. The dedication proceedings continued through Sunday, December 4. President Hinckley had dedicated a total of six new LDS temples in 1983, a milestone in and of itself.

Said he in early 1984, "As many temples will be dedicated in three years as we have built and dedicated in all the previous history of the Church.

"We will build smaller temples and more of them. They will be built of the finest materials available, on the premise that nothing is too good for the Lord.

"Temples and the blessings obtained therein are the very essence of the gospel, and correspond with eternal life and things of eternity."[53]

Six More New Temples in 1984

Temple building began in 1984 with groundbreaking for a temple in Denver, Colorado by President Hinckley on May 19, 1984. Three thousand attended the ceremony on a warm and nearly cloudless day. It was the 19th temple groundbreaking since 1980. The site was on 7 acres, a knoll in Four Lakes, a suburb of Denver 15 miles to the southeast.

President Gordon B. Hinckley & wife Marjorie Pay Hinckley
in front of the Mexico City Temple
December 2, 1983

Two years of effort had been required for favor to finally shine on the plans. Two sites had been relinquished due to building permit difficulties.[54]

The first new temple dedication was once again presided over by Gordon B. Hinckley. It was on Friday, May 25, 1984 at Boise, Idaho. The temple became the LDS Church's 27th. At 8 A.M. 1,200 attended the cornerstone ceremony and dedication. Gordon B. Hinckley had participated in 22 of the 27 operating temple dedications, an unbelievable statistic. At the dedication, President Hinckley mentioned there were two audiences there that day–those here and those on the other side of the veil. Elder James E. Faust, an LDS apostle, was also at the activities. Twenty-three dedicatory sessions were held for this temple.

Four months later, the Sydney, Australia temple was dedicated in Carlingford, a suburb 15 miles northwest of Sydney. Some drove 2,598 miles across Australia to be present at the September 20, 1984 dedication. President Hinckley offered the prayer.[55] Dedicatory sessions continued on through September 23.

Two days later found the delegation in Manila, Philippines for the dedication of the temple there. Gordon B. Hinckley laid the cornerstone and gave the first dedicatory prayer. There were nine dedicatory sessions until September 27, 1984 attended by 6,454 Latter-day Saints. The last session ended at 5 P.M. that day and the first endowment session started at 7 P.M. the same day![56] All temples were special to President Hinckley but this one especially was fond to his heart because it was here in Manila just 24 years ago he had met at the military cemetery outside Manila where there was only one native Filipino member of the LDS Church out of the whole of the Philippine Islands.

The Dallas, Texas temple was dedicated by President Hinckley on October 19, 1984. It is a smaller temple but beautiful with pillars rising on its sides to pinnacles. Next was the Taipei, Taiwan Temple. November 17, 1984 was the dedication. Then less than a month later, Guatemala got their House of the Lord on December 12, 1984.

A group of 75 Kekchi native Americans of the El Polochik area, southwest Guatemala, started their pilgrimage to the Guatemala City Temple dedication. They first hiked on foot through thick rain forests with two days bread and clothing bundles on their shoulders. Lake Isabel was reached at daybreak where they boarded small pole and paddle driven boats.

Two hours after boarding the boats, they arrived at shore and took pickup trucks to a bus station for another 14 hour bus ride to the temple site. The faithful native Americans paid $11.50 per couple for the bus ride alone, 15 days normal pay to them. stayed at a school for the night close by the Guatemala City stake president's home and next morning changed to dresses and white shirts and trousers.

Their pilgrimage was worth it. As they peered upon the gleaming steeples of the temple, they felt like they were "in the pre-existence in the presence of God." Cackchiquel, Mam and Quiche native American tribes were also at the services, many speaking only their tribal tongue. But of the 34,000 at the dedication, 9,100 came from many other surrounding areas to be serviced by the temple. Citizens of Honduras, El Salvador, Nicaragua, Panama and Southern Mexico attended as well as Guatemala.

"I am satisfied that Father Lehi smiles this day,"President Hinckley said. "He smiles after untold generations of his sons and daughters . . . have been refined in the fires of terrible adversity. Now this generation, from whose eyes have fallen the scales of darkness, have grown in beauty to understand their capacity.

"This is as tremendous a development as the coming of morning after night; it is a miracle. The Lord is remembering His ancient covenant, and what a wonderful feeling this is."[57]

Many wiped tears from eyes as they participated in this special event for their people and looked upon the temple located on 1.5 acres in the southeast hills of Guatemala City. The year 1984 ended with six more new LDS temples dedicated by President Gordon B. Hinckley.

Five Temples in 1985

The Manti, Utah Temple had been dedicated May 17, 1888 by LDS prophet Wilford Woodruff on a hill north of the small settlement. It was the third temple completed in Utah after the pioneers had arrived in 1847. The rededication after extensive renovation was accomplished by Gordon B. Hinckley on June 14, 1985.

Six days later he was at the dedication of the first temple in a communist country. In 1985, the diplomacy of LDS apostle Thomas S. Monson resulted in permission to build an LDS temple in Freiberg, East Germany. The temple was completed and dedicated on June 20, 1985 by President Hinckley. Who knows what effect this temple had on the breaking down of the Berlin Wall and reunification of divided Germany a few years later.

Then it was to Stockholm, Sweden where Gordon B. Hinckley dedicated a temple there on July 2, 1985. The groundbreaking had been started on March 17, 1984 by LDS apostle Thomas S. Monson. [58]

The Chicago Temple was ready for dedication a month later. President Hinckley was the privileged representative of the First Presidency to pronounce the dedicatory prayer on August 9, 1985.

At this temple in the state where the early LDS saints had erected their second temple in Nauvoo the beautiful, President Hinckley related the history of the early believers in the State of Illinois. He said he felt his own grandfather Ira Nathaniel Hinckley must have worked on the Nauvoo Temple.

"I feel a great emotion when I think of the past. The construction [of the Nauvoo Temple] started 2½ months after the revelation [D.&C. 124] was given to build it. The saints of Nauvoo carried construction of the temple forward to completion knowing they would be driven from the city. Men were sent back to dedicate the temple.

"I have a feeling that the erection and dedication of this House of the Lord carries something of a redemption of what happened in the past. It brings together the tradition of Nauvoo and the blessings of today. I am grateful for the environment of peace and goodwill as people look upon us with appreciation and respect–a people worthy of a House of the Lord.

"I think of those who gave their lives for a testimony and are buried in Illinois, and feel that this building by its very nature, is dedicated to those who are beyond death.

"We live after death. Every ordinance of this house carries the essentials of immortality. What happens here is for eternity, for ourselves and in behalf of the dead. This house is the link between this life and the life beyond."[59]

Johannesburg, South Africa was President Hinckley's next destination on Saturday, August 24, 1985 where he dedicated the new temple completed there. Ezra Taft Benson gave a classic discourse on the Christ in LDS General Conference in October 1985 and in a month was ordained 13th prophet of the LDS Church after the passing of Spencer W. Kimball.

But President Benson still directed Gordon B. Hinckley, President Benson's new 1st counselor, to follow through with plans for groundbreakings and temple dedications during 1985. So on to Las Vegas, Nevada the Hinckleys went, where on November 30, 1985

9,000 came to the Las Vegas Convention Center where the groundbreaking services were viewed by video in the presence of President and Sister Hinckley and LDS apostle Boyd K. Packer.[60]

Two weeks later, President Hinckley and his wife Marjorie went to Seoul, Korea for dedication of the temple there. Sister Hinckley was enchanted by the beautiful women in Korean dresses lining the halls as they came out of the dedication.[61]

The temple, although small, was designed along the lines of the Salt Lake and Washington, D.C. temples, consisting of six spires rising from the corners of a diamond form radiating light and enlightenment to the world.

10 More Temples

The Lima, Peru temple was expected to be dedicated in 1985 but it missed it by 10 days. President Hinckley was in Lima on January 10, 1986 for the cornerstone ceremony and dedicatory prayer. The dedication was unpublished, probably due to the danger of terrorist acts by anti-government or anti-American factions.

But physicians, lawyers, judges, businessmen and those with little or no education all assembled at the beautiful experience. Some came by airplane 350 miles from the northeast over the rainy Amazon forests. Some rode buses from Tacna, 400 miles to the south. A bus from Bolivia travelled past washed out bridges to reach the ceremony.

Gordon B. Hinckley wept. "I was so pleased I couldn't hold back the tears and I haven't been able to hold them back since. There stands now a House of the Lord in the nation of Peru. God be thanked for this glorious and happy day."[62]

President Hinckley also said, "Surely father Lehi has wept with sorrow over his posterity, surely he weeps today with joy.

"As I look into your faces today . . . I see men of power and capacity; I see women of strength and beauty. I know the Lord is moving among this people to redeem them and to bring light and industry in their lives, wisdom in their minds, to rear leaders among them–men who hold and honor the priesthood."[63]

After the Peru dedication, Thomas S. Monson dedicated a temple in Argentina and then new LDS prophet Ezra Taft Benson dedicated two temples in Denver, Colorado and Frankfurt, Germany. Gordon B. Hinckley conducted the cornerstone ceremony in Denver and other sessions, spoke at two and offered the dedicatory prayer at three.[64]

It was with the failing health of President Ezra Taft Benson that President Hinckley once again assumed dedication role. He next dedicated the Portland Temple in the suburb of Lake Oswego, Oregon on August 16, 1989. The temple was a showcase of six white steeples once again placed at the corners of a diamond shaped white main structure. The temple was also visible from the adjacent interstate freeway running between California and Portland. The top spire rose 189 feet among the beautiful tall pine tree surroundings.

Typical of the experiences at other temples, a young college student whose ancestry went back to early LDS pioneers in Utah went to the open house. She "felt the Spirit" in the edifice so strongly she asked for missionaries to explain LDS beliefs to her and was baptized. She then immediately became involved in searching out her ancestors and made contact with a family association for her pioneer LDS line.

Said President Hinckley in part, "I am grateful to take part in this era of temple building, the greatest temple building era in the history of the world."[65]

On Tuesday, August 23, 1988, President Hinckley participated in the temple president seminars he initiated during the last year of his Temple Committee chairmanship. President Benson talked to the nine new temple presidents as well as his counselors.

Said President Hinckley, "One of my assignments is to confer the sealing power upon others when authorized to do so by the President of the Church. I have never conferred the sealing power that I have not pondered the wonder of it all. It is the only power that reaches beyond the grave. It is eternal in its nature and everlasting and binding in its consequences."[66] President Hinckley spoke as usual at another three day seminar for 13 new temple presidents on Thursday, August 17, 1989.

The Chicago Temple was nearly doubled in size to 34,000 square feet and rededicated on Sunday, October 8, 1989 by President Hinckley before 600. The remodeling expanded the size mostly underground and was required by the activity of steadfast, faithful members after less than four years from the first dedication.[67] Marjorie Hinckley spoke at the proceedings and President Hinckley said in part, "What a marvelous thing a temple recommend is–a holder is certified as one who knows the Lord and seeks to do His will."

On December 16, 1989 an impressive edifice now stood on the mountains east of downtown Las Vegas, Nevada on Bonanza Avenue. The tall spires and cathedral ceiling added a new kind of landmark to the previous sole casinos and hotels of the bawdily lit Las Vegas Boulevard. Now there was a stark contrast–a House of the Lord in the city famous for gambling.

President Ezra Taft Benson, LDS prophet, was present and presided but Gordon B. Hinckley conducted the first session and gave the dedicatory prayer to an audience of between 9 to 10,000. "Never has there been so beautiful a day in the history of Las Vegas," said President Hinckley. "There will never be so beautiful a day as this day as we dedicate this house of the Lord, the crowning jewel overlooking the city of Las Vegas."

Eleven dedicatory sessions were held after openhouses. "Feelings were near the surface in all the sessions." After the dedication, a news reporter asked President Hinckley, "Why would you put a temple in a place like this?"

"Because our members need it."[68]

Continuing the accelerating speed in LDS temple building, the First Presidency of the LDS Church announced the building of temples in Bountiful, Utah just north of Salt Lake and also in Orlando, Florida.[69]

President Hinckley addressed 21 new temple presidents and wives in the chapel inside the Salt Lake Temple on August 15, 1990 with all of the 12 apostles, the three members of the presiding bishopric and the 7 presidents of the Seventies Quorums in attendance.[70] Ten days later, President Hinckley was in Toronto, Canada dedicating an LDS Temple there. It sat on a 10 acre lot in Brampton, 20 miles west of Toronto. President Benson was unable to attend so President Hinckley gave the dedicatory prayer. Then an additional 20 dedicatory sessions were held.

"The real test of our love for this house lies in the use of it. It isn't built as a monument, but it is dedicated to be used," said President Hinckley. He also spoke of the prophecy given by the Lord to Joseph Smith, Jr. when a young boy by the heavenly messenger Moroni on September 21, 1823 indicating Joseph's name would "be had for good and evil among all nations, kindreds, and tongues."

"Your presence here is a fulfillment of those marvelous and remarkable words of prophecy."

President Hinckley's own ancestors had come from the Toronto, Canada area in the 1800's and eventually to the Rockies of the Salt Lake Valley.

An additional 20 general authorities spoke at the ceremonies attended by over 17,000 faithful LDS members. Six languages heard the services in their own tongue–French, Spanish, Portuguese, Mandarin, Cantonese and Korean.

The next year, the Cardston, Alberta LDS Temple, first temple to have been built in Canada, was refurbished and ready for the third time. Heber J. Grant had dedicated it first, Hugh B. Brown second and now Gordon B. Hinckley the third time. Twelve sessions were held with 1,937 in the temple the first session with an overflow crowd in a nearby stake house on June 22, 1991.[71]

That evening President and Sister Hinckley were taken in a horse drawn carriage through the city of Cardston. When residents saw them, they ran out of their homes to wave.

Not only were dedications and temple president seminars part of the forte. December 8, 1991 found the Assembly Hall on Temple Square in Salt Lake City filled with 3,000 Jordan River Temple workers and family members where President Hinckley gave them a fireside address.

A video presentation depicting the last 10 years of temple building was shown and then President Hinckley said, "We give at Christmas through the Spirit of Christ . . . Somehow, unless we give and give and give, we do not worship Him in spirit and truth. . . . The true Christmas gift that exceeds anything . . . is the gift of eternal life made possible through the eternal life made possible through the Son of God with the power within us His sons and daughters to open the door and lift the gate and make way the road . . . that leads to exaltation and eternal life.

"Somehow, there is no way if we put a red box, or a green box, or silver box under the tree for [unbaptized ancestors], but there is something you can do that is far better than a red box, or green box or a silver box . . . ."

Those who serve in temples "do for others what they cannot do for themselves, and in the process, exemplify in some small measure at least the great vicarious work of the Son of God, in giving His life in propitiation for the sins of all mankind, making certain the resurrection from the dead, and opening beyond, the doors of opportunity based upon obedience for exaltation and eternal life in the highest of the glories of our Father and His beloved Son.

"I know that it isn't easy. Some of you arise very early in the morning, some travel very long distances, some of you leave work in order to go to the temple, and then have to make up for it.

"May you have joy in service and not be tired . . . When you go home so weary that you can scarcely put one foot ahead of the other, may you say to yourselves, 'This is the sweetest weariness I have ever known.'"[72]

At the groundbreaking for the Bountiful, Utah Temple on May 2, 1992, a canvas tent was prepared for LDS Church dignitaries under which was seated President Ezra Taft Benson and other general authorities with their wives. The spot was the shelf of a hill high on the Rocky Mountains east of Bountiful.

President Benson shoveled a scoop of earth for the last time as a living prophet on the earth. He was assisted by Gordon B. Hinckley and others with his wife Marjorie by his side. Next, at general LDS conference, future temples in Hartford, Connecticut and Hong Kong were announced.

The London and Berne Temples which Gordon B. Hinckley had assisted outfitting in the 1950's were updated and modernized and rededicated from October 8 to 25, 1992 also. Open houses were held during which many visitors reminiscent of the events over 40 years ago were once again witnessed by President Hinckley and it was his privilege on the second day of the rededication to announce the purchase of a site in his dear Preston in the northwest section of England for the building of a future temple.

LDS general authorities go to the temple, too. On April 1, 1993, one such occasion was a group visit by LDS authorities and wives for the same endowment session in the Salt Lake Temple as part of preparation for general conference to be held two days later.[73] Following general conference, the open houses began for the San Diego Temple. The size was larger than most recent ones, a full 82,000 square feet. The location was on a visible rise close to the San Diego I-5 Interstate Freeway. Two major towers on both sides were complemented by 10 smaller steeples of this white rock edifice.

"Strengthen us in our resolutions and guard us against failure in observing the obligations we have accepted. In thy sacred temples we make further covenants with thee. Give us the will to live above sin and selfishness. Save us from pride and arrogance. Smile with favor upon us we humbly pray thee. Bless us with a spirit of benevolence toward all who are in distress wherever they may be or whatever their circumstances,"[74] President Hinckley prayed in the dedicatory prayer.

Many Latter-day Saints from Mexico were in attendance at this temple dedication for it sat just a few miles north of the border between the United States. So two sessions were conducted in Spanish.

The Spanish sessions were attended by general authorities who knew some Spanish and then President Hinckley said, "There will be other temples in this state. More temples are coming and we're hopeful that Spanish will be spoken very extensively in some of them. What we have now is but the beginning of what we will have as the work of the Lord moves in power and majesty across the earth."[75]

President Hinckley also spoke of visiting Spain twice recently resulting in announcement of a temple to be built there. "But," he cautioned, members of the LDS faith "must never lose sight" of the purpose of temples. "The whole purpose is to provide a place where we can worship God according to the dictates of our own conscience, exercise the priesthood that has been restored in its fullness and receive the blessings that are administered only in these holy houses."[76]

Groundbreaking for the Mt. Timpanogos Temple, the second temple for the Utah Valley immediately south of Salt Lake City, was accomplished on October 9, 1993 by President Hinckley. It was explained the purpose for this temple was to relieve the pressure being placed on the Provo Temple operating at 115 percent of its capacity. Twenty percent of the work done in all of the temples was being done in the Provo and Jordan River Temples.

President Hinckley said, "You are a people who know what this temple is all about. I notice over here a sign that says 'Lost and Found.' That essentially is what this temple is about. Its chief purpose will be to bless the lives of those who otherwise would be lost or have lost to them the full benefit of the atonement of the Redeemer of the world and you are those who are working to find them and to act vicariously in their behalf. What a tremendous and unselfish and wonderful service that is."[77]

The Angel Moroni gold leaf statue blowing the trumpet of the gospel of Jesus Christ was hosted atop the Bountiful Temple spires in a special ceremony watched by 2 to 3,000 on October 18, 1993. Then at the end of October, Gordon B. Hinckley was in St. Louis, Missouri breaking ground for the temple there. St. Louis was another historic site for the Latter-day Saints for many of the early pioneers came to port in St. Louis from Europe and elsewhere and then took riverboats up the river on their way to Zion.

The air was crisp in the Fall of St. Louis. President Hinckley related the same conditions existed when numerous saints of the LDS faith came there and worked there in the 1800's before departing for the Rocky Mountains. He told of the difficulties of the Missouri saints, of the dedication of two spots for temples never built due to the persecutions which caused their exodus. Now he said, "I am satisfied that the Prophet Joseph smiles on us today. And I am satisfied that those who were with him on that long trek across Missouri in the Winter of 1838 smile upon us as they see what we begin here today."[78]

"Now, we'd better hurry to beat the blizzard and we'd better break the ground before it freezes," he said, and the ground was turned.

A historic first occurred February 13, 1994 when the LDS First Presidency announced a previous older LDS tabernacle used as a meeting hall in the town of Vernal, Utah would be renovated and turned into a temple. Nothing of this kind had ever been done before. President Hinckley also broke ground for the temple in Preston, England on June 12, 1994. At the ground breaking, he broke down and cried when he met Robert Pickles, a Latter-day Saint one year his senior who tracted with President Hinckley when President Hinckley was on his full-time mission in 1933. [79]

The Bountiful Temple was dedicated on January 8, 1995 where President Hinckley assisted wheelchair-ridden Howard W. Hunter, installed as 14th prophet of the LDS faith in June of 1994. President Hinckley did not dedicate this temple but assisted in the various dedicatory services when President Hunter's health immediately deteriorated after President Hunter uttered the first dedicatory prayer on January 8.

The site of the Preston England Temple was inspected by now prophet Gordon B. Hinckley on August 31, 1995 where he toured the city and his former missionary proselyting area while observing progress in the temple construction.

Hong Kong Temple Dedication

On May 26, 1996 in Hong Kong, President Gordon B. Hinckley dedicated the first temple he had ever dedicated as President of the Church. The temple had eight floors, one in the basement. It was of white granite with gray marble on the first floor and entrance. The top three floors and basement constituted the temple. The remaining levels housed a chapel, administrative offices and temple server and patron residences.

Said prophet Hinckley in his dedicatory prayer, "Now we pray for Hong Kong and its people. May the blessings of freedom continue to be enjoyed by those who live here . . . ." Hong Kong was to return to the Peoples Republic of China jurisdiction in 1997.

Participants traveled from Thailand, Singapore and Taiwan in addition to the local LDS saints in Hong Kong.[80]

Spain Temple Groundbreaking

Almost immediately after returning from an energetic trip to Asia and the Hong Kong Temple dedication, it was off to Europe and Spain where on June 11 he broke ground for the Madrid Spain Temple at a sight he had selected in 1992. Surrounded by many high-rise apartments on an elevated area west of central Madrid, 2,000 participants shielded themselves from the sun with umbrellas as government officials from the city and nation looked on during a prayer of dedication.[81]

The Prophet's Declaration Regarding Temple Work

At the General Priesthood Meeting of the semiannual general world conference in Salt Lake City on Saturday evening, September 30, 1995, President Hinckley talked to the LDS priesthood holders present in the Tabernacle and in halls throughout the world by closed circuit TV and satellite. His message was threefold: Missionary work, temples and family history work, and the state of the LDS Church.

After talking of missionaries and mission work, President Hinckley turned his attention to temples. He declared those of past generations are likewise deserving of the temple ordinances. Then he indicated 28 of the 47 operating LDS temples had been dedicated since 1981 when he first came to the First Presidency. Four others had been rededicated.

He talked of a possible temple in Venezuela and moving of the Hartford, Connecticut temple to Boston. Six other sites in six more areas were being considered.

"I have a burning desire that a temple be located within reasonable distance from all members," he declared.

Then the blessings of the temple would influence all Latter-day Saints. He was confident such access to temples would make believers "better people" and there would be less infidelity and divorce. But it takes time. However, he constantly prays that somehow it might be speeded up.

Temples are a persuasive tool. Temple recommends are a precious asset. All Latter-day Saints were counseled to make a greater effort to go to the temples Then we would be better women and better men. In the House of the Lord we feel His Spirit in an environment of solemnity and peace.[82]

SPREADING

Spreading the gospel he believes has always been a part of Gordon B. Hinckley's life ever since his parents imparted to him the example of sharing the message of restoration. Gordon's father performed a tremendous missionary effort himself while president of the Liberty Stake with 1,800 baptisms occurring during his tenure.

The mission to England Gordon accepted in 1933 refined his testimony and caused the desire to share more and more. Then he entered the Church Administration Building as executive secretary for the Radio, Publicity and Mission Literature Committee of the LDS Church.

The job was essentially to support the missionaries. Tracts were created, film strips produced, and numerous other efforts engaged providing unified printed and audio/visual aids for missions.

Gordon was going to find himself during his life literally fulfilling the promise of his patriarchal blessing received when he was 11. He would be testifying in numerous ways, many uncontemplated, of the faith in which he believed. And he could see the hand of the Lord in preparing him and his environment for the spreading he would exemplify and aid others do.

The LDS Church began improved coordinated efforts to share their beliefs by initiating missionary training classes in LDS wards on January 10, 1932.[1] By February 3, 1934, Seventies quorums, then existing in each stake, were told to do missionary work. And nine months after Gordon began employment for the RPML Committee of the LDS Church the LDS First Council of the 70, considered general authorities, were assigned supervisory responsibilities over stake missions in each LDS stake.[2]

By 1939, Gordon had not only produced radio scripts, pamphlets and film strips for the missions, he had organized, planned and implemented the LDS Church's exhibit at the Golden Gate Exhibition in San Francisco, California.[3] Missionaries were pulled from Germany, however, in August 1939 and later from all of Europe. But the work in other areas continued and Gordon was called upon to assist.

The Ill Missionary Sent to John Hopkins

It was at this time that Gordon was asked by the LDS First Presidency on one of these occasions to hurry to New York City. A 20 year old missionary assigned to the Argentina Mission had been diagnosed with brain cancer and sent on a boat to New York for help.

Gordon B. Hinckley
About Late 1940's

The missionary was taken to John Hopkins University Hospital while Gordon took the parents of the missionary and quickly traveled to New York. When they arrived, they found Elder Jay Ambrose Quealy, Jr. recovering not from a brain tumor but from a disease due to eating bad pork. The Argentine doctors had made a mistake.[4]

This first meeting with Jay Quealy was to develop into a lifelong friendship. Elder Quealy was soon well and reassigned to the Northern States Mission where he became mission secretary and essentially ran the entire mission when his mission president was made one of the first of the five Assistants to the Quorum of the Twelve called in 1940.

Gordon also prepared the "Picture Story of Mormonism" this year and kept records of certain investigators. Filmstrip projectors were first introduced into LDS missions the following year. An activity questionnaire pertaining to converts was also developed.[5]

On March 23, 1942, the LDS First Presidency restricted mission calls to high priests and seventies. As a result, many married men volunteered and served on missions. Gordon went to work for the railroad to aid in the war effort and then was asked to return to Church employ by his former supervisor Stephen L. Richards.

Reflecting upon his decision to return to his pre-war work, Brother Hinckley has said, "This is the Lord's work and I felt I would make my contribution in life by doing my humble part to further the cause."[6]

Gordon took a 90 day leave from his D.&R.G. Railroad executive position to contemplate and after several weeks made the decision. Help was needed with the renewed missionary work. Stephen L. Richards was still chairman of the Radio, Publicity and Mission Literature Committee of six LDS apostles and David O. McKay was liaison from the First Presidency over the RPML committee responsible for the missionary program of the LDS Church.[7]

That same year the LDS Church proposed a plan to help its members residing in war torn Europe. As a result, President Harry S. Truman met LDS prophet George Albert Smith in the White House where President Smith explained the plan of the Church to relieve the suffering LDS people in Europe.

On February 4, 1946, the newly organized United Nations met for the first time in London. Not one LDS mission president in the world drove a car.[8] Mission work was just starting to resume in many countries. But missionaries still became sick. One such missionary was sent home to a hospital and then a room near the hospital for the

Summer. But the summer was hot and humid. Brother Hinckley brought the elder his fan from the Church office to help ventilate the elder's room.[9] By the end of 1946, missionaries had been increased to 3,000 and by 1948 all previous missions were functioning again including a mission in Japan which had been closed since 1925.[10]

One of the projects Gordon spearheaded at this time was translation of the Book of Mormon into several new languages.[11] Gradually Gordon got to know every mission president's name. Another innovation was use of radio programs and music in the missions. And by December 1947, a fast day was set aside by the LDS Church for relief of the European population. Visitors at Temple Square also exceeded 1,000,000 during the year for the first time. May 12, 1949 saw the blockade of Western supplies into Berlin end. And a labor missionary program where construction work was performed by specially called "building missionaries" was started in the South Pacific.

American jets were attacked by North Korean Migs on November 8, 1950 and Gordon found himself soon involved in another responsibility. The Church desired missionaries but the government desired soldiers for the Korean War. Accordingly, certain arrangements needed to be worked out between the Church and the US Government pertaining to drafting of LDS men into the armed services. Gordon was given the task along with his other mission related work.

Many problems pertaining to the Korean War came and later President Hinckley wrote, "I would never wish to have to go through the experiences of those years again."[12]

One solution implemented was the reduction of young men called on missions and the encouragement of seventies to serve missions as was done during 1942-1945. Through this procedure, Dwayne N. Andersen volunteered for missionary work and was sent to Japan where he became a counselor to the mission president and later became the mission president himself. He had served in the US Army and carried a wireless radio onto the beaches during the battle of Okinawa.

A concession of the US Army to the LDS Church was authorization to make special LDS identifying tags for LDS servicemen. Small pocket editions of the Book of Mormon and other Standard Works were also made and distributed.

Five months after the Korean Conflict began, David O. McKay became 9th prophet of the LDS Church when George Albert Smith died April 4th at age 81. And in David O. McKay's place as previous 1st counselor in the First Presidency, President McKay chose Stephen L. Richards. Thus President Richards assumed liaison responsibility in the First Presidency for guidance of all mission work of the LDS faith.

Overseeing the "Mission Department"

There was no formal Missionary Department in the LDS Church yet. But Brother Hinckley essentially was staff supervisor of missionary work world wide.[13] His official label was "Executive Secretary to the General Missionary Committee but in effect, he *was* the "missionary department" of the LDS Church at that time.

Through seven years in this position, he really was on 24 hour call. The phone rang at his home late at night from mission presidents with problems. One morning when he arrived at his operations center with a big map of the world on the wall, before he could take his hat off, he had taken telephone calls from missions in South America, Europe and Asia.[14]

By 1952, a systematic program for teaching the gospel was published and introduced in all LDS missions.[15] This was a tremendous step forward in Latter-day Saint proselyting activity. Up to then, each mission was left essentially on its own to guide the instruction given by missionaries. The same year on March 2, 1952, a new Primary Children's Hospital was dedicated on the Avenues northeast of downtown Salt Lake. Also, LDS apostle Ezra Taft Benson became new US President Dwight D. Eisenhower's Secretary of Agriculture, service which extended through all eight years of Eisenhower's presidency.

On March 25, 1953, returning LDS missionaries no longer reported to general authorities but to their stake president for release. All of these innovations were influenced by Gordon B. Hinckley.

Visiting the Missions

Visiting the missions of the Church was another privilege of Gordon Hinckley's call. For example, on January 2, 1952, President and Sister Stephen L. Richards and Gordon B. Hinckley met with the mission presidency and 166 elder and sister missionaries of the California Mission for a mission conference.[16] This type of experience and the additional travel experience he enjoyed all helped prepare him for the days when he would be the featured visitor at hundreds of such conferences.

In 1956, a tour to Europe was taken. Brother Gordon Hinckley was with the travelers. European Missions were surveyed and conferences held.

Visit to California Mission Conference
January 2, 1952
l. to r. second row middle
Pres. Stephen L. Richards, Pres. Bryan L. Bunker
Brother Gordon B. Hinckley, Pres. Wilford C. Brimley

Mission Calls

Another choice privilege of Brother Hinckley in his executive secretary position was the privilege of attending weekly sessions where the select body of LDS apostles on the Missionary Committee met and prayed and through inspiration and delegation from the President of the Church reviewed missionary applications and called each to a specific mission. Later President Hinckley was to remark he probably has been present during his lifetime either as executive secretary or as general authority in seeing more missionary calls made than any other man living. The prophet himself was often present, too.

Woman From Scotland

One day in 1956, a small woman from Scotland visited Brother Hinckley's office. She handed Brother Hinckley a $600.00 check and said, "I would like to help a needy missionary."

"Please sit down and tell me your story," Gordon said.

The sister explained she had no sons, a meager job and was widowed. Following her first visit, she came again and again and again giving funds for a total of seven missionaries to go on missions.[17] This same year, a building was completed on the northwest corner of Administration Block at Main Street and North Temple on October 3, 1956 for use by the LDS relief society general board.

Next year in October, LDS general conference was cancelled for the first time in history due to a flu epidemic and the first satellite in history was launched successfully by the Soviet Union. A new program for convert integration was piloted in several LDS stakes.

Murdock Travel

The first flight of the Wright Brothers at Kitty Hawk, North Carolina on December 17, 1903 marked entrance into the age in which Gordon would utilize this tool almost incessantly to spread the LDS faith. Air transportation began 16 years later. The first trans-continental air mail was delivered in the United States in 1920. Gradually passenger planes developed until after the Korean War, they were smooth flying jets.

Missionaries needed to get to their fields and utilizing air transportation was smart. Gordon worked closely with Franklin J. Murdock to provide inexpensive air space for missionaries and the two worked up and presented a report to the LDS First Presidency in 1958. As a result, a travel agency called Murdock Travel was created. The agency began booking space on airlines. The LDS Church also invested in Pan American Airlines and used it heavily where possible for missionary transportation.

Missionary work often occurred through correspondence received from inquirers. One such time, a letter came from a man in a federal penitentiary in Ohio. He had stolen gas, then automobiles and then other things which finally put him in the penitentiary. He wrote, "I came across a copy of the Book of Mormon in the prison library. I have read it and when I read Mormon's lamentation over his fallen people—'O ye fair ones, how could ye have departed from the ways of the Lord, how could ye have rejected that Jesus who stood with open arms to receive you! Behold, if ye had not done this, ye would not have fallen . . .' [Mormon 6:17-18] When I read this, I felt that Mormon was talking to me. Can I get a copy of that book?"[18]

The book was sent and a few months later the man walked into Brother Hinckley's office in the Church Administration Building in Salt Lake and announced he was a new baptized member of the LDS Church. He next went to the West Coast and started an honest occupation.

LDS apostle Charles A. Callis, who had ordained Gordon a high priest and stake president's counselor, told Gordon an experience he had when president of the Southern States Mission. He said,"When I was president of the Southern States Mission, I had each missionary come into the office before he was released. One day a young man came in and I said, 'What have you accomplished?'

"He said, 'Nothing, and I am going home.'

"'What do you mean you have accomplished nothing.'

"'Well, I baptized one man in the backwoods of Tennessee. He didn't know enough or have enough sense to wear shoes. And that's all I've done. I have wasted my time and my father's money, and I'm going home.'"

Elder Callis checked on that backwoods convert six months later. He had been ordained a deacon and accepted some small callings in his branch. Elder Callis kept making regular checks on him. He was made an elder and given more responsibility. He moved from his rented farm and bought a little piece of land himself. He was made branch president. Then he sold his farm and purchased a new one in Idaho, rearing his family in the Church. His children and their children went on LDS missions.

"I have just completed a survey," Elder Callis said, "which indicates, according to the best information I can find, that over 1100 people have come into the Church as a result of the baptism of that one man by a missionary who thought he had failed."[19]

In the first devotional talk he ever delivered before the BYU studentbody, Brother Hinckley related Brother Callis' experience and then concluded, "No one can foretell the consequences of a conversion."

One day before he was called to be a general authority, Brother Hinckley was researching in the missionary records of the Church and came across David O. McKay's appraisal in 1899. The evaluation stated Elder McKay was a good speaker and writer, a very good presiding officer, possessed a good knowledge of the gospel, very energetic and emphatically discreet with a good influence. The remarks stated there was "none better in the mission."[20] The evaluation impressed Gordon with President McKay's example. Since the days of his mission he still was solidly consistent in his actions, unfailing in kindness, unwavering in his consideration and poised with ease in confronting every situation. It influenced him.

As an Assistant to the Twelve

Gordon's missionary responsibilities did not end with his installation as an Assistant to the Twelve. In many respects they just increased. During the first six months of his general authority responsibility, he visited Europe once again for the London Temple dedication and met with over 500 missionaries. He marvelled at their devotion and maturity through the missionary program and sensed the tremendous power of it all.[21]

While on the plane crossing the Atlantic, he had a conversation with a young man from England and saw he got a Book of Mormon. He read it together with other literature and corresponded with Elder Hinckley. A significant change in his attitude took place towards the LDS faith.[22]

All was not peaches, however. All missionaries were not successful. Some fell to temptations. One such young elder came to the mission home for his training before leaving for his field of labor and realized he was not worthy. He was sent to Elder Hinckley.

Elder Hinckley sat with him in the office and said, "Don't you think you'd better go home and talk this out with your father?'

"I can't talk to my father. We never get along, there is a great chasm between me and my father."[23]

Another disappointing meeting with a young man bitter in heart ended by Elder Hinckley saying, "If you had seen what I have seen, if you had experienced what I have experienced, you would not feel as you now do."[24]

A father of a missionary came to Elder Hinckley in January 1959, too. He was paying $67.00 a month to keep his son on his mission.

"My son is riding a bicycle and I am afraid he is going to get killed. Can I take a car to him?"

"You can if the mission president feels he needs one," Elder Hinckley responded.

The father went and obtained the approval and drove the 1,000 miles to his son's mission and delivered the car. He then attended a baptism and the convert bore testimony of the love he had for the missionary who had taught him. The father realized then the new member was talking about his son. Though not an emotional man, tears streamed down his cheeks.[25]

A mission president wrote Elder Hinckley the latter part of January 1959 and told of a retired couple. They were ready to come home from a mission and 50 of their converts were going to sing for them in a choir. The sacrament was also going to be blessed and passed by converts they helped come into the LDS faith. The elder said, "I thought I had made some contribution to the world during my life, but I never did anything until I was past 65 and went on a mission."[26]

In May 1959, Gordon B. Hinckley's long time mentor Stephen L. Richards passed away. Elder Hinckley expressed appreciation for his wisdom, kindly persuasion and unfailing courtesy at October conference. Henry D. Moyle had replaced President Richards as First Presidency counselor in charge of missionary work and Elder Hinckley was assigned to assist him.[27]

In January 1960, the building missionary program started on a limited basis was expanded worldwide. This program provided many with an opportunity to serve while accelerating the creation of chapels for the LDS congregations. Regular full-time missionaries had risen to 6,000 by now.

As a general authority, Elder Hinckley was now given his share of stake conferences to visit. While preparing for one of them, a phone call came from a man who said, "I need a little information. I know a widow who goes out every morning at four O'clock to milk 60 cows to keep her son in the mission field. She has just received a letter from her boy saying that he needs a new overcoat and a pair of shoes, and she doesn't know where to get the money to buy them. Is there some way I can help?"

On the way to the stake conference in Dallas, Elder Hinckley thought about the sacrifices made for giving the message of the restoration to others.

Innovations in Worldwide Spreading

It was July 26, 1961 when major innovations were announced in mission work. The first mission president seminar was held and new programs outlined at Elder Hinckley's suggestion and implementation. President Moyle also was involved. A new six lesson missionary teaching plan was officially presented. "Every member a missionary", the catchall phrase declared by President David O. McKay, was also emphasized and the division of missions throughout the world into nine areas in 1960 with eight members of the 12 apostles and assistant to the 12 Gordon B. Hinckley becoming Area Supervisors was explained.[28]

From the moment Elder Hinckley became an Area Supervisor, he made it a practice to try and interview every missionary in his area while visiting their missions. The interviews were warm and friendly, conducted under a variety of circumstances, but always in privacy. Many a missionary poured out their trials to Elder Hinckley and he encouraged them.

Some failed to live up to the commitments they had made and for various reasons were sent home. But the vast majority were true to their covenants with the Lord and made the resolve Elder Hinckley himself had made on his mission in England and finished their missions honorably.

At this time in LDS Church history, too, apostles were still the ones setting apart missionaries for full-time missions. The setting aparts occurred regularly at the Church Administration Building in Salt Lake. If the elder or sister lived within reasonable distance of Salt Lake, a short time before he or she was scheduled to enter the mission home for training, the missionary would be invited to the headquarters in Salt Lake where he or she with immediate family would meet in the assigned apostle's office, there to have an apostle lay hands upon their head and set them apart as a missionary to their specific mission. Words of counsel and blessing were then given the missionary by the apostle as he was inspired. Tears often flowed in these sacred and spiritual events.

If the missionary lived a great distance from Salt Lake, the ordinance was performed while she or he were receiving their week's training at the mission home. Elder Hinckley set many a missionary apart for her or his mission.

In the beginning days of the LDS faith, often even the prophet of the Church and his counselors set missionaries apart. As the religion grew and the volume of missionaries increased, delegation of this privilege was made to the apostles. And as the LDS Church further grew, this power was delegated to the individual stake presidents of the respective missionaries.

Missionary Training Centers

James L. Barker, a University of Utah professor of modern languages and former mission president over France, suggested to David O. McKay a language training school be organized for LDS missionaries assigned to foreign countries.[29] The first school, called the Language Training Institute, started at BYU in November 1961 for Spanish speaking calls. In 1963 the concept was expanded into a full blown Language Training Mission and in 1978 it was combined into the Mission Training Center replacing previous mission home training.[30]

The *Improvement Era* wrote when Elder Hinckley assumed the apostleship, "In all his labors he has kept close to the heartbeats of the missionaries themselves. He has been with them in the London fog, in the cold Swiss rain, in the Montana wind, and in the humid heat of the Orient. He has helped them when sick, comforted them when bereaved, encouraged them when despondent, sorrowed with them in their tragedies, and rejoiced with them in their tremendous accomplishments. He has been on his knees with many a young man in distress."[31]

One missionary in the Orient he interviewed was having a hard time learning Japanese. As he broke down and wept, he told Elder Hinckley the language was extremely difficult. Elder Hinckley encouraged him and then the elder got on his knees and plead, "I'll do it. I'll make it." He did. He not only learned the language but became a traveling elder and assistant to the mission president. He had baptisms and sweet joy. Another had great capacity and scholarship but was a missionary failure because he refused to humble himself.

Another missionary was sent home sick.

"My mission is a failure," he said.

"How do you know?" Elder Hinckley asked.

"Well, I have come home sick."

"Let's get you on your feet. Maybe you can try again."

The elder was treated three months. Then he plead to go back to his mission. He did go back for 13 months but because of his weak constitution was put in the mission home shipping packages to missionaries and branches. But when the 13 months were over, his contributions were totalled. In the 13 months of working in the days in the mission office and tracting at night, he had baptized 32 people. He had exercised the faith and reaped the rewards.[32]

In the Summer 1962, President Henry D. Moyle and Elder Hinckley toured 21 missions in Europe in 23 days, holding day long seminars in each mission.[33] That previous March, the age for missionary service by male members of the LDS Church was reduced from age 20 to age 19. In visits to the Orient it was not uncommon to meet in Seoul, Korea in concrete meeting rooms not warmer than 26° F.[34]

Personal Finding

Elder Hinckley has never just preached. He has practiced. Whenever occasion has arisen, he has shared his testimony. One time he was in a first class lounge on a jet plane with three gentlemen. Everyone was smoking but one man and Elder Hinckley.

All were smart looking businessmen with self evident education. But one lit up a cigarette. Another became disturbed at seeing it. Then the other lit up and offered Elder Hinckley one. When Elder Hinckley declined, he offered the agitated man and he also declined saying, "I'm trying to quit, and it's nearly killing me."

All four then started a conversation. The first to light up said, "I decided to quit after hearing the Surgeon General's report in '64. It was agonizing. I couldn't sleep," he said as he inhaled and let his bowed head slowly release the captured smoke. "I couldn't lick it."

The second who lit up volunteered, "I almost quit. I'd been burning two packs a day. I thought I could taper off. I cut down to one cigarette after each cup of coffee. That was my formula. It lasted for a time, but I found myself drinking too much coffee. Now I'm back to a pack a day.

"I read the SG's report, too, and it frightened me. But then I read contrary opinion. Perhaps the relationship between cancer and smoking is coincidental. Exhaust fumes could just as easily cause it".

He crushed his half burnt cigarette in the tray and said, "Just the same, I wish I could quit."

The other whose fist had clenched and face reddened when the smoking started said, "I'm convinced there's some truth in what I've seen and read on the subject.

"We take the government's word for an awful lot these days, conclusions based on less convincing evidence than this. I don't believe you can deny the facts. There is a hazard in smoking. But I'm having a terrible fight. I never dreamed a habit could be so tough to break."

Turning to Elder Hinckley, he said, "What about you?"

"I've never used them," Gordon said.

"How lucky can you be!" the struggling man said.

Gordon thought to himself, truly, "How lucky can you be!" and thought of the fervent address he had heard from President Heber J. Grant while Gordon listed in the Tabernacle as a boy when President Grant spoke of the "Little White Slaver" as he declared the LDS doctrine called "The Word of Wisdom", a divine law with promises, and gave Gordon the resolution never to smoke.[35]

The men looked upon Elder Hinckley with envy and respect. Seeds of truth had been planted.

The Mormon Pavilion patterned after the shape of the Salt Lake LDS Temple opened at the New York World's Fair in April 1964. New murals depicting the dispensations of the gospel of Jesus Christ from Adam to Noah to Abraham to Moses and then depictions of Isaiah's foretelling of the birth of Christ 700 years before His birth and phases of the Savior's mortal ministry hung from the exhibit hall's walls. Statements of the ancient apostles and early Protestant reformists predicting an apostasy and then a restoration of the gospel of Jesus Christ were also included complemented with a film themed "Man's Search for Happiness."

The pavilion marked a decided improvement in quality and professionalism and as a result began to reap numerous inquiries into the beliefs and doctrines of the Latter-day Saint faith. Elder Hinckley had his input in guiding the pavilion to its success.

Elder Hinckley was back at another BYU Devotional, held at that university every Thursday morning during each semester. His October 13, 1964 speech to the thousands of students focused on selfishness. Said he in furtherance of the missionary concepts of his church, "We have on this campus some 2 or 3,000 returned missionaries. I think that if nothing else came of our missionary program than to take out of the lives of our young people the vicious selfishness which is so prone to afflict young men, all that we put into it would be worth it. What a marvelous thing it is to have a boy go out into the world, at the time of life when he is most prone to think of himself alone, and lose himself in the service of others and in the service of God."[36]

On November 3, 1969, a father of a full-time missionary visited with Elder Hinckley in the evening.

"I've just been talking with my son in another land. He is beaten; he is destroyed. He is lonely; he is afraid. What can I do to help him?" the father asked.

Elder Hinckley immediately remembered his own experience and empathized greatly with the loneliness of missionary work or leadership or LDS membership or personal testimony.

"How long has he been there?" Gordon asked.

"Three months."

"I guess that is the experience of almost every missionary who has been there three months. There is scarcely a young man or woman who is called to go into the world in a position of great responsibility to represent The Church of Jesus Christ of Latter-day Saints who does not feel much of the time, I am sure, in the early months of his or her mission, the terrible loneliness of that responsibility. But he also comes to know, as he works in the service of the Lord, the sweet and marvelous companionship of the Holy Spirit which softens and takes from him that feeling of loneliness."[37]

A representative of the hippie generation sat down in a South American airport by Elder Hinckley in 1970 as both waited for delayed planes. Elder Hinckley did not care about his beard, his long hair, large round glasses, sandals and disrupted clothing. He seemed "earnest and evidently sincere."

A conversation taught he was traveling on his father's money and was a graduate of a great North American university.

"What are you after in life?" Elder Hinckley asked.

"Peace—and freedom."

"Do you use drugs?"

"Yes. They give me the peace and freedom I seek."

"How about morality?"

"Now our new morality gives so much more freedom, more than

any previous generation."

The young man knew Elder Hinckley was a religious leader from introductions and condescendingly said, "Your Christian idea of morality is a joke. How can you honestly defend personal virtue and moral chastity?"

"Your freedom is a delusion. Your peace is a fraud. And I will tell you why," Gordon said.

Elder Hinckley's humble response sort of shocked the lad as their flights were called before Elder Hinckley could go into detail..[38] Later President Hinckley talked to the lad through one of his general conference addresses hoping he would somehow hear or read it. This is the valiant way Elder Hinckley constantly stood up for and in meekness and sobriety declared the convictions of his heart.

During September 1972, Elder Hinckley travelled with the new 11th LDS prophet Harold B. Lee to the Holy Land. On their return through New York, a press conference for the new prophet was arranged at the Waldorf Astoria Hotel. A journalist posed a question regarding the LDS Church's missionaries and Elder Hinckley responded.

"I think with very few exceptions, you will find them to be extremely active, strong. A young man cannot go out into the world and teach this gospel and lose himself in it for a few years without coming back with something having happened to him that remains with him and stays with him for the rest of his life. There are few exceptions."[39]

While attending a conference in the Eastern United States, testimony was borne by an engineer in Elder Hinckley's presence. The engineer was unreceptive to the LDS missionaries but his wife soon expressed a desire for baptism. The engineer flew into a rage. She didn't know what this meant. It would mean time, payments, loss of friends, no more smoking.

He threw on his coat and left the house. Swearing at his wife, the missionaries and himself for permitting them to teach his family, he walked the streets. Then fatigue cooled his anger and a reverse spirit entered his heart. He felt compelled to pray. He plead to God for answers. Then the realization came. "It's true, it's true, it's true." Peace filled his bosom. As he returned home, his wife was on her knees praying. Gladness came into their home and lives. They found with a little scheduling, they could share their substance, their time, their responsibility. A little careful budgeting was all that was required.[40]

Shortly after hearing this testimony, Elder Hinckley was on a plane from San Francisco to Sydney, Australia. He noticed a young male passenger reading a book entitled *Joseph Smith, An American Prophet*.

Elder Hinckley opened his mouth, "Hello. I notice you are reading a book. I know the author. What interest do you have?"

The young man answered, "Among other things, I have an interest in prophets. A modern prophet intrigues me. I picked the book from the library."

The two had a long talk and Elder Hinckley bore his testimony to the man.[41] Another seed had been planted because Brother Hinckley just opened his mouth and was a friend.

Elder Hinckley spoke to the university students at BYU once more on April 8, 1976. He entitled his talk that morning "Things are Getting Better" and displayed his constant optimism about the work of the Latter-day gospel. He made a point of reduced cultural shock in the world by noting a shrinking world, rising educational levels, an increasing knowledge of foreign languages, good men of experience presiding as mission presidents and erosion of cultural paths.

"People are essentially the same everywhere, all over the earth," he said. "Husbands love wives, and wives love husbands. Parents love children. An appreciation for beauty in whatever form it may take is found among people everywhere. They also have a concern with suffering, the ever-present conscience, the sense of right and wrong, and the universal recognition of a higher power to whom men may appeal for help, who sits in judgment upon us, and to whom, someday, each of us must make an accounting."

That is why when he was once asked by a person whether the LDS Church used different lessons for teaching Christians as opposed to non-Christians, he answered, "We use the same lessons because we teach the same kind of people, whose hearts are touched by the same eternal truths. Because we all come of the same parentage, we all respond in the same way to the same truths. Men the world over respond in the same way. They seek warmth when they are cold, they all know the same kinds of pain, they experience sadness, and they know joy. Everywhere they look to a superior power."[42]

He went on to say to the 5,000 assembled in the Smith Fieldhouse about the marvelous growth which has occurred in the Philippines where there was only one native member of the LDS faith in May 1961 and recently he attended an area conference there attended by 18,000.

Such phenomenal growth presents the future's challenge. With the great populace in China, the tremendous humanity in India, the millions in Russia and the billions in the Mideast, the LDS Church's invitation is great. Elder Hinckley expressed this challenge.[43] He could see the rapidly shrinking world. The greater understanding of ways and customs, increased study of languages, and the merging of age old customs helping the work to proceed.[44]

About April 1977, Elder Hinckley boarded a plane with a young man seated beside him. They conversed and reached the subject of religion. He was an IBM sales representative, an active member of a Christian denomination, and professed a reading knowledge of the Latter-day Saints. But then he said, "I admire Mormon practices but I cannot condone the story of your church's origin and particularly Joseph Smith."

"Where did you get your information?" Elder Hinckley asked.

"From my church."

"Would you think it fair for your customers to learn of the qualities of IBM products from a Xerox representative?"

Smiling, he said, "I think I get the point of what you're trying to say."

Elder Hinckley then removed his copy of the Doctrine and Covenants from his briefcase and read a few of the revelations received by Joseph Smith, Jr. forming the basis for many of the LDS practices the passenger admired.

"I'll send you some of our pamphlets. Will you read them?"

"Yes."

"I promise you if you will do so prayerfully, you will know the truth not only of our doctrines and practices, but also of the man through whom they were introduced."

Elder Hinckley then bore testimony to the acquaintance of his conviction concerning the prophetic calling of Joseph Smith.[45]

Nauvoo, Illinois, site of the beautiful city founded by the prophet Joseph Smith, Jr. from a disease infested swampland in the Spring of 1839, was scene of a 12 mission presidents' seminar on Sunday, October 21, 1979 presided over by apostle Hinckley. Haze, warm days, cool nights, and Autumn leaves enhanced the beauty of the environment.

The mission presidents, Elder Hinckley and two members of the First Quorum of the 70 used the old restored 70's Hall for their first meeting. The 70's Hall was essentially the first mission home for early LDS elders preparing for proselyting. Elder Hinckley envisioned the early stalwart leaders of the fledgling church—Joseph Smith, Jr., his older brother Hyrum, Brigham Young, Heber C. Kimball, John Taylor, Wilford Woodruff, brothers Orson and Parley P. Pratt, and many others, all seemed there.

The experience was exhilarating to him. He thought of the forces which ultimately brought the LDS saints there to Nauvoo. He contemplated the works of his predecessor Joseph Smith and the book he brought forth providing a second witness of the Savior Jesus Christ. He mused regarding the increased accumulation of evidence stimulating scholars dig up validating the history contained in Mormon's book as time progresses.[46] He came home renewed and refreshed with new vigor from that seminar.

Shanghai and the Christian Church Visit

No missionaries have formally proselyted in China since brief visits by LDS elders in the 1800's. But the opportunity to plant seeds of the restoration among the current generation came during the Summer of 1980. Two weeks were spent by Elder Hinckley and Sister Hinckley in May touring the Peoples Republic of China with BYU Young Ambassadors, a variety singing and dancing group of university students. The Chinese government had officially invited the young ambassadors for the first formal visit following a very impressive private tour the year before.

When the group arrived in Shanghai, they learned a 50 year old Methodist Gothic arched cathedral closed as a result of the cultural revolution for over 10 years had recently been reopened by the government. The ambassadors' visit fell on Sunday so the Hinckleys made arrangements for the entire delegation of 32 to meet with them.

The run down Mo An Church used for a high school during weekdays and by several combined Christian denominations for three separate capacity sessions on Sundays was filled with 1,500 visitors who heard a beautiful sermon regarding Christ's injunction to Peter to feed His sheep. So many attended, 10 separate rooms were piped the proceedings through remote speakers. "But they didn't really understand," Sister Hinckley said. "They didn't really know the extent of the Savior's mission and what He really did for us."

Following the services, 10 to 12 leaders of the congregation visited in one of the classrooms with the Hinckleys and group. They were very congenial and candid for the 45 minute to hour get together. When it was over, Elder Hinckley said, "I want to tell you something."

He then bore witness to the dozen Chinese Christians that God lives and Jesus is his living Son and Redeemer. Lastly he told them of Joseph Smith and the restoration of the ancient gospel of Jesus Christ in all its pristine purity. This small dozen leaders of Christian faith in a nation of over a billion population heard a Latter-day Saint apostle bear his special witness of the divinity of Jesus Christ and the restoration of His church on the earth in their day.[47]

Sister Marjorie Hinckley says, "Sometimes the desire to spread the truth of the gospel burns so heavily with us that we feel burdened with it. I know that people who are nonmembers may think that we're a little offensive. But it isn't that we're trying to force our feelings or our ways of thinking on them. It's just that we have such a desire to share with the world the beautiful, beautiful things that we have. And how blest we are to have them. How blessed we are!"

October 1980 found the Hinckleys in Tokyo awaiting the dedication of the Tokyo Temple and as Marjorie took a stroll along the beach by their hotel on a beautiful Saturday morning a little before 6 A.M., she experienced one of those yearnings to be an angel so she could proclaim the gospel to everyone.

She was delighted to see so many beautiful families on the sand having picnics with their children even at 6 in the morning and felt like getting on a soapbox and shouting, "Listen, all you beautiful families, I want to tell you something. We have something important to tell you. We can be families forever—forever![48]

About this time, a stake conference assignment took Elder Hinckley to a rural town where a freckled 18 year old boy with a big smile rose and talked about preparation for his mission. The 10 points impressed Elder Hinckley so much he later printed them in a First Presidency message of the *Ensign*. "I have never heard a better summary of missionary preparation, " he said.

The ten points were: 1. Have great parents to help you, 2. Attend church, 3. Be a scout and become an eagle scout, 4. Earn the Duty to God Award, 5. Be a priest quorum assistant, 6. Attend seminary, 7. Be a primary teacher, 8. Take part in family home evenings from the time you are a child, 9. Try to live a clean life, and 10. Take responsibilities in school to lead and serve.[49]

In the LDS general conference in October 1981, then President Hinckley, as a counselor in the First Presidency, declared his vision of the future of the LDS missionary work. "Many gates are now closed against us. But I am convinced that the Lord in his own time will open them, provided we constantly seek and pray for such openings and are prepared to take advantage of them. I do not know specifically the time frame of the Lord's work, but I do know that we must be anxiously engaged."[50]

Unbelievable as it was to the world, from that time forward the momentum of the forces which would crumble the Berlin Wall and Iron Curtain began to grow and grow, opening the vast East European and Soviet Union nations to LDS mission work by the end of the decade.

LDS Church membership reached the plateau of 5,000,000 on Sunday, April 4, 1982. The term of service for male LDS missionaries had been two years up to that time but in order to provide an easier financial burden on missionaries and families, who largely paid for their missions, length of service was reduced to 18 months at the same time. But this change proved to be a trial balloon. Two and a half years later, the length of male full-time missionary service was once again returned to 24 months.[51]

As BYU's football team prepared to play a bowl game in San Diego determining 1984's college national champions, Gordon B. Hinckley was still doing missionary work. He and Marjorie, together with 2nd counselor in the First Presidency, Thomas S. Monson, met and spoke with missionaries assigned to the San Diego area.

"You and I are ordinary people who have been given an extraordinary call. The success of the work in this area depends on us," he said.[52]

Mission work has always seemed to be Elder Hinckley's "first love."[53] He has always spoken fervently and ardently about it. Regional representatives (representing the Quorum of the LDS 12 Apostles in certain regions comprising several stakes until 1995 when they were replaced by area authorities) heard his fervor, too.

In a large auditorium on the northeast side of the Church Administration Building and in the Tabernacle on Temple Square on Friday morning and evening, President Hinckley reported 197,640 convert baptisms in 1985. Seventy nine new stakes were created. "This is a remarkable thing," but he said it is not enough. Missionaries in the field were now 27,225 but more are needed.

A missionary of the future should start to save for it in his youth. "It is the responsibility of the individual and the family to provide support for the missionary even though there may necessarily be some delay in departure for the field. Better that a young man delay his mission for a year and earn money toward his support than that he rely entirely on others," he said.[54]

"A boy who serves a mission is never the same. He returns home with qualities and strengths that seem to surface from no other experience. He knows to a degree he never knew before that this work is true and that it is the most important work on the face of this earth."[55]

Two months later a new "teaching from the heart" set of missionary discussions was approved for English speaking missions July 6, 1986.[56] Then six months later, President Hinckley once again spoke of the excitement of missionary work, quoting much of his regional representatives address of eight months before. He said the LDS missionaries were young, handsome and beautiful. They were vital, alive and enthusiastic. They were not easily daunted and enthusiastic and dedicated, committed to a cause and willing to fortify one another. They create lifelong friendships and constantly bring an infusion of new blood into the work. "I am one who believes missionary work is primarily a priesthood responsibility," he wrote.[57]

After this First Presidency Message in the *Ensign*, President Hinckley once again took up the gauntlet less than a year later with another mandate from the First Presidency for all LDS members to be involved in spreading the message and preparing themselves and children to fill missions.[58] February 1988 found President Hinckley emphasizing spreading the gospel once again in his *Ensign* First Presidency Message.[59] Three strikes in 14 months!

Could it be President Hinckley foresaw the increased need for missionaries in new fields which would burgeon in just two years? On June 1, 1988, the LDS religion was officially recognized in Hungary. Soon other walls would fall in Eastern Europe and Russia.

The President of Brazil Jose Sarvey was greeted by President Hinckley on behalf of the First Presidency on Saturday, July 2, 1988 and true to form, the opportunity was not lost without presenting him a specially leather bound copy of the Book of Mormon and some Tabernacle Choir tapes. President Hinckley also explained the purposes of the LDS faith.[60]

Also, in 1988 President Hinckley visited the Philippines once again. He noted, "Phenomenal as the present growth is here (in convert baptisms), the *real* growth will be when our missionaries return home, marry in the temple, and raise up righteous second or third generation Mormons."[61]

A similar experience was had in the Canandaigua Ward Chapel in the New York Rochester Mission by Cumorah on Saturday, July 23, 1988. At the meeting missionaries presented President Hinckley a cross section of a 370 year old tree cut down in the Sacred Grove of Palmyra, New York, where Joseph Smith, Jr. was said to have been visited by God the Father and His Son Jesus Christ as two distinct personages in the form of men.

The opening performance entitled "America's Witness for Christ", a newly revised Hill Cumorah Pageant, depicting the message and bringing forth of Mormon's book, was attended by President and Sister Hinckley the night before and President Hinckley presided at a Sunday service on the Hill Cumorah Sunday, July 24, the day the pioneers entered the Salt Lake Valley in 1847.[62]

In missionary conferences President Hinckley attended, he often quoted the words of the 4th section of the Doctrine & Covenants, second verse. The thoughts touched him: "Therefore, O ye that embark in the service of God, see that ye serve him with all your heart, might, mind and strength, that ye may be found blameless before God at the last day."

Speaking of this verse in his First Presidency Message of January 1989, he penned, "There will be a day of reckoning. There will be a time of confession and accounting. Each day in mortality we are writing the text of that accounting."[63]

This has been his theme throughout his life: Go forth and serve and write that play which the Maker will accept when the curtain falls. Go and serve even though you can't seem to put one foot in front of the other from fatigue. Go and serve as the Master served, selflessly and constantly.

On Friday, March 31, 1989, President Hinckley encouraged regional representatives to see converts were fellowshipped with sincere love.[64] But then the LDS Church suffered three tragedies in its missionary efforts. Two missionaries were killed by terrorists in LaPaz, Bolivia on May 24, 1989. Ghana then abruptly expelled all missionaries from four Christian sects, including those of the Latter-day Saints, on Friday, June 23, 1989.[65] And Thailand's top security agency refused registration of the LDS Church as a recognized religion in its borders saying it had "not received wide recognition among Thais."[66] This was typical opposition to the work as its message continued to penetrate every continent.

But in contrast, Czech, Hungary and Poland branches were established July 1990, part of 29 for the year. September saw mission work begin in East Germany and Russia in September 1990. And a branch was officially recognized in Leningrad (soon to revert to its former name of "St. Petersburg") in Russia.[67]

Up to this time, each full-time missionary was paying different costs for their missions depending upon their place of service. Costs ranged from as low as $65.00 a month in some missions in Mexico to $800.00 or more in areas like Geneva or Japan. But on January 1, 1991, the funds began to be pooled and divided equally between all missionaries worldwide at the average rate of $350.00 a month.[68]

June 18, 1991 saw 81 new mission presidents come for the now annual seminar held just before July when they began three years service in missions throughout the world. President Hinckley was a key speaker at the Missionary Training Center established at Provo, Utah. Then 2,000 missionaries received addresses from President Hinckley, President Monson, and three other apostles and seventies.

President Hinckley said to perform "solid and well-done" work. "The work at best is slow. It must be solid and well done. We cannot afford the kind of teaching that leads to unstable membership and weak and flagging testimony."

Mission presidents go "as leaders, inspired and dedicated and selfless in your service to those whom you lead," he said. They are ambassadors of the Lord Jesus Christ. The responsibility is "almost terrifying," he said, but "You go with our love and confidence to do the work of the Lord."[69]

Implemented for the first time in LDS history was a satellite missionary conference on November 26, 1991 participated in by 16,000 missionaries located throughout the United States and Canada meeting in "many zones" linked by beams from the Tabernacle on Temple Square to space and back to earth.[70]

Planting Seeds Among Kings and Rulers

The Palacio de la Zarzuela, residence palace north of Madrid, Spain was the location President Hinckley went after two days of regional conferences. Here he met the King and Queen of Spain for the second time and gave them a leather bound copy of the Book of Mormon. At the end of the reception on March 9, 1992, the King made an appointment with the Madrid Stake President Faustino Lopez to talk about the LDS principles in more detail.[71]

Two days later, President Hinckley was at the Vatican Library of the Roman Catholic Church in Rome, Italy presenting a five volume set of a recently completed *Encyclopedia of Mormonism* to the Reverend Leonard Boyle. Rev. Boyle received them with pleasure and said, "I can assure you they will be a valued asset to our collection."

In return, Rev. Boyle presented Gordon with a copy of Rev. Boyle's book called *The Vatican Library.*[72]

Back at home, President Hinckley served as keynote speaker at the mission presidents seminar for 1992. "I assure you that the Lord will not let you down if you walk with faith and humility. I have no hesitancy in promising you that."

President Hinckley emphasized mission presidents are better trained now than ever before. Still, hesitancy as to ability will never change. Mission presidents have smaller areas and better transportation now. But the responsibility of mission presidents to help their missionaries, be their friend and helper, have not changed. The most important message to present is a certain knowledge that Jesus is the Christ and Redeemer.

"Of all the victories in human history, none is so great," President Hinckley said, "none so universal in its effect, none so everlasting in its consequences as the victory of the crucified Lord who came forth in the resurrection that first Easter morning."[73]

Cambodia recognized LDS humanitarian service missionaries on March 6, 1994. Shortly thereafter, President Hinckley once again spoke at the annual mission president's seminar on June 22, 1994. That August, it was announced that ⅓ of the United States had been visited by representatives of the LDS Church and 36% of United States citizens had LDS friends or relatives. The "spreading" of the message of the LDS faith had progressed but still ⅔ of the work remained.

After President Hinckley assumed the position of 15th prophet of the Church of Jesus Christ of Latter-day Saints, he did not diminish his zeal for missionary work. June 21-24, 1995, he was sharing one of his favorite scriptures from the Doctrine & Covenants, Section 112:10:"Be thou humble and the Lord thy God shall lead thee by the hand and give thee answers to thy prayers."[74] Then on September 30, 1995, he gave a ringing challenge to every young man. "Prepare to serve a mission for the Church of Jesus Christ of Latter-day Saints."

The legacy of Gordon B. Hinckley's contributions to the mission work of the LDS Church is great. No man has contributed more in innovation and motivation for spreading the restoration message. Indeed, President Hinckley has never been without an official assignment concerning missionary work since he entered the mission home on Administration Block in Salt Lake City that Summer in June 1933.[75]

HUMOR

At the core of Gordon B. Hinckley's personality is the principle of humor. "Humor is a very important element in life–wonderful to be able to laugh–to laugh at ourselves, particularly–not to have fun at the expense of others, but to see the bright side of things. There is an element, a little streak of humor in almost every situation, and it's the thing which makes life sparkle and makes life tolerable, really. What a great thing is a little humor," he says.[1]

President Hinckley has manifested this belief all his life. His mate Marjorie states, "He never took himself or other things too seriously, except things which should be taken seriously. He never has been a worrier."[2]

This philosophy has been a part of his home life. Memories of fun around the dinner table have often been recalled by his children. There was fun there. There was lots of laughing. When Elder Hinckley was a Missionary Department leader, a stake president, and in charge of temple ceremonies in Europe all at once, still he exhibited no great deal of pressure because of his ability to laugh.

Around the dinner table, he would often relate to his family something that happened at the office and then laugh and laugh until he was red in the face and couldn't breathe. This has never ceased.

Helping a Little Lady in the Pre-existence

Going back to the first acceptance speech of his life when called to be an assistant to the twelve apostles, he started his ministry off with a joke. At the podium, President David O. McKay had just introduced Elder Gordon B. Hinckley as the newest assistant-to-the-twelve apostles. President McKay, in his silver white hair, then turned to the right of the podium in the Salt Lake Tabernacle and glanced at his new general authority as he made way for Elder Hinckley to assume the microphone. Elder Hinckley passed President McKay on the way to the stand, then turned towards the audience.

His tongue licked his lower lip as he assumed a stare directly into the middle of the tabernacle participants. He swayed to the right and then the left, clasped his hands and leaned his elbows on the platform.

"I'm reminded of a statement made by my first missionary companion when I received a letter of transfer from the European Mission Office. After I'd read it, I turned it over to him and, he read it. And he said, 'Well, you must have helped an old lady across the street in the pre-existence. It isn't anything you've done here.'" The congregation roared as Elder Hinckley straightened and beamed right along with the congregation with a hearty smile.[3]

Then he became somber. He knows how to laugh when it's right to laugh and be sober when it's right to be so.

A Chip off the Old Block

In a BYU Devotional address on January 10, 1967, Elder Hinckley recalled how a man met him and his father once and said to Gordon, "You're a chip off the old block."

Gordon's father then reminded his son, "Remember, Gordon, the chip is never as big as the block."[4]

The Lost Umbrella

In October 1969 general conference, Elder Hinckley began his address by saying, "I suppose you have heard the story of the absent-minded professor who went shopping and lost his umbrella. Discovering his loss, he retraced his steps. At the first three stores on which he called, the clerks denied having found his umbrella. At the fourth store the clerk handed him the missing umbrella. He grumbled, 'Thank goodness for an honest man. The other three told me they didn't have it.'"[5]

Your Former State

At a BYU Devotional on November 4, 1969, Elder Hinckley remarked after the BYU Symphonic Band had completed an opening number, "I appreciated very much the music of the band directed by Richard Ballon. You are all awake after that. I will do my best to restore you to your former state."[6]

Toolhouse

While leading into his talk at the General Priesthood Meeting of October 1970 general conference, Elder Hinckley talked about a thornless honey locust he had planted. He looked out of his window and noticed how terribly misshapened it had become, leaning ungracefully to the West.

"I went to my toolhouse," he quipped, "where I save things for two years before throwing them away . . ."[7]

Climbing the Ladder

For General Priesthood at the October 7, 1972 general conference, Elder Hinckley told a story of a lad who came down to breakfast one morning and said, "Dad, I dreamed about you last night."

"About me? What did you dream?"

"I dreamed I was climbing a ladder to heaven and on the way up I had to write one of my sins on each step of the ladder."

"And where did I come into your dream?" asked the father.

"When I was going up, I met you coming down for more chalk."[8]

The Freshman Team

As the 34th speaker just before the closing remarks of LDS prophet Harold B. Lee at October 1943 conference, Elder Hinckley stepped up to the pulpit and said, "It is not a new experience for me to speak immediately preceding President Lee. I have had that privilege a score of times recently. Each time I have felt like the freshman team before the varsity comes out for the big game."[9]

Fasting

Speaking to an evening 12 stake fireside at BYU on March 6, 1977, following Fast Day, Elder Hinckley began, "I suppose that most of you have been fasting today. I would suppose that on this campus at least 20,000 people have been fasting and that you have accompanied your fasting with earnest prayer. I think that's a most remarkable phenomenon. Most of you, I assume, have fasted and prayed with a purpose—that you might find answers to perplexing personal problems or the needs of others, or that moisture might fall upon these arid western lands. I hope you haven't prayed for snow with the hope that you could go skiing on Sunday."[10]

The Bus

The sessions of a conference in Johannesburg, South Africa on October 24, 1978 had been hot in the arena and very chilly in the tent where President of the LDS Church Spencer W. Kimball and Elder Hinckley had addressed priesthood bearers in the evening until 9 P.M. Elder Hinckley then announced the bus scheduled to take everyone to the hotel had developed mechanical problems and would be delayed.

Turning to President Kimball, he said, "I'm sure these men would want you to continue talking while they're fixing the bus."

The several hundred priesthood holders present burst into spontaneous applause.

President Kimball then replied, "Thank you," and then with a smile said, "but you couldn't do anything else."[11]

Family Reunions

Elder Hinckley accepted the invitation of his friend Jay Ambrose Quealy, Jr. to speak at Brother Quealy's McCune Family Association reunion on September 11, 1980 in the Lion House in Salt Lake City.

As Elder Hinckley started his talk after dinner he quipped, "Well, I feel very much like a gentile tonight among all these McCunes who are of the House of Israel. I never come to a group of this kind who are interested in their forebears without I think of the statement of an Englishman who said, 'People are like potatoes. The best part of them are underground.'"[12]

He then acknowledged that his wife Marjorie who was there was related through her grandfather George Francis Paxman to the McCunes in some way and said, "I'll let her chart it out when I get home and I will go to bed."

Hong Kong

Elder Yoshihiko Kikuchi, the first native Japanese general authority in the LDS Church, brought laughter in a priesthood session of an Area Conference in Hong Kong on October 20, 1980 by saying, "If each member living in Hong Kong brings just one convert into the Church each year as we are asked to do by the prophet, then the whole city could be baptized in 11 years."

Elder Hinckley then rose to announce more of the proceedings and said, "You have just listened to Elder Kikuchi who has been using one of those Japanese calculators."[13]

Stuffed Pork

One time in an early afternoon budget meeting of the Church Education System feelings became intense between the managers present. Another general authority present turned to President Hinckley, "What do you think?"

With his chin resting on the palms of his hand, President Hinckley said, "I think I am never again going to have stuffed pork chops for lunch." The laughter of everyone immediately dispelled all tenseness.[14]

In the Flesh

While overflow crowds of University of Utah Institute students listened December 7, 1980 on remote TV transmissions in two other chapels while Gordon spoke at an institute fireside in the main multi-purpose center of the LDS Institute complex, President Hinckley remarked, "I was at a stake conference last Sunday and a woman came up after the meeting and said, 'I'm so glad to meet you and look at you in the flesh. You look so much better than your pictures.'

"So if you in the other chapels don't get the right picture, it's because that's the way it goes."[15]

Dallas Temple Groundbreaking

At the Dallas Temple groundbreaking on Saturday, January 22, 1983, 90 regional representatives and stake presidents assembled with President Hinckley and other general authorities present.

"I don't know when I've ever met so many presidents. There are more presidents per square mile in this Church than anywhere else in the world," President Hinckley said.[16]

Absent First Presidency Members

President Hinckley spoke to a mission presidents seminary of 61 new mission presidents on June 24, 1983 but LDS prophet Spencer W. Kimball and his first counselor Marion G. Romney were not with him.

Regarding their absence, he said, "We excuse them. I know how they feel. I had a birthday myself yesterday."[17]

Jet Lag

At a BYU Devotional while still suffering from jet lag and great fatigue from an all night flight from Santiago, Chile where he had delivered 15 speeches during the last 10 days without a speech writer, President Hinckley said, "I do not have a speech writer. I only have the opportunity to pray and work. When I have talked today you may think I should have prayed more and written less."[18]

Mysteries

Speaking to the University of Utah LDS Student Association members in a young adult devotional, President Hinckley said, "I refuse to fret over the mysteries. I do not worry whether the pearly gates swing or slide. I am only concerned that they open."[19]

Convocation

The 109th annual convocation exercises for BYU graduates occurred on a blistering Spring morning, Friday, April 20, 1984. It was a large graduating class clutching their tasseled caps, battling billowing gowns. But they marched dutifully to the convocation location.

President Hinckley arose and said, "There is nothing quite so slow as an academic procession on a cold day."[20]

Broadcast House

At dedication services for a new state-of-the-art television and radio studio for LDS Church owned KSL broadcasting, President Hinckley sparked, "This facility ought to be good—it cost enough."[21]

National Champs

Glen C. Tuckett, Athletic Director for BYU, conducted a special banquet on January 19, 1985 honoring the new 1984 National Football

Champions for American colleges—the BYU Cougars. President Hinckley remarked when he was asked to make some remarks, "I don't like to confess this, but I haven't applauded this vigorously since Washington beat Oklahoma."[22]

Eight months later on Thursday, September 17, President Hinckley was speaking at another BYU Devotional. He asked where you could find a more beautiful campus, better facilities, better qualified faculty and then said, "Where a football team more worthy of cheering about?"[23]

The Gray Eagle

Before Gordon B. Hinckley's opening remarks at a fireside in Soldotna, Alaska in conjunction with the first ever regional conference of LDS members in Alaska, an announcement was made that a gray Eagle automobile had left its lights on in the parking lot. Gordon said, "What's a gray eagle? Is that one of those Alaskan mosquitoes we saw?"[24]

Iosepa

On a desert 60 miles southwest of Salt Lake City where Hawaiian LDS converts had established a settlement a hundred years before, President Hinckley spoke to an audience while dedicating a monument to them on May 24, 1987. He said that if you put a leaf in the ground in Hawaii, before long you have a tree. "You put a leaf in the ground here and before long you have a dry leaf. And that's the difference."[25]

Maturity

Speaking of youth and maturity in April 1988, President Hinckley remarked, "Once we danced and sang with noisy delight. We now enjoy peace and quiet and a comfortable chair."[2627]

The Choir

Remarking on the Tabernacle Choir's return from the South Pacific President Hinckley remarked regarding their televised "Music and the Spoken Word" via satellite from Australia, "Our prayers have been with you, and to see you all here indicates that they have been answered. God be with you, and g'day mates."[28]

Handling a Telephone Call in Japan

Through his long association with Japan for over a decade, President Hinckley had been in many offices and homes there. The Japanese acknowledge what they are hearing frequently by words such as "Eeee" or "Hai", which also means "yes."

One time while extending a call to a brother to serve as a mission president in one of the LDS Church's numerous missions there, President Hinckley said not to worry about the language. He would tell the prospective mission president how to carry a conversation on the phone in Japanese.

Then he proceeded to demonstrate. "Just do this," as he raised his right arm like he was holding a telephone receiver to his ear and repeated over and over again with one second pauses in between each word, "Hai . . ., hai . . ., hai . . ., hai!"[29]

At Phoenix

At a Phoenix, Arizona North Regional Conference on Sunday, January 13, 1991, after Sister Hinckley's remarks, President Hinckley stepped to the microphone for his address and said, "I have done something I have never done before. I have prepared a talk. I ask the Saints to stay awake."[30]

Moisture Received

At the rededication of the Cardston, Alberta, Canada Temple in June 1991, referring to the moisture the community had just received, President Hinckley smiled and said, "The Lord has baptized the entire area with the recent storms. I've been in Cardston a number of times, but have never seen it as washed and polished as it is now."[31]

The next day was President Hinckley's birthday. At the 6th dedication session in Cardston he smiled, "Today's my birthday. The rivets are popping and the solder's wearing thin, but I'm here."[32]

That evening at a dinner honoring his 81st birthday, President Hinckley said, "This evening has been a piece of cake."[33]

Missionary Training Center

At the October 24, 1991 ceremony shoveling soil with six other authorities for expansion of the already too small Missionary Training Center, on Provo, Utah, President Hinckley talked of the planned huge cafeteria to be part of the enlargement and said, "Think of that—a 40,000 square foot cafeteria. No one has greater appetites than missionaries. My father used to say a missionary is like a threshing machine when it comes to his power to consume food."[34]

Cove Fort Dedication

The Cove Fort was restored for preservation and touring on May 9, 1992 in inclement weather. With umbrella over head, President Hinckley went to a stand placed for the occasion and said, "It's raining."[35]

Grandson Peter

Six year old grandson Peter visited Salt Lake in the Summer of 1992 with his parents. President Hinckley related the experience in April 1993 general conference.

Peter's parents pointed out the temple and explained it took 40 years to build. Peter asked, "Why did it take the pioneers 40 years to build the temple when it took the Lord six days to create the whole world?"[36]

Choir & National Guard Army Band

While speaking at the special joint concert with the Tabernacle Choir and the National Guard Army Band on September 13, 1992, President Hinckley explained the construction of the Tabernacle contained no nails. The splits "they bound with green rawhide. Rawhide shrinks when it dries, as any good cavalryman would know." The audience of national guardsmen laughed.[37]

General Priesthood

At the beginning of President Hinckley's address to the General Priesthood session of April 3, 1993 conference, he said, "I think I would like to say a few things to the boys. You older men may listen or sleep."[38]

"Bless You Dear"

At October 1993 LDS conference, Spencer J. Condie, a member of the Seventy general authorities whose appearance resembles President Hinckley, spoke of an experience at the conclusion of a general conference a few years before. After the meetings, two who were attending saw Elder Condie outside the Tabernacle and thought he was President Hinckley. He did not say anything to the first but when the second sister gave the same greeting calling him President Hinckley, he blurted out, "Bless you my dear, have a nice day."

Several months later at a regional conference in Portugal, Elder Condie confessed his sin to President Hinckley.

Said President Hinckley, "Well, Spencer, if you're going to impersonate me, I hope you behave yourself."

A huge laugh reverberated from the Tabernacle congregation. Then after Brother Condie finished his address, President Hinckley rose to announce the next speaker and said, "I must get a new pair of glasses so Brother Condie will no longer be embarrassed." Another hearty laugh emanated from the audience present and from those watching on television, too.[39]

Hinckley's Law

Daughter Virginia remarked in the September 1994 *Ensign* regarding her father, the "Real entertainment is watching Dad tell [jokes]. He laughs so hard as he approaches the punch line that he can hardly speak."[40]

At one of these occasions in talking about the building of new temples and other edifices for the rapidly growing LDS Church he expounded "Hinckley's Law"—"It will cost more and take longer than they said it would."[41]

On Becoming "Emeritus"

After the final speeches of Elders Horacio A. Tenorio and Hartman Rector, Jr. following their respective releases and new emeritus status from the 2nd and 1st Quorums of the Seventy, President Hinckley said, "These two delightful and impressive men have spoken to us out of their hearts as they leave their service as general authorities. That doesn't mean they're through . . . [some laughter from the congregation]

"Brother Tenorios' native tongue is Spanish [from Mexico]. Brother Rector's native tongue is Missourian," as he said "is" in a high tone. There was heavy laughter from the congregation.[42]

At the end of conference sessions on Saturday the day before daylight savings time begins, President Hinckley has often taken the opportunity to suggest the congregation and broadcast listeners should take note of the change and turn their clocks up an hour. "If you don't, you'll find yourself late." Laughter always follows.

He always gets a good laugh when he also says, "Nobody in his right mind—nobody asks to be a general authority—nobody in his right mind would ask to be a general authority."

Microphones

At the funeral address for Sister Eudora Widtsoe Durham, wife of President Hinckley's boyhood friend George Homer Durham, March 10, 1995, President Hinckley stepped up to the microphone and said as the mike emitted some static, "I have spoken at this pulpit before and sometime I'm gonna get that fixed. My first duty when I speak is to raise the microphone."

Later in his address he talked of dinner he had enjoyed at the Durhams' home "which was long on salads and short on sweets" but was always pleasant and very delightful.[43]

A Joke About Jokes

On May 1, 1995 at the groundbreaking ceremony for the new law library addition to the J. Reuben Clark Law School at Brigham Young University, newly sustained 2nd Counselor in the First Presidency James E. Faust, a former lawyer, mentioned in his remarks, "When President Hunter became president of the Church, he did away with all the law jokes."

Picking up on this, President Hinckley repeated President Faust's statement and then said, "Would you like to hear a few?" The crowd burst into laughter.[44]

I'll Trade You Places

At a speech in August 1995, President Hinckley came up to a static mike and said, "I hope this sound improves. It's been acting as if its a little bit upset tonight. There was a situation like this once. People asked what the speaker said. They found a loose screw in the speaker.

"One to the front also said, 'I can't hear,' and a man on the back row said, ' I can and I will trade you places.'"[45]

Trade In

While on his trip in August 1995 to England and Ireland, as President Hinckley was scurrying from a radio interview just ended with a British newscaster to another meeting with 200 waiting missionaries, he quipped, "My voice is tired. I think I'll trade it in on a new one."[46]

Quips with Brother Pickles

During the same trip to England on August 31, 1995 President Hinckley visited his old mission days friend Bob Pickles, then 86, in his living room in Nelson, Lancashire County.

"You look great!" said President Hinckley. "I remember you when you were young," he said as he smiled. "I just wanted to come and say hello. You are the one man left of all the people I knew here."

"All the young ladies thought I was a handsome lad then, didn't they?" Brother Pickles remarked.

President Hinckley laughed.

Brother Pickles then said, "Congratulations on your new call as President of the Church. I'm proud of you. What are you doing in your spare time?"

"Sleeping," President Hinckley said.

When the jovial 20 minute visit ended, Brother Pickles said as they moved outside, "Take good care of him; you know he needs it."[47]

Elder Doxey who accompanied President Hinckley on this trip said the people in Dublin were equally friendly to the prophet. They loved his humor and his being down to earth. The counsel he gave was felt very personal—just for them.

Conference

Before the priesthood in General Priesthood on September 30, 1995, President Hinckley recounted he had recently spoken to the women at their Relief Society Conference, an inspiring experience, and now was speaking to the general priesthood. "I leave to you the judgment of which was the most attractive audience."[48]

During the same meeting before the priesthood, President Hinckley spoke of a question from a British journalist during the LDS president's recent trip to England. The reporter had asked President Hinckley how the LDS Church could use such "callow" youth in their proselyting.

"Yes, they are lacking in sophistication. What a great blessing this is."[49]

After a standing rest song had been sung, President Hinckley said, "I knew you needed that rest. I don't know what your fathers can stand for. I will say it before I get through."

When the conference session Sunday, October 1, 1995 convened, President Hinckley said as he entered, "I'm still here." Then before his closing talk at the Sunday A.M. session, Elder Jeffrey R. Holland of the 12 referred to the hymn "Awake and Arise."

When President Hinckley arose to give the last address of the morning, he said, "It is all right to awake but please don't arise until I get through speaking."

Then in Sunday P.M. session as LDS prophet Gordon B. Hinckley walked into the Tabernacle he said, "We've decided to come back."

The Smile

While talking of outgoing BYU President Rex E. Lee at the BYU Devotional on October 17, 1995, President Hinckley said, "He has even brought a smile to the rock-jawed visage of [BYU football coach] LaVell Edwards, a great accomplishment in and of itself."[50]

When you are around President Hinckley, there is an ease from tension. You know you are in the presence of a prophet but a prophet comparable to Joseph Smith, Jr. - a prophet who is not curt, over somber or stoic, but a prophet who loves life and understands what it is all about.

These are only a sampling of the many sunbeams of humor President Hinckley interjects into every day of life's activities. As 15th prophet in this dispensation, he makes a solemn occasion more sacred by showing mankind God has a sense of humor and so should we. He has always been this way from long, long before he accepted the mantle of an official full-time-authority with general worldwide responsibility. We could do well to learn a mighty lesson about life and its joys from him.

He summed it up himself when he said on September 1, 1995, "We have got to have a little humor in our lives. You had better take seriously that which should be taken seriously but, at the same time, we can bring in a touch of humor now and again. If the time ever comes when we can't smile at ourselves, it will be a sad time."[51]

STAKE PRESIDENCY

Grant LDS Stake was divided on June 17, 1945 while Gordon B. Hinckley's family still lived in Denver, Colorado.[1] The community of East Mill Creek was formed into a new stake covering that area and when the Hinckleys returned to Salt Lake City following World War II, they returned to their home at 3703 South 2700 East on the East bench of the Valley as members of East Mill Creek Stake.

It was not long after Brother Hinckley and family were back in their home before a call came to him to fill the shoes of the second counselor to East Mill Creek LDS Stake President Lamont B. Gunderson. The call was an executive position in the LDS Church requiring ordination to the office of high priest in the Melchizedek Priesthood.

The ordination occurred on July 21, 1946 under the hands of Elder Charles A. Callis, an LDS apostle visiting the East Mill Creek Stake at the time of the installation. Elder Callis first conferred the office of high priest upon Brother Hinckley and then set him apart as the new second counselor to President Gunderson. Thus began almost 12 years service for Brother Hinckley in the stake presidency until he was called to be an assistant to the twelve and became a general authority.

Gordon was just shy of one month into his 37th year, having turned 36 on June 23rd of 1946. He was two years younger than the prophet Joseph Smith, Jr. when Joseph Smith was assassinated by a mob in Carthage, Illinois. He had seen his father faithfully fulfill the same assignment as counselor and then president of the Liberty Stake of Zion all through his developing years and into his mission to England. Now he was fulfilling the same responsibility.

The office of counselor in an LDS stake presidency involved numerous duties. In addition to assisting the stake president with administrative matters, the counselor spoke regularly at meetings within the wards of the stake, interviewed members requesting new temple recommends, sat in counsel with the stake president, his counselors and the stake clerk and executive secretary praying and fasting regarding the selection of stake members to numerous callings in the priesthood and auxiliaries, met with the stake presidency and the stake high council of 12 men weekly, set the example of faithfulness through daily living, planned and spoke at stake conferences, and involved himself in many other activities. It was an exacting job, one that well prepares a man for serving in additional quorums which he would do as a general authority in the future.

As for administration, each counselor served on several committees in the stake, a preview to the numerous committees and boards Gordon would serve on in the future overseeing activities of the entire LDS body. He was on the High Priest Committee, the Stake Board of Education, the Stake Welfare Committee and was Employment Placement Counselor for some time.[2]

Every stake in the LDS Church was similarly organized. Each stake had the full program of the LDS faith which included a full high council with each high councilor visiting the wards within the stake on a rotating basis speaking at Sacrament meetings, attending one or two wards within the stake, and serving on high council committees which included the ones Gordon served on as well as all of the auxiliaries and priesthood branches of the faith.

By November 14, 1948, just two years after becoming 2nd counselor in the stake presidency, another reorganization occurred. This time Gordon was installed as first counselor to President Gunderson and H. Cecil Baker was made second counselor. This makeup of the stake presidency continued until 1950 when H. LeRoy Erickson replaced H. Cecil Baker as second counselor.

Call to Be Stake President

President Lamont B. Gunderson had served as the initial stake president for over 11 years when a reorganization installing a new stake president occurred. Stake Conference met at the large facility on 2005 South 900 East in the Sugarhouse area on Sunday, October 28, 1956 where there was a large meeting hall with rear cultural hall and balcony capable of accommodating many more people than regular chapels. The facility was the Salt Lake Granite Stake Tabernacle built in the mid 1930's and originally dedicated by President Heber J. Grant. It was one of the last tabernacles built by the LDS Church around the early stakes of Zion before smaller stake centers, larger than regular chapels but smaller than tabernacles, were built.

The day was started early in the morning with the Sunday A.M. session. The congregation was favored with the attendance of two LDS apostles, Elder Harold B. Lee, 57, and Elder George Q. Morris, 82. Announcement was made there would be a new stake president called

Salt Lake Granite Stake Tabernacle
2005 South 900 East, Salt Lake City, Utah
Where Gordon B. Hinckley Was Made East Mill Creek Stake President

Interior Tabernacle Meeting Hall
of Salt Lake Granite Stake Tabernacle
Where Gordon B. Hinckley was Made a Stake President
Sunday, October 28, 1956

that day in the East Mill Creek Stake. Elder Harold B. Lee presented the name. When he asked for a sustaining vote from the congregation for Gordon B. Hinckley as the new president of East Mill Creek Stake, a murmur of approval could be heard reverberating from the crowd as they raised their right hands in a unanimous show of approval.

President Hinckley had proven himself for 10 years in the stake presidency as a man of ability, a good leader, administrator and anxiously engaged saint.[3] He had also been involved in the civic affairs of East Mill Creek as its economic and community development president and member of the local water board.

The immediate challenge of the new stake president was meeting facilities for the rapidly developing area of East Mill Creek, quickly becoming a burgeoning adjunct to downtown Salt Lake City. Through the division, only the one meeting house established on the banks of the Mill Creek stream remained in the new stakes's geographical boundary. Numerous homes were constantly being constructed in the community and LDS membership rising. New chapels were needed.

Normally the stake would go on an annual excursion to Lagoon, an outdoor amusement park established in the community of Farmington in the 1870's on the shores of the adjacent Great Salt Lake and later moved to the shores of a small fresh water lagoon by Farmington. This year, however, Gordon cancelled the event and in lieu thereof placed the saved expenditure in a building fund for the stake.

Gordon was a doer. Meetings never were a drag. Although one teenager said President Hinckley's speeches as a stake president were boring to him, President Hinckley ripened into an eloquent orator. He was a man of activity, of inspiration to his stake membership, exhibited humor, had fun and had a way of making you feel good.[4]

The Reluctant Stake Supporter

In addition to the meeting house problem, the new stake had a welfare farm within its boundaries. Accordingly, the interests of the Grant Stake and one other stake organized from the Grant boundaries in the welfare farm would have to be purchased.

"I walked the floor for hours," President Hinckley said. "I didn't know what to do. Then I realized it wasn't my problem, but the Lord's problem and the problem of every priesthood holder in the stake."

A Million Dollar fundraising campaign was launched at a special meeting called for every priesthood holder in the stake. President Hinckley rose and explained the new stake needed buildings. It needed to purchase the interests in the stake farm of the other two stakes from which East Mill Creek had been formed. And every member was a "stockholder" in this venture.

A brother on the front row rose and said, "Ever since I moved into this stake all I've heard from President Gunderson and you is money, money, money. When is it going to stop?"

"Not for a while," was the answer.

One other brother rose and said he was going to move from the stake because of this and two more similarly voiced opposition. Then a small man rose, a postman by vocation.

"Brethren", he remarked, "this isn't President Hinckley's church. It isn't my church. It's the Lord's Church. This problem has to be taken care of and has to be looked at. I'm a postal carrier without very much money; but my wife and I have a savings of $200 or $300 we could give. I'm sure she will back me, and I'm sure we will be blessed for what we do."

A hush came over the congregation. The first brother who voiced his opposition then rose and asked that his remarks be removed from the minutes of the meeting and the other three priesthood holders who had disputed did also.

The fund raising was successful and a new modern red brick edifice was started somewhat above the old Hinckley farm during President Hinckley's presidency which relieved the pressure on the fledgling stake's meeting capacity. Over $50,000.00 came within 28 days, the remaining amount required by Church headquarters at that time for church building construction to commence.[5]

LDS Church headquarters provided a building policy at that time matching every dollar of stake or ward generated funds for chapel construction. As a result of the faithfulness of Gordon's stake members six new chapels were constructed and ward budgets for maintenance and activities paid by financially stressed but faithful saints.[6]

Saving a Marriage

Stake presidents and LDS bishops frequently are called upon to give counsel to struggling couples and families, too. One such occasion arose for Stake President Hinckley with a phone call from a distressed bishop in the stake wondering what to do with a couple seeking divorce who had become deeply in debt and argued over their financial dilemma incessantly to the point of divorce.

Notice of foreclosure had been received on the couple's home and collection judgments were being garnished from the husband's wages. The wife refused to remain at the family house for fear bill collectors would harass. Shouting flew in their mutual frustration.

Emergency needs had been provided by the bishop from the welfare program of the LDS Church where resources from stake welfare farms and canneries and other storehouses reserved for the poor could be tapped. But the long term strategic financial problem needed attention.

President Hinckley asked, "Does the brother belong to a priesthood quorum."

"Yes, he's an elder."

President Hinckley suggested the brother's priesthood quorum become involved in helping one of their brothers. The bishop arranged a confidential meeting with the elder's quorum presidency of the brother. They in turn organized a committee of quorum members to aid the brother and his family. A lawyer, an accountant and a credit manager happened to be in the quorum. They were asked to assist.

The family was called in by the bishop and elders quorum presidency and asked if they would agree to put their financial affairs in the hands of their brethren. They broke down in tears at the sight of willing fellow members so eager to help them.

Monthly payment obligations for the family were double monthly income. But the committee members were used to such problems in their daily professions. They worked with creditors and negotiated satisfaction plans and assured each obligee they would manage the assets and disburse the payments. It worked. The creditors were won over and the family was saved. Their budget habits were patiently changed. Months were necessary but the story ended in success.[7]

President Hinckley later used the experience of the overspending couple to teach the principle of unselfish brotherhood. "The priesthood must look at their needy brethren as a continuing problem until not only his temporal needs are met, but his spiritual ones also. . . A priesthood quorum sets him up in work and tries to see that he goes along until fully self-supporting and active in his priesthood duties," President Hinckley quoted from remarks made by President J. Reuben Clark, Jr. in 1941.[8]

The Temple Recommend Seeker

Before a Latter-day Saint may enter any of the LDS temples to perform ordinances for himself or ancestors there, she or he must be interviewed and found worthy on an annual basis not only by their respective bishop but also by a member of their stake presidency. A recommend is signed by the bishop or his delegated counselors and then is taken to the stake presidency for additional interview and signature by the stake president or his delegated counselors. Then it may be used for 12 months after which it must be renewed.

A brother came to Stake President Hinckley for his temple recommend approval and was asked the usual questions including, "Are you paying an honest tithing?"

The Latter-day Saint said, "No, President, I cannot afford to because of my many debts."

President Hinckley felt impressed to impart, "You will not be able to pay your debts until you pay your tithing."

The brother continued the same for a couple of years and then came and told President Hinckley, "What you told me when you interviewed me for my recommend has proved to be true. I felt I could not pay my tithing because of my debts. I discovered that no matter how hard I tried, somehow I could not manage to reduce my debt. Finally my wife and I sat down together and talked about it and concluded we would try the promise of the Lord.

"We have done so. And somehow in a way we can't quite understand, the Lord has blessed us. We have not missed that which we have given to him, and for the first time in many years we are reducing our debt. We have come to the wisdom of budgeting our expenditures and of determining where our funds have been going.

"Because we now have a higher objective, we are able to curtail some of our appetites and desires. And above all of this, we feel we can now go to the house of the Lord with clear consciences as those deserving of this wonderful blessing."[9]

On April 6, 1958, Gordon B. Hinckley was called to be a general authority for the LDS Church and was released from his stake presidency service in the East Mill Creek Stake.

Stake President Reunion

Nineteen years after Gordon became a general authority for the LDS Church, the surviving former stake presidents who had served over the East Mill Creek Stake met in a fireside at East Mill Creek Stake facilities honoring their service. Six of the 8 stake presidents were present and President Hinckley spoke of his remembrances during that two years of stake president church service prior to being sustained as an assistant to the twelve.[10]

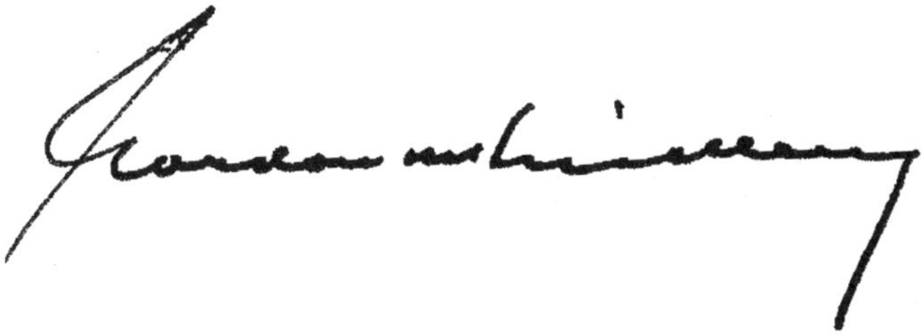

Signature of Gordon B. Hinckley

FAR EAST SUPERVISION

President Henry D. Moyle, new 2nd counselor in the First Presidency as of June 12, 1959, met with Elder Gordon B. Hinckley, Assistant to the Twelve, sometime between that time and April 1960. The subject of consultation was organization of the expanding mission work of the LDS Church.

Area Supervision

The two leaders pounded out a proposal for the creation of area supervision by each member of the Twelve Apostles. The world was divided up, but one area remained – Asia. Elder Hinckley was asked if he could be a supervisor along with the 12. The proposal was approved by the full First Presidency. And Gordon B. Hinckley began his odyssey as Supervisor of the Far East.

He did not waste any time. A trip to the Orient was planned. It was Elder Hinckley's first visit to that part of the world. The travesty of war had been a tool opening doors. Japan was opened to the work by American servicemen after a long lull during the war years. The first converts after the war were the future revisor of the early 1900's translations of the Book of Mormon and Doctrine in Covenants texts, Tatsui Sato and his first wife Chiyo on July 7, 1946 in the old swimming pool of an otherwise bombed out Sannomiya University campus.

A bombed out Japan Government Welfare Ministry building in Hiroo-cho, Tokyo was purchased for a mission home, several other intact homes bought for missionary quarters and meeting houses and the mission formally reopened in 1948. But there were no wards, stakes nor permanent meeting houses in Japan by 1960 even though LDS Church membership had then risen to several thousand.

There was little stability in leadership at the time. "They were baptizing them but no faster than they were walking out the back door," Elder Hinckley later said.[1]

Korea had been largely untouched until the Korean War when another American presence of LDS servicemen swung the doors open for missionary work. But no permanent structures or chapels existed there either.

In truth, no permanent buildings for worship existed in all of Asia. The gospel message had been preached. But the leadership was weak. The sustaining Church influence was the continuing presence of LDS Servicemen active in the faith.

Elder Hinckley surveyed the compass of his responsibility. It covered virtually all the vast reaches of Asia from India on the south to Japan on the north—over one-third the world's population with China included. Many of these areas were yet untouched by the gospel since minor efforts by the early elders in the 1800's.

The nations in the Far East were divided at that time into only 2 missions: The Southern Far East Mission, comprising all the nations from India, Burma, Singapore, Malaysia, Indonesia, Cambodia, Laos, Vietnam, Hong Kong, China, Taiwan and everything between; and the Northern Far East Mission, comprising Korea, Japan and Okinawa. Both missions had been organized in 1955 splitting the Japanese Mission.

Elder Hinckley was well acquainted with the work which had been going on here. His work as virtually the head of the missionary department of the Church had taught him. He also had coordinated re-translation of the standard works in Japanese. But he had never set foot in that part of the world in his 50 years.

First Trip to Asia

Now the vast reaches of Asia were before him–and his responsibility. A seven week exploratory visit to all of the nations where any LDS presence existed, native or American military, was planned.

Gordon and his wife Marjorie had travelled as far as Hawaii before on a propeller-driven plane but never further. And on that occasion an engine had stopped. The plane had dipped and all aboard about to meet their Maker. But the plane was able to fly on the remaining engine.[2] Now he boarded a Boeing 707 jet to Hawaii and then on to the Far East. The date was April 29, 1960.

His first stop was Hawaii where his now long-time friends Jay and Virginia Quealy met him. Brother Quealy had been made the Honolulu Stake President about the time of the war after serving as a bishop in his home ward. Now the Quealy's, who ran an air conditioning company franchise, greeted their brother-in-the gospel with open arms.

Then it was on to Hong Kong. The growing Hong Kong skyscrapers were amazing. The teaming swarms of humanity amazed him, and the faith of the handful of Latter-day Saints encouraged him. He held member and missionary conferences wherever he went. If LDS military groups or districts existed, he was at their side, greeting, encouraging and getting a feel for the territory.

Next it was to the Philippines. Not one native baptized member of the Church could be found. Unbelievable! But the LDS serviceman was there. Then it was to Japan.

In Japan, servicemen's conferences were held. Land was examined for potential sites for permanent chapels. Even the possibility of purchasing a plot of ground for an LDS cemetery was brought to his consideration.

At this time, he first met the first convert to the Church in Japan following World War II, Brother Tatsui Sato, who was now working full time for the Church as its native Japanese translator. Brother Sato's re-translation of the Book of Mormon and Doctrine & Covenants and Pearl of Great Price has gone past Elder Hinckley's desk in the early 1950's when he had been in charge of foreign translations of the standard works.

The members were met and conferences held. Little did Elder Hinckley know that this trip would be the commencement of over 40 trips to the Orient before he was ordained seer, revelator and prophet 35 years later, trips which if added up would total over 3 years of his life, the equivalent of a full-time mission president's tenure. Missionaries were not forgotten. They were met, interviewed, and encouraged in missionary conferences. The some odd 20 branches interspersed throughout the islands of Japan and Okinawa were visited. Elder Hinckley was beginning to get a more sure picture of the strengths and the needs of the Far Eastern church.

Then off to Korea. This visit encouraged him. He sat in a high school gymnasium where a sandy haired full-time missionary from a Southern Utah farm conducted a meeting for 500 Korean Latter-day Saints and friends investigating the LDS faith. Only two married couples were then members of the LDS Church in all the city of Seoul. The members were young, oh so young. But their faces were "forward looking." After the meeting, the Koreans came up to the missionary filling the shoes of District President in Seoul and embraced him. He embraced them. Elder Hinckley marveled at the power of Jesus Christ's gospel which alters the hearts of humanity.

He then visited Pusan, a city on the south tip of the shoe shaped peninsula which is Korea. Gordon called it a "sad city" at that time. The harbor park was the scene of a street meeting with missionaries and 150 curious but intelligent looking men and women a few feet from a large anti-aircraft gun, remnant of the recent Korean War. Elder Hinckley walked into the crowd with an LDS US Army sergeant as an LDS elder from Florida began to speak.

A spectator in the crowd stopped them and in broken English asked, "How long that young man been here?"

"Two years."

"No—he here longer. Americans here 15 years and not speak our language. Americans no speak Korean like that."

But the sergeant and Elder Hinckley assured him the missionary had only been there two years. At that time foreign missions were three years in length.

Elder Hinckley thought of the Savior's words, "They shall speak with new tongues."[3]

At the conclusion of doing the same things he had been doing in every other nation he had visited, he wrote in his tour notes, "This has been a most interesting and faith-promoting experience to meet with our missionaries and members in Korea. While the missionaries have been wonderful everywhere, I felt that we had a finer spirit in our testimony [meetings] here than anywhere I have been. These young men love the people among whom they are laboring. This is one reason for their success. For the most part they are doing good work and are very happy in it."[4]

Then it was back to Japan, the last leg of his trip. Rising as usual at 4:30 or 5:30 in the morning, he conducted his concluding visits to church leaders, missionaries and servicemen.

Northern Far East Mission President Paul C. Andrus took Elder Hinckley to Hiroshima, site of the first Atom Bomb explosion in 1945, where they met an LDS businessman living in Hiroshima who had served in the Imperial Army of Japan nine years. The brother from Hiroshima was now an elder in the Melchizedek Priesthood.

"Thank God for the missionaries," the brother said. "Last night my wife and I were on our knees, as we are each night, to express gratitude for the coming of these two young men who have literally saved our lives. We had nothing to live for, no hope here or hereafter, and we were drinking ourselves to death. They came. They taught us. They brought purpose into our lives. The change in me has been so noticeable that my business partner became curious. I have been teaching him the gospel, and I am now going to baptize him."[5]

At a missionary testimony meeting, Elder Hinckley witnessed a full-time LDS elder stand to his feet with a letter in his hand. "I think I am happier than I have ever been in my life," he said. "I have had many wonderful experiences here, and they have made me happy, but it is this letter that has really warmed my heart."

He told of his father, a drinker before his son left for his mission who said to him as he left on his mission, "My son, I am going to try to live worthy of you."

Now the letter in his hand from his father reported his father had been ordained a high priest and was set apart as a counselor in the bishopric.[6]

At the conclusion of his tour on June 18, 1960 he dictated, "We have many problems in our missionary work in this part of the world, but I think they are essentially no different from those found in other areas. As a matter of fact, the missionaries are generally happier. This is difficult to understand in view of the circumstances under which they are living. They are in the midst of filth and have lack of the comforts to which they are so accustomed when they go. However, they are well and happy and devoted and it has been inspiring to see them at work."[7]

It was seven weeks since Elder Gordon B. Hinckley had left home. He had traveled over 25,000 miles and had laid the groundwork for serious construction of several of the first permanent chapels in Asia.

He was so impressed with his first visit to Asia, his entire general conference talk that October 1960 was devoted to the "miracle" he had witnessed there.

From this first trip, other flights to the same areas ensued. Pan American Airlines, in which the LDS acquired an interest, were used by him many times. He flew to Tokyo, other cities in the Pacific Rim, Australia, India and even Switzerland, Germany, Britain, South America and other places serviced by Pan Am until it sold its routes and dissolved.[8]

Elder Hinckley kept a tight reign on the missionaries. Hardly ever did a general conference roll by but what President Hinckley was back visiting with his missionaries and mission presidents and the servicemen and saints.

When he interviewed the missionaries he often said, "Are you the kind of missionary your mother hopes you are?"

If there was a strong "Yes", he often felt other questions unnecessary. He felt living up to the hopes and expectations of one's mother showed integrity in performance.[9] One time he interviewed an elder in Japan, the elder expressed frustrations and feelings of inadequacy.

Elder Hinckley forcefully and powerfully said, "Elder, you just need to live one day at a time. You don't need to worry about yesterday or tomorrow."[10]

Philippines Dedication for the Gospel

Following LDS general conference the first part of April 1961, Elder Hinckley recorded one of the major events in his life. He has referred to it at least 12 times in public addresses and articles since the experience.

Southern Far East Mission President Robert S. Taylor accompanied Elder Hinckley to Manila, Philippines on April 28, 1961 where the US Embassy in Manila provided a meeting place on the porch of the marble memorial of the American Military Cemetery at Fort McKinley on Manila's outskirts for a sunrise service.

The service began at 6:30 A.M. Sister Maxine Grimm had been the catalyst for it. She was from Tooele, Utah, a member of the Red Cross during World War II who carried a strong conviction of the LDS faith and a little portable organ with her all through the war campaigns of the Pacific.

When the war ended, Maxine and her US Army officer husband established a home in Manila and introduced the gospel every time they could. The center of the Latter day Saints in the Philippines became the Grimm home. Meetings were held there and baptisms performed in the swimming pool. But the converts were all US military personnel.

Maxine believed in the Filipino people. She had grown to love them dearly and knew many of them would readily accept the restored gospel message if missionaries could just knock on their door. So when Elder Hinckley came to the Philippine Islands in 1960, she was one of the first ones to greet him with her plea to send missionaries. Elder Hinckley took her request to the LDS First Presidency who authorized the establishment of mission work there and the sunrise meeting had been organized with that purpose in mind.[11]

One lone Filipino member of the Latter-day Saint Church had been found since Gordon's first visit in 1960. The boy had discovered a copy of the *Reader's Digest* in a garbage can which contained a condensed book about the LDS faith and spoke of Joseph Smith, Jr. as a prophet. The word "prophet" did something to him. He lost the magazine but wondered and wondered all during the war and oppression.

He obtained work at Clark Air Base following the war. He soon found his supervisor, a US Air Force officer, was LDS. For some time he was hesitant to ask but finally exerted the courage and said, "Are you a Mormon, sir?"

"Yes, I am."

"Do you believe in a prophet? Do you have a prophet in your church?"

"We do have a prophet, a living prophet, who presides in this church and who teaches the will of the Lord," the officer replied.

The brother was baptized and eventually became an elder.

Both Sister Grimm and this brother were at the sunrise services where the small group organized formal LDS proselyting in the Philippines. Sister Grimm brought her well used portable organ and played the music as the small group sang amidst the 5,000 white crosses surrounding the monument where they met, graves of part of the 30,000 American servicemen who had died during WW II. Full-time missionaries arrived from Hong Kong that same day to start the work.

A baptism soon was performed for Miss Filipinos Ping, age 29, who had become involved in assisting Sister Grimm's husband as he did the legal work and Sister Ping obtained Philippine Government approval for establishment of mission work there. Sister Ping eventually married a Brother Bachelor and lived in Buena Park, California in 1984 when a Philippine LDS Temple became a reality. The Grimms' swimming pool at the Spanish style home continued to serve as a nice baptismal font for 2,000 or more converts!

Elder & Sister Hinckley became even closer to that sacred ground in the military cemetery when they saw the name of a man on a marble memorial Marjorie Hinckley knew who had grown up in the same neighborhood with her. As a captain he and his airplane had plunged into the ocean during World War II. Marjorie took a picture of the stone tablet and presented it to the deceased son's mother after they returned to the States. The mother wept, this time in gratitude.[12]

Building Missionaries

President Hinckley could see the Church members in Asia deserved permanent chapels in which to worship. The building missionary program was worldwide now. So he tapped into its organization and secured approval for chapels in Japan and Taiwan. A building supervisor was sent to the Far East and local inexperienced builders as well as construction-experienced men with their families from America were called and brought together to work as a team filling building missions. Chapels were begun in north, east, and west Tokyo and in Yokohama, Osaka and Okinawa.

A stake center in Taiwan was begun in 1961. Elder Hinckley recalls seeing the local members excavate the foundations. The relief society president sat on a pile of lumber removing her shoes and silk stockings, then hoisted a pole across her shoulders with a bucket hanging on each end. She walked barefoot through the mud and grease squeezing between her toes. Then she entered the trenches and began bringing dirt up out in her shoulder balanced buckets.[13]

Organizing the Korean Mission

Elder Hinckley came back as a newly ordained LDS apostle when he visited Asia in 1962. This time one of his major objects was the formation of a separate mission in Korea. Recommendation had been approved by the First Presidency. On July 8, 1962, the Korean Mission separated from the Northern Far East Mission.

Work in Korea had been generated by several forces. There was the influence of the LDS military during the Korean conflict from 1950-1953. But, also, the first native Korean baptized was Brother Kim Ho Jik in the United States. Oliver Wayman and Don C. Wood met Kim as fellow college students at Cornell University.

All three were graduate students pursuing masters and doctorate degrees. The Book of Mormon was introduced to Kim. Examples were shown. Genuine love was expressed. And Kim took two titles back with him to Korea after baptism in the LDS chapel he attended in Ithaca, New York—that of "Doctor of Philosophy" and "Brother." Through the prestige of Dr. Kim's educational credentials and the responsible position he acquired in Korea, his LDS label established a beachhead for the LDS faith in his nation through the first formal work in 1956.[14]

Added Excitement in the Nations

Additional experiences in 1962 excited Elder Hinckley. The 8,000 members throughout Asia were steadily rising. In Hong Kong sang hymns in Cantonese. Native Chinese elders served there now. One said, "I hated Americans. I hated all foreigners until I met the missionaries."

"As I look at foreigners," another said, "I think: He is not American; he is not British; he is not Canadian; he is my brother."

In an upstairs room in Tsim Sha Tusi, Kowloon, a 13 hour marathon testimony meeting greeted Elder Hinckley. Missionary after missionary expressed love for his Chinese brothers and sisters.

Kwok Yuen Tai received an invitation from a fellow friend to attend LDS Sunday School with him in 1962. A year later he was baptized. Later Elder Hinckley met him as he studied in Sydney, Australia for a chemistry degree. Next Elder Hinckley saw him in London working for a great chemical organization. In April 1993, he became the first LDS general authority from Hong Kong.[15]

Taiwan produced the same spirit. Meetings there brought a brilliant and handsome young Chinese Latter-day Saint to Elder Hinckley's acquaintance as the Chinese brother spoke of the gospel in Mandarin. A missionary in Taipei from warm Hawaii was expressive of his blessing to teach the gospel to the Taiwanese even though he stood in a very barren and cold meeting room where his breath vaporized as he spoke. Thirty other missionaries heard him.

Four thousand native LDS were in Japan and 1,300 in Korea.[16]

President Quealy's Miracle

Gordon's good friend Jay A. Quealy, Jr. was the mission president over the Southern Far East Mission now. He and his family had come into the field in August 1962 with headquarters in Hong Kong. Two years of his three year mission still remained.

At 6 A.M. on a morning in July 1963, President Quealy took a motorscooter to visit some lazy elders who were not rising at the appointed time. On the way back to board the Kowloon ferry, rain slickened the streets. He collided with a police van taking 30 police officers to their beats around the city.

He awoke in the Hong Kong University Medical Center Hospital with no recollection of the collision. One leg was broken in four places, the other in three. Nine ribs were broken as well as his left wrist and jaw. And he was suffering from a concussion. A Catholic nurse from England was holding President Quealy in a stretcher in the hospital hall. No authority to treat had yet been obtained. They had notified the Mission Home but his wife was shopping for groceries.

The Mission Office notified Elder Hinckley in Salt Lake City. He and wife Marjorie were all packed to pick up their son Richard from his mission in Germany. "I'll get there," Elder Hinckley told the office staff. He cancelled his trip to pick up his son and was in Hong Kong in 36 hours.

Elder Hinckley arrived after one operation had already been performed on the president's legs. Others were needed. Elder Hinckley had been given instructions to bring President Quealy home. A member of the Quorum of the 70 would take his place in the interim while a permanent replacement could be found.

Elder Hinckley said, "Jay, what would you like to do?"

"Well, I would really like to stay here, Brother Hinckley. I'm sure if I stay here I'll be out of the hospital faster than they tell you I'll be because I heal quickly. From past experience, I know.

"They tell you it will be a year and two to three months. I'm sure I'll be out of here in nine months."

Elder Hinckley then laid his hands on the mission president's head and blessed him. "You will have all the use of your limbs," he promised. He next talked to both the president and his wife.

Next Gordon got on the telephone to President Henry D. Moyle, First Presidency counselor responsible for LDS missionary work. "Brother Quealy is broken up from head to toe. But there's one thing that isn't broken and that's his heart. If we bring him home, I'm afraid we'll break that."

Following the phone call, Jay Quealy said, "If you can come out twice every three months during nine months, Virginia can visit the missionaries in between." The arrangements were finalized.

Gordon B. Hinckley did come back and visited all of the zones of the mission including the 590 missionaries within the vast Southern Far East Mission area. There were missionary counselors in each of the three zones. Each had separate offices and counselors due to the language difficulties. President Quealy's wife Virginia would substitute for the president's presence.

President Quealy phoned each of the 110 missionaries in Hong Kong weekly and wrote to the rest in the mission each week using a dictating machine from his hospital bed. He could not raise his head for seven months. So he used a glass stand placed above his head on which the weekly report letters of the missionaries were placed face down so he could look up and read them and then respond to them.

Two nurses attended the president round the clock. The doctors first wanted to amputate President Quealy's right leg. Gangrene had developed. But President Quealy told them Elder Hinckley blessed him he would have use of all of his legs. So the nurses massaged his legs gently every day and night for a month. Then the legs mended. The blessing of Elder Hinckley had been realized and President and Sister Quealy finished their term of service.[17]

Missionary Conference in Tokyo

By this time chapels were taking shape. The special building missionaries had been working hard.

The first two permanent chapels in Japan neared completion and Elder Hinckley notified President Dwayne N. Andersen, then presiding over the Northern Far East Mission, he would come to dedicate the first two chapels on April 26, 1964 with a special invitation to missionaries in the Tokyo Area to gather with him to fast and bear testimony the day before.

The spirit of the missionaries privileged to participate in this event was one of happy anticipation in view of the purpose of President Hinckley's visit. They arrived early at Central Branch in Tokyo. As Elder Hinckley came walking in the door, they sang in loud unison a special song for him to the tune of "Welcome, Welcome, Sabbath Morning."

Welcome, welcome, Elder Hinckley,
Welcome, welcome, to Japan,
We are gathered here to greet thee,
And to share the Gospel plan.
From your words of inspiration,
Our efforts are renewed,
And we go forth greatly strengthened,
This mission work to do.

Welcome, welcome, Elder Hinckley,
We are glad to have you here,
We are thankful for your guidance,
And the spirit that you share.

Welcome, welcome, Elder Hinckley,
We have brought our buckets here,

To be filled with inspiration,
From your words so true and dear.
We are thankful to be servants,
In this our Father's work.
We will try to march on,
Stronger never to waver or shirk.

Welcome, welcome, Elder Hinckley,
We are glad to have you here,
We are thankful for your guidance,
And the spirit that you share.

The Sacrament was passed to all present, following which Elder Hinckley asked each missionary to introduce themselves and tell how many people they had the privilege of teaching the gospel and seeing them come into the Church and how many of those people were still active. The missionaries then began their testimonies.

Then Sister Andersen and President Andersen, mission parents, spoke. At the conclusion, Elder Hinckley rose and talked.

"This is the 7th time I have been here. I never know when it will be the last. I have gained a love for the Japanese. I rejoice in the strength that is coming to the Church here. I visited East Branch and saw the new building. I was thrilled. When I came before I saw an old dusty, dirty warehouse. I am looking forward to tomorrow when we will dedicate the first two of our buildings constructed from the ground up in Japan.

"I was in Hong Kong on the 12th for a conference at Hong Kong City Hall. A thousand saints were there.

"The Church has now purchased an expensive property. It is on a hill and looks over Hong Kong Harbor.

"We then went to the Philippines and had a conference with 250-300 members who were not members 3 years ago when the mission was opened there. Then we went to Formosa and held a series of meetings with our people. The work is going well in the Republic of China.

"Then I went on to Korea. The sadness of Korea is heartbreaking. The poverty of the people. The terrible poverty of the people. You can't believe it 'til you see it. Rice is $30.00 a bag. Potatoes $10.00 a 100. Sugar $100.00 a pound, bread 80¢ a loaf. But I don't know any place where I feel the spirit of the Lord more strongly than in Korea. It was a conference there with a wonderful spirit.

"Then we went to a servicemen's meeting. Then here. I have one regret and that is that I don't feel I am taking enough time to see the other missionaries here. The only thing I can do is to assure you that the Church feels concerned about you. We are concerned for your welfare, and your parents are concerned. Be the kind of missionary your mother thinks you are.

"Young men, you didn't come to Japan to get a wife. The Japanese girls are not for you. And I say to the Japanese girls, the missionaries are not for you. Because of customs and for other reasons both you and they, and your children, will be happier if you marry within your race. Don't get involved. You are here to preach the gospel and not to find a wife.

"Happiness lies in obedience. Three weeks ago 4 missionaries were excommunicated from the Church. President McKay said, 'No missionary gets into trouble in a moment.' The thought is always father to the deed. These young men know better. They had been to the temple of the Lord and had made solemn covenants with the Lord. You don't get in trouble in the moment.

"Be careful of people you baptize. Be careful of baptizing the mentally retarded. These people are not of a capacity to understand what they are doing. They are likely to become difficult problems to the Church. Spend time with those who will add strength to the Church. We must have people with faith and ability to build the Church in the last days. We should not be looking for people who are going to be potential problems. I am shocked at the convert mortality rate. We are not holding enough of the people who are baptized. Do not leave those you have baptized without seeing that the Priesthood of the branch will fellowship and continue to teach them.

"We grow under responsibility. If we have responsibility and take it seriously, we will grow under it. Give every convert a responsibility commensurate with his ability.

"Here are some steps of proselyting:

1. Be certain your investigators are adequately prepared for baptism.
2. Use fellowshipping lessons following baptism.
3. Assign every convert some responsibility.
4. 'Nurture with the good word of God.'
5. Help every man to live worthy to receive the Priesthood."[18]

These were the significant statements made by Elder Hinckley at this historic meeting prior to dedication of the first chapel in Asia.

Tokyo North Branch Dedicatory Service
First Chapel Dedicated in Asia

The next morning, Sunday, April 26, 1964, on a beautiful Spring day, members from the surrounding Tokyo branches gathered to witness the dedication of the first permanent chapel in Japan and Asia. The snow-white walls of the North Branch chapel blended with the white steeple. It rose in a triangle from the entrance way at the chapel front to a sharp point in the sky.

The main chapel and extended recreation hall was filled to capacity with happy and rejoicing members. Many American members from surrounding servicemen's branches joined in the jubilation—to witness this moment in Church history. Numerous flowers decorated the pulpit and surrounding area. The guest of honor, Elder Gordon B. Hinckley, and other leaders wore distinguishing corsages as added commemoration of the occasion.

Brother Katwyk

The first speaker was Brother Katwyk, one of the building supervisors. To his side stood a native interpreter who translated. Speakers spoke a sentence or two and then paused while the interpreter conveyed the words in Japanese.

"Many buildings have been built in the Church. When I came to Japan, I had mixed emotions. I fought against these people and had a great deal of hatred for the Japanese young men. I prayed to the Lord when I was placed over eight Japanese boys that I would control what feeling of hatred I had for them. He has done it. I love these boys like I do my own sons. These young boys should get the credit here today. I am real proud of them and I would like to show them off to you today. I would like them to come up today."

The building missionaries stood and began walking to the front.

"When we started this building, the Japanese Government said it would never happen. 'You can never build a building like this with unskilled labor,' they said. These young men didn't know how to build when they started on this job. I can't even talk to them. But we had a partner. That was our Lord and Savior Jesus Christ and the Holy Ghost communicated between us—me and these young men. You can look around and compare this structure to any other structure in Japan and these young men have done it.

"My brothers and sisters, a great deal of praise should be given to these young men. They are giving up 2 years of their life to work for the Lord. There are many others that we should thank at this time, all the fine brothers and sisters of the branch here. The sisters that came out faithfully and worked. Also the servicemen that came down here and donated their time. There are many of them that can go back to the States and say boastfully, 'I put the concrete in.'

By this time the 21 Japanese labor missionaries had assembled before the congregation and were recognized. Brother Katwyk, a Paul Bunyan of a man, began weeping for joy as he recognized them.

"I am a pretty big man. I am getting upset with myself. I would like to thank my Heavenly Father for the many blessings he has given me and the wonderful association that I have had all the time I have been here. I would like to bear you my testimony that I know this is the Lord's work, that Jesus Christ lives, that if we are faithful to the end, we may receive this reward if we are worthy. I would like to ask your forgiveness at this time. If I said something to hurt you or offend you or anything, I am deeply sorry. I would like to ask your forgiveness."

Brother Chenney

Brother Chenney, Far East Construction Supervisor, then rose.

"The Lord says, 'This is my work and my glory to bring to pass the immortality and eternal life of man.' The purpose of our meeting here today is to give this building to the Lord. He also tells us that he who is greatest among you shall be a servant.

"I give thanks to the labor missionaries for their dedication to the Lord. There are many who feel that if you are laboring with your hands, you are belittling yourself. This is not so. If you recall, the Savior of the world worked with His hands for the first 20 or 30 years before He went into the mission field as a carpenter. King Benjamin in the Book of Mormon is a classic example of a person who worked with his hands in order that he did not have to tax the people for his support.

"When he became an old man, he had all of the people in the kingdom called together. Among many things which he said under the direction of the spirit of the Lord is that the natural man is an enemy of God. And he said that we would have to put off this pride and put it to one side and overcome the natural man. And he said unless we become spiritual to the enticings of the Holy Spirit and become dependent on the Kingdom of the Gospel, we do not find place in the

Kingdom of God.

"The author-master of this earth was Jesus Christ under the direction of our Father in Heaven. He built this because he wants to see us progress. And he commanded that we meet together often that we may worship him often. This is the purpose of this building. Now we are giving the Lord this building that we may become dedicated to the Lord. There is the scripture that says unless we build it to the Lord the building is in vain and I might say that this edifice is not only to the Saints here but to our Lord. I pray that we will put forth the effort in our lives to do this I pray in the name of Jesus Christ. Amen."

A choir of relief society sisters rose and sang "Bless This House" after which Mission President Dwayne N. Andersen stood to speak.

President Dwayne N. Andersen

"Today I can see a fulfillment of something still a miracle. I can see the hand of the Lord in gathering out the young in heart in His people. I suppose you can say that this starts an era or opening era of the work of the Lord in the Orient.

"I was greatly thrilled by the musical number given by these fine young singers of the relief society of this district. I was pretty happy to have them sing that beautiful song "Bless This House" and to labor so diligently to sing it in English. Now I think there are a lot of people responsible for this great edifice and I would like to just mention a few today of them.

"I wish President Grant could look upon this group—this congregation. This would thrill his heart as he labored so diligently here in the first years of the mission. President Grant, then an Apostle, labored in Tokyo in 1901 with the small handful of missionaries. They were met with disgrace and disappointment and failed in being able to firmly establish the Kingdom of God in this land. And it became necessary in 1923 to close the work of the Lord in this land. But I think we owe a great deal of gratitude to those pioneers who opened the work and got it started for they had a great deal to do with what you witness today.

"The second group of people in 1948, another group of missionaries, were sent to unlock the doors and open the work of the Lord again. So it is with a great deal of gratitude we thank those missionaries who from 1948 until the present have been gathering out the honest in heart and bringing them to God's Kingdom.

"Then we owe a great deal to those who have come here to labor and to a foreign land to help build the Kingdom in this wonderful country. They have come to a world different than what they are accustomed to and a language they cannot understand and to a people they know little about. But as you can see, the Lord has melted the bond that was between them or the thing that holds people apart and through love and cooperation, this has melted to make it possible for this wonderful building. And I think that no greater love can be shown among men than is found with those supervisors and these young men with whom they work.

"Then we owe a great deal of gratitude to these young men who have given up 2 years of their life to come and work for the Lord. They have laid aside all of their own individual plans and all their own individual desires and put their hand to the building of the Kingdom of God.

"Along with these young men, there are two families which I would like to pay tribute to at this time. Brother and Sister Nara and now Brother and Sister Niita helped look after these young men, looking after their needs. We have one other group which we owe a great deal to. This is the American servicemen who have come to this land from the close of the war 'til this time. Without their help, this building would not be standing here today. Out of their meager alms, the wages they have received, they have contributed thousands of dollars to this program. And with this money, we have been able to start the building program.

"Many of these young men contributed much money who knew they would never see the buildings which would be built for the honest in heart and that they would be gathered together and taught that they would become strong together in this land. And when these buildings were started, the servicemen were the first to contribute and labor to erect these buildings. They have worked hand in hand in establishing the work of the Lord in this land.

"Then we owe a great deal of gratitude to the members who have also helped with finances and labor of their own hands and I wish to express appreciation to the fine people, friends of the Church, who have provided money for the building of these buildings.

"I would like to draw your attention to the fact that this is a modern miracle, this building is a modern miracle that these young men, unskilled, with the help of a supervisor, could build such a beautiful edifice as we have here, especially when the language is completely new and no knowledge is had by the supervisors. These buildings were built by faith and courage of dedicated men to the Lord. President Hinckley entitled one of his articles or talks, I guess it was, with a scripture and I would like to quote because it is one of my favorites. Psalms 127:1. 'Except the Lord build the house, they labour in vain that build it. . .'

"I would like to say that the Lord built this house and that those who labored here did not labor in vain. I mentioned this once before but I would like to mention it again today. When we were talking to one of the architects about what we were doing, we told him that we had inexperienced boys that were working. He just couldn't believe it. He would keep shaking his head, 'It can't be done.'

"We had an occasion to bring him out before the building was completed. He banged on the walls and examined the walls and then he talked to these young labor missionaries. He said, 'I can't believe it. The workmanship is better than what they are putting in the skyscrapers in New York.'

"He worked there for 8 years. And he said, 'There is something different about those boys. I have talked to them. They are different.'

"Of course they are different. They are Priesthood bearers. They are building the house of the Lord and the Lord is working with them. Not one part has been built from the woodwork to the plaster without feeling the Lord and His Spirit. Everyone that enters this house in the future will feel something different about it. It is because this is the Lord's house and His Spirit is here. It has the mark of divinity stamped upon it.

"Now I would like to just pay tribute again to some of these young men. It is thrilling to hear the testimonies of these young construction missionaries. They came to this mission with soft hands. And many times they hit those thumbs and fingers with their hammers. Many times I have been on the job seeing bandages all over their hands. Many of them did not say a word about their hurt fingers. They are strong enough to work harder everyday.

"But if you look at their hands now, they are broad and thick and calloused but I don't see any sores anymore. And the Lord has blessed them in health and strength and their bodies have stood up to this work. And so it is a testimony to me to see what they have done. And it thrills me to know that these men have grown and developed along with the building of this chapel. And with them will come a chapel where thousands of Japanese people will be taught and instructed in things pertaining to eternal life and exaltation. Thousands of lives will be changed. And like Elder Jones said, they will no longer be Japanese particularly but will be Mormons, children of God. Our loads will be lessened and lighter and our eyes will be opened. And their heart will be happier because of what has taken place here today.

"I would like to bear testimony that this is the work of God, that it is the most important thing that is taking place on the earth today, that the leaders and missionaries are working in all the lands possible today, gathering the faithful, honest in heart, to come listen to the word of the Lord. I pray that you will continue to support this building program. Now because you have a building doesn't mean you should stop

"We need to help in all of the buildings constructed here upon this land. You should be working more diligently now to be able to make this kind of thing possible for the other branches in the mission. And you should be taking good care of this building so that all who come here will know it to be the house of the Lord, so that the investigators who come here will feel something different and stay to learn. Now I love and appreciate each of you and the fine work you are doing and pray that the Lord will continue to bless you as He has done up to now. And I say these things humbly in the name of Jesus Christ. Amen."

The time then came for Elder Hinckley to dedicate the chapel. He went to the podium with his interpetor standing by his side.

Elder Gordon B. Hinckley

"My beloved Brethren and Sisters, this is a day for which I have long prayed. This day is an answer to many prayers. This is a day which will be remembered in the history of the Church in Japan. This is the day on which we dedicate two buildings. These are the first two buildings to be built by the Church in the great and ancient lands of Asia. God be thanked for this day.

"President Andersen has mentioned President Grant. I believe that President Grant is with us this day. The dedication of these buildings is the fulfillment of the prayer of dedication of this land. On a Sunday in August of 1901, he and his associates went on to a hill to the south of Yokohama. There these first four missionaries gathered and sang "We Thank Thee Oh God for a Prophet", and there in the authority of the holy apostleship, President Grant dedicated the land of Japan for the preaching of the restored gospel of Jesus Christ. He invoked the blessings of the Lord upon this land, and he prayed that the spirit of darkness might be lifted from this land. He asked that the spirit of God would touch the hearts of the people.

"The Lord did not see fit to answer that apostolic prayer with a harvest at that time. Sixty-three years have passed since then. You and I are witnessing the day of the fulfillment of that prayer. God is now touching the hearts of the people. This building is solemn witness of that fact, my Brothers and Sisters. And this is but the dawn of a great and marvelous day for the Church in this part of the world.

"If you are faithful and if you continue to pray and be diligent, the Lord will pour out his blessings without measure upon this land. You shall see the fulfillment of all the promises of old in behalf of the people. The hearts of the fathers shall turn to the children and the hearts of the children to the fathers and the spirit of the gospel will spread among the people, and whereas there are now thousands of members, the day will come when there will be tens of thousands of members.

"Now to every man and woman here this day, I want to say: Pray for the outpouring of the spirit of the Lord upon the people. Get on your knees night and morning in your secret places. Pray to the Lord to bless this land. Pray to the Lord with your families that His spirit will rest upon this land. Be faithful in doing all that you are asked to do in the Church. The Lord will not ask you to do anything that you cannot do. These young missionaries who have stood here this day are evidence of that fact. When they were called, they did not think they had the ability to build. But the bricks and mortar which you see are evidence of the fulfillment of the promises given them by the servants of the Lord.

"Support and sustain the missionaries who are sent to your land. Their lot is not easy. Their burdens are not light. Their fathers and mothers love them. They weep for them when they say goodbye as they leave to come to this distant part of the world. They sacrifice much to send them here.

"They struggle to learn this difficult language. They are rebuked by most of the people they meet. They need your help and your prayers and your blessings. Sustain them in their work, my Brothers and Sisters, and pray for them constantly. Pray for those who investigate the gospel. Pray that the spirit of the Lord will touch their hearts and enlighten their minds. And when they come into your midst, reach out the hand of fellowship toward them. Put your arms about them and embrace them in the spirit of the gospel of Christ. Let them know that they are welcome and wanted.

"Only as you serve others will you grow in faith and testimony. I give you the words of John the Revelator, 'Be thou faithful unto death and I will give you a crown of life.'

"Now my Brethren and Sisters, I am grateful for all who have made this possible. I think of all in this land who have labored to build this house to the Lord. And I think of the faithful saints throughout the earth. Most of the money that has gone to build this structure has come from the contributions of those in other lands. The Lord's tithing in the United States, Canada and South America is all here. Let us remember that this building stands because of the faith of people in many lands. Let us work with grateful hearts, my Brothers and Sisters. Let us never enter this building with evil in our hearts. Let us leave at the *genkan* (entrance) our spirit of backbiting and evil speaking. Let there be no gossip in this house of the Lord. Let the spirit of love dwell in our hearts.

"God bless you, my Brethren and Sisters. God bless you that you may have peace in your hearts and in your homes. God bless you that as we dedicate this building this day we shall dedicate our lives to this service. God bless that you shall assist in building his kingdom in this great and beautiful land of Japan that the people of this land will become one with the peoples of all lands in worshipping the Lord Jesus Christ. And now I ask that all of you bow your heads and close your eyes and join with me in a prayer of dedication to the Lord.

Dedicatory Prayer for First LDS Chapel in Asia

"Our Holy Father in Heaven, in the name of thy Son, the Lord Jesus Christ, we bow our heads before thee this day. Our hearts are full of gratitude, Father. We thank thee for the knowledge we have that we are thy sons and daughters and that thou art our Father. We thank thee that we are truly brethren and sisters. We thank thee for the outpouring of thy Holy Spirit. We thank thee for the gift of thy Son who gave His life that we might live.

"Father, we love thee. We love thy Son, our Lord and Savior. We thank thee that thou didst reveal thyself to the boy Joseph Smith. We honor him as thy chosen prophet in this dispensation of time. We thank thee for the gift of revelation. We thank thee that thou art still speaking to thy children through thy prophet, President David O. McKay. We thank thee for the faith of all who have gone before us. Dear Father, we thank thee for all who have come to this land to teach the restored gospel. Our hearts are touched when we think of the sorrows they have borne. May we always walk in gratitude concerning them.

"And now, Father, we thank thee for this building, for all who have made it possible, for those who were led by the Holy Spirit to buy the ground on which it stands, for those who in a spirit of consecration have erected it. May we walk in appreciation while here.

"Father, we give it unto thee as thy house. It is paid for and free of debt. We give it unto thee without restriction.

"Now, our Father in Heaven, in behalf of all who are gathered here this day, in the authority of the holy apostleship, I dedicate this the North Tokyo Branch building of the Northern Far East Mission unto thee our Father and our God. Wilt thou accept it as a gift of thy children.

"Let thy spirit dwell here. Preserve it by thy power. May it be blessed from the footings to the top of the tower. May it be preserved from the ravages of nature. May it be a house of worship. May it be a house of learning. May it be a house of faith. May it be a place of amusement where thy children shall gather together and enjoy one another's company.

"May thy holy truths be taught from this pulpit. May anthems of praise be sung unto thee in this chapel. May it be a place from which missionaries will go forth to the world. May it be a place in which those who lose loved ones may mourn in faith. May the classrooms be places where learning concerning thy work shall take place. May all those who come here do so with clean hands and pure hearts.

"We rebuke the powers evil that they shall not have place here. May this be a gathering place for ever increasing numbers of people. May this branch increase in such numbers that it shall have to be divided again and again. And may thy work spread from this beginning across this land that this shall be the first of many beautiful houses of worship.

"Let thy spirit dwell upon these surrounding grounds. May they be kept beautiful, and may there always be an invitation to those on the outside to come in and learn and worship.

"Now Father, we invoke upon this sacred structure every good blessing, and as we dedicate it unto thee, we rededicate our lives to thy service. Bless the missionaries who labor here, bless thy faithful saints, bless even those who are indifferent to the faith that they may turn back unto thee. For these and every other good gift, we humbly pray this day of dedication, asking that thou will bless thy work throughout the world. We pray as we testify of thee and invoke thy blessings upon thy chosen servants, the honest in heart everywhere, and ask that thou wilt pour out thy blessings upon this land that peace may dwell here and that thy work may grow and prosper, in the name of thy Son, the Lord Jesus Christ. Amen."[19]

The first of numerous chapel dedications under the hands of Gordon B. Hinckley in Asia had been accomplished.

Tracting in Tokyo

While in Tokyo, Sister Hinckley participated in a cottage meeting and tracted with the missionaries.

"I always find spiritual refreshment among the Oriental people, who have the gifts of humility and sincerity. They are receptive to the message that assures them of the existence of a personal God and Savior. Their many talents and their fine cultivated natures seem to unfold like flowers as they apply the gospel to their lives."[20]

Elder Hinckley interviewed an elder with astigmatism two or three times. He had difficulty with sight but Elder Hinckley saw something in his sense of devotion, a certain humility above all, and a reliance on the Lord. He made anxious, prayerful pleadings for success and was blessed. He grasped the difficult language and spoke with power. In 1965 Elder Hinckley was privileged to seal this elder to a spouse for time and all eternity in an LDS temple.[21]

Similarly Elder Hinckley met a sister missionary during several interviews. She displayed a wonderful spirit, deep faith and a moving sense of duty. These were beautiful fruits of his labors to him.

A Ray of Light in India

In June 1964, Elder Hinckley was in Hong Kong meeting with the Chinese saints there and Gordon's good friend Jay A. Quealy, Jr. was now well. A referral had been received from Paul Thiruthuvadoss in Quanluator, Bangalore, South India asking for someone with authority to come baptize him.

For all intents and purposes, LDS proselyting in and among the vast masses in India had terminated in 1856 just before the famous

Elder Gordon B. Hinckley greets Sister Sagawa, shakes hand of Bro. Sagawa looking on l. to r. Bryant Hinckley Wadsworth, nephew of Elder Hinckley through his youngest sister Sylvia; Goro Yamada, translator & counselor to the Northern Far East Mission President; President Dwayne N. Andersen, Northern Far East Mission, at first LDS chapel dedicated in Asia, April 26, 1964

North Branch Dedication
Tokyo, Japan, April 26, 1964
Walking out after Ceremony

Elder Gordon B. Hinckley at North Branch Dedicatory Service
Tokyo, Japan, April 26, 1964
l. to r. Rex Chenney, Far East Construction Supervisor; ?, Labor Missionary Supervisor; Dwayne N. Andersen, Northern Far East Mission President, Elder Gordon B. Hinckley; Brother Watabe with corsage in background.

Sepoy Mutiny. Some British soldiers had been converted in 1851 by testimonies of some recently converted sailors visiting Calcutta—Matthew McCune and his best friend James Patrick Meik, wife Mary Ann Meik and Maurice White—and as a result several full-time missionaries sent to preach in India and Burma but converts were for the most part military personnel from England and not natives.

Elder Robert Skelton, the last missionary to leave India in May 1856, was so disappointed when he left India he had washed his feet in the Hoogly River as a testimony against the entire nation. In the late 1880's additional LDS missionaries went to India for a short time including Matthew McCune's oldest son Henry Frederick McCune but soon moved on to New Zealand after little success in the land where Henry had been born and spent his boyhood.

Now there was a man in India desiring baptism. He had come across a pamphlet *Joseph Smith Tells His Own Story.* It touched him and he wrote letters pleading for baptism. He knew he would be cast out of the society of his community and nation but his letters showed a warm testimony. When Elder Hinckley returned to the Orient for his next visit, President and Sister Quealy and Elder and Sister Hinckley decided to visit him.

A plane was taken from Singapore to Madras arriving at night. The heat was tremendous everywhere they went. The party then took a taxi way out in the country to an old hotel evidently built in the days of Queen Victoria. The party took two rooms with ants all over the place—1½ inches long it seemed. The beds had a single old khaki sheet on them and a sleezy bedspread. And the place was filthy. The two couples had prayer together and went to bed.

They arose early for a 6 A.M. flight to Bangalor, then to Quanluator. At the airport, the group asked, "Isn't there a better hotel in town?"

"Oh, yes, a number of them," was the reply. "But Pan American said you were vegetarians and should be put in a vegetarian hotel." So much for that!

The delegation did arrive in Quanluator, however and met a little man, dark as anthrocite, waiting for them. He explained in more detail. He had been investigating the LDS faith for 10 years after picking up a tract.[22] He had written to LDS headquarters in Salt Lake City and they sent him more literature. He had incessantly asked for baptism.

Paul took them by taxi to an English club built in Queen Victoria days to stay. But nothing much had been done to it since. Paul could not come in, however, because he was the wrong caste. The entourage talked to him. He was an angelical sort of man but Elder Hinckley worried about him all night. He thought about whether he should be baptized. He needed to be helped. He did not yet have a sufficient foundation of basic gospel principles. If they baptized him then, it would have been to leave a sheep in a pack of wolves.

Next morning they decided they would get two missionaries in six months to teach him, then he could be baptized. He was elated.

Several months later, President Quealy returned and baptized Paul T. and Paul lost himself in service for others. He purchased a small parcel of land with his meager savings and erected a school. It was of simple and rough construction but served well. This accountant for a cement factory had a heart large and overflowing. His humble home was smaller than the living room of an average American home. But his school took in 400 poverty stricken illiterate children.

He constructed another building nearby with his own hands and organized an orphanage for 45 additional children, some infants, some as old as 5. Elder and Sister Hinckley visited again and saw this progress. Sister Hinckley's eyes watered as she watched the orphans sleeping on boards for beds because cots and mattresses were too expensive.

Through Brother Paul T., five small LDS branches also were established in rural villages near his home. Neat and clean buildings were constructed with the name of the LDS Church placed over them in the Tamil and English languages. Concrete floors were prepared for seating by mixing cow dung with water, spreading it on the concrete and then polishing it when dry to a shiny gloss. Elder Hinckley met with the 200 LDS members of five branches on the floor, partook of the Sacrament with them and shared testimonies.[23]

"I think somehow by the power of the Lord and the exercise of the priesthood, we have to remove the curse Elder Skelton put on the land of India because the work has to go forward there. We have to preach the gospel to those people. The gospel is to be preached to every nation, kindred, tongue and people. There's so many of them. They must be taught in India," President Hinckley later said.[24] "Somehow, someday, under the plan of the Lord, the time will come when the gospel will be preached in that land with power, and the harvest will follow."[25]

Vietnam

Not only was Elder Hinckley in charge of supervising missionary work in the Far East but also the welfare of all of the members of the LDS faith living in that vast expanse. This responsibility took on new meaning after the Gulf of Tonkin Resolution was passed by the U.S. Congress on August 7, 1964 authorizing the American president to take steps to "maintain peace" in Vietnam. American servicemen in Vietnam increased from 23,000 to 184,000 over 1965. The troops level continued to increase and increase and increase until a peak of about 525,000 in 1968. And among these servicemen were many Latter-day Saints.

Elder Hinckley found himself organizing the servicemen districts for LDS soldiers as well as visiting them in the war zones all up and down Vietnam. He had already had exposure to conflict when gunfire passed outside his hotel once in Korea. Also, he was awakened at 4 A.M. by artillery fire on a visit to a country in Asia during a government coup one time.

Several LDS chaplains found their way to Vietnam and Elder Hinckley traveled with them at times, sometimes on his own. The Latter-day Saint servicemen pled for Sacrament meeting. They also asked for Church publications.[26]

Elder Hinckley was in Thailand and organized a servicemen's district on March 27, 1966.[27] Gradually, servicemen spread the good news of their LDS faith to local Vietnamese and baptisms ensued. Other faithful brethren taught and baptized Korean, Chinese, Filipino and American acquaintances. Military representatives from many nations were in the fray. They included Great Britain, Australia, New Zealand, Korea and the Philippines and there were LDS members amongst them, too.

The zone president of the LDS military in Saigon then suggested the extra combat pay received by servicemen be contributed to a local building fund for a permanent chapel in Vietnam. In one day in Saigon, $3,000.00 was collected and $18,000.00 throughout Vietnam in 30 days.[28]

Not only did Elder Hinckley meet with the servicemen, he also interviewed them. [29] Hundreds received the wisdom of his counsel as the US trrops in Vietnam reached 300,000 by the end of 1966. Vietnam became another zone of the Southern Far East Mission presided over by a presidency of three with three district presidencies and 30 branches or groups with presidencies disbursed among areas such as Saigon, Bien Hoa, Phu Loi, Cam Ranh Bay, Bac Lieu, Chu Lai, Plei Ku.

The increasing involuntary draft in the United States brought many Latter-day Saints with wide church experience into the American Armed Forces. Numerous bishops, bishopric counselors, high counselors, branch presidents and active and experienced Latter-day Saints became part of the military effort and part of the Church effort of the LDS presence in Vietnam and Thailand.

Later Elder Hinckley was to remark that there is a little of a "silver thread" running through the travesty of war, a tool in some way of the Almighty in bringing His children to a knowledge of His plan of salvation. Such was the experience among the dark jungles, the humid heat and the stench of death in war torn Vietnam.

"I am confident that today, out of the misery of that fearful, tragic, vicious war in Southeast Asia, will come some measure of good as the Lord, working through faithful men, turns the evil snares of the adversary to blessings in the lives of many of his children," Elder Hinckley said.[30]

Dedication of Seoul East Chapel

On October 6, 1966, Elder Hinckley boarded Pan Am flight 845 at Noon from San Francisco to Tokyo. He was greeted by President Adney Y. Komatsu, successor for the past year to previous president Dwayne N. Andersen, over the Northern Far East Mission. Sister Judy Komatsu and about 25 other Latter-day Saints were also at the Haneda Airport to meet them.

Elder Hinckley lost a day in travel across the International Date Line and arrived in Tokyo October 7. The next day, while still suffering from the eight hours of jet lag between Utah and Japan, he arrived in Korea, a Saturday. Sunday was spent in an 8 A.M. testimony meeting with missionaries. "I wept as I heard them speak and saw them weep," Elder Hinckley wrote in his journal.[31]

Then he met with the LDS Servicemen's District at 1 P.M. in the 8th Army Chapel. Enthusiastic members brought non-member friends. At 4 P.M. it was out by automobile, past the remnants of a great wall which had once served as enclosure for the city of Seoul in pre-airplane days, to the new East Chapel where boys dressed in their boy scout uniforms greeted the visitors.

Gordon B. Hinckley Enjoys
Friendship with Youth in Korea

Many dignitaries were present along with Latter-day Saints as the capacity congregation sang hymns of Zion along with a choir. The new chapel was then dedicated by Elder Hinckley. It was the first chapel dedicated on the mainland soil of Asia, chapels on the islands of Japan having been dedicated in 1964.

Okinawa

Elder Hinckley had traveled 1,000's of miles up and down Japan with a faithful Brother Kan Watanabe from the second largest city of Osaka, including visits to Okinawa. The next Sunday, October 16, 1966 it was Elder Hinckley's privilege to be in Okinawa once again, this time up early after only four hours sleep the night before.

A great American military staging area for Vietnam operations was developing on that small island 1,000 miles south of Tokyo as meetings were attended at the long white stucco LDS chapel with steeple located just across the street of the US Marine base in Futenma. The LDS servicemen asked Elder Hinckley to build another chapel for them further north by the major Kadena US Air Force Base located just west of Koza City.

In the afternoon, the new white building of Naha Branch by the side of an ancient Sogenji Mon (gate) near Kokusai Dori (International Street), the main shopping area in Okinawa's capital city, was dedicated before 350 LDS saints and friends packed into the new worship place.

Taipei Chapel, Taiwan

Then after shaking hands, Elder Hinckley was whisked off down Ichigosen (Highway 1) to the Naha Airport where a plane was waiting to fly him the 400 miles south to Taipei, Taiwan. At 5 P.M. the same afternoon, a new chapel was there dedicated by Gordon B. Hinckley before 500 saints and guests, the first chapel for the LDS people in the realm of China. Eight years previous, LDS missionaries first started proselyting there. Now membership was at 3,000 among 15 branches.

Elder Hinckley was very tired that evening as he climbed into bed.

Manila Chapel, The Philippines

The next Sunday, October 26, 1966 Elder Hinckley penned in his journal, "This is a day to remember. We are in the Philippines. This island republic holds a special place in my affections. It was only five years ago that we gathered a few of our American brethren and sisters together here to invoke the blessings of the Lord upon the missionary work we were about to commence."[32]

As US President Lyndon B. Johnson arrived in Manila for a Summit with leaders from five other countries regarding the Vietnam conflict, Elder Gordon B. Hinckley dedicated the first permanent LDS chapel in the Philippines before 1,050 LDS members and guests in Manila. Membership had grown to 2,000 local Filipinos and additional chapels were needed in such places as Quezon City where there were now 400 local members. "How great is the promise of the future," Elder Hinckley recorded.[33]

Hong Kong Missionary Testimonies

The next Friday, October 28, Elder Hinckley met with 84 missionaries in Hong Kong where he listened to testimonies from 8 A.M. until 3 P.M. He remembered a similar meeting a few years before where a non-member sailor dropped in on the testimony meeting of missionaries and was so touched he joined the LDS Church. Elder Hinckley ran into him in the Eastern United States a short time before this trip to Asia and found him serving in a branch presidency.

As he wrote his journal entry prior to flying to Vietnam the next morning, Elder Hinckley thought, "I wonder how many of the good young men with whom I have talked today will, in the next year or two, find themselves in the hot jungles of that sad land as soldiers of war."[34]

Northern Vietnam District Conference

Cathay Pacific Airways carried Elder Hinckley, Elder Marion D. Hanks of the Council of the Seventy, and President Keith E. Garner of the Southern Far East Mission to Saigon on Saturday, October 29. The flight path traversed Vietnam to Phom Penh, Cambodia, over the Mekong River, over plush green vegetation and trees and into the Tan San Nhut Airport.

South Vietnam Zone President, Major Allen C. Rozsa, and his associates met the three elders at which time each was asked to sign waivers of liability for their safety and welfare before they exited the airport and climbed aboard a C-47 "Gooney Bird" furnished by the US Air Force. The door was kept open to ventilate from the sultry heat.

In mid-flight a motor began to sputter and Elder Hinckley wondered how to put on the camouflage coveralls and use the survival gear hanging on the rack at the rear of the plane if they should go down in the Viet Cong controlled jungle they were now crossing. But luckily the propeller commenced purring again.

C-rations provided lunch before arriving at DaNang. "If we're going to get shot, this is where it will happen as we come in for a landing, " Major Rozsa encouraged the group. But the plane of LDS saints safely landed at the same time an admiral with five helicopters "riding shotgun" with marines fingering machine guns similarly touched down.

Many baby faced youth had come down from the "Rock Pile" and "Marble Mountain", nicknames assigned by the soldiers to their potential death beds in the DMZ where fearce fighting and the stench of death and burnt gun powder reigned. "We loved them the minute we looked into their eyes," Elder Hinckley wrote.[35] Their muddy boots and fatigues covered hearts of faith and hope as they piled their M-16 rifles along the back two rows and seated for the Northern Vietnam LDS Servicemen's District Conference.

Elder Hinckley ate with the men in the same chow line following the meeting and stood and talked to the soldiers for hours. It was wonderful but it was discouraging. These men have come from clean sheets and warm showers to fields of mud, sweat and tears. They should be in colleges and universities gaining knowledge and skills to benefit mankind and themselves. Here they walk in dark jungles on patrol ever succeptible to instant death. "I thought of the terrible inequality of sacrifice involved in the cause of human liberty," Elder Hinckley penned.[36]

Little good sleep was obtained in DaNang as F-4 Phantom jets roared incessintly one after another on takeoff heading north. "Will he come back?" Elder Hinckley thought as he lay sleepless in the unfinished hospital provided for lodging.[37]

Central Vietnam District Conference

On Sunday, October 30, 1966 Elder Hinckley was up at 4 A.M. in a warm rain making the earth soft and slippery. A military ambulance had been obtained to transport the three elders across the bumpy, muddy road to the airstrip where the same "Gooney Bird" lifted them up from DaNang and across "as beautiful a beach as I had seen anywhere in the world" over Cam Ranh Bay. But it was deserted and seemingly lifeless.

At Nha Trang a conference was held in the unfinished mess hall, largest gathering place on the base. Many LDS brethren Elder Hinckley had previously met at various places such as Frankfurt and Paris and Tokyo and Taipei were there along with numerous others.

Elder Gordon B. Hinckley Meets With
American GI's in Southeast Asia

The Sacrament was blessed and passed at the request of First Cavalry soldiers who had not had it for weeks.

Dedication of Vietnam for the Preaching of the Gospel

Elders Hinckley and Hanks and President Garner were flown to Saigon next for a conference of 200 from the Southern Vietnam District. The meeting place was the roof garden of the Caravelle Hotel. Converts and guests were present. President Twede of the Southern Vietnam Servicemen's District conducted. Clyde Hart played the music. Jesse Laterite was chorister as the congregation sang "Israel, Israel, God is Calling" after which Brother Minh, whom Elder Hinckley had ordained the first ever native Vietnamese Latter-day Saint elder earlier that day, offered an opening prayer.[38]

Then President Keith E. Garner spoke followed by Elder Marion D. Hanks. And "The Spirit of God" was sung.

Elder Gordon B. Hinckley then rose and began talking. About 30 minutes into his talk, he stopped and said, "President McKay has authorized me to dedicate this land for the teaching of the Gospel."[39]

At that moment he asked everyone to join him in prayer and offered a prayer of dedication of Vietnam for the preaching of the restored gospel of Jesus Christ.

In part, he said, "May there from this time forward, Father, come upon this land an added measure of the Holy Spirit to touch the hearts of the people and the rulers thereof. May they open their hearts to the teaching of the truth and be receptive to the gospel of thy Son. May those who have these blessings feel a new urge in their hearts to share with others the great gifts and powers and authority which are theirs, which have come from thee . . . ."[40]

Following the prayer, he continued speaking. That evening a testimony meeting was held in the apartment of a Brother Hart where one by one each bore their testimonies of the divinity of the LDS religion as mortar and artillery fire was heard on the outskirts of Saigon. One officer present at the dedication of the land of Vietnam for preaching the gospel that day was killed in action four days later as he was "carrying his wounded men to safety."[41]

Singapore & Thailand

Singapore was visited the next day where Australia and British Armed Forces felt the spirit of the Lord as Elder Hinckley and Elder Hanks and President Garner met with and bore witness to them. The brethren then flew to Bangkok, Thailand.

l. to r. Elder Marion D. Hanks, of the Seventy &
Elder Gordon B. Hinckley, LDS Apostle
On the Streets of Saigon, Vietnam

It was Wednesday, November 2, 1966 in Lupini Park by a clock tower at 6:30 A.M. when Elder Hinckley, with his commission from the LDS prophet David O. McKay, similarly dedicated that nation, the former Kingdom of Siam, for the preaching of the restored gospel of Jesus Christ. He prayed for a softening of the hearts of the people of Thailand so the missionaries could come, that the missionaries would be able to learn the language and that "thousands, yea and tens of thousands" would harken to the LDS message.[42]

Later Elder Hinckley and his other two companions met with the Minister of Education and Religion of Thailand. Considerable conversation ensued after which the minister agreed to authorize missionaries from the LDS faith in his nation.[43] One year and three months later, the first LDS full-time missionaries were admitted to Thailand.

As Elder Hinckley completed this momentous trip to the Far East, he reflected upon the promise of the Lord given to the young prophet Joseph Smith, Jr.:

> "The ends of the earth shall inquire after thy name, and fools shall have thee in derision, and hell shall rage against thee; while the pure in heart, and the wise, and the noble, and the virtuous, shall seek counsel, and authority, and blessings constantly from under thy hand (D.&C. 122:1-2)."[44]

Furtherance of the Work in the Far East

At times the problems and difficulties and disappointments of the work in the Far East seemed insurmountable barriers.[45] "We wondered what we were doing, whether anything could become of what we were doing . . .," President Hinckley said. "Today we are seeing a miracle being accomplished and prophecy fulfilled."[46]

The Book of Mormon translations in Chinese and Korean were accomplished. The dark, unheated, partially unlighted meeting facilities of the LDS members in Asia gradually began to turn to bright, white, shining edifices topped with sparkling steeples. It was wonderful, peaceful to see the look on the faces of the saints in that great section of the earth.

Elder Hinckley was privileged to seal a couple from Korea in the temple for time and all eternity in Salt Lake City on Monday, April 10, 1967.[47] The Philippine LDS Mission was formally organized on June 28, 1967. Brother Minh, whom Elder Hinckley had ordained the first native Vietnamese elder, requested permission to translate the Book of

Mormon. Elder Hinckley and he walked together under an umbrella on the streets of Saigon as he made his plea. By April 1968, LDS membership in Asia had grown to 25,000.[48]

In October 1969, the first broadcast of the Tabernacle Choir in Okinawa was arranged through a serviceman and returned missionary from Japan now stationed there. Elder Hinckley authorized a 30 minute broadcast via satellite. Then on March 15, 1970, although LDS apostle Ezra Taft Benson had been assigned to replace Elder Hinckley in area supervision of the Far East at that time, Elder Hinckley was present when the first LDS stake in Asia was organized in Tokyo, Japan, the 505th stake in the LDS Church.[49]

The LDS Taiwan Mission was formally created on December 5, 1970 with 4,500 LDS members already among the 14½ million population.[50] Three more years later, Elder Gordon B. Hinckley was once again asked to be area supervisor over the Far East after three years supervising Europe. The Seoul LDS stake was organized March 8, 1973, number 604 in the LDS faith. The Manila stake followed on May 20, 1973, number 613 worldwide.

Taking the general authorities out and amongst the people started in the 1970's, eventually resulting in the organization of area presidencies comprised of members of the Quorums of the Seventy positioned with residency in areas throughout the world. An area conference convened in Hong Kong on August 5, 1975 in the Lee Theatre with 40 other church leaders and a vast congregation of LDS faithful.

"The primary church activity for the foreseeable future in Hong Kong and Asia will be the building of chapels for its members," Elder Hinckley told the newsmen. Education, social services or mass media are not the job of the Church. The job of the LDS Church is to spread the teachings of Jesus Christ. Members are to help themselves, be self reliant, with help from family if needed. Only when the individual and immediate family cannot help does the Church step in and assist his welfare needs.[51] This is the way of the Kingdom of God in the Latter-day Saint doctrine and has been from the beginning.

The first Area Conference in Japan was then held on Saturday, August 9, 1975 in the Tokyo Budokan Hall. President Spencer W. Kimball, LDS prophet at that time, was present as he had been in Hong Kong. A breathtaking announcement was made by him at the conference. A temple was to be built in Tokyo.[52] Extensive Far Eastern news coverage resulted from this announcement. Articles appeared in every major news organ in Japan.

While in Manila two days following the Tokyo area conference, Elder Hinckley was left to substitute at a news conference originally scheduled for LDS prophet Spencer W. Kimball when President Kimball's plane had been delayed. At that time, the wife of then US President Gerald Ford was being scrutinized by the press for recent remarks she made where she appeared to condone pre-marital affairs.

A Filipino newsman asked the LDS Church's views on morality.

"We very much deplore the deterioration of moral standards throughout the world," Elder Hinckley replied. "We advocate strongly and seriously adherence to moral standards. We teach our young people chastity—not only our young women but also our young men.

"We decry the ever loosening standards of morality which seem to be affecting the world. We cannot expect a great and good society unless morality resides in people.

"We feel very strongly about this. Chastity is to be observed before marriage and fidelity after marriage."[53]

On sending missionaries to China and socialist countries, President Hinckley said, "We hope the way will be open to send missionaries there," and recalled the Savior's charge to take the gospel worldwide. "We hope the day will come when we might be permitted to send a mission to those countries where we are now not permitted." [54]

Area conferences were then held in Manila and Seoul and Taipei. Eighteen thousand members assembled in the Araneta Coliseum in the Philippines. Elder Hinckley wept for joy as he reflected upon the little beginnings that morning in 1961 at the military cemetary in the suburbs of Manila.

By the time the last vestiges of American presence were withdrawn from Vietnam in 1975, 200 local Vietnamese and 1,000 servicemen had joined the LDS Church.[55] One hundred forty thousand refugees left the country, too, and many of them found their way to the United States for asylum, settlement and introduction to the LDS faith. Vietnamese branches of LDS converts sprang up in many cities in America.

The Residual Fruits

Back at the United States, Elder Hinckley, Bernard P. Brockbank, Adney Y. Komatsu, Hartman Rector, Jr., David M. Kennedy and their wives together with President Nathan Eldon Tanner of the LDS First Presidency and his wife were present in San Franciso as the Japan

Society of San Francisco hosted Japan's Emperor Hirohito (his reign being called the "Showa Period" or "enlightened peace" era) at the St. Francis Hotel.

LDS member John Ritchie, and president of the Japan Society of S.F., conducted. The Emperor had arrived with his entourage of three planes including 22 aides that day and returned to Japan via Hawaii on October 14.

At the luncheon, the aging emperor addressed those attending, paying tribute to the San Francisco people who were first visited by a delegation from Japan in 1860. President Tanner, Elder Rector and Bro. Kennedy, then serving as World Ambassador for the LDS Church, met with the emperor prior to the luncheon and shook hands.[56]

Elder Hinckley continued his trips to the Far East. Shortly before April 1976, he visited Korea, Thailand, Indonesia and Singapore and after April LDS general conference visited Japan, Taiwan, the Philippines and Hong Kong.[57] By this time B-747 jet airliners carried Elder Hinckley to Japan in 9-10 hours. In Taipei, stake No. 755 of the LDS Church was organized April 22, 1976.

Back in Salt Lake City, Elder Hinckley received 12 businessmen from Kyoto, Japan, their city's Committee for Economic Development. They had begun in Boston, moved to New York City and seen Washington, D.C. Now they visited the Rocky Mountains of Utah. When Gordon B. Hinckley met them at the Church Office Building, he told the business delegation he had himself visited Japan 29 times and that the Latter-day Saint Church had contributed more money to Japan in a temple being built, chapels, and missionary labor in Japan than was received from Japan sources.

The group were taken to dinner at the Roof Restaurant on the 10th floor of the Hotel Utah overlooking the Salt Lake Temple. The tall pinnacles shined brilliantly in the night with the golden leafed statue of the trumpet blowing heavenly messenger Moroni on the top of the middle steeple.

The delegation was then guided through Zions National Park, one of Utah's 5 national parks, located 260 miles southwest of Salt Lake City and 30 miles from St. George. United Way representatives of Salt Lake City also met with them as well as executives of the local natural gas provider Mt. Fuel.

In 1977, the Hinckleys returned to visit Paul T. in India and saw the 220 members. They sang "God Be With You 'Til We Meet Again."

Privileged to accompany the BYU Young Ambassadors to Mainland China in May 1979, they found those of the billion-plus Chinese people in their nation warm, curious, kind, loving intelligent and marvelous. Then they met with a Christian group in an old Methodist cathedral in Shanghai and bore testimony to 10-12 officers of the group following the services.

Elder Hinckley recalled the 1921 visit of Elder David O. McKay to Peking, China dedicating that vast nation for the preaching of the gospel, the miracle of the gospel expansion in Hong Kong started with the Quealy administration in 1962-65, and felt "there is a little sliver of light as if a door had just opened with a tiny crack with a light that's visible in China."[58]

The enclave in China strengthened as the second stake in Hong Kong was organized by Elder Hinckley in June 1980, "nothing short of a miracle," Elder Hinckley said.[59] In Japan, he saw a new dimension to the dynamics of it all when he met a man in Japan from Fiji whose heritage was from India. Truly the diversity of God's children was gradually being unified worldwide.

September 6, 1980 found Elder Hinckley witnessing more of this melting pot when he talked at the local Vietnamese Branch in Salt Lake City. There were 100 there. Four were sustained to receive the priesthood, alert, sharp, clean, good and handsome men.

"The gates of Vietnam will be open if not for you, for your children or your grandchildren or your great-grandchildren," Elder Hinckley promised. Then a Vietnamese brother baptized the night before bore his testimony of escape from the land of his birth. He was on a boat 10 feet wide and 30 feet long with 135 others. Pirates boarded and threatened the terrified passengers. Then they drifted ashore in Thailand but were rejected and pushed out to sea again. Three times more they were attacked by pirates. They were in storms and with tears on his cheeks the new brother told of finally reaching Malaysia. Eventually they were permitted to come to America because of a cousin already admitted there.

"I say again," Elder Hinckley said, "we're prone to look at things in the short term. I said to myself, 'The Lord is answering that prayer. These people, these Vietnamese, they are joining the Church here and sometime in the future, I don't know the generation, I don't know the generation, but sometime they will have the privilege of going back there.'"[60]

On September 11, 1980 Elder Hinckley said about China, "I don't know when it will happen. The Lord will have to turn some keys and help influence some people and a lot of things will have to happen, but it will happen in the future because a quarter of the people on the earth live in that nation and area. I believe that sometime, somehow, some way the great nation of the People's Republic of China will be opened to the preaching of the gospel.

"To me a great miracle is happening in Asia. The Lord is putting his hand on those nations and marvelous things are happening. Soon a stake in Zion will be formed on Okinawa. That to me is a miracle. The eighth stake to be organized in the Philippines was approved today."[61]

The next month Elder Hinckley participated in area conferences in Asia, the first such since 1975, and the dedication of the Tokyo Temple in company with President Spencer W. Kimball and other general authorities. First, he revisited the American Memorial Cemetery outside Manila during humid meetings in the Philippines. Then he was in Hong Kong in a new meetinghouse where 1,856 attended.

Then it was to Taipei where 2,550 met. Then he attended the area conference at the Seoul US Army Retreat Center towards the latter part of October, then at the Seoul 4th Ward chapel in 28° F. windy weather where the general authorities were in coats and blankets. The next day they were in Tokyo dedicating the first LDS temple in Asia. And lastly they travelled to Osaka for a two day conference on the first days in November. The trip of three weeks covered 18,000 miles.

In the Korean conference, Elder Hinckley said, "While we're walking in the sunlight of peace, we cannot afford to lose a day or an hour in opportunities to share the gospel."

In the Philippines, Elder Hinckley exclaimed that when he dedicated the Philippines for the preaching of the gospel only one native member existed in all the Philippines. Then he called the mission president of the Philippine Manila Mission to the stand. Putting his arm around him he then told the audience of the Philippine progress. Then he suggested a silver anniversary goal of 100,000 members in 1986.[62]

At the area conference in Tokyo 10,000 attended and in Osaka at the Matsushita Center 6,387 came. Elder Hinckley set the tone of the conferences when he quoted the words of Heber J. Grant, the first missionary and LDS apostle to live and work for any length of time in Japan: "This work will be slow at first, but the harvest is to be something great and will astonish the world in years to come."

Then Elder Hinckley said, "This land is called the 'Land of the Rising Sun.' I have felt this is the land of the rising Church. This is a place where the Church has a tremendous future." Then he challenged the membership to be 100,000 by 1985. Membership in Japan was then 48, 627.

Following the sessions the general authorities shook hands with members for 45 minutes and on the way to Osaka, Elder Marion D. Hanks encouraged the members and general authorities to sing hymns while riding the 200 miles by bus. The members and general authorities joined in unison singing "I'm a Child of God", "Abide with Me" and "Come, Come, Ye Saints." A welding bond was created as tears flowed freely.[63]

On March 7, 1982, over 300 Laotian Latter-day Saints and missionaries met in Sandy, Utah for a West Regional Conference. President Hinckley told them they had been "led through a great refining process and brought here for a great and marvelous purpose."

The Sandy Branch President Thongdeang Douargmais conducted.

President Hinckley said he hoped those there would "turn your backs to the past." "We cannot change the past, but must go forward. This is your day of opportunity." He urged them to read the Book of Mormon, hold family home evening, pray, read the other scriptures, improve their skills, teach obedience to law and teach their children to speak their native tongue as well as English.

"I believe in my heart that not only have you been beneficiaries of the goodness and kindness of the people of America in bringing you here as refugees, but in a larger sense are beneficiaries of Almighty God in rescuing you from the fire of war, bringing you to this land and giving you the gospel of Jesus Christ. That is the greatest gift that God can give to man."

President Hinckley then said they probably would not have availed themselves of this gift in their homeland and wouldn't have listened but here God has softened their hearts and given them understanding.[64]

Sunday, September 11, 1983 found President Hinckley at the Long Beach Convention Center at an LDS Seminary and Institute Fireside. Present were 4 Vietnamese sisters from the Huntington Beach 5th Ward baptized in Saigon.[65]

On Thursday, September 27, 1984, President Hinckley was once again back at the American War Memorial Cemetery in Manila. There he offered a prayer of gratitude for the marvelous success the LDS people had experienced in that land since 1961.[66] Ten days later he bore testimony on Sunday, October 7, 1984, "I have been a part of the miracle of the Philippines." There are 7,000 islands in that nation, he said. The harvest has been greatest there in the shortest period of time. Then with emotion he said, "The Lord has remembered His people on the isles of the sea."[67]

Nineteen eighty eight found President Hinckley visiting Japan and the Philippines again. "The attitude of its people" had made Japan an economic power he said on Wednesday, September 7, 1988 in Japan.[68] The nine day whilrlwind tour of the Philippines took him to regional conferences and leadership meetings before 20,000 members and 1,400 missionaries, ending in Cacalod before 7,000.[69]

On July 1, 1990, the tenth mission in Japan was organized on Okinawa covering the entire archipelego of the Ryukyu Islands from Japan's island of Kyushu to the north to islands only 40 miles away from Taiwan to the south. And in October or November of that same year Elder Hinckley had a nostalgic meeting in the Abeno Branch building completed in the 1960's during his first years visiting the Far East. He met with stake presidents and numerous district presidents and became very teary eyed a couple of times. His greatest sorrow he had was the falling away and inactivity of some of the leaders of the LDS local branches and wards he once knew during those first years supervising the Far East area.

Between April and June 1991, Elder Hinckley visited Korea and met with the ministers of government, business executives and 150 LDS members. He discussed strong family relations in a luncheon as guest of the National Assembly Chairman Pak Joon Kyu.[70]

1996 Visit as Prophet

It was May 1996 when now "President Hinckley" first visited the land that he loved as prophet of his church. In another pacesetting blitz of 18 days, he visited many nations. Okinawa, the little island in the sea 400 miles from Taiwan and 1,000 miles southwest of Tokyo, was visited May 20—the first time a prophet of the LDS faith had visited the Ryukyu Islands or its capital.

Then it was to the main islands of Japan where he met with tear eyed saints as they basked in the light of what they considered a representative of the Lord like Moses among them.

Hong Kong awaited the prophet for their temple dedication, the 48th operating temple dedicated. It was the first temple Gordon B.

Hinckley had dedicated as full President of the Church. May 26 the cornerstone was cemented with mortar and the initial of seven dedications accomplished by President Hinckley. Marjorie was by his side. The day before in his typical meeting with the full time LDS missionaries serving in the area, he remarked, "This temple represents one of the great dreams of my life."

The temple was the exact square footage of the Tokyo Temple—18,000 square feet. But uniquely it shared room in an eight level white granite building in Kowloon with a chapel, administrative offices and housing for temple servers and patrons on the first four ground floors containing another 10,000 square feet.

On May 28, through an invitation arranged by the LDS Polynesian Cultural Center in Hawaii, President Hinckley and his entourage of four other general authorities and wives visited the Chinese Town and Chinese Folk Villages in Shenzhen on the mainland of China.

Also called "Splendid China" (folk villages) & "Windows of the World" (recreations of world wonders such as the Grand Canyon, the Eiffel Tower, and the Egyptian Pyramids), the idea for the "cultural center" had come from viewing the LDS Church's Polynesian Cultural Center in Laie, Hawaii, a display of South Pacific nation villages.

Then President Hinckley visited his fond islands–the Philippines. He luxuriated in the fellowship of 30,000 Filipino Latter-day Saints as they met together in the Araneta Coliseum on May 30th.[71]

President Hinckley's Legacy in the Far East

Spencer J. Palmer, former mission president and temple president in Korea has said, "President Gordon B. Hinckley is without question the father of the Church in Asia."[72]

President Hinckley has said himself, "It is an area I greatly love."

Prior to becoming the 15th prophet of the Church of Jesus Christ of Latter-day Saints, Gordon B. Hinckley officially presided over the work in the Far East area of the world for 11 years and unofficially ever since his first trip there in April 1960. His influence had been monumental. His problems had seemed insurmountable at times. But satisfaction and joy had been endless as he had seen the membership in Japan alone top his challenged 100,000 members in the early 1990's.

Totalling the time he had actually been in the Orient since 1960, it was over three years and more like three and a half years. At least 45 times he had travelled across the International Date Line in 30 years from 1960 to 1990 and added more visits since.[73]

MINISTRY

Ever since Gordon B. Hinckley knelt before the Lord in that second story flat in England in the latter part of 1933 and resolved to forget himself, he has been a follower of the Savior in selfless service. His ministry is replete with numerous sacrifices, unknown fatigue, compassion for acquaintances, relatives and complete strangers and constancy in the midst of different voices.

In the complex of Gordon's service has been a quiet dignity, a deference to others coupled with a strength of conviction. It seems Elder Hinckley has a sixth sense. He has keen insight into problems and can isolate the central question of almost any problem. His way with words and writing also were free flowing and convincing.

Sunday School Service

David O. McKay recognized this. Elder McKay had been serving as the first assistant on the LDS General Sunday School Union in charge of text creation and administration of the Church's Sunday schools ever since 1917. Gordon's father Bryant S. Hinckley understood the same traits in his son.

So when Gordon returned from his mission, one of the very first things he was asked to do was to serve on the Liberty Stake Sunday School Board in 1935. Within a year, he was made Liberty Stake Sunday School Superintendent in 1936. He was 25 and 26 years of age.[1]

His encounter with the First Presidency reporting affairs of the European Mission and subsequent employment in the mass communications work of the developing church similarly proved his skills so much that not only the stake over which his father presided but also the church for which he served saw great penmanship talent in this young man, so much so that at age 27 he was called to serve on the LDS Deseret Sunday School Union in 1937 and served there until made a counselor in the East Mill Creek stake presidency in 1946.[2].

The general Sunday school board assignment was a position in addition to his full time employment for the Church. It entailed travel to almost every ward and stake in the Church during the nine years he served and the co-authorship of textbooks for use in the Sunday schools of LDS congregations. The main concern of the Sunday school board was high quality teaching in its wards and branches.[3]

Gordon worked with Marion G. Merkley, a prolific writer from Scandinavia, on lessons published as *Leaders of the Scriptures*, 47 chapters & 126 pages. Gordon's love for the LDS prophet Joseph Smith, Jr. certainly helped him in this project. In addition, the lives of 30 men and one woman, mainly from the Book of Mormon, were treated in brief life sketches, including a few who were not so valiant. This class manual was translated into several languages and republished for active use in LDS Sunday school classes until 1962.[4]

Selective Service

Selective Service in the United States (a polite word for involuntary draft into the US military) was another important facet of Gordon's earlier selfless service. He negotiated with the government arranging many a young man's opportunity to serve a full-time mission while still satisfying his obligation for military induction if needed.[5] Many a young man counseled with him free of charge. It was grueling and challenging and Gordon later said he hoped he never had to go through that experience again. His state and federal liaison with the Selective Service bureau of the US government during the Korean War helped many a young man and the Church.[6]

Polynesian Cultural Center

Many do not know Gordon B. Hinckley also had an integral part in the creation of the Polynesian Cultural Center adjacent to the Church College of Hawaii. The LDS Church acquired a large parcel of land from the King of Hawaii in 1865 through tremendous good will created by Joseph F. Smith and those following him when they served LDS missions there. The land used to be a safe haven for fugitives. If the fugitives could make it to Laie before being caught, they were allowed to live there in peace.

The property was located to the North on the opposite side of Oahu Island from Honolulu and in early years of LDS ownership was used as a plantation. In 1919, an LDS temple was completed on a portion of the 6,000 acres owned by the Church and on September 26, 1955, a college for the vast Polynesian membership of the LDS Church was established adjacent to the temple.

By the 1960's, population at the college was increasing so it was difficult for students to find employment to maintain their studies. For some time a group of students had been performing Polynesian song and dance and the idea of creating a theme park where students could perform while attending school was suggested. Elder Hinckley was on committee to study the recommendations. A three day and two evening round of meetings was held in November 1961 regarding the Bishop's museum, Ulu Mau Hawaiian Village, Traders Hall Curio Shop, Pat's Dining Hall and other facilities with LDS apostle Delbert L. Stapley and Elder Hinckley but the recommendation to President David O. McKay at that time was to defer building of a village and the focus on enhancing the Hawaiian Temple grounds.[7]

The concept was remembered, however, and reconsidered later at which time a village composed of various areas for Tonga, Fiji, Hawaii, New Zealand, Samoa and other Polynesian cultural displays together with a live music and dance program was given approval and completed October 12, 1963. The name chosen was the "Polynesian Cultural Center." The center has become one of the major attractions for visitors to Hawaii and provides a way for the students of the college, which is now a branch of Brigham Young University, to fund their educations while attending school.

Stake Organizing

Another part of Gordon B. Hinckley's ministry has been the regular organizing and reorganizing of scores of stakes throughout the world. In such reorganizations, the financial worth of a proposed candidate to serve as a stake president has been the least of all considerations. The Lord's will has been paramount.[8]

Just one of many such experiences is related. It occurred in Salt Lake City during the reorganization of the Wilford Stake leadership. Elder Hinckley was at the Wilford Stake to choose a new president. He spent the entire day on Saturday interviewing stake members to establish the right choice.

Brother Lee H. Nelson was brought in for his first interview in the morning. Four hours later he was brought in again. His wife Dorothy and he were then brought in for the third interview at the end of the day and Elder Hinckley said, "You will be called as the 4th president of the Salt Lake Wilford Stake."[9]

The release of a faithful stake president occurred in Idaho on Sunday, February 28, 1977. Elder Hinckley stayed in the president's home the evening before and rose with the family to read John 12:24-25 before morning prayer.

"Verily, verily, I say unto you, Except a corn of wheat fall into the ground and die, it abideth alone; but if it die, it bringeth forth much fruit. He that loveth his life shall lose it; and he that hateth his life in this world shall keep it unto life eternal."

It was the Jerome Stake. The stake president had served there for 13 years. He had spent 1,000's of hours neglecting personal affairs to assist needful members within his stake and travelled 10's of 1,000's of miles in all kinds of weather. Elder Hinckley later, for more reasons than one, remembered Phillips Brooks' statement "How carefully most men creep into nameless graves, while now and again one or two forget themselves into immortality" as he spoke of the event.

The love and appreciation bestowed on the outgoing president was significant not only to the unity within the stake and the outgoing president, but also to a small man serving as the outgoing president's stake clerk. That clerk, a mail carrier, had years before persuaded in patient gentleness and kindness that future stake president to come out of inactivity into the light. Tears fell down the clerk's face as the leader he had unselfishly helped was honorably released.[10]

Such were examples of myriad experiences in the stakes. Likewise, bishops were ordained and set apart by general authorities at that time. One such faithful brother was Al "Olie" Langston, a neighbor in East Mill Creek. Said Elder Hinckley of Bishop Langston as he spoke at his funeral, "Money was only a means to an end and the end was to help those who needed it more."[11]

Claudious Bowman's Funeral

In June 1958, Elder Hinckley, newly called assistant to the LDS 12 apostles, attended the funeral of former Mexican Mission President Claudious Bowman. As the remains were lowered in the earth of the Dublan Cemetery, Gordon was dismayed but as quickly knew as the sun would rise over the dry mound the next morn that Brother Bowman had but graduated to a new life. His still slow smile and strong hand would never be forgotten.[12]

Moral Bankruptcy

At the same time, Elder Hinckley picked up a magazine while riding an airplane and read a sick description of the moral bankruptcy of society that year. "What's in it for me?" the individuality seemed to be saying at the time. Elder Hinckley spoke on that subject at an assignment, first in a long string to come, at Brigham Young University. He had heard a man tell him his story of returning to activity. He said in the course of the conversation, "Until death do you part" was a ceremony of marriage, but it was also a bill of divorcement and encouraged in his address to the BYU students June 5, 1958 to seek for something better.

Stephen L. Richards had told Gordon once of a talk delivered by LDS prophet Joseph F. Smith in which he said the Lord intends his people to enjoy the good things of the earth. The next April he said at his regular general conference talk, "As I look into your faces, I see the fulfillment of prophecy. In your presence I see a realization of the words of Jeremiah: '. . . I will take you one of a city, and two of a family, and I will bring you to Zion. And I will give you pastors according to mine heart, which shall feed you with knowledge and understanding (Jer. 3:"14-15).'"[13] Elder Hinckley likes that scripture and has used it often since.

Gordon spoke at his mentor's funeral on May 22, 1959.[14] Stephen L. Richards had been an LDS apostle for 42 years when he died at age 71. Elder Hinckley had associated with him for 24 of those years.

On July 9, 1959, Gordon attended the 86th birthday party for his father. Gordon had a bow tie, an increasingly receding hairline, thin wire glasses, his characteristic white "2 peak" handkerchief in his left suit coat pocket marking his appearance.[15]

He then spoke November 4, 1959 at a BYU Devotional on building an eternal home. Stake conference visits and speaking assignments continued unending, too.

Lesson in Compassion

In 1960, Elder Hinckley made an appeal to President David O. McKay regarding a member who was being excommunicated. He said to President McKay he thought the brother had been trapped in a moment of weakness. David O. McKay replied, "The thought was father to the act." The prophet counseled Elder Hinckley that this transgression had not happened in a moment of weakness but over an extended period of thinking about it.[16]

Shortly after this, Gordon's good friend G. Homer Durham was made president of Arizona State University. Then Gordon attended the funeral in December 1960 of a returned missionary, a brilliant young man, who had been killed in a head on collision. He stood at the pulpit and looked in the faces of the brother's father and mother. There came into his heart a conviction never felt before with such assurance. "As I looked at the casket, he had not died but had only been transferred to another field of labor to commence his mission so well begun here."[17] The same month, his ministry took him to a stake conference in Idaho.

The next year, Gordon's father died of a disabling stroke. He was one month shy of turning 94 when he passed away June 5, 1961. The next month the Berlin Wall was erected in Germany. Elder Hinckley's apostleship began in October of this year, ordained under the hands of President David O. McKay. That December, he was talking to a young man who had attempted suicide. The fellow was defeated. Elder Hinckley's advice was, "Believe in yourself."[18]

A grandmother came to visit him at this time, too. She was bereft and heartbroken with a conscience of guilt over something which happened when she was 19. The new apostle consoled and reassured her to believe in herself, put the past behind her and forget it.

Sylvia's Cancer

Gordon's youngest sister Sylvia was diagnosed with cancer about 1962. She was only 42. Gordon requested the First Presidency and Quorum of the 12 to pray for her in their weekly Thursday meetings in the Salt Lake Temple. His mother's same fight with this affliction flooded back to his mind. In 1966 the doctor said Sylvia had about five months to live but her life continued on. She was outstanding, brilliant, a woman of courage, patient and valiant.[19]

During the next eight years, Elder Hinckley made untold of trips and communications to his sister in remote Panaca, Nevada giving comfort and priesthood administrations. He gave her a blessing in the hospital in Cedar City, Utah shortly before her demise. Finally on February 6, 1970, Sylvia passed away in the Cedar City Hospital just about a month before turning 50, the same age their mother Ada passed away in 1930 exactly 40 years before.

Elder Hinckley and Marjorie were in the car to Panaca, Nevada for the memorial services and he spoke to the congregation. Less than two years later, Sylvia's husband Don was seriously ill with a cerebral hemorrhage and Gordon soon returned to speak at the additional funeral for Sylvia's husband. The Summer of 1972, Elder and Sister Hinckley visited the cemetery in Meadow Valley, now Panaca, Nevada where Sylvia and Don rest.

These were the kinds of compassionate expenditures Elder Hinckley constantly was disbursing for family, friends and acquaintances. He was never too busy to change schedules and drop plans for the same types of compassionate service exemplified by the Savior. That was where the Savior would be and that, therefore, was where Elder Hinckley was going to be. He would later speak at numerous funerals, many for his friends and others for beloved brethren of the general authorities.

President Kennedy Visit to Tabernacle

John F. Kennedy visited Salt Lake City and spoke at the LDS Tabernacle on Temple Square about this time.[20] Elder Hinckley picked up a book from the BYU Bookstore with a forward by Charles Malik, former president of the UN General Assembly. It "impressed him tremendously." Mr. Malik wrote, "In this fearful age you must transcend your system. You must have a message to proclaim to others. You must mean something in terms of ideas and attitudes and fundamental outlook on life. This something must vibrate with relevance to all conditions of man."[21]

French Polynesia

In May 1963, Elder Hinckley received assignment to dedicate an LDS meeting house on the Island of Huahini, Tahiti, 2,300 miles southeast of the Hawaiian Islands and 1,000 miles south of the Equator. He flew to the island by seaplane and saw the beautiful little chapel situated on the crest of a hill overlooking the bay. The chapel was packed with members, the curious and government officials. Following the dedication, members boarded boats to return to their homes while Elder Hinckley went to Papeete, capital of Tahiti, for a missionary conference on May 22nd.

Waves heaved the *Manuia,* a boat containing all but two of the Maupiti Branch relief society with children and a nurse named Clair, onto a reef. The boat tossed to and fro expelling its passengers into the sea where they were further battered by the surf. Clair hung on to a pole for three hours until rescued. The Maupiti relief society was not so blessed. Fifteen died, 10 of them relief society sisters, five of them mothers. Three babies and a 5 year old girl also perished. Clair prayed to God while clinging to her life saving pole, "O God, please save us and show me Thy Church. I will follow you."

A fisherman named Andre Manea spotted the distressed boat passengers and pulled Clair and eight other survivors into his boat. When Clair arrived on Maupiti, LDS missionaries requested she notify Elder Hinckley and the other church leaders.

Knowledge of the tragedy in Maupiti came by telegram to the mission home in Papeete from the surviving nurse Clair. The missionary conference was immediately postponed. Elder Hinckley cancelled his flight home and began searching with leaders for a boat and food to carry them the 24 hour journey by sea to Maupiti Island.

Gordon B. Hinckley with wife Marjorie
and two Polynesians examine
Wood Dagger

When the converted PT boat arrived in Maupiti, Elder Hinckley began walking the streets and holding the children and husbands of the lost mothers and children in his arms. He wept with them and hugged the children. He spoke words of comfort.

Clair was emotionally distraught. Elder Hinckley said, "Would you like a blessing?"

"What is that?"

They explained the ordinance of anointing the sick and ill in the household of faith. She consented. Hands were placed on her head and a priesthood blessing given her by Elder Hinckley. In the blessing, in addition to encouraging her in her recovery he encouraged her to join the Church of Jesus Christ of Latter-day Saints and serve the Lord.

That evening, Elder Hinckley wrote in his journal, "This has been a terrible day. I'm glad I came. I shall never forget Maupiti."

As the Tahiti LDS Temple was being dedicated by President Gordon B. Hinckley 20 years later, Clair Manea came up and greeted him. Both shed tears together as Elder Hinckley learned she had joined the LDS faith, married the sailor who had rescued her, he had also joined the church shortly after Elder Hinckley blessed her, and he was then serving as a counselor to the mission president in Tahiti. She believed his blessing an answer to her pleading prayer while in the raving ocean.[22]

Elder Hinckley and the contingent from Papeete returned to the mission home where a missionary out six months approached Elder Hinckley for a special blessing before leaving for a new assignment in a remote island with a "green bean" companion. The elder was feeling anxious about his abilities to perform. Elder Hinckley consented and laid his hands on the elder's head at the mission home.

After stating the elder's name, Elder Hinckley started to pronounce his blessing. "You will be successful on your mission . . . ," then he suddenly halted and went to the mission president. "This elder is not to go to Rimatera Island. Please give him a new assignment."

President Young assigned the elder closer to the mission headquarters. Two months later, President Thomas R. Stone replaced the previous mission president and chose the elder as an assistant. The elder then authored textbooks, including a dictionary, in the Tahitian language during his remaining two years and organized two temple excursions for the Tahitian LDS saints to New Zealand.[23]

On another occasion, Elder Hinckely was in Peru when a deadly earthquake hit. In like manner he dispensed comfort and consolation to those injured and bereaving.[24]

Moral Campaigns

Although the LDS church does not take sides regarding normal political issues, when they involve morals, the Church speaks its mind. And often Elder Hinckley has been the major spokesman regarding the LDS position.

Nineteen sixty four found Elder Hinckley speaking out on the months of recent research substantially supporting the Church's stand on the harmfulness of tobacco. He reasoned that all the research, study and counsel is great but the simple revealed word of the Lord has been around since the early 1830's. "Let it be remembered," Elder Hinckley declared. "'the things of God are understood by the Spirit of God,' and revelation is fruitless unless it be listened to and obeyed."[25]

In October 1968, Elder Hinckley campaigned against alcohol by the drink being considered by the legislature of the State of Utah. In an articulate article entitled "Rise, and Stand Upon Thy Feet", Elder Hinckley said, "There is now a proposal, under the guise of better control, to greatly expand the availability of liquor, providing for public bars where people of all ages could be admitted. We are convinced that this would mean a much wider exposure of youth to alcohol, with, as we believe, subsequent tragic results." Then he closed by quoting three questions from the Jewish Theological Seminary text:

> "How shall we pass on our heritage?
>
> "Will it be diminished or increased?
>
> "Will we be the grandfathers, or only the grandsons of great men?"[26]

10 Years of Apostleship

Elder Hinckley talked to a young man in the Summer of 1964. "How are you getting along?" Elder Hinckley asked.

"I'm getting along wonderfully! I'm back at the Y. I have a good place to live, nothing fancy, but decent, comfortable, and fairly cheap. I got the classes I want from the teachers who know their stuff. And I have my eyes on a wonderful girl."

"How lucky can you be!" Elder Hinckley replied.[27]

Elder Hinckley strolled the BYU campus after that encounter and looked at the students. He was impressed. They were clean, well dressed and with no cigarettes in their mouths.

Elder Gordon B. Hinckley
At a Typical Commemoration Service

In contrast, he had the unpleasant experience of interviewing two people divorced. They professed they loved one another but they talked about the negative amongst the positive. In individual interviews, the husband sobbed and sobbed. The wife cried, too and then called her former husband "stingy."

Elder Hinckley then brought them together. "There is only one thing wrong with you. You're just too miserably selfish. You are unwilling to sacrifice for one another. You are unwilling to lay aside your own little comforts in order to accommodate one another."[28]

Shortly thereafter, Elder Hinckley rode the airplane over New York City to Chicago and the plains of Nebraska and Wyoming at 600 miles an hour, thinking of his grandfather Ira Nathaniel Hinckley and the slow 15-20 miles a day he had travelled in such adverse conditions while traversing the same plains to the Rocky Mountains.

Joshua 24:13 came to his mind and he pulled his Bible to review. "And I have given you a land for which ye did not labour, and cities which ye built not, and ye dwell in them; of the vineyards and oliveyards which ye planted not do ye eat."

"Our generation did not make the land—our ancestors did," he thought. What debt of gratitude we have to them.[29] The tremendous pressure he had been laboring under for the past months did not seem as heavy to him when he reflected upon the immolations of his forebears.

The experience of a young man at the New York World's Fair at the time also rung in his heart. The man had tried churches galore. When he found prophets taught in Judaism, he joined them. Then he visited the 1964 World's Fair in New York. There he saw a building in the shape of the Salt Lake Temple and went in. On the walls were beautiful murals of the prophets recorded in the Old Testament but not only dead prophets—living prophets!

His heart warmed and he was baptized. Later he served a mission in South America and became the instrument bringing his family and others to the same knowledge that God does not change, that He treats his children the same whether in the past or the present. Living prophets live today as well as in the past.[30]

A student asked Elder Hinckley in 1965 whether he believed in evolution. He replied, "I know little about organic evolution, but I am very much concerned with the evolution of man, the child of God." He then quoted D.&C. 50:23-24 "And that which doth not edify is not of

God, and is darkness. That which is of God is light; and he that receiveth light, and continueth in God, receiveth more light; and that light groweth brighter and brighter until the perfect day."

Regardless of the reasonings of philosophers, moralists or public opinion shapers, Elder Hinckley stated the principle of "edifying" is eternal in application and benefit.[31]

During the course of Elder Hinckley's ministry he has received much correspondence and has always been attentive to it. Many replies under his personal stationery have been penned and dictated as well as official church communication. He always has been willing to listen.

He has been a man of great openness, both in written and personal communication. The door to his office has always been open and his life has been an open book. He has never been hesitant to have anything he says or does recorded and disseminated.

This is a stark contrast to the great majority of the world.

Many unsigned letters have been received on his desk, too. One contained a $20.00 bill with a confession and an apology of repentance. The anonymous writer revealed 25 years ago he had entered the Hinckley home and found currency on a dresser. Elder Hinckley used the experience to teach the principle of honesty in the workplace as well as home. He asked how many anonymous takers of envelopes, stamps, etc. are in businesses or other places.[32]

The Berkley riots of 1965 were raging in the Spring of 1965 and with it great division throughout the rest of the United States. But missionaries of the LDS Church still preached peace and forgiveness on the same streets and throughout the world and many others performed unfeigned acts of love. Elder Hinckley, even with busy schedules he had, still found time to visit others such as Tatsui Sato and his second wife Tomiko and invited them to come over and visit their home.[33]

At a BYU Devotional address on January 10, 1967, Elder Hinckley drew from his personal journal for the subject of his address called "Asian Journal" and suggested the keeping of a diary was a good thing, commending the practice to his listeners. On the same day, Israel completed its Six Day War taking territory surrounding the Holy Land four times its previous size. To Latter-day Saints, the events were merely an unfolding of prophecy concerning the Latter-days.

A son of one of Elder Hinckley's friends phoned his office in 1967. The frantic voice on the other end said, "Elder Hinckley, I need to see you."

"Well, Brother, I'm quite involved with appointments the remainder of the day. Can you come tomorrow?"

"I need to see you at once, Brother Hinckley."

"All right, come on over and we'll talk."

The secretary changed Elder Hinckley's remaining appointments and shortly the boy with a "hunted and haunted look" arrived. He had long hair and looked in complete disarray.

"Come on in, Brother. Let's talk openly and frankly. I have your interest at heart. My only desire is to help."

The youth told his distressing and miserable story. He had been unclean and broken the law. Now the realization of his predicament was weighing upon him and he needed help.

"Does your dad know of this?"

"No. I can't talk to him. He hates me."

Elder Hinckley knew the contrary was true but that the father had an uncontrollable temper. When disciplining his children he lost control and destroyed rather than mended. He looked across the desk at the trembling and broken young man and thought of the true order of parental love. Kindness, gentleness, persuasion, long-suffering, meekness, love unfeigned were the tools.

"Reproving betimes with sharpness when moved upon by the Holy Ghost, and then showing forth afterwards an increase of love toward him whom thou hast reproved, lest he esteem thee to be his enemy. (D.&C. 121:41-44)"[34]

Elder Hinckley next spoke at the BYU Devotional on December 5, 1987 about Joseph the Seer who had received that great revelation while languishing six months in a dark and dingy basement dungeon in Liberty, Missouri.

Former US President Dwight D. Eisenhower's funeral in March 1969 impressed Elder Hinckley. He saw the "matchless wonder of the Son of God" in his mind as he witnessed the pageantry, the dignitaries, the eulogies and the legions of military filing by the TV camera on that Monday.

As he looked into the faces of the mourners, the comfort which all sought became clear to him—the example of the simple life and testimony of the resurrected Man of Peace, "He who never lifted the sword of war, who never ruled as head of state, who walked among the poor, who died on the cross and was buried in a borrowed tomb" [35]

While the memorial service for President and General Eisenhower unfolded, Gordon reached for his book containing an interview by Bruce Barton with H.G. Wells and reviewed a signet fond to him. Mr. Barton asked Wells, after all of the prominent men and women Wells had studied in authoring his *Outline of History*, which of them deserve to be called great?

H.G. Wells pondered the question for two days and then submitted a list of six names to Mr. Barton. At the top of the list was Jesus of Nazareth.

By the time eight years of his apostolic ministry had passed, Elder Hinckley's friend G. Homer Durham was chosen to be Utah State's first Commissioner of Education. The news was still full of rot and filth. President Richard M. Nixon wiped perspiration from his face as he spoke to the Nation on November 3, 1969 and Elder Hinckley thought of the terrible loneliness of leadership. He remembered Queen Victoria's statement, "Uneasy rests the head that wears the crown," and made "Loneliness of Leadership" the theme of his talk the next day before the BYU studentbody devotional.[36]

About April 1970, Elder Hinckley read early LDS apostle Parley P. Pratt's poetic statement of obligation to advance the work. He also clipped an article by Sidney Harris from the *Deseret News* about men who had problems but became great. The statements gave him inspiration and refreshing support to move on.

Two university freshmen came to him for counsel in 1970. The young woman sobbed. The handsome, tall and manly man was penitent. They confessed they had cheated themselves. They were to be married in a week but not in the temple. The ways of the world had caught them. Three years remained of education for the beautiful, sensitive and perceptive woman, an excellent student, but now faced with motherhood. The man declared he would take responsibility even though it blighted the future he once dreamed.

Elder Hinckley admired his courage but his heart ached as he watched both weep and sob. The world had told them of "freedom" but now all they found were shackles. They did not know peace, especially the peace of self respect.[37]

Such were some of the hundreds of joyful and sorrowful experiences this apostle of the LDS faith witnessed through his ministry as his 10th anniversary as a special witness for Jesus Christ neared.

Elder Gordon B. Hinckley
In a Familiar Pose at the Pulpit

On February 25, 1971, in the Union Ballroom of the student center on the University of Utah campus, Elder Hinckley was awarded the Distinguished Alumnus Award at the University Founder's Banquet.[38] These awards were going to be almost commonplace as the ministry of Gordon B. Hinckley progressed.

Elder Hinckley enjoyed visiting the grave of his older brother Stanford in the military cemetery in France where he had died during World War I. He thanked the Lord for the sacrifices those who gave their lives made for liberty.

Elder Hinckley sat with his elbows on the left and right armrests, his two index fingers extended supporting his lower lip, hands clasped, fingers intertwined, with a black onyx ring on his left second finger looking forward with glasses and a confident look in his chair at the morning session of the LDS Primary Conference convened Thursday, April 1, 1971. He was present as a new member of the Primary Correlation Committee of general authorities.

When he rose to talk, he said in part, "Don't ever sell short a boy or a girl. Your great task as Primary teachers is to help each child fulfill the potential that lies within him."[39]

Elder Hinckley talked about divorce in his April 1971 general conference address. He declared divorce was the root cause of soaring public welfare, a denial of the family ordained by God. The reason: No parental love, consequent child insecurity, and the bitter fruits—6 million divorced or separated adults in the United States alone.[40]

By the time Elder Hinckley's 10th anniversary as an LDS apostle had ended, he had tallied two trips around the world, visits to all areas of the Far East allowed to U.S. citizens, seven trips to South America, seven trips to Europe, and additional visits to wide areas of the United States, Canada, Mexico, the Pacific Islands, Australia and New Zealand.[41] He was also serving as a director of the Utah Agencies, a coordinating organization of representatives of the State of Utah, Salt Lake City, various chambers of commerce, and other organizations dealing with airline service to Utah.

Reflecting upon his experiences for the past 10 years, Gordon had to say his "most rewarding" was the meetings he had in the presence of his brethren, the other 11 members of the Quorum of 12 Apostles, and the First Presidency in the room specially furnished for their weekly quorum meetings each Thursday in the Salt Lake Temple.[42]

When he watched the King Family on local Salt Lake TV during a Christmas special December 14, he reflected on the first morning of Christmas as "I'm Dreaming of a White Christmas" and "I'll be Home for Christmas" were sung. He had just returned from more conferences and meetings in the Midwest the night before. Soon he would find himself on one of the most significant trips of his life with the future prophet of the LDS church, Harold B. Lee, as they walked for the first time the actual soil where Jesus had walked.

Pilgrimage to the Holy Land

Joseph Fielding Smith's tenure as 10th prophet of the LDS Church did not last quite 2½ years when he passed away on July 2, 1972 at age 95. LDS apostle Harold B. Lee, who had presented Gordon's name to the congregation of East Mill Creek Stake in 1956 to be its second president, was next in line to assume the presidency as senior member of the 12 apostles. The new president soon asked Elder Gordon B. Hinckley to accompany him on a trip to the Holy Land.

There were 3,200,000 members of the Latter-day Saint Church at the time.[43] The trip was to last three weeks and take the two couples to Italy, Greece, Jerusalem, Bethlehem, Jericho, Jacob's Well, the Garden of Gethsemane and sacred spots in between.

President and Sister Lee met Elder and Sister Hinckley about September 7, 1972 in England. There they first reorganized the London Stake, attended the London Temple, held meetings with the missionaries and interviewed with prominent government and other business and professional people not only in England but also in Switzerland and Italy.[44] The installation of a new LDS prophet had increasingly attracted the attention of high officials in addition to the media.

They then flew to Athens, Greece where they met President and Sister Edwin Q. Cannon, Jr., presiding over the Swiss Mission, then covering the nation of Greece. Meetings were held with the members.

Early in the morning of the 19th of September, they took a taxi and rode to the Acropolis. The Parthenon sits on the top of "Mars Hill" where a view of all of Athens and its surrounding emerald seas can be seen. A few LDS saints were also with them. On the hill where Paul the Apostle had declared the gospel to the Greeks they testified to each other. President Lee re-read the account of Paul's words uttered there. Elder Hinckley said, "As we came down from that historic hill . . . we were all quickened in our faith."[45]

That evening they flew to Tel Aviv, then up to Jerusalem. "The Spirit bore witness of His divinity, of His life and death and resurrection and of His living reality," Elder Hinckley reported.

Next they visited Bethlehem with guide Elder David B. Galbraith. With great appreciation they saw in their mind the shepherds in the field, the angels in song, and the manger as Elder Galbraith read the scriptures pertaining to that sacred night when the Messiah was born. The feeling was subdued.

On September 20 and several days thereafter, they visited the road to Bethany the Savior had walked, the tomb of Lazarus, Caiphas' courtyard where Jesus was sentenced. Pictures were taken by reverent faces in suits and dresses. Then Jericho and the Mount of Temptation, the Hall of the Last Supper, and the waters of the River Jerico were seen.

"I reflected on the fact that even He who was perfect, suffered Himself to be baptized, for thus it becometh Him to fulfill all righteousness," Elder Hinckley wrote.

From Galilee, the party climbed to the scene of the Sermon on the Mount and reflected on the Beatitudes uttered by the Savior and His divinity. From Nazareth, the group moved south to the Mount of Transfiguration, to the site of Samaria where wind continued to blow dust over columns of the past.

At Jacob's Well, the party drank water together and remembered the Lord's meeting with the Samarian woman. At Jerusalem's sites, they reflected on the Savior's final days, entry, supper, betrayal and institution of the Sacrament in His remembrance at the Hall of the Last Supper.

At the Garden of Gethsemane they reverently looked at the old gnarled and shaggy 3,000 year old olive tree which was over a 1,000 years old when Jesus made his most infinite sacrifice in that garden atoning for the sins of mankind. They read together the scripture regarding the event and meditated in somber thought reflecting upon how Judas had arrived with the guards and taken Jesus captive.

They followed the terraced path down from the garden to the Kedron Valley where the Sisters of Zion Monastery now stands over the ancient Courtyard of Caiphas. They then thought of the three crosses and the physical and emotional torture the Savior had endured for them and the rest of humanity.

The Prophet's Declaration at the Garden Tomb

Special permission was obtained to visit the Garden Tomb in the evening after the day's tourists had departed. There was moonlight through the trees of olives as the small group of Latter-day Saints stood there and sang hymns of praise and bore testimony to each other as they organized a Jerusalem Branch with Elder David B. Galbraith as branch president. A Jewish member bore testimony and children sang a song and a chorus of "I am a Child of God."

President Cannon spoke truth and President Lee, Elder Hinckley and President Galbraith each bore their testimonies. Then they had prayer and sang "God Be With You 'Til We Meet Again."[46]

When President Lee, the new LDS prophet, stood for the first time at the tomb with his wife and Elder and Sister Hinckley, he was very quiet. Then he declared, "Here Christ's body lay. Here the first Easter morn occurred."[47]

It was a wonderful experience. The certitude expressed by the living prophet brought great joy into the heart of Elder Hinckley.

But what was more wonderful was the power of God expressed in the special sacred experience had by the group in Jerusalem. President Lee became quite ill. At night Elder Hinckley could hear him coughing incessantly through the thin walls between their hotel rooms. The next morning, President Lee asked for an administration at the hands of Elder Hinckley.

Through the power of the same priesthood through which Gordon had blessed Jay Quealy's legs to heal and Sister Clair Manea on the Tahitian Island of Maupiti to be comforted and join the Church, Elder Hinckley laid his hands upon the head of the living oracle of God on the earth at that time and blessed him to get well. He had been coughing up blood the night before. President Lee later remarked to Elder Hinckley, "We had to go to the Land of Miracles to experience our own miracle."

News Conference at Waldorf Astoria

The contingent returned from the Holy Land to New York City in the evening on September 27, 1972 and stayed at the Waldorf Astoria Hotel. The next day at 2 P.M., despite their unbelievable fatigue, they held a historic press conference in the hotel before media from the Associated Press, United Press, the New York Times, Time Magazine, the New York Daily News, the Washington Post, CBS and others.

Elder Gordon B. Hinckley Talks
at a
Typical Regional Conference

Elder Hinckley began the conference. President Lee, Elder Hinckley, Lee S. Bickmore and Wendell J. Ashton met the press. Questions were asked and candidly answered and a great step made in understanding and cordial relations with the mass media of major news and television.

At the news conference, President Lee announced that Elder Hinckley and Elder Mark E. Petersen, also an LDS apostle, were now the contact men for the External Communications of the LDS Church, in other words, the "Public Relations" heads of the Church.[48] Through this new responsibility, new editors and managers were appointed for the *Deseret News* in December.

Conferences & Dedications

Elder Hinckley was back at quarterly conferences at BYU on March 22, 1973. Sessions for two stakes were held at 10 A.M., another for 5 stakes at 1:30 P.M. and two stakes met at 6 P.M. for a priesthood leadership meeting to top a full Sunday.

In May, he helped Spencer W. Kimball, Marion G. Romney and J. LeRoy Kimball of the Nauvoo Mission dedicate the Joseph Bates Noble home, the Jonathan Browning Home & Workshop, the Webb Wagon & Blacksmith Shop and the Seventies Hall in Nauvoo, Illinois after their restorations.[49] He also visited President Harold B. Lee's ancestor's home with President Lee, a home which in 1844 looked towards the Nauvoo Temple on the hill. A youth conference was attended in South Africa in August.

Elder Hinckley was ministering to the family of a husband and four children, including a boy of 6, in March 1974 at the bedside of their terminally ill wife and mother.

Elder Hinckley was in Washington, D.C. in October 1974 when President Nixon was granted a pardon by his successor Gerald Ford. That December he spoke at the funeral of Harold B. Lee who had died of a heart attack only a year and a half after becoming prophet.

The ministering went on. A prayer was given by Elder Hinckley at the unveiling of the 16 foot high, 66 foot long mural depicting Christ and the remaining 11 disciples placed in the foyer of the Church Office Building on July 31, 1974. He was at the ground breaking of the six story addition to the BYU Library on October 25 of that year. Fourteen men and women, including Elder Hinckley, wielded gold plated shovels as they turned the first earth.

Letters of appreciation were sent to friends who sent the Hinckleys a gift at Christmas. "It was so generous and kind of you to give us that beautiful dish at Christmas. We are grateful for the gift, but more grateful for your friendship," Elder Hinckley wrote. At the 65th anniversary of the Hotel Utah, Gordon served as master of ceremonies. On July 24, 1975, he spoke at the sunrise service for patriotism. He told of the faith of the pioneers and compared the Israelites coming to the promised land to the LDS pioneers coming to the Rocky Mountains.

At this time, Salt Lake City was taking on a new face. The Hotel Utah was being remodeled. A Main Street beautification project replacing sidewalks and planting trees was in progress. The ZCMI Center mall was under construction with cranes in place.[50]

The next year new LDS prophet Spencer W. Kimball discontinued assistants to the 12 and reorganized the seventies. Seventies would now take responsibility for assisting the 12 apostles.[51] Elder Hinckley spoke of the expanding Church by subject assignment at the BYU on April 8, 1976. Two months later, area supervision was placed under Quorum of the 12 "advisors" and Seventies became the "supervisors." Elder Hinckley was to advise Elder Adney Y. Komatsu, who had become a seventy, Elder DeJager, 17 missions, seven stakes and 42 districts.[52]

Elder and Sister Hinckley attended the last performance of the Hill Cumorah Pageant on July 31, 1976. A record 100,000 attended. Two green and white tents were filled with supplemental visitor centers containing plaques depicting Nephi's vision of the Savior's birth, His mission and His death. King Lamoni's conversion was also depicted as well as the destruction of Zarahemla and the appearance of the Savior in America, all recorded in Mormon's book. Elder Hinckley spoke at the public Church Service the next day.[53]

In February 1977, the Hinckleys were on another journey around the world. They met in Dublin, Ireland at a small branch. On their return, Elder Hinckley spoke at BYU 12 stake fireside about "Forget Yourself." That April at general conference, Gordon's boyhood friend G. Homer Durham was called to the First Quorum of the Seventy. At his devotional talk at BYU February 14, 1978, Elder Hinckley said that the great challenge is self-centered lives.

Revelation on the Priesthood

The First Presidency and Quorum of the Twelve assembled as usual on Thursday in June 1978. They stood in a circle and President Spencer W. Kimball plead with the Lord for guidance on what to do about eligible men holding the priesthood. Elder Hinckley felt the spirit of revelation on that occasion and shortly it was announced all worthy men would be eligible for the priesthood.[54]

A new visitor's center on the south side of Temple Square in Salt Lake was next completed and dedicated June 10, 1978. Elder Hinckley explained the history of Temple Square and said, "One of the most remarkable prophecies ever uttered was that this would become the great highway of nations, and that kings and emperors and the noble and wise of the earth would visit us here. It is of singular importance that the beautiful visitor's center to the north of the square, as large as it is, has become inadequate to accommodate the crowds of visitors who come every day of the year.

"They include some of the rulers of the earth, and the learned, the noble and the weak. Two and a half million of them came last year and that figure should be exceeded in 1978."[55]

Elder Hinckley was with President Kimball in Johannesburg, South Africa on October 22, 1978, arriving at 10 A.M. After resting just four hours, Elder Hinckley spoke at 2 P.M. about the loneliness of membership. "In the days and months and the years to follow, you will find yourselves very much in the minority, whether it be in business, politics, in the professions, in education, in whatever your chosen vocation. You will feel loneliness in your faith."[56]

Twelve thousand attended. It was the first time in history more than one general authority of the LDS faith was present at the same time in the nation of South Africa. There was polite, dignified and reserved attendance shaking the prophet's hand. In the P.M., members lined up and reverently sang "We Thank Thee, O God, for a Prophet", as the President walked along the path and then "Come, Come, Ye Saints." President Kimball shook many hands as they were singing.

During a 10 hour layover, Elder Hinckley and President Kimball took a cable car to the top of Table Mountain, then had a "moving meeting" with 12 missionaries.

Back at Salt Lake City, Elder Hinckley received an honorary degree of Doctor of Humanities from Brigham Young University on April 20, 1979 as he delivered the commencement address at 9:30 A.M. as chairman of the Executive Committee of the Board of Trustees.[57]

In his October 1979, LDS general conference address, Elder Hinckley challenged members and friends everywhere to read the Book of Mormon once again or for the first time by April 6, 1980, the 150th anniversary of the LDS religion.[58] That November, he read a letter from a New York evangelist expressing a diatribe of hate against Joseph Smith, Jr., calling him an imposter, fraud, fake and deceiver and saying he was launching a national campaign to prove it.

Elder Hinckley took up the challenge to prove the evangelist a hoax. Two days later, he spoke of the prophet Joseph Smith at the BYU fireside November 4, 1979. He reviewed recent "word print" analysis through computer providing substantial evidence there really were 24 different authors to the various books in the Book of Mormon. He showed Joseph Smith influenced strong men and women to follow him, even unto death.

And he noted the prophecy Joseph Smith made in 1832, 29 years before the American Civil War which told the exact location where it would begin. He also told of Joseph Smith's prophecy in August 1842 that the members of the LDS faith would move to the Rocky Mountains where they would become a mighty people.

The LDS Church started a new meeting program in March 1980. Previous to this, Sunday meetings had normally been spaced throughout the day on Sundays. Sunday School was held at one time and then at another time Sacrament meeting and priesthood and relief society would be held. The new meeting program provided for a "consolidated schedule" of three hours in the United States and Canada.

150th Anniversary of the Church

One of the memorable experiences of Gordon B. Hinckley was the anniversary commemoration of the 150th birthday of the LDS Church. Elder Hinckley made the arrangements and prepared the physical facilities. He directed removal of the chapel located on the spot where the old Whitmer home porch area stood, saw the home's reconstruction and visited the scene a number of occasions before completed.

He drove to the scene in Fayette, New York where the David Whitmer home had been reconstructed as a church history site. As he drew near the house on April 6, 1980, he had difficulty restraining the strong emotions welling within him. Here the LDS Church had begun.

He was particularly emotional when standing in the reconstructed Whitmer home and thought of the whole panorama of Church history since the Smith and Mack families lived in Sharon County, Vermont; the first vision of the prophet Joseph Smith, Jr.; the restoration of the priesthood; the translation of the Book of Mormon and the tremendous forces which that set in motion.

On that day as a special segment of general conference was broadcast by television satellite from the log house in Fayette, New York, a spirit of gratitude for the wonderful ways of the Almighty and terrible prices made together with a spirit of testimony "welled within me," he wrote.[59]

A strong and certain reaffirmation came to him that day that God lives, Jesus is the Christ, Joseph Smith saw the Father and Son, the priesthood and keys were restored, and the Book of Mormon is true. He rejoiced over the opportunity to be a participant in the great and eternal work restored directly by the Father and Son.

"I felt particularly emotional over standing in the restored Whitmer home under circumstances designed to simulate the meeting which occurred 150 years earlier where the Prophet Joseph Smith with his associates stood. On that occasion there passed through my mind the whole panorama of the history of the Church with the events that culminated in that meeting held April 6, 1830."[60]

The Today Show

The next day, Elder Hinckley appeared on the NBC Today Show with J. Willard Marriott, Jr. Tom Brokaw interviewed them. Elder Hinckley said the Church is an "anchor in an uncertain world." All people worldwide respond because humanity's needs are the same. He described the missionary program and stated the Church had 30,000 missionaries in the field. A brief film was shown of the history of the Church and its persecutions at the beginning.[61]

The ministry of Elder Hinckley continued with a speech before the Salt Lake City Rotary Club on Tuesday, April 15, 1980. Then Gordon and Marjorie spent time with the BYU Young Ambassadors touring Mainland China. *PSA Magazine* next interviewed Elder Hinckley. Hard questions were posed to him but he handled them well. Major misconceptions, polygamy, the recent discipline of ERA advocate Sonja Johnson for apostacy from LDS doctrine all came out.[62]

The Psalm of Gordon B. Hinckley

It is not uncommon for men and women with sincere testimonies of the Savior to feel so strongly about their emotions they pen their own psalms to the Lord. Elder Hinckley did the same around December 7, 1980.

I know that my Redeemer lives,
Triumphant Savior, Son of God,

Victorious over pain & death,
My King, my Leader, & My Lord.

He lives, my one sure Rock of faith,
The one bright hope for me on earth,
A beacon to a better way,
The light beyond the veil of death.

Oh, give me Thy sweet spirit still,
The peace that comes alone from Thee,
The faith to walk the lonely road,
That leads to Thine eternity.[63]

In an hour of thoughtful reflection, Elder Hinckley had penned the words to a future hymn—his psalm. In March 1983, Beth S. Rasmussen, secretary to G. Homer Durham, took the 1983 *New Era* magazine to him at Room 240-C in the Historical Department of the Church Office Building in Salt Lake City. Elder Durham, Gordon's boyhood friend, was now managing director of the Historical Department of the LDS Church. His secretary suggested he read the magazine while traveling to a stake conference assignment. Elder Durham placed it in his briefcase before leaving the office.

The next Tuesday, Elder Durham buzzed his secretary in mid-morning on the intercom. "Come see something."

He had the *New Era* opened on the desk to page 49 and pointed, "Look."

There were eight measures of "rough" music sketched underneath the printed psalm of Gordon B. Hinckley. Sister Rasmussen worked on the music and submitted it to the LDS Music Department on the 12th Floor who were at that time selecting hymns to include in a new LDS Hymnbook revision. The music was first played at a LDS Historical Department devotional on September 13, 1983. The song was selected for inclusion in the new hymn book. After Elder Durham received a list of proposed titles for the hymn, he could not improve on the title President Hinckley gave it and it remained "My Redeemer Lives."[64]

In 1988, inspiration came to Elder Hinckley again while attending the funeral for a friend and he penned another psalm on death.[65]

SOUTH AMERICA SUPERVISION

After eight years supervising the Far East, Elder Gordon B. Hinckley was assigned in 1968 to watch over the LDS Church in South America. LDS apostle Melvin J. Ballard had opened South America for spreading the LDS gospel by opening a mission in Buenos Aires, Argentina on December 6, 1925. By 1968, LDS missions numbered about eight. There were two in Brazil, two in Argentina, two in the Peru/Ecuador area, a Chilean and a Uruguay mission. Fifteen hundred missionaries carried on the work.[1]

Elder Hinckley was on the soil of his new area soon. On July 1, 1968, the Colombia-Venezuela Mission was organized. Four days later, the Brazillian North Mission was organized from the Brazillian and Brazillian South Missions.

Before October conference 1969, he met 154 missionaries in Montevideo, Uruguay, 1,050 miles down the Eastern coast of South America from Rio de Janeiro, Brazil and interviewed every one of them. He discovered 58 of them came from homes where parents were not LDS or were inactive. They so impressed him he talked of them in his conference talk that Fall.

He also visited Sao Paulo, Brazil where he met an elder who had been the instrument of the Lord so far in bringing 43 new members into the LDS Church. He was a convert himself, financing his mission at great sacrifice. One of his 43 converts was a sister who caught the fire of the gospel message so intensely she referred 300 acquaintances to the missionaries in seven months and 60 had joined so far.[2]

Two new stakes were organized in Brazil. The first had been formed in 1966. On February 22, 1970, the first stake in Peru was organized by Elder Hinckley in Lima, the capital city. Elder A. Theodore Tuttle of the Seventy accompanied him. There were 10,771 members in the nation at that time. That same year, the Peru Mission was formed from the Chile-Andes Mission .

Six months later, Elder Hinckley organized the Ecuador Mission on August 1, 1970. Elder Hinckley went to Chile to organize a stake about May 1972 but found the leaders not prepared. Disappointedly, he postponed the organization and waited six months. Then he returned and found leaders were ready and organized the stake in Santiago in 1972.[3]

As when in the Far East, Elder Hinckley took every opportunity to meet with the leaders and missionaries in leadership sessions and conferences. Saturdays were usually the workshop and missionary testimony days. Sunday was the organizing day.

Elder Hinckley also examined missionary density and implemented measures disbursing missionaries throughout every area in South America allowed. By the time of July 1971 when he received a new assignment to supervise the European area, the three areas of Guyana at the middle of the north coast of South America were the only areas where LDS missionaries were not yet proselyting.[4] On July 1, 1971, the day Elder Hinckley officially assumed supervision of his new area of Europe, the new Venezuela Mission started operation.

Post Area Supervision Visits

Once Elder Hinckley moved on to supervision of the area in Europe, he still did not lose touch with South America. He came back in the 1980's to dedicate temples, first in Santiago, Chile where 11 years before the leaders were not ready for the planned organization of their stake. Now they had an LDS temple!

President Hinckley, as a member of the First Presidency, also had the privilege of dedicating the temples in Lima, Peru and Buenos Aires, Argentina in January 1986.

April 19 and 20, 1986 also saw President Hinckley back in Buenos Aires for a Regional Conference where he presided. Elders J. Thomas Fyans and Spencer H. Osborn, Seventies, accompanied him. They were two of the new Area Presidencies of the seventy quorums assigned by 1986 worldwide in strategic areas around the earth as resident general authorities. Following the regional meeting, President Hinckley went to the LDS temple in Buenos Aires and held a seminar with the temple workers.[5]

November 17 and 18, 1986, mission presents and their wives from Venezuela, Peru, Colombia, Ecuador and Bolivia went to Quito, Equador for an annual mission presidents' conference with President Gordon B. Hinckley and Elder Richard G. Scott of the Seventy. By that time, Chile was fast approaching 50 stakes. Argentina had 23, Bolivia 8, Brazil 50. Colombia membership was 45,800, Ecuador 43,000. Peru had 23 stakes. Uruguay membership was drawing near 50,000. Venezuela had 23,516 members in five stakes.

EUROPEAN GERMANIC ADVISOR

On July 1, 1971, Elder Gordon B. Hinckley officially took over advising and directing the European-Germanic Area. The area actually encompassed more than traditional Europe. Germany, Switzerland, Austria and Italy were in the area. But also members in disbursed and scattered locations in the Middle East as well as Africa were his territory.[1] In reality, Elder Hinckley was advising and directing locations in the continents of Europe, Asia and Africa.

On May 29, 1971, the LDS First Presidency announced members of the Quorum of the 12 would be advisors of areas in a "director" roll and assistants to the 12 and members of the 1st Council of the 70 would be made "supervisors" over the areas first created by President Moyle and Elder Hinckley in 1959. Elder William H. Bennett, an assistant to the 12, was placed under Elder Hinckley as area supervisor and Elder Hinckley was the member of the 12 in charge of advising and directing Elder Bennett.

The missions within the area were the Austria, Germany Central, Germany North, Germany South, Germany West, Switzerland, Italy North, and Italy South.[2]

The official responsibility continued for two years although Elder Hinckley was involved in numerous other activities, including returning to South America to form a stake in Chile in 1972 and continued contact with the Far East.

Elder Hinckley had in reality been involved with Europe ever since his first visit to the continent with his two missionary companions in the Summer of 1935 at the end of their missions to Britain. The preparation, dedications and follow-up inspection of the Swiss and London LDS Temples had also afforded him additional visits to Europe. In 1956 he had also traveled Europe while serving essentially as the head of the unofficial "Missionary Department" yet to be formally formed by the LDS Church.

In 1967, Gordon visited the countries of Iran, Turkey, Lebanon, Greece, Italy, Spain and most of the countries in Europe even though he was still officially the supervisor over the Far East. But he did not visit the Holy Land. He gathered with the enclaves of saints in these nations and shared testimony with them.

December 5, 1967 also found him in the Bavarian Alps even though he was still officially the supervisor over the Far East. He was at Berchtesgaden in the shadow of Hitler's "Eagle's Nest" meeting at possibly the same hall where 25 years before evil men met to plan conquest and genocide.

Now Elder Hinckley and a group of American servicemen met in the hall and made its chamber ring with the hymn "Praise to the Man" which had played such an important part in Gordon B. Hinckley's testimony when he was 12 years old. The saints bore testimony. A well publicized hero of the Vietnam war who saved many fellow air force soldiers battling for the Atau Airstrip, Vietnam bore a "quiet and measured" testimony of the priesthood, Jesus Christ, and the prophet Joseph Smith, Jr.

To the world he was a decorated Lieutenant Colonel in the US Air Force but to the group who met with him he was one of their brothers, a quiet, sandy-haired, freckle-faced man.[3]

Elder Hinckley already had a tangible love for the people in Europe when he was officially designated to advise the LDS work there. His shared faith during the next two years was to further lift them and strengthen them.[4]

Youth Conference in Switzerland

One of the first things Elder Hinckley was found doing in 1971 was meeting with the youth in Switzerland. The German speaking Swiss youth of the LDS faith met. Elder Hinckley saw leaders of the future, solid in faith and testimony and set in the right direction. They expressed their ambitions and desires, ambitions and desires to serve in the Church as well as in society in responsible positions of trust. They expressed desires for knowledge and education. They seemed good and optimistic.[5]

Tour With the Prophet

The major tour for Elder Hinckley in Europe and the Mid-East in 1972 was with newly ordained LDS prophet Harold B. Lee. The tour lasted three weeks. First, they installed two new regional representatives in Britain. Then they met with LDS members in Switzerland, in Italy where two missions were flourishing, and in Greece and Israel.

Elder Hinckley got to visit the Holy Land for the first time in his life and was at the side of the living prophet of his church at the time.

A great conference of youth similar to the one Elder Hinckley had experienced in Switzerland the year before met just outside Rome, Italy in September 1972. The young men and women of the LDS faith came from many areas. Testimonies were heard. Similar future leaders were seen. The Church was in good hands in Italy for the future.[6]

A group of children assembled around President Harold B. Lee at Lausanne, Switzerland during Elder Hinckley's tour with him. Elder Lee imparted a childhood experience to them. As a little boy, some old farm buildings appeared across a fence of the family fields after his father left work for the day. Harold was caught with curiosity to explore them. But as he began going through the fence, he heard a quiet voice say, "Harold, don't go in there."

He looked around for his father but no one was around. He did not question the voice he had heard. He turned around and hurried home. He took the prompting as a warning of the still small voice of the Holy Ghost guiding him in his life.[7]

During the three week tour with President and Sister Lee and his own wife Marjorie, Elder Hinckley was tutored by a prophet. Gordon found this intimate association a reservoir of intelligence further refining him for his future role in the same position. Elder Hinckley saw President Lee as humble, without arrogance, no officiousness in him, never haughty or noisy or offensive. He also, although holding the mantel of Presiding High Priest over the entire LDS Church, was teachable. He listened to others.[8]

The Brilliant Female Doctor

In early 1973, Gordon attended a conference of LDS servicemen in Berchtesgaden, Germany. A female US Army Major, also a medical doctor highly respected in her profession, spoke.

"More than anything else in the world," she said, "I wanted to serve God. But try as I might, I could not find him. The miracle of it all is that he found me.

"One Saturday afternoon in September 1969 I was at home in Berkeley, California, and heard my doorbell ring. There were two young men there, dressed in suits, with white shirts and ties. Their hair was neatly combed. I was so impressed with them that I said: 'I don't know what you're selling, but I'll buy it.'

"One of the young men said, 'We aren't selling anything. We're missionaries of The Church of Jesus Christ of Latter-day Saints, and we would like to talk with you.'

"I invited them to come in, and they spoke about their faith. This was the beginning of my testimony. I am thankful beyond words for the privilege and honor of being a member of The Church of Jesus Christ of Latter-day Saints. The joy and peace this glad gospel has brought to my heart is heaven on earth. My testimony of this work is the most precious thing in my life, a gift from my Heavenly Father, for which I will be eternally thankful."[9]

South Africa Youth Conference

In South Africa, Elder Hinckley also attended a great youth conference. Hundreds of bright and clean-cut Latter-day Saints participated. Educated, refined, and clean, they were just as articulate in speaking about their faith as the LDS youth of Europe.

A conference was also held in Munich, Germany focusing on the Church in Europe. The major challenges Elder Hinckley saw in Europe were four fold. The LDS faith was not as well known on the European Continent and therefore still lacked the good image it deserved. There was great moral temptation for youth. Communication was more difficult with scattered membership, fewer telephones, fewer cars and long distances of bus and train travel required to attend meetings. And as a result, youth members of the faith "feel a little more lonely than they do where there are substantial numbers."[10]

Church membership numbers were still not significant enough to create the image desired. Permanent chapels existed but were still scarce due to lack of numbers. And the Church had not yet received the "good press" then enjoyed in North America although that was changing as knowledge of the Church of Jesus Christ of Latter-day Saints increased.

The Swiss Temple dedication in 1955 provided a new sense of pride among European resident Latter-day Saints. The Tabernacle Choir visit then also portrayed the LDS religion in a new light. Cultural arts were portrayed as important to the LDS people.

However, during Gordon B. Hinckley's two year directing of the work in Europe, his expectations for the future were high. "I look for the time when the missions and stakes of Europe will produce most of the missionaries needed in those countries. I think that day is coming. I look for an increase in the number of stakes—a steady increase as districts become strong and local leadership is developed.," Elder Hinckley declared.[11]

He also felt the growing youth would meet the challenge of responsibility, developing talents and holding positions of responsibility in the community as well as the developing Church. "We have every reason to be optimistic about the future of the work in Europe," Elder Hinckley said. "More and more of our people are saying, 'Here is where we and our children and our children's children will build our Zion and strengthen the cause of the Lord and be a party to sharing the gospel with legions of others who, through our efforts, our sacrifices, and our enthusiasm, will come to know the sweetness of the restored gospel of the Lord Jesus Christ.'"[12]

After two years advising and directing the European-Germanic Area, Elder Hinckley once again returned to advising and directing the Far East Area of the LDS Church.

June 1996 Visit to Europe

After visiting eight nations on an 18 day tour of Asia between May 16-June 2, 1996, now prophet Hinckley, whisked off to Europe on June 11 to first break ground for the new LDS temple to be reared in Madrid. Spain.

Next he went to Brussels, Belgium where the US ambassador and NATO representative from the United States met him at the airport. In the evening, he spoke to 1200 Latter-day Saints at the Palais des Congres. No prophet of the LDS Church had visited that country in 59 years since President Heber J. Grant. Belgium is an ancient city of many cathedrals, castles, monuments and cobble streets, thin and winding.

The Netherlands was his next stop. Here 2,000 LDS faithful greeted him at the Nederlands Congresgeooow Den Haag at The Hague. "We are all part of the same family, sons and daughters of God, who have taken upon ourselves the name of the Lord Jesus Christ and made solemn covenants," he told them.

Denmark was reached on June 14. The spiritual experience of seeing "some of the finest" paintings ever made of the Savior was enjoyed by President Hinckley at the Fredricksborg Castle. The artist was Carl Bloch. The gallery was a penumbra like room seeming to accentuate the works of art.

Equally edifying was the view of the original *Christus*, a replica of which stands in the North Visitors Center on Temple Square in Salt

Lake City. The original sits above the altar in an alcove at the Vor Fruc Kirke church in Copenhagen. President Hinckley looked silently at the statue with his wife Marjorie Pay Hinckley. Then they viewed the large statues depicting the ancient Twelve Apostles of the Lamb of God situate around the same chapel.

President Hinckley remarked the church attendant did not know why the statue of Peter was carved with a ring of keys in his hands. Latter-day Saints believe Peter was given the "keys of the Kingdom" by Christ before his crucifixion and became the first President of the ancient Church of Christ with apostles James and John as his counselors. The keys in the hand of the statue symbolically would memorialize that conveyance of authority and power to act for and on behalf of the Messiah following His sacrifice.

At two firesides in the evening, President Hinckley challenged the membership to "double the membership of the Church here in five years."

Then President Hinckley visited Berlin, Germany. He mingled with 3722 LDS saints at the Berlin Regional Conference on June 15 and 16. In attendance, also, were many Latter-day Saints from former East Germany. He spent four hours in a priesthood leadership meeting and one hour and fifteen minutes in a special meeting for missionaries.

Reporters interviewed him from the two major Berlin newspapers. One asked, "What is your message for Germany?"

Replied President Hinckley, "I would say to return to God and look to Him for guidance . . . My message to the people is to strengthen your families. Have families with a mother and father, and children who are loved, a family who prays together to achieve a common good.

"No nation can rise higher than its family life."

When President Hinckley had completed his Far East and European tours, he had in 24 days visited 13 nations.[13]

OPTIMISM

"I am by nature an optimist."[1]

Such has been the statement of Gordon B. Hinckley even in the throes of adversity. He has recognized the difficulties in world society. But He has seen them as stepping blocks to higher things.

In 1963, Elder Hinckley browsed at a newsstand. He first saw the beautification magazines in four color print inviting redecoration and improvement of homes and gardens. Then he saw a magazine with a blaring header, "Will city streets ever be safe again?"

He read on regarding the rising assault, robbery and other crime in American society. The Chief of Police International Association president Stanley R. Schrotel of Cincinnati, Ohio was interviewed.

"Are you saying that parents are to blame, really, for juvenile delinquency?" the interviewer asked.

"I'd have to say that there is a woeful need today for greater strength in the home, greater respect for parents as the authority symbol, and more parental guidance."[2]

Elder Hinckley commented in his April LDS general conference talk on the chief's interview, "I find only one interpretation of this—serious failure in the homes of the people. There is failure in cultivating those virtues which lead to respect for law, respect for associates, even respect for self."

Elder Hinckley then proclaimed, "Only as we build back into the fiber of our lives the virtues which are the essence of true civilization will the pattern of our times change. That building process must begin in the homes of the people. It must begin with recognition of God as our Eternal Father, of our relationship to him as his children, with communication with him in recognition of his sovereign position, and in supplication for his guidance in our affairs."[3]

"Prayer, family prayer in the homes of this and other lands, is one of the simple medicines that would check the dread disease that has eroded the fiber of our character. It is as simple as sunshine and would be as effective in curing our malady."

"Can we make our homes more beautiful? Yes, through addressing ourselves as families to the source of all true beauty. Can we strengthen our society and make it a better place in which to live? Yes, by strengthening the virtue of our family life through kneeling together and supplicating the Almighty in the name of his Beloved Son. This simple practice, a return to family worship, spreading across the land and over the earth, would in a generation largely lift the blight that is destroying us . . . ."[4]

While recognizing the problem, Elder Hinckley stated it can be changed.

Good in America

October 1968 general conference found Elder Hinckley once again proclaiming his optimism. "I am not one who believes that all is wrong with this land," he declared. "There is so much that is right and so much that is good . . . The course can be changed. We can bring about a regression of the dread disease which seems to trouble us . . . .

"Problems of the kind we have today are not new . . . . The place to begin is with oneself . . . From self, the next step is the family . . . Fathers and mothers are needed who will rise and stand upon their feet to make of their homes sanctuaries in which children will grow in a spirit of obedience, industry, and fidelity to tested standards of conduct."[5]

"Be Not Afraid, Only Believe"

Gordon B. Hinckley's little card given him by his wise father when leaving for his mission contained five simple words spoken by the Savior to a worried parent who thought her daughter was dead. "Be not afraid, only believe (Mark 5:36)," it said.

"I should like to express a few thoughts on that theme," Elder Hinckley said in November 1969 LDS conference. "I believe in the triumph of the gospel of Jesus Christ and the triumph of the Church and kingdom of God on the earth . . . . I believe, my friends, that the cause we have the honor to represent is that kingdom which shall stand forever . . . . I see the miracle of its strength and of its growing influence in the lives of thousands across the earth . . . .

"I do not want to boast. Heaven knows we have problems among us. We are far from perfection. And yet I have seen so much of good that my faith constantly strengthens . . . . I believe in our youth. I believe in their goodness and decency. I believe in their virtue. I have interviewed thousands of them on a personal and individual basis. Yes, there are some who have succumbed to evil, but they are a minority."[6]

Elder Hinckley has used the five words given him on a little card by his father in 1933 numerous times in his discourses to emphasize his objectivity and optimism. In the February 1996 *Ensign* First Presidency Message, he once again called upon this theme and expressed his great positiveness in the work of the Lord.

Funeral of Prominent Individual

Elder Hinckley was speaking at a prominent business leader's funeral not long before April 1972.

"It was a time for mourning, yes. But it was also a time for reassurance. And shining through the tears of the wonderful little woman and her children who that day were bereaved was a smile of peace that came of an overriding conviction that their husband and father had merely gone hence to prepare for reunions that will follow," said Elder Hinckley as he spoke of the resurrection, of the atonement, of the hope which abides in every devoted Latter-day Saint.

Following the funeral, Elder Hinckley received a letter from a non-LDS business leader. He wrote:

> "You people have a positive approach that is truly impressive. You come to comfort and not to mourn—to praise life rather than curse death. The depth of your faith surely must tide you over many of the vicissitudes of life, not the least of which is death."[7]

Don't Be a Pickle Sucker

At the pardon of US President Richard M. Nixon in 1974, Elder Hinckley read the commentators' remarks about that and the Nation. Though very incisive and brilliant editorialists and commentators, their words were full of invective, anger, judging "as if all wisdom belonged to them." After a week of these newspaper diatribes Elder Hinckley admitted he too succumbed to "a negative observation." Said he, "Surely this is the age and place of the gifted pickle sucker."[8]

Before the BYU devotional on October 19, 1974 he talked of this and made a plea that "we stop seeking out the storms and enjoy more fully the sunlight." Accentuate the positive, look a little deeper for the good, still our voices of insult and sarcasm, compliment virtue and effort. "I am not suggesting that our conversation be all honey and blossoms. Clever expression that is sincere and honest is a skill to be sought and cultivated."

But he asked that "we turn from the negativism . . . and look for the remarkable good in the land and times in which we live, that we speak of one another's virtues more than we speak of one another's faults, that optimism replace pessimism, that our faith exceed our fears."[9]

The American Constitution was then praised as the keystone of the nation of the United States. Lifting sites to build strength and goodness in the American nation and world will carry America and the world forward. Elder Hinckley then encouraged to count our blessings, associate with one another, building strength in one another, for "No man is an island; no man stands alone." Compliment, strengthen, encourage, bear one another's burdens. "Don't be a 'pickle sucker.' There is so much of the sweet and the decent and the good to build on."[10]

Elder Hinckley ended by quoting another favorite scripture: "Let not your heart be troubled, neither let it be afraid (John 14:27)."

Things Are Getting Better

Elder Hinckley stood before the BYU studentbody in a weekly devotional on April 8, 1976. "Things Are Getting Better" was his theme. Elder Hinckley recounted the efforts of the early missionaries of the LDS gospel, the shrinking cultural barriers in modern missionary work and the success of the missionary effort. "Truly we are engaged in a marvelous work and a wonder," he said.

Some 134 missions then dotted the earth. The Philippines which had only one native member in May 1961, held a conference with 18,000 members in a large coliseum recently. Looking back on the formidable tasks 50 or 25 years ago and seeing the mushrooming stakes and missions in South America, the South Pacific, Mexico and Central America "has brought to pass [a] miracle, and what we have seen is but a foretaste of greater things to come."[11]

Growth of the LDS Church

April 1978 brought another statement of excitement for the work. "Be Not Faithless" was Elder Hinckley's conference talk title. He recounted the tremendous growth of the LDS Church since he became an LDS general authority 20 years before.

In 1958 LDS membership was just over 1,000,000. There were 273 stakes and about 2,500 wards. Now church membership in the LDS faith was 4,000,000, a 166% increase in two decades. Stakes were 937 and wards 7,500.

"This remarkable growth has come about because there has been the courage to teach and the faith to listen . . ." Elder Hinckley proclaimed.

To doubting disciple Thomas, the risen Lord told him to thrust his finger in his hands and side "and be not faithless, but believing (John 20:27)."

"Can any man who has walked beneath the stars at night, can

anyone who has seen the touch of spring upon the land doubt the hand of divinity in creation?"

"All of beauty in the earth bears the fingerprint of the Master Creator, of those hands which, after they took the form of mortality and then immortality, Thomas insisted on touching before he would believe."[12]

Then Elder Hinckley told his audience to believe in him who was the God of Abraham, Isaac, and Jacob. Doubt not. Believe that John the Baptist spoke by the power of revelation when he said, "Behold the Lamb of God, which taketh away the sin of the world (John 1:29)."

Positive

In his first general conference talk as a member of the LDS First Presidency, Elder Hinckley declared on October 3, 1981, the Church has "moved out across the world in a remarkable way. They have been years in which millions of members have benefited. They have also been years in which strident voices have been raised against us. We have been criticized, but this criticism has in no way deterred the progress of the work. In fact, it has brought many to our defense and our support . . .

"I have been touched by the warmth of good people in travels around the world. All are children of our Father in Heaven. True, there are vast chasms of political and ideological differences. But innately people are the same.

"The church has a great and compelling responsibility to teach the everlasting gospel to the peoples of the earth. Although many gates are now closed, I am convinced that the Lord in His own time will open them provided we constantly seek and pray for such openings and are prepared to take advantage of them."[13]

Good Cheer

Good cheer has been a vital message of President Hinckley's life.[14] To the priesthood on Saturday evening, April 7, 1984, President Hinckley told the brethren assembled that many said the Church would fall. When the Book of Mormon came off the press they said the work would die.

But Elder Hinckley said those who are trying to undermine the Church will fail. Church membership had risen to 5,400,000. "The work has gone forward. The church has never taken a backward step since it was organized in 1830, and it never will," 2nd Counselor in the First Presidency Gordon B. Hinckley pronounced.[15]

Diplomat

The steady, quiet growth of the Church amidst opposition was again addressed in April 1986.[16]

His message on June 27, 1989 was one of reconciliation, a more tolerant day, at the dedicatory address for the newly refurbished and restored Church Historical grounds at Carthage Jail, Carthage, Illinois.

"All of us are grateful for the reconciliation which has come with the passage of time," he declared. There was a new "sunshine of goodwill" shining. We have a duty to forgive and put behind us the troubles of the past, to rise above old animosities, and build well on the foundation laid long ago.[17]

The Greater Picture & the Smaller Field

Later at BYU in September 1989, President Hinckley expressed, "It is a marvelous thing to sit where one can see, at least in some measure, the whole broad encompassing picture of this great throbbing, mobil, growing phenomenon the Lord has called the Church of Jesus Christ of Latter-day Saints."[18]

He expanded upon this at October conference. He had stood on the top of the hill called "Ensign Peak" northeast of Salt Lake City that Summer and contemplated the early LDS pioneers who used a bandanna handkerchief as a flag and a stick as a pole when they first implanted what they considered an "ensign to the nations," a little symbol of the great work about to increase and spread throughout the world.

"Sometimes in our day, as we walk our narrow paths and fill our little niches of responsibility, we lose sight of the grand picture," President Hinckley declared. "We catch nothing of the broader vision."

But the program of the Lord is of great breadth, depth, height, grand and wonderful, all-encompassing. "We ought to recognize" this and then "work with diligence to meet our responsibility for our assigned portion of that program . . . Each of us has a small field to cultivate. While so doing, we must never lose sight of the greater picture, the large composite of the divine destiny of this work."[19]

Pioneer Strength

A constant theme of President Hinckley's ministry has been his gratitude and appreciation for those who have gone before, the strength of the LDS pioneer heritage. An appreciation for the past brings expectations for the future.

Before dedicating the former Valley Music Hall as a Bountiful,

Utah Regional Center for LDS Church meetings and functions Sunday, February 3, 1991, President Hinckley said, "The Lord has a way of turning adversity to the good of His people and His work . . . . I thank the Lord that I am living in this great day of the history of the world when the God of heaven through His almighty power has brought to pass the Dispensation of the Fullness of Times, when there has been brought together in one all of the power and blessings and principles and standards of all the previous dispensations of the gospel."

The center had run into financial problems after serving as a center for the performing arts and concerts. Then it was purchased by the LDS Church for conferences and other Church and cultural functions.

In his dedicatory prayer, President Hinckley said, "We thank thee for the faith of our fathers . . . . They came to these valleys of the mountains, and here again planted thy work, and it has grown and goes forth to the nations of the earth with power and conviction and testimony spoken from the mouths of thy servants who have dedicated themselves and have been set apart to this divine and holy work."[20]

It Is the Best Period

To the LDS Business College Devotional on Tuesday, February 5, 1991, President Hinckley said this period in time is not the darkest period. It is the best.[21] Manifesting his belief in this, he spoke in a hoarse voice drained of energy for the October 13, 1992 BYU devotional address substituting for then LDS prophet Ezra Taft Benson in the first devotional of the 1992-1993 school year and said, "And so, I come to you this morning looking on the bright side."[22]

At the BYU Management Society chapter in Washington, D.C. on March 5, 1994, he similarly indicated that these are not dark days—these are great days.[23]

"All of us occasionally feel fed up with life," he said to 6,000 single adults of the LDS faith on July 28, 1991. "We feel alone and discouraged. If you are experiencing such feelings, if you feel that you are worthless, go out and look up somebody who is in worse condition than you are—and you will find very many of them. Read to the blind. Read to the aged. Help those in distress. Comfort those who are in sorrow. Give a little of your substance to those who are in need. Share. And the world will become a sweeter, more delightful place for you. Look to God and listen to Him, and lose yourself in the service of others, which is of the very essence of His divine work."[24]

Vitality of This Work

"There has never been a time when the Latter-day Saint people have been more highly respected, well regarded and doing better than at this time," President Hinckley said at a large group of new mission presidents on June 26, 1993 at the Missionary Training Center in Provo, Utah. A full 136 mission presidents and their wives were present.

"There is a vitality about this work that is wonderful and just keeps growing and strengthening and you are part of it—an important part of it. You are what makes it grow. You have been called by the Lord to strengthen His Church. What a wonderful call that is."

In St. Louis, Missouri before youth gathered at a multi-stake fireside, President Hinckley told them, "This is the greatest age in history and a wonderful time to live. This age is, however, fraught with temptations and traps that can be avoided by wise youth who keep the commandments . . . It is an age of challenge and opportunity, just a wonderful time to be alive."[25]

Following assumption of the LDS presidency, President Hinckley was as equally optimistic about the religion he so dearly loved. He said there was no place in this work for those who are pessimistic. "The gospel is good news." It is a message of gladness. "It should be emblazoned with enthusiasm."[26]

The example of Gordon B. Hinckley regarding attitude is marvelous. Even in the face of known discouragement, obstacles, tragedies and adversity, his panoramic vision truly has been that of a prophet who sees beyond the moment as if into the joys of the future. Optimistic outlook on life. It is a value well worth solidifying.

COUNCILS

Councils are the life blood of the Church of Jesus Christ of Latter-day Saints. The method of performing the mandate Latter-day Saints believe they have to carry the message of a fully restored pristine Church of Jesus Christ to everyone, help them to perfect their lives in the household of faith and bring the same blessings to their ancestors has been use of "councils" in every level of Church government.

A "council" includes quorums and committees. It also encompasses business executive groups such as boards of directors. And it can extend to community service organizations.

Gordon B. Hinckley's involvement on ecclesiastical as well as business "councils" has been great. By the very nature of the isolationism which the early LDS Church experienced with its seemingly "foreign" concepts of Christianity and novel society, the Latter-day Saints were pushed from one region of the United States to another from 1820 to 1847 when they ended up in the Valleys of the Rocky Mountains and established their Zion.

Food had to be cultivated and raised. Clothing had to be spun from cotton and wool. Furniture was made. Publishing companies had to be created if the Latter-day Saints were to communicate with one another. Education of children was needed. Virtually every facet of existence needed their own personal attention.

Accordingly, numerous commercial enterprises, including newspapers, banks, cooperatives, schools and later radio and television stations were formed by the LDS Church to fill the needs of its people. Many of these business entities or their successors exist today. And the method of overseeing these business enterprises has been the regular placement of ecclesiastical leaders of the LDS Church on the various governing boards.

In addition, the governmental structure of the LDS Church consisted of a First Presidency, forming a quorum in and of itself of at least three or more men vested with the titles of prophet, seers and revelators, the president of the quorum being the Presiding High Priest and prophet.

Next came the Quorum of 12 Apostles presided over by the senior member who had served longest on the quorum. This body of 12 men, numbering the number of the disciples first chosen by Jesus Christ when on the earth, and similarly equalling the number of tribes of the ancient House of Israel, were charged with the responsibility of being special witnesses of Jesus Christ and watching over and caring for the church. They were, as you will, the Lord's executive board subject to the direction and control of the First Presidency and are also sustained as prophets, seers and revelators by their Church members.

The growth of the Church caused the First Presidency to establish assistants for the Quorum of the 12. And then there were priesthood quorums of Seventies, whose calling according to LDS revelations found in the Doctrine & Covenants and the statements of the ancient Church preserved in the Bible, was to prepare the way for the 12 and to assist in the administration duties of carrying out Church objectives.

A body of at least three men was also in place to oversee the temporal affairs of the LDS faith. These men were designated a Presiding Bishopric and essentially were full-time authorities charged with overseeing the collection of tithes and offerings and the provision of physical facilities and welfare programs for the Church.

The Church also had numerous "auxiliary organizations" such as the relief society for women, the primary for children, the young men's and young women's mutual improvement associations for youth and the Sunday school union for coordinating instruction in principles of the LDS faith.

But in order to provide an orderly implementation of the vast duties of the councils, quorums and auxiliaries, a system of management and administration was needed. That system was the use of "councils" in the form of committees. Committees evolved in their application as the LDS Church evolved in its growth.

When Gordon B. Hinckley was born in 1910, the LDS Church membership was relatively small but during his lifetime, the membership had increased almost twenty fold. And the membership continued to climb.

The 12, their assistants and the 70, along with the presiding bishopric and auxiliaries all were assigned to various committees. At first they were just called committees, whether entirely composed of general authorities or mixed with general authorities and others. But gradually the word "Executive" was added at some place in names of major committees composed only of members of the Quorum of the 12 Apostles and First Presidency.

President Hinckley has served on numerous of these "councils" in his life.

Ecclesiastical Councils

Almost every calling President Hinckley has received in the LDS Church has been a "council" of one type or another. Probably his first council appointment was his calling as his Deacon's Quorum's president. At the age of 12 to about 14 he served as the president of three Aaronic Priesthood holders holding the office of deacon. He had just as much presiding authority over that quorum of up to 12 deacons as anyone presiding over other priesthood quorums.

In addition to these main councils, numerous special "councils" have been part of his experience. Prior to becoming LDS prophet, these included:[1]

BYU Board of Trustees and Church Board of Education. Oversees operations of the LDS Church's major university, Brigham Young University, same as traditional regents of an institution of higher learning, while also overseeing other educational institutions operated by the LDS Church. The President of the LDS Church chairmans this committee.

Institutions have included Ricks College, Rexburg, Idaho; the branch of BYU located in Laie, Hawaii called BYU-Hawaii; the LDS Business College, Salt Lake City, Utah, remnant of the former LDS University; elementary and secondary education schools in New Zealand; and the Institute and Seminary programs of the LDS Church.

President Hinckley had served in one position on this council since 1961. On April 10, 1975, he was made chairman of an executive sub-committee for BYU and BYU-Hawaii. The seminary and institute programs of the LDS faith expanded remarkably during this time.

Church Information Committee. Public relations arm for the LDS Church and eventually created the Public Communications Department of the Church.

Committee on the Disposition of Tithes. Makes decisions on the disbursement of tithing funds. This council is composed of the entire First Presidency, the entire Quorum of the 12, and the entire Presiding Bishopric.

Correlation Executive Committee. Directs correlation of all services of the LDS Church including unified use of subject material in Sunday schools, auxiliaries and priesthood quorums.

Chairman, Children's Correlation Committee. Correlated work for infants and children of the LDS Church.

Finance Committee. Recommended financial policies.

President Hinckley was a major influence promulgating recommendations approved by the First Presidency and Quorum of the 12 easing financial burdens upon LDS members.

Historical Department Advisor. Oversaw the operation of the Historical Department whose mission was the preservation of history pertaining to the Church and the Latter-day Saint people.

Melchizedek Priesthood Executive Committee. In charge of all matters regarding the Melchizedek Priesthood.

The committee was one of four established in the Quorum of the 12.

The other three committees, also composed of three members of the 12, were the Temple and Genealogy Executive Committee, the Missionary Executive Committee, and the Correlation Executive Committee.

The Melchizedek Priesthood Executive Committee, in addition to other Melchizedek Priesthood matters, was responsible for nominating regional representatives and training regional representatives and area presidencies.

When there were common matters needing the input of others, organizations such as the Primary, Young Women, Aaronic Priesthood, Relief Society and the Presiding Bishopric would be included in the committee activities.

Elder Hinckley was assigned chairman of the committee on June 5, 1976. LDS apostles L. Tom Perry and David B. Haight were additional committee members.

Military Relations Committee. Liaison with the Selective Service of the US Government and similar bodies in other nations.

Missionary Executive Committee. This council oversees the missionary program of the LDS Church including the designation of calls to specific missions as delegated by the LDS prophet.

President Hinckley served as executive secretary for the committee and its predecessors since 1935 for 20 years and then since about 1962 as an apostle. He stated in 1971, ". . . and in this capacity I think I have been present when more missionaries have been called to various fields of labor than any other man in the history of the world."[2]

Primary Advisor Committee. Oversaw correlation of primary curriculum and programs for three to 11 year children.

Elder Gordon B. Hinckley

Elder Hinckley was appointed to the committee on December 5, 1970 and worked with Elder Robert L. Simpson of the Quorum of Seventy.

Reinstatement Committee. Considered requests by previously excommunicated members for restoration of blessings including membership, priesthood and temple ordinances.

Elder Hinckley served with "sympathetic love" and with great empathy for the innocent affected.[3]

Special Affairs Committee. Special liaison on governmental and political matters. It handled criticism of the Church, a First Presidency responsibility.

Sunday School Advisor Committee. Assisted the General Sunday School Board in its ongoing programs for improving Sunday school curriculum and teaching.

Elder Hinckley was appointed on December 5, 1970 together with additional LDS apostles Thomas S. Monson and Boyd K. Packer.

Temple Ceremony Presentation Committee. Development of video and other innovations for use in temple ordinances.

Temple Committee. Supervises temple building and operations worldwide.

Elder Hinckley became chairman of the committee from October 1972 to May 1976. O. Leslie Stone was secretary to the committee. LDS apostle Howard W. Hunter, and future president of the Church immediately prior to President Hinckley's administration, became the next chairman of the committee following Elder Hinckley.

Special Committee on Church Activities for African Races. Provided African Americans and Africans in other areas of the earth activities and programs for Church activity prior to the 1978 revelation received by President Spencer W. Kimball on the priesthood.

Business & Community Institutions

All board of director or executive officer positions President Hinckley has held have been for LDS Church owned entities or entities in which the LDS Church has held a major interest. They have included:

Beneficial Life Insurance Company. Board of directors for the Church owned insurance company providing private as well as LDS Church protection.

Bonneville International Corporation. Board of directors for the holding of all mass media holdings of the LDS Church including radio and TV and audio/visual productions. Broadcast facilities were located in Salt Lake City, Seattle, San Francisco, Los Angeles, Dallas, Kansas City, Chicago and New York City.

Elder Hinckley served as chairman of the Executive Committee for many years.

Deseret Management Corporation. Board of directors for the LDS Church's real property holdings company.

Deseret News Publishing Company. Board of directors of the LDS Church owned newspaper. The newspaper started publication in the 1800's after arrival of the LDS pioneers. It continues to be the newspaper voicing LDS standards and views on issues. It also publishes the official *Church News*, a weekly supplement to the regular newspaper setting forth current news of the Latter-day Saints. It owned the largest daily circulating newspaper and printing plant in the intermountain West.

President Hinckley served on the board many years. Then on June 29, 1971, he was named president and chairman of the Executive Committee succeeding LDS apostle Mark E. Petersen in a special meeting of the board of directors. LDS apostle Thomas S. Monson was named vice president of the Executive Committee. He served as president for six years.

East Mill Creek Betterment League. Community organization designed to improve citizen environment and standard of living.

Gordon served as president prior to moving to Denver, Colorado in 1942.

East Mill Creek Water Company. Board of directors for the local water rights of citizens of the East Mill Creek area.

Newspaper Agency Corporation. Board of directors overseeing joint circulation and subscriptions for the two major newspapers in Salt Lake City—the *Salt Lake Tribune* and the *Deseret News*.

KIRO, Inc. Board of directors for a Church owned television and radio station located in Seattle, Washington.

Elder Hinckley served as a member of the Executive committee.

KSL, Inc. Board of directors for the main LDS Church radio and TV station located in Salt Lake City.

Elder Hinckley was a member of the Executive Committee.

Radio World Wide New York Inc. Board of directors for Church owned short wave radio stations WNYW and WRFM located in New York City, New York.

Recording Arts, Inc. Board of directors for a phonograph record production company.

Elder Hinckley was on the board and also vice president.

Utah Agencies. Coordination board of government authorities working on improving air service to Utah.

Utah Power & Light Company. Board of directors for the major electric power supplier in Utah.

Zions First National Bank. Board of directors for the LDS Church owned bank established by Brigham Young.

SHOULDER

Realizing their growing infirmities, the LDS First Presidency in 1981 looked for a man who could sustain the burdensome, growing administrative demands of leadership. President Spencer W. Kimball, his first counselor Nathan E. Tanner, and even his second counselor Marion G. Romney just could not function as they needed in this important steering mechanism of the latter-day Church.

Their meditation and pondering led them to prayer regarding Gordon B. Hinckley. Solid in fabric. Brilliant in diplomacy. Open minded and yet uncompromising on doctrinal principles. Inviolable with management. Rich in comprehension and vision. And, most importantly, unwavering in the testimony of Jesus Christ and the prophet Joseph Smith. The credits could go on and on.

Elder Hinckley had in truth been the help-meet of every LDS First Presidency he had known in one way or another from the eras of Heber J. Grant, increasing greatly with his shouldering President Harold B. Lee on their joint pilgrimage in 1972 to the Holy Land before President Lee had even been sustained as new prophet leader of the LDS faith in solemn assembly by the general membership.

So it was the direction of the Spirit from on high to bring Elder Gordon B. Hinckley officially into the fold of the presidency. Now the Lord needed him even more officially to help shoulder His Kingdom.

Although there were normally only two counselors to the LDS prophet in the First Presidency, there was precedent for calling an additional counselor. Joseph Smith, Jr. had more than two at one time including an assistant president. In more recent time, Hugh B. Brown had become a third counselor for David O. McKay as well as Joseph Fielding Smith, Thorpe B. Isaacson and Alvin R. Dyer during David O. McKay's declining years.

Events were already happening which would shape President Hinckley's challenge as a shoulder for the Lord. President Kimball's first reported illness was a bout with the flu on March 10, 1976 just 18 days before turning 81.[1] On September 1977, he was admitted to the hospital for observation and again was admitted for observation on July 15, 1979. He was then 84 years old.

Two months later he suffered his first subdural hematoma operation September 6 and 7 requiring him to miss a scheduled Area Conference in Atlanta, Georgia on September 15. He received his second subdural hematoma operation on November 17 of the same year and was recovering until December 1st. On December 12, President Kimball was re-admitted to the hospital and released December 17, 1979.[2]

The Forged Copy of the Gold Plates Characters

At the same time a young Utah State University college student by the name of Mark Hofmann started five years of deception by creating a forged document purported by him to be the original sheet of characters the prophet Joseph Smith, Jr. copied from hieroglyphics engraved on the "gold plates" he had been entrusted by the heavenly messenger Moroni for translation into the English language.[3]

According to documented Latter-day Saint Church history, an early disciple named Martin Harris took the copy of hieroglyphics to two learned scholars in New York City, Dr. of Philosophy Samuel L. Mitchell and Columbia College Professor Charles Anthon, in February 1828 together with a short translation from the prophet Joseph for verification.

When both scholars verified the authenticity of the translation, Martin Harris hurried back to Palmyra, New York and became the first scribe for Joseph Smith, copying the translation of the first 116 pages from the plates into English as the prophet Joseph dictated them to him. If the sheet had been the original, it would have been an invaluable historical relic for the LDS faith.

Since the age of 15, Hofmann had engaged in forgeries. As a very young boy he showed interest in coin collecting. He grew up in Salt Lake City with his family and was integrated into the LDS Church through his LDS parents. But during adolescence, he inwardly turned from belief although outwardly still following the LDS routine, attending meetings and accepting priesthood offices.

His fascination with coins gave him the idea of adding a mint mark to a coin through electrography. The finished fake was taken to a coin dealer who submitted it to the US Treasury for authentication. The forensic examination by the Treasury said the coin was authentic. At that time, Hofmann gained confidence in his ability to fool even the experts and embarked on a tragic course.

Mark Hofmann's circle of victims included his parents and ecclesiastical leaders. He continued to outwardly do what they expected and desired even to the extent of filling a full-time mission for the LDS Church in southwest England. During the mission, he and his companions enjoyed visiting book dealers with old books, purchasing old Bibles and turning around and selling them for a profit.

Hofmann's lies expanded. His whole life was ultimately consumed with them. He had been doing it so long by the time he was over his mission and into college at Logan, Utah, his method of speech and manners conveyed a believable air when in effect he was outright lying. His deceptions began to excite and enthrall him. He revelled in his ability to lead others along a false path. He was not dumb. His mind was gifted but his channel was cut in the wrong direction.

He studied the LDS Church's history vociferously, acquiring knowledge of little known historical facts hardly anyone else knew. He also acquired a library on document forgery including one on the world's greatest forgers. No one but himself knew of this at the time, however.

At university libraries, he cut sheets of paper dated during the years he desired from the front and back leafs of rare books, then created his own ink from burnt ashes and linseed oil, aging it to the right period of time with chemicals he had learned from his forgery library. He then went about creating his false sheet of characters he would purport to be those penned by Joseph Smith, Jr. about the first part of 1828. Then he went Bible hunting, obtaining an old Bible as he had done with his missionary companions in England. The forged sheet of characters was glued into the inside leaf and additional signatures purported to be those of Joseph Smith, Jr.'s family members forged inside the Bible's covers.

Hofmann then tested his work on the special collections department director at the Utah State University Library. A.J. Simmonds trusted the student's find completely. He even helped remove the sheet from the Bible. Hofmann then took the forged sheet to Daniel Bachman, an LDS Institute teacher at Utah State University. Bachman contacted the LDS Historical Department about the supposed "find."

The LDS Historical Department managing director at the time was Elder Hinckley's boyhood friend G. Homer Durham. Elder Hinckley was also at that time a member of the Historical Department Advisory Committee of LDS apostles. So it was within Elder Durham and Elder Hinckley's responsibilities at the time to oversee such matters.

The Historical Department of the LDS Church was always interested in acquiring documents pertaining to its history. If the sheet of characters Hofmann claimed to have found was in fact the original penned by Joseph Smith, Jr., it was not only just a document of Church history, it was one hinging on one of the two key episodes forming the foundation of the LDS Church's claim to divine authority—the vision of the Father and the Son to 14 year old Joseph Smith, Jr. and the entrusting and translation of a sacred scriptural record of the ancient inhabitants of the American people by a heavenly messenger to Joseph Smith, Jr. for translation providing another witness besides the Bible to the divinity of Jesus Christ.

But any responsible curator of ancient records requires proof of the "provenance" (or chain of possession and title) for documents before their authenticity is believed. The Historical Department asked Hofmann to provide provenance to the document.

Hofmann then concocted his story. To make it look legitimate, he claimed he had acquired the Bible from a book dealer who told him they had acquired it from a descendant of the family of Lucy Mack Smith, Joseph Smith, Jr.'s mother, in the Midwest United States. USU's special collections director A.J. Simmonds believed Hofmann implicitly even though Hofmann was the only one who told him of the provenance. Hofmann showed Simmonds what Hofmann purported to be a statement from the members of the Lucy Mack Smith family he had "visited." Hofmann & Simmonds both signed affidavits to the false facts, Hofmann with knowledge of fraud and Simmonds ignorantly.

When the affidavits were submitted to G. Homer Durham along with the purported sheet of characters, Elder Durham contacted his long time friend Elder Hinckley and disclosed the possibility they had found the characters written by Joseph Smith, Jr. given to Martin Harris when he visited New York City in 1828. At that time, Elder Hinckley was probably very excited as was everyone else. Even if the find was not true, they wanted it to be true. Elder Hinckley was anxious to see the sheet and meet with the finder.

When Mark W. Hofmann first met Elder Hinckley in April 1980, he felt a little bit of fear but also excitement in "duping" even LDS general authorities.[4] Elder Hinckley was told by Historical Department personnel that Hofmann was a student at Utah State University in Logan, Utah and that in the pursuit of a hobby in collecting early LDS documents, he had secured an old Bible with the signature in it of Samuel Smith (one of four younger brothers of Joseph Smith, Jr. and one of the eight men who signed a statement saying they had seen the gold plates from which the Book of Mormon was translated). The characters written by Joseph Smith, Jr. for Martin Harris to take to New York City were in it, he was told.

Hofmann agreed to let the LDS Historical Department have

possession of the document for two years.[5]

Installation of New President at BYU-Hawaii

On February 20, 1981, Elder Hinckley was at the BYU-Hawaii campus in Laie, Hawaii as a member of the Church Board of Education Trustees and Executive Committee over BYU and BYU-Hawaii installing J. Elliot Cameron as its new president in the new Activity Center capable of accommodating 2,000 people.

He told the students, largely of Polynesian and Asian descent, to marshall their resources, open their minds, enlarge their understanding, think with intellectual integrity, act with moral responsibility, stand as examples, and build faith in God. Elder Thomas S. Monson, also on the same executive committee, was present and conducted.[6]

The Forged Blessing to Joseph Smith III

Almost a month later, back in Salt Lake City, the Historical Department executives came to Elder Hinckley's office again with Mark Hofmann. This time Hofmann had forged a purported blessing transcript on its face given by the prophet Joseph Smith, Jr. to his son Joseph Smith III supposedly dated June 17, 1844, just 10 days before Joseph Smith, Jr. had been killed in Carthage, Illinois. The handwriting was supposed to have been that of Thomas Bullock, the prophet Joseph's scribe at the time, whose signature Hofmann had also forged.[7]

Hofmann had drafted each word of the blessing in such a way as to give the impression Joseph Smith, Jr. had designated his son Joseph Smith III, although only a child at the time, to be his successor as prophet of the LDS faith. When this was announced to the press, it created a great fervor of speculation by many in and outside of the LDS faith. Those antagonistic to the Church were elated. Apostate members were elated. Publicity quickly mushroomed worldwide.

While Hofmann reveled in the notoriety he was receiving in the press and the furor he was creating in and outside the Latter-day Saint faith regarding documents he and he alone at the time knew were forgeries, President Spencer W. Kimball was hospitalized once again, this time for weakness and dizziness on August 26, 1980. By December 16, 1980, he was in surgery having his prostrate partially removed.[8]

Elder Hinckley was penning his April 1980 conference address to set the record straight as to divine authority as Hofmann planned his next forgery. This masterful discourse by Elder Hinckley articulately showed every faithful Latter-day Saint and reasoning person what really was important and how to look at such a document as the "Joseph

Smith III blessing" even if it was authentic.

"I think I should like to say a few words this afternoon about the recently discovered transcript of a blessing reported to have been given January 17, 1844, by Joseph Smith to his 11 year old son. This has received much attention in the media of late."

Then Elder Hinckley premised his treatise, "Our Historical Department secured it in pursuit of their practice of obtaining artifacts of many kinds related to our early history. We determined that we would give full publicity to the discovery, even though we were confident that critics, knowing little of the factual history of the Church, would seize upon it as suggesting a flaw in our line of authority.

"Furthermore, and this is of significant importance, we recognized the wording of the document as a father's blessing, having great sentimental value for the Reorganized Church of Jesus Christ of latter-day Saints, whose presidents have been lineal descendants of Joseph Smith."[9]

The LDS Church by that time had given Hofmann certain holdings in the possession of the church historical department in exchange for the Joseph Smith III blessing. And then the First Presidency and 12 Apostles had determined to offer it to the Reorganized Church and the Reorganized Church offered the LDS Church a valuable artifact they had in exchange.

Elder Hinckley then masterfully explained the distinction between a blessing and an ordination and indicated the purported transcript acquired from Hofmann was in the form of a blessing—not an ordination. He then quoted statements actually made in a US Federal Court in 1893 by Joseph Smith III stating he never was ordained a prophet by his father.

He then indicated that most of the early leaders of the Church were all mentioned by Joseph Smith, Jr. before his death as possible successors to his calling as prophet. Elder Hinckley then stated, "We in the Church recognize that the fulfillment of all blessings given under authority of the priesthood is conditioned upon two things: one, the worthiness and faithfulness of the recipient, and two, the overriding will and wisdom of God."

Then he reviewed numerous parts of the revelations received by Joseph Smith, Jr. forming the Doctrine and Covenants stating that the Quorum of the Twelve Apostles hold the keys of the Kingdom of God on the earth when the president of the church dies. He cited D.&C. 107:24 and D.&C. 112:30 and D.&C. 124:127-128 and minutes of a conference in September 1841 published in the church publication *Times and Seasons.*

The actions and course of conduct of the leaders of the Church at the time Joseph Smith was martyred were next reviewed. Brigham Young had spoken on behalf of the 12 Apostles where many who saw him testified he looked and sounded like the martyred prophet Joseph. Thomas Bullock, who was purported by Hofmann's forgery to have signed the copy of the false blessing, had been captured by mobbers trying to leave Nauvoo.

The mobbers told him if he would renounce "Mormonism" he could stay in Nauvoo and they would protect him. His reply was, "I am a Mormon, and if I live, I shall follow the Twelve." He later kept a faithful record of the pioneer company's crossing of the plains to the Rocky Mountains, returned East again in 1848 and came back to Salt Lake and served a mission to England from 1856-1858, conduct inconsistent with a man who was supposed to have recorded a blessing which purported to designate Joseph Smith, Jr.'s son Joseph Smith III his successor as prophet.

The question naturally follows, Elder Hinckley reasoned, that would Thomas Bullock have "paid such a heavy price for his membership in the Church and to have suffered so much to advance its cause as a missionary at the call of Brigham Young if he had any doubt that President Young was the proper leader of the Church and that this right belonged to another according to a blessing which he had in his possession and which he had written with his own pen?"[10]

The closing argument was powerful and the conclusion was compelling. Such a blessing as Hofmann had forged, even if authentic, could not alter the true order of things. All canonized revelation and course of conduct from 1844 to the present precipitated in direct opposition to such.

New Museum of Art at BYU

As co-chair for the Executive Committee over BYU, Elder Hinckley met with BYU president Rex Lee regarding a first proposal for construction of a Museum of Art on the campus. Elder Hinckley saw the benefit but felt tithe payers would not receive the benefit in a proportionate way. But Rex Lee promised the art gallery would be built by donations. Thus the construction commenced in 1981.[11]

LDS prophet Spencer W. Kimball next received a heart pacemaker implant on May 16, 1981.[12]

June found Elder Hinckley in Europe. He visited the Latvia concentration camp where Nazis killed 100,000 Jews during World War II. He visited the Dachau camp near Munich, Germany and said later, "Anyone who has been there senses the horrors of the days, months, years of those who lived and died in the concentration camps."[13]

At the Federal Heights Ward, Salt Lake City, Elder Hinckley spoke at the funeral of Freda Joan Lee on July 6, wife of deceased LDS president Harold B. Lee. He said she had showed love to children and thus to the Lord. "Death is not the end, but only the transition to something better for those who have served the Lord," he said. She might have lived longer, "But for what purpose? She had completed her work on earth."[14]

President Hinckley was officially called to be an additional counselor in the LDS First Presidency on July 23, 1981.

Tour of Yugoslavia, Rumania and Russia

That Summer, President Hinckley and Marjorie once again accompanied the BYU Young Ambassadors on a historic tour, this time to Yugoslavia, Rumania and Russia. At the Summer Graduation for BYU, Gordon presided for the First Presidency before 2,100 graduates while Elder Boyd K. Packer conducted on August 21st. Two days later, President Hinckley gave the dedicatory address and prayer for the Sons of the Utah Pioneers new 18,000 square foot building on the south edge of eroded flood plains of the ancient water flows from Parley's Canyon.

"In our environment of abundance, it is good to occasionally be taken back to earlier days, to have our minds refreshed on the struggles of our forebears, to remind us of the necessity of labor if the earth is to be made to yield, of the importance of faith if there is to be lasting achievement," President Hinckley stated as he stood square at the podium, both hands holding the left and right sides.[15]

These dedications were going to become routine to him. About and around Salt Lake City and in many areas of the world, he would dedicate just about every Church related edifice of temples and major historical significance from that time on until and after called as 15th prophet of the LDS faith.

The False Letter from Martin Harris to W.W. Phelps

Hofmann's next forgery was a purported letter written by Martin Harris, the disciple who had taken the sheet of characters copied from the "gold plates" to the two scholars in New York City in 1828. The letter was purportedly addressed to W.W. Phelps, the author of the hymn "Praise to the Man" which played such a key ingredient in Elder Hinckley's own first conviction of the truth of the work. This powerful hymn revealed a powerful man who idealized the prophet Joseph Smith, Jr. & the author Brother Phelps had remained true and faithful to death.

In his new position as an additional third counselor in the First Presidency, President Hinckley received a visit from Mark Hofmann on Friday, September 4, 1981.

"Hello, what can I do for you?" President Hinckley said.

"I'm surprised at the way people are reacting to Joseph Smith's blessing," Hofmann said.

"Oh, you might expect some such reactions. People are too prone to accept such a document without considering the context—circumstances under which given."

"Thanks for your conference talk in April. I've told several people to read it."

"Thank you."

"I offered the document to the Church two weeks before the Reorganized LDS Church. I'm disappointed word has got out on the exchange."

"How did word get out?"

"A reporter told me someone at the Historical Department."

"I know nothing of this."

"I got 36 other documents with the Joseph Smith III blessing. The Historical Department has bought some of them. One of them I still have relates to the blessing. Here it is."

Gordon B. Hinckley read the false letter purportedly from Martin Harris to W.W. Phelps.

"I'm a believing, active Latter-day Saint. I want to give this to you. I don't want to blackmail the Church," Hofmann lied.

"Are you telling me that you wish to give this document to the Church without cost?"

"Yes. I have no copy."

"Thank you. The First Presidency will be advised and also Elder Durham."

The two shook hands and President Hinckley said, "Thank you and the Lord bless you."

Mark Hofmann Committing Fraud
on the LDS First Presidency
and Elder Boyd K. Packer

l. to r. Mark Hofmann, Nathan Eldon Tanner, President
Spencer W. Kimball, Marion G. Romney,
Elder Boyd K. Packer, Gordon B. Hinckley

President Hinckley first showed the letter to Elder G. Homer Durham, managing director of the Historical Department. Then they gave it to Francis Gibbons, secretary to the First Presidency. On Tuesday it was discussed with counselors in the first presidency, Nathan Eldon Tanner and Marion G. Romney. President Kimball had received additional surgery August 29, the Saturday before, and was operated on again on September 5 to remove fluid from the skull.[16]

Hofmann was later to reveal his motive in creating and presenting the letter to the Church was to "demonstrate concern for the Church" to prepare for future deals.

The false letter was supposedly indicating that Joseph Smith, according to Martin Harris, had obtained the "gold plates" from which the Book of Mormon was translated from a "white salamander" typical of folk magic beliefs going about the New England States of the upper Northeastern United States during the early 1800's. This dart of the Adversary shot through the Hofmann bow created an additional furor of national press and media coverage regarding the fundamental foundations upon which the restored gospel rested when Elder Hinckley made the decision to disclose it publicly.[17]

Spencer W. Kimball experienced respiratory distress on September 10, 1981 and his condition worsened on September 30, 1981.

Albeit, despite the concerns of the first presidency counselors for their prophet leader, President Hinckley went to the task once more. He refuted the hecklers concisely and profoundly with the same inspiration received regarding the false Joseph Smith III blessing. "The real test of the faith both Martin Harris and W.W. Phelps had in Joseph Smith and his work is found in their lives, in the sacrifice they made for their membership in the Church and in the testimonies which they bore to the end of their lives.

"Martin Harris died in 1875 in Clarkston, Utah in full fellowship in the Church and bearing a fervent testimony of the divine authenticity of the Book of Mormon. W.W. Phelps passed away in Salt Lake City in 1872 as an active high priest with a distinguished career of Church service."

Elder G. Homer Durham and Elder Theodore M. Burton, both of the 70, were hospitalized during general conference as well as recovering President Spencer W. Kimball. President Hinckley remarked his new calling of two months was a "worrisome responsibility but a satisfying experience."[18]

Increasing Responsibility in the Presidency

A few days after October LDS general conference, LDS prophet Spencer W. Kimball had additional surgery on his urinal tract on October 12, 1981. He convalesced until November 7 when he began slight work and was still recovering on December 31.[19]

With President Kimball only slightly functioning in administrative paperwork, Gordon B. Hinckley spoke as the First Presidency representative at the annual First Presidency Christmas Devotional on December 10. His theme was "peace." It was unseasonably warm outside the Temple Square Tabernacle as the Poinsettia strewn Tabernacle stands framed the Tabernacle Choir and general authorities attending. Elder Mark E. Petersen, of the 12, also talked but President Nathan E. Tanner and President Marion G. Romney, additional First Presidency counselors, were present but did not talk.[20]

President Kimball still remained seriously ill on March 9, 1982. The counselors in the First Presidency frequently visited him in the hospital and at his condominium. That day, President Hinckley continued his ceremonial representation for the First Presidency by dedicating the Kimball Tower, the tallest building yet built on the campus of Brigham Young University, to Spencer W. Kimball's honor. President Hinckley said of the new faculty office building of 10 stories, it was a "symbol of a man who has centered his life in learning spiritual things." Eighteen thousand heard his message and dedicatory prayer in the Marriott Center on the BYU campus in Provo, Utah.[21]

President Hinckley was designated First Presidency liaison for missionary work as the chairman of the Missionary Executive Council on March 18, 1982. The two other counselors took similar liaison duties for the Priesthood Executive Council and the Temple Executive Council.[22]

President Kimball restricted his communication and was not present at the Regional Representatives meeting on Friday evening, April 2, 1982 at 7 P.M. in the Salt Lake Tabernacle the night before general conference began. Infirmities of Presidents Tanner and Romney, although they attended the meeting, put President Hinckley in the major conducting role. Significant changes were made shortening length of service for full-time male missionaries to 1½ years worldwide. He cautioned LDS membership about investment schemes then causing a problem among LDS circles, especially in Utah. Loans were discontinued on all LDS buildings except where real property sellers required long term payment contracts.

Local wards, branches, districts and stakes were to be provided with full maintenance of buildings in the US and Canada through central LDS Church funds for the first time. Elder Hinckley also stated the faithfulness in payment of tithes would be a new condition for approval of temple construction in areas. Difficulty in financing missions, long absences from college studies, and labor organizations law were cited as the reasons for shorting the missionary service time.[23]

At the major sessions of Saturday and Sunday general conference, it was President Gordon B. Hinckley who conducted. Normally First Presidency counselors and the prophet would take rotating turns in such function. President Kimball attended the opening session on Saturday morning and last session on Sunday afternoon but otherwise watched proceedings from TV at his home.

President Marion G. Romney was able to deliver an address along with Elder Bruce R. McConkie and Victor L. Brown of the Presiding Bishopric. The capacity crowd in the Tabernacle was also joined for the Saturday evening General Priesthood meeting by 2,200 other congregations at various sites by telephone and satellite channels.

President Hinckley said in his talk to the general priesthood that paying tithes bring a reward for our needs and ancillary blessings not always financial or material. He declared wealth and financial success are not a consideration for extending calls—personal worthiness is along with spiritual anchors and some administrative ability.[24]

President Hinckley also gave the opening address at the Sunday morning session of general conference, normally an address delivered by the president of the Church. He declared that membership in the LDS faith was now over 5,000,000. He said that this was not a summit, but a milestone. "We walk today in the sunlight of good will," he said. He emphasized this sustaining growth will be insured if Latter-day Saints hold fast to the doctrine, implement the Church in their lives, cultivate love and charity among men, strengthen and sustain the membership and leaders and move forward in faith.[25]

President Kimball attended the closing session of general conference on Sunday afternoon and made brief remarks. He said, "All is well. I have waited for this day and hoped for it and believed for it."

First Counselor Tanner, also ill with Parkinson's disease, spoke shortly.[26]

President Gordon B. Hinckley
Discoursing
Side View
President Hinckley is Said to
Favor His Mother's Features to the Right

Side View
Gordon B. Hinckley's Mother
Ada Bitner Hinckley
1880-1930

Harmon Building Devotional

Gordon B. Hinckley was at the BYU campus again on April 13 giving the dedicatory prayer for the Caroline Hemenway Harmon Building to house the Division of Continuing Education. Dr. Henry Eyring was at the dedication, too. In 1995, he was to be designated an LDS apostle, the first apostle chosen by President Hinckley after becoming president of the LDS Church. President Hinckley also met with Pete Harmon at this time, founder of the first Kentucky Fried Chicken franchises. The first Kentucky Fried Restaurant franchised by Colonel Sanders was located in Salt Lake City at the corner of 3900 South and State Street in the 1950's.

President Hinckley represented the LDS First Presidency on Tuesday, April 20, 1982 at ceremonies before the Governor of the State of Utah in the Rotunda of the Utah State Capitol remembering the 39th anniversary of Jewish imprisonment and genocide. Seventy-five were present. Scott M. Matheson was state governor at the time and Ted L. Wilson was the mayor of Salt Lake City. Dan Marriott was one of Utah's representatives in the United States Congress.

President Hinckley said, "Don't say it can't happen again. We must work constantly to subdue hate because actions such as the holocaust begin with a handful of emotional men. Wherever one voices hate, we are sowing the seeds of holocaust."[27]

By about this time, the LDS Church had purchased the forged document of purported characters written by Joseph Smith, Jr. from the "gold plates" from Mark Hofmann for $20,000.00 worth of documents in exchange. Hofmann continued to churn out small forgeries and presented them to personnel at the LDS Historical Department who continued to be excited about them and interested in adding them to their collections documenting Church chronology.

The non-profit inter-faith organization of American Mothers held their conference in Salt Lake City and were hosted as guests at a reception and dinner sponsored by the LDS Church on April 29, 1982. President Kimball was well enough at this time to greet the participants and President Hinckley, by his side, welcomed the visitors.[28]

Advancement in the young women programs of the LDS faith were changed in June 1982 to conform with advancement ages for young men in the Aaronic Priesthood. Young women started at 12 in a group designated "Beehives". At 14 they would advance to a group named "Mia Maids." And finally at age 16, they would move into the top group of "Laurels" until they reached age 18 and integrated into relief society for adult women.[29] Sometimes relief society groups are set up for the youngest segment of sisters age 18 and above so they may identify more readily with their peer groups.

Mission presidents were once again instructed at the Church Office Building with their wives on President Hinckley's 72nd birthday, June 23, 1982. Fifty-two mission presidents and wives were present. President Hinckley said that we should "convert"—don't seek just numbers. "With all the powers of persuasion that I am capable of, I plead with you to train and motivate your missionaries to the point of view that it is converts they are out to win, rather than numbers of baptisms for the sake of good statistics."[30]

Elder Durham's Illness

About July 1982, President Hinckley's boyhood friend Elder G. Homer Durham became ill. Through faith and skilled treatment, he recovered.[31] At this time President Spencer W. Kimball was reported in the press as alert but weak. A couple President Hinckley knew with their children now grown departed on a full-time mission at this time. They sold their home and car. President Hinckley thought of the following words of the Savior: "Everyone who has forsaken . . . for my sake shall receive an hundred fold. (Matthew 19:20)"[32]

". . . generally speaking, the most miserable people I know are those who are obsessed with themselves; the happiest people I know are those who lose themselves in the service of others."

This belief of President Hinckley appeared when President Hinckley heard complaining students, who in their youth are prone to murmur about housing, food and the pressures of study.

President Hinckley read the words of Edgar Lee Masters' *Spoon River Anthology* which in part stated "What is this I hear of sorrow and weariness, anger, discontent and drooping hopes? Degenerate sons and daughters, life is too strong for you—it takes life to love life."[33]

Then he counseled those complaining youth if they felt the pressures and food and housing were too much for them, there was a cure for them. "Lay your books aside for a few hours,leave your rooms, and go visit someone who is old and lonely, or someone sick and discouraged. By and large, I have come to see that if we complain about life, it is because we are thinking only of ourselves."[34]

With this advice fresh on his mind, President Hinckley went to Nauvoo to dedicate 16 restored buildings renovated by the Nauvoo

Restoration Association. Through the "crucible of Mormonism" of Nauvoo, President Hinckley said the church has strength, a good name, and constantly growing membership. At the dedication on Saturday, August 14, 1982, President Hinckley said, "Nauvoo was a crucible of vision, a crucible of loyalty, a crucible of integrity, a crucible of leadership and a crucible of faith."[35]

The Burden of the Presidency

In every practical since, President Gordon B. Hinckley was becoming the sole steering force in the First Presidency. But he reassured the membership on September 14, 1982 while dedicating the John Taylor Building at Brigham Young University, "I assure you that no major decisions reached by the First Presidency and the Council of the 12, and no policy is implemented that impacts upon the membership of the Church without [President Kimball's] approval."[36]

President Kimball and counselors Tanner and Romney were all unable to attend. BYU had become the largest private university in America.

US Constitution Week, the 195th anniversary of its signing, was supported by the LDS First Presidency in September 1982. In October conference, President Kimball was present but a message from him was read by his private executive secretary Arthur Haycock. Gordon B. Hinckley talked of raising the sights of the saints. And at the closing session President Nathan Eldon Tanner gave a closing talk but President Kimball, although present, did not speak.[37]

During this conference, President Hinckley also talked of morals, drugs, lust, child abuse, and spouse abuse. The subtitle "Another Witness of Jesus Christ" added underneath the main title *The Book of Mormon* was also announced.

Luncheon with Lutheran Ministers

A historic luncheon hosting 12 Lutheran ministers was held for two hours in the west dining room on the 26th floor of the LDS Church Office Building in Salt Lake City on Monday, November 8, 1982. Elder G. Homer Durham, managing director of the Historical Department, Heber G. Wolsey, managing director of the Public Communications Department of the LDS Church, Richard P. Lindsay, director of the Special Affairs Committee, and Clark N. Stohl, director of Hosting were also present.

President Hinckley, in his typical familiar style, performed a masterful feat of diplomacy expressing appreciation for the life of

Martin Luther and commending the Lutheran ministers on the "measured temperance" of a four page pamphlet just prepared by them comparing the LDS Church with the Lutheran Church. Slight misinterpretations in two places were pointed out but overall he said it was a "splendid statement" and expressed appreciation for it.

A copy of President Hinckley's small book *Truth Restored* together with a pamphlet prepared for the April 6, 1980 Sesquicentennial for the LDS religion and a copy of the Topical Guide included in the recently published LDS annotated Kings James version of the English Bible were distributed to each minister visiting as President Hinckley held up the LDS Scriptures to the Topical Guide section and explained how to find any quote listed in all four of the canonized LDS Standard Works.

The responding Lutheran Minister Auer expressed appreciation for the luncheon and requested response to the inaccuracies pointed out by President Hinckley. He said the pamphlet was prepared to give Lutherans moving into predominantly LDS Utah an understanding of the doctrinal positions of the LDS Church. As far as he knew, the occasion was the first time so many Lutheran Ministers had sought opportunity to promote further understanding of the LDS faith.[38]

Honoring Utah Governor Matheson

Utah Governor Scott M. Matheson and his wife Norma were honored at Promised Valley Playhouse, a restored theater on State Street a block or so south of the Beehive House, on Friday, December 10, 1982 for his support of the arts in Utah. A festive atmosphere prevailed as President Hinckley presented the governor with a black wool jacket to go with a kilt the governor already had from Scotland made of the "Matheson" clan tartan.

Made Second Counselor in First Presidency

President Nathan Eldon Tanner passed away of his Parkinson's disease on November 27, 1982. On December 11, 1982, Marion G. Romney moved from second counselor to first counselor and Gordon B. Hinckley was installed as second counselor in the LDS First Presidency. President Hinckley was now 72 years old. He had been a third counselor in the First Presidency for 1⅓ years.[39]

Now there were even less helpers in the First Presidency as President Romney's health continued to deteriorate. But there was the Lord and there were the 12 and other general authorities. These were called upon to assist from time to time in functions normally handled by the First Presidency.

President Hinckley said of these times the day to day responsibility fell largely on him. It was almost a terrifying load at times. He felt overwhelmed on occasion. Then one day he went to his office and fell to his knees. He asked God's help in a very difficult crisis. As he prayed, there came into his mind, "Be still and know that I am God (Psalms 46:10 & D.&C. 101:16)."

He was immediately reassured that this is His work. He would not let it fail. We just need to work and do our very best.[40]

Shouldering the Load

Dr. Barney B. Clark was the first person in the world to receive an artificial heart when he was operated on at the University of Utah Medical Center on December 22, 1982 in Salt Lake City, Utah. The plastic and metal device was designed by Dr. Robert K. Jarvik.[41] The operation put the University of Utah Medical School before the world and literally "on the map" from that time forward.

Leonid Brezhnev died the month before in the Soviet Union and Walensa was given the Noble Peace Prize in 1983. The forces of liberty were beginning to smolder in Europe. Eventually communism would topple in Eastern Europe and the Union of Soviet Socialist Republic.

President Kimball remained seriously ill by March 9, 1983 reports. Exactly one month later, President Marion G. Romney was hospitalized with a urinary track problem and by June 23 was suffering pneumonia and heart problems.[42] President Hinckley was asked to take charge of April LDS general conference. General new welfare principles were announced in the Friday, April 1, 1983 meeting in the Tabernacle with regional representatives and stake presidents.

President Hinckley outlined the increase in personal and family self-reliance, spiritual growth and Christian service would include funding from fast-offering contributions rather than cash assignments from Church Headquarters and procurement of welfare farms and facilities by general church funds. Wards and stakes would continue to manage production projects and provide volunteer service.[43]

The next day, President Hinckley was the only member of the First Presidency present at the opening session of general conference. "It is the prerogative of the Lord not to counsel him but to follow him . . . Our imperative need is to be found doing our duty individually," President Hinckley declared.

President Gordon B. Hinckley
Makes a Point by Pointing
His Right Hand and Finger

We do not need to fear, worry, or speculate. "President Kimball dresses each day. But he is weak and his body is tired," President Hinckley assured. "There is no gap in leadership. No work of the presidency is being neglected."

To those concerned over the elderly leadership, Gordon said, "What a blessing. While the church needed young, malleable men in its early history, the advantages of wisdom are now serving the organization well.

"The basics of our doctrine are now well in place, and we are firmly established as a people, at least until the Lord should mandate another move. We do not need innovation. We do need devotion and adherence to divinely spoken principles. We need loyalty to our leader, whom God has appointed."[44]

On Saturday evening, he spoke again, this time to the general priesthood. He talked about avoiding the goliaths of alcohol, tobacco, drugs and pornography. He told the priesthood to discipline themselves, guard their homes, keep affections within the home, fulfill the role as shepherds of the flock, guide home inactives and remember the "crook of the shepherd's staff is a loving arm." From the home teacher to the stake president to the father, all new converts should be welcomed, home teaching performed and care given each priesthood holder's individual family.[45]

President Hinckley showed his guiding wisdom in use of mass communications by also announcing general priesthood meetings would be changed from 7 P.M. to 6 P.M. for East Coast time zone viewers.

The final address of general conference was also given by President Hinckley on Sunday afternoon, April 3, 1983. Senior member and president of the Quorum of the 12, Ezra Taft Benson, was called upon to conduct the P.M. session. President Hinckley closed by saying the church was the "greatest society of friends."[46]

Normally this would be the end of a very busy conference week, but President Hinckley then re-dedicated the newly refurbished Assembly Hall originally dedicated by Joseph F. Smith when President Smith was second counselor to 3rd LDS prophet John Taylor.

Two days later, President Hinckley was the featured speaker and offered the dedicatory prayer at the dedication of the Nathan Eldon Tanner Business Building at BYU. The building had been completed entirely from contributions. In his speech, President Hinckley reviewed the traits he had seen in President Tanner, especially his will to work, genius of delegation and ability to listen and treat people with care and kindness.[47]

President Kimball was next hospitalized on April 9, 1983 for a further urinary problem.[48]

The last official act of a busy April was representing the First Presidency at the graduation of the largest convocation ever assembled at Brigham Young University on April 22, 1983 for 2,772 graduates. The Tabernacle Choir also performed for the historic occasion.

Floods Stream Down Salt Lake City State Street

The Spring of 1983 brought strong runoff from the rapidly melting snows of the warm weather and with it overflowing streams from several creeks and rivers all along the Wasatch Range of the Rocky Mountains stringing from the south to the north on the east side of the Utah, Salt Lake and Weber Valleys. So much water rushed down City Creek northeast of Salt Lake, a diversion stream was created with sandbags down State Street (100 East) in Salt Lake. The street was blocked off and the curbs sandbagged. It was a unique site to see the main north and south thoroughfare in Salt Lake become a river of running water. The Great Salt Lake reached its highest level in recorded history on June 2, 1983.[49]

The next challenge was "intellectuals" and "humanists" criticizing the LDS Church. President Hinckley said regarding them on June 18, 1983, "The humanists who criticize the Lord's work, the so-called intellectualists who demean, speak only from ignorance of spiritual manifestation. They have not heard the voice of the Spirit. They have not heard it because they have not sought after it and prepared themselves to be worthy of it. Then, supposing that knowledge comes only of reasoning and of the workings of the mind, they deny that which comes by the power of the Holy Ghost."[50]

At the same time, speaking of himself as well as others, President Hinckley said, "We are in a period of stress across the world. There are occasionally hard days for each of us. Do not give up. Look for the sunlight through the clouds. Opportunities will eventually open up to you."[51]

President Hinckley tried to read two to three newspapers a day and sometimes examine the columnists and TV and radio. But as articulate as they might be, they seemed to have the attitude of criticizing. And letters to the editor seemed to contain venom. President Hinckley encouraged at this very difficult time in his responsibilities that "we stop seeking out the storms and enjoy the sunlight. "I am suggesting as we go through life we accentuate the positive."[52] This statement was made just five days before 1st counselor Marion G. Romney was hospitalized for pneumonia and heart problems.

In addition to administrative paperwork and public addresses, President Hinckley was called upon to pen numerous First Presidency Messages for the LDS Church Magazines. His resoluteness and great zeal for the work continued to ring through these messages and uplift and strengthen the LDS Church readership.

Statesmanship

The last day of mission presidents' seminar was presided over by President Hinckley on June 24, 1983. President Kimball and President Romney were both absent. Gordon told of the letter received from his father while on his mission suggesting Gordon forget himself and go to work. July and August were spent dedicating three temples in Atlanta, Georgia, Samoa and Tonga. From September 10 to September 20, President Hinckley spoke to 15 different groups in 10 days all the way from California to Santiago, Chile dedicating the LDS temple there, and to Detroit, Michigan.

One of the visits was before 14,000 youth at the Long Beach, California Convention Center composed of 68 seminaries and institutes and 500 part time seminary and institute teachers. His wife Marjorie and then LDS Church Commissioner of Education Henry B. Eyring were with him. He told the audience in the hot facility, only slightly cooler than the humid air outside, that everyone is discouraged at times. He then quoted John 11:35 where the record said, "Jesus wept." To him this passage showed even the Savior became discouraged at times.

Then he related times when the prophet Joseph Smith, Jr. had been discouraged and personal experiences seeing LDS prophets George Albert Smith, David O. McKay, Harold B. Lee and Spencer W. Kimball weep. Do not let discouragement beat you, he told them. The remedy he proposed was turning to the scriptures, particularly the Book of Mormon.

Suggestions on choosing a companion to marry turned him to Alma 37:37 in the Book of Mormon where is said, "Counsel with the Lord in all thy doing, and He will direct thee for good." He further advised to keep themselves chaste and virtuous for their eventual eternal companion. Education was also lauded as well as prayer. "Get selfishness out of your lives by doing what the Lord wants you to do."[53]

At the Chile Temple dedication, President Hinckley said, "I feel deeply touched as I reflect on President Kimball's condition. He is the prophet of the Lord. He came here two years ago and stood in a heavy rainstorm to break ground for this temple. At 88, he is weak and largely unable to leave his apartment, yet with a great desire to do as he has always done—build the kingdom of God. I have felt a terrible loneliness in his absence. It would have been so wonderful to have him here."[54]

He spoke to the studentbody of Brigham Young University on September 20, 1983 after travelling all night the night before from Chile. He still joked about the fact he hadn't had time to write a speech and spoke positively of the associations, the large and small problems, the discouragement, the rich challenges and the exhilaration of achievement.

Speaking at the General Women's Meeting on September 24, 1983 before a Tabernacle congregation and 552 other satellite receiver locations, President Hinckley told the sisters, "No legislation can alter the sexes. Legislation should provide equality of opportunity . . ., compensation . . . [and] political privilege . . . . I wish with all my heart we would spend less of our time talking about rights and more talking about responsibilities." Women present brushed tears from their eyes.[55]

At the Saturday evening general priesthood session of general conference on October 1, 1983, President Hinckley presided, conducted and spoke. Then the next morning he conducted the A.M. session. President Kimball and President Romney attended the morning session but not the afternoon one. President Hinckley talked about the "Glorious History of Faith" and ended the conference by saying, "Carry with us the great feeling of uplift we have received because of our participation together."[56]

After general conference was over, it was off to England where the first ever regional conference (multi-stake) was held by the LDS Church there in London on October 16, 1983. Nine days later US Marines and Rangers invaded Grenada and deposed the ruling dictator.

At a young adults and high school seminaries fireside sponsored by the LDS Student Association at the University of Utah, President Hinckley spoke along with Dr. Chase N. Peterson on Sunday, November 6, 1983. Three days later, President Hinckley was at the new north addition to the Salt Palace convention facilities dedicating them.[57]

Back at BYU, another new building, the David M. Kennedy Center for International Studies, was dedicated by President Hinckley on Thursday, November 17, 1983. The next evening, he continued his representative activities speaking of Ezra Taft Benson at the 66th annual Utah Farm Bureau Federation's dinner.

By the end of the month, a letter from the First Presidency went out dated Thursday, December 1, 1983 to LDS leaders asking for them to take advantage of criticism of the LDS faith in a positive way providing information about the church, its members and doctrines.

At the Christmas Devotional sponsored by the LDS First Presidency on Sunday, December 18, 1983, President Hinckley once again was the key speaker. For the first time, the proceedings were carried to 605 stake centers in the United States. President Kimball, President Romney and Quorum of the 12 president Ezra Taft Benson were all excused. Gordon's emotions made it difficult reading a letter about President Kimball helping a mother with a small child in a Chicago airport.[58]

President Hinckley's delivery from the podium typically was eloquent, like melodic prose. Occasionally he would get a rough throat but a slight cough about twice seemed to clear it most of the time.

Leaders of the World

In President Hinckley's lifetime, he has met with many great leaders of the world. People of prominence and power have regularly visited Salt Lake City. They also have met President Hinckley in their own native lands or at other spots of the world. Whenever they have greeted President Hinckley, he never put on airs. He was always expert in breaking the ice and relaxing the parties by making a disarming remark. Then at the right moment, he returned to serious moments. He almost always presented Book of Mormons specially bound in leather to the guests and otherwise plants seeds of the restored gospel, reading passages from the book or otherwise explaining LDS tenets.[59]

Elder Mark E. Petersen Funeral

President Hinckley prepared and delivered a talk at the funeral for Elder Mark E. Petersen of the LDS apostles on Monday, January 16, 1984. He also conducted the services. On January 29, 1984, he was principal speaker at a Satellite Fireside to many LDS meetinghouses. The theme was promoting successful marriage. A dramatization was shown by video and then addresses were given. One of the numerous dignitaries visited Church headquarters on Tuesday, February 14, 1984.

Sir Oliver Wright, British Ambassador to the US together with his wife Lady Wright spoke in Salt Lake City. President Hinckley gave the ambassador and his wife some albums of Tabernacle Choir music and some books.

President Hinckley told him of his 19 months in London in the 1930's and the contribution made to the LDS membership from British converts during that century. "The converts have been of real substance ever since, " he said. "We feel a great kinship with the British Isles."

"The LDS missionary program is a unique feature of the Church. Did you have a successful stay?" asked Ambassador Wright.

"Eminently successful, " replied President Hinckley. "My mission was a great thing. I spent a great 24 months in England. The marvelous thing is that those young men and women who go on missions never get over them as long as they live.

"The British were described by one person I knew as being stubborn, difficult and obtuse, but you can't sell them short in my book because I came to know them, not as a tourist, but as one who sat at their firesides and felt of their hearts and strength. I just love that part of the world. I love the English."[60]

Selecting the Denver Temple Site

President Hinckley asked President Ezra Taft Benson, senior presiding member of the Quorum of the 12, to accompany him to Denver on a snowy, overcast and bitter cold day about March 1984 to tour a temple site. They admired the view of Pike's Peak to the south, the rolling prairies to the east, the Rocky Mountains to the west and the Denver skyline to the north and prayerfully and carefully deliberated. "We determined this should be the site," President Hinckley said.[61]

Growth of the LDS Church was creating difficulties housing all historical records from wards and branches. So on April 2, 1984, directions were given to deposit only records on a stake, mission and district level. The keeping of personal journals was expected to continue.

Shortly thereafter, President Hinckley spoke and dedicated the new LDS Church Museum of History and Art on the west side of West Temple Street immediately across the street from Temple Square in Salt Lake. He told of the importance of preserving the history of people dedicated to building faith and strong community.[62]

April 1984 General Conference

The Regional Representatives and stake presidents met for their conference on Friday, April 6, 1984 and heard President Hinckley say, "The infirmity of President Kimball has served as a catalyst to draw the general authorities of the Church closer together in a great sense of love and loyalty. The misfortune of President Kimball has become our opportunity in our love, one to another, and our dedication to advance this great cause."[63] Two thousand leaders were in the Tabernacle for the meeting including 210 regional representatives.

At the Saturday, April 7 general priesthood meeting, as keynote speaker, President Hinckley indicated "the Church has never taken a backward step since it was organized in 1830 and it never will."[64] Several LDS temples to be constructed in Bogota, Columbia, Toronto, Las Vegas, Portland, and San Diego were announced that day also before general authorities and regional representatives in the Church Office Building Auditorium.

Sunday, President Hinckley once again conducted. President Kimball and President Romney attended the Saturday afternoon and Sunday sessions but did not talk. Two new members of the 12, Elder Russell M. Nelson, a heart surgeon, and Dallin H. Oaks, former BYU president and current Utah Supreme Court justice, were called as LDS apostles with no prior experience serving as general authorities. Said President Hinckley regarding the appointments, "The two new members of the 12 were called because the Lord wants them to serve, not because the First Presidency wanted those men. I want to give you my testimony that they were chosen and called by the spirit of prophecy and revelation."[65]

During the Sunday afternoon session, President Hinckley leaned over to President Kimball and said, "This is a large congregation. All those people love you."

"And I love them," President Kimball replied.

President Hinckley could always be seen aiding President Kimball walk to and from the sessions of general conference he attended. His concern for the LDS prophet and his counselor Marion G. Romney were always well known. Included in these concerns was regular contact at the president's apartment when he was unable to come to the office.

Setting Apart New Seventies

Seventies were also called at this conference for three to five year terms and President Hinckley set six of them apart Sunday afternoon at 4:30 P.M. following regular general conference. The new seventies consisted of a mission president, temple president, temple presidency counselor, and three regional representatives.

Their wives gathered. with them on the left side of the long table in the West Board Room of the Church Administration Building. The Seven Presidents of the 70 and Elder Ezra Taft Benson, president of the quorum of the 12, sat on the right side of the table with Elder G. Homer Durham, Historian and Recorder. President Hinckley sat at the head of the table.

This very sacred occasion in the lives of new general authorities was over in an hour. President Hinckley explained first the nature of their call and their full status and responsibilities as general authorities. "You will serve for three to five years and releases will follow," he said.

"There were many worthy, capable, experienced brethren from which to choose, but for reasons but known to the Lord, you have been called and will have apostolic authority and commensurate responsibility to testify, as special witnesses, of the divinity of the Lord Jesus Christ in all the world, wherever you might be assigned."

President Hinckley also explained they would receive assignments from the Twelve under whom the Seventy and the 7 Presidents of the Seventy work. Under standards in place, their wives would have the privilege of accompanying their husbands from time to time. Strict confidentiality was to be maintained regarding their work. Not even their spouses were to be told. Truthfully, they can say "I don't know," if confronted by inquisitors.

Then each brother called came to the front where President Hinckley laid his hands on their head followed by President Benson and the 7 Presidents of the Seventy standing in a circle. Pronouncing each new elder's blessing, if they had not previously been given the office of a seventy in a stake before stake seventies quorums were dissolved, they were given that office. They then were set apart as members of the First Quorum of the Seventy and as LDS general authorities with apostolic authority and responsibility to testify of the divinity and mission of the Lord Jesus Christ in all the world. Blessings of each were extended to their wives, families and interests together with health, safety in traveling and enjoyment of the blessings of "mingling with the people" throughout the world wherever assigned.

Once the ordinations and setting apart blessings were completed, the meeting was opened for questions. They were asked to attend the 70's quorum meeting Thursday morning 11 days later at 8 A.M. Release with smooth transition from their previous positions would take some time but if they could attend the quorum meeting the next Thursday on April 12, they should do so. Special orientation meetings were to be scheduled by the 7 Presidents of the 70.[66]

7 Stake Conference at University of Illinois Pavilion

President Ezra Taft Benson of the Quorum of the 12 and President Hinckley accompanied each other as companions on April 15, 1984 to a seven stake fireside before 5,350 in the University of Illinois Pavilion. Despite a rainstorm, the gathering was the largest of a group of Latter-day Saints in Illinois since the LDS pioneers left Nauvoo in 1846.

President Hinckley recalled his father's service for five years in the Chicago area during the mid 1930's. He indicated his father had taught him to "lose yourself in the work." Then he held up a credit card and a temple recommend. "This card authorizes financial expenditures," he said as he held up the credit card. "This card is a temple recommend that certifies its bearer for much more important work. I challenge each of you to prepare for the completion of the Chicago Illinois Temple by qualifying for a temple recommend."[67]

Five days later, President Hinckley conducted the commencement ceremonies at Brigham Young University and delivered the concluding remarks. He next was found at the Spectrum Building at the Utah State University on Saturday, May 12, 1984, talking to 9,000 youth and young adults age 14 to 24. It was a Youth Temple Fireside. When he rose to the podium he told the group he was laying aside his prepared text. "It is not quite what I want to say to you tonight." Then he spoke extemporaneously about the recent temple building in the Latter-day work. His delivery was with warm eloquence and good humor.[68]

Special Fast to Control Spring Floods

The First Presidency called upon their people to enter into a special fast on May 13, 1984 to control Spring flooding. The year before had seen wide flooding and damage. Thirteen Area Presidencies were appointed from the Seventies Quorums to reside in areas of their responsibilities effective July 1 of 1984. Each presidency was composed of a president and two counselors as with other presidencies in the LDS framework.

The mission presidents seminar on Tuesday June 19 was attended by President Hinckley and 11 of the 12 members of the 12 apostles. Ezra Taft Benson gave the keynote address. President Hinckley talked about the miracle of missionaries. It is "an absolute miracle. There is no greater miracle in the world than to see these boys and girls who come out of the little dusty towns . . . go out with freckles on their faces and dirt under their fingernails, and, not knowing much about it, become giants.

"There isn't anything like it in all the world; they come back with convictions in their hearts concerning this work, they come back with a love for people, they come back with a knowledge of God and of the Lord Jesus Christ that is absolutely of priceless benefit to them. They will shed light upon their families, and many others, all of their days. The miracle of the missionary is a miracle to behold."

At this meeting, the new mission presidents were told of the new Area Presidency network being implemented. President Hinckley said the men appointed over each mission president's area would be there close to them to help direct the details of the work. "We can't lick every postage stamp and make every decision in Salt Lake City. We have to do something about decentralizing authority."[69]

New "Broadcast House"

KSL TV and Radio had been housed in broadcast facilities dubbed "Broadcast House" for many years on an avenue directly east of where the old Social Hall of pioneer days used to stand. Now new facilities had been completed as part of a refurbishing of the west side of downtown Salt Lake City. The new facility was in the Triad Center at 100 North and 300 West in Salt Lake City.

July 12, 1984 was the ribbon cutting day. It was a hot sunny day. As chairman of the Bonneville International Corp. board of directors, President Hinckley was at the occasion and did the cutting honors. A month later 13 new temple presidents and wives met in the auditorium of the Church Office Building Auditorium at 8 A.M. where Gordon B. Hinckley called the gathering to order. "Come, O Thou King of Kings" was sung and Ezra Taft Benson gave the opening prayer. President Hinckley then introduced the presidents and their wives and talked. The group then sang "High On the Mountain Top" and the opening session ended.

The Newel K. Whitney store in Kirtland, Ohio, a historic site where early LDS saints in Kirtland frequented and where the prophet Joseph Smith, Jr. first visited when he went to Kirtland in a snow sleigh in February 1831, was dedicated by Ezra Taft Benson with President Hinckley present on Saturday, August 25, 1984.

Visit by President Ronald Reagan

On September 4, 1984, US President Ronald Reagan visited Salt Lake City. He met 20 minutes with President Hinckley, Quorum of the 12 President Ezra Taft Benson, all 12 members of the Quorum of the 12, and the three women presidents of the LDS general boards of the primary, young women and relief society.

"This woman presides over an organization of a million and a half women," remarked President Hinckley as he introduced the general relief society president.

"A million and a half?" the United States president remarked in unbelief.

"And even more," President Hinckley responded.

President Hinckley, true to form, presented President Reagan with a special leather bound copy of the LDS scriptures including the Book of Mormon. He then turned to the book of Ether in the Book of Mormon and read verse 12 in chapter 2:

"Behold, this is a choice land, and whatsoever nation shall possess it shall be free from bondage, and from captivity, and from all other nations under heaven, if they will but serve the God of the land, who is Jesus Christ, who hath been manifested by the things which we have written."

"In the Church's view, personal honesty, integrity and a reliance on the Creator form the foundation of the needed strength to confront the overwhelming problems the nation faces," President Hinckley told the statesman. He affirmed the LDS Church is non-partisan and cited a need for men and women of judgment and wisdom from all walks of life to join in efforts to serve the prophetic promise of freedom cited in Mormon's book.

President Hinckley toured the LDS Church Welfare Square Cannery with the American President and the LDS General Relief Society President Barbara W. Winder. They explained the LDS concept of helping oneself while helping others. The LDS concept of self-reliance was explained. President Reagan also visited the Church Administration Offices. All of these tours were guided by President Hinckley.[70]

US President Ronald Reagan Visits
with General Relief Society President
Barbara W. Winder and President Gordon B. Hinckley
Salt Lake City, Utah, September 4, 1984

The next day, President Reagan's opponent, Democrat Walter Mondale, also visited the LDS Church headquarters and met with President Hinckley. Both presidential campaigners addressed the American Legion Convention. President Hinckley did also.

Following the convention, the former national commander of the American Legion J. Milton Patrick wrote to the editor of the *Deseret News*, "Our recent stay with you during the National Convention of the American Legion will long be remembered. It was the finest convention city that I have ever attended since World War II.

"The friendliness of the people from the taxi cab drivers, the cafe waitresses, the Mayor, and President Hinckley's was most remarkable. President Hinckley's patriotic message to us, along with the Tabernacle Choir, was one of the most remarkable events of my lifetime. I have it on tape, which I intend to share with my friends here in Oklahoma."[71]

Miss America

The next week, the LDS Church was honored in another way when BYU junior coed Sharlene Wells, also a daughter of LDS general authority Robert E. Wells of the Seventy, was crowned Miss America for 1985 before a television audience of 100,000,000 on September 23, 1984.[72]

The Arizona Chapter of the National Association of Christians visited with President Gordon B. Hinckley, two of the LDS apostles and Elder Marion D. Hanks of the 70. Also significant was the presence of Henry B. Eyring, Church Board of Education Chairman, and Jeffrey R. Holland, BYU president.[73] Both of these men were to be called into the 12 apostles within 10 years.

The October 1984 Conference

President Kimball was absent from the General Women's Meeting held September 29, 1984 so President Hinckley substituted with a discourse on Doctrine & Covenants Section 25. This section records a revelation received in July 1830 by Joseph Smith, Jr. for his wife Emma Smith. It is one section which most significantly touches upon women.

"Past mistakes should be repented of, then forgotten, not dwelt upon to the detriment of further progress. Be happy. The gospel is a thing of joy. It provides us with a reason for gladness. Of course, there are times of sorrow. Of course, there are hours of concern and anxiety. We all worry, but the Lord has told us to lift our hearts and rejoice," President Hinckley told the sisters. Optimistic attitudes and faith and awareness of goodness of nature and humankind should be cultivated.[74]

At a special LDS employees department heads meeting on Thursday, October 4, 1984 at 3 P.M., for 45 minutes President Hinckley explained the new Area Presidency deployment. He made a plea for simplicity in the Church. We must accomplish our purpose—not the ends—working together to build the kingdom. "The people are hungry for the spiritual things," President Hinckley told the heads of the employees for the administrative departments of the faith. He then gave the executives a blessing and prayed for their well being and performance.[75]

President Hinckley continued on with the regular sessions of LDS general conference. President Hinckley greeted the assembly on Saturday morning. He confirmed that President Kimball has become feeble but he said there was no need to worry. In the afternoon session, President Hinckley firmly gripped attending LDS prophet Spencer W. Kimball's left hand with his right. President Kimball was now 89½.

That evening, Gordon B. Hinckley delivered the keynote address before the general priesthood session. He revealed the burden he was under when he said, "I cannot say enough in appreciation for you. Your sustaining vote in this conference means more than I can express. Sometimes, when I think the load is heavy and the burdens are many, I think of you who not only raise your hands in affirmation, but also give of your hearts, time and substance in loyal support."[76]

The next morning as he spoke at the Sunday morning session of conference on October 7, 1984, he expressed delight that President Kimball was in attendance. "I am not here as a substitute for the president of the Church. President Kimball is the prophet of the Lord. None other can or will take his place for so long as he lives. When he passes, there will be another ready, a man who through long years of experience and service has been . . . refined and prepared to fill that sacred and awesome responsibility."[77] Such seems now a prophecy about himself 10½ years later.

Even with the burden he was bearing, Gordon spoke that "a life of service in the Church of Jesus Christ of Latter-day Saints is a rewarding route to contentment and fulfillment."[78] Although both Marion G. Romney and Spencer W. Kimball both attended the last sessions of the conference, both had to be assisted on both sides by other men. The infirmity of the president and his first counselor was progressing.

Gordon B. Hinckley
Reading from a Book

BYU National Football Championship

Although the burdens were great, still the bright and positive experiences were seemingly multiplying. President Hinckley had been dedicating not only historical sites and public buildings, he had been privileged to dedicate numerous temples during the year. Also, the BYU football team was on its way to a perfect season of 11 straight games and the designation as the number 1 college football team in the United States for 1984.

President Hinckley and 10 of the LDS apostles attended a banquet in honor of their Western Athletic Conference title win on December 12, 1984 at the Lafayette Ballroom in the Westin Hotel in Salt Lake. Next he attended the Holiday Bowl game in San Diego on December 20 where he stated he was a perennial optimist.

"I think the chances of BYU coming out on top are reasonably good. But pride goeth before the fall," he said. BYU did come back from behind to defeat Michigan and preserve its perfect record for the year, however, on December 21st after Gordon B. Hinckley and Thomas S. Monson attended a California San Diego Mission conference, saw a potential temple site and attended a luncheon.

The Emery County Mine Disaster

"Our lives are to be used in service to others," President Hinckley said at the First Presidency Christmas Devotional on December 23, 1984, four days after there was a rumble at the coal mines in southeastern Utah's Emery County mine trapping 27 coal miners in death.

Three days later he was at the side of the grieving widows and families of those who perished. The memories of the Peru quake and the Maupiti Tahitians over 20 years ago certainly flowed in his mind. Now a tragedy almost twice that of Maupiti had hit home just a very short distance southeast of Salt Lake City. The miners who perished had been trapped in fire and smoke at the Wilberg Mine. It was the 4th worst mining catastrophe in Utah history.

On that day after Christmas in 1984, a hush came over the high school auditorium in the little mining community of Castle Dale when President Gordon B. Hinckley walked in. It seemed as if a special presence had come into the midst of the mourning congregation. Seventeen hundred had assembled from mostly Emery and Carbon Counties from which the dead miners came. One woman and 26 men had been lost.

The bonds of faith became strong in such situations. President Hinckley brought peace and consolation. "It's cold and gray outside, but there is a spirit of peace and warmth and love in this auditorium.

"No human can understand why such catastrophes occur. In the history of the race there have been many . . . They are always overwhelming, and their after-effects are felt for years and years by those most intimately affected. . .

"There will be loneliness—much of it—but for those who believe in the mercy of our Eternal Father, there will also be comfort. Great as is the present tragedy, it would be even greater if it meant oblivion for those who are gone.

"Their mortal bodies have expired. But the spirit lives on. They are as much individuals today as they were a week ago. To deny this would be to deny the very essence of Christmas which we are celebrating."

Following the services, Ann Bell, a mother of one of the dead miners, came close. In spontaneity, President Hinckley and the sister embraced in the bond of mourning for those who have cause to mourn, comforting those who stand in need of comfort.[79]

Death of a Close Friend

In little over two weeks, President Hinckley was called upon to mourn the loss of his boyhood friend G. Homer Durham and to speak at his funeral. "Our lives have been closely intertwined, " President Hinckley said on Friday, January 11, 1985 at a memorial service of 70 Historical Department employees in the conference room of the Church Office Building's east wing. President Hinckley conducted. Elders Boyd K. Packer and J. Thomas Fyans, LDS general authorities, spoke. Then it was President Hinckley's turn.

"Our lives have been closely intertwined," Gordon said. "Homer and I have known each other from boyhood to manhood.

"As a young teen, he wrote a message in my high school yearbook with a slight grammatical error. Then he grew physically, intellectually and spiritually until he achieved positions of importance, among them being a university president, the first Utah Commissioner of Higher Education.

"But he never lost the common touch; a 'giant' among men."

Then modestly Gordon B. Hinckley said, "Modestly but proudly I am happy to say our hymn will be published in the new hymnbook, where once again I and my dear friend, Homer, will be together—this time in song."[80]

Strong and powerful and trembling with emotion, President Hinckley spoke at the funeral of his childhood friend George Homer Durham on January 14, 1985.

Grid Champs Salute

Clapping and cheering fans of the successful BYU Cougar football team died down when President Hinckley rose to speak to a crowd of 15,000 gathered in the BYU Marriott Center on January 19, 1985 to "reminisce about a year to remember and honor a team to remember."

Regarding the 1st place National Football Champions of 1984, President Hinckley remarked, "As much as we appreciate what we celebrate tonight, I don't think any of us can realize the full import of what has happened.

"The university located in a little town in the West and sponsored by a church that expects a high standard of behavior from its students to become No. 1 is tremendous. And there has been a tremendous spillover.

"Not only has BYU become famous and Provo become widely known, but the sponsoring institution has become honored and respected and widely known as an institution that expects much from its people and gets much from its people."

President Hinckley said his ending remarks and was received with a standing ovation from the crowd. Earlier Coach LaVell Edwards had credited him as a major contributor to the success of the team. Said he, "He was with us long before we became famous. Through him, we received approval to expand the stadium, without which this never would have happened tonight."[81]

The Non-Existent McLellin Papers

January 27 found President Hinckley speaking at a parenting fireside. President Kimball and 1st counselor Marion G. Romney were absent and President Hinckley said they were "greatly missed." But he said in his satellite fireside address, "Never quit trying."

One hundred American flags were draped from the Temple Square Tabernacle balcony for the commemoration of the 75th anniversary of the Boy Scouts of America on Monday, February 11.

Back in Mark Hofmann's little world, he was still churning out his homemade forgeries. Many businessmen, including a coin collector, attorney, investment company executives, historical libraries and the LDS Church had been duped by him. Such forgeries as early handwritten notes supposed to be the first money created by the isolated LDS pioneers when they arrived in the Salt Lake Valley, later LDS currency printed by LDS pioneers, a contract for printing of the first copies of the Book of Mormon, a supposed letter by Betsy Ross, maker of the first American flag, and purported correspondence from Martin Harris reaffirming his testimony in the Book of Mormon and from Joseph Smith, Jr. the day before he was killed were just a few of the forgeries, all taken as authentic and bringing Hofmann thousands of dollars.

The LDS Church had purchased the false Joseph Smith III blessing in exchange for other historical items worth $20,000.00. President Hinckley had purchased on behalf of the Church the false letter Hofmann created to counter the previous fraudulent letter purportedly written by Martin Harris to W.W. Phelps for $10,000.00. The purported Harris to Phelps letter had been purchased by a 30 year old investment manager named Steven Christensen for $40,000.00 as a representative for Gary Sheets & Associates who donated it to the LDS Church. President Hinckley had also purchased a purported letter from Joseph Smith, Jr. to a Josiah Stowell for $15,000.00 "on behalf of the Church."

In 1982, Hofmann thought of William E. McLellin, one of the original 12 apostles of the LDS Church appointed in 1835. McLellin had been a doctor of medicine when converted to the LDS faith, had been zealous enough to be chosen as one of the select 12 men of the first Quorum of the 12, but was a man of murmurs, critical of even the First Presidency in a letter of censure while proselyting with the rest of the 12 in the Eastern States. He declared no confidence in the First Presidency, including Joseph Smith, Jr., and was excommunicated for his apostasy and unbelief on May 11, 1838.

From his date of excommunication, McLellin joined the Missouri mobs, robbing and driving the LDS faithful from Missouri. He also plundered Joseph Smith, Jr.'s home and stable and vindictively asked to flog Joseph when the prophet was imprisoned in a dungeon in Richmond, Missouri but the sheriff would not allow it unless both men were allowed to fight on equal terms. McLellin then tried to form his own church but without success.[82]

Mark Hofmann had gotten his information regarding McLellin, as with other ideas for his forgeries, from historical records of the LDS people as well as from anti-Mormon literature. He knew that papers of this kind of an apostate would raise interest in not only the Latter-day

Saint Church but also its splinter sect the Reorganized Church and those antagonistic to LDS doctrines.

Hofmann first talked of a "McLellin Collection" to attorney Brent Ashworth. He then talked of it to Deseret Book Company, major publishing company for the LDS Church. He spiced up interest by saying it included a missing piece of Egyptian papyrus containing the original pictograph which had been printed in the LDS Church's scripture called the *Pearl of Great Price*, part of what is said to be translations of an autobiography written by the ancient patriarch Abraham found on Egyptian papyrus in the 1830's. He also said it contained affidavits by Joseph Smith, Jr.'s wife Emma pertaining to the prophet Joseph's polygamous marriage relationships.

These feelers resulted in no money for Hofmann but he saw how the eyebrows raised. Whenever he needed it, he could draw upon this bait and they would bite. In February 1985, he told Deseret Book the McLellin papers had been sold to a third party and donated to the LDS Church.

The Oath of a Freeman

Then he concocted the scheme to create the earliest printed document in America, a typeset statement of the freeman's oath taken by the early inhabitants of the 17th century New England pilgrims. Ironically, President Hinckley's ancestor Samuel Hinckley had taken the real oath of a freeman shortly after arriving in the Plymouth Colony. The oath gave its takers special privileges of voting and participating in the government created from the compact signed on the *Mayflower* vessel before its passengers disembarked to the soil of New England.

Hofmann's elaborate but, in retrospect, moronic actions included creating a master for a printing plate of the freeman's oath purportedly printed in a 1653 book of Quaker catechisms. He then used a pseudonym "Mike Hansen" to order a plate from Debouzek Engraving company in Salt Lake City on March 8, 1985, but used his own phone number on the paperwork. "Mike Hansen" was assumed by Hofmann before this for previous plates to complete forged early Deseret money notes, a forged page purportedly from the first LDS hymnal organized by the prophet Joseph Smith, Jr.'s wife Emma, and a "Jack London" signature with a "small letter."[83]

Hofmann then took paper from a library book of the same time period and created his ink and hand pressed the oath. It took him only one day of work in his home basement. The image was only 4" X 7" with a border around the statement. He then got on an airplane to New York City. On the island of Manhattan, he wandered up and down the streets and avenues until he spotted an old book store like the kind he and his missionary companions had visited in England when buying old Bibles.

The unsuspecting book dealer was Argosy Books at 16 East 59 Street. Mark went in and assumed browsing mode. When he found an appropriate old book, he pasted the fake Oath of a Freeman in its covers and then went to the employee in the store, showed him the book and pasted sheet inside and said he would like to purchase it.

"Twenty-five dollars," the employee said.

Upon receiving the funds, a receipt for the book dated March 13, 1985 was written and given Mark as he left the store. Mark had now established his provenance and created a witness for the fake "oath" of a freeman. This was his big game. He was going for big bucks this time.

Next he found an agent willing to believe his story and approach the US Library of Congress for sale. He got his wish and the agent eagerly worked on the project. This was big business if real. No copies of the oath in print were known to exist. The Library of Congress told Mark's agent "we might display this along with the Constitution and Bill of Rights in the National Archives." Asking price was $1,000,000.00. Back in Salt Lake City, Mark was in dire need of funds to tide him over until his "Oath of a Freeman" forgery could be sold. As a stop gap measure to appease creditors, he now embarked on a scheme to obtain advances for purchase of an imaginary group of manuscripts supposedly belonging to William E. McLellin,

Tragedy

The sale of the "oath" forgery appeared to be going well, the Library of Congress appeared willing to purchase, and Mark expected to be a millionaire for a day when the check was cut. He had to wait only a short time and he could repay the advances received on the McLellin papers when the "oath" sale money was received. It all sounded like a fool proof plan.

Hofmann mentioned his "McLellin Collection" to Salt Lake coin collector Alvin Rust in February or March 1985, an "important" document collection in New York. But Rust declined to lend $185,000.00 for its purchase. In the Soviet Union, the youngest member of the Politburo, Mikhail Gorbachev, was chosen chairman.

April LDS conference arrived. One hundred eighty two mission presidents were brought from all over the world and met with another 60 new mission presidents on Wednesday, April 3, 1985. A "mighty renewal" challenge was given all mission presidents. Ezra Taft Benson drew from quotes of ailing President Kimball pertaining to mission work. Announcement was made of a new improved set of missionary discussions to be tested beginning in July. Less structured and more flexible, these lessons would place "reliance upon the Spirit and emphasis on the Book of Mormon." The goal to increase missionaries soon to 35,000 was also announced.[84]

This month LDS Church membership reached 6 million. The Church also announced they accepted the Harris to Phelps letter as authentic and the LA Times soon published articles about it as well as a report from Hofmann that he had seen a history written by Oliver Cowdery. His statement was false.

Hofmann went back to Alvin Rust in April 1985 talking about the bogus McLellin papers. "This is 20 times more important than anything we have bought before," he said. Rust, based upon past dealings he thought legitimate, advanced $150,000.00 to Hofmann for its purchase on the condition his son accompany Hofmann to pick up the "collection" in New York City.

Hofmann used the funds to relieve pressure from his creditors and looked for another taker. He went with Mr. Rust's son to New York, told him to wait and he will go get the collection, came back with three purported insured shipment receipts and said the collection had been mailed by insured mail to protect against loss.

When the pair returned to Salt Lake, Hofmann failed to meet Alvin Rust at his coin shop the next day and Mr. Rust went looking for him. When confronted by Rust, Hofmann lied and said the LDS Church was buying the collection for $300,000.00 "but it is confidential and President Hinckley is acting as agent." Rust was made to believe his money would be returned in two weeks.

Hofmann looked for money to satisfy pressuring Rust. He went to Arizona with another scheme, a purported non-existent manuscript of Charles Dickens. He and an acquaintance Shannon Flynn persuaded Wilford Cardon to "invest" $110,000.00 in a ⅓ interest to the manuscript.

Now it's to the LDS Church for what Hofmann hopes will give him the extra money needed to satisfy Rust. Hofmann contacted Steve

Christensen who had previously negotiated purchase of the Harris to Phelps letter which was later donated to the LDS Church. Christensen took Hofmann to Hugh W. Pinnock, a 70, and member of the new Utah South Area Presidency. A month went by and Rust was anxious. He wrote President Hinckley a letter indicating he had lent money to Hofmann to purchase the "McLellin Collection" and wondered when the purchase by the LDS Church would be complete.

The next day, in June 1985 Hofmann came to see President Hinckley and indicated he had access to what he called the "McLellin Collection." President Hinckley had never heard of it and asked what it contained. Hofmann indicated it had correspondence, affidavits and related items. Hofmann indicated he desired to donate the collection to the Church. At that time, President Hinckley let Hofmann know he had received a letter the day before from Mr. Rust indicating he had lent Hofmann money.

"Have you paid Mr. Rust the money borrowed?"

"No, but I will do so."

"When you have settled your account with Mr. Rust, then we can discuss the contribution of the McLellin papers."[85]

President Hinckley then left for Europe. On June 28, the pressure from Rust and others was getting unbearable. Hofmann went to Elder Hugh W. Pinnock, a 70, and one of the new Utah South Area Presidency, who took Hofmann to Elder Dallin H. Oaks, a member of the 12 apostles responsible for directing the Utah South Area Presidency. Hofmann told the two LDS general authorities he had an "option" to purchase the McLellin papers but it would run out in a week unless he paid the owner $185,000.00.

Elder Oaks knew nothing of past knowledge or discussions between Hofmann and President Hinckley regarding such a historical collection and told Elder Pinnock in his judgment the Church shouldn't be involved even indirectly in the acquisition of the McLellin papers. Hofmann had said he expected a million dollars coming from the Library of Congress for a document sold to them at which time the $185,000.00 would be returned and the collection donated to the Church.

"If Hofmann has a million dollars receivable from the Library of Congress, why wouldn't a bank simply loan him $185,000.00?" Elder Oaks asked Elder Pinnock.

"Would it be appropriate if we put him in touch with banking officials?"

"I see no harm in that provided it is clearly understood by all parties that the Church is not a party or a guarantor and that you are not a party or guarantor," Elder Oaks replied.

Elder Pinnock then referred Hofmann to Interstate Bank where Hofmann applied for a loan using the receivable from the Library of Congress as collateral. The bank loaned the funds and Hofmann had his money. But now he had to some way either produce forgeries he could say were the McLellin papers or buy time to create them. He didn't have anything but one forgery he claimed came from the collection.

Meanwhile, President Hinckley had returned from his trip to Europe and Elder Oaks reported the meetings with Hofmann. President Hinckley was interested in the purported McLellin papers but took no action. Then he went to the commemoration of the 50th year since the Moroni Monument at the Hill Cumorah in Palmyra, New York had been dedicated. He remembered the day 50 years before when he and Elder G. Homer Durham were there to see President Heber J. Grant dedicate the memorial. That evening, Sunday, July 28, 1985, he spoke to 8,000 people regarding the original dedication.[86]

Hofmann tried to get out of the deal with the LDS Church for the McLellin papers by indicating it was stored in a safety deposit box but the Library of Congress sale was not then worth the $1,000,000.00 and he wasn't in the position to donate the collection to the Church. Hofmann then said or implied he would have to sell the collection in pieces. Elder Pinnock was told this by Hofmann and Elder Pinnock told Elder Oaks.

J. W. Marriott, the faithful LDS member who had moved to Washington, D.C. in the 1920's and established Hot Shoppes, in flight meals for airlines, and an international hotel empire, died on August 13 and President Hinckley flew to Washington, D.C. for his funeral at the local LDS chapel in Kensington, Maryland overlooking the Washington, D.C. LDS Temple on August 17, 1985. Former US President Richard M. Nixon, Elder Boyd K. Packer, Billy Graham and President Ezra Taft Benson spoke along with President Hinckley.

"Now that he is gone, he will become a legend. His faith was simple and his love of God profound. No one will know of the vast good he did. It seems the more he gave away, the more he prospered," said President Hinckley.[87]

It was sometime in September 1985 when Elder Pinnock asked

Elder Oaks, "I know at least two individuals who might be interested in purchasing the McLellin papers. Is there any harm in calling its availability to their attention?"

"No, I don't see any harm in that, but we must stress to them that the Church is not involved as a purchaser or a guarantor and caution them we haven't see any of the collection."

One of the potential buyers notified by Elder Pinnock indicated he was interested in purchasing the collection if it was what Hofmann represented and its value was at least $185,000.00. Steve Christensen was asked to examine the collection for authenticity and value.

The walls were closing in on Hofmann. How was he going to get out of this one? He had told everyone he had a collection but there really was nothing in a safe deposit box other than a piece of blank papyrus he had obtained on loan. Now there was a legitimate buyer who wanted to have Steve Christensen examine the collection. They wanted to close the deal soon.

The Utah National Parks Council of the Boy Scouts of America honored Gordon B. Hinckley for his support of scouting on September 13, 1985. He was presented a handcrafted porcelain figurine commemorating the 75th anniversary of scouting. Reflecting upon his life, President Hinckley remembered the many friends he had acquired during his life. They had been faithful with few exceptions. They had lived happy and productive lives. Most were not "worldly wealthy" but in faithful things they were not wanting.[88]

By this time, Hofmann had accumulated a debt of $455,000.00.[89] Additional investors were upset at Hofmann. He had not performed and had given them checks that bounced. A check for $132,000.00 delivered Rust also bounced and Rust started collection. One of the investors actually confronted Hofmann and knocked Hofmann down with a punch when he displayed "detached arrogance" to the debt owed. The short term note with Interstate Bank also became delinquent and Elder Pinnock was informed of the default. Steve Christensen was informed and confronted Hofmann. He was suspicious now himself and pressured Hofmann for answers.

President Hinckley spoke at the BYU Devotional on September 17, 1985, then at the General Women's meeting for primary girls 10 & 11 and young women and relief society members. He said "emphasize the positive."

Luckily for Hofmann, Rust was out of town when the buyer found for the McLellin hoax was found. Hofmann fabricated the story Rust had the key to the safe deposit box as security for debt Hofmann still owed him. But he would be back in a few days and a "closing" was scheduled for Tuesday, October 15, 1985 at which time Steve Christensen would examine the "collection" and if it was genuine and of value in Mr. Christensen's eyes, the anonymous buyer would authorize his attorney to deliver a check for $185,000.00 already in the attorney's trust for the payment.

General conference convened on Saturday, October 5, 1985. LDS prophet Spencer W. Kimball was present but did not speak. At the priesthood session in the evening, President Hinckley answered commonly asked questions by posing the questions to himself. Ninety year old President Kimball is suffering from infirmities of age but is still the prophet.

The Church is not afraid of research of its history provided it is done with balance and integrity. The BYU Jerusalem Center being constructed on the slopes of the Mount of Olives will not be a center for proselyting if not authorized by the local Government of Israel. The LDS Church has many assets in temples, chapels, schools, welfare projects and colleges "but it should be recognized that all of these are money-consuming assets and not money-producing assets."

Why is the church in commercial business of any kind? They are outgrowths of enterprises established in pioneer times when church members were isolated and fulfilled the needs of the people. He noted, also, that allowances given general authorities come from the income of church businesses and not from tithes. Child abuse and non-payment of child support were denounced. Members were urged to pray for a peaceful solution to the nuclear-arms race. Lotteries in the states were denounced by him as a deterioration of public and political morality.[90]

The noose was tightening. Hofmann went to the hardware stores and Radio Shack and bought nails, pipes, gunpowder, batteries, rocket igniters and mercury switches for bombs. He built one and secretly detonated it out at the south end of the Great Salt Lake in the area of Grantsville. It worked and he knew if he doubled its potency, it would kill. He thought the victim would be Thomas Wilding, a financial consultant pressing to produce some purported documents or return $300,000.00 given for them. Another possible was attorney Brent Ashworth who also was pressuring for performance on promises.

President Gordon B. Hinckley
A Familiar Pose at General Conference

Bombs

Two bombs were made by October 14. He concluded his victim had to be Steve Christensen to prevent the McLellin collection closing. The other bomb would be a diversion at the Sheets residence since Hofmann knew their business was having problems and it would put the police checking that business rather than Hofmann.

Early in the morning on October 15, Hofmann took one of his death packages to the Judge Building in Salt Lake City where Steve Christensen's office was located. He placed it outside the office door. He then went to the Gary Sheets home and placed the second bomb on a walk by the house.

After delivering the bombs, he had second thoughts. He tried to call the Sheets family but both Gary and his wife Kathleen had already left for exercise and a visit to the bank. He called the Steve Christensen office but no one was there, just a telephone answering machine.

Steve Christensen arrived at the Judge Building shortly before 8 and saw the package at his office door. He touched it and it exploded. A huge door was knocked off its hinges. An insurance company woman close by heard the explosion and Mr. Christensen's final groans.

Gary Sheets, at the YMCA for a morning workout, heard radio broadcasts of Steve Christensen's murder. He immediately thought of Steve's wife and father and headed to visit them. Meanwhile, his wife Kathleen Sheets returned home at 9:45 A.M. from the bank and saw the brown package by a walkway running on the side of their home. She reached down to pick it up and the explosion instantly killed her.

The bomb blasts were a sensation. They quickly become national and international news. The media spent most of their day covering the tragic deaths. Hofmann, meanwhile, headed to the LDS Church Administration Building. Shortly before 3 P.M., he asked to see Elder Pinnock. He was not in so Elder Oaks saw him. The 10 minute conversation went like this:

"I think the police will question me," said Hofmann. "What should I say?"

"You should simply tell them the truth. You don't have any reason to believe that this bombing has anything to do with you, do you? Simply tell them the truth," said Elder Oaks.

"Well, should I tell them about the McLellin papers?"

"Look, that's been handled on a confidential basis, but there's a murder investigation underway. You should tell the police everything you know and answer every question—and I intend to do the same."

Hofmann went home and took a third bomb and placed it in his car together with a few documents such as the receipt for the book he had purchased in New York in which he had planted the purported "oath" of a freeman so it would look as though the McLellin papers had been there, too.

Then he drove his car to downtown Salt Lake City on the morning of the 16th of October and parked in front of the Deseret Gymnasium on Main Street and about 155 North, the new gym completed in the 1960's replacing the older gym where Elder Hinckley had worked when under his father's management. There he self detonated his third bomb with intentions, he says, of suicide. The bomb this time did not kill, although it did maim. Hofmann was found quite injured and rushed to a hospital.

Salt Lake City was in a frenzy. The news of the third bombing in three days hit international news immediately. Elder Oaks soon heard and immediately called the FBI. He told them everything which had transpired in his conversation with Hofmann the day before.

On Thursday, Hofmann's acquaintance Shannon Flynn came to the Church offices to see President Hinckley who was unavailable. So Elder Oaks saw him. He wanted to know what he should do. "Tell the truth," was the reply. The next day, Alvin Rust came to the Church offices and was similarly referred to Elder Oaks.

"I know some more things," Rust said.

"Whatever you haven't told the police, tell them. Give them everything. Make a complete disclosure on this matter. This is a murder investigation. The Church has nothing to hide. Tell them everything."

The weekend news raised conjectures and innuendo directed at the LDS Church and its possible involvement in the murders. By the next Wednesday, eight days after the first bombings, the Church had scheduled a news conference at which President Hinckley, Elder Oaks and Elder Pinnock would speak "to set the record straight."

Diplomacy

Three women from the Soviet Central Committee visited Salt Lake City on Thursday, October 17, 1985 and were hosted by President Hinckley the following day. "If women of the world became aroused in the interest of peace, there would develop a will for peace that could be felt across the earth for great good," President Hinckley said.

"May I say that the people of this church seek for peace and pray for peace. We know something of the threat that hangs over the world. I have been to Hiroshima many times to see that small reminder of what could happen on a very large scale with some misadventure. I hope and pray that there will be peace in the world—peace with honor; peace with respect; peace with mutual appreciation for the basic good that is found in people across the world."[91]

News Conference

The news conference was a hard experience for President Hinckley. Although innocent procurement of historical documents in furtherance of the LDS Church's mandate to keep a record of the history of its people had been taking place, now there was a possible cloud on the integrity of the Church which appeared to directly hinge on associations he had had with Hofmann.

The news conference was convened Wednesday, October 23 at 8:30 A.M., an hour and a half before scheduled dedication services of the LDS Church's new Genealogical Library were to take place immediately west of Temple Square to the south of the Church Museum of Art dedicated not long before.

After Richard P. Lindsay, the director of the Public Communications Department of the Church, greeted everyone and made introductions, President Hinckley and then Elder Oaks read prepared statements. Then the meeting was turned over to questions. President Hinckley's voice cracked with emotion as he answered some of the questions directed at him. But the innocence of any actions on their part was displayed and the conference ended 5 minutes before the dedication time of 10 A.M. when President Hinckley was to be at the Genealogical Library facility.

First Counselor

Spencer W. Kimball passed away on Tuesday, November 5, 1985. His long bout with numerous ailments had been an inspiration to LDS faithful. Gordon B. Hinckley had been put to the test, too. He had been rounded, and smoothed and polished in the hands of the Lord. Due to President Marion G. Romney's continuing convalescence, the new LDS president Ezra Taft Benson chose President Hinckley as his first counselor with LDS apostle Thomas S. Monson as his second counselor.

The roles had been changed. Now President Hinckley was working under Ezra Taft Benson rather than the reverse. Such is the common case in LDS callings. During the course of a lifetime, the hats of responsibility change often and each member receives numerous chances to serve. Oftentimes, roles are reversed. When President Hinckley assumed the 15th place as prophet in the Church of Jesus Christ of Latter-day Saints, he spoke of this principle.

"This church does not belong to its President. Its head is the Lord Jesus Christ, whose name each of us has taken upon ourselves. We are all in this great endeavor together. We are here to assist our Father in His work and His glory, 'to bring to pass the immortality and eternal life of man (Moses 1:39).'

"Your obligation is as serious in your sphere of responsibility as is my obligation in my sphere. No calling in this church is small or of little consequence. All of us in the pursuit of our duty touch the lives of others . . . .

"The progress of this work will be determined by our joint efforts. Whatever your calling, it is as fraught with the same kind of opportunity to accomplish good as is mine. What is really important is that this is the work of the Master. Our work is to go about doing good as did He."[92]

At the funeral for President Kimball, Gordon B. Hinckley conducted and spoke briefly. It was Saturday, November 9, 1985. The next evening there was the first ever Young Women Satellite Fireside Broadcast at 6 P.M. New president Ezra Taft Benson attended and presided but it was Gordon B. Hinckley who spoke on "The Wonderful Thing That Is You — The Wonderful Good You Can do."

"Your Father in Heaven smiles upon you . . . . You are very important . . . . You give assurance of new generations yet to come—generations of strength and goodness and faith. So very much depends upon you," he declared.

"Selfishness can become a consuming disease that destroys character and makes one unattractive."[93] Serve others was President Hinckley's remedy, the lesson he learned that day when a scripture was read and a letter came and a young Elder Hinckley dropped to his knees in that flat in Preston, England in 1933.

The ordination of Ezra Taft Benson as 13th LDS prophet took place in the Salt Lake Temple on Monday, November 11. All of the apostles laid their hands upon his head as Howard W. Hunter, new senior member and new president of the Quorum of the 12, acted as voice. Then it was President Hinckley's turn. He sat in the chair and similar hands were laid upon his head as he was set apart as 1st counselor in the First Presidency.

Awards International Executive Award

Gordon was at BYU on November 24, 1985 presenting the international executive award of the BYU School of Management to billionaire Trammell Crow, 70. He was praised by President Hinckley as a Mehodist who represents the "boldness that comes with the spirit of the entrepreneur."[94]

President Hinckley also conducted the annual First Presidency Christmas Devotional. New prophet Ezra Taft Benson talked. About December 10, 1985, President Hinckley said, "The Church is being attacked on many sides. A few dissidents, apostates and excommunicants have marshalled their resources in an effort to belittle and demean this work—its history, its doctrine, its practices. We are in another peak era of this criticism."[95]

As the American Challenger spaceship rose into the sky on January 28, 1985, a malfunctioning O ring caused the explosion and disintegration of the ship and all aboard. The next day the First Presidency of the LDS Church expressed sorrow to the families and friends of the crew that perished.

Then on February 4, 1986, after 3½ months investigation, Mark Hofmann was charged with two murders. President Hinckley was awarded the Silver Beaver by the Boy Scouts of America on Thursday, February 20, 1986. Forces were moving towards free enterprise in March when Soviet Union's Mikhail Gorbachev declared, "The essence of *perestroika* is for people to feel they are the country's master."

"Giant in Our City"

On the rostrum was Gordon B. Hinckley for a Tuesday, March 11, evening presentation of the "Giant in Our City" award to Arch L. Madsen, 1964 founder of Bonneville International Corporation, holding company for the LDS Church broadcast media and stations.

Back at Church headquarters, however, it was not hard for President Hinckley to "grumble" at misused authority, domineering executives, academic elitism, unreasonable conduct in family life and worldly pretensions. "Brethren, it is almost enough to take the joy out of our callings," he remarked.[96]

When visitors would knock on President Hinckley's door early in the morning, they would wait a time for President Hinckley to rise from his knees and get to the door. His scriptures were also well used.[97]

President Benson's General Conference

President Benson was 86 years old when he first presided at LDS general conference April 1986. Following conference, President Hinckley met with 300 Manti Temple workers in Manti, Utah on Sunday April 13, 1986. He said, "We need more faith, which is what makes this work grow. Also, be happy. We can all use more smiles. Let people know you are happy. It helps them a lot."[98]

Those chosen as temple workers, he also said, are special. They are carefully chosen because of faithful work done in the past.

General authority O. Leslie Stone died at age 82 and President Hinckley conducted his funeral on Wednesday, April 30, 1986 while new President Benson presided and spoke. The Hofmann murder trial was in preparation at this time and President Hinckley met with his defense lawyers to determine stipulated testimony. Judge Paul G. Grant conducted a preliminary hearing for Hofmann on May 6, 1986. He was charged with 32 felony counts involving bombing and murder. Thirty additional counts of fraud, theft and bomb-making were also on the list.

William Flynn, a document dealer in Phoenix, Arizona, toók the stand and testified he found unique flaking of ink on a Hofmann document. He told the court methods oxidizing ink to make it appear older causes similar cracking in laboratory tests. His conclusion was 12 documents he examined, including the Martin Harris letter to W.W. Phelps, were forgeries.[99] The preliminary hearing continued for 11 days during which it was agreed to stipulate to testimony President Hinckley would give even though he was not reluctant to testify.

Hofmann was bound over for trial for murder and related charges.

National Conference of Christians & Jews

President and Sister Hinckley joined seven other LDS general authority couples at the Westin Hotel in Salt Lake for an annual awards reception of the Utah Chapter of the National Conference of Christians and Jews on Thursday evening, May 22, 1986. Then on Saturday, May 31, President Hinckley himself was presented an honorary doctorate from Westminster College, Salt Lake City, Utah. Then he went to Utah State University in Logan, Utah where one week later he received an honorary doctor degree in the humanities on June 7, 1986.

The funeral of Elder James A. Cullimore, 80, emeritus member of the First Quorum of 70, was held at the Assembly Hall on Temple Square in Salt Lake City Wednesday, June 18, 1986. President

Hinckley conducted and read a message from president Ezra Taft Benson who was confined to home after a brief hospitalization for "flu like distress." But President Benson spoke at the mission presidents seminar on June 25.

On President Hinckley's 76th birthday, he was working with a short break for cake and punch June 23, 1986. The new mission presidents seminar found him speaking on Friday, June 27 to the 68 fresh mission presidents at the Missionary Training Center in Provo, Utah. Two days later he was speaking with Elders Neal A. Maxwell and A. Theodore Tuttle, apostle and 70 respectively, at a conference of the North America Area in Soldotna, Asusks, Alaska where many members had to fly by plane since there were no roads from their homes to the meeting location. A 180 member choir also sang to the group.

Roy W. Simmons was honored at the annual convention of the Utah Bankers Association on Tuesday, July 1, 1986, at which President Hinckley and wife were present. Simmons was CEO and chairman of Zion Utah Bancorp and Zions 1st National Bank. When one looks at all of the activities LDS general authorities attend, one immediately realizes the schedule of an LDS leader is indeed very demanding.

In his August 1986 First Presidency message, President Hinckley talked about the demands of the First Presidency and wrote, "I have frequently reflected on how Joseph Smith must have felt at times."[100] He noted a book written by unbelievers designated a "history" of the LDS faith and remembered that day in London, England when he confronted the publisher about a similar re-print of an earlier work of fiction disguised as history. He thought, "They know nothing of the prophetic mission of the Church."

Nine new temple presidents and their matrons were trained at a seminar for three days beginning Tuesday, August 19, 1986. President Hinckley was with President Benson and President Monson as he said to make the temple a spot of spirituality where it might be "a place of refuge . . . where testimonies are strengthened, where spirituality is enhanced."

"Never lose sight" of the fact that the temple is "the bridge over the river between death and immortality."[101]

New York-New Jersey Bi-Regional Conference

Fifty-five wards met in the Nassau Coliseum at Uniondale, New York on Sunday, September 14, 1986 for a bi-regional conference of New York and New Jersey saints. This was a unique conference.

Fifteen wards were non-English speaking, including Spanish, Korean, Mandarin, and Chinese members. Sign language and voice transmission for the deaf were also provided. Then President Hinckley broke ground for the Portland Temple when Ezra Taft Benson was unable to attend.

President Hinckley went to a stake conference without assignment on September 23, 1986, a practice he would take up once he became prophet in 1995. He went to Southeastern Utah and met with some saints. As general conference convened Saturday, October 4, President Hinckley said the saints were fighting a battle with Satan. Recently opposition had come over escalated temple construction and over seemingly minor issues, things the lay members of the LDS Church did not hear much about except in a small reference here and there now and again in a public discourse by a general authority. But the battle was raging.

That Saturday, announcement was made that 70's quorums which had been functioning in LDS stakes ever since stakes were organized in the 1830's would be discontinued and the only Seventies who would be ordained thereafter would be to general authority status. The First Quorum of the Seventy, traditionally a general authority quorum, would be expanded and additional general authority 70 quorums organized when needed.

The Sunday morning LDS conference session began with a talk by President Hinckley. "I believe without equivocation or reservation in God," he stated. "Though some feel it demeans God to say that man is created in his image, it should rather elevate mankind and engender within the heart of every man and woman a greater appreciation for himself or herself as a son or daughter of God."[102]

Just two weeks following conference, President Howard W. Hunter, president of the Quorum of the 12, had open-heart surgery. This weakness in the upper leadership of the Church once again placed great pressures on President Hinckley and his co-counselor Thomas S. Monson. The rigors of ceremonial services continued.

A new Eagle Gate Plaza skyscraper of 22 stories had been erected on the spot of the old Presiding Bishopric Offices on the south side of the street immediately across the street from the Beehive House on South Temple and State Street. It was equipped with state-of-the-art heating, lighting, communication and transportation technology. President Hinckley offered the dedicatory prayer although LDS prophet Benson was there. Reflective glass windows came from Belgium and crushed granite from Colorado formed the exterior walls. The office tower contained 385,000 square feet of space with retail space on the ground floor. Another design could have produced greater lease space but "we determined to give up an economic advantage for beauty and create a building that is complementary to the Beehive and Lion Houses across the street and the new Eagle Gate Apartments," President Hinckley said.[103]

The First Presidency Vault

During this time, a controversy relating to the lies of Mark Hofmann had arisen concerning a First Presidency Vault said to exist. The vault had been established by Brigham Young and Hofmann had planted the idea that certain documents casting unfavorable light on the LDS Church were housed there. Hofmann had spun one of his lies about a manuscript written by Oliver Cowdery, the lawyer and school teacher who was the first baptized Latter-day Saint.

A search by the Historical Department and First Presidency turned up no history written by Oliver Cowdery.

At a conference in Houston, Texas on Sunday, November 9, 1986, President Hinckley was interviewed by the *Houston Chronicle*. The reporter asked, "How do you account for the growth of the Church in Texas?"

"I could simply say that people receive truth wherever they are."[104]

Young Women's Anniversary Celebration

November 25, 1986 saw the 117th anniversary celebration of the founding of the Young Women's organization in the LDS Church. The First Presidency and wives were present on the 26th floor of the Church Office Building together with members of the 12 and 70 and the general presidencies and board members of the young women and relief society. Elder A. Theodore Tuttle's funeral was held at the Sandy Utah Cottonwood Creek Stake Center on Tuesday, December 2, 1986. President Hinckley spoke.

"He was accorded a measure of renown by reason of the fact that he was the Marine who went back [to a landing craft] to get the flag to give the men who planted it atop Mount Suribachi on Iwo Jima." That flag planting was immortalized by the famous photograph showing Marines placing the American flag on that hill.

Forgeries Declared Hoax

Mark Hofmann plea bargained with officials on his two charges of first degree murder and 28 counts of theft by deception. On January 23,

1987 an arrangement was made for his guilty plea to two counts of second-degree murder and two counts of communication fraud pertaining to the "Harris-Phelps letter" and also the "McLellin collection" which never existed even in forged form. He also agreed to a thorough deposition disclosing everything about his fraud and forgery schemes.[105]

Shortly he was committed forthwith to the Utah State Penitentiary and the lengthy interrogation of his schemes ensued. During the interviews, he detailed his fraud and forgeries from the time he was a young adolescent and disclosed that all of the documents he had sold regarding LDS Church history were frauds. The chapter in deception of the historically minded of the LDS Church was ended.

New BYU-Hawaii President

Decision was made in 1987 to close the Hotel Utah and convert it into a Church office building, theater and genealogy computer search facility. Internationally, forces continued to move towards collapse of communism in Eastern Europe and the Soviet Union. Negotiations were successful to destroy two nuclear missile classes. January 16 found President Hinckley speaking at a symposium on the British Isles Mission.

President Hinckley substituted for LDS prophet Ezra Taft Benson installing new BYU-Hawaii president Alton L. Wade on February 20, 1987 because it was too much travel for the aging president. Then on February 27, he spoke with President Benson and President Monson at the funeral for Elder Henry D. Taylor, a former 70, at the Salt Lake Eagle Gate Stake Center. He also spoke at the BYU 16 stake fireside on March 1, 1987.

Gordon B. Hinckley presided at the first regional conference ever held by the LDS faith in Jacksonville, Florida on March 30, 1987. Elder Marvin J. Ashton of the 12 and Elder Rex D. Pinegar of the 70 assisted in speaking to the 6,000 attending from eight LDS stakes.

General Conference April 1987

President Hinckley was the first speaker at the Sunday morning general conference session April 6, 1987. "There was never a brighter day than today," he said. The Salt Lake Chamber of Commerce banquet was attended by President Hinckley on April 15 together with 600 others. He wore a tux and a bow tie. The comic strip character Superman turned 50 in May of this year. And President Hinckley conducted commemorative services for the restoration of the Aaronic

Priesthood at a fireside May 17. LDS prophet Benson was in Helsinki, Finland at the time.

A revolution in LDS Church correlation and proselyting was about to take place. Launching the changes was a teleconference from Church headquarters broadcast by satellite on June 28, 1987 by President Hinckley and several other general authorities. "Accomplishing the Mission of the Church" unveiled a new policy to interact with priesthood quorums and utilize full-time missionaries in certain cases to reactivate less active LDS members.

July 4 President Hinckley spoke at the Ft. Moore Monument in Los Angeles, California commemorating 500 members of the "Mormon Battalion" who had marched to the coast in a show of force in the 1847 American war with Mexico securing the California Territory for United States possession. He also dedicated a monument in Birmingham, England that same month where 400 attended. Then in September of the same year, the Eagle Gate was dedicated by President Hinckley.

Camilla E. Kimball Funeral

LDS prophet Spencer W. Kimball pre-deceased his wife Camilla by just two years. On October 1, 1987, President Hinckley was at Camilla's funeral speaking. And on October 3, he attended the Jon M. Huntsman appreciation banquet.

During the October 1987 general conference, President Hinckley noticed all of the speakers were not using up all of their allotted time. Elder Franklin D. Richards of the 70 was sitting on the row just in front of Elder Hinckley and Gordon saw his head. All of a sudden, "I had an impression—a strong impression, and a voice—to call on Brother Richards [because] this would be the last time he would bear his testimony to the Church," President Hinckley said.

President Benson was asked, "I'd like to call on Frank Richards to speak."

"Go ahead," was the reply from the LDS prophet.

That was the last testimony Elder Richards would bear to the body of the LDS Church for he passed away at age 86 on November 13 after a short illness. President Hinckley was at his funeral relating this experience on November 17.[106] President Benson had experienced a mild heart attack shortly before so President Hinckley was presiding.

President Benson appeared for the first time since general conference for the annual First Presidency Christmas Devotional. President Hinckley declared, "Thank you, president, for coming."

In his talk, President Hinckley related the first Christmas of the LDS pioneers where work occupied the day with a little dancing in the evening and boiled rabbit and a little bread for dinner. He then said, "There is no other season like Christmas. All of us stand a little taller at this time. All of us feel a little more generous, a little more forgiving. All of us are disposed to be a little more kind. And this is of the very essence of the gospel of Jesus Christ."

He then held up in his hands some "gifts which I have received." He said, "I regard them as gifts of Christ because they are really gifts from him. He has revealed them to us. They speak words of promise concerning his coming. His voice is heard rising from their pages. They testify of his living reality."

The "gifts" were then identified as a Bible given him 30 years before when he became a general authority and a Book of Mormon given him 54 years before when he was called to go to Britain on a mission. The others were the Doctrine and Covenants and its companion the Pearl of Great Price.[107]

"Gift of Life" Award Dinner

US Senator Jake Garn from Utah was honored at a black-tie dinner given by the Utah National Kidney Foundation on December 30, 1987 for donating one of his kidney's to his daughter Susan Horne. President and Sister Hinckley together with 5 LDS apostles and wives and Elder William R. Bradford of the 70 attended in the Grand Ballroom of the Sheraton Hotel & Towers before more than 500.

President Hinckley received a magazine called *Leadership* periodically from South Africa. He also regularly kept abreast of other publications and TV and radio news. This helped crystallize his empathy and vision of mankind and its destiny.

He travelled to Mesa, Arizona on February 13, 1988 and addressed a group at the dedication of a monument to the LDS pioneers in the Pioneer Park. The next evening, he conducted a fireside honoring the 75th anniversary of the Boy Scouts of America broadcast to 1,800 stake centers. The next Saturday, February 27, he was at the management meeting for the BYU Management Society in Washington, D.C.

Impressive Youth Conference

On a Saturday morning in a large auditorium in the Spring of 1988, President Hinckley was impressed as he attended a regional conference meeting. On the front row below the stand were a group of beautiful girls, well-groomed, clean, lovely, vivacious and bright. Some had their scriptures. All were attentive. Scriptures were opened and read with the speakers. It was evident they were seminary students and probably had to travel early to their religious seminary. It was apparent they had learned to love the Lord.

"They impressed me as representing what this marvelous work is all about," President Hinckley wrote.[108]

Regional Representatives Seminar

Then it was back to Salt Lake City for April LDS general conference. On April 1, the concept of three dimensions of the mission of the LDS Church was explained before 200 regional leaders in their annual seminar. Three LDS apostles, Ballard, Ashton and Packer, explained the three dimensions to be proclaiming the gospel, perfecting the saints, and redeeming the dead.

President Hinckley spoke about spreading the gospel and the young women's program in his church. "We now have more [missionaries] servicing in the field than we have ever had, but we do not have enough. The world, with its 4 billion plus people, is a very large world. And while we do not have access to many millions of these, the numbers we are free to work with are still very large. Truly the field is white, and the laborers are few."

Couples were encouraged to fill missions if they were financially stable, reasonably healthy and their children were grown. Regarding local missionary work, he said, "Missionary work is the responsibility of each of us. Stake missionaries can assist in a wonderful way the work of the full-time elders and sisters."

Greater emphasis should be given on the process of fellowshipping. "Our people must reach out with greater diligence, with greater love to those who come into the Church as converts."

Young girls in the LDS Church need an opportunity for and motivation to develop their skills, increase their self-worth, and broaden their knowledge of the restored glad tidings.

"Of all the creations of the Almighty, there is none more beautiful, none more inspiring, than a lovely daughter of God who walks in virtue, with an understanding of why she should do so, who honors and respects her body as a thing sacred and divine, who cultivates her mind and constantly enlarges the horizon of her understanding, who nurtures her spirit with everlasting truth."[109]

He gave an address on "Christ's Victory" in the Sunday, April 9 session.

Redeeming the Dead Painting

President Marion G. Romney died May 20, 1988 at age 90 after several years convalescing. In addition to speaking at his funeral, President Hinckley attended the funeral of an inactive sister he had known most of his life. He was disappointed she had not appeared as strong as her pioneer grandparents and great-grandparents who would have given their life for the restored gospel.[110]

May 28 found President Hinckley at the new Genealogy Library building where a large painting was unveiled in the foyer of the main floor depicting the spheres of existence in Latter-day Saint doctrine.

The pre-existence where LDS believe they lived as spirits with God and his son Jesus Christ were depicted on the left, then the mortal life of earth where those living on the earth searched records for their ancestors and helped them obtain the same blessings they realized living at a time when priesthood authority restored allowed for the receipt of baptism recognized and sanctioned by Jesus Christ and temple endowments and sealings binding the fathers to the children and the children to the fathers in one eternal chain, and on the right the entrance into eternal existence with their Father in Heaven.[111]

That day the LDS First Presidency also made an official statement regarding the new AIDS plague. The words of President Hinckley delivered in the April 1987 LDS general priesthood meeting of general conference were then quoted: "The observance of one clearly understandable and divinely given rule would do more than all else to check this epidemic. That is chastity before marriage and total fidelity in marriage."[112]

Britain & Israel

President Hinckley returned from another trip to Britain and Israel about June 19, 1988. Meetings were held every Wednesday in the Salt Lake Temple with the general authorities. The new mission presidents arrived Friday, June 24, 1988 for their instruction. The entire First Presidency, 12 and additional general authorities met with the 68 men and their wives. Counsel was given to love, motivate, forget, and bless.

The American Freedom Festival in Provo, Utah held a special meeting in the BYU Marriott Center on Sunday, June 26, 1988 where Gordon was the featured speaker. Attendance was 14,203. The next day he dedicated stones from the old Territorial Prison where many LDS leaders had been incarcerated for polygamy. Now plaques were affixed to the stones as a memorial to their sacrifice for their beliefs.

The 19th Party Conference was held in Moscow, Russia on June 28. A man by the name of Yeltsin was there. Party chairman Mikhail Gorbachev had called for immediate changes in Soviet commerce immediately after his installation as March 1985 Politburo chief. Intensive economic development had been his focal point.

Now Gorbachev launched proposals which would place the USSR on a nonreversible course to free enterprise. The Secretariate would no longer supervise government ministries. The Supreme Soviet would be abolished and replaced with a 2,250 member Congress of People's Deputies. The head of the 400-450 member Supreme Soviet chosen by the People's Deputies Congress would be in charge of the government, foreign policy and defense.

The televised dramatic debate before the Party Conference included Boris Yeltzin who insisted on speaking the last day of the convention. He argued for faster "democratization", a faster track towards the democratic process and genuine elections.

President Hinckley was in Brazil at regional conferences about this time on Saturday, July 2, 1988. Three days later, he welcomed home the Tabernacle Choir from their successful Hawaii and South Pacific Tour. Then he attended the opening performance of the newly revised Hill Cumorah Pageant in Palmyra, New York on July 22 and spoke at the Sunday morning services at Cumorah on Pioneer Day, July 24.

August found President Hinckley out of the United States. Much of the United States was in drought at the time. Then on August 13, Gordon attended the 13th annual City of Joseph Pageant in Nauvoo, Illinois. Vice presidential candidate Dan Quayle and wife Marilyn visited with President Benson, President Monson and President Hinckley on Friday, August 26, 1988. Opponents Michael Dukakis and Jesse Jackson met with President Monson earlier the same day.

President Hinckley announced the LDS Church membership was now 6,000,000 when he spoke to the Governor's Conference on Utah's Future at the University of Utah campus on Wednesday, September 7, 1988. He indicated that the LDS Church was still careful to speak only on moral issues in politics while defending Latter-day Saints' right to involve themselves individually in political affairs and indicated through the facilities at BYU, Temple Square, the Eagle Gate Plaza Tower and Apartments & the Gateway Apartments that the LDS Church was the 4th largest Salt Lake County taxpayer and otherwise funnels millions of dollars into the Utah economy.[113]

The Traits of Bishops

As if a modern Paul writing to Timothy, President Hinckley advised the 11,000 bishops then in the Church via the Saturday evening general priesthood meeting on October 1, 1988 to avoid even the appearance of evil. Avoid the pitfalls. Be better examples to their members. Be men of integrity. Be wise with inspired wisdom. Be a counselor, a comforter, a teacher. Be sure no false doctrine creeps into the Church. Confidences placed must be held absolutely inviolate. Watching too much TV, poor sportsmanship, gambling and risque literature, visual media and sound must also be shunned.[114]

The next morning he declared there is sickness of sin, conflicts, quarrels and arguments. Avoid them. Turn the other cheek or go the extra mile when attacked, he advised.

Substitute

President Hinckley substituted for LDS prophet Ezra Taft Benson at the opening devotional at BYU on October 11, 1988 after having attended a Sacrament meeting in St. George, Utah shortly before. His subject was the "Uniqueness of BYU." Then he unveiled the J. Willard & Alice S. Marriott School of Management plaque at the BYU Tanner Business Building on Friday, October 28.

Special meetings were held in Argentina in addition to a regular regional conference for Rosario and Salta on November 12 and 13. Then he went to San Rafael on November 16, Mendoza and Godoy Cruze on November 17, and the Salta Region on November 19 and 20. Elder L. Tom Perry of the 12 accompanied after which the two returned to Salt Lake after 10 days in the country.[115]

President Benson requested Gordon B. Hinckley to read his address at the Sunday, December 4, 1988 Christmas Devotional. President Hinckley escorted the LDS prophet Benson on his left arm. Senator Orrin G. Hatch from Utah was next honored at the Grand Ballroom of the Hilton Hotel in Salt Lake City on Thursday, December 15, 1988 with the "Gift of Life Award" with President Hinckley present.

"I look with wonder at the farm boy of Palmyra," President Hinckley said in his First Presidency Message in the *Ensign* magazine of January 1989. "The variety of matters the [Doctrine & Covenants] deals with is amazing . . . It is evident from reading the Doctrine and Covenants that Joseph Smith had an all encompassing understanding of the eternal purposes of God. I love the language of the book. I love the tone of its word. I marvel at the clarity and strength of its statements."[116]

Regional Conferences

The first months of 1989, the Utah State Legislature had on its calendar a bill which would have allowed alcoholic consumption on "fun buses" traveling to Nevada from cities in Utah. The LDS Church took a stand on this moral issue and called key legislators stating their disapproval of the bill. The bill was defeated.

On February 26, 1989, President Hinckley spoke to single Latter-day Saints about their lives. President Monson conducted while President Benson attended and presided. Following President Howard W. Hunter's address, Gordon B. Hinckley said, "Somehow we have put a badge on this large group. It reads 'singles.' I wish we would not do that. You are individuals, men and women, sons and daughters of God, not a mass of 'look-alikes' or 'do-alikes.' Because you do not happen to be married does not make you essentially different from others."

The four main groups of single Latter-day Saints were identified as returned missionaries, single sisters, single parents and those who have lost companions in death. The natural process of dating and courting will take care of most RM's, he counseled. Sisters should serve.

"The best antidote I know for worry is work. The best medicine for despair is service. The best cure for weariness is the challenge of helping someone who is even more tired."

Single parents have a lonely duty, but "need not be entirely alone." Many are understanding and are sensitive. The widowed and alone may also enrich other lives.[117]

A St. George, Utah regional conference was attended by President Hinckley with Elder Dallin H. Oaks and Elder Paul H. Dunn and two regional representatives. Twelve stakes participated on March 18 & 19, 1989. President Ezra Taft Benson attended the regional representatives seminar in the Church Office Building on Friday, March 31 where President Hinckley spoke.

The next day, announcement was made at the first session of Saturday general conference, April 1, 1989, that a 2nd Quorum of 70 would be organized. More growth demanded more general authorities to oversee the work. President Hinckley told the LDS faithful to "magnify" their callings, "strengthen themselves and bring themselves closer to and strengthen others."

Following conference, President and Sister Hinckley both spoke to 4,500 attending the Pikes Peak Center, Colorado on Sunday, April 23, 1989. The theme of President Hinckley's talk was "Look on Us" as recorded in Acts 3 of the New Testament.

Jeffrey R. Holland, President of BYU, was given a standing ovation sendoff as he became one of the new 70 general authorities when President Hinckley started applauding at graduation activities for the 114th convocation at Brigham Young University on April 28, 1989. The new children's primary songbook was announced Thursday, May 11, 1989. President Hinckley spoke during the special program in the Assembly Hall on Temple Square.

Rex E. Lee was chosen the next BYU president and installed by Gordon B. Hinckley on Friday, May 12, 1989. Twenty three months before President Lee had been diagnosed with non-Hodgkins lymphoma but still assumed the position. President Hinckley stated he had been called by the apostleship as well as the BYU Board of Trustees.

The "Jets", an LDS group of pop singers and dancers, were at the top of their popularity at the time. They were from Tonga and ages 16, 23, 19, 18, and 15.

President Hinckley talked at the time of a friend he had who had been consumed with lust for greater and greater riches. This friend helped some of his friends to the same but then the economy dropped. His friends became his violent and hateful accusers. President Hinckley recommended to the University of Utah Institute students in a speech to them on May 21, 1989 to watch greed.

Watch being a slave to fashion, too. Don't go to wild excess. Some individuality is good but be modest in physical wants. Have the virtues of thrift and industry. Such makes a nation and people strong and makes family independent. Do not borrow beyond your ability to pay for education or home. Avoid egotism and greed and cultivate self-discipline and self-restraint.

Gorbachev of the USSR was visiting China at the same time period after 30 years of strained diplomatic relations between the two countries. Students eager for freedom had taken courage before and started demonstrations for reforms similar to those going on in Eastern Europe and the Soviet Union. The demonstrations and marches then mushroomed in April into a "hunger strike" demonstration in the vast Tiananmen Square outside and in front of the Great Hall in Beijing, China where China's communist leaders officed.

The demonstrators set up camps and built a beautiful white papier-mache "Godess of Democracy", the symbol of their hopes and dreams for freedom. Gorbechev visited Beijing as the students demonstrated. Workers joined. But in June 1989 loyal Chinese military crushed the students' and workers' demonstration with military force and tanks. Many were killed and the Godess of Democracy toppled and destroyed. Students and other dissidents were arrested if they couldn't escape. Many were later executed. But something miraculous had happened with the human spirit of the billion of humanity in that great nation.

President Hinckley talked about *glasnost* and *perestroika* and Tiananmen Square in part of his remarks to the U of U institute students on May 21. Four days later in the Soviet Union, the 1st Congress of People's Deputies met.

President Hinckley spoke at the Utah State University in honor of Elder David B. Haight, LDS apostle, who was receiving that university's Most Distinguished Alumnus award on May 23, 1989.

Eulogy for Slain Missionaries

At Wellington, Morgan County, Utah on Tuesday, May 30, 1989, President Hinckley spoke at one of two funerals for two full-time missionaries killed in LaPaz, Bolivia. President Thomas S. Monson spoke at the other memorial service in Coalville, Utah. The missionary Todd Wilson, and his companion had been gunned down by an assassin as they returned to their apartment.

President Hinckley told Elder Wilson's parents, "Your son has become part of a small number who will be remembered always in the records of The Church of Jesus Christ of Latter-day Saints. Many have died in this cause. Many have given their lives—thousands—for their testimony of the truth, but only few have been gunned down by hateful men who loved not the Lord nor His works.

"He might have given his life in other causes. He could not have given it in a greater cause than this. We wonder why it happened, why a strong and faithful and good young man who responds to a call to go into the mission field should lose his life while in the service of the Lord. We cannot explain it. We can only say the wisdom of God is greater than our wisdom, that mortal life . . . is only a passing episode in an eternal journey and that it really doesn't matter whether we are here for a long time or a short time in this probation."[118]

Founder's Day Award

The Founder's Day Award from Weber State College in Ogden, Utah was accepted on behalf of the LDS Church by President Hinckley on June 9, 1989. Weber State College was originally one of the LDS Academies. Nine days later, President Hinckley was at the 1st ever regional conference in Missoula, Montana held at the University of Montana's Adams Fieldhouse on June 19. Then he returned to Salt Lake City to meet with 75 new mission presidents on Wednesday, June 21, at the Missionary Training Center in Provo, Utah.

"In missionary work, all else is secondary to the testimony that Jesus is the Christ, the Son of God; that He lives, our resurrected Lord and Savior, the Redeemer of the world," President Hinckley stated. "I speak to you as an apostle, called and ordained to be a special witness of the name of Christ in all the world. I am sobered by that charge. At times I feel overwhelmed by the magnitude of this responsibility. It is my constant prayer that I shall always speak as one who knows, and as one who has the courage to bear witness for all. For if we deny Him, He will also deny us.

"You likewise are called to be special witnesses to the name of Christ in that part of the world where you labor. Likewise, those missionaries who labor under your direction have that responsibility."[119]

Nauvoo Pioneer Cemetery

President Hinckley read the names and causes of death of those in the Nauvoo Pioneer Cemetery on a visit there in 1989. He thought of the grieving mothers who went to Nauvoo for refuge and whose lives were threatened. President Ezra Taft Benson was present but President Gordon B. Hinckley spoke and dedicated the newly refurbished Carthage Jail complex in Carthage, Illinois on Tuesday, June 27, 1989, exactly 145 years to the day following the martyrdom of Joseph Smith, Jr. and his older brother Hyrum Smith at the jail.

"I'm always deeply affected when I walk where Joseph walked and when I stand where he was shot and killed," President Hinckley said.[120]

Tabernacle Choir Broadcast 60th Anniversary

The LDS Tabernacle Choir was honored at a banquet in the Marriott Hotel on Friday, July 14, 1989 celebrating three years of weekly broadcasts on NBC and 57 years on CBS radio. President Hinckley was the keynote speaker before 744 people. Fourteen general authorities and wives also attended including many from the 12 apostles.

President Hinckley lauded their music talent. "Beyond these qualities the choir has a thing of the spirit," President Hinckley spoke. "There is faith unwavering in God our Eternal Father and in His Beloved Son, the Savior of the world. They sing anthems to the Almighty with a conviction of His reality as the Father of all mankind. They sing praises to His Begotten Son with love and certain knowledge of Him as the Savior and Redeemer of mankind."[121]

In Confidence With Acknowledged Leaders

Ezra Taft Benson was honored on his 90th birthday Sunday, July 30, 1989 with a video from US President George Bush awarding him the Presidential Citizens Medal. And the next month the first non-communist premier was appointed in Poland. President Hinckley was with Thomas S. Monson at a reception for LDS prophet Ezra Taft Benson on Friday, August 4, 1989. Then he went to dedicate the monument paying honor to the Hawaiian Latter-day Saints who founded a little community called Iosepa in the desert west of Salt Lake City. He was draped in leis in a long white sleeve shirt grasping the tall metal mike with his right hand, left hand dropped straight to his left side on Monday, August 28, 1989.

Many world leaders had passed by Salt Lake City or met him in their own nations. Other prominent women and men had similarly met him for one occasion or another. In all of these meetings, he reflected, "What a rewarding experience to stand in confidence with acknowledged leaders." Then he thought, "What a wonderful thing to stand with confidence, unafraid and unashamed and unembarrassed, in God's presence."[122]

Reflection on the Summer of 1989

Gordon sat down at the end of August and pondered his activities of the Summer. He had not been on the beach or sand. He had not been at resorts or places of fun. Except for six days, he had been at the office. He had spent a few days "perspiring in the sun, stirring the earth, and witnessing the miracles of nature" at his orchard planting, cultivating, irrigating, pruning, and eating fruit from his own produce.

At sunset & darkness, he looked into the heavens, saw the stars and sensed in some small degree the majesty and wonder and magnitude of the universe, the greatness of creations, including his own place as a child of God. His world was in the trees of fruit and it reminded him of Revelation 7:2-3, explained by the prophet Joseph Smith, Jr. in the D.&C. 77, "Hurt not the earth, neither the sea, nor the trees."[123]

President Gordon B. Hinckley Visits
With Actor Jimmie Stewart
Thomas S. Monson Present on the Right

He also spent a few days in the Rocky Mountains and watched the replay of the landing on the moon 20 years ago with awe. At 3 A.M. he got up to watch the pictures relayed to earth of Neptune as Voyager II moved within 3,000 miles. It had left in 1977 traveling at 61,000 miles per hour. It was an awesome feeling. He reflected on the wonders of the human mind when devoted to the constructive and not the destructive.

He also looked at the eclipse of the moon through the trees and revelled in the celestial clockwork of the Master Creator, the wonderful pattern. He was excited at the discovery of the gene which might lead to cure of cystic fibrosis and thought of a little boy he knew with that dread malady. He also received enjoyment reading good books a little and listening to good music and associating with treasured friends and family.

He then read the *Wall Street Journal* report of US State Department's officer Francis Fukayama but did not believe his cynicism about the future. He felt rather that youth should reach out to the challenges of improving the soul and personality and fill their minds with all learning of the past and face the challenges. He spoke of this "wonderful summer" before the studentbody of Brigham Young University on September 3, 1989, now 17 stakes strong.

He revealed the burden of his responsibility when he disclosed to the students, "The Church is now established in more than a hundred nations. There are decisions to be made every day, and some of these are difficult. The guidance of the Lord is sought in all of these deliberations. The work is demanding, but there is something wonderfully stimulating in the very challenge of it."[124]

Fall of the Berlin Wall

President Hinckley spoke at the general women's meeting on Saturday, September 23, 1989 on educating their hands and minds, keeping marriage and motherhood in perspective and inculcating prayer, faith, charity and love in their lives. Hurricane Hugo destroyed the Caribbean Islands up to and including September 23 for six days. Then on Saturday, September 30, 1989 in general conference, President Gordon B. Hinckley made a stirring plea to stay away from medicines and drugs not needed for medicinal purposes.

Following conference, President Hinckley went to Nauvoo, Illinois and dedicated four more restoration projects on Saturday, October 7, 1989. He then attended a reception at a Catholic cathedral on October

11 to kickoff a $6.3 Million fund-raising project to refurbish the Salt Lake City edifice. The Fall convocation on October 27, 1989 installed BYU's 10th president, Rex E. Lee where President Hinckley conducted.

President Hinckley was on the receiving end on Wednesday, November 8, 1989 when he was given one of 10 George Washington Honorary Medal Awards from the Freedom Foundation at Valley Forge. And the next day, freedom loving East Berliners ripped and knocked down the Berlin Wall.

Integrity

About this time a developer was negotiating for a piece of real estate in which several stakes had an interest. Contracts of sale were signed and a closing set. Then some of the stake presidents expressed second thoughts and desired to withdraw from the purchase or negotiate new terms. The developers went to LDS Church Headquarters. Soon a call came from Church Headquarters to all of the stake presidents concerned to meet with President Hinckley at the Church Administration Building in Salt Lake to discuss the matter with the developers.

All of the stake presidents and the developers were sitting in a conference room waiting for President Hinckley when he came in. He sat down and asked each stake president, "Did you agree to sell this property to these gentlemen?"

"Yes," was the reply from each stake president.

"Then let's get it done."

President Hinckley then left the room.[125] The point was forcefully made. When you agree to do something, keep your promise.

New Ricks College President

On Friday, November 10, 1989, President Hinckley installed the new 13th president of Ricks College, Steven D. Bennion. This was unique because President Bennion had grown up in the same East Mill Creek area where the Hinckley Farm and President Hinckley's later family home was located. He had known the Bennions of East Mill Creek from early years.

The Ricks College then had 7,700 students from the 50 States of the US and from an additional 40 countries. It was also significant that Henry D. Eyring was also with President Hinckley and spoke there, too.

A week after the installation of the new Ricks president, a large student demonstration took place in Prague, Czechoslovakia.

Then the Hinckleys went to Sydney, Australia for a regional conference. Young Women celebrated in a meeting of 200, too. Tapes were presented with messages from President Benson and Ardeth G. Kapp, Young Women's president.

Bells rang at the 120th annual Young Woman's organization founding birthday on November 18, 1989. At the time, 400,000 LDS teen girls worldwide made a commitment to home, religion, integrity, morality, no drugs and no alcohol by ringing bells simultaneously at the same moment. President Hinckley and Sister Hinckley were with James E. Faust and joined ringing the bells with the young women at the Sydney Parramatta Stake.

At the Greenwich Stake Center in Sydney at Baulkham Hills, 560 priesthood leaders assembled on Saturday for a leadership meeting. "Resist the tendency to judge people for past actions," President Hinckley counseled.

On Sunday, more than 5,000 from the Sydney LDS Region met at general sessions in the recently completed Convention Center at Darling Harbor.[126]

The contingent next went to New Zealand for a November 26 regional conference in the Michael Fowler Centre in Wellington. Two thousand were present as President Hinckley and Elder Faust spoke. They also conducted seminars for New Zealand, Tahiti and Fiji priesthood leaders and mission presidents from Australia.

Christmas First Presidency Devotional 1989

Back at home, President Hinckley gave the sole address at the Christmas devotional. President Monson conducted. President Benson was present but was frail. President Hinckley spoke of the crumbling of European communism and was melodious in his statement on the Savior.

Said he, this year is "a Christmas present of gigantic proportions to millions who have been under a yoke of bondage." During the United States' celebration of the 200th anniversary of the US Constitution, "another bill of rights is being crafted as the spirit of Christ broods over great areas of Europe and millions of her people.

"Like a glorious sunburst through dark clouds, there is emerging freedom of worship, freedom of assembly, freedom of expression, freedom of choosing those who will govern. In these nations, where new chapters of law and new constitutions of liberty are being written, there is a strong residual of faith in the Lord Jesus Christ . . . From this seed will spring new truth as the revealed word of the Lord Jesus Christ is taught as opportunity comes. and come it will. This is a season of rejoicing. It is a season of peace."

The Savior was then praised. "There is none other to compare with Him. In His birthright as the Son of God, in His divinity as the worker of miracles, in His humility in submitting to the torture of His death, in His Godhood in bringing to pass His resurrection and the salvation of the human family," the family stands supreme.

"He is the author of our salvation. He is the source of the good news of the gospel. He is our hope in our season of desperation, our guide in the wilderness of life through which we walk, our source of comfort and consolation in seasons of distress, our assurance of the eternity of the soul of man."[127]

One half million men and women had demonstrated in Prague, Czechoslovakia in a non-violent revolt.

President Hinckley informally accepted the Utah Heritage Foundations's Preservation Award on Monday, December 18, 1989 for preserving the Brigham City Tabernacle. Then he spoke at the Elder Theodore M. Burton funeral on Wednesday, December 27, 1989 at the Salt Lake Central Stake, 11th Ward.

New Unit Budget Allocations

President Hinckley spoke in a satellite broadcast to the LDS Church on February 18 indicating from now on no budget funds to maintain and provide utilities to Church buildings or for clerical overhead or ward activities would be needed in the United States and Canada, saying that LDS members in those areas now are faithful enough in their tithes to handle the expenses.

From that time forward, such expenses would be paid from general tithe funds and each church unit would be allocated a certain amount quarterly to cover local clerical expenses and activity expenses.[128]

Fall of Communist Monopoly in Russia

On February 7, 1990, acceptance of a Western-style presidency and cabinet government organization was approved by the Soviet Communist Party which also consented to relinquish its monopoly as the sole party in Russia.[129]

Opposition

A statement made by Joseph Smith, Jr. said when you do increased good, expect increased opposition. In reverse, if opposition is an indication of good being done by the LDS Church, it surely saw it in

1990. Contention arose in Utah over many issues. In Utah County, opposition was raised to graduation prayer ceremonies.

In Salt Lake and Duchesne Counties, opposition was raised to using Church chapels as voting sites. In St. George and Logan cities, opposition was raised to use of public funds to light the temples, the major landmarks in both cities. Logan City removed the Logan Temple from the official city seal.[130] Such was the flavor.

But another statement by Joseph Smith, Jr. also seemed solidifying. "The truth of God will go forth boldly, nobly, and independent . . ." And so it seemed. President Hinckley did not let up. He was speaker in competition with Linda Ellerbee at the Belle S. Spafford Endowed Chair of the University of Utah Graduate School of Social Work on Friday, February 23, 1990 talking about working women.

President Hinckley indicated working mothers have been sent off to work due to rising expenses, but said that was at a terrible price. The working mother comes home often too tired and exhausted to give her children attention they crave and need. He still encouraged women to obtain as much education as they can. "Training will unlock the doors to your dreams," he said. But "keep marriage and motherhood in perspective."

"Men ought to be fathers,." and women "ought to be paid in accordance with their work, their contribution . . . . One of our great efforts has been to educate, and at the same time teaching that the home is the anchor point of society."[131]

First Ethnic African General Authority

March 30, 1990 found President Hinckley speaking to the Regional Representatives seminar. He reminded those attending of President Benson's December 1985 call to estranged LDS members to "come back." He also once again reviewed the traits of bishops. The following morning, Saturday, March 31, the first black LDS general authority was presented for sustaining vote as a 70. He was Helvicio Martins, age 59, from Brazil. President Hinckley talked on temple recommends and on Sunday was the keynote speaker, talking on "Mercy".

"I am confident that a time will come for each of us when, whether because of sickness or infirmity, of poverty or distress, of oppressive measures against us by man or nature, we shall wish for mercy," he stated. "And if, through our lives, we have granted mercy to others, we shall obtain it for ourselves."[132]

President Benson felt too feeble to deliver the closing remarks at the Sunday afternoon session being in his 91st year so President Hinckley gave closing remarks.

First Soviet Ambassador Visits Salt Lake City

On April 27, 1990, the first Soviet Ambassador to ever visit the LDS Church dined at Jon M. Huntsman's home in Salt Lake City, creator of a special project to provide relief for the Armenian earthquake victims of December 1988. President Hinckley greeted him along with LDS apostle Boyd K. Packer, Utah's governor Norm Bangerter and Salt Lake City mayor Palmer DePaulis.

In just a year, the Soviet empire was to crumble. Interesting that such a meeting should take place in Salt Lake City prior to this. Ambassador Yuri Dubinin said, "What [Jon Huntsman's] company is doing and what the Mormon Church is doing will continue to be a symbol of the special friendship between the Soviet and American people. This is one of the best manifestations of a new era in Soviet American relations."

Then he turned to President Hinckley and said, "Our friendship with your church is not so long, but it began in a very important moment for us and for the Armenian victims of the earthquake. It was a wonderful and very touching manifestation that all of us are human beings."

"We're delighted to have you here," President Hinckley responded. "You do us a great favor by your presence."

"I am delighted to be here. It is an absolutely new region for us. I was told it is a wonderful part of the country. It's true, and it's very special for Liana and for me because we are both from Soviet mountains. The mountains separated our birthplaces, but they were unable to separate us."[133]

General Authorities Fast Meeting in Salt Lake Temple

The next day following meeting with the Soviet Ambassador, President Hinckley and all of the other general LDS authorities met in the Salt Lake Temple. They bore testimonies to each other and partook of the Sacrament.

President Ezra Taft Benson rose with tears in his eyes and conviction and in his characteristic high pitched voice said, "I love you, my brethren. I bless you in your great ministry."[134]

Sons of the American Revolution Medal

The Sons of the American Revolution Utah Society recognized President Hinckley at the Alta Club in Salt Lake City on May 4, 1990 with a silver "good citizenship medal" Following presentation of the medal, Gordon spoke to the audience of the Bill of Rights to the United States Constitution, the first 10 amendments to the original document.

"One who stands where I stand knows something of the constant threat of the heavy hand of government against religion . . . In recent years it has grown in strength and the attacks have increased in frequency."

After commenting on all 10 of the Bill of Rights, President Hinckley declared they are "so basic and fundamental in guaranteeing to all citizens those natural rights which come from God, and over which the federal government has neither authority nor jurisdiction."[135]

The same day in Salt Lake City, an upset limousine driver and other limousine companies filed a lawsuit against the Latter-day Saint Church claiming conspiracy in the recent defeat of legislation which would have allowed alcoholic consumption while inside their limousines.

New Primary Childrens Medical Center

President Hinckley gave the First Presidency's talk at the fireside celebrating the 161st anniversary of the restoration of the priesthood on Sunday, May 6, 1990 in the Tabernacle and 2,600 additional congregations meeting throughout the United States, Canada, Puerto Rico and the Dominican Republic.

The song "I Am a Mormon Boy" was song by a choir of young men. President Benson used to sing that song when he was a youth and began mouthing the words with the choir. President Hinckley and President Monson then joined in quietly.

The body of 900,000 Aaronic Priesthood then in the LDS faith and 800,000 Melchizedek Priesthood constitute "a royal priesthood" with "wondrous powers and prerogatives . . ."

"There is no other power or authority comparable to it," President Hinckley said. "We are prone to take it for granted. It deserves more than this. It deserves the very best within us."[136]

The new Primary Children's Medical Center was then dedicated by President Gordon B. Hinckley on Thursday, May 17, 1990 on the top of the hill immediately west of the University of Utah Medical Center hospital overlooking the Salt Lake City skyline. The new four story hospital shined beautifully in its light peach and cream exterior facing.

The new hospital replaced the hospital built in 1952 on the avenues of northeast Salt Lake City. The dedication took place on the helipad on top of the facility with 450 in attendance.

Permanent Church Restoration Display

A permanent display of artifacts, original paintings and historical narrative of the restoration of the gospel of Jesus Christ in the Fullness of Times was completed on Thursday, May 17, 1990 at the LDS Church Museum of Art & History on the corner of West Temple and North Temple Streets in Salt Lake City.

The mass media were first shown the display including the original press upon which the first Book of Mormons were printed, the death masks of the prophet Joseph Smith, Jr. and his martyred elder brother Hyrum Smith and the pocket watch worn by John Taylor in the Carthage Jail which stopped a bullet from piercing his heart during the assault on the LDS leaders June 27, 1844.

Dublin, Ireland Missionary Killing

The almost 150 years since mobs had murdered Joseph Smith, Jr. and his brother Hyrum Smith, LDS missionaries were still in the same perils. Another LDS full-time missionary was stabbed to death by an 18 year old assailant as he and his companion returned to their flat in Dublin, Ireland May 27. President Hinckley spoke at Elder Gale Stanley Critchfield's funeral on June 2 in Payson, Utah. At the end of the services, President Hinckley could be seen embracing the slain elder's younger brother Scott.

"All we know for certainty is that death is not the end, that life continues. We lay aside our mortal bodies, yes. But all of the accumulated learning of all the days of our lives goes with us," President Hinckley said. "I am satisfied that the labors of a good missionary are never completed. There is such a tremendous work, so much greater work beyond the veil than there is here on earth."[137]

President Benson Hospitalized

As LDS prophet Ezra Taft Benson was put in intensive care at the LDS hospital for a bacterial infection, President Hinckley spoke to the largest ever mission presidents seminar of 124 with spouses June 19-22, 1990.

"Lose yourselves in the work so that your lives might be filled with light," President Hinckley counselled. "You husbands and wives must become great exemplars before your missionaries in following this standard. It is a constant challenge to keep the eye of the missionary on the glory of Him whom he serves."

Speaking of missionaries he said, "This Church is producing men of tremendous quality and accomplishment all over the world. They are being recognized far and wide for their abilities . . . . The roots of their accomplishments in so very many cases are found in the habits they acquired while serving as missionaries."[138]

On Saturday, September 15, 1990, President Hinckley spoke to 2,000 about a dark day in LDS history when some Arkansas immigrants passing through Southern Utah were massacred by some local native Americans from the Paiute tribe supported by some misguided LDS pioneers. In order to heal the wounds of that tragic day in September 1857, President Hinckley spoke of the peaceful "Mountain Meadows" Valley where the killings occurred and where John D. Lee, an LDS convert, was executed by a firing squad for involvement.

A new plaque was placed on a new marker setting forth a straight forward account of the tragedy without casting blame. President Hinckley said the events which occurred are "something we do not and cannot understand" on this "hallowed ground."

With severe headaches and swallowing difficulty, LDS prophet Ezra Taft Benson was hospitalized again on September 18, 1990, this time for subdural hematomas. He had not recovered by general conference time on October 5 and was suffering gastrointestinal bleeding, also. He underwent two subdural hematoma operations on September 19 and September 23, the second when one hematoma re-formed. He had not missed a general conference up to this time but hadn't personally talked at conference since 1988.[139]

Number 1 City in US for Business

Salt Lake City received some national and international attention when *Fortune* magazine named the growing metropolis the number one city in which to do business among all US cities.[140] President and Sister Hinckley attended a luncheon on October 5 on the 26th floor of the Church Office Building honoring Prime Minister Tofilan E. Alesana and his wife Pitoula from Western Samoa. Three of the 12 LDS apostles and spouses were also there as President Thomas S. Monson conducted. President Hinckley was presented a large kava bowl for placement in the Church Museum of Art & History. Reciprocal gifts were given to the prime minister and expressions of gratitude extended by both President Hinckley and President Monson to the prime minister for all the kindnesses his government extends to LDS missionaries laboring in his nation.

President Hinckley presided over the general LDS conference which began Saturday, October 6, 1990 with President Benson in serious but stable condition in the intensive care unit of the LDS Hospital. He quoted President Benson's past addresses. President Hinckley always delicately observed the prophet's position.

President Hinckley spoke of his beliefs regarding "counselors" in the Kingdom of God. He stated they were partners and provided a safety valve, sometimes acting as proxy but they "should never move ahead of the leader." He said, "A leader chooses his own counselors because they must be compatible. He must have absolute confidence in them. They must have absolute confidence in him. They must work together in a spirit of mutual trust and respect."[141]

The Sunday morning session of conference heard President Hinckley talk about the motto "Mormon means 'more' good." Such a thought when we remember the man "Mormon" would strengthen family lives, bring more tolerance, bring more mutual respect and foster more helpfulness.

Ambassadorial Functions

October 15, 1990 found President Hinckley meeting the Ambassador from Iceland Ingni S. Invarsson. Then he spoke at the BYU Devotional the next day. It was one of the largest crowds ever—13,577. The visiting Ambassador from Uganda Stephen K. Katenta-Apuli visited LDS Church Headquarters on October 18. Then President Hinckley gave the dedicatory prayer for the new law offices of the Church's general counsel and firm Kirton, McConkie & Poelman on the 17th & 18th floors of the Eagle Gate Tower on Tuesday, November 6, 1990. Describing the relationship between the Church and the law firm "would be integrity," President Hinckley said.

Next he spoke with President Thomas S. Monson at the funeral of former Deseret News general manager O. Preston Robinson. Robinson had married Gordon B. Hinckley's older sister Christine Hinckley. Christine had been bed ridden several years and at the services on Tuesday, November 13, 1990, President Hinckley expressed appreciation for Preston Robinson's devoted care for his sister.

President Hinckley became the first member of an LDS First Presidency to visit Portugal in December 1990 at a regional conference in Lisbon. Elders Richard G. Scott and Spencer Condie accompanied him with their wives. An assembly of 3,500 attended. Poland's election selected Walesa as president and Romania discontinued communism the same month.

Then in January, President Hinckley presided at two regional conferences in Arizona with Elder David B. Haight of the 12 and wife accompanying him. The Phoenix North and West regions met in the Sundome in Sun City, Arizona on Sunday, January 13, 1991.

Sister Marjorie Hinckley spoke at the conferences about hearing President Heber J. Grant speak once repeating the word "comfort" over and over again in his talk. She spoke of a young boy she knew, now a young man in a tank division being deployed to the Gulf War in Saudi Arabia who received comfort from his mother when he skinned his knee as a child and who hugged him when he flew to see her to say good-bye.

In the condominium where the Hinckleys now reside, many others live of her same age. The relief society president of her ward was 80 years old but still goes around "giving comfort to those in need of it." Prayer is the ultimate comfort, Sister Hinckley told the audience.

President Hinckley assured the congregations, President Benson is, "reasonably well for 91. He dresses himself every day, and attends the Presidency meetings some days. He is the prophet and nothing is done without his approval. We singly must do the work we need to do."[142]

Family Prayer

President Hinckley's First Presidency message in the *Ensign* magazine of February 1991 focused on "family prayer." He saw a billboard once which said "A nation at prayer is a nation at peace." He believed in this.

James H. Moyle made a statement to his grandchildren concerning the family prayers held in Brother Moyle's boyhood home. It always impressed President Hinckley. Mr. Moyle's statement said: "We have not gone to bed before kneeling in prayer to supplicate divine guidance and approval. Differences may arise in the best governed families, but they will be dissipated by the . . . spirit of prayer . . . . Its very psychology tends to promote the more righteous life among men. It tends to unity, love, forgiveness, to service."[143]

The Bountiful Regional Center was re-dedicated by President Hinckley on Sunday, February 3, 1991 after additional modification. Then he spoke two days later at the Tuesday LDS Business College Devotional. "This is a great and marvelous age in which to be alive," he said. The Gulf War was raging at the time. "This isn't the darkest period in the history of the world. It is the best. This is the greatest age in the history of the world and you are a part of it. What a wonderful and tremendous thing that is."[144]

Former President Ronald Reagan visited the LDS Church headquarters once again on Friday, February 1991. He had left the office of the presidency in 1988. The meeting lasted 45 minutes at the Church Administration Building North Board Room in Salt Lake City. Then the former US president visited Brigham Young University as a forum assembly speaker at the invitation of university president Rex E. Lee, USA Solicitor General from 1981-1985.[145]

Tempe & Mesa Regional Conferences

Sister Hinckley spoke along with President Hinckley before 14,000 at the Arizona State University Activity Center at Tempe and Mesa regional conferences on Sunday, February 17, 1991. The capacity crowd was double the number who could fit in the Salt Lake Temple Square Tabernacle.

The regional representative seminar in April 1991 was themed to "simplicity." "When all is said and done, our goals are relatively simple and straightforward. Our procedures in achieving those goals ought likewise to be simple and straightforward."[146] The success of the first year of unit budget allowances was also discussed. President Hinckley remarked, "There can be an increase of faith in simple activities that will not result from more costly and elaborate activities."

On June 8, 1991, the Tabernacle Choir started a 21 day tour to Hungary, Austria, Czechoslovakia, Poland and the Soviet Union for the first time. They also visited three other nations in Europe.

The Ellen "Nellie" Pucell Monument was dedicated on the Southern Utah University campus in Cedar City, Utah by President Hinckley on August 3, 1991. She was an unsung heroine who lost her feet to frostbite while crossing the plains. "I know it's hot here today," President Hinckley said. "That's good. It's good to suffer a little on an occasion of this kind as a reminder of those who suffered so terribly, so deeply."[147]

Dressed in college commencement robes, President Hinckley conducted the summer graduation exercises at BYU on August 15, 1991. Four days later, communists made their last ditch efforts to avert freedom in Russia by kidnapping Gorbechev and his wife. On August 21 the kidnappers either surrendered or committed suicide. On the 1st day of September 1991, LDS Church membership increased to 8,000,000.

Visit by US President George Bush

Elaine J. Jack was introduced to US President George Bush in Salt Lake City on September 18, 1991 by President Hinckley. Said he, "This woman presides over 3 million women in well over a hundred nations." President Bush was impressed.[148] Ten days later, President Hinckley spoke to the general women's meeting for women 12 years of age and older.

A Mother in Heaven

"Logic and reason would certainly suggest that if we have a Father in Heaven, we have a Mother in Heaven. That doctrine rests well with me," President Hinckley quoted from an address given before regional representatives in April 1991. "However, in light of the instruction we have received from the Lord Himself, I consider it inappropriate for anyone in the Church to pray to our Mother in Heaven. I suppose those who use this expression and who try to further its use, are well-meaning, but they are misguided. The fact that we do not pray to our Mother in Heaven in no way belittles or denigrates her."[149]

Following general conference, President Hinckley was at the Missionary Training Center in Provo, Utah on October 25, 1991 breaking ground for the new three building addition to be built there.

November 3, 1991 he spoke to 285 LDS students from UCLA and USC campuses in California at a devotional service. The smaller audience allowed President Hinckley to speak softly, almost intimately, to the students. He spoke of the National Debt of the United States and compared it to bankruptcy in moral values in America.

He told the students the Lord did not justify himself when he wrote the 10 Commandments. There are moral attributes which are absolute. "You who have come to earth in this dispensation, be true, be faithful, be decent, be honest, be virtuous, be worthy of the tremendous birthright that is yours," President Hinckley taught.[150]

George Washington Honor Medal

On November 8, 1991, President Hinckley was given the George Washington Honor Medal for public communications in bringing about a better understanding and appreciation of the United States and its principles of human dignity and freedom in President Hinckley's address to the Sons of the American Revolution about the Bill of Rights on May 4. On December 1, 1991, freedom continued to be declared in the former Soviet Union when the Ukraine declared independence.

President Hinckley spoke of the Messiah at the First Presidency Christmas Devotional on December 1.

"Particularly at this Christmas season, we remember Him with a special sense of gratitude. We look to Him with love as the ideal we seek to emulate. Our efforts are stumbling and awkward and so often result in failure because of our selfishness, our greed, our pride, our arrogance. But we try. And the world is better for our effort."[151]

Two days later, President Hinckley received the Queen of Tonga Mala`aho at the Salt Lake City church headquarters. Also the Book of Mormon tied with 6th & 7th place as the most influential book in America in the Book of the Month Club poll in 1991.

Joseph Smith Symposium

February 22, 1992 President Hinckley spoke to a 2,500 overflow crowd at the Joseph Smith Auditorium at Brigham Young University. "I thank and love the Prophet," he told his audience. "I grew up in an environment of appreciation for the Prophet. I am now growing old and I know that in the natural course of events before many years, I will step across the threshold to stand before my Maker and my Lord and give an accounting of my life. And I hope that I shall have the opportunity of embracing the Prophet Joseph Smith and of thanking him and of speaking of my love for him"[152]

The next month, President Hinckley wrote in the March 1992 *Ensign* First Presidency message about the 150th anniversary of the relief society organization founded in Nauvoo, Illinois two years before Joseph Smith, Jr.'s death. He stated he believed the relief society to be the largest, most efficient organization of its kind in the world dedicated to acts of charity.

At his BYU 18 Stake Fireside at Provo, Utah on Sunday, March 1, 1992, President Hinckley revealed his 10 beliefs. "Behavior is governed by beliefs," he said, as he listed his personal 10. They were belief in: 1. the wonders of the human body and the miracle of the human mind, 2. beauty, 3. work, 4. honesty, 5. service, 6. family as the most important unit in society, 7. thrift, 8. myself, 9. God and His Beloved Son, and 10. prayer.[153]

President Hinckley was with Elder M. Russell Ballard and Elder Spencer W. Condie in Madrid, Spain on March 7 & 8, 1992 for a regional conference. Then on March 24, 1992, he spoke at the funeral of Edward Y. Okazaki, a former mission president in the late 1960's in Japan. The returned missionaries from his mission in Kobe/Okinawa sang the opening song in Japanese at the Salt Lake Wasatch Stake Center at Noon.

Said President Hinckley, "This has been a very interesting service—the opening numbers by these returned missionaries sung in Japanese and the singing of the Hawaiian love songs we will hear, songs of fire and affection. I was very interested to listen to a bishop with a Polish name and see him pronounce these names in Japanese. [laugh from audience] You did very well. [another heartier laugh from the audience]

"As I was with the family in the other room, I thought how wonderful, how sweet that a man can leave behind sons who can speak with authority by the power of the priesthood to walk in the example of their father as a guide in their lives."[154]

Three days later, he was speaking at the funeral of his long time friend Jay Ambrose Quealy, Jr. "I look at these beautiful flowers on his pier, these roses which speak of love, these beautiful lilies that speak of Easter and the resurrection, and still as remarkably these magnificent leis which come out of the spirit of Hawaii, the spirit of love, the spirit of Aloha, the spirit of kindness and goodness . . . .," President Hinckley said as his voice cracked and tears and emotion halted his speech for 19 seconds. ". . . . . deep and strong affection, ardent.

"I'm growing old and my friends are dying, and he was one of them. His love and respect will live on and be admired. I will miss him."[155]

117th Ricks College Commencement

Three members of the 12 LDS apostles and three of the 70 plus President Monson accompanied President Hinckley to the 117th Ricks College commencement. It is interesting that Henry B. Eyring spoke along with some concluding remarks by President Hinckley. He had been president of Ricks from 1972 to 1977 and was former LDS Commissioner of Education. In 1995, President Hinckley, as new 15th prophet of the LDS Church, called Henry B. Eyring to be an LDS apostle.

On several occasions it appears presidency over one of the LDS educational institutions has served as a grooming ground for future LDS apostles.

Bountiful Handcart Days were celebrated on July 19, 1992 in the Bountiful LDS Regional Center where President Hinckley spoke. Then on July 20, 1992 he visited Toronto, Ontario, Canada with the LDS Tabernacle Choir. An audience of 13,087 attended.

Hurricane Andrew caused significant damage in Florida from August 23 to 26, 1992. Then presidential candidate Bill Clinton stopped for 20 minutes at LDS headquarters September 15 and was presented with a porcelain sea gull, symbol of the event shortly after the first LDS pioneers entered the Salt Lake Valley. Sea gulls saved their crops from destruction by crickets. Clinton expressed appreciation for LDS Church help given victims of the Florida hurricane. President Hinckley responded by explaining the LDS practice of fasting and offering the unused value of the two meals or more for relief of the poor.

The 500th anniversary of Columbus' voyage to America was celebrated on October 12, 1992. Once again, President Hinckley substituted for President Benson as the speaker at the beginning devotional of the BYU school year on October 13. His voice, however, was hoarse from speaking at general conference and he said he was without subject matter. "How did I ever agree to come here today?" he asked himself. But he still performed.

President Hinckley left for a regional conference in London and rededication of the London and Swiss LDS temples on October 15. Recently he had read the dual biographies of Robert E. Lee and Ulysses S. Grant, the two major generals of the US Civil War.

During December 1992, President Hinckley remarked he had seen 100's of statues and paintings of great men and women of history. But no man was greater in his eyes than Jesus the Christ. On the 1st of December, also, the LDS Church reached 20,000 wards and branches. Church leaders toured Welfare Square, the LDS Church center for welfare services, the next day with President Hinckley and President Monson. They visited the sorting center for used items, the LDS social services office, and the employment center, all designed to aid in assisting LDS saints in need.

At the First Presidency fireside on December 6, 1992, President Hinckley conducted and spoke along with a speech by President Thomas S. Monson. President Hinckley reflected in March 1993 he almost every day has been able while living in Salt Lake City to feast on the Salt Lake Temple's architectural beauty. The temple turned 100 years old in April of that year.

April 9, 1993 found President Hinckley once again substituting for President Ezra Taft Benson due to President Benson's poor health. The new Science Center to be named in LDS prophet Benson's name was officially started with ground breaking ceremonies. Henry B. Eyring was also present three seats to the right of President Hinckley.

Said President Hinckley, "The fact is that you can't stand still. In the world in which we live, you have to keep up with the world; in fact, you have to stay a little ahead. That's the purpose of this building, a science building, in which primarily chemistry will be taught."[156]

Two daughters of President Ezra Taft Benson as well as President Monson, US Senator from Utah Orrin Hatch, and BYU president Rex E. Lee each wielded a shovel along with President Hinckley as the ground was turned.

Social Hall Memorial Walkway

The foundations of the historic Social Hall built by the LDS pioneers just a few years after the first group arrived in the Salt Lake Valley were uncovered during construction of an underpass across State Street to the ZCMI Center and refurbished and made part of the walkway. On June 9, 1993, President Hinckley dedicated the facility. He read a stanza from "Praise to the Man" in his speech, halting with emotion at times.[157]

Then it was speaking at the largest mission presidents seminar in history on June 22, 1993, one day before President Hinckley turned age 83.

The Joseph Smith Memorial Building

The Church was getting ready to dedicate the newly renovated Hotel Utah and the edifice needed a new name. It was originally thought to name it Utah Plaza but a new skyscraper on Main Street had taken almost the identical name and to avoid confusion, another title was sought.

President Hinckley was unable to sleep. Then he gazed out a window from his condominium overlooking the Salt Lake Temple. Inspiration came that the structure ought to be named in honor of the prophet Joseph Smith, Jr. There was another Joseph Smith Memorial Building on the BYU campus but that would not detract. In fact, it would enhance the memory of the great prophet.

He thought then he wished a building named after Joseph Smith could be in every city. So President Hinckley took the idea to his co-counselor Thomas S. Monson and he approved. The Quorum of the 12's approval was similarly given and the name "Joseph Smith Memorial Building" replaced the name of the old Hotel Utah.[158]

On the 149th anniversary of the martyrdom of Joseph Smith, Jr., the Joseph Smith Memorial Building was dedicated by President Hinckley who also conducted and spoke at the dedication on June 27, 1993. A large statue of the prophet Joseph Smith which had been in storage for a long time was brought out of moth balls and placed on the west side of the lobby of what used to be the most elegant hotel in the State of Utah.

In his First Presidency message of October 1993, President Hinckley told how he had seen time and time again love of God bridging the chasm of fear. That month, he went to BYU with Marjorie and dedicated the new art museum at BYU which Rex E. Lee had asked be constructed from private contributions. The task had been accomplished and now BYU and the communities in Utah County had another museum of art in which to display antiquities and masterpieces from around the globe.

The Solo First Presidency Christmas Devotional

On December 5, 1993, President Hinckley visited President Ezra Taft Benson and then Thomas S. Monson about 5 P.M. Both were unable to attend the Christmas devotional. Elder Boyd K. Packer was asked to substitute for President Monson's speech while Gordon B. Hinckley presided and addressed the satellite broadcast from the Temple Square Tabernacle. President Hinckley read from the scriptures.

"As most of you know," President Hinckley said, "I have spoken a number of times on these occasions concerning the Lord whom I love. Tonight I wish to let Him speak for Himself."

He then read selections from the Standard Works of the LDS religion as Christmas music was played in the background.[159]

The account of the Savior visiting the Nephites following his resurrection was first read from the Book of Mormon in 3rd Nephi 1:13-14. Then the account of his birth was explained as found in Luke 2:40. Then passages regarding his life were read from the Bible.

"Behold your Little Ones" was a special satellite broadcast aired January 23, 1994 regarding the holy accountability to raise children in love and truth. Anger, abject selfishness and the worst form of evil towards children must be replaced with "an increased awareness of the terrible offense toward God, our Eternal Father, that is given whenever a child is made to suffer," said President Hinckley.[160]

The BYU combined stake fireside now included 19 separate stakes when President Hinckley spoke to the studentbody on March 6, 1994 about being positive. Four days later, the new additions to the Missionary Training Center were dedicated by President Hinckley before an assembly of 3,000. TV monitors were required in overflow rooms on March 10, 1994. The Hall of Fame plaque from the University of Idaho Alumni Association was received on behalf of Ezra Taft Benson by Presidents Hinckley and Monson in the First Presidency Board Room in Salt Lake on May 13, 1994. The two counselors presented it personally to President Benson in his apartment later. The 27th of May, President Hinckley was awarded the Silver Buffalo award from the Boy Scouts of America National Convention in Salt Lake for his influence on youth and exemplary service.[161]

President Ezra Taft Benson died May 30, 1994 at the age of 94. In the interim between his passing and reorganization of the First Presidency, President Hinckley moved ahead with his baccalaureate address to the graduates of Southern Utah University in Cedar City on June 3, 1994. Then on June 5, 1994, Howard W. Hunter was ordained 14th LDS prophet, Gordon B. Hinckley was set apart as President of the Quorum of the 12 and 1st counselor and Thomas S. Monson was set apart as 2nd counselor. Elder Boyd K. Packer was set apart as acting President of the Council of the Twelve, he being next in seniority to Thomas S. Monson. The two senior members of the 12 were thus taken into the First Presidency.

On June 26, 1994, a Sunstone from the original Nauvoo Temple was unveiled at Nauvoo, Illinois. It had been carved by the early Latter-day Saints in the early 1840's together with several others attached to the temple. A commemoration of the 150th anniversary of the death of the prophet Joseph Smith, Jr. was held the following day. The Minuteman Award was given to President Hinckley two days later at the Little America Hotel in ceremonies of the 33rd Annual Awards Banquet June 29, 1994.

July 2, 1994 found President Hinckley back just seven miles south of Nauvoo, Illinois at Boy Scout Camp Eastman. There he spoke to a group of young women from St. Paul Minnesota Stake. July 25, 1994, a statue of Brigham Young was unveiled to sit in the Capitol Rotunda in Washington, D.C. It was one of two statues allowed from each of the 50 states of the Union displayed there.

A 5 stake fireside was packed with an overflow crowd at Ricks College in Rexburg, Idaho on Sunday evening, August 28, 1994 where President Hinckley gave his "5 Be's" to the group—Be grateful, be smart, be clean, be true, be humble.

On January 4, 1995, President Hinckley stated the Latter-day Saints must become "more acceptable of the destiny among its people." LDS prophet Howard W. Hunter revealed he was suffering from cancer immediately after dedicating the Bountiful LDS Temple on January 8, 1995. Less than two months following this statement, President Howard W. Hunter passed away on Friday, March 3, and the keys of the Kingdom according to Latter-day Saint beliefs fell upon the body of the Council of the 12. With Gordon B. Hinckley the senior apostle in that body, the burden of direction fell upon his shoulders.

March 8, 1995 the general authorities and a packed Tabernacle witnessed the vacant chair of Howard W. Hunter and a somber faced President Hinckley sat in white long sleeved shirt, tie and dark suit coat in the chair immediately to the right of the chair for the prophet. It was memorial services for President Howard W. Hunter, 87½ years old at time of passing. President Hinckley praised President Hunter for his devotion to the truth and his testimonies of the Savior. In four days, President Hinckley would sit in President Hunter's chair as 15th LDS prophet.

PROPHET

Gordon B. Hinckley, now 84¾ years old, was not idle. Two days following Pres. Hunter's funeral on March 10, 1995, he spoke at the Eudora W. Durham's funeral at Bonneville Stake, Yalecrest 2nd Ward.

On March 12, 1995, the 14 remaining LDS apostles met in the Salt Lake Temple to reorganize the First Presidency. President Gordon B. Hinckley had hands of all of the remaining 13 apostles placed upon his head and Thomas S. Monson, acting as mouth, ordained him as the 15th prophet of The Church of Jesus Christ of Latter-day Saints.

President Hinckley chose President Thomas S. Monson as 1st counselor and Elder James E. Faust as 2nd. Elder Faust had been an assistant to the twelve from 1972 to 1976, one of the 7 presidents of the 70 from 1976 to 1978 and an LDS apostle since then. He was past Utah Bar president, lawyer, and long time friend of President Hinckley.

Thomas S. Monson was set apart as President of the Quorum of the Twelve, being senior member in the quorum and Elder Boyd K. Packer as Acting President of the Quorum of the Twelve as next in seniority among the LDS apostles. Ordination date and age determined seniority.

Monday, March 13, 1995, President Hinckley, the master communicator, moved the normal new presidency press conference from its usual place at the Church Administration Building in Salt Lake to the Joseph Smith Memorial Building lobby. The new First Presidency and President Packer were seated at a table strategically located immediately in front of the large statue of Joseph Smith, Jr. in the middle west side lobby area. Press and other invited guests were located to the east of the main table.

President Hinckley then entered into a press conference lengthier than any held for decades. First President Hinckley, dressed in long sleeve white shirt, tie, dark suit, and white handkerchief in his left suit coat pocket, stood and read a prepared statement before a microphone.

"Thank you for your presence this morning, and thank you for the manner in which you handled the passing of our beloved friend and leader, Howard W. Hunter. His death has deeply affected all of us. The memories of his great virtues will long linger with us.

"One cannot come to this sacred office without almost overwhelming feelings of inadequacy. Strengthened resolution to go forward comes from the knowledge that this is the work of God, that He is watching over it, that He will direct us in our efforts if we will be true and faithful, and that our accountability is to Him.

Administration Block, Salt Lake City, Utah
From State Street Looking Northwest on South Temple Street
Where Gordon Bitner Hinckley Spent 60 Years of His Life
Before Being Called as 15th Prophet of the LDS Church

l. to r. Old Utah Hotel (now Joseph Smith Memorial Building), Administration Building (Home of Offices of the LDS First Presidency and Quorum of the Twelve Apostles), Lion House and Beehive House

"With that assurance we reach out to our own people and to those of good will throughout the world, in that spirit of love and brotherhood which comes from the Lord Jesus Christ . . . .

"As the Church moves forward on its divinely appointed mission, I do not anticipate any dramatic change in course. Procedures and programs may be altered from time to time, but the doctrine remains constant. We are dedicated, as have been those before us, to teaching the gospel of peace, to the promotion of civility and mutual respect among people everywhere, to bearing witness to the living reality of our Lord Jesus Christ, and to the practice of His teachings in our daily lives."[1]

President Hinckley said quality of family life is a concern. He said they were grateful for faithful Latter-day Saints, then numbering 9,000,000 in 150 nations. They were proud of their youth. "I think we have never had a stronger generation of young men and women than we have today," he remarked. He then asked for forgiveness of any he or the others had offended and expressed "our only desire is to cultivate a spirit of mercy and kindness, of understanding and healing. We seek to follow the practice of our Lord who 'went about doing good.'"

"Carry On"

After short extemporaneous statements from Presidents Monson and Faust, questions were entertained for 30 minutes. In response to various questions, President Hinckley displayed his characteristic familiarity, humor and astute diplomacy. He stood with the tips of his fingers of both hands touching the table top in front of him.

To a question regarding his health, he said he had been in a hospital so far just once—overnight at age 75. "That doesn't mean I am ready to run a 100-yard dash," he added.

To a question regarding the LDS Church's greatest challenge, he replied "growth." To a question regarding travel, President Hinckley said he didn't like it much, but "we want to get out with the people. It is important for us to meet with the people and feel of their pulse, out across the world. And they do great things for us. And we hope that it will be of some benefit to them."

To a question regarding the theme of his presidency, he spontaneously responded, "Carry on," a favorite Latter-day Saint hymn.

He said the best ingredient for youth to be successful is education of mind and hands, "the family is the basic element of society", and the Church will go through the front door of all nations as soon as proper government authority allows. Leaders needed can be found everywhere.

The young women's general meeting was held March 25, 1995 where President Hinckley's second daughter Virginia H. Pearce spoke as 1st Counselor in the YWMIA General Presidency and President Hinckley spoke last. Satellite carried the proceedings to North America.

"My beloved associates in this great work, you wonderful young women and your mothers," the LDS prophet began. He said he was not a scheduled speaker but welcomed the opportunity to say a few words.

In past years when he and Marjorie "were much younger and less stiff and brittle" they danced to a 1932 tune "Somebody Loves You." Following marriage, President Hinckley didn't do much dancing. He loved his wife's company "more than I enjoyed the dancing." he said.

But he desired to tell the young ladies he loved them. Their Father in Heaven loved them. And God desired his Spirit to be near them wherever if they "invite it and cultivate it."[2]

"Some of you may feel that you are not as attractive and beautiful and glamorous as you would like to be. Rise above any such feelings, cultivate the light you have within you, and it will shine through as a radiant expression that will be seen by others."[3]

Young women never need feel inferior, he said. Just try a little harder. "Awake and arouse your faculties," as Alma said. (Alma 32.27)

Implementing His Expressed Beliefs

The traditional Solemn Assembly of the entire LDS faith sustaining a new LDS prophet was convened during the Saturday morning session of LDS general conference in Salt Lake City, Utah on April 1, 1995.

President Thomas S. Monson read the name of Gordon B. Hinckley for sustaining vote as prophet, seer and revelator of The Church of Jesus Christ of Latter-day Saints. All right hands raised. Elder Henry B. Eyring replaced the vacant LDS apostle spot.

"I do not know why in His grand scheme one such as I would find a place," President Hinckley said shortly after stepping to the pulpit in the Salt Lake Tabernacle in the Saturday afternoon session of conference for the first time as a sustained LDS prophet.

"But having this mantle come upon me, I now rededicate whatever I have of strength or time or talent or life to the work of my Master in the service of my brethren and sisters."[4]

"We are becoming a great global society. But our interest and concern must always be with the individual . . . Out great responsibility is to see that each is 'remembered and nourished by the good word of

God' (Moroni 6:4), that each has opportunity for growth and expression and training in the work and ways of the Lord, that none lacks the necessities of life, that the needs of the poor are met, that each member shall have encouragement, training, and opportunity to move forward on the road of immortality and eternal life."

President Hinckley further counseled, "President Lee told us on more than one occasion to survey large fields and cultivate small ones.

"He was saying that we must know the big picture and then assiduously work on the particular niche assigned to each of us, and that in doing so we concentrate on the needs of the individual."[5]

Everyone can and may obtain a "strong and secure testimony" of the restored gospel and Jesus Christ, quoting the Messiah's promise in John 7:17. "Service in behalf of others, study, and prayer lead to faith in this work and then to knowledge of its truth. This has always been a personal pursuit, as it must always be in the future."[6]

Newly sustained President Hinckley ended his first general conference address as LDS prophet, seer and revelator with testimony of Christ after saying, "Now in conclusion, may I say that I glory in the wonderful, courageous, victorious past of this great work. I marvel at the present when you and I stand as watchmen upon the towers. I envision the future with hope, assurance, and certain faith."[7]

Two More Addresses at Conference

President Hinckley gave two more significant addresses during his first general conference as prophet. To the priesthood he said:

"Mine has been the special privilege to serve as a counselor to three great Presidents. I think I know something of the meaning of heavy responsibility," the new prophet said. President Hinckley was "overwhelmed with feelings of inadequacy and total dependence upon the Lord," the general authorities and world members. He realized the total import of his talk years ago on the loneliness of leadership. But he was resolute, and the mantle of the prophet shined upon him.

President Hinckley announced the replacement of "regional representative" with "area authority," high priests with church experience, residing at their homes with about six year terms of service. "They will be closely tied to the area presidencies," a fewer number.

D.&C. 107:98 gave authority: "Whereas other officers of the church, who belong not unto the Twelve, neither to the Seventy, are not under the responsibility to travel among all nations, . . . notwithstanding they may hold as high and responsible offices in the church."

He next reviewed inspirational points of his family heritage, and expressed his love for children and youth, for prayer in homes, and for the elderly "who have faced into the storms of life and who, regardless of the force of the tempest, have gone forward and kept the faith."

Callings were articulately defined and then he said, "The progress of this work will be determined by our joint efforts."[8]

The estranged from the Church, for whatever reason, were invited back to partake of happiness once known. Apology was expressed for any offence President Hinckley had made to anyone throughout his life.

"Now, my brethren and sisters, the time has come for us to stand a little taller, to lift our eyes and stretch our minds to a greater comprehension and understanding of the grand millennial mission of this The Church of Jesus Christ of Latter-day Saints," the prophet said.

It is a season to be strong, to move forward without hesitation, to do what is right regardless of the consequences, to be found keeping commandments, to reach out with kindness and love, to be considerate and good, decent and courteous toward one another in all relationships. In other words, "to become more Christlike."

Sunday, April 2, 1995, P.M., President Hinckley once more emphasized work. "The Church needs your strength. It needs your love and loyalty and devotion. It needs a little more of your time and energy," the prophet said. "I am not asking anyone to do so at the expense of your employer" or "at the expense of your families . . .

"But I am suggesting that we spend a little less time in idleness, in the fruitless pursuit of watching some inane and empty television programs. Time so utilized can be put to better advantage, and the consequences will be wonderful. Of that I do not hesitate to assure you."[9]

Off to the Saints

His personal dislike for travel, with jet lag and temporary quarters aside, desire to be among and strengthen the people took President Hinckley on numerous trips the next six months.

On April 15 and 16 he was with newly sustained LDS apostle Henry B. Eyring in St. Louis, Missouri visiting a six stake regional conference. He talked of the Savior and his resurrection on Easter Sunday. Anyone lacking a testimony could and had the obligation of getting a firm conviction of the truth by following John 17:17.

The St. Louis LDS temple site 20 miles west of St. Louis was visited also. He recalled the bitter cold day and frozen earth when he and President Monson had broken ground 1½ years ago for the temple.

President Hinckley was back in Utah on April 18 for presentation of the Exemplary Manhood Award to him by the students of BYU.

He was at the new center for the arts to be named Tuacahn by Snow Canyon State Park near St. George, Utah on April 23 dedicating the facility. Two hundred of the Tabernacle Choir also sang.

On June 12, 1995, President Hinckley broke ground for the Pioneer Handcart Park located just east of the northeast corner of Administration Block. City Creek resurfaced and flowed through it.

"This park is established to remind us of those who discovered this land," President Hinckley said. "This ground is broken as a reminder of those very difficult times."[10]

June 17th to the 23rd, 1995 found the prophet visiting Alaska, the first time an LDS prophet had visited that state. Seven thousand seven hundred members attended the regional conference in Anchorage at the Sullivan Arena on Sunday, June 18. In the afternoon, President Hinckley had his traditional missionary conference and fireside.

A fireside attended by 850 was held in the city of Juneau. The prophet greeted most of the 18 LDS members in the small branch in Gustavus on June 19. On Thursday, June 22, he delivered a fireside message in Ketchikan to 3,007. Marjorie accompanied him.[11]

"Be Willing and Obedient"

President Hinckley's initial First Presidency message in the *Ensign* as LDS prophet focused on willingness to follow the Lord and His prophets. The equivocating of King Saul in not being fully obedient to the Lord's commands was reviewed.

He told his readers that they may feel inadequate and assignments received may be difficult as was his assignment by his mission president to visit a publisher in England and ask him to correct the misimpression of a reprint of fiction made to appear history. He said he came to know "that when we try in faith to walk in obedience, . . . the Lord opens the way, even when there appears to be no way."[12]

The prophet was in Tacoma, Washington before some 17,328 on August 20 speaking to a regional conference. Elder Oaks and his wife and Elder Pace, a 70, and his wife were also present. President Hinckley tried to shake many hands during his visit. "I hope it conveys a sense of friendship and love and appreciation and respect," he said.[13]

"I wish my brothers and sisters, we could get more enthusiastic about temple work," he said. "Great are the promises of the Lord. The marvelous thing to me is that the Lord never asks us to do anything that He does not attach to it a blessing." He declared the progress, the prosperity and the happiness of the LDS people lies in following God's commands.[14]

President Hinckley commented he misses some of his privacy but you "can't have it with this assignment. So you make adjustments."[15] Overseas, he liked to speak in dedicated chapels rather than large halls. He said he felt a better response with the people as he spoke there.

International travel took him to England from August 25 to September 1, 1995. Canterbury Cathedral was visited August 25, also the silt filled Sandwich Port, once bustling, where ancestor Samuel Hinckley left with his family for America in the 1630's.

On August 26, he had a BBC interview, a missionary conference with London South Missionaries & a fireside in Crawley before 1,100.

Sunday, August 27 found him at the Wandsworth Stake Conference, the Maidstone Stake Conference, the creation of Canterbury Stake and setting apart three stake presidencies. But the day was not over until he traveled an hour to the rededication of the Hyde Park Chapel. That same day in America, his older sister Carol from the Johnson line passed away in Bountiful at 93. Rather than slowing down, President Hinckley was accelerating his pace even more than the day he dedicated two chapels in Okinawa and Taipei on the same day.

August 28, President Hinckley was at the London Temple, did two radio interviews, a missionary conference address at the London Mission and traveled two hours north. August 29 he toured three Church farms, traveled two hours to Solihull for missionary meetings and was at a conference at Harbourne with a fireside in the evening.

August 30 the prophet visited the Europe North Area offices in Solihull, spoke to employees in two separate devotionals, travelled to Nottingham and the small town of Hinckley with its ancient chapel. That evening he spoke at a fireside at the Nottingham Stake Center.

The group travelled northeast to Preston, England August 31, saw the temple site, President Hinckley's first missionary apartment, visited Bob Pickles in Nelson, and spoke at a Liverpool fireside to 1100.

September 1 the group visited the Maritime Museum at Albert Docks, Liverpool for a tour.[16] President and Sister Hinckley then flew to Ireland where they spoke to 160 missionaries and another 1100.

It was the first time since David O. McKay had visited in August 1953 that a member of the LDS First Presidency had been on Irish soil.

About 7,730 had heard the prophet's voice and seen him in person in the short week he had been in England. He gave 14 addresses.

"I'm so optimistic about this work," President Hinckley said.

"I have a great desire in my heart to get out among the people and to express my appreciation and my love and to leave a blessing upon them," he said in Dublin, Ireland. "I don't like long plane rides, but I love the people," he had said earlier at the Crawley, England fireside.[17]

Many members of the LDS faith wept. Area President Graham W. Doxey, said of the prophet's visit, "They love his humor and his being down to earth. He understands their problems, and you can just see that they are drinking in every thing that he said. It is a marvelous thing."[18]

"What touched us most was the way he talked about the Irish people and the way he spoke," said the Dublin Ireland Stake president. "He knew so much about our circumstances. It was special that he was here. He deeply touched the Irish people by the way he spoke to us."[19]

Sister and Missionary Friend's Funerals

Before his jet lag could hardly wear off, President Hinckley was speaking at Wendell J. Ashton's, funeral in SLC on September 4. "I know of no other single individual during my lifetime who has done more for the good of this community than has he," said the prophet.

Brother Ashton and President Hinckley had served in the same mission in the 1930's at the same time where Wendell edited the British LDS Church magazine the *Millennial Star*. President Hinckley had come back and began work in mass communications work for the LDS Church and Brother Ashton also became involved in journalism.

The next day President Hinckley was speaking at his older sister Carol Hinckley Cannon's funeral at Colonial Hills LDS 2nd Ward.

Visit of the Ambassador from Japan

The Ambassador of Japan Takakazu Kuruyama and his wife Masako visited with the LDS First Presidency on September 11, 1995 in Salt Lake City and then the First Presidency issued a proclamation to the world at the Women's Conference on September 23, 1995 reaffirming the family and urging LDS members to study and be careful, thoughtful and prayerful. Such proclamations had been made by First Presidencies on important subjects in years past.

On September 28, President Hinckley was awarded the Distinguished Service to Humanity Award from the Association of Mormon Counselors and Psychotherapists. On September 29, 1995, President Hinckley declared the call of president of the Church is different from counselor "because you have total reliance on the Lord."

Fall LDS General Conference

The second general LDS conference of President Hinckley's presidency gathered September 30-October 1, 1995. At the general priesthood session, President Hinckley displayed a "widow's mite" given him by David B. Galbraith. He keeps it as a reminder that we are dealing with the consecration of the widow as well as the wealthy.

He gave a masterful discourse on benefits of missionary work, temples, and the state of the Church.

Sunday, President Hinckley talked of broad vision, of involvement, of liveliness. He scorned the indifferent, the narrow thinking and those busily doing nothing of positive advancement. "This gospel is good news. It is a message of triumph. It is a cause to embrace with enthusiasm," the prophet said. "The Lord never said there would not be troubles . . . But faith has shown through all . . . sorrows."[20]

President Hinckley marvelled at the faith of the early emigrants from Liverpool, England, tens of thousands of them, who walked over the stone walks at Liverpool Harbor to their ships for an unknown land. He "could scarcely comprehend the magnitude of Brigham Young's faith in leading thousands of people into the wilderness."

"Today we walk in the sunlight of goodwill. There is a tendency on the part of some to become indifferent . . . . This is His work. Never forget it. Embrace it with enthusiasm and affection. Let us not be afraid. Jesus is our leader, our strength, and our king."

Reaffirm faith. Strengthen it by the manner you live. "How glorious is the past of this great cause. It is filled with heroism, courage, boldness, and faith. How wondrous is the present as we move forward to bless the lives of people wherever they will hearken to the message of the servants of the Lord. How magnificent will be the future . . . .

"To me it is exciting. It is wonderful . . . . I invite every one of you, wherever you may be as members of this church, to stand on your feet and with a song in your heart move forward, living the gospel, loving the Lord, and building the kingdom. Together we shall stay the course and keep the faith, the Almighty being our strength. In the name of Jesus Christ, amen."[21]

Church Donation to Huntsman Cancer Institute

On October 2, the LDS Church donated $1,000,000 to Huntsman Cancer Institute and President Hinckley made remarks at the U of U. He also dedicated the Brigham Young Historic and City Creek Park.

The subject of faith and certitude was taken as President Hinckley's First Presidency message in the October *Ensign*. The majority of the text was taken from his earlier address to the BYU studentbody years before. He took exception to one writer that "Certitude is the enemy of religion." President Hinckley said, "Certitude, which I define as complete and total assurance, is not the enemy of religion. It is of its very essence." Then he quoted prophets and cited John 7:17 again.[22]

Surprise Visits

On Sunday, October 15, 1995 the 35 members of the Promontory Branch in Promontory, Utah, at the north of the Great Salt Lake, were excited with a surprise visit by President Hinckley and his wife Marjorie. "I'm here to keep my word," the prophet said. He had met the branch president Brent H. Larsen at a meeting on May 10, 1994, never knew a branch existed at Promontory and said, "I'll visit you one day." The hymn, "We Thank Thee O God, for a Prophet" was sung for the opening song. Almost everyone was in tears.[23]

The next day a large group of African Americans marched in Washington, D.C. in the "Million Man March." On October 17, the LDS prophet spoke at a BYU devotional honoring retiring university president Rex E. Lee. The audience laughed when he said, "[President Lee] has even brought a smile to the rock-jawed visage of [BYU football coach] LaVell Edwards."

"What does the Church expect of each of us—you and me? It expects the kind of behavior which has been exemplified in the life of the man of whom I have spoken today . . . . We have a mandate to work at it, to keep trying constantly to improve."[24]

Then on October 19, 1995, Wallace B. Smith, current president of the Reorganized Church, visited President Gordon B. Hinckley in the President's Board Room at Church headquarters. This was a monumental feat, a furtherance of mutual respect fostered by Gordon.

The Reorganized Church is a splinter group of about 243,000 from the LDS Church formed about 20 years after the death of the prophet Joseph Smith, Jr.[25]

President Hinckley then dedicated the Ezra Taft Benson Science Building at BYU October 20, 1995. The building was "dedicated to the cause of chemistry, to explore the great secrets of the mighty Creator. I doubt there is anything superior to it in all the world. I wonder what the Curies and the Pasteurs would have thought of this."[26]

The next day a third runway opened at the Salt Lake City

International Airport.

President Hinckley next surprised the Magna South Stake on Sunday, October 22, 1995 with a visit during their conference. Only the stake president knew he was coming. "I did not come here to preach," the LDS prophet said. "I just came to tell you that I love you."[27]

President William R. Walker's stake in Sandy, Utah was also visited. Only the stake president knew in advance he was visiting. President Walker had been one of those thousands of missionaries interviewed by then Elder Hinckley in the late 1960's in Japan. At the time Elder Hinckley had told Bill Walker and the other assistant to the mission president W. Emery Smith, "Get ready to be stake presidents." Both elders had since served as mission presidents in Japan and now Bill Walker was in deed a "stake president."

Next on November 8, 1995 President Hinckley made an unannounced visit to Beehive Clothing Mills, the LDS Church owned temple clothing factory. "Thank you for all you do, and may the Lord bless you and your families," President Hinckley said.

"I think it's a great honor and so exciting to see the living prophet of God right here. It's wonderful!" said receiving clerk Sandra Balle.[28]

Visit at White House with US President Clinton

American President Bill Clinton invited President Hinckley to come visit the White House after hearing about the recent LDS First Presidency proclamation on the family. President Hinckley accepted and arranged a trip to visit missionaries, the president and prominent executives beginning November 12. A lot precipitated from that visit.

The meeting with the full-time missionaries was held first. Elder Neal A. Maxwell, chairman of the Executive Committee on Public Affairs, was also present. President Hinckley told the missionaries, "You never can foretell the consequences of your service as a missionary. Don't get discouraged.

"Do you know what an ambassador plenipotentiary is? One with full powers and authority granted by his government to act in its behalf. That's what you are. Each of us is an ambassador of the Lord Jesus Christ with authority given by Him to represent Him in this work of teaching the gospel to others."[29]

Following the missionary meeting, President Hinckley met with LDS members of Congress. The LDS prophet said he had not come to talk politics with President Clinton but to assure him he was praying for him. All government officials and congress need our prayers.

On November 13, LDS prophet Hinckley and Elder Neal A. Maxwell, of the 12, met with the United States President at the White House for 30 minutes. President Hinckley presented President Clinton with a copy of the First Presidency's Proclamation on the Family.

Responsible citizens and officers of government were urged in the proclamation to "promote those measures designed to maintain and strengthen the family as the fundamental unit of society."

President Hinckley expressed appreciation to President Clinton for his recent statements on family values. Six generations of the president's and his wife Hillary Rodham's pedigrees were presented to the President along with another copy for their daughter Chelsea. President Clinton was very appreciative and grateful for the history.

"We advocate in the Church a program we call family home evening, reserving one night a week where father, mother and children sit down together and talk—talk about the family and about one another and study some together. You might get Hillary and Chelsea and sit down with those books and have a family home evening."

President Clinton said he would take the family history books with him to Camp David for Thanksgiving and "discuss our heritage."

Business & Media Executives Reception

Following President Hinckley's meeting with the United States president, he and Elder Maxwell traveled to New York City to the Harvard Club where Edelman Public Relations World Wide had arranged a luncheon with major media leaders and business executives.

Newsweek, Hearst Magazine Enterprises, CBS Evening News, Associated Press, and International Radio and Television Society executives were there along with Mike Wallace of CBS television's documentary program "60 Minutes."

President Hinckley began by telling the group as a young missionary he spoke on a soap box in Hyde Park, London, where hecklers were constant. He then turned to Mike Wallace and said, "After an experience like that, Mike Wallace doesn't look too formidable." Mr. Wallace had a nice laugh along with the rest of the group, the tone was set for a friendly meeting, and President Hinckley launched into a media blitz pertaining to his church.

Missionaries, LDS welfare, disaster relief, the LDS health code, education, strong family relationships, seminary and institute and the extensive LDS building program were explained.

After the luncheon, Mike Wallace asked President Hinckley if he could visit Salt Lake City and interview him. "Sure," Gordon replied.

Interview with Mike Wallace

Mr. Wallace, a prominent journalist in America, interviewed President Hinckley in Salt Lake City on December 18. His news crew first did a documentary on recent gang problems in the United States, focusing on a couple of Utah young men and boys with delinquency problems who had received successful help at an East Coast school.

He also went to a missionary conference of all LDS full-time missionaries working in the Salt Lake City Mission. President Hinckley stood beaming proudly as the missionaries were interviewed impromptu on camera by Mr. Wallace. The cameramen became so involved, they let their cameras run out of film and scrambled to reload.

One elder couldn't wait during the interviews. He jumped up and said, "I'm Elder Rotnum. I was Hindu. Our family moved from Sri Lanka to Tonga. I joined the Church there. My father died after I was called to the Salt Lake City Mission from Tonga. I went home and organized his funeral. I baptized my mother while there.

"When I returned here, my mother had a heart attack. The Holy Ghost saved her. The Holy Ghost told her to go see a doctor. She never went to the doctor. But this time she went because the Holy Ghost told her to. That's what the Church does."

At the end of the missionary conference, Mr. Wallace, standing in between two sister missionaries, sang the hymn "Called to Serve" with the missionaries. Then he said to the warm group surrounding him the true story of the LDS faith needs to be told and added, "I'm a Jew. I'm 73. I'm not a practicing Jew. I've been looking all my life for peace."

President Hinckley then quickly spoke, "Mike, you just found it."[30]

President Hinckley's 60 minute interview with Mike Wallace was "incisive." They then strolled through Temple Square. Mr. Wallace returned again to Utah in February 1996 for a followup visit and attended a BYU married student Sacrament meeting. He then returned to New York City and finished the final touches on his documentary.

Continued Ministry

On January 4, 1996, Utah celebrated its 100th birthday reenacting the celebration held a century before. President Hinckley appeared and offered brief remarks. He expressed appreciation for those of the past who worked harder than any other people to obtain statehood.

He stated as the state moved into its second century, its people must retain individuality while working "cooperatively to maintain and enhance those elements of our common culture, . . . arts which refine and elevate the human spirit." Improve education, guard and wisely use precious water, and safeguard natural wonders, he also counseled.[31]

On January 6 & 7, 1996, a group of 3,600 Latter-day Saints assembled at the Pan-American Auditorium, Corpus Christi, Texas for a multi-stake conference. President Hinckley encouraged every man and woman, every boy and girl to reread the Book of Mormon. Place a check mark by each reference to Jesus Christ. Then "there will come to you a very real conviction as you do so that this is in very deed another witness for the Lord Jesus Christ,"— the Book of Mormon.

Sister Marjorie Hinckley, Elder and Sister Jeffrey R. Holland, and Elder F. Enzio Busche of the 70 and wife attended.

President Hinckley told of recently acquiring land in Monterrey, Mexico for another LDS temple. Those in Corpus Christi will also be benefited by the temple to be only 150 miles south of McAllen, Texas.

On January 13, President Hinckley was in Parowan, 240 miles south of Salt Lake City, for the town's 145th birthday celebration and dedicated the Pioneer Heritage Park, "dropped in" on the stake conference of Pine View Stake in St. George Sunday and spoke to 10,000 at a youth fireside in the Dixie Center Burns Arena on the Dixie College campus. "Choose the right," the LDS prophet proclaimed. Youth stood in line for seats as adults relinquished seats for them.

Sister Hinckley also spoke and Earl C. Tingey of the 70 conducted. "I know why there are 1,800 in that choir," President Hinckley said. "They knew they could get a reserved seat if they sang in the choir."

The prophet received many letters from the St. George area. He said, "I suppose you thought I'd never read them, but I did. Some of you should have taken another class in penmanship. It wasn't easy.

"You've come on the scene of the world in the greatest age in the history of mankind. Nobody else who ever lived on this earth has had quite the advantages that you have. It's marvelous to be alive in this day and time," President Hinckley said.

A question asked by TV anchor Mike Wallace was related. The TV announcer asked, "How does Jesus speak to you?"

President Hinckley said he replied, "The voice of the Lord doesn't come in dramatic fashion, but as with the prophet Elijah through the still small voice."

President Hinckley closed by saying, "I leave my blessing upon you that you may grow in faith and faithfulness as you go forward with your lives, making the right choices at all times and in all circumstances, and invoke every good blessing upon you." Tears were in the eyes of many as the closing songs were sung.

On January 15, 1996, Robert Dole, Majority Leader in the US Senate, and US Presidential candidate, visited the First Presidency.

Mexico

The Salt Lake Valley institutes met for a January 21, 1996 fireside in the Salt Lake Tabernacle. A grandson of President Hinckley, Michael Hinckley, conducted the meeting as president of the U of U LDSSA.

President Hinckley suggested the Church stands as an anchor of stability and values in a world of shifting values. The LDS Church stands for something. Self discipline is the answer to pressures of sexual promiscuity. Marriage is ordained of God and is the institution designed for the bringing of offspring into the world. Those who profane or use uncouth language "only advertise the poverty of their vocabularies and a glaring paucity in their powers of expression." Keep a balance in studies between critical academic analysis and criticism of the Church and leaders. Be positive in thinking of the Lord's work.

"The Church is the great reservoir of eternal truth from which we can constantly drink. It is the preserver from which we can constantly drink. It is the preserver of standards, the teacher of values. Latch onto those values. Bind them to your hearts, let them become the lodestar of your lives to guide you as you move forward in the world of which you will become an important part."[32]

On January 27 and 28, 1996, the LDS prophet visited Veracruz, Mexico on the southeast coast where he met with 9,000 Latter-day Saints and then trained 1,200 priesthood leaders and full-time missionaries. He also met with top government leaders.

"I hope, my brothers and sisters, that you are having your family home evenings with your children," said President Hinckley. You cannot afford to postpone this. The days, the months, and the years pass so quickly and before long it will be too late."[33]

The prophet visited 6,000 married students at BYU gathered from 5 married student stakes. On February 10, 1996, he told them to use the soft answer at home. "Quiet speech is the speech of peace. Quiet speech is the speech of harmony. Quiet speech is the speech of love," he said.[34]

Such was the first year of the LDS prophet Gordon B. Hinckley's example in fulfilling his belief—only through service to his fellowmen is he fulfilling his mandate from God to love Him and His children.

LEGACY

As is stated in the latter-day saint scripture, the Book of Mormon, regarding the events chronicled therein, even a 100th part of the great and marvelous things which transpired have not been written herein, so with the ministry of selfless service of Gordon Bitner Hinckley. Herein only a sampling of his life and experiences has been written.

But the prophet Gordon Bitner Hinckley has never been afraid to lay his life out on the table for examination. Truly his life is an open book. Always permissive of recording his every word, his every movement, this has undoubtedly been one of his greatest traits, because it mirrors not only his mastery of a listening ear, not only to the Spirit of the Lord but also to men, but to other cardinal traits of deity: Patience, gentleness, kindness, godliness, love unfeigned. You add the extras.

A man whose life has largely been lived with a home base in the Valley of the Everlasting Hills with a central station on Administration Block. A man who has known in youth not only one but two environments of daily life–metropolitan and rural.

A man whose ancestors come from Gaul, Switzerland, Germany, Britain and the Americas, whose blood flows with not only gentile blood, but the rich blood of Ancient Abraham, Isaac, Jacob and Joseph of Egypt. A man who has met with kings, princes, emperors and presidents, who has supped with the most prominent of men in the eyes of man but who has yet sat at the paupers table, dined with the meek, succored the poor, lifted up the heart of the grieving and accepted every request to serve the common man, his kinsmen, associates, friends, and neighbors where the priority was ever possible.

Truly Gordon Bitner Hinckley was prepared from the foundations of the world as was Abraham to assume leadership of the Kingdom of God on earth in 1995. Truly he is one of the noble and great ones spoken of by the Lord to Abraham. Truly he is the "Shoulder for the Lord" in the dispensation of the fullness of times.

The Lord has given him challenge, the Lord has given him heartache, the Lord has given him pressure beyond the height of imagination. But the Lord has been merciful to him, the Lord has given him ability, the Lord has blessed him with faith, and the Lord has capped him with vision.

His eyes have beheld the unfolding of a great work, in its rudimentary growth when he passed through the veil to mortality. He has seen virtually the entire sphere of our planet. Edom has made its mark on him but he has made his mark on Edom. Such is the legacy of the prophet of God whom the Lord called to His holy station on March 12, 1995.

Twenty one years before Gordon B. Hinckley ascended to the presidency of his church, he spoke of prophets and their polishing in preparation. Speaking of the dear prophet Joseph Smith, Jr., whom he dearly loved, President Hinckley said, "The corners of that rough stone *were* knocked off, and he became a polished shaft in the hand of the Almighty.

"It has been so with those who have succeeded him. Through long years of dedicated service, they have been refined and winnowed and chastened and molded for the purposes of the Almighty. Could anyone doubt this after reading the lives of such men as Brigham Young, Wilford Woodruff, and Joseph F. Smith?"[1]

Prophetically, Gordon B. Hinckley was also speaking of himself. He was put through some very unique refiner's fires. But he weathered them all.

As early as 1974, President Hinckley spoke of the lyrics to the hymn "We Thank Thee O God for a Prophet." Said he regarding them, "They have become a grateful expression of appreciation for millions over the earth. I myself have heard them sung in 21 different languages as a reverent prayer of thanksgiving for divine revelation."[2]

The Refiner placed Gordon in a golden crucible. Through His divine providence Gordon was born to "goodly parents" who truly "taught him in the ways of the Lord" and through that experience Gordon developed a compassion, an empathy for others, which would bless the lives of all he ever met. "I don't think father ever laid hand on me except to bless me, placing hands on my head."[3] What a legacy Gordon received from goodly parents. And he has used this legacy to build his own legacy of love and compassion for his fellowman.

The *Deseret News* editorial spoke of President Hinckley in January 1982, he is "a man whose quiet and almost incredibly effective work behind the scenes of the Church administration is known to comparatively few."[4] Then the editorial continued explaining President Hinckley was incredibly successful in paying attention to details, concerned, an implementer of "big plans" and "imaginative plans." He was "a strong right arm to the brethren."

President Howard W. Hunter, a mentor, said of President Hinckley, "I appreciate his wisdom and judgment. Men of his ability are rare." President Hinckley's co-counselor Thomas S. Monson spoke of him, "He has an unequalled blend of knowledge coupled with compassion. His mind grasps quickly the details of any matter put before the Council [of the 12 apostles]. Justice is always tempered with mercy. He is a tireless worker and has demonstrated his belief that one should put first the Kingdom of God and His righteousness."

Jeffrey R. Holland, then BYU president, said of President Hinckley in January 1982, "He is farsighted, fair and forgiving. He has a sense of grace even under unusual pressure."

Elder Neal A. Maxwell, in writing an article about President Hinckley said he had a great love of America but no "Americanization" and an unusual capacity to communicate. President Hinckley's talks use stories and experiences, general wisdom which can be applied to different situations. He can challenge data with respect and merely clarify the truth. He is willing to stand alone if needed and knows the value of silence.[5]

Equally it must be said of Sister Marjorie Pay Hinckley, she is a gleaming example of a helpmate par excellence, a woman who realizes who she is and has been faithful and true to her God as well as her eternal mate in great and untiring service and sacrifice throughout all of the Hinckleys' married lives.

President Hinckley, when he was ordained prophet of the LDS Church, was the only LDS prophet to that time who had been an LDS Church staff employee to prophets. He has always considered himself one member of a team, a team which is ever growing larger and larger. Fear and inadequacy have frequented him but also "his confidence has waxed strong" as he has without rest performed his duties and service.[6]

His slow, distinct, deliberate speech is trademarkable. It has always been an inspiration to those who hear him. It is humble and sincere speech but accented with conviction and admonition when exactly appropriate. His drawing out of the last words of his sentences, his mellow soft traits, straight cadence, bring home his words.

You knew when you heard him he spoke his heart, many times tapering his volume at the end of a point in distinctive style. An LDS scripture from the Doctrine and Covenants says in part, "He that speaketh, whose spirit is contrite, whose language is meek and edifieth, the same is of God if he obey mine ordinances (D.&C. 52:3:16)," a

President Gordon Bitner Hinckley
Sincere and Sober Expression
at the Podium

perfect description of President Hinckley.

President Hinckley has written his own epitaphs in the melodic and eloquent tributes he has given on many occasions to his colleagues of the general authorities and prophets.

As to the prophet Moses, so to President Gordon Bitner Hinckley, the Lord speaks: "Blessed art thou, Gordon, for I, the Almighty, have chosen thee, and thou shalt be made stronger than many waters; for they shall obey thy command as if thou wert God.

"And lo, I am with thee, even unto the end of thy days."[7]

THE BEGINNING

FOOTNOTES

Tokyo

1. George M. McCune, *Testimony* (Provo: B.Y.U. Press, 1967), 92-93.

Heritage

1. *Improvement Era*, June 1958, p. 456.
2. "Vikings," *Encyclopedia Britannica*, 1960, Vol. 23:615-616; "Normandy," *Encyclopedia Britannica*, 1960, Vol. 16, 493; "Normans," *Encyclopedia Britannica*, 1960, Vol. 16, 494-496; "William I," *Encyclopedia Britannica*, 1960, Vol. 17, 615; "Henchman," *The New Merriam-Webster Dictionary*, 1989, 347.
3. Lorin A. Hinckley, *Arza Erastus Hinckley and Ira Nathaniel Hinckley Descendants & Ancestors*, (Salt Lake City: Lorin A. Hinckley, 1979), xxi.
4. Marlene Alma Hinkley Groves, *Hinckleys of Maine*, (Blue Hill, Maine: Penobscot Press, 1993), p. 1. This work not only contains transcripts but also copies of original wills and other vital statistic documents of several of the earliest known Hinckleys in England and America.
5. Vera Norton, *Some Descendants of Samuel Hinckley who came to America in 1635 and Some Ancestors of Their Wives*, (Lake Worth, Florida: Vera Norton, 1976), p. 9.
6. Groves, *Hinckley's of Maine*, p. 2-5.
7. *Matthews' American Armory and Blue Book*.
8. Groves, *Hinckley's of Maine*, pp. 7-12; Norton, *Some Descendants of Samuel Hinckley*, pp. 7-8, 25, 27-31.
9. E. Charles Hinckley, *Hinckley Heritage and History*, 3rd ed., (Ft. Worth, Texas: E. Charles Hinckley, 1982), pp. 16-22.
10. Lorin A. Hinckley, *Arza Erastus Hinckley and Ira Nathaniel Hinckley Descendants & Ancestors, p. xxvii.*
11. Norton, *Some Descendants of Samuel Hinckley*, p. 37.
12. Groves, *Hinckleys of Maine*, p. 14.
13. Norton, *Some Descendants of Samuel Hinckley*, p. 34.
14. E. Charles Hinckley, *Hinckley Heritage & History*, p. 27.
15. Groves, *Hinckleys of Maine*, p. 287.
16. Groves, *Hinckleys of Maine*, pp. 14-17; Norton, *Some Descendants of Samuel Hinckley*, p. 40: Hinckley, *Hinckley Heritage & History*, p.
17. L. Richard "Dick" Bentley & Marjorie Dutson Bentley, *Personal History of Ira Noble Hinckley (1860-1942)*, (Alpine, Utah: Dick & Marge Bentley, 1988), p. 4.

Heritage
Mayflower & the Wampanoags

1. Alvin G. Weeks, *Massasoit of the Wampanoags*, (Fall River, Mass.: A.G. Weeks, 1920), p. 130.
2. Henry M. Dexter, *Mourt's Relations*, 1865, p. 73.
3. Alvin G. Weeks, *Massasoit of the Wampanoags*, (Fall River, Mass.:A.G. Weeks, 1920), p. 113, 129.
4. *Mayflower Families Through Five Generations*, (General Society of Mayflower Descendants, 1992), Vol. 6, p. 3; Leon Clark Hills, *Mayflower Planters at Plymouth, Mass. 1620 and Other Newcomers to Ye Olde Colonie*, (Hills Publishing Co., 1936), Vol. 1.
5. Eugene Aubrey Stratton, *Plymouth Colony Its History & People 1620-1691*, (Salt Lake City, Utah:Ancestry Publishing, 1986), p. 21.
6. Eugene Aubrey Stratton, *ibid.*
7. Eugene Aubrey Stratton, *Ibid.*
8. John S. C. Abbott, *Makers of History*, (New York:Harper & Brothers, 1902), p. 60.
9. Marsh & Clark, *Story of Massachusetts*, (New York:American Historical Society, 1938), Vol. 1, p. 51.
10. Henry M. Derter, *Mourt's Relations*, 1865.
11. Leon Clark Hills, *Mayflower Planters at Plymouth, Mass. 1620*, (Hills Publishing Co., 1936), Vol. 1.
12. Eugene Aubrey Stratton, *Plymouth Colony Its History & People 1620-1691*, (Salt Lake City, Utah:Ancestry Publishing, 1986), pp. 308-309.
13. Richard and Marge Bentley, *Ira Noble Hinckley History*, (Alpine, Utah:Dick & Marge Bentley, 1989), p. 7.

Heritage
Pres. F.D. Roosevelt Relationship

1. Samuel Crompton, *The Presidents of the United States*, (New York:Smithmark Publishers Inc., 1992), pp. 48-49, 56-59.

Heritage
Grandfather Ira Nathaniel Hinckley

1. Ileen Judd Johnson & Hilga Judd Frier, *Ontario to Chihuahua:The Story of Hyrum Judd Mormon Pioneer 1824-18894*, (Murray, Utah:Roylance Publishing, 1991), pp. 3-5.
2. Dick & Marge Bentley, *Ira Noble Hinckley History*, (Alpine, Utah: Dick & Marge Bentley, 1989), pp. 4-5.
3. 2 Thessalonians 2:3.
4. Acts 3:19-21.
5. Arza Erastus Hinckley, "Diary", *Arza Erastus Hinckley & Ira Nathaniel Hinckley*, (Salt Lake City, Utah:Lorin A. Hinckley, 1982), p. 9 of diary.
6. 4 Generation Family Group Sheet of Nathaniel Hinckley, 1794-1831, and Lois Judd on file at the Family History Library, Joseph Smith Memorial Building Branch, Salt Lake City, Utah.
7. 4 Generation Family Group Sheet of Nathaniel Hinckley, 1794-1831, and Lois Judd on file at the Family History Library, Joseph Smith Memorial Building Branch, Salt Lake City, Utah.
8. Ileen Judd Johnson & Hilga Judd Frier, *Ontario to Chihuahua:The Story of Hyrum Judd Mormon Pioneer 1824-18894*, (Murray, Utah:Roylance Publishing, 1991), pp. 5-8.
9. Parley P. Pratt, quoted in George M. McCune, *Personalities in the Doctrine and Covenants and Joseph Smith-History*, (Salt Lake City, Utah: Hawkes Publishing, Inc., 1991), p. 117.
10. Arza Erastus Hinckley, "Diary", *Arza Erastus Hinckley & Ira Nathaniel Hinckley*, (Salt Lake City, Utah: Lorin A. Hinckley, 1982), p. 9 of diary.
11. *Church History in the Fullness of Times*, (Salt Lake City, Utah: Church of Jesus Christ of Latter-day Saints, 1989), p. 205.
12. *History of the Church*, (Salt Lake City, Utah: Church of Jesus Christ of Latter-day Saints, 1980), Vol. 5, p. 137.
13. Arza Erastus Hinckley, "Diary", *Arza Erastus Hinckley & Ira Nathaniel Hinckley*, (Salt Lake City, Utah: Lorin A. Hinckley, 1982), p. 9 of diary.
14. 4 Generation Family Group Sheet of Nathaniel Hinckley, 1794-1831, and Lois Judd on file at the Family History Library, Joseph Smith Memorial Building Branch, Salt Lake City, Utah.
15. Arza Erastus Hinckley, "Diary", *Arza Erastus Hinckley & Ira Nathaniel Hinckley*, (Salt Lake City, Utah: Lorin A. Hinckley, 1982), p. 9 of diary.
16. Dick & Marge Bentley, *Ira Noble Hinckley History*, (Alpine, Utah: Dick & Marge Bentley, 1989), p. 11.
17. Parley P. Pratt, quoted in George M. McCune, *Personalities in the Doctrine and Covenants and Joseph Smith-History*, (Salt Lake City, Utah: Hawkes Publishing, Inc., 1991), p. 117.
18. Bryant S. Hinckley, *Autobiography of Bryant Stringham Hinckley*, (Salt Lake City, Utah:Ruth Hinckley Willes, 1971), p. 2.
19. Dick & Marge Bentley, *Ira Noble Hinckley History*, (Alpine, Utah: Dick & Marge Bentley, 1989), p. 6.
20. Dick & Marge Bentley, *Ira Noble Hinckley History*, (Alpine, Utah: Dick & Marge Bentley, 1989), p. 6.
21. Bryant S. Hinckley, *Autobiography of Bryant Stringham Hinckley*, (Salt Lake City, Utah: Ruth Hinckley Willes, 1971), p. 2.
22. Dick & Marge Bentley, *Ira Noble Hinckley History*, (Alpine, Utah: Dick & Marge Bentley, 1989), p. 6.
23. Dick & Marge Bentley, *Ira Noble Hinckley History*, (Alpine, Utah: Dick & Marge Bentley, 1989), p. 8.
24. Letter of Ira Nathaniel Hinckley to his son Ira Noble Hinckley dated August 14, 1884, quoted in Dick & Marge Bentley, *Ira Noble Hinckley History*, (Alpine, Utah: Dick & Marge Bentley, 1989), p. 17.
24. Dick & Marge Bentley, *Ira Noble Hinckley History*, (Alpine, Utah: Dick & Marge Bentley, 1989), p. 16.
25. Dick & Marge Bentley, *Ira Noble Hinckley History*, (Alpine, Utah: Dick & Marge Bentley, 1989), p. 17.
26. Letters of Angeline Wilcox Noble Hinckley to her son Ira Noble Hinckley in New Zealand dated December 7, 1883; February 29, 1884; and March 29, 1884 quoted in Dick & Marge Bentley, *Ira Noble Hinckley History*, (Alpine, Utah: Dick & Marge Bentley, 1989), p. 16.

27. Dick & Marge Bentley, *Ira Noble Hinckley History*, (Alpine, Utah: Dick & Marge Bentley, 1989), p. 5.
28. Dick & Marge Bentley, *Ira Noble Hinckley History*, (Alpine, Utah: Dick & Marge Bentley, 1989), p. 13.
29. Dick & Marge Bentley, *Ira Noble Hinckley History*, (Alpine, Utah: Dick & Marge Bentley, 1989), p. 11.
30. Dick & Marge Bentley, *Ira Noble Hinckley History*, (Alpine, Utah: Dick & Marge Bentley, 1989), p. 5.
31. Dick & Marge Bentley, *Ira Noble Hinckley History*, (Alpine, Utah: Dick & Marge Bentley, 1989), p. 6.
32. Dick & Marge Bentley, *Ira Noble Hinckley History*, (Alpine, Utah: Dick & Marge Bentley, 1989), p. 11.
33. Dick & Marge Bentley, *Ira Noble Hinckley History*, (Alpine, Utah: Dick & Marge Bentley, 1989), p. 11.
34. Letter of Ira Nathaniel Hinckley to his son Ira Noble Hinckley in New Zealand dated March 2, 1883 quoted in Dick & Marge Bentley, *Ira Noble Hinckley History*, (Alpine, Utah: Dick & Marge Bentley, 1989), p. 14.
35. Dick & Marge Bentley, *Ira Noble Hinckley History*, (Alpine, Utah: Dick & Marge Bentley, 1989), p. 13.
36. Letter of Angeline Wilcox Noble Hinckley to her son Ira Noble Hinckley in New Zealand dated May 28, 1884 quoted in Dick & Marge Bentley, *Ira Noble Hinckley History*, (Alpine, Utah: Dick & Marge Bentley, 1989), p. 16.
37. Letter of Angeline Wilcox Noble Hinckley to her son Ira Noble Hinckley in New Zealand dated March 28, 1884 quoted in Dick & Marge Bentley, *Ira Noble Hinckley History*, (Alpine, Utah: Dick & Marge Bentley, 1989), p. 16.
38. *Church History in the Fullness of Times, (Salt Lake City, Utah:The Church of Jesus Christ of Latter-day Saints, 1989), p. 427.*
39. Dick & Marge Bentley, *Ira Noble Hinckley History*, (Alpine, Utah: Dick & Marge Bentley, 1989), p. 20.
40. *Journal History of the LDS Church*, Wednesday, April 13, 1904, p. 3, taken from the *Deseret News* of April 14, 1904.

Heritage
Uncle Arza Alonzo Hinckley

1. Karl D. Butler, *Mighty Men of Zion*, (Salt Lake City: Karl D. Butler, 1974), pp. 264-265.

Heritage
Parents
Bryant S. & Ada B. Hinckley

1. 4 Generation Family Group Sheets of Ira Nathaniel Hinckley and his wives Adelaide Cameron Noble and Angelina Wilcox Noble at Family History Library Branch, Joseph Smith Memorial Building, Salt Lake City, Utah.
2. Dick & Marge Bentley, *Ira Noble Hinckley History*, (Alpine, Utah:Dick & Marge Bentley, 1989), p. 10.
3. Dick & Marge Bentley, *Ira Noble Hinckley History*, (Alpine, Utah:Dick & Marge Bentley, 1989), p. 10.
4. Bryant Stringham Hinckley, *Autobiography*, (Salt Lake City, Utah:Ruth Hinckley Willes, 1971), p. 11
5. Andrew Jensen, *LDS Biographical Encyclopedia*, (Salt Lake City, Utah:The Church of Jesus Christ of Latter-day Saints, 1901), Vol. 1, p. 778.
6. Dick & Marge Bentley, *Ira Noble Hinckley History*, (Alpine, Utah:Dick & Marge Bentley, 1989), p.10.
7. D. & C. 27:2.
8. D.& C. 20:53-55.
9. *BYU Speeches of the Year*, November 19, 1953, p. 2.
10. John 15:16.
11. *BYU Speeches of the Year*, November 19, 1953, p. 3.
12. Bryant Stringham Hinckley, *Autobiography*, (Salt Lake City, Utah:Ruth Hinckley Willes, 1971), pp. 20-25.
13. Missionary Index, Book B132, 1892:197, LDS Historical Department, Salt Lake City, Utah.
14. Andrew Jensen, *LDS Biographical Encyclopedia*, (Salt Lake City, Utah:The Church of Jesus Christ of Latter-day Saints, 1901), Vol. 1, p. 778.
15. Joseph Simmons Willes, *The Story of Ada Bitner Hinckley*, (Salt Lake City, Utah:Ruth Hinckley Willes, 1980), p. 49.
16. "Gordon B. Hinckley, Man of Integrity," aired by KSL TV, Salt Lake City, Utah, April 1, 1995.
17. Lynn M. Hilton, *The History of LDS Business College*, (Salt Lake City, Utah:LDS Business College, 1995), p. 110.
18. Joseph Simmons Willes, *The Story of Ada Bitner Hinckley*, (Salt Lake City, Utah:Ruth Hinckley Willes, 1980), p. 39.
19. Andrew Jensen, *LDS Biographical Encyclopedia*, (Salt Lake City, Utah:The Church of Jesus Christ of Latter-day Saints, 1901), Vol. 1, p. 778.
20. *Church History in the Fullness of Times*, (Salt Lake City, Utah:Church of Jesus Christ of Latter-day Saints, 1989), p. 407-410.
21. *1995-96 Church Almanac*, (Salt Lake City, Utah:Deseret News, 1994), p. 376.
20. Dick & Marge Bentley, *Ira Noble Hinckley History*, (Alpine, Utah:Dick & Marge Bentley, 1989), p. 10.
21. John Simmons Willes, *The Story of Ada Bitner Hinckley*, (Salt Lake City, Utah:Ruth Hinckley Willes, 1980), p. 48.
22. John Simmons Willes, *The Story of Ada Bitner Hinckley*, (Salt Lake City, Utah:Ruth Hinckley Willes, 1980), p. 63.
23. Proverbs 31:11.
24. John Simmons Willes, *The Story of Ada Bitner Hinckley*, (Salt Lake City, Utah:Ruth Hinckley Willes, 1980), p. 61.
25. John Simmons Willes, *The Story of Ada Bitner Hinckley*, (Salt Lake City, Utah:Ruth Hinckley Willes, 1980), p. 49.
26. John Simmons Willes, *The Story of Ada Bitner Hinckley*, (Salt Lake City, Utah:Ruth Hinckley Willes, 1980), p. 80.
27. John Simmons Willes, *The Story of Ada Bitner Hinckley*, (Salt Lake City, Utah:Ruth Hinckley Willes, 1980), p. 49.
28. LDS Ancestral File Computer Database on file at the LDS Family History Library, Salt Lake City, Utah, 1995.
29. LDS Ancestral File Computer Database on file at the LDS Family History Library, Salt Lake City, Utah, 1995.
30. John Simmons Willes, *The Story of Ada Bitner Hinckley*, (Salt Lake City, Utah:Ruth Hinckley Willes, 1980), p. 23.
31. John Simmons Willes, *The Story of Ada Bitner Hinckley*, (Salt Lake City, Utah:Ruth Hinckley Willes, 1980), p. 23.
32. John Simmons Willes, *The Story of Ada Bitner Hinckley*, (Salt Lake City, Utah:Ruth Hinckley Willes, 1980), p. 24.
33. LDS Ancestral File Computer Database on file at the LDS Family History Library, Salt Lake City, Utah, 1995.
34. LDS Ancestral File Computer Database on file at the LDS Family History Library, Salt Lake City, Utah, 1995.
35. John Simmons Willes, *The Story of Ada Bitner Hinckley*, (Salt Lake City, Utah:Ruth Hinckley Willes, 1980), p. 24.
36. John Simmons Willes, *The Story of Ada Bitner Hinckley*, (Salt Lake City, Utah:Ruth Hinckley Willes, 1980), p. 20.
37. John Simmons Willes, *The Story of Ada Bitner Hinckley*, (Salt Lake City, Utah:Ruth Hinckley Willes, 1980), p. 25.
38. John Simmons Willes, *The Story of Ada Bitner Hinckley*, (Salt Lake City, Utah:Ruth Hinckley Willes, 1980), p. 25.
39. John Simmons Willes, *The Story of Ada Bitner Hinckley*, (Salt Lake City, Utah:Ruth Hinckley Willes, 1980), p. 29.
40. John Simmons Willes, *The Story of Ada Bitner Hinckley*, (Salt Lake City, Utah:Ruth Hinckley Willes, 1980), p. 26 & 60.
41. John Simmons Willes, *The Story of Ada Bitner Hinckley*, (Salt Lake City, Utah:Ruth Hinckley Willes, 1980), p. 25.
42. John Simmons Willes, *The Story of Ada Bitner Hinckley*, (Salt Lake City, Utah:Ruth Hinckley Willes, 1980), p. 27.
43. John Simmons Willes, *The Story of Ada Bitner Hinckley*, (Salt Lake City, Utah:Ruth Hinckley Willes, 1980), p. 17.
44. John Simmons Willes, *The Story of Ada Bitner Hinckley*, (Salt Lake City, Utah:Ruth Hinckley Willes, 1980), p. 17.
45. John Simmons Willes, *The Story of Ada Bitner Hinckley*, (Salt Lake City, Utah:Ruth Hinckley Willes, 1980), p. 20.
46. John Simmons Willes, *The Story of Ada Bitner Hinckley*, (Salt Lake City, Utah:Ruth Hinckley Willes, 1980), pp. 20-21.
47. John Simmons Willes, *The Story of Ada Bitner Hinckley*, (Salt Lake City, Utah:Ruth Hinckley Willes, 1980), p. 86.
48. John Simmons Willes, *The Story of Ada Bitner Hinckley*, (Salt Lake City, Utah:Ruth Hinckley Willes, 1980), p. 87.
49. John Simmons Willes, *The Story of Ada Bitner Hinckley*, (Salt Lake City, Utah:Ruth Hinckley Willes, 1980), p. 66.
50. John Simmons Willes, *The Story of Ada Bitner Hinckley*, (Salt Lake City, Utah:Ruth Hinckley Willes, 1980), p. 39; *Improvement Era*, December 1961, p. 978.
51. John Simmons Willes, *The Story of Ada Bitner Hinckley*, (Salt Lake City, Utah:Ruth Hinckley Willes, 1980), p. 5.
52. *1995-1996 Church Almanac*, (Salt Lake City, Utah:The Deseret News, 1994), p. 376.
53. LDS Ancestral File Computer Database on file at the LDS Family History Library, Salt Lake City, Utah, 1995.
54. *Journal History of the Church*, The Church of Jesus Christ of Latter-day Saints, April 14 and 22, 1910.
55. *Journal History of the Church*, The Church of Jesus Christ of Latter-day Saints, April 21, 1910.
56. Bryant Stringham Hinckley, *Autobiography*, (Salt Lake City, Utah:Ruth Hinckley Willes, 1971), p. 34.

Boyhood
Birth

1. *Doctrine Covenants* 122:9.
2. *Population Abstract of the US*, Vol. 1, (McLean, Virginia:Andriot Associates, 1983), pp. 799, 801.
3. *1995-1996 Church Almanac*, (Salt Lake City, Utah:The Church of Jesus Christ of Latter-day Saints, 1994), pp. 376-377.
4. *BYU Speeches of the Year*, (Provo, Utah:BYU Press, 1992), March 1, 1992, p. 77.
5. *1995-1996 Church Almanac*, (Salt Lake City, Utah:The Church of Jesus Christ of Latter-day Saints, 1994), pp. 376.
6. Bryant Stringham Hinckley, *Autobiography*, (Salt Lake City, Utah:Ruth Hinckley Willes, 1971), p. 36.
7. Bryant Stringham Hinckley, *Autobiography*, (Salt Lake City, Utah:Ruth Hinckley Willes, 1971), p. 35.
8. *Ensign*, (Salt Lake City, Utah:The Church of Jesus Christ of Latter-day Saints, 1993), May 1993, p. 52.
9. John Simmons Willes, *The Story of Ada Bitner Hinckley*, (Salt Lake City, Utah:Ruth Hinckley Willes, 1980), p. 54.
10. John Simmons Willes, *The Story of Ada Bitner Hinckley*, (Salt Lake City, Utah:Ruth Hinckley Willes, 1980), p. 53.
11. John Simmons Willes, *The Story of Ada Bitner Hinckley*, (Salt Lake City, Utah:Ruth Hinckley Willes, 1980), p. 86.
12. John Simmons Willes, *The Story of Ada Bitner Hinckley*, (Salt Lake City, Utah:Ruth Hinckley Willes, 1980), p. 53.
13. John Simmons Willes, *The Story of Ada Bitner Hinckley*, (Salt Lake City, Utah:Ruth Hinckley Willes, 1980), p. 53.
14. *Ensign*, May 1993, p. 52.
15. *Journal History*, The Church of Jesus Christ of Latter-day Saints, June 17, 1971.
16. John Simmons Willes, *The Story of Ada Bitner Hinckley*, (Salt Lake City, Utah:Ruth Hinckley Willes, 1980), p. 79.
17. John Simmons Willes, *The Story of Ada Bitner Hinckley*, (Salt Lake City, Utah:Ruth Hinckley Willes, 1980), p. 78.
18. John Simmons Willes, *The Story of Ada Bitner Hinckley*, (Salt Lake City, Utah:Ruth Hinckley Willes, 1980), p. 59.
19. John Simmons Willes, *The Story of Ada Bitner Hinckley*, (Salt Lake City, Utah:Ruth Hinckley Willes, 1980), p. 57-73.
20. John Simmons Willes, *The Story of Ada Bitner Hinckley*, (Salt Lake City, Utah:Ruth Hinckley Willes, 1980), p. 80.
21. John Simmons Willes, *The Story of Ada Bitner Hinckley*, (Salt Lake City, Utah:Ruth Hinckley Willes, 1980), p. 86; *Ensign*, February 1986, p. 7, May 1993, p. 52, September 1994, p. 7.
22. *1995-96 Church Almanac*, (Salt Lake City, Utah:Deseret News, 1994), p. 377.
23. *1995-96 Church Almanac*, (Salt Lake City, Utah:Deseret News, 1994), p. 377.
24. *Journal History*, The Church of Jesus Christ of Latter-day Saints, February 11, 1985, p. 1.
25. *1995-96 Church Almanac*, (Salt Lake City, Utah:Deseret News, 1994), p. 377.
26. John Simmons Willes, *The Story of Ada Bitner Hinckley*, (Salt Lake City, Utah:Ruth Hinckley Willes, 1980), p. 54.
27. John Simmons Willes, *The Story of Ada Bitner Hinckley*, (Salt Lake City, Utah:Ruth Hinckley Willes, 1980), p. 85 and "Autobiographical Sketch" of Gordon B. Hinckley written June 23, 1971, in Lorin A. Hinckley, *Arza Erastus Hinckley and Ira Nathaniel Hinckley Descendants & Ancestors*, (Salt Lake City, Utah:Lorin A. Hinckley, 1979).
28. *New York City Documentary*, PBS Channel 7, Salt Lake City, Utah, August 23, 1995.
29. *Journal History*, The Church of Jesus Christ of Latter-day Saints, Friday, November 10, 1989, p. 3.
30. John Simmons Willes, *The Story of Ada Bitner Hinckley*, (Salt Lake City, Utah:Ruth Hinckley Willes, 1980), p. 85.
31.John Simmons Willes, *The Story of Ada Bitner Hinckley*, (Salt Lake City, Utah:Ruth Hinckley Willes, 1980), p. 86.
32. John Simmons Willes, *The Story of Ada Bitner Hinckley*, (Salt Lake City, Utah:Ruth Hinckley Willes, 1980), p. 81
33. *Ensign*, May 1993, p. 54.
34. John Simmons Willes, *The Story of Ada Bitner Hinckley*, (Salt Lake City, Utah:Ruth Hinckley Willes, 1980), p. 84.
35. John Simmons Willes, *The Story of Ada Bitner Hinckley*, (Salt Lake City, Utah:Ruth Hinckley Willes, 1980), p. 78
36.John Simmons Willes, *The Story of Ada Bitner Hinckley*, (Salt Lake City, Utah:Ruth Hinckley Willes, 1980), p. 79
37. Marjorie Pay Hinckley & Gordon Bitner Hinckley, *The Wonderous Power of a Mother*, (Salt Lake City, Utah:Deseret Book, 1989), p. 2.
38. John Simmons Willes, *The Story of Ada Bitner Hinckley*, (Salt Lake City, Utah:Ruth Hinckley Willes, 1980), p. 61.
39. Marjorie Pay Hinckley & Gordon Bitner Hinckley, *The Wonderous Power of a Mother*, (Salt Lake City, Utah:Deseret Book, 1989), p. 4-5.
40. *Church News*, June 24, 1995, p. 7.
41. *Ensign*, May 1982, p. 42.
42. John Simmons Willes, *The Story of Ada Bitner Hinckley*, (Salt Lake City, Utah:Ruth Hinckley Willes, 1980), p. 48.
43. John Simmons Willes, *The Story of Ada Bitner Hinckley*, (Salt Lake City, Utah:Ruth Hinckley Willes, 1980), p. 87.
44. John Simmons Willes, *The Story of Ada Bitner Hinckley*, (Salt Lake City, Utah:Ruth Hinckley Willes, 1980), p. 81.
45. Letter of Bryant Stringham Hinckley to Ada Bitner Hinckley, Salt Lake City to California, in John Simmons Willes, *The Story of Ada Bitner Hinckley*, (Salt Lake City, Utah:Ruth Hinckley Willes, 1980), p. 66.
46. *Standard American Encyclopedia*, Vol. 8, Chicago,1939.
47. *1995-96 Church Almanac*, (Salt Lake City, Utah:Deseret News, 1994), p. 378.
48. Bryant S. Hinckley, *Autobiography of Bryant Stringham Hinckley*, (Salt Lake City, Utah:Ruth Hinckley Willes, 1971), appendix.
49. *Journal History*, The Church of Jesus Christ of Later-day Saints, April 21, 1916.
50. *Ensign*, May 1993, p. 54.
51. John Simmons Willes, *The Story of Ada Bitner Hinckley*, (Salt Lake City, Utah:Ruth Hinckley Willes, 1980), p. 82.
52. *Ensign*, February 1986, p. 7.
53. John Simmons Willes, *The Story of Ada Bitner Hinckley*, (Salt Lake City, Utah:Ruth Hinckley Willes, 1980), p. 59-60.
54. *Ensign*, May 1993, p. 52.
55. *Church News*, December 5, 1987, p. 6.
56. *Ensign*, January 1982, p. 8.
57. John Simmons Willes, *The Story of Ada Bitner Hinckley*, (Salt Lake City, Utah:Ruth Hinckley Willes, 1980), p. 80.
58. *Ensign*, November 1989, p. 52.
59. John Simmons Willes, *The Story of Ada Bitner Hinckley*, (Salt Lake City, Utah:Ruth Hinckley Willes, 1980), p. 59.
60. *Church News*, June 24, 1995, p. 7.
61. John Simmons Willes, *The Story of Ada Bitner Hinckley*, (Salt Lake City, Utah:Ruth Hinckley Willes, 1980), p. 79.
62. John Simmons Willes, *The Story of Ada Bitner Hinckley*, (Salt Lake City, Utah:Ruth Hinckley Willes, 1980), p. 86.
63. *Journal History*, The Church of Jesus Christ of Latter-day Saints, October 8, 1916.
64. *Ensign*, January 1982, p. 8.
65. *Ensign*, May 1993, p. 59.
66. "Autobiographical Sketch of Sherman Bitner Hinckley" in *Lorin A. Hinckley, Arza Erastus Hinckley and Ira Nathaniel Hinckley*, (Salt Lake City, Utah:Lorin A. Hinckley, 1979), appendix..
67. John Simmons Willes, *The Story of Ada Bitner Hinckley*, (Salt Lake City, Utah:Ruth Hinckley Willes, 1980), p. 82.
68. John Simmons Willes, *The Story of Ada Bitner Hinckley*, (Salt Lake City, Utah:Ruth Hinckley Willes, 1980), p. 83.
69. John Simmons Willes, *The Story of Ada Bitner Hinckley*, (Salt Lake City, Utah:Ruth Hinckley Willes, 1980), p. 83.
70. *1995-96 Church Almanac*, (Salt Lake City, Utah:Deseret News, 1994), p. 377.
71. "Autobiographical Sketch of Gordon Bitner Hinckley" written June 23, 1971.
72. *Ensign*, May 1993, p. 52-53.
73. *Ensign*, May 1993, p. 53.
74. "Autobiographical Sketch of Gordon Bitner Hinckley" written June 23, 1971.
75. John Simmons Willes, *The Story of Ada Bitner Hinckley*, (Salt Lake City, Utah:Ruth Hinckley Willes, 1980), p. 83.
76. *Ensign*, May 1982, p. 40.
77. Genesis 14:20; Malachi 3:30.
78. *Journal History*, The Church of Jesus Christ of Latter-day Saints, November 17, 1985, p. 11.
79. *BYU Speeches of the Year*, February 14, 1978, p. 21; *Ensign*, March 1984, p. 3.
80. *Ensign*, February 1986, p. 5; John Simmons Willes, *The Story of Ada Bitner Hinckley*, (Salt Lake City, Utah:Ruth Hinckley Willes, 1980), p. 83; "Autobiographical Sketch of Sherman Bitner Hinckley" in *Lorin A. Hinckley, Arza Erastus Hinckley and Ira Nathaniel Hinckley*, (Salt Lake City, Utah:Lorin A. Hinckley, 1979), appendix..
81. *1995-96 Church Almanac*, (Salt Lake City, Utah:Deseret News, 1994), pp. 377-378.
82. *Church News*, June 9, 1993, p. 2.
83. *Ensign*, January 1982, p. 9.
84. Record of Members 1836-1970, 1st Ward, Liberty Stake, The Church of Jesus Christ of Latter-day Saints, Salt Lake City, Utah, CR 375-8.
85. *Journal History*, October 19, 1919.
86. *1995-96 Church Almanac*, (Salt Lake City, Utah:Deseret News, 1994), p. 378.
87. *Church News*, February 29, 1992, p. 10.
88. *Ensign*, May 1993, p. 52.
89. John Simmons Willes, *The Story of Ada Bitner Hinckley*, (Salt Lake City, Utah:Ruth Hinckley Willes, 1980), p. 83.
90. *Ensign*, May 1993, p. 54.
91. John Simmons Willes, *The Story of Ada Bitner Hinckley*, (Salt Lake

City, Utah:Ruth Hinckley Willes, 1980), p. 60.
92. *Ensign*, November 1994, p. 53.
93. *Ensign*, November 1978, p. 18.
94. *Church Newsl, March 12, 1994, p. 3;* Bryant S. Hinckley, *Autobiography of Bryant Stringham Hinckley*, (Salt Lake City, Utah:Ruth Hinckley Willes, 1971), p. 50.
95. *Ensign*, May 1993, p. 52.
96. *Ensign*, November 1978, p. 18.
97. John Simmons Willes, *The Story of Ada Bitner Hinckley*, (Salt Lake City, Utah:Ruth Hinckley Willes, 1980), p. 85-86.
98. *Church News*, June 24, 1995, p. 7.
99.*Journal History*, The Church of Jesus Christ of Latter-day Saints, Sunday, April 2, 1989, p. 2.
100. Gordon B. Hinckley, LDS Church Satellite Fireside Message, Sunday, May 1985.
101. John Simmons Willes, *The Story of Ada Bitner Hinckley*, (Salt Lake City, Utah:Ruth Hinckley Willes, 1980), p. 58.
102. John Simmons Willes, *The Story of Ada Bitner Hinckley*, (Salt Lake City, Utah:Ruth Hinckley Willes, 1980), p. 86.

Boyhood
Age 10-18

1. Bryant Stringham Hinckley, *Autobiography*, (Salt Lake City, Utah:Ruth Hinckley Willes, 1971), p. 31.
2. John Simmons Willes, *The Story of Ada Bitner Hinckley*, (Salt Lake City, Utah:Ruth Hinckley Willes, 1980), p. 57.
3. *Ensign*, May 1993, p. 53.
4. "Gordon B. Hinckley, Man of Integrity" documentary aired on KSL TV, Salt Lake City, Utah April 1, 1995.
5. *Ensign*, February 1986, p. 7; *Journal History*, The Church of Jesus Christ of Latter-day Saints, November 12, 1986, p. 2; *Church News*, September 9, 1995, p. 11.
6. *Ensign*, February 1986, p. 7; *Journal History*, The Church of Jesus Christ of Latter-day Saints, November 12, 1986, p. 2.
7. Joseph Smith-History 1:28, *Pearl of Great Price*, (Salt Lake City, Utah:LDS Church, 1981).
8. *Journal History*, The Church of Jesus Christ of Latter-day Saints, Saturday, November 19, 1988, p. 8; *1995-96 Church Almanac*, (Salt Lake City, Utah:Deseret News, 1994), p. 378.
9. *BYU Speeches of the Year*, (Provo, Utah:BYU Press, 1979), p. 202.
10. *Journal History*, Monday, February 11, 1985.
11. Doctrine and Covenants 13.
12. *BYU Speeches of the Year*, (Provo, Utah:BYU Press, 1979), p. 202.
13. *Ensign*, February 1986, p. 5.
14. *BYU Speeches of the Year*, (Provo, Utah:BYU Press, 1979), November 4, 1979, p. 202.
15. "Praise to the Man," *Hymns of the Church of Jesus Christ of Latter-day Saints 1985*, (Salt Lake City, Utah:The Church of Jesus Christ of Latter-day Saints, 1985), Hymn No. 27.
16. *Ensign*, May 1977, p. 66.
17. "Gordon B. Hinckley, Man of Integrity," KSL TV Channel 5 broadcast, April 1, 1995.
18. *Ensign*, January 1992, p. 7.
19. "Autobiographical Sketch of Gordon Bitner Hinckley" written June 23, 1971 in Lorin A. Hinckley, *Arza Erastus Hinckley and Ira Nathaniel Hinckley*, (Salt Lake City, Utah:Lorin A. Hinckley, 1979), appendix.
20. *Ensign*, May 1993, p. 52.
21. *Journal History*, The Church of Jesus Christ of Latter-day Saints, Saturday, October 6, 1990, p. 8.
22. *Journal History*, The Church of Jesus Christ of Latter-day Saints, May 6, 1990, p. 2.
23. *1995-96 Church Almanac*, (Salt Lake City, Utah:Deseret News, 1994), p. 378.
24. *Fifty Years of Public Education*, (Salt Lake City, Utah:[Utah] Board of Education, 1940), p. 135.
25. "New York City Documentary," PBS Channel 7, Salt Lake City, Utah, August 23, 1995.
26. Gordon B. Hinckley talk aat G. Homer Durham Funeral, Assembly Hall, Salt Lake City, Utah, January 14, 1985.

College

1. *University of Utah, A History of Its First 100 Years - 1850-1950*, (Salt Lake City, Utah:U of U Press, 1960), p. 408.
2. *Catalog & U. of U. Directory*, (Salt Lake City, Utah:U of U Press, 1928).
3. Marjorie Pay Hinckley & Gordon B. Hinckley, *The Wondrous Power of a Mother*, (Salt Lake City, Utah:Deseret Book, 1989), p. 2.
4. "Autobiographical Sketch of Gordon Bitner Hinckley" written June 23, 1971.
5. *Chronicle of the 20th Century*, (Mount Kisco, New York:Chronicle Publications Inc., 1987), pp. 362-363.
6. *Catalog & U. of U. Directory*, (Salt Lake City, Utah:U of U Press, 1928), pp. 166-169.
7. *Catalog & U. of U. Directory*, (Salt Lake City, Utah:U of U Press, 1928), pp. 61, 166.
8. University of Utah Archives Records.
9. *Church News*, June 24, 1995, p. 7.
10. *Ensign*, July 1984, p. 4.
11. *Catalog & U. of U. Directory*, (Salt Lake City, Utah:U of U Press, 1928).
12. *Catalog & U. of U. Directory*, (Salt Lake City, Utah:U of U Press, 1928),p. 268.
13. *BYU Speeches of the Year*, January 3, 1962.
14. *1995-96 Church Almanac*, (Salt Lake City, Utah:Deseret News, 1994), p. 379.
15. 4 Generation Family Group Sheets for Bryant Stringham Hinckley, LDS Family History Library, Joseph Smith Memorial Building, Salt Lake City, Utah.
16. Bryant S. Hinckley, *Autobiography of Bryant Stringham Hinckley*, (Salt Lake City, Utah:Ruth Hinckley Willes, 1980), p. 34.
17. Record of Members, LDS Historical Department Archives, Salt Lake City, Utah, CR 375-8.
18. Doctrine & Covenants 42:48.
19. John Simmons Willes, *The Story of Ada Bitner Hinckley*, (Salt Lake City, Utah:Ruth Hinckley Willes, 1980), p. 72.
20. John Simmons Willes, *The Story of Ada Bitner Hinckley*, (Salt Lake City, Utah:Ruth Hinckley Willes, 1980), p. 73.
21. *Ensign*, May 1994, p. 54.
22. *Ensign*, May 1994, p. 54.
23. John Simmons Willes, *The Story of Ada Bitner Hinckley*, (Salt Lake City, Utah:Ruth Hinckley Willes, 1980), p. 83.
24. John Simmons Willes, *The Story of Ada Bitner Hinckley*, (Salt Lake City, Utah:Ruth Hinckley Willes, 1980), p. 60.
25. John Simmons Willes, *The Story of Ada Bitner Hinckley*, (Salt Lake City, Utah:Ruth Hinckley Willes, 1980), pp. 61-62.John Simmons Willes, *The Story of Ada Bitner Hinckley*, (Salt Lake City, Utah:Ruth Hinckley Willes, 1980), p. 83.
26. John Simmons Willes, *The Story of Ada Bitner Hinckley*, (Salt Lake City, Utah:Ruth Hinckley Willes, 1980), pp. 63-64.
27. John Simmons Willes, *The Story of Ada Bitner Hinckley*, (Salt Lake City, Utah:Ruth Hinckley Willes, 1980), p. 64-65.
28. John Simmons Willes, *The Story of Ada Bitner Hinckley*, (Salt Lake City, Utah:Ruth Hinckley Willes, 1980), p. 66.
29. John Simmons Willes, *The Story of Ada Bitner Hinckley*, (Salt Lake City, Utah:Ruth Hinckley Willes, 1980), p. 70-71.
30. John Simmons Willes, *The Story of Ada Bitner Hinckley*, (Salt Lake City, Utah:Ruth Hinckley Willes, 1980), p. 67.
31. Doctrine and Covenants 76.
32. John Simmons Willes, *The Story of Ada Bitner Hinckley*, (Salt Lake City, Utah:Ruth Hinckley Willes, 1980), p. 72-73.
33. John Simmons Willes, *The Story of Ada Bitner Hinckley*, (Salt Lake City, Utah:Ruth Hinckley Willes, 1980), p. 74.
34. *1995-96 Church Almanac*, (Salt Lake City, Utah:Deseret News, 1994), p. 5.
35. Marjorie Pay Hinckley & Gordon B. Hinckley, *The Wondrous Power of a Mother*, (Salt Lake City, Utah:Deseret Book, 1989), p. 1.
36. *Utonian*, (Salt Lake City, Utah:U of U Press, 1931).
37. Lynn M. Hilton, *The History of LDS Business College & Its Parent Institutions, 1886-1993*, (Salt Lake City, Utah:LDS Business College, 1995), p. 27.
38. *University of Utah, A History of Its First 100 Years - 1850-1950*, (Salt Lake City, Utah:U of U Press, 1960), p. 413.
39. Franklin D. Roosevelt, *Franklin Delano Roosevelt Fireside Chats*, (New York:Penquin Books, 1995), p. 65.
40. *BYU Speeches of the Year*, (Provo, Utah:BYU Press, 1992), March 1, 1992, p. 75.
41. *Journal History*, The Church of Jesus Christ of Latter-day Saints, May 23, 1964, p. 7.
42. *1995-96 Church Almanac*, (Salt Lake City, Utah:Deseret News, 1994), p. 379.
43. *University of Utah, A History of Its First 100 Years - 1850-1950*, (Salt Lake City, Utah:U of U Press, 1960), p. 391.
44. Sylvia Hinckley Wadsworth Funeral Service, Panaca, Nevada, February 6, 1970.
45. *BYU Speeches of the Year*, (Provo, Utah:BYU Press, 1992), March 1, 1992, p. 75.
46. *Journal History*, The Church of Jesus Christ of Latter-day Saints, Tuesday, February 5, 1991, p. 3.
47. *BYU Speeches of the Year*, (Provo, Utah:BYU Press, 1977), March 6, 1977, p. 46; Ensign, September 1985, p. 3; October 1993, p. 5.
48. *BYU Speeches of the Year*, (Provo, Utah:BYU Press, 1958), June 5, 1958, p.6.
49. "Gordon B. Hinckley, Man of Integrity," KSL TV Channel 5 broadcast, April 1, 1995.

50. *BYU Speeches of the Year*, (Provo, Utah:BYU Press, 1979), November 4, 1979, p. 203.
51. *Improvement Era*, December 1970:123; *Ensign*, July 1995, p. 2.
52. *Improvement Era*, October 1960.
53. *Ensign*, May 1982:40.
54. *Improvement Era*, 1965:520.
55. *Ensign*, September 1985, p. 3.
56. *Utonian*, (Salt Lake City, Utah:U of U Press, 1933), p. 13.
57. *Utonian*, (Salt Lake City, Utah:U of U Press, 1933), p. 200-205.
58. *Utonian*, (Salt Lake City, Utah:U of U Press, 1933), p. 320-328, 352.
59. *1995-96 Church Almanac*, (Salt Lake City, Utah:Deseret News, 1994), p. 379.
60. Bryant S. Hinckley, *Autobiography of Bryant Stringham Hinckley*, (Salt Lake City, Utah:Ruth Hinckley Willes, 1980), p. 45.
61. *1995-96 Church Almanac*, (Salt Lake City, Utah:Deseret News, 1994), p. 379.
62. *1995-96 Church Almanac*, (Salt Lake City, Utah:Deseret News, 1994), p. 379.
63. *Ensign*, September 1994, p. 8.
64. *Utonian*, (Salt Lake City, Utah:U of U Press, 1933), p. 57.
65. *BYU Speeches of the Year*, (Provo, Utah:BYU Press, 1958), June 5, 1958 Baccalaureate Address, p. 6.
66. *BYU Speeches of the Year*, (Provo, Utah:BYU Press, 1958), June 5, 1958 Baccalaureate Address, p. 6.
67. *Ensign*, September 1994, p. 8.
68. *Chronicle of the 20th Century*, (Mount Kisco, New York:Chronicle Publications Inc., 1987), p. 407-409.
69. *Chronicle of the 20th Century*, (Mount Kisco, New York:Chronicle Publications Inc., 1987), p. 418.
70. Franklin D. Roosevelt, *Franklin Delano Roosevelt Fireside Chats*, (New York:Penguin Books, 1995), p. 1.
71. Franklin D. Roosevelt, *Franklin Delano Roosevelt Fireside Chats*, (New York:Penguin Books, 1995), p. 1.

Mission

1. *Improvement Era*, December 1961, p. 906; "Autobiographical Sketch of Gordon Bitner Hinckley" written June 23, 1971.
2. *Journal History*, The Church of Jesus Christ of Latter-day Saints, April 5, 1986.
3. *Journal History*, The Church of Jesus Christ of Latter-day Saints, Friday, April 2, 1982, p. 3.
4. Funeral of Franklin Dan Wadsworth, Panaca, Nevada, July 1971.
5. "Autobiographical Sketch of Sherman Bitner Hinckley" in Lorin A. Hinckley, *Arza Erastus Hinckley and Ira Nathaniel Hinckley*, (Salt Lake City, Utah:Lorin A. Hinckley, 1979), appendix; Marjorie P. Hinckley and Gordon B. Hinckley, *The Wondrous Power of a Mother*, (Salt Lake City, Utah:Deseret Book, 1989), p. 1.
6. 4 Generation Family Group Sheets of Bryant Stringham Hinckley and Gordon Bitner Hinckley, LDS Family History Library, Joseph Smith Memorial Building, Salt Lake City, Utah.
7. Missionary Index, LDS Historical Department, Salt Lake City, Utah, Book F, p. 54, line 2160; "Autobiographical Sketch of Gordon Bitner Hinckley" written June 23, 1971 in Lorin A. Hinckley, *Arza Erastus Hinckley and Ira Nathaniel Hinckley*, (Salt Lake City, Utah:Lorin A. Hinckley, 1979), appendix.
8. *Church News*, March 19, 1994, p. 11.
9. *Improvement Era*, December 1969, p. 98.
10. *Ensign*, April 1989, pp. 2-5.
11. "Gordon B. Hinckley, Man of Integrity," KSL TV Channel 5 broadcast, April 1, 1995.
12. *BYU Speeches of the Year*, (Provo, Utah:BYU Press, 1958), June 5, 1958, p. 14.
13. A Century of Progress Personal Scrapbook of James Paxman McCune's visit to 1933 Chicago World's Fair in possession of the author, Salt Lake City, Utah.
14. *Church News*, September 9, 1995, p. 6.
15. *Church History in the Fullness of Times*, (Salt Lake City, Utah:The Church of Jesus Christ of Latter-day Saints, 1989), pp. 174-175; *1995-96 Church Almanac*, (Salt Lake City, Utah:Deseret News, 1994), p. 364.
16. *Church News*, September 9, 1995, p. 11.
17. *Ensign*, July 1987, p. 9.
18. "Autobiographical Sketch of Gordon Bitner Hinckley" written June 23, 1971 in Lorin A. Hinckley, *Arza Erastus Hinckley and Ira Nathaniel Hinckley*, (Salt Lake City, Utah:Lorin A. Hinckley, 1979), appendix; *Improvement Era*, 1961:907.
19. *Church News*, September 9, 1995, p. 5.
20. *Ensign*, July 1987, p. 6.
21. *Journal History*, The Church of Jesus Christ of Latter-day Saints, January 4, 1987, p. 7.
22. *Ensign*, July 1987, p. 7; September 1994, p. 7; "Gordon B. Hinckley, Man of Integrity," KSL TV Channel 5 broadcast, April 1, 1995; *Church News*, September 1995, p. 4.
23. *Church News*, September 16, 1995, p. 3.
24. *BYU Speeches of the Year*, (Provo, Utah:BYU Press, 1959), January 28, 1959.
25. *BYU Speeches of the Year*, (Provo, Utah:BYU Press, 1959), January 28, 1959.
26. *Ensign*, July 1987, p. 7.
27. *Church News*, September 16, 1995, p. 3.
28. *Ensign*, September 1994, p. 7.
29. KSL TV Channel 5, Salt Lake City, Utah interview with President Gordon B. Hinckley, Noon, October 1, 1995.
30. *Journal History*, The Church of Jesus Christ of Latter-day Saints, October 14, 1933.
31. Andrew Jenson, *LDS Biographical Encyclopedia*, (Salt Lake City, Utah:Western Epics, 1971), Vol. 1, p. 784.
32. Franklin D. Roosevelt, *Franklin Delano Roosevelt Fireside Chats*, (New York:Penguin Books, 1995), p. 33.
33. *BYU Speeches of the Year*, (Provo, Utah:BYU Press, 1958), June 5, 1958 Baccalaureate Address, p. 8.
34. *1995-96 Church Almanac*, (Salt Lake City, Utah:Deseret News, 1994), p. 379.
35. *Improvement Era*, December 1961, p. 978; *Ensign*, September 1994, p. 7.
36. Mrs. Alec Tweedie, *Hyde Park, Its History & Romance*, (London:Besant & Co., Ltd., 1930).
37. Mrs. Alec Tweedie, *Hyde Park, Its History & Romance*, (London:Besant & Co., Ltd., 1930), p. 197.
38. *Ensign*, July 1987, p. 9; G. Homer Durham Funeral, January 14, 1985, Salt Lake City, Utah.
39. KSL TV Channel 5 Interview with President Gordon B. Hinckley broadcast at Noon, October 1, 1995.
40. *Improvement Era*, 1964:109; *Ensign*, August 1988, p. 2.
41. KSL TV Channel 5 Interview with President Gordon B. Hinckley, Noon, October 1, 1995; *Church News*, September 16, 1995, p. 3.
42. KSL TV Channel 5 Interview with President Gordon B. Hinckley, Noon, October 1, 1995.
43. *Church News*, September 9, 1995, p. 6.
44. Gordon B. Hinckley, "New Mission Methods in Britain," *Deseret News*, August 10, 1935, in *Journal History*, The Church of Jesus Christ of Latter-day Saints, August 10, 1935, p. 6.
45. Gordon B. Hinckley, "New Mission Methods in Britain," *Deseret News*, August 10, 1935, in *Journal History*, The Church of Jesus Christ of Latter-day Saints, August 10, 1935, p. 7.
46. Gordon B. Hinckley, "New Mission Methods in Britain," *Deseret News*, August 10, 1935, in *Journal History*, The Church of Jesus Christ of Latter-day Saints, August 10, 1935, p. 7.
47. Gordon B. Hinckley, "New Mission Methods in Britain," *Deseret News*, August 10, 1935, in *Journal History*, The Church of Jesus Christ of Latter-day Saints, August 10, 1935, p. 7.
48. Gordon B. Hinckley, "New Mission Methods in Britain," *Deseret News*, August 10, 1935, in *Journal History*, The Church of Jesus Christ of Latter-day Saints, August 10, 1935, p. 7.
49. Gordon B. Hinckley, "New Mission Methods in Britain," *Deseret News*, August 10, 1935, in *Journal History*, The Church of Jesus Christ of Latter-day Saints, August 10, 1935, p. 7.
50. Gordon B. Hinckley, "New Mission Methods in Britain," *Deseret News*, August 10, 1935, in *Journal History*, The Church of Jesus Christ of Latter-day Saints, August 10, 1935, p. 7.
51. G. Homer Durham Funeral, January 14, 1985, Salt Lake City, Utah.
52. *Church News*, September 2, 1995, p. 4.
53. *Ensign*, December 1971, pp. 124-125; "Gordon B. Hinckley, Man of Integrity," KSL TV Channel 5 broadcast, April 1, 1995; *Ensign*, July 1995, p. 5.
54. *BYU Speeches of the Year*, (Provo, Utah:BYU Press, 1969), November 4, 1969, p. 4-5; *Journal History*, The Church of Jesus Christ of Latter-day Saints, August 29, 1971.
55. *Ensign*, November 1976, p. 97.
56. *Journal History*, The Church of Jesus Christ of Latter-day Saints, August 29, 1971, Manchester Area Conference.
57. University of Utah Institute Fireside Address, December 7, 1980.
58. *Church News*, December 27, 1950; G. Homer Durham Funeral, January 14, 1985, Salt Lake City, Utah; Eudora W. Durham Funeral, March 10, 1995, Salt Lake City, Utah.
59. Franklin D. Roosevelt, *Franklin Delano Roosevelt Fireside Chats*, (New York:Penguin Books, 1995), p. 65.
60. Marjorie P. Hinckley and Gordon B. Hinckley, *The Wondrous Power of a Mother*, (Salt Lake City, Utah:Deseret Book, 1989), p. 8.
61. *Journal History*, The Church of Jesus Christ of Latter-day Saints, July 28, 1985, p. 14.
62. "Autobiographical Sketch of Gordon Bitner Hinckley" written June 23, 1971 in Lorin A. Hinckley, *Arza Erastus Hinckley and Ira Nathaniel Hinckley*, (Salt Lake City, Utah:Lorin A. Hinckley, 1979), appendix.
63. *Journal History*, July 28, 1985, p. 14.

64. "Gordon B. Hinckley, Man of Integrity," KSL TV Channel 5 broadcast, April 1, 1995.
65. *Ensign*, September 1985, p. 3.
66. *Era*, December 1958, p. 925.
67. McCune Family Association Reunion, Lion House, September 11, 1980.
68. *Ensign*, September 1994, p. 7; "Gordon B. Hinckley, Man of Integrity," KSL TV Channel 5 broadcast, April 1, 1995.
69. *Ensign*, November 1995.

Mass Communications

1. *Ensign*, September 1994, p. 8.
2. "Autobiographical Sketch of Gordon Bitner Hinckley" written June 23, 1971 in Lorin A. Hinckley, *Arza Erastus Hinckley and Ira Nathaniel Hinckley*, (Salt Lake City, Utah:Lorin A. Hinckley, 1979), appendix.
3. *Utah Magazine*, August 1938, p. 10.
4. Wilburn D. Talbot, *The Acts of the Modern Apostles*, (Salt Lake City, Utah:Randall Book Co., 1985).
5. Stephen L. Richards Files, Radio, Publicity and Mission Literature Committee, LDS Historical Department Archives, CR 21-11.
6. Stephen L. Richards Files, Radio, Publicity and Mission Literature Committee, LDS Historical Department Archives, CR 21-5.
7. *Ensign*, February 1986, p. 5.
8. Gordon B. Hinckley Files, Radio, Publicity and Mission Literature Committee, LDS Historical Department Archives, CR 21-5.
9. *Journal History*, The Church of Jesus Christ of Latter-day Saints, November 17, 1985, p. 11.
10. Gordon B. Hinckley Files, Radio, Publicity and Mission Literature Committee, LDS Historical Department Archives, CR 21-2 & 3.
11. "Gordon B. Hinckley, Man of Integrity," KSL TV Channel 5 broadcast, April 1, 1995.
12. *Journal History*, The Church of Jesus Christ of Latter-day Saints, June 17, 1971.
13. *Forgotten Empires* script, 1936. on file at LDS Historical Department Library, Salt Lake City, Utah.
14. Landmarks of Church History script, 1936, on file at LDS Historical Department Library, Salt Lake City, Utah.
15. Gordon B. Hinckley Files, Radio, Publicity and Mission Literature Committee, LDS Historical Department Archives, CR 21-4.
16. *Chronicle of the 20th Century*, (New York:Chronicle Publications Inc., 1987), p. 451.
17. Missionary Index, LDS Historical Department Archives, Book F, p. 112, line 7.
18. Bryant S. Hinckley, *Autobiography of Bryant Stringham Hinckley*, (Salt Lake City, Utah:Ruth Hinckley Willes, 1980), p. 32.
19. Gordon B. Hinckley Files, Radio, Publicity and Mission Literature Committee, LDS Historical Department Archives, CR 21-14.
20. *Chronicle of the 20th Century*, (New York:Chronicle Publications Inc., 1987), p. 452-461.
21. *Chronicle of the 20th Century*, (New York:Chronicle Publications Inc., 1987), p. 463-469.
22. Gordon B. Hinckley Files, Radio, Publicity and Mission Literature Committee, LDS Historical Department Archives, CR 21-14.
23. *Utah Magazine*, September 1938, p. 27.
24. *1995-96 Church Almanac*, (Salt Lake City, Utah:Deseret News, 1994), p. 380.
25. *Chronicle of the 20th Century*, (New York:Chronicle Publications Inc., 1987), p. 507-510.
26. Franklin D. Roosevelt, *Franklin Delano Roosevelt Fireside Chats*, (New York:Penguin Books, 1995), p. 49.
27. 1995-96 Church Almanac, (Salt Lake City, Utah:Deseret News, 1994), p. 380.
28. Franklin D. Roosevelt, *Franklin Delano Roosevelt Fireside Chats*, (New York:Penguin Books, 1995), p. 64-75.
29. *Church Almanac*, (Salt Lake City, Utah:Deseret News, 1994), p. 381.
30. *Church History in the Fullness of Times*, (Provo, Utah:The Church of Jesus Christ of Latter-day Saints, 1989), 533.
31. Gordon B. Hinckley Files, Radio, Publicity and Mission Literature Committee, LDS Historical Department Archives, CR 21-3, 4, 6, 10, 14.
32. "Autobiographical Sketch of Gordon Bitner Hinckley" written June 23, 1971 in Lorin A. Hinckley, *Arza Erastus Hinckley and Ira Nathaniel Hinckley*, (Salt Lake City, Utah:Lorin A. Hinckley, 1979), appendix.
33. *Journal History*, June 17, 1971.
34. Gordon B. Hinckley Files, Radio, Publicity and Mission Literature Committee, LDS Historical Department Archives, CR 21-5 through 14.
35. Gordon B. Hinckley, *What of the Mormons?* (Salt Lake City, Utah:The Church of Jesus Christ of latter-day Saints, 1953), p. 223.
36. *1995-96 Church Almanac*, (Salt Lake City, Utah:Deseret News, 1994), p. 382.
37. *1995-96 Church Almanac*, (Salt Lake City, Utah:Deseret News, 1994), p. 383.
38. *BYU Speeches of the Year*, (Provo, Utah:BYU Press, 1960), December 14, 1960.
39. Gordon B. Hinckley Files, Radio, Publicity and Mission Literature Committee, LDS Historical Department Archives, CR 21-14.
40. *1993 Information Please Student Almanac*, (New York:Houghton Mifflin Company, 1992), P. 9.
41. Gordon B. Hinckley, *James Henry Moyle, the Story of a Distinguished American and an Hornored Churchman: Based in Part on the Research and Manuscript Writings of John Henry Evans*, (Salt Lake City, Utah:Deseret Book, 1951), p. 325.
42. Missionary Committee, LDS Historical Department Archives, CR 301-38.
43. *1995-96 Church Almanac*, (Salt Lake City, Utah:Deseret News, 1994), p. 383.
44. *1995-96 Church Almanac*, (Salt Lake City, Utah:Deseret News, 1994), p. 384.
45. *Church News*, September 1995, p. 6.
46. *Journal History*, The Church of Jesus Christ of Latter-day Saints, August 18, 1985.
47. *Journal History*, The Church of Jesus Christ of Latter-day Saints, September 9, 1971, p. l.
48. *Journal History*, The Church of Jesus Christ of Latter-day Saints, September 9, 1971, p. 4.
49. *Ensign*, January 1982, p. 7.
50. *Ensign*, November 1981, p. 5.
51. *Journal History*, The Church of Jesus Christ of Latter-day Saints, April 2, 1983, p. 1.
52. *Ensign*, February 1986, p. 9.
53. *1995-96 Church Almanac*, (Salt Lake City, Utah:Deseret News, 1994), p. 393.
54. *Church News*, March 28, 1992, p. 2.
55. *Church News*, May 2, 1992, p. 5.
56. "Gordon B. Hinckley, Man of Integrity," KSL TV Channel 5, broadcast April 1, 1995.
57. KSL Editorial, March 14, 1995.
58. KSL Editorial, March 14, 1995.
59. *Ensign*, November 1995, Opening Address.
60. *Ensign*, January 1982, p. 8.
61. *Church News*, September 9, 1995., p. 5.

Marriage

1. "Gordon B. Hinckley, Man of Integrity." KSL TV Channel 5 broadcast, April 1, 1995.
2. "Gordon B. Hinckley, Man of Integrity." KSL TV Channel 5 broadcast, April 1, 1995.
3. Record of Members, LDS Historical Department Archives, CR 375-8.
4. *Poke's Salt Lake City Directory*, 1916-1920; 4 Generation Sheets of LeRoy Phillip Pay, LDS Family History Library, Joseph Smith Memorial Building, Salt Lake City, Utah.
5. University of Utah Institute Speech delivered December 7, 1980, p. 3.
6. *Church News*, September 9, 1995, p. 11.
7. *Church News*, October 2, 1995, p. 7.
8. Richard Pay, "History of Richard Pay" autobiographical sketch manuscript on file in the records of the Juab County Daughters of the Utah Pioneers Museum, Nephi, Utah; Mary Goble Pay, "History of Mary (Goble) Pay 1843-1909" autobiographical sketch manuscript on file in the records of the Juab County Daughters of the Utah Pioneers Museum, Nephi, Utah.
9. Richard Pay, "History of Richard Pay" autobiographical sketch manuscript on file in the records of the Juab County Daughters of the Utah Pioneers Museum, Nephi, Utah; Mary Goble Pay, "History of Mary (Goble) Pay 1843-1909" autobiographical sketch manuscript on file in the records of the Juab County Daughters of the Utah Pioneers Museum, Nephi, Utah.
10. James W. Paxman, *William Paxman, a Brief Biographical Sketch*, (Nephi, Utah:James W. Paxman, 1935); Alice Ann Paxman McCune, *Biographical Sketch of the Life of Ann Rushen Keys Paxman*, (Nephi, Utah:Alice P. McCune, 1930).
11. *Journal History*, The Church of Jesus Christ of Latter-day Saints, May 23, 1964, p. 7.
12. *Poke's Salt Lake City Directory, 1921-1961.*
13. Marjorie Pay Hinckley & Gordon B. Hinckley, *The Wondrous Power of a Mother*, (Salt Lake City, Utah:Deseret Book, 1989), p. 10-15.
14. *Journal History*, The Church of Jesus Christ of Latter-day Saints, May 23, 1964, p. 7.
15. LDS Historical Department Audio Visual Tape, AV1824.
16. *Journal History*, The Church of Jesus Christ of Latter-day Saints, May 23, 1964, p. 7.
17. *BYU Speeches of the Year*, March 1, 1992, p. 78.

18. *Journal History*, The Church of Jesus Christ of Latter-day Saints, May 12, 1984, p. 2.
19. *Journal History*, The Church of Jesus Christ of Latter-day Saints, April 4, 1971.
20. *Utah Magazine*, August 1937, p. 13.
21. *Ensign*, September 1985, p. 3-4.
22. *Journal History*, The Church of Jesus Christ of Latter-day Saints, May 23, 1964, p. 7.
23. *Journal History*, The Church of Jesus Christ of Latter-day Saints, April 4, 1971.

Family

1. *Ensign*, September 1994, p. 8.
2. Record of Members, LDS Historical Department Archive, Salt Lake City, Utah, CR 375-8.
3. *University of Utah Institute Speeches*, May 21, 1989.
4. Record of Members, LDS Historical Department Archive, Salt Lake City, Utah, CR 375-8.
5. "Autobiography of Gordon B. Hinckley" written June 23, 1971.
6. "Autobiography of Gordon B. Hinckley" written June 23, 1971.
7. *Journal History*, The Church of Jesus Christ of Latter-day Saints, May 23, 1964, p. 7; *Ensign*, September 1994, p. 8; "Gordon B. Hinckley, Man of Integrity," KSL TV Channel 5 broadcast, April 1, 1995.
8. *Deseret News Church News Section*, January 24, 1942; *Church News*, September 16, 1995, p. 6.
9. *Church News*, July 1, 1995, p. 7.
10. Olie Langston Funeral, Audio Tape, c.a. 1970, LDS Historical Department Archives.
11. *Journal History*, The Church of Jesus Christ of Latter-day Saints, May 23, 1964, p. 7;
12. "Gordon B. Hinckley, Man of Integrity," KSL TV Channel 5 broadcast, April 1, 1995.
13. Record of Members, LDS Historical Department Archives, Salt Lake City, Utah, CR 375 8, reel 1778, p. 612, line 27.
14. Marjorie P. Hinckley and Gordon B. Hinckley, *The Wondrous Power of a Mother*, (Salt Lake City, Utah:Deseret News, 1989), p. 15.
15. *East Mill Creek Stake Carnival Program*, August 23 and 24, 1946.
16. *Ensign*, September 1994, pp. 8-9; "Gordon B. Hinckley, Man of Integrity," KSL TV Channel 5 broadcast, April 1, 1995.
17. *Journal History*, The Church of Jesus Christ of Latter-day Saints, Saturday, August 13, 1988, p. 6.
18. "Gordon B. Hinckley, Man of Integrity," KSL TV Channel 5 broadcast, April 1, 1995.
19. *Chronicle of the 20th Century*, (New York:Chronicle Publications Inc., 1987), p. 755.
20. "Gordon B. Hinckley, Man of Integrity," KSL TV Channel 5 broadcast, April 1, 1995.
21. Doctrine and Covenants 128:22.
22. *Journal History*, The Church of Jesus Christ of Latter-day Saints, May 23, 1964.
23. *Ensign*, February 1986, pp. 9, 3.
24. *Ensign*, September 1994, p. 11.
25. *Ensign*, September 1994, p. 11.
26. *Ensign*, September 1994, p. 11.
27. *Ensign*, January 1982, pp. 10-11.
28. *Ensign*, February 1991, p. 4.
29. *Ensign*, September 1994, p. 11.
30. *Ensign*, January 1982, pp. 10-11.
31. BYU Baccalaureate Address, June 5, 1958, p. 14.
32. *BYU Speeches of the Year*, (Provo, Utah:BYU Press, 1959), November 4, 1959
33. Bryant S. Hinckley, *The Autobiography of Bryant Stringham Hinckley*, (Salt Lake City, Utah:Ruth Hinckley Willes, 1971), pp. 48-52.
34. *Journal History*, The Church of Jesus Christ of Latter-day Saints, May 8, 1983, p. 14.
35. "Gordon B. Hinckley, Man of Integrity," KSL TV Channel 5 broadcast, April 1, 1995.
36. *Chronicle of the 20th Century*, (New York:Chronicle Publications Inc., 1987), p. 864.
37. *Ensign*, September 1994, p. 8.
38. Barbara Smith and Shirley W. Thomas, *Women of Devotion*, (Salt Lake City, Utah:Bookcraft, 1990), p. 4; *Ensign*, September 1994, p. 10.
39. *Ensign*, September 1994, p. 10.
40. *1993 Information Please Student Almanac*, (New York:Houghton Mifflin Company, 1992), P. 10.
41. *Improvement Era*, 1966, p. 530.
42. John Simmons Willes, *The Story of Ada Bitner Hinckley*, (Salt Lake City, Utah:Ruth Hinckley Willes, 1980).
43. "Autobiography of Gordon B. Hinckley" written June 23, 1971.
44. *Ensign*, September 1994, p. 8.
45. *BYU Speeches of the Year*, (Provo, Utah:BYU Press, 1989), September 3, 1989, p. 12.
46. *Ensign*, November 1978, p. 18.
47. *BYU Speeches of the Year*, (Provo, Utah:BYU Press, 1982), September 14, 1982, p. 15.
48. *Women of Devotion*, (Salt Lake City, Utah:Bookcraft, 1990), p. 5.
49. *Journal History*, The Church of Jesus Christ of Latter-day Saints, June 18, 1983, p. 3.
50. *Journal History*, The Church of Jesus Christ of Latter-day Saints, May 8, 1983, p. 14.
51. *Ensign*, September 1994, p. 10.
52. *Church News*, June 27, 1987, p. 6.
53. *1995-96 Church Almanac*, (Salt Lake City, Utah:Deseret News, 1994), p. 91.
54. *Journal History*, The Church of Jesus Christ of Latter-day Saints, June 23, 1990, p. 3.
55. *BYU Speeches of the Year*, (Provo, Utah:BYU Press, 1992), March 1, 1992, p. 78.
56. *1995-96 Church Almanac*, (Salt Lake City, Utah:Deseret News, 1994), p. 91.
57. *Church News*, June 27, 1992, p. 5.
58. KSL TV Channel 5 Broadcast, 12 Noon, October 1, 1995.

Temples

1. *1995-96 Church Almanac*, (Salt Lake City, Utah:Deseret News, 1994), p. 383.
2. *Ensign*, November 1995.
3. "Gordon B. Hinckley, Man of Integrity, KSL TV Channel 5 broadcast, April 1, 1995.
4. Gordon B. Hinckley, "Autobiographical Sketch of Gordon B. Hinckley," written June 23, 1971.
5. *Church News*, March 7, 1987, p. 6.
6. *Journal History*, May 5, 1971.
7. *Improvement Era*, August 1973, p. 7.
8. *BYU Speeches of the Year*, (Provo, Utah:BYU Press, 1958), June 5, 1958, p. 9.
9. *BYU Speeches of the Year*, (Provo, Utah:BYU Press, 1969), November 4, 1969, p. 1; *Journal History*, The Church of Jesus Christ of Latter-day Saints, May 5, 1971.
10. *BYU Speeches of the Year*, (Provo, Utah:BYU Press, 1960), December 14, 1960.
11. *Ensign*, January 1972, p. 91.
12. *BYU Speeches of the Year*, (Provo, Utah:BYU Press, 1958), June 5, 1958, p. 9.*BYU Speeches of the Year*, (Provo, Utah:BYU Press, 1958), June 5, 1958, p. 9.
13. *Improvement Era*, May 1974, p. 24.
14. *Journal History*, The Church of Jesus Christ of Latter-day Saints, August 11, 1983, p. 4.
15. *Improvement Era*, December 1958, p. 924.
16. *Improvement Era*, May 1974, pp. 23-24.
17. *Improvement Era*, May 1974, pp. 22-23.
18. *BYU Speeches of the Year*, (Provo, Utah:BYU Press, 1959), November 4, 1959.
19. *Improvement Era*, June 1969, pp. 425-426.
20. *Improvement Era*, December 1958, p. 924.
21. *Improvement Era*, December 1958, p. 925.
22. *BYU Speeches of the Year*, (Provo, Utah:BYU Press, 1959), January 28, 1959.
23. *Improvement Era*, December 1967, p. 87.
24. *Journal History*, The Church of Jesus Christ of Latter-day Saints, February 9, 1972.
25. *Improvement Era*, August 1974, pp. 37-41.
26. *Journal History*, The Church of Jesus Christ of Latter-day Saints, September 9, 1974, pp. 2-5.
27. *Journal History*, The Church of Jesus Christ of Latter-day Saints, September 12, 1974, pp. 1-2.
28. *Ensign*, July 1990; *Improvement Era*, November 1974, p. 98.
29. *Improvement Era*, November 1974, p. 100.
30. *Journal History*, The Church of Jesus Christ of Latter-day Saints, September 14, 1974, p. 6.
31. *Journal History*, The Church of Jesus Christ of Latter-day Saints, September 14, 1974, p. 4.
32. *Journal History*, The Church of Jesus Christ of Latter-day Saints, November 22, 1974, p. 4.
33. *Ensign*, July 1990.
34. *Journal History*, The Church of Jesus Christ of Latter-day Saints, March 22, 1975; *University of Utah Institute Fireside*, December 7, 1980.
35. *Journal History*, The Church of Jesus Christ of Latter-day Saints, March 22, 1975.

36. *Journal History*, The Church of Jesus Christ of Latter-day Saints, April 16, 1975, pp. 4 & 9.
37. *Journal History*, The Church of Jesus Christ of Latter-day Saints, April 19, 1975, p. 12.
38. *Journal History*, The Church of Jesus Christ of Latter-day Saints, August 10, 1975.
39. *Journal History*, The Church of Jesus Christ of Latter-day Saints, October 14, 1975, p. 2.
40. *Journal History*, The Church of Jesus Christ of Latter-day Saints, March 17, 1979, pp. 1 & 17.
41. *Journal History*, The Church of Jesus Christ of Latter-day Saints, April 18, 1980.
42. *Journal History*, The Church of Jesus Christ of Latter-day Saints, November 1, 1980; *University of Utah Institute Fireside*, December 7, 1980.
43. *Journal History*, The Church of Jesus Christ of Latter-day Saints, August 15, 1981, p. 3.
44. *Journal History*, The Church of Jesus Christ of Latter-day Saints, August 4, 1981, pp. 1-2.
45. *Ensign*, February 1982, p. 4.
46. *Journal History*, The Church of Jesus Christ of Latter-day Saints, August 20, 1982, p. 1.
47. *Journal History*, The Church of Jesus Christ of Latter-day Saints, January 22, 1983, pp. 1-2.
48. *Journal History*, The Church of Jesus Christ of Latter-day Saints, October 28, 1984, p. 8.
49. *Journal History*, The Church of Jesus Christ of Latter-day Saints, Wednesday, June 1, 1983, p. 2.
50. *Journal History*, The Church of Jesus Christ of Latter-day Saints, August 21, 1983.
51. *Journal History*, The Church of Jesus Christ of Latter-day Saints, September 15, 1983, p. 2.
52. *BYU Speeches of the Year*, (Provo, Utah:BYU Press, 1983), September 19, 1983, p. 8.
53. *Journal History*, The Church of Jesus Christ of Latter-day Saints, April 15, 1984, p. 3.
54. *Journal History*, The Church of Jesus Christ of Latter-day Saints,Saturday, May 19, 1984, p. 3.
55. *Journal History*, The Church of Jesus Christ of Latter-day Saints, October 7, 1984, p. 13.
56. *Journal History*, The Church of Jesus Christ of Latter-day Saints, October 7, 1984, pp. 9-10.
57. *Journal History*, The Church of Jesus Christ of Latter-day Saints, December 12, 1984, p. 3.
58. *Journal History*, The Church of Jesus Christ of Latter-day Saints, Thursday, July 4, 1985.
59. *Journal History*, The Church of Jesus Christ of Latter-day Saints, August 9, 1985, p. 5.
60. *Journal History*, The Church of Jesus Christ of Latter-day Saints, Saturday, November 30, 1985, p. 2.
61. *Ensign*, September 1994, p. 10.
62. *Journal History*, The Church of Jesus Christ of Latter-day Saints, Friday, January 10, 1986, p. 2.
63. *Journal History*, The Church of Jesus Christ of Latter-day Saints, Saturday, November 30, 1985, p. 9 & 2.
64. *Journal History*, The Church of Jesus Christ of Latter-day Saints, Friday, October 24, 1986, p. 6.
65. *Journal History*, The Church of Jesus Christ of Latter-day Saints, Saturday, September 20, 1989, pp. 3 & 5.
66. *Journal History*, The Church of Jesus Christ of Latter-day Saints, Tuesday, August 23, 1988, p. 3.
67. *Journal History*, The Church of Jesus Christ of Latter-day Saints, Sunday, October 8, 1989, p. 3.
68. *Journal History*, The Church of Jesus Christ of Latter-day Saints, Saturday, December 16, 1989, p. 5.
69. *Journal History*, The Church of Jesus Christ of Latter-day Saints, December 29, 1990, p. 13.
70. *Journal History*, The Church of Jesus Christ of Latter-day Saints, August 15, 1990, p. 1.
71. *Church News*, June 29, 1991, p. 3.
72. *Journal History*, The Church of Jesus Christ of Latter-day Saints, December 14, 1991, p. 7.
73. *Ensign*, May 1993, p. 72.
74. *Church New*, May 1, 1993, p. 4.
75. *Church New*, May 1, 1993, p. 3.
76. *Church New*, May 8, 1993, p. 8.
77. *Church New*, October 9, 1993, p. 3.
78. *Church New*, October 30, 1993, p. 2.
79. *Ensign*, September 1994, p. 7.
80. *Church News*, June 1, 1996, pp. 3-5, 8-9.
81. *Church News*, June 22, 1996, pp. 3, 10.
82. *Ensign*, November 1995.

Spreading

1. *1995-96 Church Almanac*, (Salt Lake City, Utah:Deseret News, 1994), p. 379.
2. *1995-96 Church Almanac*, (Salt Lake City, Utah:Deseret News, 1994), p. 380.
3. *Journal History*, The Church of Jesus Christ of Latter-day Saints, June 17, 1971.
4. "Oral Video Interivew with Jay A. Quealey, Jr., Salt Lake City, Utah, January 20, 1990.
5. Records of the Radio, Publicity and Mission Literature Committee, LDS Historical Department Archives, Salt Lake City, Utah, CR 21 10.
6. "Gordon B. Hinckley, Man of Integrity," KSL TV Channel 5 broadcast, April 1, 1995.
7. *Church News*, March 19, 1994, p. 11
8. *Church News*, June 27, 1992, p. 4.
9. *Ensign*, January 1982, p. 10.
10. *1995-96 Church Almanac*, (Salt Lake City, Utah:Deseret News, 1994), p. 382.
11. *Journal History*, The Church of Jesus Christ of Latter-day Saints, June 17, 1971.
12. "Autobiographical Sketch of Gordon B. Hinckley" written June 23, 1971.
13. *Ensign*, January 1982, p. 7.
14. "Gordon B. Hinckley, Man of Integrity," KSL TV Channel 5 broadcast, April 1, 1995.
15. *1995-96 Church Almanac*, (Salt Lake City, Utah:Deseret News, 1994), p. 383.
16. Photo Files, LDS Historical Department Archives, Salt Lake City, Utah, PH 4277.
17. *BYU Speeches of the Year*, (Provo, Utah:BYU Press, 1959), January 28, 1959.
18. *Improvement Era*, September 1959, p. 960.
19. *BYU Speeches of the Year*, (Provo, Utah:BYU Press, 1959), January 28, 1959, pp. 4-5.
20. *Improvement Era*, December 1958, p. 925.
21. *Improvement Era*, December 1958, p. 925.
22. *Improvement Era*, April 1959, p. 478.
23. *BYU Speeches of the Year*, (Provo, Utah:BYU Press, 1959), November 4, 1959, p. 6.
24. *Improvement Era*, December 1958, p. 925.
25. *BYU Speeches of the Year*, (Provo, Utah:BYU Press, 1959), January 28, 1959.
26. *BYU Speeches of the Year*, (Provo, Utah:BYU Press, 1959), January 28, 1959, p. 5.
27. *Improvement Era*, November 1959, p. 958.
28. *1995-96 Church Almanac*, (Salt Lake City, Utah:Deseret News, 1994), p. 385.
29. *Church News*, March 19, 1994, p. 11
30. *Encyclopedia of Mormonism*, Vol. 2, p. 917.
31. *Improvement Era*, December 1961, p. 978.
32. *BYU Speeches of the Year*, (Provo, Utah:BYU Press, 1962), January 3, 1962, pp. 3-4.
33. "Autobiographical Sketch of Gordon B. Hinckley," written June 23, 1971.
34. *BYU Speeches of the Year*, (Provo, Utah:BYU Press, 1964), October 13, 1964.
35. *Improvement Era*, 1965, p. 520.
36. *BYU Speeches of the Year*, (Provo, Utah:BYU Press, 1964), October 13, 1964, p. 4.
37. *BYU Speeches of the Year*, (Provo, Utah:BYU Press, 1969), November 4, 1969, p. 4.
38. *Improvement Era*, December 1970, pp. 71-72; *Ensign*, January 1982, p. 13.
39. *Journal History*, The Church of Jesus Christ of Latter-day Saints, October 10, 1972, p. 13.
40. *Improvement Era*, July 1973, p. 50.
41. *Improvement Era*, January 1974, p. 124.
42. *BYU Speeches of the Year*, (Provo, Utah:BYU Press, 1976), April 8, 1976, p. 89.
43. *Journal History*, The Church of Jesus Christ of Latter-day Saints, April 17, 1976, p. 12.
44. *Ensign*, December 1976, pp. 16-17.
45. *Ensign*, May 1977, pp. 64-65.
46. *BYU Speeches of the Year*, (Provo, Utah:BYU Press, 1979), November 4, 1979, pp. 203-204.
47. *Journal History*, The Church of Jesus Christ of Latter-day Saints, Saturday, August 23, 1980, p. 5; *University of Utah Institute Address*,

December 7, 1980, pp. 1-2, 8.
48. *University of Utah Institute Address*, December 7, 1980, p. 2.
49. *Ensign*, December 1986, pp. 4-5.
50. *Ensign*, November 1981, p. 6.
51. *Ensign*, April 1982, p. 42; *Journal History*, The Church of Jesus Christ of Latter-day Saints, November 30, 1984, p. 1.
52. *Journal History*, The Church of Jesus Christ of Latter-day Saints, December 21, 1984, p. 5.
53. *Ensign*, February 1986, p. 5.
54. *Journal History*, The Church of Jesus Christ of Latter-day Saints, Friday, April 4, 1986, p. 1.
55. *Journal History*, The Church of Jesus Christ of Latter-day Saints, Friday, April 4, 1986, p. 1.
56. *1995-96 Church Almanac*, (Salt Lake City, Utah:Deseret News, 1994), p. 392.
57. *Ensign*, December 1986, p. 3.
58. *Ensign*, October 1987, p. 2.
59. *Ensign*, February 1988, p. 3.
60. *Journal History*, The Church of Jesus Christ of Latter-day Saints, Saturday, July 2, 1988, p. 5.
61. Elliott & Margaret Richards Christmas Letter, December 1989.
62. *Journal History*, The Church of Jesus Christ of Latter-day Saints, Saturday, July 30, 1988, p. 7.
63. *Ensign*, January 1989, p. 5.
64. *Journal History*, The Church of Jesus Christ of Latter-day Saints, Friday, March 31, 1989, p. 8.
65. *Journal History*, The Church of Jesus Christ of Latter-day Saints, May 30, 1989, p. 2; *Journal History*, The Church of Jesus Christ of Latter-day Saints, Friday, June 23, 1989, p. 6.
66. *Journal History*, The Church of Jesus Christ of Latter-day Saints, June 30, 1989, p. 1.
67. *1995-96 Church Almanac*, (Salt Lake City, Utah:Deseret Book, 1994), p. 394.
68. *1995-96 Church Almanac*, (Salt Lake City, Utah:Deseret Book, 1994), p. 394.
69. *Church News*, June 22, 1991, p. 4.
70. *Church News*, November 26, 1991.
71. *Church News*, March 28, 1992, p. 2.
72. *Church News*, March 28, 1992, p. 2.
73. *Church News*, June 27, 1992, p. 4.
74. *Church News*, July 1, 1995, p. 4.
75. *Church News*, March 19, 1994, p. 11.

Humor

1. "Gordon B. Hinckley, Man of Integrity," KSL TV Channel 5 broadcast, April 1, 1995.
2. "Gordon B. Hinckley, Man of Integrity," KSL TV Channel 5 broadcast, April 1, 1995.
3. *Improvement Era*, June 1958, p. 456.
4. *BYU Speeches of the Year*, (Provo, Utah:BYU Press, 1967), January 10, 1967, p. 1.
5. *Improvement Era*, December 1969, p. 97.
6. *BYU Speeches of the Year*, (Provo, Utah:BYU Press, 1969), November 4, 1969, p. 2.
7. *Improvement Era*, December 1979, p. 97.
8. *Ensign*, January 1973, p. 91.
9. *Ensign*, January 1974, p. 122.
10. *BYU Speeches of the Year*, (Provo, Utah:BYU Press, 1977), March 6, 1977, p. 43.
11. *Journal History*, The Church of Jesus Christ of Latter-day Saints, November 4, 1978, p. 4.
12. "McCune Family Association Reunion," video, Lion House, Salt Lake City, Utah, September 11, 1980.
13. *Journal History*, The Church of Jesus Christ of Latter-day Saints, November 1, 1980, p. 2.
14. *Ensign*, September 1994, p. 10.
15. University of Utah Institute Fireside, December 7, 1980.
16. *Journal History*, The Church of Jesus Christ of Latter-day Saints, Saturday, January 22, 1983, p. 2.
17. *Journal History*, The Church of Jesus Christ of Latter-day Saints, June 24, 1983, p. 3.
18. "Gordon B. Hinckley, Man of Integrity," KSL TV Channel 5 broadcast, April 1, 1995.
19. *Journal History*, The Church of Jesus Christ of Latter-day Saints, Sunday, November 6, 1983, p. 16.
20. *Journal History*, The Church of Jesus Christ of Latter-day Saints, Friday, April 20, 1984, p. 3.
21. *Journal History*, The Church of Jesus Christ of Latter-day Saints, July 12, 1984, p. 4.
22. *Journal History*, The Church of Jesus Christ of Latter-day Saints, January 19, 1985, p. 1.
23. *Journal History*, The Church of Jesus Christ of Latter-day Saints, Thursday, September 17, 1985, p. 1.
24. *Journal History*, The Church of Jesus Christ of Latter-day Sunday, July 6, 1986, p. 4.
25. *Church News*, May 30, 1987, p. 10.
26. Church News, April 9, 1988, p. 16.
27.
28. *Church News*, Tuesday, July 5, 1988, p. 3.
29. Interview of George M. McCune with William Walker, March 1995.
30. *Church News*, Sunday, January 13, 1991, p. 4.
31. *Church News*, June 29, 1991, p. 4.
32. *Church News*, June 29, 1991.
33. *Church News*, June 29, 1991.
34. *Church News*, November 2, 1991, p. 4.
35. *Church News*, May 16, 1992, p. 9.
36. *Ensign*, May 1993, p. 72.
37. *Church News*, September 19, 1992.
38. *Ensign*, May 1993, p. 52.
39. *Ensign*, November 1993.
40. *Ensign*, September 1994, p. 10.
41. *Ensign*, September 1994, p. 10.
42. LDS General Conference broadcast on KSL TV Channel 5, October 1, 1994.
43. Audio Recording of Eudora Widtsoe Durham funeral, March 10, 1995, LDS Historical Department Archives, AV 1824.
44. BYU New Law Library Groundbreaking, Provo, Utah, May 1, 1995.
45. KSL TV Channel 5, Salt Lake City, Utah, 12 Noon, October 1, 1995.
46. *Church News*, September 2, 1995, p. 3.
47. *Church News*, September 16, 1995, p. 3.
48. *Ensign*, November 1995.
49. *Ensign*, November 1995.
50. *Church News*, October 21, 995, p. 4.
51. *Church News*, September 9, 1995, p. 5.

Stake Presidency

1. Record of Members 1836-1970, LDS Historical Department Archives, Salt Lake City, Utah, CR 375-8.
2. Record of Members, LDS Historical Department Archives, East Mill Creek Stake, CR 375-8.
3."Gordon B. Hinckley, Man of Integrity," KSL TV Channel 5 broadcast, April 1, 1995; Autobiographical Sketch of Gordon B. Hinckley written June 23, 1971.
4. "Gordon B. Hinckley, Man of Integrity," KSL TV Channel 5 broadcast, April 1, 1995;
5. *Church News*, December 5, 1987, p. 6.
6. *Journal History*, The Church of Jesus Christ of Latter-day Saints, Sunday, February 1990, p. 2.
7. *Ensign*, November 1977, pp. 84-85.
8. J. Reuben Clark, Jr., "Bishops and Relief Society," *Improvement Era*, July 9, 1941, pp. 17-18.
9. *Ensign*, May 1982, pp. 40-41.
10. *Church News*, December 5, 1987, p. 6.

Far East Supervision

1. Gordon B. Hinckley Address at McCune Family Association Reunion, Lion House, Salt Lake City, Utah, McCune Family Association video, September 11, 1980, LDS Historical Department Arvhices, McCune Family Association Manuscript Collection.
2. *Improvement Era*, December 1964, pp. 1092-1093.
3. "I Have Witnessed Miracles," *Improvement Era*, 1960.
4. Gordon B. Hinckley Unpublished Tour Notes of the Southern Far East and Northern Far East Missions, LDS Historical Department Archives, Salt Lake City, Utah, 1960.
5. "I Have Witnessed Miracles," *Improvement Era*, 1960.
6. "I Have Witnessed Miracles," *Improvement Era*, 1960.
7. Gordon B. Hinckley Unpublished Tour Notes of the Southern Far East and Northern Far East Missions, LDS Historical Department Archives, Salt Lake City, Utah, 1960.
8. *BYU Speeches of the Year*, (Provo, Utah:BYU Press, 1992), March 1, 1992, p. 81.
9. Marjorie P. Hinckley & Gordon B. Hinckley, *The Wondrous Power of a Mother*, (Salt Lake City, Utah:Deseret Book, 1989), p. 1.
10. George M. McCune, *Testimony*, (Provo, Utah:BYU Press, 1967), p. 29.

11. *BYU Speeches of the Year*, (Provo, Utah:BYU Press, 1977), March 6, 1977, p. 46; *Journal History*, The Church of Jesus Christ of Latter-day Saints, Sunday, October 7, 1984, p. 9; *Ensign*, September 1991, p. 3-4..
12. Marjorie P. Hinckley & Gordon B. Hinckley, *The Wondrous Power of a Mother*, (Salt Lake City, Utah:Deseret Book, 1989), p. 8.
13. *Journal History*, The Church of Jesus Christ of Latter-day Saints, August 26, 1982, p. 1.
14. *BYU Speeches of the Year*, (Provo, Utah:BYU Press, 1977), March 6, 1977, p. 46; *Ensign*, August 1982, p. 5; *Journal History*, The Church of Jesus Christ of Latter-day Saints, December 14, 1985, p. 3.
15. *Ensign*, May 1993, pp. 93-94.
16. *Improvement Era*, June 1962, pp. 461-462.
17. Jay Ambrose Quealy, Jr. oral history video interview by George M. McCune, Salt Lake City, Utah, January 20, 1990, in McCune Family Association Collection, LDS Historical Department, Salt Lake City, Utah.
18. George M. McCune, *Testimony*, (Provo, Utah:BYU Press, 1967), pp. 17-18.
19. George M. McCune, *Testimony*, (Provo, Utah:BYU Press, 1967), pp. 18-28.
20. *Journal History*, The Church of Jesus Christ of Latter-day Saints, May 23, 1964.
21. *Ensign*, November 1982, pp. 8-9.
22.Gordon B. Hinckley Address at McCune Family Association Reunion, Lion House, Salt Lake City, Utah, McCune Family Association video, September 11, 1980, LDS Historical Department Archives, McCune Family Association Manuscript Collection.
23. *BYU Speeches of the Year*, (Provo, Utah:BYU Press, 1977), March 6, 1977, p. 44; *Ensign*, August 1982, p. 4.
24. Gordon B. Hinckley Address at McCune Family Association Reunion, Lion House, Salt Lake City, Utah, McCune Family Association video, September 11, 1980, LDS Historical Department Archives, McCune Family Association Manuscript Collection.
25. *BYU Speeches of the Year*, (Provo, Utah:BYU Press, 1977), March 6, 1977, p. 44.
26. *Ensign*, January 1982, pp. 8-10.
27. *Ensign*, September 1995, p. 52.
28. *Improvement Era*, July 1968, p. 49.
29. *Improvement Era*, December 1969, p. 98.
30. *Improvement Era*, December 1966, p. 1122.
31. *BYU Speeches of the Year*, (Provo, Utah:BYU Press, 1967), January 10, 1967, p. 3.
32. *BYU Speeches of the Year*, (Provo, Utah:BYU Press, 1967), January 10, 1967, pp. 4-5.
33. *BYU Speeches of the Year*, (Provo, Utah:BYU Press, 1967), January 10, 1967, p. 5.
34. *BYU Speeches of the Year*, (Provo, Utah:BYU Press, 1967), January 10, 1967, p. 5.
35. *BYU Speeches of the Year*, (Provo, Utah:BYU Press, 1967), January 10, 1967, p. 6.
36. *BYU Speeches of the Year*, (Provo, Utah:BYU Press, 1967), January 10, 1967, p. 7.
37. *BYU Speeches of the Year*, (Provo, Utah:BYU Press, 1967), January 10, 1967, p. 7.
38. *BYU Speeches of the Year*, (Provo, Utah:BYU Press, 1967), January 10, 1967, p. 5.
39. A. David Allen letter dated December 2, 1974 from Rexburg, Idaho, LDS Historical Department Archives, Salt Lake City, Utah, Ms. 4689.
40. *Improvement Era*, June 1968, p. 49.
41. *BYU Speeches of the Year*, (Provo, Utah:BYU Press, 1967), January 10, 1967, p. 8.
42. *Ensign*, September 1995, p. 53.
43. *BYU Speeches of the Year*, (Provo, Utah:BYU Press, 1967), January 10, 1967, p. 9.
44. *BYU Speeches of the Year*, (Provo, Utah:BYU Press, 1967), January 10, 1967, p. 10.
45. *Church News*, July 24, 1993, p. 6.
46. Gordon B. Hinckley Address at McCune Family Association Reunion, Lion House, Salt Lake City, Utah, McCune Family Association video, September 11, 1980, LDS Historical Department Archives, McCune Family Association Manuscript Collection.
47. *Improvement Era*, June 1967, p. 55.
48. *Improvement Era*, June 1968, p. 50.
49. *Improvement Era*, June 1970, p. 39.
50. *Journal History*, The Church of Jesus Christ of Latter-day Saints, December 5, 1970.
51. *Journal History*, The Church of Jesus Christ of Latter-day Saints, August 5, 1975, p. 3.
52. *Journal History*, The Church of Jesus Christ of Latter-day Saints, Saturday, August 9, 1975, p. 7.
53. *Journal History*, The Church of Jesus Christ of Latter-day Saints, Saturday, August 11, 1975, p. 3.
54. *Journal History*, The Church of Jesus Christ of Latter-day Saints, Saturday, August 11, 1975, p. 3.
55. Gordon B. Hinckley Address at McCune Family Association Reunion, Lion House, Salt Lake City, Utah, McCune Family Association video, September 11, 1980, LDS Historical Department Archives, McCune Family Association Manuscript Collection.
56. *Journal History*, The Church of Jesus Christ of Latter-day Saints, October 18, 1975, p. 18.
57. *BYU Speeches of the Year*, (Provo, Utah:BYU Press, 1976), April 8, 1976, p. 87.
58. Gordon B. Hinckley Address at McCune Family Association Reunion, Lion House, Salt Lake City, Utah, McCune Family Association video, September 11, 1980, LDS Historical Department Archives, McCune Family Association Manuscript Collection.
59. Gordon B. Hinckley Address at McCune Family Association Reunion, Lion House, Salt Lake City, Utah, McCune Family Association video, September 11, 1980, LDS Historical Department Archives, McCune Family Association Manuscript Collection.
60. Gordon B. Hinckley Address at McCune Family Association Reunion, Lion House, Salt Lake City, Utah, McCune Family Association video, September 11, 1980, LDS Historical Department Archives, McCune Family Association Manuscript Collection.
61. Gordon B. Hinckley Address at McCune Family Association Reunion, Lion House, Salt Lake City, Utah, McCune Family Association video, September 11, 1980, LDS Historical Department Archives, McCune Family Association Manuscript Collection.
62. *Journal History*, The Church of Jesus Christ of Latter-day Saints, November 1980, pp. 1-3.
63. *Journal History*, The Church of Jesus Christ of Latter-day Saints, October 18, 1975, p. 18.
64. *Journal History*, The Church of Jesus Christ of Latter-day Saints, March 7, 1982, p. 1.
65. *Journal History*, The Church of Jesus Christ of Latter-day Saints, Sunday, September 11, 1983, p. 11.
66. *Journal History*, The Church of Jesus Christ of Latter-day Saints, Thursday, September 27, 1984.
67. *Journal History*, The Church of Jesus Christ of Latter-day Saints, Sunday, Octobr 7, 1984, p. 9.
68. *Journal History*, The Church of Jesus Christ of Latter-day Saints, Wednesday, September 7, 1988, p. 3.
69. *Journal History*, The Church of Jesus Christ of Latter-day Saints, October 1, 1988, p. 1.
70. *Church News*, June 8, 1991, p. 12.
71. *Church News*, June 1, 1996, pp. 3-5, 8-9.
72. "Gordon B. Hinckley, Man of Integrity," KSL TV Channel 5 broadcast, April 1, 1995.
73. *Journal History*, The Church of Jesus Christ of Latter-day Saints, June 23, 1990, p. 3.

Ministry

1. "Gordon B. Hinckley Autobiographical Sketch" written June 23, 1971.
2. *Journal History*, The Church of Jesus Christ of Latter-day Saints, May 5, 1971.
3. *Ensign*, January 1982, p. 8.
4. "Gordon B. Hinckley, Man of Integrity," KSL TV Channel 5 broadcast, April 1, 1995.
5. *Ensign*, February 1986, p. 5.
6. *Ensign*, January 1982, p. 7.
7. Letter to President David O. McKay dated November 29, 1961, LDS Historical Department Archives, Salt Lake City, Utah, Ms. 6198.
8. *Ensign*, May 1982, p. 41.
9. Oral Interview of President Lee H. Nelson by Lauritze S. Peterson, July 14, 1976, LDS Historical Department Archives, Salt Lake City, Utah, Ms. 9277.
10. *BYU Speeches of the Year*, (Provo, Utah:BYU Press, 1977), March 6, 1977, pp. 43-44.
11. Al Langston funeral services audio tape, LDS Historical Department Archives, Salt Lake City, Utah.
12. *BYU Speeches of the Year*, (Provo, Utah:BYU Press, 1948), June 5, 1958, p. 9.
13. *Improvement Era*, 1959, p. 476.
14. Stephen L. Richards Funeral Services audio tape, LDS Historical Department Archives, Salt Lake City, Utah, AV 103, segment 1.
15. *Ruth Hinckley Willes, The Autobiography of Bryant Stringham Hinckley*, (Salt Lake City, Utah:Ruth Hinckley Willes, 1971).
16. *BYU Speeches of the Year*, (Provo, Utah:BYU Press, 1965), pp. 4-5.
17. BYU Speeches of the Year, (Provo, Utah:BYU Press, 1960), December 14, 1960.
18. BYU Speeches of the Year, (Provo, Utah:BYU Press, 1962), January 3, 1962.
19. Joseph Simmons Willes, *The Story of Ada Bitner Hinckley*, (Salt Lake City, Utah:Ruth Hinckley Willes, 1980), p. 74.
20. *Improvement Era*, 1967, p. 53.
21. BYU Speeches of the Year, (Provo, Utah:BYU Press, 1964), October 13, 1964.
22. *Journal History*, The Church of Jesus Christ of Latter-day Saints, Salt Lake City, Utah, October 29, 1983, p. 2; "Gordon B. Hinckley, Man of Integrity," KSL TV Channel 5 broadcast, April 1, 1995.
23. *Church News*, February 3, 1996, p. 4.

24. *Ensign*, February 1986, p. 7.
25. *Improvement Era*, June 1964, p. 478.
26. *Improvement Era*, December 1968, p. 70.
27. BYU Speeches of the Year, (Provo, Utah:BYU Press, 1964), October 13, 1964.
28. BYU Speeches of the Year, (Provo, Utah:BYU Press, 1964), October 13, 1964, p. 5.
29. BYU Speeches of the Year, (Provo, Utah:BYU Press, 1964), October 13, 1964.
30. *Ensign*, September 1991, p. 4.
31. BYU Speeches of the Year, (Provo, Utah:BYU Press, 1964), October 26, 1965, pp. 7-8.
32. *Ensign*, October 1990, p. 2.
33. Oral interview of Tatsui and Tomiko Sato with George M. McCune, Salt Lake City, Utah, March 15, 1995.
34. *Improvement Era*, December 1987, p. 87.
35. *Improvement Era*, June 1969, p. 73.
36. BYU Speeches of the Year, (Provo, Utah:BYU Press, 1969), November 4, 1969, p. 2.
37. *Improvement Era*, December 1970, p. 71.
38. *Journal History*, The Church of Jesus Christ of Latter-day Saints, Salt Lake City, Utah, February 25, 1971.
39. *Journal History*, The Church of Jesus Christ of Latter-day Saints, Salt Lake City, Utah, April 1, 1971.
40. *Journal History*, The Church of Jesus Christ of Latter-day Saints, Salt Lake City, Utah, April 4, 1971.
41. Autobiography of Gordon B. Hinckley written June 23, 1971.
42. *Improvement Era*, December 1971, p. 125.
43. *Journal History*, The Church of Jesus Christ of Latter-day Saints, Salt Lake City, Utah, October 10, 1972, pp. 16 & 18; *Time Magazine*, October 23, 1972.
44. *Journal History*, The Church of Jesus Christ of Latter-day Saints, Salt Lake City, Utah, September 1972, p. 7.
45. *Journal History*, The Church of Jesus Christ of Latter-day Saints, Salt Lake City, Utah, September 1972, p. 7.
46. *Journal History*, The Church of Jesus Christ of Latter-day Saints, Salt Lake City, Utah, September 1972, p. 8.
47. "Gordon B. Hinckley, Man of Integrity," KSL TV Channel 5 broadcast, April 1, 1995.
48. *Journal History*, The Church of Jesus Christ of Latter-day Saints, Salt Lake City, Utah, October 10, 1972, p. 7.
49. *Journal History*, The Church of Jesus Christ of Latter-day Saints, Salt Lake City, Utah, May 25 & 26, 1973.
50. *Journal History*, The Church of Jesus Christ of Latter-day Saints, Salt Lake City, Utah, August 10, 1975.
51. *Ensign*, September 1981, p. 73.
52. *Journal History*, The Church of Jesus Christ of Latter-day Saints, Salt Lake City, Utah, June 26, 1976, p. 6.
53. *Journal History*, The Church of Jesus Christ of Latter-day Saints, Salt Lake City, Utah, July 31, 1976, p. 8.
54. *Ensign*, March 1993, p. 2.
55. *Journal History*, The Church of Jesus Christ of Latter-day Saints, Salt Lake City, Utah, June 10, 1978, p. 20.
56. *Journal History*, The Church of Jesus Christ of Latter-day Saints, Salt Lake City, Utah, November 4, 1978.
57. *Journal History*, The Church of Jesus Christ of Latter-day Saints, Salt Lake City, Utah, April 12, 1979, p. 1.
58. *Journal History*, The Church of Jesus Christ of Latter-day Saints, Salt Lake City, Utah, November 1979, p. 8.
59. *Journal History*, The Church of Jesus Christ of Latter-day Saints, Salt Lake City, Utah, April 6, 1980.
60. Gordon B. Hinckley statement on 150th anniversary of the Church, LDS Historical Department, Salt Lake City, Utah, Ms. 6431.
61. *Journal History*, The Church of Jesus Christ of Latter-day Saints, Salt Lake City, Utah, April 19, 1980, p. 8.
62. *PSA Magazine*, June 1980, p. 1.
63. University of Utah Institute Fireside, December 7, 1980.
64. "A Hymn is Born," manuscript in LDS Historical Department Archives, Salt Lake City, Utah, Ms. 9008.
65. *Church News*, June 24, 1995, p. 7.

South America Supervision

1. *Improvement Era*, December 1969, p. 98.
2. *Improvement Era*, December 1969, p. 98.
3. *Journal History*, The Church of Jesus Christ of Latter-day Saints, September 17, 1983, p. 1.
4. "Autobiographical Sketch of Gordon B. Hinckley" written June 23, 1971.
5. *Journal History*, The Church of Jesus Christ of Latter-day Saints, April 27, 1986, p. 4.

Europe Advisor

1. "Autobiographical Sketch of Gordon B. Hinckley" written June 23, 1971.
2. *Journal History*, The Church of Jesus Christ of Latter-day Saints, July 1, 1971.
3. *BYU Speeches of the Year*, (Provo, Utah:BYU Press, 1967), December 5, 1967, p. 6.
4. "Gordon B. Hinckley, Man of Integrity" KSL TV Channel 5 broadcast, April 1, 1995.
5. *Ensign*, August 1973, p. 8.
6. *Ensign*, August 1973, p. 8.
7. *Ensign*, January 1973, p. 93; June-July 1974, p. 88.
8. *Ensign*, June-July 1974, pp. 88-90.
9. *Ensign*, July 1973, p. 50.
10. *Ensign*, August 1973, p. 7.
11. *Ensign*, August 1973, p. 8.
12. *Ensign*, August 1973, p. 9.
13. Church *News*, June 22, 1996, pp. 3-4.

Optimism

1. *BYU Speeches of the Year*, (Provo, Utah:BYU Press, 1982), September 14, 1982, p. 16.
2. *Improvement Era*, June 1963, pp. 529-530.
3. *Improvement Era*, June 1963, p. 530.
4. *Improvement Era*, June 1963, pp. 531-532.
5. *Improvement Era*, December 1968, p. 69.
6. *Improvement Era*, December 1969, p. 98.
7. *Ensign*, July 1972, p. 73.
8. *BYU Speeches of the Year*, (Provo, Utah:BYU Press, 1974), October 29, 1974, pp. 265-266.
9. *BYU Speeches of the Year*, (Provo, Utah:BYU Press, 1974), October 19, 1974, p. 266.
10. *BYU Speeches of the Year*, (Provo, Utah:BYU Press, 1974), October 29, 1974, p. 273.
11. *BYU Speeches of the Year*, (Provo, Utah:BYU Press, 1976), April 8, 1976, p 91.
12. *Ensign*, May 1978, p. 59.
13. *Journal History*, The Church of Jesus Christ of Latter-day Saints, *October 3, 1981, pp. 9-10.*
14. *Ensign*, January 1982, p. 13.
15. *Journal History*, The Church of Jesus Christ of Latter-day Saints, Saturday, April 7, 1984, p. 6.
16. *Journal History*, The Church of Jesus Christ of Latter-day Saints, Sunday, April 6, 1986, p. 12.
17. *Journal History*, The Church of Jesus Christ of Latter-day Saints, Tuesday, June 27, 1989, p. 3.
18. BYU Speeches of the Year, (Provo, Utah:BYU Press, 1989), September 3, 1989, p. 12.
19. *Ensign*, November 1989, pp. 52-53.
20. *Journal History*, The Church of Jesus Christ of Latter-day Saints, Sunday, February 3, 1991, p. 3.
21. *Journal History*, The Church of Jesus Christ of Latter-day Saints, Tuesday, February 5, 1991, p. 3.
22. BYU Speeches of the Year, (Provo, Utah:BYU Press, 1992), October 13, 1993, p. 22.
23. *Church News*, March 12, 1995, p. 5.
24. *Church News*, August 3, 1991, p. 4.
25. *Church News*, November 6, 1993, p. 4.

Councils

1. *BYU Speeches of the Year*, (Provo, Utah:BYU Press, 1969), November 4, 1969, p. 1; "Biographical Sketch of Gordon B. Hinckley" written June 23, 1971; "Resume of the Life of Gordon B. Hinckley" written September 1977; *Ensign*, February 1986, pp. 8-9; *Journal History*, The Church of Jesus Christ of Latter-day Saints, December 5, 1970; *Journal History*, The Church of Jesus Christ of Latter-day Saints, May 5, 1971; *Journal History*, The Church of Jesus Christ of Latter-day Saints, June 23 & 29, 1971; *Journal History*, The Church of Jesus Christ of Latter-day Saints, April 10, 1975; *Journal History*, The Church of Jesus Christ of Latter-day Saints, June 5, 1976, p. 1; *Journal History*, The Church of Jesus Christ of Latter-day Saints, October 23, 1985, p. 3; *BYU Speeches of the Year*, (Provo, Utah:BYU Press, 1988), October 11, 1988, p. 47; *Ensign*, January 1982, p. 7.

2. "Autobiographical Sketch of Gordon B. Hinckley" written June 23, 1971.
3. *Ensign*, February 1986, p. 7.

Shoulder

1. *Journal History*, The Church of Jesus Christ of Latter-day Saints, March 10, 1976, p. 4.
2. Spencer W. Kimball, Journal History Subject Catalog Card Index, LDS Historical Department Library.
3. *Journal History*, The Church of Jesus Christ of Latter-day Saints, February 4, 1986, p. 1.
4. *Journal History*, The Church of Jesus Christ of Latter-day Saints, August 1, 1987.
5. *Journal History*, The Church of Jesus Christ of Latter-day Saints, Wednesday, October 23, 1985, pp. 2-3.
6. *Journal History*, The Church of Jesus Christ of Latter-day Saints, February 20, 1981, p. 5.
7. *Journal History*, The Church of Jesus Christ of Latter-day Saints, October 23, 1985, p. 3.
8. *Journal History*, The Church of Jesus Christ of Latter-day Saints, August 26, 1980, p. 1.
9. *Ensign*, May 1981, p. 20.
10. *Ensign*, May 1981, pp. 20-23.
11. *Journal History*, The Church of Jesus Christ of Latter-day Saints, April 4, 1984, p. 1; *Church News*, October 23, 1993.
12. *Journal History*, The Church of Jesus Christ of Latter-day Saints, May 16, 1981, pp. 1-2.
13. *Journal History*, The Church of Jesus Christ of Latter-day Saints, April 20, 1982, pp. 1 & 3.
14. *Journal History*, The Church of Jesus Christ of Latter-day Saints, July 6, 1981, p. 1.
15. *Journal History*, The Church of Jesus Christ of Latter-day Saints, August 23, 1981, p. 1.
16. *Journal History*, The Church of Jesus Christ of Latter-day Saints, September 5, 1981, p. 9.
17. *Journal History*, The Church of Jesus Christ of Latter-day Saints, October 23, 1985, p. 3.
18. *Ensign*, November 1981, p. 5.
19. *Journal History*, The Church of Jesus Christ of Latter-day Saints, October 12, 1981, p. 1; November 7, 1981, p. 4; December 31, 1981, p. 1.
20. *Journal History*, The Church of Jesus Christ of Latter-day Saints, December 10, 1981, p. 1.
21. *Journal History*, The Church of Jesus Christ of Latter-day Saints, March 9, 1982, p. 1.
22. *Journal History*, The Church of Jesus Christ of Latter-day Saints, March 18, 1982, pp. 1-5.
23. *Journal History*, The Church of Jesus Christ of Latter-day Saints, April 2, 1982.
24. *Journal History*, The Church of Jesus Christ of Latter-day Saints, April 3, 1982.
25. *Journal History*, The Church of Jesus Christ of Latter-day Saints, April 4, 1982.
26. *Journal History*, The Church of Jesus Christ of Latter-day Saints, April 4, 1982, p. 3.
27. *Journal History*, The Church of Jesus Christ of Latter-day Saints, Tuesday, April 20, 1982, p. 1.
28. *Journal History*, The Church of Jesus Christ of Latter-day Saints, April 29, 1982, p. 3.
29. *Journal History*, The Church of Jesus Christ of Latter-day Saints, June 23, 1982, p. 1.
30. *Journal History*, The Church of Jesus Christ of Latter-day Saints, July 3, 1982, p. 1.
31. *Journal History*, The Church of Jesus Christ of Latter-day Saints, July 3, 1982, p. 1.
32. Edgar Lee Masters, *Spoon River Anthology*, (New York:MacMillan Publishing Co., 1944), p. 221.
33. *Ensign*, August 1982, p. 5.
34. *Ensign*, August 1982, p. 5.
35. *Journal History*, The Church of Jesus Christ of Latter-day Saints, Saturday, August 14, 1982, p. 1.
36. *Journal History*, The Church of Jesus Christ of Latter-day Saints, Tuesday, September 14, 1982, pp. 1 & 15..
37.*Journal History*, The Church of Jesus Christ of Latter-day Saints, October 2, 1982, p. 9; and October 3, 1982, p. 6.
38. *Journal History*, The Church of Jesus Christ of Latter-day Saints, Monday, November 8. 1982, pp. 1-2.
39. *Journal History*, The Church of Jesus Christ of Latter-day Saints, December 11, 1982, p. 1.
40. "Gordon B. Hinckley, Man of Integrity," KSL TV Channel 5 broadcast, April 1, 1995.
41. *Chronicle of the 20th Century*, (Mount Kisco, New York: Chronicle Publications, Inc., 1987), p. 1213.
42. *Journal History*, The Church of Jesus Christ of Latter-day Saints, April 8, 1983 & June 23, 1983..
43. *Journal History*, The Church of Jesus Christ of Latter-day Saints, April 1, 1983, p. 1.
44. *Journal History*, The Church of Jesus Christ of Latter-day Saints, April 2, 1983, p. 2.
45. *Journal History*, The Church of Jesus Christ of Latter-day Saints, Saturday, April 2, 1983, p. 6.
46. *Journal History*, The Church of Jesus Christ of Latter-day Saints, Sunday, April 3, 1983, p. 3.
47. *Journal History*, The Church of Jesus Christ of Latter-day Saints, Tuesday, April 5, 1983, p. 1.
48. *Journal History*, The Church of Jesus Christ of Latter-day Saints, April 9, 1983, p. 2.
49. *Journal History*, The Church of Jesus Christ of Latter-day Saints, June 2, 1983, p. 1.
50. *Ensign*, April 1986, p. 6.
51. *BYU Hawaii Commencement*, First Presidency Message, April 1986, p. 2.
52.*Ensign*, April 1986, pp. 2-5.
53. *Journal History*, The Church of Jesus Christ of Latter-day Saints, September 11, 983, p. 11.
54. *Journal History*, The Church of Jesus Christ of Latter-day Saints, Sunday, September 17, 1983, p. 1.
55. *Journal History*, The Church of Jesus Christ of Latter-day Saints, September 24, 1983, p. 1.
56. *Journal History*, The Church of Jesus Christ of Latter-day Saints, Sunday, October 2, 1983, p. 1.
57. *Journal History*, The Church of Jesus Christ of Latter-day Saints, Wednesday, November 9, 1983, p. 5.
58. *Journal History*, The Church of Jesus Christ of Latter-day Saints, Sunday, December 18, 1983, p. 4.
59. *Ensign*, February 1986, p. 7.
60. *Journal History*, The Church of Jesus Christ of Latter-day Saints, Tuesday, February 14, 1984.
61. *Journal History*, The Church of Jesus Christ of Latter-day Saints, Saturday, May 19, 1984, p. 3.
62. *Journal History*, The Church of Jesus Christ of Latter-day Saints, Wednesday, April 4, 1984.
63. *Journal History*, The Church of Jesus Christ of Latter-day Saints, Friday, April 6, 1984, p. 1.
64. *Journal History*, The Church of Jesus Christ of Latter-day Saints, Saturday, April 7, 1984, p. 6.
65. *Journal History*, The Church of Jesus Christ of Latter-day Saints, Sunday, April 8, 1984, p. 1.
66. *Journal History*, The Church of Jesus Christ of Latter-day Saints, Sunday, April 8, 1984, pp. 25-28.
67. *Journal History*, The Church of Jesus Christ of Latter-day Saints, Sunday, April 15, 1984, p. 6.
68. *Journal History*, The Church of Jesus Christ of Latter-day Saints, Saturday, May 12, 1984, p. 2.
69. *Journal History*, The Church of Jesus Christ of Latter-day Saints, Sunday, July 1, 1984, p. 2.
70. *Journal History*, The Church of Jesus Christ of Latter-day Saints, September 4, 1984, p. 1; *Ensign*, March 1992, p. 2.
71. *Journal History*, The Church of Jesus Christ of Latter-day Saints, Thursday, September 27, 1984, p. 2.
72. *Journal History*, The Church of Jesus Christ of Latter-day Saints, September 23, 1984, p. 17.
73. *Journal History*, The Church of Jesus Christ of Latter-day Saints, Friday, September 7, 1984, p. 8.
74. *Journal History*, The Church of Jesus Christ of Latter-day Saints, September 29, 1984, pp. 5-6.
75. *Journal History*, The Church of Jesus Christ of Latter-day Saints, Thursday, October 4, 1984, p. 6.
76. *Journal History*, The Church of Jesus Christ of Latter-day Saints, Saturday, October 6, 1984, p. 13.
77. *Journal History*, The Church of Jesus Christ of Latter-day Saints, Sunday, October 7, 1984, p. 3.
78. *Journal History*, The Church of Jesus Christ of Latter-day Saints, Sunday, October 7, 1984, p. 5.
79. *Journal History*, The Church of Jesus Christ of Latter-day Saints, December 26, 1984, p. 1; Sunday, December 30, 1984, pp. 3-4.
80. "Memorial Service at Historical Department for Elder Durham," LDS Historical Department Archives, Salt Lake City, Utah, Ms. 6008.
81. *Journal History*, The Church of Jesus Christ of Latter-day Saints, Saturday, January 19, 1985, p. 1.
82. George M. McCune, *Personalities in the Doctrine & Covenants and Joseph Smith-History*, (Salt Lake City, Utah:Hawkes Publishing, Inc., 1991), pp. 76-77.
83. *Journal History*, The Church of Jesus Christ of Latter-day Saints, August 1, 1987; *Salt Lake Tribune*, August 1, 1987, p. 6A.

84. *Journal History*, The Church of Jesus Christ of Latter-day Saints, Wednesday, April 3, 1985, p. 6.
85. *Journal History*, The Church of Jesus Christ of Latter-day Saints, October 23, 1985, p. 3.
86. *Journal History*, The Church of Jesus Christ of Latter-day Saints, July 28, 1985, p. 14.
87. *Journal History*, The Church of Jesus Christ of Latter-day Saints, Saturday, August 17, 1985, p. 4.
88. *Ensign*, September 1985, p. 4.
89. *Journal History*, The Church of Jesus Christ of Latter-day Saints, May 6, 1986, p. 4.
90. *Journal History*, The Church of Jesus Christ of Latter-day Saints, Saturday, October 5, 1985, p. 11.
91. *Journal History*, The Church of Jesus Christ of Latter-day Saints, Friday, October 18, 1985, p. 1.
92. *Ensign*, May 1995, p. 71.
93. *Journal History*, The Church of Jesus Christ of Latter-day Saints, Sunday, November 10, 1985.
94. *Journal History*, The Church of Jesus Christ of Latter-day Saints,Sunday, 24 November 1985, p. 2.
95. *Journal History*, The Church of Jesus Christ of Latter-day Saints, December 10, 1985, p. 2.
96. *Ensign*, February 1986, p. 7.
97. *Ensign*, February 1986, p. 9.
98. *Journal History*, The Church of Jesus Christ of Latter-day Saints, Sunday, April 13, 1986, p. 9.
99. *Journal History*, The Church of Jesus Christ of Latter-day Saints, August 14, 1986, p. 1.
100. *Ensign*, August 1986, p. 4.
101. *Journal History*, The Church of Jesus Christ of Latter-day Saints, August 19, 1986, p. 4.
102. *Journal History*, The Church of Jesus Christ of Latter-day Saints, Sunday, October 5, 1986, p. 5.
103. *Journal History*, The Church of Jesus Christ of Latter-day Saints, Wednesday, October 15, 1986, p. 5.
104. *Journal History*, The Church of Jesus Christ of Latter-day Saints, Sunday, November 9, 1986, p. 2.
105. *Journal History*, The Church of Jesus Christ of Latter-day Saints, August 1, 1987.
106. *Church News*, November 21, 1987, p. 3.
107. *Deseret News*, December 7, 1987, p. B2.
108. *New Era*, September 1988, pp. 45-46.
109. *Church News*, April 9, 1988, p. 4.
110. *New Era*, September 1988, p. 47.
111. Church News, *May 28, 1988, p. 11.*
112. *Church News*, May 28, 1988, p. 7.
113. *Deseret News*, September 8, 1988; *Journal History*, The Church of Jesus Christ of Latter-day Saints, pp. 1-2.
114. *Journal History*, The Church of Jesus Christ of Latter-day Saints, Saturday, October 1, 1988, p. 17.
115. *Journal History*, The Church of Jesus Christ of Latter-day Saints, November 13, 1988, pp. 3-6 & Sunday, November 20, 1988.
116. *Ensign*, January 1989, pp. 3-4.
117. *Journal History*, The Church of Jesus Christ of Latter-day Saints, Sunday, February 26, 1989, p. 3.
118. *Journal History*, The Church of Jesus Christ of Latter-day Saints, Tuesday, May 30, 1989, p. 7.
119. *Journal History*, The Church of Jesus Christ of Latter-day Saints, Friday, June 23, 1989, p. 3.
120. *BYU Speeches of the Year*, (Provo, Utah:BYU Press, 1989), September 3, 1989, p. 14.
121. *Journal History*, The Church of Jesus Christ of Latter-day Saints, Friday, July 14, 1989, p. 1.
122. *Ensign*, August 1989, p. 6.
123. *BYU Speeches of the Year*, (Provo, Utah:BYU Press, 1989), September 3, 1989, p. 12.
124. *Journal History*, The Church of Jesus Christ of Latter-day Saints, Sunday, September 3, 1989, p. 2.
125. Interview of George M. McCune with one of the developers present at the meeting with the stake presidents and President Hinckley.
126. *Journal History*, The Church of Jesus Christ of Latter-day Saints, March 1990, p. 8.
127. *Journal History*, The Church of Jesus Christ of Latter-day Saints, Sunday, December 3, 1989, p. 3.
128. *Journal History*, The Church of Jesus Christ of Latter-day Saints, February 18, 1990, p. 1.
129. Bernard Gwertzman and Michael T. Kaufman, editors, *The Decline and Fall of the Soviet Empire*, (New York:The New York Times Company, 1992), p. 233.
130. *Journal History*, The Church of Jesus Christ of Latter-day Saints, October 5, 1990, p. 6.
131. *Journal History*, The Church of Jesus Christ of Latter-day Saints, Friday, February 23, 1990, p. 9.
132. *Journal History*, The Church of Jesus Christ of Latter-day Saints, Sunday, April 1, 1990, p. 5.
133. *Journal History*, The Church of Jesus Christ of Latter-day Saints, Friday, April 27, 1990, p. 1.
134. *Journal History*, The Church of Jesus Christ of Latter-day Saints, Thursday, April 28, 1990, p. 8.
135. *Journal History*, The Church of Jesus Christ of Latter-day Saints, Friday, May 4, 1990, p. 3.
136. *Journal History*, The Church of Jesus Christ of Latter-day Saints, Sunday, May 6, 1990, p. 2.
137. *Journal History*, The Church of Jesus Christ of Latter-day Saints, Saturday, June 2, 1990, p. 17.
138. *Journal History*, The Church of Jesus Christ of Latter-day Saints, Friday, June 22, 1990, p. 9.
139. *Journal History*, The Church of Jesus Christ of Latter-day Saints, September 18, 19, and 23, 1990.
140. *Journal History*, The Church of Jesus Christ of Latter-day Saints, Sunday, October 7, 1990, p. 3.
141. *Journal History*, The Church of Jesus Christ of Latter-day Saints, October 6, 1990, p. 8.
142. *Journal History*, The Church of Jesus Christ of Latter-day Saints, Sunday, January 1991, p. 4.
143. *Ensign*, February 1991, p. 5.
144. *Journal History*, The Church of Jesus Christ of Latter-day Saints, Tuesday, February 5, 1991, p. 3.
145. *Journal History*, The Church of Jesus Christ of Latter-day Saints, Friday, February 15, 1991, p. 8.
146. *Church News*, April 13, 1991, p. 6.
147. *Church News*, August 10, 1991, p. 3.
148. *Ensign*, March 1992, p. 2.
149. *Church News*, October 5, 1991, p. 6.
150. *Church News*, November 16, 1991, p. 4.
151. *Church News*, December 7, 1991, p. 4.
152. *Church News*, February 29, 1992, p. 10.
153. *Church News*, March 14, 1992, pp. 10-11.
154. Edward Y. Okazaki Funeral shorthand notes of George M. McCune, Tuesday, March 24, 1992, Salt Lake Wasatch Stake Center, Salt Lake City.
155. Funeral of Jay Ambrose Quealy, Jr. funeral, Friday, March 27, 1992, 11:00 A.M., Monument Park North Ward, 2795 Crestview Drive, Salt Lake City, Utah, audio tape.
156. *Church News*, April 17, 1993, p. 3.
157. *Church News*, June 9, 1993, pp. 2-3.
158. *Church News*, Saturday, July 3, 1993.
159. *Church News*, December 11, 1993, p. 3.
160. *Church News*, January 23, 1994, p. 4.
161. *Church News*, June 18, 1994, p. 4.

Prophet

1. *Church News*, March 18, 1995 p. 3.
2. *Ensign*, May 1995, p. 99.
3. *Ensign*, May 1995, p. 99.
4. *Ensign*, May 1995, p. 51.
5. *Ensign*, May 1995, p. 53.
6. *Ensign*, May 1995, p. 53.
7. *Ensign*, May 1995, p. 53.
8. *Ensign*, May 1995, p. 71.
9. *Ensign*, May 1995, p. 89.
10. KSL Radio broadcast, 12:08 P.M., June 12, 1995.
11. *Church News*, July 1, 1995, p. 7.
12. *Ensign*, July 1995, pp. 2-5.
13. KL TV, Noon broadcast, October 1, 1995.
14. *Church News*, August 26, 1995, p. 4.
15. KL TV, Noon broadcast, October 1, 1995.
16. *Church News*, September 9, 1995, pp. 2-11.
18. *Church News*, September 9, 1995, p. 11; September 2, 1995, p. 3.
18. *Church News*, September 9, 1995, p. 11.
19. *Church News*, September 9, 1995, p. 3.
20. *Ensign*, November 1995, p. 71.
21. *Ensign*, November 1995, p. 72.
22. *Ensign*, October 1995, pp. 2-5.
23. *Church News*, October 21, 1995, p. 7.
24. *Church News*, October 21, 1995, p. 4.
25. *Church News*, October 19, 1995, p. 2.
26. *Deseret News*, October 21, 1995, p. B-1.
27. *Church News*, October 28, 1995, p. 7.
28. *Church News*, November 18, 1995, p. 6.
29. *Church News*, November 18, 1995, p. 3.
30. President David Christensen, Salt Lake City Mission, speaking at monthly Partnership Meeting with Stake Mission Presidencies, Tuesday, February 20, 1996, SL Granite Stake Tabernacle, Salt Lake City, Utah.
31. *Church News*, January 13, 1996, p. 4.
32. *Church News*, January 27, 1996, p. 3.

33. *Church News*, February 3, 1996, p. 3.
34. *Church News*, February 17, 1996, p. 3.

Legacy

1. *Improvement Era*, January 1974, p. 124.
2. *Improvement Era*, January 1974, p. 122.
3. *Church News*, October 28, 1995, p. 7.
4. *Ensign*, January 1982, p. 11.
5. *Ensign*, January 1982, pp. 11-13.
6. *Ensign*, May 1978, p. 58.
7. Moses 1:25-26.

INDEX